Free in the USA:

1800+ parks, museums, collections, and roadside attractions where admission is always free

Neala McCarten
Compass Rose Publishing
Jacksonville, FL

ISBN-13: 978-0-9973322-2-3

Cover design and logo by Barbara Rosen

Note: Hours of operation are included, however, not all places indicate that they are closed on holidays, and hours often change. It is advised to verify before you go. Moreover, places that are currently free can decide to change their admission policy. Free tours can suddenly become fee-based or morph into something quite different. Before you make a special trip to visit one of these attractions, call or check their website for the latest information.

Also by Neala McCarten:
Offbeat New Mexico: Places of unexpected history, art, and culture. Available on Amazon. https://www.amazon.com/Offbeat-New-Mexico-Unexpected-History/dp/0997332212

Table of Contents

Preface

Many people are a bit suspicious of free things. We wonder how good something can be if there's no charge. But across the USA there are places to visit, and things to do that are both outstanding and 100% free. Not low-cost. Not free on Tuesday afternoons, or special Fridays but free . . . always.

Why would bona fide attractions be free? Often, organizations cover the running expenses because public education and access are parts of their mission.

Other places are privately owned (or endowed) and opened at no cost because there's sufficient resources without charging – and the owner wants to share the joy of the collection. The Karpeles Library is the world's largest private holding of important original manuscripts and documents. The changing exhibits are displayed in historic buildings across 16 cities in the continental USA. Admission is always free. http://www.rain.org/~karpeles/index.php.

A successful business may use the attraction as a form of public relations, or even marketing. Classic car dealerships are a repository of beloved icons from muscle cars to speedway pace cars.

Some of the places included offer additional fee-based experiences. It is becoming more common for museums to open their permanent collection for free but to charge for special exhibits. We've included these places but indicated what's free, and what isn't.

Many places say they are free, but then set an amount for a *voluntary* donation, or say that admission is by *free will* donation. However much we understand their need to keep the doors open, these places aren't included. Requiring a donation or telling you how much you should donate isn't free.

The Recreation Enhancement Act allows the government to charge a fee for recreational use of public lands managed by the Bureau of Land Management (BLM), the Bureau of Reclamation (BOR), the Fish and Wildlife Service (FWS), the National Park Service (NPS), and the Forest Service (USFS). So some places are free others are not. Currently, fish hatcheries are all free. But that the situation can change.

Remember, as J. R. R. Tolkien said, "Not all those who wander are lost." Sometimes that's the best way to explore. Especially when it's for free.

Alabama

Alabama played a key role in the Civil War with Montgomery as the Confederacy's first capital, but it was also the state that gave us the Tuskegee Airmen. The first Black flying unit in the U.S. military was trained in Alabama. The Saturn V rocket that made it possible for humans to land on the moon was designed in Huntsville. This is a state that offers a rich diversity of history and experiences.

Anniston, AL
Greyhound Bus Station was the site of the 1961 attack by segregationists on the bus carrying the Freedom Riders. The side of the building that borders the bus station's driveway features a mural and educational panels about the events of May 14, 1961. 1031 Gurnee Ave; Anniston, AL 36202; https://www.nps.gov/frri/planyourvisit/index.htm

Auburn, AL
Donald E. Davis Arboretum features native trees, shrubs, and wild flowers, including 150 different tree species native to Alabama and the Southeast. No charge for admission. Open daily from sunrise to sunset. 181 Garden Dr; Auburn, AL 36830; Phone: (334) 844-5770; http://www.auburn.edu/cosam/arboretum/about_us/index.htm

Birmingham, AL
Alabama Museum of the Health Sciences represents 700 years of medicine and disease through instruments, equipment, specimens, and models used by healthcare professionals around the world. There is no admission fee. Currently under renovation, check the website for updates. Lister Hill Library of the Health Sciences; Third floor; 1700 University Blvd; Birmingham, AL 35233; Phone: (205) 934-4475; https://www.uab.edu/amhs

Birmingham Botanical Gardens encompasses over 60 acres filled with more than 30 gardens. Admission is free. Open daily from dawn to dusk. 2612 Lane Park Rd; Birmingham, AL 35223; Phone: (205) 414-3950; https://bbgardens.org

Birmingham Museum of Art presents a diverse collection of paintings, sculpture, prints, drawings, and decorative arts dating from ancient to modern times as well as the Charles W. Ireland Sculpture Garden. General admission is free. Admission may be charged for special exhibitions. Open Tuesday through Saturday from 10 AM to 5 PM and Sunday from Noon to 5 PM. 2000 Rev Abraham Woods, Jr

Blvd (formerly Eighth Avenue N); Birmingham, AL 35203; Phone: (205) 254-2565; https://artsbma.org

Don Kresge Memorial Radio Museum, named after retired General Electric engineer Don Kresge, celebrates WSY radio station of Alabama Power Co. and the historic radios of the 1920s through 1950s. The displays are located inside the Alabama Power Building. Open Monday through Friday from 9 AM to 5 PM. 600 N 18th St; Birmingham, AL 35203; Phone: (205) 822-6759; http://alabamahistoricalradiosociety.org/Museum.html

Museum of Fond Memories is actually Reed Books, specializing in antiquarian objects, including rare volumes. It is filled with objects beloved by Jim Reed. Open Tuesday through Friday from 10:30 AM to 5:30 PM and Saturdays from 11 AM to 4 PM. 2021 Third Ave N; Birmingham, AL 35203; Phone: (205) 326-4460; https://jimreedbooks.com/index.php

Sloss Furnaces created the iron-industry boomtown of Birmingham. Although nothing remains of the original furnace complex there are remnants from a later part of the complex dating from 1902. The museum is free to enter. Stop by the visitor center for a self-guided tour brochure, and a short video. Open Tuesday through Saturday from 10 AM to 4 PM. Open Sunday from Noon to 4 PM. Closed major holidays. 20 32nd St N; Birmingham, AL 35222; Phone: (205) 324-1911; http://www.slossfurnaces.com

Bridgeport, AL
Russell Cave National Monument mixes nature with geology and prehistory. The park's museum features artifacts and reproductions found in Russell Cave which would have been used from 10,000 BC to 1650 AD. Programs include guided cave shelter tours (tours are only led into the cave shelter and not inside the cave itself) nature walks, even lantern hikes. Admission and all activities are free. Open daily 8 AM to 4:30 PM. Closed Thanksgiving, Christmas, and New Year's Day. 3729 County Rd 98; Bridgeport, AL 35740; Phone: (256) 495-2672; https://www.nps.gov/ruca/index.htm

Calera, AL
Heart of Dixie Railroad Museum is the official railroad museum of the state of Alabama, located just south of Birmingham. The museum features historic railway locomotives, cars, and artifacts from late 1800s to the 1950s in the 100-year-old depot and the railroad yard. Museum admission is free but there is a charge for the train rides. Open mid-March through mid-December on Tuesday through

Saturday from 9 AM to 2 PM. 1919 Ninth St; Calera, AL 35040; Phone: (205) 757-8383; https://www.hodrrm.org

Columbiana, AL

Karl C. Harrison Museum of George Washington focuses on the Colonial period to 1865 and contains everything from paintings and letters to furniture and jewelry. Highlights include Martha Washington's prayer book (printed in 1783), writing instruments and tools from George Washington's survey case, and even an original tintype depicting Robert E. Lee in his uniform. Admission is free. Open Monday through Friday 10 AM to 3 PM. Mildred B. Harrison Regional Library; 50 Lester St; Columbiana, AL 35051; Phone: (205) 669-8767; http://www.washingtonmuseum.com

Danville, AL

Oakville Indian Mounds Museum contains five Indian mounds of which two are still intact. The museum is a seven-sided modified design of a Cherokee council house. Admission is free with donations appreciated. Open Monday through Friday from 8 AM to 4 PM. Open Saturday from 10 AM to 4 PM and on Sunday from Noon to 4 PM. Closed on some holidays. 1219 County Rd 187; Danville, AL 35619; Phone: (256) 905-2494; http://oakvilleindianmounds.com/Museum.html

Daphne, AL

American Sport Art Museum & Archives provides one of the largest collections of sport art in the world, including paintings, sculptures, assemblages, prints, posters, and photography. The museum is free. Open Monday through Friday from 9 AM to 4 PM. 1 Academy Dr; Daphne, AL 36526; Phone: (251) 626-3303; http://www.asama.org/visitor-info

Daviston, AL

Horseshoe Bend National Military Park goes back to 1814 and the battles for the land held by Creek Native Americans. Andrew Jackson's troops won the war and the Creeks had to cede their ancestral home. In 1828 Jackson signed the Indian Removal Bill that forced the southeastern tribes and their allies to move west. However, it wasn't implemented until the fall and winter of 1838 and 1839. That long murderous journey came to be known as the infamous *Trail of Tears*. Trails skirt the edge of the battlefield, and lead visitors to the site of a 1880s Creek Indian camp. Open daily. Closed Thanksgiving, Christmas, and New Year's Day. The visitor center is open 9 AM to 4:30 PM. 11288 Horseshoe Bend Rd; Daviston, AL 36256; Phone: (256) 234-7111; https://www.nps.gov/hobe/index.htm

Foley, AL

Holmes Medical Museum, at the site of the original first hospital in Baldwin County, illustrates medicine as it was practiced in the 1920s through the 1950s with actual equipment. There's also a collection of hoax and quackery medical devices. Admission is free but donations are appreciated. Open Monday through Saturday from 10 AM to 3 PM. 111 W Laurel Ave; Foley, AL 36535; Phone: (251) 970-1818; https://www.facebook.com/HolmesMedicalMuseum

Fort Rucker, AL

U.S. Army Aviation Museum displays 50 aircraft, selected from their collection of over 160 airplanes, helicopters, and other vertical flight aircraft. There is no admission charge but donations are accepted. Open Monday through Friday from 9 AM to 4 PM and Saturday from 9 AM to 3 PM. Bldg 6000; Novosel St; Fort Rucker, AL 36362; Phone: (334) 598-2508; http://www.armyaviationmuseum.org

Huntsville, AL

North Alabama Railroad Museum preserves over 30 pieces of rolling stock (both freight and passenger equipment) and three historic locomotives. Self-guided tours are free. Open April through October on Wednesday and Saturday from 9 AM to 2 PM. 694 Chase Rd NE; Huntsville, AL 35811; Phone: (256) 851-6276; http://northalabamarailroadmuseum.com/wp

Jacksonville, AL

Dr. Francis Medical Museum was formerly a doctor's office and apothecary shop and houses items from the mid-19th to the mid-20th century. It is free to visit. Note: The library strongly suggests calling ahead to make sure the museum is open. Open Tuesday through Friday from 8 AM to 5:45 PM. Open Saturday from 8 AM to 3:45 PM. 200 Pelham Rd S; Jacksonville, AL 36265; Phone: (256) 435-6332; http://www.jacksonvillepubliclibrary.org/Francis_Museum.html

Mobile, AL

Archaeology Museum University of South Alabama covers over 12,000 years of prehistory and history. Life-size scenes depict archaeologists at work to show the different ways of ancient Woodland cultures, mound-building Mississippian peoples, early French settlers, and a Black family after the Civil War. Visits are self-guided and the museum is free of charge. Open Tuesday through Friday from 9 AM to 4 PM. 6052 USA Drive S; Mobile, AL 36688; Phone: (251) 460-6106; http://www.southalabama.edu/org/archaeology/museum

Phoenix Fire Museum is filled with turn-of-the-century horse-drawn steam engines and early motorized vehicles. Admission is free. Open Monday through

Friday from 9 AM to 5 PM. 203 S Claiborne St; Mobile, AL 36602; Phone: (251) 208-7508; http://www.historymuseumofmobile.com/phoenix-fire-museum

Montgomery, AL

Alabama State Capital is a museum of state history and politics. The Confederacy began in the senate when delegates from southern states voted to secede from the Union in February 1861, and the President of the Confederacy, Jefferson Davis, was inaugurated there. Open Monday through Friday from 8 AM to 4:30 PM. Saturday from 9 AM to 3 PM. Enter at 1 N Union St. 468 S Perry St; Montgomery, AL 36130; Phone: (334) 242-3184; http://ahc.alabama.gov/alabama-state-capitol.aspx

First White House of the Confederacy was the residence of Confederate President Jefferson Davis and his family while the capitol of the Confederacy was in Montgomery. It is furnished with original period pieces. Admission is free. Open Monday through Friday from 8 AM to 4:30 PM and Saturday from 9 AM to 4 PM. Closed state holidays. 644 Washington Ave; Montgomery, AL 36130; Phone: (334) 242-1861; http://www.firstwhitehouse.org

Hyundai Motor Manufacturing Plant Tour – Alabama (HMMA) offers a tram tour through the plant. There is no cost for the tour but reservations are required and a confirmation must be presented. 700 Hyundai Blvd; Montgomery, AL 36105; Phone: (334) 387-8019; https://www.hmmausa.com/tours/about-hmma-tours

Montgomery Museum of Fine Arts displays American art through the 21st century as well as regional art from the 1930s. American Art glass is a particular focus. Admission is free. Open Tuesday through Saturday from 10 AM to 5 PM, Thursday from 10 AM to 9 PM, Sunday from Noon to 5 PM. Closed major holidays. 1 Museum Dr; Montgomery, AL 36117; Phone: (334) 240-4333; http://www.mmfa.org

Museum of Alabama at the Department of Archives and History tells the story of the people of Alabama using more than 800 artifacts including hundreds of images, letters, speeches, and songs. Admission is free. Open Monday through Saturday from 8:30 AM to 4:30 PM. Closed on all state holidays. 624 Washington Ave; Montgomery, AL 36130; Phone: (334) 242-4435; http://www.museum.alabama.gov/plan-your-visit.html

Muscle Shoals, AL

Wilson Dam was once the largest hydroelectric installation in the world. The visitor center displays panels describing the struggle between private and public power interests for ownership of the facility. The lock is sometimes open for tours.

Check the website or call for information. 3985 Reservation Rd; Muscle Shoals, AL 35660; Phone: (800) 882-5263; https://www.tva.gov/Energy/Our-Power-System/Hydroelectric/Wilson-Reservoir

Pickensville, AL
Tom Bevill Lock and Dam & Visitor Center is housed in a reproduction of a Greek Revival antebellum home and describes life in the Tombigbee River Valley. A highlight is the Snagboat Montgomery, one of last steam-powered stern-wheel snagboats to ply Southern rivers. No fee to visit. Open Wednesday through Saturday from 9 AM to 5 PM. 1382 Lock and Dam Rd; Pickensville, AL 35447; Phone: (205) 373-8705; https://alabama.travel/places-to-go/tom-bevill-visitor-center-snagboat-montgomery

Selma, AL
The site of crucial Civil Rights history, most of the museums in Selma exploring those events charge admission.
Edmund Pettus Bridge became a powerful Civil Rights symbol when marchers were violently confronted by law enforcement personnel on March 7, 1965. The day became known as Bloody Sunday. The **Selma Interpretive Center** at the foot of the bridge provides history and background. Free to visit. Open Monday through Saturday from 9 AM to 4:30 PM. 2 Broad St; Selma, AL 36701; Phone: (334) 872-0509; https://www.nps.gov/semo/learn/historyculture/edmund-pettus-bridge.htm

Heritage Village is the site of several 1800s structures that were donated to the Selma-Dallas County Historic Preservation Society. Note: Some are now private residences. It is free to stroll through the area. 622 McLeod Ave; Selma, AL 36702; http://historicselma.org/heritage-village

Tensaw, AL
Fort Mims State Historic Site was the setting for battles between settlers and Native American tribes. In 1813 over 700 Creek Native Americans destroyed Fort Mims, where American settlers, allied Creeks, and enslaved Blacks had sought refuge. The attack is considered the beginning of the Creek War of 1813-14. A log stockade marks the fort's location, and a replica of an 1800s blockhouse was constructed at what would have been one corner. Admission is free, although a small fee may be required during living history weekends. Open daily dawn to dusk. Fort Mims Rd; Tensaw, AL 36579; Phone: (251) 533-9024; http://ahc.alabama.gov/properties/ftmims/ftmims.aspx

Tuscumbia, AL
Key Underwood Coon Dog Memorial Cemetery is likely the world's only Coon Dog cemetery. It began when Key Underwood buried his beloved dog, Troop, on

the site in 1937. There is no charge to visit. Open dawn to dusk. 4945 Coon Dog Cemetery Rd; Phone: (256) 412-5970; http://www.coondogcemetery.com

Tuskegee, AL

Legacy Museum at Tuskegee University has two very different exhibits – one focuses on art and antique furniture, the other tells a story of the misuse of public health. That exhibit includes a serious investigation of two seemingly disparate experiences. One part refers to the cell line of Henrietta Lacks whose story has been made into the movie *The Immortal Life of Henrietta Lacks*. The other exhibit focuses on a controversial study that observed the progression of untreated syphilis in rural Black men in Alabama. When the study began, there was no cure for the disease, but even after penicillin was found to be successful the men were never treated. Admission is free but donations are gratefully accepted. Open Monday through Friday from 10 AM to 4 PM. Closed during official university holidays. 1 Benjamin Payton Dr; Tuskegee, AL 36088; Phone: (334) 727-8888; https://www.tuskegee.edu/libraries/legacy-museum

Tuskegee Airmen National Historic Site focuses on the famous Tuskegee Airmen from World War II. About 16,000 men and women ultimately became air traffic controllers, bombardiers, flight instructors, and mechanics. Exhibits in two major buildings depict the soldiers' experiences. There are also two videos and a full-sized replica of the Red-Tail P-51 Mustang. Outside over 20 wayside exhibits provide additional information. Admission is free. Open Monday through Saturday 9 AM to 4:30 PM. Closed Thanksgiving, Christmas, and New Year's Day. 1616 Chappie James Ave; Tuskegee, AL 3608; Phone: (334) 724-0922; http://www.nps.gov/tuai

Tuskegee Institute National Historic Site honors Booker T. Washington who came to the Tuskegee Institute in the 1880s to provide an education to future teachers. The most famous student was George Washington Carver. Visitors can peruse the exhibits at the George Washington Carver Museum, and tour both the Tuskegee University campus, and the home of Booker T. Washington. There is no charge to visit the historic campus, the museum, or tours. Open Monday through Saturday from 9 AM to 4:30 PM. Closed Thanksgiving, Christmas, and New Year's Day. 1212 W Montgomery Rd; Tuskegee, AL 36088; Phone: (334) 727-3200; https://www.nps.gov/tuin/index.htm

Vance, AL

Mercedes-Benz Visitor Center displays classic, concept, and race cars. Admission is free. Open Monday through Friday 8:30 AM to 4 PM. Closed all major holidays. Call for current schedule of plant tours. 6 Mercedes Dr; Vance, AL 35490; Phone: (888) 286-8762; https://mbusi.com/visitorcenter/vc-museum

Alaska

Bigger than Texas in size (although not population), this 49th state nicknamed The Last Frontier is still isolated. Many places can only be visited by small plane, or by ship. Given the sparse population spread out over so much territory, there are only a few population centers. Anchorage tops the list with almost 300,000 people. Juneau and Fairbanks barely make it over 30,000. Travel is notoriously difficult. Weather further complicates visiting and many attractions are only open seasonally.

Anchorage, AK can be reached by air, water, and highway.
Campbell Creek Science Center offers access to a variety of creeks, trails, forests, and meadows as well as many free-of-charge programs. The Center is on the Bureau of Land Management Campbell Tract in Anchorage. Open all year. In summer open Monday through Friday from 7:30 AM to 5:30 PM. In winter open Monday through Friday from 8 AM to 4 PM. 5600 Science Center Dr; Anchorage, AK 99507; Phone: (907) 267-1247; https://www.blm.gov/node/7797

Fraternal Order of the Alaska State Troopers (FOAST) Law Enforcement Museum is Alaska's only collection of historical law enforcement memorabilia. Featured items include an authentically restored 1952 Hudson Hornet automobile as well as antique radios and communications devices. Admission is free. Open Monday through Friday from 10 AM to 4 PM and on Saturday from Noon to 4 PM. 245 W. 5th Ave; Suite 113 (underneath the 5th Avenue parking garage); Anchorage, AK 99501; Phone: (907) 279-5050; http://www.alaskatroopermuseum.com

Potter Marsh treats visitors to views of the scenic Turnagain Arm at the southern end of the 16-mile Anchorage Coastal Wildlife Refuge. There's a mountain-lined waterway, and ½-mile wooden boardwalk with interpretative signs starting at the parking area and wending through the marsh habitats. There are no entry fees to the refuge. The entrance is located just past the Rabbit Creek exit of the New Seward Highway. 2999 E 154th Ave; Anchorage, AK 99516; http://www.adfg.alaska.gov/index.cfm?adfg=viewinglocations.pottermarsh

Tony Knowles Coastal Trail has been developed for bikes, horses, and hikers. Considered to be one of the most beautiful coastal trails in the nation, it provides views of downtown Anchorage, the Chugach Mountains, Denali, Mount Susitna (Sleeping Lady), and Fire Island. The trail runs from W Second Avenue in downtown Anchorage to Kincaid Park. https://www.anchorage.net/discover/trails-and-local-parks/coastal-trail

Wells Fargo: The Heritage Library and Museum presents an extensive collection of Native artifacts, fine art by Alaskan artists, as well as a three-quarter size stagecoach. Free to visit. Open Monday through Friday from Noon to 4 PM. 301 W Northern Lights; Anchorage, AK 99503; Phone: (907) 265-2834; https://www.wellsfargohistory.com/museums/anchorage

Bartlett Cove, AK (See also Gustavus, AK) can only be reached by water or by highway from Gustavus.

Glacier Bay National Park is one of the most popular tour stops on Alaska's Inside Passage, but the park itself is essentially roadless. Visitors must see the park from the water, generally from a cruise ship, or private hire. However, Glacier Bay National Park is free to visit. Both Bartlett Cove and Gustavus can only be reached by air or water (including Alaska Marine Highway System), although a road does link the two towns. https://www.nps.gov/glba/index.htm

Coldfoot, AK can be reached by highway. Located at the edge of the Gates of the Arctic National Park and Preserve, Coldfoot is the farthest north truck stop in the United States. Its population in the 2010 census was 10 and it was featured in the third and fourth seasons of Ice Road Truckers.
Arctic Interagency Visitor Center explores the Arctic Circle through exhibits, walks along the nearby nature trails, and special evening programs on the unique landscapes and history of the Far North. Admission is free. Open Memorial Day through Labor Day from 11 AM to 10 PM but call ahead or visit the website to verify hours. Dalton Hwy; Milepost 175; Coldfoot, AK 99701; Phone: (907) 678-5209; https://www.blm.gov/learn/interpretive-centers/arctic-interagency-visitor-center

Copper Center, AK can be reached by highway.
Wrangell-St. Elias National Park & Preserve encompasses Kennecott Mines National Historic Landmark located near McCarthy. This is about seven or eight hours from Anchorage and about 3 ½ hours from the town of Copper Center.
Copper Center Visitor Center Complex, 10 miles south of the intersection of the Glenn Highway and the Richardson Highway, hosts an exhibit hall, a theater, the Ahtna Cultural Center, scenic overlooks, and short hiking trails. Park rangers provide guided talks and daily walks. There is no charge to enter the park. The park is open year round but the center is open from mid-May through September from 9 AM to 6 PM. Lodging is available in both Copper Center and McCarthy

but planning ahead is advised. Mile 106.8 Richardson Hwy; Copper Center, AK 99573; Phone: (907) 822-7250; https://www.nps.gov/wrst/index.htm

Fairbanks, AK can be reached by highway from Canada and Washington State as well as by air.

Morris Thompson Cultural & Visitors Center introduces visitors to Alaska, showing films on the state's history, nature, and cultures. Admission is free. Open daily in summer from 8 AM to 9 PM. In winter from 8 AM to 5 PM. Closed on Christmas, and New Years' Day. 101 Dunkel St; Fairbanks, AK 99701; Phone: (907) 459-3700; https://www.morristhompsoncenter.org

Pioneer Park is billed as Alaska's only historic theme park. Although there's no cost to enter Pioneer Park, the site mixes free and fee-based places. Open Memorial Day to Labor Day. Here are the free-to-visit places. 2300 Airport Way; Fairbanks, AK 99701; Phone: (907) 459-1087; https://www.alaska.org/detail/pioneer-park

The stern-wheeler **Riverboat Nenana** is the second largest wooden vessel in existence. There is no charge to walk through the interior of the boat, and view the 300-foot diorama of life along the Tanana and Yukon rivers. Open only in the summer. **Kitty Hensley House** is furnished with authentic pieces from the period. No fee but donations appreciated. **Tanana Valley Railroad Engine #1** is part of the Tanana Valley Railroad Museum. Dating back to 1899, it is the oldest operating steam locomotive in Alaska and the Yukon Territory. There's no charge to view and explore the Engine #1, but there is a charge for taking a ride on the historic train. **Wickersham House** was the first house in Fairbanks built with milled lumber. In 1904 Judge James Wickersham personally built the house. The story goes that he hauled the lumber down the street on his back. There is no charge to enter, but donations are appreciated.

Gustavus, AK (See also Bartlett Cove, AK) can only be reached by air and water.

Glacier Bay National Park Visitor Center is on the second floor of Glacier Bay Lodge. Open daily from Memorial Day through Labor Day. Park naturalists and Hoonah Indian Association cultural interpreters provide a variety of free activities. Ranger-led walks meet in the lodge lobby. 179 Barlett Cove Rd; Gustavus, AK 99826; Phone: (907) 697-2661; https://www.nps.gov/glba/planyourvisit/join-a-park-ranger.htm

Haines, AK is accessible by air, water, and highway.

Historic Fort Seward was the first permanent army fort built in Alaska. It was started in 1904 with the goal of keeping the peace between settlers, miners, Native Americans, and fish canneries as well as with the nearby Canadians. The fort is now an arts community with art studios, galleries, and businesses as well as restaurants. One of the major organizations is **Alaska Indian Arts** which is open in summer on Monday through Friday from 9 AM to 5 PM. 13 Ft Seward Dr; Haines, AK 99827; Phone: (907) 766-2160; http://www.alaskaindianarts.com

Homer, AK can be reached by air, water, and highway.
Islands & Ocean Visitor Center offers inside exhibits focused on marine life, and outdoor interpretive trails on the center's 60-acre site. There's also naturalist-led walks to Bishop's Beach on Kachemak Bay held June through August. Admission is free. Memorial Day to Labor Day open daily from 9 AM to 5 PM. Open Tuesday through Saturday from Noon to 5 PM the rest of the year. Closed federal holidays. 95 Sterling Hwy; Homer, AK 99603; Phone: (907) 235-6961; https://www.fws.gov/refuge/alaska_maritime/visit/visitor_center.html

Hope, AK is about 2 hours away by highway from Anchorage.
Hope and Sunrise Historical and Mining Museum recalls the Turnagain Arm Gold Rush of 1896, the development of Hope, and the decline of Sunrise. The site hosts the 1904 schoolhouse, three 1917 gold mine buildings, a 1950 Forest Service cabin, and a full-size pit saw display. Admission is free. Donations welcomed. Open Memorial Day to Labor Day from Noon to 4 PM. 64851 Second St; Hope, AK 99605; Phone: (907) 782-3115; https://sites.google.com/site/hopehistoricalsite2/home

Juneau, AK can only be reached by air and water. Ferry service from Washington State is available.
Alaska State Capitol welcomes visitors to a lobby featuring sculptures and carvings representing the importance of hunting and fishing for the local population. When the Legislature is in session (mid-January through mid-April), the Capitol is open daily 7 AM to 9 PM. When the Legislature is not in session, the Capitol is open Monday through Friday from 7 AM to 5 PM. The website provides links to a downloadable brochure and videos. Fourth Ave and Main St; Juneau, AK 99801; Phone: (907) 465-4648; http://w3.legis.state.ak.us/pages/capitol.php

Aunt Claudia's Doll Museum highlights indigenous dolls, toys, and miniatures. There's also a working doll artist studio. There is no fee to visit although donations are welcomed. Generally open Tuesday through Saturday from Noon to 5 PM. 114 S Franklin St; Suite 103; Juneau, AK 99801; Phone: (907) 586-4969; http://auntclaudiasdolls.com

Mendenhall Glacier is one of the prime attractions of Juneau. It is the most easily accessed glacier on the Tongass. Located 13 miles from downtown Juneau along a paved road. The area is a mix of free and fee-based places. There is a seasonal $5 fee for several trails and the visitor center. However the following trails are currently exempt from the fee: Nugget Falls Trail, East Glacier Trail, Powerline Trail, Moraine Ecology Trail, Trail of Time, all the trails around Dredge Lakes, all the trails the West Glacier area, and the parking area. The Trail of Time is a ½-mile paved interpretive walk, with signs marking the glacier's recession. Glacier Spur Rd; Juneau, AK 99801; Phone: (907) 789-0097;
http://www.alaska.org/assets/content/related_items_pdfs/mendenhall_glacier/men denhall.glacier.pdf
For more information on fees go to:
https://www.fs.usda.gov/detail/tongass/about-forest/offices/?cid=fseprd502109

Perseverance National Recreation Trail starts at Basin Road (near the fee-based Last Chance Mining Museum) then up to the old gold mine ruins, and past waterfalls. There are numerous trails to be explored along the way.
http://www.alaska.org/detail/perseverance-trail

Ketchikan, AK is located on the Inside Passage and can only be reached by air and water.
The city offers Native American totem poles, living culture, clan houses. Many Native American totem poles are on display throughout town. You can pick up a map at the Visitor's Bureau at 131 Front St, Ketchikan, AK. Their phone is (907) 225-6166. You can download the map here:
http://www.experienceketchikan.com/ketchikan-walking-tour.html
Potlach Park has a collection of totem poles, and clan house. If you time it right, you may watch an artist carving new totem poles. Privately owned, you can do a bit of shopping in their gift shop. There are also displays of antique firearms, and classic cars. Currently there's no admission charge. 9809 Totem Bight Rd; Ketchikan, AK 99901; Phone: (907) 225-4445;
http://www.alaska.org/detail/potlatch-totem-park

Nome, AK can only be reached by air from Anchorage.
Bering Land Bridge National Preserve is about 100 miles from Nome at the western most point in Alaska. There are no fees (or services) within Bering Land Bridge National Preserve. The visitor center on the first floor of the Sitnasauk Building on Front Street and is open throughout the year. There are programs offered in June, July, and August. Phone: (800) 471-2352. Access to the preserve is by small airplane, boat, or foot. https://www.nps.gov/bela/index.htm

Prince of Wales Island, AK can be reached by water, either the ferry from Ketchikan or the Alaska Marine Highway. Once on the island, all towns are linked by road. The island is famous for its Native Haida carvers and the totem parks. Some charge a fee to visit.

Hydaburg Totem Park is an open-air park and free to visit. There's also a Native carving shed. Fifth St; Hydaburg, Prince of Wales Island, AK 99925.

Klawock's Totem Park displays original and replica totems from the old village of Tuxekan. Visitors are welcome to drop by to see the carvers at work. There is no admission fee. Bayview St; Klawock, Prince of Wales Island, AK 99925; Phone: (907) 755-2261; http://www.cityofklawock.com/vst_info.htm

Port Alsworth, AK can only be reached by air.

Lake Clark National Park and Preserve is known for outdoor activities and Dick Proenneke's cabin. Proenneke (1916-2003) built the cabin by hand using tools and techniques he developed, living there for almost 30 years. The documentary *Alone in the Wilderness* tells his story. There are no roads to his lake-side cabin, but visitors can backpack in from other areas of the park, or come in by floatplane. The cabin is open summers only. https://www.nps.gov/lacl/index.htm

Sitka, AK can only be reached by air or water. It is part of the Alaska Marine Highway System and regular ferry service is available to and from Juneau and other Inside Passage destinations.

Baranof Castle State Historic Site (also known as Castle Hill) uses a fully accessible walkway to lead visitors to the top of the hill and views of downtown Sitka and waterfront. Interpretive panels focus on the history of this site. There is no fee to explore the park. 101 Harbor Dr; Sitka, AK 99835; http://www.alaska.org/detail/castle-hill-trail

Saint Michael's Cathedral was the first Russian Orthodox church in North America. Constructed in traditional style it was built between 1844 and 1848. Although it burned down in 1966, an exact replica was built and many of the artifacts that had been saved are on display in the new cathedral. 240 Lincoln St; Sitka, AK 99835; Phone: (907) 747-8120; https://stmichaelcathedral.org

Sitka National Historical Park is a day-use urban park with several hiking trails. The Totem Trail and the adjacent grounds feature 18 replica and original totem poles carved by Alaska Native carvers. The park is also home to the extraordinary collection of photographs by Elbridge W. Merrill who photographed Sitka and its Tlingit population for 30 years between 1899 and 1929. Visitors can learn about early Russian colonial history and its legacy at the restored Russian Bishop's

House. There is no entrance fee. The visitor center is open all year with seasonal days and hours. Russian Bishop's House is open summers only. 103 Monastery St; Sitka, AK 99835; Phone: (907) 747-0110; https://www.nps.gov/sitk/index.htm

Skagway, AK is generally reached by air or water. Although it is possible to drive to Skagway from Juneau visitors will need to go part of the way by ferry.
Gold Rush Cemetery, located four miles out of town, is the final resting place of many of the town's famous Gold Rush characters. Walk to the cemetery from town or take the SMART bus shuttle to a stop ½ mile from the cemetery. Pick up a trail map from the Skagway Visitor Information Center open Monday through Friday 8 AM to 5 PM. Note: Hours are seasonal. 245 Broadway; Skagway, AK 99840; Phone: (907) 983-2854. The National Park Visitor Center for the Klondike Gold Rush National Historic Park listed below also provides this information.

Klondike Gold Rush National Historic Park encompasses over 20 historical buildings with four museums illuminating the story of the Alaskan Gold Rush and the life in early Skagway. Open seasonally early to mid- May through mid-September. The National Park Service offers several free walking tours. Note: Tours of some buildings will incur a fee. The visitor center screens a 30-minute overview of the area and its gold rush history. Admission is free. May through late September open daily from 8:30 AM to 5:30 PM. October through April open Monday through Friday 8 AM to 3 PM. Closed federal holidays. 291 Broadway; Skagway, AK 99840; Phone: (907) 983-9200; https://www.nps.gov/klgo/index.htm

Valdez, AK is accessible by highway from Fairbanks, and Anchorage, or by air from Anchorage.
Maxine & Jesse Whitney Museum offers a large collections of Native Alaskan art and artifacts. Admission is free. Open daily Memorial Day through Labor Day from 9 AM to 7 PM. Call ahead if you wish to visit in winter. 303 Lowe St; Valdez, AK 99686; Phone: (907)834-1690; http://www.mjwhitneymuseum.org

Arizona

> *Best known for the popular and fee-based Grand Canyon, Arizona also has rich cowboy, outlaw, and Native American history, and its ghost towns attest to its mining boom past.*

Anthem, AZ
Anthem Veterans Memorial can be visited free any time during the year, but every Veteran's Day at 11:11 AM the sun shines through the five marble pillars representing the military branches and creates a representation of the mosaic medallion of the Great Seal of the United States at the foot of the pillars. Designed and engineered by Renee Palmer-Jones and Jim Martin of Anthem, Arizona, the memorial is free and open to visitors Monday through Sunday from 6 AM to 10 PM. 41703 N Gavilan Peak Pkwy; Anthem, AZ 85086; Phone: (623) 742-6050; http://www.onlineatanthem.com/visitors/veterans_memorial/index.php

Bowie, AZ
Fort Bowie National Historic Site invites bird-watching, hiking, and wildlife viewing. But there's also the ruins of Fort Bowie and exhibits inside the visitor center. The cemetery which actually predates the fort is still there. There is no admission fee. The park is open daily sunrise to sunset. 3500 S Apache Pass Rd; Bowie, AZ 85605; Phone (520) 847-2500; https://www.nps.gov/fobo/index.htm

Chinle, AZ
Canyon de Chelly National Monument was the home of the Ancestral Puebloans. Two paved drives shadow the rim and lead to the overlooks which provide excellent views of the canyon below. There are fee-based tours available from private companies, but there's also scheduled free events by park rangers. Visitor center is open daily from 8 AM to 5 PM. Closed on Thanksgiving, Christmas, and New Year's Day. The park entrance and visitor center is about 3 miles from Highway 191. Phone: (928) 674-5500; https://www.nps.gov/cach/index.htm

Coolidge AZ
Casa Grande Ruins National Monument preserves an Ancestral Sonoran desert people's farming community and Great House. Stop by the visitor center museum and pick up a copy of the park's official map and guide. The auditorium screens a 22-minute orientation film. Guided tours are offered from late November to mid-April. Take a self-guided tour around the Casa Grande following wayside signs.

Admission is free. Open 9 AM to 4 PM daily. October through the end of April open daily until 5 PM. Closed Thanksgiving, Christmas, and July 4th Independence Day. 1100 W Ruins Dr; Coolidge, AZ 85128; Phone: (520) 723-3172; https://www.nps.gov/cagr/index.htm

Deer Valley, AZ

Gateway Classic Cars is a classic and exotic car dealership – one of several across the country. Their back showroom is filled with gorgeous classic cars and they welcome browsers. 22275 N 23rd Ave; Deer Valley, AZ 85027; Phone: (623) 900-4884; http://gatewayclassiccars.com/locations?location=SCT

Flagstaff, AZ

Flagstaff offers visitors urban hiking with over a dozen trails. The most popular is the Nate Avery Trail that makes a two-mile loop around Buffalo Park atop the ancient lava flow now known as McMillan Mesa. The trail offers panorama views. https://www.flagstaff.az.gov/1763/FUTS-Trail-Descriptions

Art Museum at Northern Arizona University specializes in curated exhibitions and diverse collections. Admission is free. Open during exhibitions Tuesday through Saturday Noon to 5 PM. Closed all university holidays. Building 10; Old Main; 620 S Knoles Dr; Flagstaff, AZ 86011; Phone: (928) 523-3471; https://nau.edu/artmuseum

Florence, AZ

Florence Copper Site Tour showcases their mining operation. Tours are held several times per month, lasting about two hours. Reservations are required but there is no charge. Phone: (520) 374-3984; https://florencecopper.com/show-your-support/tour-our-site

Ganado, AZ

Hubbell Trading Post is the oldest operating trading post on the Navajo Nation. Visitors come to admire and shop for the art, jewelry, and rugs. The Hubbell family operated the trading post until 1967 when it was sold to the National Park Service. The visitor center offers interpretive exhibits on the Hubbell family, the trading post, and the Long Walk. The visitor center is free to visit but there is a fee to tour the Hubbell home. Note: When a park ranger is conducting a house tour the visitor center will be temporarily closed. Milepost 446.3 on AZ- 264; Ganado, AZ 86505; Phone: (928) 755-3475; https://www.nps.gov/hutr/index.htm

Glendale, AZ

Historic Sahuaro Ranch offers a look at Arizona ranch life from the late 1800s to the 1930s. Explore the 13 original buildings set amid 17 acres including a rose garden, barnyard, and historic orchards. Admission and tours are free. The site is open 6 AM to sunset. Tours are provided September through May on Friday,

Saturday, and Sunday. June and July tours are available on Friday and Saturday. 9802 N 59th Ave; Glendale, AZ 85302; Phone: (623) 930-4200; https://www.glendaleaz.com

Mesa, AZ
Mesa Arts Center Museum showcases curated and juried exhibitions of contemporary art. Admission is free. Open Tuesday, Wednesday, Friday, and Saturday from 10 AM to 5 PM. Open late Thursday until 8 PM. Open Sunday from Noon to 5 PM. Closed major holidays. 1 E Main St; Mesa, AZ 85201; Phone: (480) 644-6560; https://www.mesaartscenter.com/index.php/museum/visit

Page, AZ
Carl Hayden Visitor Center at Glen Canyon Dam provides interactive exhibits, introductory films, and a relief map of the entire Glen Canyon area. Visitors can view the dam and exhibits about the Ancestral Puebloans, and the dam's construction. Tours of the dam will incur a fee. Open daily 8 AM. November through February closes at 4 PM. Mid-May through mid-September closes at 6 PM. The rest of the year closes at 5 PM. US-89; Page, AZ 86040; Phone: (928) 608-6072; https://www.nps.gov/glca/index.htm

Phoenix, AZ (See also Tempe, AZ)
Arizona State Capitol Complex includes the Arizona Capitol Museum and the State Library. The museum highlights the story of the government of the 48th state and features four floors filled with more than 20 exhibition areas. Although admission is nominally free they request a donation of $1 to $5 per person. Note: This would disqualify inclusion, but it is the State Capitol. Open Monday through Friday from 9 AM to 4 PM. From May to September it is also open on Saturday from 10 AM to 2 PM. 1700 W Washington St; Phoenix, AZ 85007; Phone: (602) 926-3620; https://azlibrary.gov/azcm

Penske Racing Museum enables visitors to peruse the cars, trophies, and racing memorabilia amassed by the Penske family. There is no admission charge. Open Monday through Saturday from 8 AM to 4 PM and Sunday from Noon to 5 PM. 7125 E Chauncey La; Phoenix, AZ 85054; Phone: (480) 538-4444; http://www.penskeracingmuseum.com/the-penske-racing-museum.aspx

South Mountain Park is home to thousands of petroglyphs created by the Hohokam people. There is no admission fee. Open daily 5 AM to 7 PM. Trails are open later. Note: Bring water. Temperatures during the summer can top 100

degrees. 10919 S Central Ave; Phoenix, AZ 85042; Phone: (602) 262-7398; https://www.phoenix.gov/parks/trails/locations/south-mountain

Wells Fargo History Museum offers a large display of N.C. Wyeth's western-themed work. There's also an authentic 19th century stagecoach, and a replica stagecoach for kids to climb. No entrance fee. Open Monday through Friday from 9 AM to 5 PM. 100 W Washington St; Phoenix, AZ 85003; Phone: (602) 378-1852; https://www.wellsfargohistory.com/museums/phoenix

Scottsdale, AZ
McDowell Sonoran Preserve is famous for the magnificent Sonoran Desert which covers a whole swath of the Southwest and is home to two unique and fascinating species of cacti – the saguaro and the organ pipe cacti. The preserve has over 180 miles of well-maintained trails. There is no charge for access. Open daily from sunrise to sunset. Note: Remember to bring lots of water. Phone: (480) 998-7971; https://www.mcdowellsonoran.org

Sedona, AZ
Although several of the iconic places in Sedona charge admission, driving through the mountains and valleys is free, and spectacular. One favorite is the Coconino National Forest. If you park and hike, you'll have to pay a fee, but drives are lovely and the pull-offs offer rich vistas. Arizona State Route 89A, starting just south of Flagstaff takes you through switchbacks into scenic Oak Creek Canyon, known for colorful rocks and unique formations. Tlaquepaque Arts and Crafts Village is the place to go for shopping. Set up like a sprawling, charming town, it's filled with shops, galleries, restaurants, and fountains. Well worth a look. https://www.tlaq.com

Amitabha Stupa and Peace Park inspires calm contemplation. There are two stupas (or temples) – 36-foot Amitabha Stupa and the smaller Tara Stupa. The Peace Park is free although donations are accepted. Open daily dawn until dusk. 2650 Pueblo Dr; Sedona, AZ 86336; Phone: (877) 788-7229; https://www.tara.org/featured_post/amitabha-stupa

Chapel of the Holy Cross is a place of quiet reflection. Its striking architecture and spectacular views have made it a popular tourist destination. 80 Chapel Rd; Sedona, AZ 86336; Phone: (928) 282-4069; https://www.gatewaytosedona.com/the-chapel-of-the-holy-cross-sedona-architectural-landmark

Shonto, AZ
Navajo National Monument is tucked into the northwest portion of the Navajo Nation in northern Arizona. The cliff dwellings of the Ancestral Puebloan date back 1250 to 1300 AD. Three trails, open sunrise to sunset, start at the visitor

center. There is no admission fee. The park offers free guided tours during the summer season. Open daily all year from 8 AM to 5:30 PM. Highway 564; Shonto, AZ 86054; Phone: (928) 672-2700; https://www.nps.gov/nava/index.htm

Tempe, AZ (See also Phoenix, AZ)
Arizona State University operates two very different spaces to explore visual and performance art. Admission to both is free. **ASU Art Museum at Nelson Fine Arts Center** is a visually striking building designed by famed Albuquerque-based architect Antione Predock. It provides three floors of year-round exhibitions that rotate seasonally. Open Tuesday through Saturday from 11 AM to 5 PM. During the academic semester it closes at 8 PM on Thursday. Closed university holidays. 51 E 10th St; Tempe, AZ 85281; Phone: (480) 965-2787; https://asuartmuseum.asu.edu/visit/asu-art-museum **Ceramics Research Center at Brickyard** displays the museum's almost 4,000 piece ceramic collection. Admission is free. Note: Use the free parking at the ASU Art Museum and visit both museums without parking charges. 699 S Mill Ave; Suite 108; Tempe, AZ 85281; Phone: (480) 727-8170; https://asuartmuseum.asu.edu/visit/ceramics-research-center

Tucson, AZ
Center for Creative Photography highlights some of the 20th century's most important photographers as well as collects individual photographs from over 2,200 artists. Free to visit. Open Tuesday through Friday 9 AM to 4 PM and Saturday from 1 PM to 4 PM. 1030 N Olive Rd; Tucson, AZ 85721; Phone: (520) 621-7968; http://www.creativephotography.org

Fort Lowell Museum replicates the Commanding Officers quarters, circa 1885, displaying permanent and changing exhibits of military artifacts. Free admission, donations welcome. There is a charge for guided tours. Open Thursday through Saturday 10 AM to 4 PM. 2900 N Craycroft Rd; Tucson, AZ 85712; Phone: (520) 885-3832; http://www.arizonahistoricalsociety.org/tucson

Kitt Peak Visitor Center is the public face of the Arizona location of the National Solar Observatory. It's actually 56 miles outside of Tucson on the Tohono O'odham Nation. Admission is free to the visitor center as well as to the observatory grounds but a guided tour will incur a cost. The 7,000-foot mountaintop also offers 100-mile views of Arizona. The free activities include interpretative exhibits as well as viewing galleries. Open 9 AM to 3:45 PM. Closed Thanksgiving, Christmas, and New Year's Day. Note: They suggest calling "before ascending the mountain." Route 386; Tohono O'odham Nation; Phone: (520) 318-8726; https://www.noao.edu/kpvc/Plan

Pharmacy Museum provides a unique glimpse into the country's pharmaceutical past. There's even a replica of an old-time drugstore. Admission is free. Free guided tours are generally available January to March on Monday through Friday from 8 AM to Noon or by appointment. University holidays excluded. Skaggs Pharmaceutical Sciences Center & Drachman Hall; 1295 N Martin Ave; Tucson, AZ 85721; Phone: (520) 626-1042; http://www.pharmacy.arizona.edu/centers/history-pharmacy-museum

Yuma, AZ

Pivot Point Interpretative Plaza celebrates Yuma's history at the exact site where the first railroad train entered Arizona in 1877. The centerpiece is the 1907 Baldwin locomotive sited on the original track alignment. An audio system re-creates the atmosphere. Informative panels and photographs round out the experience. Pivot Point Interpretative Plaza is a free city park at the river, open daily from 6 AM to 11 PM; Madison Ave; http://www.visityuma.com/pivot-point.html

Willcox, AZ

Chiricahua National Monument is famous for its pinnacles of rhyolite rock. A volcanic explosion 27 million years ago spewed ash and debris that compacted and eroded into the park's signature *tuff* pillars. Explore the park through the eight-mile paved scenic drive and 17 miles of day-use hiking trails. Visit the Faraway Ranch Historic District and the home of the Erickson family who worked to establish the Chiricahua National Monument. There is no entrance fee. The park is open all day year round. Visitor center is open daily 8:30 AM to 4:30 PM. Follow the signs to the monument from the junction of Highway 186 and Arizona State Highway 181. Willcox, AZ 85643; Phone: (520) 824-3560; https://www.nps.gov/chir/index.htm

Arkansas

Bentonville, AR
Crystal Bridges Museum of American Art was designed by Moshe Safdie to include a series of pavilions. Among the must-see art is the Norman Rockwell 1943 painting of Rosie the Riveter and the famous Gilbert Stuart painting of George Washington. There's also a Frank Lloyd Wright classic Usonian house located on the grounds and more than 3½ miles of trails winding through the Ozark landscape. The museum is free to visit, although there may be a fee to view special exhibitions. Crystal Bridges trails and grounds are open from sunrise to sunset daily. Museum is open Monday from 11 AM to 6 PM. On Wednesday, Thursday, and Friday open from 11 AM to 9 PM. Open Saturday and Sunday from 10 AM to 6 PM. 600 Museum Way; Bentonville, AR 72712; Phone: (479) 418-5700; http://crystalbridges.org

Gann Museum of Saline County remains the only building in the country made of bauxite ore. Beyond this unusual material, the 1893 building was the medical office of Dr. Dewell Gann. In addition to items of historical interest the Gann hosts an extensive collection of Niloak Pottery -- an art ceramic created in Benton from 1910 through 1947. Free admission with donations welcomed. Open Thursday through Saturday from 9 AM to 3 PM. 218 S Market St; Benton, AR 72015; Phone: (501) 778-5513; https://www.gannmuseum.com

Museum of Native American History delivers a glimpse into life as experienced by Native Americans with artifacts dating back 14,000 years – from the mammoths and Clovis man through the Mississippian villages, and farmsteads. Free admission. Open Monday through Saturday from 9 AM to 5 PM. 202 SW O St; Bentonville, AR 72712; Phone: (479) 273-2456; http://www.monah.us

Walmart Museum lets visitors see where the Walmart phenomenon started. It's filled with the history of Sam Walton and Walmart, including a video of Sam doing a hula on Wall Street and the reason why. There's also plenty of retro toys, candy, and souvenirs. 105 N Main St; Bentonville, AR 72712; Phone: (479) 273-1329; https://www.walmartmuseum.com

Eureka Springs, AR
Thorncrown Chapel is considered an architectural treasure with 425 windows and over 6,000 square feet of glass atop over 100 tons of native stone and colored

flagstone. There is no admission fee, but donations are accepted. Open daily from April through November from 9 AM to 5 PM. Note: On weekends and some weekdays the chapel occasionally closes early for special events. Closed all day on Saturdays in November. Reduced hours in March and December. The public is invited to attend Sunday services. Check the website for schedule. 12968 Hwy 62 W; Eureka Springs, AR 72632; Phone: (479) 253-7401; https://thorncrown.com

Fayetteville, AR

University of Arkansas Museum display selections from its 7 million objects from the fields of archeology, ethnography, geology, history, and zoology. No admission fee. Open Monday through Friday from 8 AM to 5 PM. University of Arkansas Collection Facility (enter through the Arkansas Archeological Survey) 2475 N Hatch Ave; Fayetteville, AR 72704; Phone: (479) 575-3456; https://fulbright.uark.edu/university-museum

Fort Smith, AR

Bass Reeves Monument honors the lawman believed to be the first black U.S. deputy marshal west of the Mississippi. Reeves was born a slave but served for 32 years under Federal Judge Isaac C. Parker. Parker was believed to have sentenced 160 people to death, and for 14 years he did so while the condemned had no right of appeal – giving him the appellation of *Hanging Judge* of the American Old West. 200 Garrison Ave; Fort Smith, AR 72901; Phone: (479) 783-8888; https://www.fortsmith.org/bass-reeves-monument

Camp Chaffee Barbershop Museum is the original barbershop of the military post Camp Chaffee, and where Elvis Presley received his famous G.I. haircut. Restored to its 1958 condition, it also depicts the 70-year history of Fort Chaffee and the people who were there over the decades. Admission is free. Open Monday through Saturday from 9 AM to 4 PM. Closed on national holidays. 7313 Terry St; Fort Smith, AR 72916; Phone: (479) 785-1839; http://chaffeecrossing.com/index.php?page=museums

Fort Smith Air Museum honors pioneer and military aviators from western Arkansas and eastern Oklahoma. The display cases are located across from the ticket counters, near the main entrance, and by the baggage claim area. There is no admission fee. Open Monday through Sunday from 5:30 AM to 11 PM. Fort Smith Regional Airport; 6700 McKennon Blvd; Fort Smith, AR 72903; Phone: (479) 785-1839; http://www.fortsmithairmuseum.com

Miss Laura's Social Club and Visitors Center started as a brothel, and by all accounts a very successful one. The house of ill repute flourished until it closed permanently in 1948. The building then became the official Visitors Center for Fort Smith. It's been restored and is open for tours. Admission is free. Open Monday through Saturday from 9 AM to 4 PM. Open Sunday from 1 PM to 4:30 PM. 2 N B St; Fort Smith, AR 72901; Phone: (479) 783-8888; http://www.fortsmith.org/miss-lauras-visitor-center

Gillette, AR

Arkansas Post Museum contains five exhibit buildings that explore life on Arkansas's Grand Prairie and in the Arkansas Delta from 1877 to today. Admission to the museum is free. Open Tuesday through Saturday from 8 AM to 5 PM and on Sunday from 1 PM to 5 PM. 5530 Hwy 165 S; Gillett, AR 72055; Phone: (870) 548-2634; https://www.arkansasstateparks.com/parks/arkansas-post-museum

Heber Spring, AR

Greers Ferry Lake National Fish Hatchery offers self-guided tours and free admission. Open daily from 7 AM to 3 PM including weekends and most major federal holidays. Closed Thanksgiving and December 24th and 25th. 49 Hatchery Rd; Heber Springs, AR 72543; Phone: (501) 362-3615; https://www.fws.gov/greersferry

William Carl Garner Visitor Center presents the history of early exploration of the area, the events that led to the building of Greers Ferry Dam, and detailed information on the purpose and history of the Greers Ferry Lake, dam, and power plant. Admission is free. Open daily from 8 AM to 4:30 PM from mid-May to mid-September. Open the rest of the year Monday to Friday from 8 AM to 4:30 PM. 700 Heber Springs Rd N; Heber Springs, AR 72543; Phone: (501) 362-9067; https://www.swl.usace.army.mil/Missions/Recreation/Lakes/Greers-Ferry-Lake

Helena, AR

Delta Cultural Center presents the history and music of the Arkansas Delta and its counties through interactive exhibits, restored historic buildings, and interpretive outdoor sites.
Delta Cultural Center Depot provides visitors with an overview of Delta history. Admission is free. Open Tuesday through Saturday from 9 AM to 5 PM. 95 Missouri St; Helena, AR 72342; Phone: (870) 338-4350; http://www.deltaculturalcenter.com/venues/depot

Delta Cultural Center Visitors Center is comprised of three interconnected buildings and is home to Delta Sounds, a state-of-the-art music area dedicated to the music of the Arkansas Delta. There's also an operating radio studio within the museum. Admission is free. Open Tuesday through Saturday from 9 AM to 5 PM. 141 Cherry St; Helena, AR 72342; Phone: (870) 338-4350; http://www.deltaculturalcenter.com/venues/visitors-center

Museum of Phillips County highlights a large collection from the Thomas A. Edison Foundation, a growing assemblage of military uniforms and equipment from U.S. wars. Admission is free with donations gladly accepted. Open Wednesday through Friday from10 AM to 4 PM and on Saturday from 10 AM to 2 PM. 623 Pecan St; Helena, AR 72342; Phone: (870) 338-7790; http://www.helenamuseum.com

Hope, AR
President William Jefferson Clinton Birthplace Home celebrates the history of the man who became 42nd President of the United States of America. Tours of the Clinton Birthplace Home are offered every 30 minutes, beginning at 9 AM. There is no charge to tour the home. 412 Division St; Hope, AR 71801; Phone: (870) 777-4455; https://www.nps.gov/wicl/index.htm

Hot Springs, AR
Hot Springs National Park harkens back to an era of wealth and elegance. There is no charge to stroll past the graceful buildings and tours of the once opulent Fordyce Bathhouse are also free, as is the outdoor guided tours offered in summer. Note: Spa services and bathing in the hot springs incurs a cost. 369 Central Ave; Hot Springs, AR 71901; Phone: (501) 620-6715; https://www.nps.gov/hosp/index.htm

Jonesboro, AR
Arkansas State University Museum highlights the lives of early settlers with artifacts from the farming and timber industries as well as everyday household tools. There's also the Crowley's Ridge Mastodon, several specialized galleries, and recreated lanes lined with shops and stores. All are free to the public. Open Monday through Friday from 9 AM to 5 PM. Open Tuesday until 7 PM. Open Saturday from 10 AM to 5 PM. Closed university holidays. 320 University Loop W; Jonesboro, AR 72401; Phone: (870) 972-2074; https://www.astate.edu/a/museum

Lincoln, AR
Arkansas Country Doctor Museum served as the home of three doctors and as a primary clinic from 1936 to 1973. The museum focuses on the life of a small town doctor and the history of medicine as it was practiced in the early 20th century. Admission is free. Open Wednesday through Saturday from 1 PM to 4 PM. 109

N Starr Ave; Lincoln, AR 72744; Phone: (479) 824-4307;
http://www.drmuseum.net

Little Rock, AR (See also Scott, AR)

Arkansas Arts Center offers an international collection of art including drawings, contemporary craft, paintings, photographs and prints. Admission is free with the exception of special ticketed exhibitions. Open Tuesday through Saturday from 10 AM to 5 PM and on Sunday from 11 AM to 5 PM. 9th & Commerce; MacArthur Park; Little Rock, AR 72203; Phone: (501) 372-4000;
http://www.arkansasartscenter.org

Arkansas State Capitol invites visitors to watch legislators at work when in session. Changing exhibits and permanent installations focus on the construction of the building, and the people of Arkansas. The free tours of the Capitol Building are offered weekdays 9 AM to 3 PM. Pick up self-guided tour booklets at the visitor center on the first floor of the Capitol. 500 Woodlane St; Little Rock, AR 72201; Phone: (501) 682-1010;
http://www.sos.arkansas.gov/stateCapitolInfo/Pages/default.aspx

Little Rock Central High School National Historic Site gained notoriety in 1957 when Black students attempted to attend the previously all-white school. It was the implementation of the Supreme Court decision Brown v. Board of Education (1954) that stated separate is inherently unequal. Still used as a school, the only way into Central High School is with a Ranger-guided tour. These tours are by reservation only and are offered twice a day on weekdays except holidays and school breaks. Tours start at the visitor center. There is no charge to enter the visitor center, grounds of Little Rock Central High School National Historic Site or to take any of the guided tours. 2120 W Daisy Gatson Bates Dr; Little Rock, AR 72202; Phone: (501) 374-1957; https://www.nps.gov/chsc/index.htm

MacArthur Museum of Arkansas Military History preserves the contributions of Arkansas men and women who served in the armed forces. Located in the Tower Building of the Little Rock Arsenal. Admission is free with donations appreciated. Open Monday through Saturday from 9 AM to 4 PM, and Sunday from 1 PM to 4 PM. Closed Thanksgiving, Christmas Eve, Christmas Day, and New Year's Day. 503 E Ninth St; Little Rock, AR 72202; Phone: (501) 376-4602;
https://www.littlerock.gov/for-residents/parks-and-recreation/macarthur-museum-of-arkansas-military-history

Old State House saw Arkansas admitted to the Union, and it was within its walls that the state voted to secede from that union. Exhibits focus on the history of the

Old State House and on aspects of politics and culture. For fashion-oriented visitors *First Ladies of Arkansas: Women of Their Times* contains the largest exhibition of First Ladies' gowns outside the Smithsonian. Admission is free. Open Monday through Saturday from 9 AM to 5 PM. Open Sunday from 1 PM to 5 PM. Closed Thanksgiving, Christmas Eve, Christmas, and New Year's Day. 300 W Markham St; Little Rock, AR 72201; Phone: (501) 324-9685; http://www.oldstatehouse.com

Testament: The Little Rock Nine Monument stands to honor the Little Rock Nine, the Black students who integrated Little Rock Central High School in 1957. Located at Arkansas State Capitol. 1 Capitol Mall; Little Rock, AR, 72201; https://civilrightstrail.com/attraction/little-rock-nine-memorial-at-state-capitol

University of Arkansas Art Galleries features work by emerging and established artists. Admission is free and open to the public. Open Monday through Friday from 9 AM to 5 PM. From Labor Day to mid-May the gallery is also open Saturday from 10 AM to 1 PM, and Sunday from 2 PM to 5 PM. Closed university holidays. 2801 S University Ave; Little Rock, AR 72204; Phone: (501) 569-3182; http://ualr.edu/art/galleries

Vogel Schwartz Sculpture Garden and Sculpture at the River Market presents over 90 works of public art along the banks of the Arkansas River. Most of the sculpture is installed in the Vogel Schwartz Sculpture Garden. Admission is free. Riverfront Park; Little Rock, AR 72201; Phone: (501) 539-0913; http://sculptureattherivermarket.com

Wildwood Park for the Arts delivers themed gardens. Several times a year Wildwood creates art exhibits that are also free and open to the public. There is a charge for festivals and special events. Open Monday through Friday from 9 AM to 5 PM. Open Saturday from 10 AM to 5 PM, and on Sunday from Noon to 5 PM. 20919 Denny Rd; Little Rock, AR 72223; Phone: (501) 821-7275; http://www.wildwoodpark.org

Witt Stephens Jr. Central Arkansas Nature Center overlooks the Arkansas River within the Julius Breckling Riverfront Park and features live native animals, interactive exhibits, cypress swamps, delta marshlands and a bottomland hardwood forest. Open Tuesday through Saturday from 8:30 AM to 4:30 PM. Open Sunday from 1 PM to 5 PM. Closed major holidays. 602 President Clinton Ave; Little Rock, AR 72201; Phone: (501) 907-0636; http://www.centralarkansasnaturecenter.com

Lonoke, AR

Joe Hogan State Fish Hatchery is one of the United States' largest fish hatcheries, with 56 ponds that produce nearly 4 million fish each year. Lee Brady Visitor Center has displays including aquariums and mounted species native to the area. Free tours available. The visitor center is open Monday through Friday from 8 AM to 4 PM. The hatchery grounds are open daily from daylight to dark. 23 Joe Hogan Ln; Lonoke, AR 72086; Phone: (877) 676-6963; https://www.stateparks.com/hogan_state_fish_hatchery_in_arkansas.html

Pine Bluff, AR

Arkansas Entertainers Hall of Fame showcases the careers of famous Arkansas sons and daughters in the entertainment world, and their musical instruments and costumes. There's also an animatronic Johnny Cash singing his hits. Free admission. Inside the Pine Bluff Convention Center. Open Monday through Friday from 9 AM to 5 PM. Closed major holidays. 500 E Eighth Ave; Pine Bluff, AR 71601; Phone: (870) 536-7600; https://www.arkansas.com/attractions-culture/arkansas-entertainers-hall-fame

Arkansas Railroad Museum started with Engine 819 but today includes passenger cars, cabooses, and baggage cars as well as many artifacts from that era. Admission is free, however donations are appreciated. Generally open Monday through Saturday from 9 AM to 2 PM however extreme heat or cold can affect hours of operation. 1700 Port Rd; Pine Bluff, AR 71601; Phone: (870) 535-8819; http://www.arkansasrailroadmuseum.org

Pine Bluff/Jefferson County Historical Museum has Civil War and World War II artifacts, Victorian furniture, clothing, quilts, and antique dolls, plus tools and cotton farming implements. The M=museum is located in the restored Union Station train depot. There is no admission fee. Open Monday through Friday from 9 AM to 4 PM. Open Saturday from 10 AM to 2 PM. 201 E Fourth St; Pine Bluff, AR 71601; Phone: (870) 541-5402; https://www.arkansas.com/pine-bluffjefferson-county-historical-museum

Rogers, AR

Rogers Historical Museum explores the history of northwest Arkansas from the pioneers to the beginning of the urbanization and more recent past. A special children's area makes this a family-friendly place as well. A middle class Victorian house has been restored to the early 1900s time period with furnishings displayed as it would have been when the Hawkins family called it home. Temporary exhibits provide a deeper look into the history. Admission is free. Open Monday through Saturday from 10 AM to 5 PM. 313 S Second St; Rogers, AR 72756; Phone: (479) 621-1154; http://www.rogershistoricalmuseum.org

Scott, AR (See also Little Rock, AR)

Plantation Agriculture Museum is housed in a series of buildings. The main museum was a general store in 1912. The Dortch Gin Exhibit contains a 1916 cotton gin. Visitors can also explore the Seed Warehouse #5 and a historic tractor exhibit. Open Tuesday through Saturday from 8 AM to 5 PM and on Sunday from 1 PM to 5 PM. Closed major holidays. 4815 AR Hwy 161 S; Scott, AR 72142; Phone: (501) 961-1409; https://www.arkansasstateparks.com/parks/plantation-agriculture-museum

Toltec Mounds Archeological State Park dates to the prehistoric Late Woodland period and protects an 18-mound complex with the tallest surviving prehistoric mounds in Arkansas. Visitors may also be able to watch actual archeological research. The visitor center exhibits and self-guided tours are free. Any guided activities require a fee. Open Tuesday through Saturday from 8 AM to 5 PM and on Sunday from 1 PM to 5 PM. Closed major holidays. 490 Toltec Mounds Rd; Scott, AR 72142; Phone: (501) 961-9442; https://www.arkansasstateparks.com/parks/toltec-mounds-archeological-state-park

Smackover, AR

Arkansas Museum of Natural Resources celebrates the pioneers of south Arkansas's oil, and brine industries. Visitors can see operating examples of the historic oil producing methods. Inside the museum, tour a reproduction of a boomtown with an old jail and cafe. There is no fee to visit. Open Monday through Saturday 8 AM to 5 PM. Open Sunday from 1 PM to 5 PM. Closed several major holidays. 3853 Smackover Hwy; Smackover, AR 71762; Phone: (870) 725-2877; http://www.amnr.org/index.html

Springdale AR

Shiloh Museum of Ozark History takes its name from the pioneer community of Shiloh (which became Springdale in the 1870s). Along with exhibits, visitors can explore six historic buildings on the museum grounds. Admission is free. Open Monday through Saturday 10 AM to 5 PM. Closed major holidays. 118 W Johnson Ave; Springdale, AR 72764; Phone: (479) 750-8165; http://www.shilohmuseum.org/index.php

Stuttgart, AR

Museum of the Arkansas Grand Prairie depicts the life of the pioneers who farmed the Grand Prairie from the 1800s to 1921 with five furnished buildings and a recreation of Stuttgart with dirt streets, wooden sidewalks as well as stores, and shops. Admission is free. Open Tuesday through Friday from 8 AM to 4 PM. Open on Saturday from 10 AM to 4 PM. Closed legal holidays. 921 E Fourth St;

Stuttgart, AR 72160; Phone: (870) 673-7001;
http://www.grandprairiemuseum.org

Wilson, AR
Hampson Archeological Museum State Park interprets the lifestyles of the
farming-based people who lived there between 1400 and 1650 AD. Admission is
free. Open Tuesday through Saturday from 8 AM to 5 PM. Open Sunday from 1
PM to 5 PM. Closed major holidays. 33 Park Ave on the Town Square; Wilson,
AR 72395; Phone: (870) 655-8622;
https://www.arkansasstateparks.com/parks/hampson-archeological-museum-state-
park

California

Home state to the rich and famous, California has more to offer than just their lifestyles.

Chico, CA
National Yo-Yo Museum is dedicated to that once popular toy with memorabilia displays and even a working, 256-pound wooden yo-yo. With the assistance of a large crane and a skilled operator, Big-Yo can go up and down along its string. Free and open Monday through Saturday from 10 AM to 6 PM and on Sunday from Noon to 5 PM. 320 Broadway St; Chico, CA 95928; Phone: (530) 893-0545; https://nationalyoyo.org

Colma, CA
Colma's fame as the city of cemeteries started in 1900 when nearby San Francisco forbid new burials within city limits. Where were the dead to go? Many went to Colma.

Holy Cross Catholic Cemetery is the oldest and largest cemetery and provides a walking tour brochure of its famous and infamous residents. Pick up a copy at the reception desk in the main office. 1500 Mission Rd; Colma, CA 94014; Phone: (650) 756-2060; http://www.holycrosscemeteries.com/locations/colma.htm

Culver City, CA (also see Los Angeles, CA)
Wende Museum has amassed art, artifacts, and personal histories that record life, expression, and political developments in Eastern Europe and the Soviet Union during the Cold War. Admission to all exhibitions, tours, and public programs is free. Open Friday from 10 AM to 9 PM. Open Saturday and Sunday from 10 AM to 5 PM. 10808 Culver Blvd; Culver City, CA 90230; Phone: (310) 216-1600; https://www.wendemuseum.org

Stoneview Nature Center provides scenic views, garden spaces, artwork, a demonstration garden, and visitor center. Admission is free. Open daily from 8 AM to 5 PM. 5950 Stoneview Dr; Culver City, CA 90232; Phone: (310) 202-3001; http://bhc.ca.gov/stoneview-nature-center

El Cajon, CA
Taylor Guitar Factory is open for free, guided tours that cover the manufacture of these prized instruments. No advance registration is required but visitors must check-in at the receptionist desk in the lobby at least 10 minutes before the tour time. Tours are currently given Monday through Friday at 1 PM, although these

times are subject to change. 1980 Gillespie Way; El Cajon, CA 92020; Phone: (619) 258-1207; https://www.taylorguitars.com/contact/factory-tours

Fairfield, CA
Jelly Belly Factory invites visitors to take the free self-guided tour along a ¼-mile path above the factory. There are interactive exhibits, videos, and games along the way as wells as free samples. Visitor center is open 9 AM to 5 PM with factory tours from 9:15 AM to 4 PM. Closed major holidays. Note: There is a fee-based guided tour option as well. 1 Jelly Belly La; Fairfield, CA 94533; Phone: (800) 953-5592; https://www.jellybelly.com/california-factory-tours

Joshua Tree, CA
Noah Purifoy Desert Art Museum of Assemblage Art is constructed entirely from junked materials and fills ten acres with large-scale sculptures. It is considered one of California's great folk art historical wonders. Free of charge. Open daily from sunrise to sunset. Sign in at the welcome kiosk near the mailboxes and take a brochure for a self-guided tour. 63030 Blair La; Joshua Tree, CA 92252; http://www.noahpurifoy.com

Los Angeles, CA (See also Culver City, CA)
Berlin Wall Project is an outreach of the Wende Museum and is part of the museum's permanent collection. Ten of the wall segments are currently on public display. The Wende commissioned four artists to paint on five of their segments. 5900 Wilshire Blvd; Los Angeles, CA 90036.

Fowler Museum at UCLA emphasizes works from Africa, Asia, the Pacific, and the Americas. Admission is free. Open Wednesday through Sunday from Noon to 5 PM with extended closing until 8 PM on Wednesday. Closed major holidays. Sunset Blvd and Westwood Plaza; Los Angeles, CA 90095; Phone: (310) 825-4361; https://www.fowler.ucla.edu

Getty Center offers beautiful gardens, open spaces, spectacular views of Los Angeles, and art indoors and out. Indoors enjoy photography, paintings, drawings, sculpture, even illuminated manuscripts, and decorative arts. Outside, stroll among 28 pieces of contemporary sculptures. The **Getty Research Institute Gallery** offers changing exhibitions of rare books, manuscripts, artists' notebooks, and other materials from its special collections. Admission to the Getty Center is free. Open Tuesday through Friday from 10 AM to 5:30 PM, and Saturday from 10 AM to 9 PM. Closed Thanksgiving, Christmas, and New Year's Day. There is a charge for parking, but the Getty can also be reached using public transportation.

1200 Getty Center Dr; Los Angeles, CA 90049; Phone: (310) 440-7300; http://www.getty.edu/visit

Getty Villa is itself a work of art – inspired by the first-century Villa dei Papiri in Herculaneum, Italy. Over 1,200 works covering ancient art from the end of the Stone Age to the end of the Roman Empire are maintained there. Admission is free but an advance timed-entry ticket is required. These can be reserved online. Open Wednesday through Monday from 10 AM to 5 PM. Closed Thanksgiving, Christmas, and New Year's Day. 17985 Pacific Coast Hwy; Pacific Palisades, CA 90272; Phone: (310) 440-7300; http://www.getty.edu/visit/villa/plan

Griffith Observatory has been poetically described as Southern California's *Gateway to the Cosmos*. Admission to the observatory, grounds, access to telescopes, exhibits, and monthly star parties are free. Open Tuesday through Friday from Noon to 10 PM. Open Saturday and Sunday from 10 AM to 10 PM. Note: There is a fee to see the programs in the Samuel Oschin Planetarium. 2800 E Observatory Rd; Los Angeles, CA 90027; Phone: (213) 473-0800; http://www.griffithobservatory.org

Hammer Museum includes European and American paintings and drawings that reflect the interests and passion of the museum's founder, Armand Hammer as well as a growing collection of international contemporary art. Admission to all exhibitions and public programs is free. Open Tuesday through Friday from 11 AM to 8 PM, and on Saturday and Sunday from 11 AM to 5 PM. Closed major holidays. 10899 Wilshire Blvd; Los Angeles, CA 90024; Phone: (310) 443-7000; https://hammer.ucla.edu

Hollywood Forever Cemetery is the final resting place of many of Hollywood's founders and stars including Johnny Ramone, Cecil B. DeMille, Jayne Mansfield, Rudolph Valentino, and Douglas Fairbanks. Admission is free. Attending special events will incur a charge. The cemetery is open daily from 8:30 AM to 5 PM. 6000 Santa Monica Blvd; Los Angeles, CA 90038; Phone: (323) 469-1181; http://www.hollywoodforever.com

Music Center is composed of several architecturally distinctive buildings. The Walt Disney Concert Hall, designed by Frank Gehry, is open for free self-guided and docent-led tours.135 N Grand Ave; Los Angeles, CA 90012; Phone: (213) 972-4399; https://www.musiccenter.org/visit/Exploring-the-Center

Pierce Brothers Westwood Village Memorial Park & Mortuary contains the graves of some of the most famous stars in Hollywood. It's a designated Los

Angeles Historic-Cultural Monument. 1218 Glendon Ave; Los Angeles, CA 90024; Phone: (310) 474-1579.

Wells Fargo Center includes an original Concord coach, the 26-ounce Challenge nugget, a panoramic painting of Los Angeles in 1859, a historically recreated agent's office, and the story of Wells Fargo and Hollywood. Admission is free. Open Monday through Friday from 9 AM to 5 PM. 333 S Grand; Los Angeles, CA 90071; Phone: (213) 253-7166; https://www.wellsfargohistory.com/museums/los-angeles

Nipomo, CA
Monarch Dunes Butterfly Habitat is the winter home of as many as 60,000 monarch butterflies. When the area was developed 19 acres surrounding the Monarch's historic area were preserved as a sanctuary. The Butterfly Habitat is open free daily from sunrise to sunset. The butterflies begin arriving in September with peak viewing in the weeks around Thanksgiving. By mid-February, they have moved on. Note: There are no restroom or drinking water facilities on site. The Trilogy at Monarch Dunes; 1610 Kingston Dr; Nipomo, CA 93444; http://www.monarchdunesbutterflies.org/index.html

Oakland, CA
Bonsai Garden at Lake Merritt features over 75 beautiful bonsai and many viewing stones (suiseki). Many of the trees change color with the seasons. Admission is free with donations gratefully accepted. Open Tuesday through Friday from 11 AM to 3 PM. Open Saturday from 10 AM to 4 PM, and Sunday from Noon to 4 PM. 650 Bellevue Ave; Oakland, CA 94610; Phone: (510) 763-8409; https://bonsailakemerritt.com

Crucible is an industrial art school that offers free guided tours of their facility. Tours are given twice a month: the first Tuesday at 6 PM, and the third Saturday at 3 PM, except holidays and special events. 1260 Seventh St; Oakland, CA 94607; Phone: (510) 444-0919; https://www.thecrucible.org

Palmdale, CA
Blackbird Airpark and Joe Davies Heritage Airpark has been the site of research, development, final assembly, and flight testing for the U.S. Air Force and NASA. Today it hosts several flight-related museums. The **Blackbird Airpark Museum** is part of Air Force Flight Test Museum and free to visit. **Joe Davies Heritage Airpark**, operated by the City of Palmdale, is also free. Both facilities are open Friday, Saturday, and Sunday from 11 AM to 4 PM. 2503 E Ave P; Palmdale, CA

93550; Phone: (661) 274-0884; http://www.afftcmuseum.org/blackbird-airpark; http://www.cityofpalmdale.org/Airpark

Roseville, CA
Roseville Telephone Museum has an extensive collection of antique telephones and memorabilia as well as local history. Admission is free. Hours are limited to the first Saturday of the month from 10 AM to 2 PM. 106 Vernon St; Roseville, CA 95678; Phone: (916) 786-1621; https://www.consolidated.com/about-us/history/telephone-museum

Richmond, CA
Rosie the Riveter/World War II Home Front National Historical Park celebrates America's affection for the spunky young woman who stepped into crucial jobs needed to maintain the United States efforts in WWII. This unusual urban national park celebrates all the Rosies, telling the stories of the home front across the country. Free to visit. Visitor center is open daily 10 AM to 5 PM. Closed Thanksgiving, Christmas, and New Year's Day. Rosie the Riveter Memorial in Marina Bay Park is open all year, dawn to dusk. 1414 Harbour Way S; Suite 3000 (Oil House); Richmond, CA 94804; Phone: (510) 232-5050; https://www.nps.gov/rori/index.htm

Sacramento, CA
California State Capitol looks like a mini replica of the U.S. Capitol in Washington, DC and houses both the California State Capitol Museum and the seat of California's government. Take a free tour to learn about the 1869 building's architecture and history. If legislators are in session, ask about access to public galleries. Open daily for self-guided tours. Free guided tours are also available. Public tours are conducted daily on the hour from 9 AM to 4 PM. Open Monday through Friday from 7:30 AM to 6 PM. Open Saturday and Sunday from 9 AM to 5 PM. Closed Thanksgiving, Christmas, and New Year's Day. On weekends enter through the N Street entrance. 1315 10th St; Sacramento, CA 95814 Phone: (916) 324-0333; http://www.capitolmuseum.ca.gov/the-museum/general-info

California State Capitol Museum provides revolving exhibits and restored historic rooms. A theater on the lower level presents films. Admission is free. Free tours are available daily on the hour between 9 AM and 4 PM. Visitors are also welcomed to take self-guided tours. Open Monday through Friday from 7:30 AM to 6 PM. Open Saturday and Sunday from 9 AM to 5 PM. 1315 10th St; Sacramento, CA 95814; Phone: (916) 324-0333; http://www.capitolmuseum.ca.gov/the-museum/the-museum

Historic City Cemetery offers beautiful statues, dramatic markers, and lush gardens. There is no fee to visit the cemetery. Open daily from 7 AM to 7 PM. Closes at 5 PM in winter. 1000 Broadway; Sacramento, CA 95818; Phone: (916) 448-0811; https://www.historicoldcitycemetery.org

Old Sacramento Schoolhouse Museum replicates a traditional, 19th-century one-room schoolhouse, with costumed interpreters. Admission is free. Open Monday through Saturday from 10 AM to 4 PM. Open Sunday Noon to 4 PM. Note: Hours are dependent on staffing availability. 1200 Front St; Sacramento, CA 95814; Phone: (916) 483-8818; http://oldsacschoolhouse.scoe.net/index.html

Wells Fargo Capitol Mall features an authentic stage coach, and the Livingston letter cover collection. Admission is free. Open Tuesday through Saturday from 10 AM to 4 PM. Closed Independence Day, Thanksgiving, Christmas, and New Year's Day. 400 Capitol Mall; Sacramento, CA 95814; Phone: (916) 440-4161; https://www.wellsfargohistory.com/museums/sacramento

Wells Fargo Old Sacramento State Historic Park is second of two Wells Fargo exhibitions in the city presenting authentic artifacts, documents, photographs, and interactive exhibits. Open daily 10 AM to 5 PM. Closed Thanksgiving, Christmas, and New Year's Day. 1000 Second St; Sacramento, CA 95814; Phone: (916) 440-4263; https://www.wellsfargohistory.com/museums/old-sacramento

San Diego, CA

The city offers two major destinations that are a blend of free and fee-based attractions.

Balboa Park sprawls across 1,200 acres with free admission to the park. Free tours of the park meet at the visitor center at 11 AM every Tuesday. Phone: (619) 239-0512; https://balboaparkconservancy.org/project/visitors-center. Built for the 1915-16 Exposition, the **Botanical Building** is free to visit with over 2,100 permanent plants. Open Friday through Wednesday from 10 AM to 4 PM. Closed holidays. Located near the Timken Museum of Art listed below. https://www.balboapark.org/gardens/botanical-building.

San Diego Mineral and Gem Societies' Museum features fine mineral, gem, lapidary and fossil specimens. It is free to visit. Open daily from 11 AM to 4 PM. 1770 Village Pl; Balboa Park; San Diego, CA 9210; https://www.sdmg.org/sdmg-public/about-sdmg/sdmg-museum. **Timken Museum of Art** houses a collection of European old masters, 19th-century American art and Russian icons. Admission is free. Open Tuesday through Saturday from 10 AM to 4:30 PM and on Sunday from Noon to 4:30 PM. 1500 El Prado; Balboa Park; San Diego, CA 92101; Phone: (619) 239-5548; http://www.timkenmuseum.org

Old Town San Diego State Historic Park blends restored original historic buildings, reconstructed sites, and early 20th-century buildings. 4002 Wallace St; San Diego, CA 92110; Phone: (619) 220-5422; http://www.oldtownsandiegoguide.com/index.html. **San Diego Sheriff's Museum** features exhibits from the 150-year history of the Sheriff's Department. Displays include guns, badges, handcuffs, uniforms, patrol car, helicopter, motorcycle, jail cell, and courtroom. Admission is free. Open Tuesday through Saturday from 10 AM to 4 PM. **Mormon Battalion Historic Site** commemorates the Mormon Battalion's historic journey from the Council Bluffs area of Iowa to San Diego, California. Free admission and free interactive tours. Open daily from 9 AM to 9 PM. **Veterans Museum and Memorial Center** honors the men and women who served in the United States military. Located in the former WWII-era Navy Chapel adjacent to the Veterans Memorial Garden. Open Tuesday through Sunday from 10 AM to 4 PM. http://www.oldtownsandiegoguide.com/history.html

San Francisco, CA

Cable Car Museum showcases these iconic pieces of San Francisco's transportation history. Visitors can stand on the deck and peer down at the huge engines and wheels that pull the cables, and then head downstairs to view the mechanical devices that make this feat possible. There's a large collection of historic photographs, and three antique cable cars from the 1870s. Admission is free. Open daily April through October from 10 AM to 6 PM. Closes at 5 PM November through March. Closed Thanksgiving, Christmas, and New Year's Day. 1201 Mason St; San Francisco, CA 94108; Phone: (415) 474-1887; http://www.cablecarmuseum.org/index.html

Fort Point National Historic Site is located within the sprawling grounds of the Presidio (listed below) at the southern end of Golden Gate Bridge. Visitors can see films on Fort Point history and the making of the Golden Gate Bridge. Self-guided and guided tours are available. Admission and all programs are free. Generally open Friday through Sunday from 10 AM to 5 PM, but visitors are advised to check the website for current days and times. Building 999; Marine Dr; San Francisco, CA 94129; Phone: (415) 504-2334; https://www.nps.gov/fopo/index.htm

Golden Gate Bridge Welcome Center delivers an in-depth look at the famous architectural icon through authentic artifacts including hard hats and rivets from the bridge's construction in the 1930s as well as videos, and the 12-foot test tower once used to evaluate the bridge's design. Located on the visitor plaza at the span's southern end on the grounds of the Presidio. Open daily from 9 AM to 6 PM.

Closed Thanksgiving, and Christmas Day. Phone: (415) 426-5220; http://goldengatebridge.org/visitors/whattodo.php

Grace Cathedral has two labyrinths (including a replica of the 13th-century stone maze on the floor of Chartres Cathedral. The cathedral also offers the beautiful Ghiberti doors cast from his Gates of Paradise, an Evensong service, the Keith Haring altar, and NAMES AIDS Quilt. There is a charge to take a guided tour, but the self-guided cellphone tour is free. The cathedral is open 8 AM to 6 PM most days. 1100 California St; San Francisco, CA 94108; Phone: (415) 749-6300; https://www.gracecathedral.org/plan-your-visit/

Museo Italo Americano highlights contemporary and historical Italian and Italian-American artworks. Admission is free. Open Tuesday through Sunday from Noon to 4 PM. Fort Mason Center; 2 Marina Blvd; Building C; San Francisco, CA, 94123; Phone: (415) 673-2200; https://museoitaloamericano.org

Pier 39 has street performers, shops, restaurants, admission-based attractions, and sea lions. One of the popular and free activities is their **Musical Stairs**, the interactive art exhibit created by Remo Saraceni. To enjoy the music, take a walk up or down the stairs found at Building O, Level 1 & Level 2. Pier 39's West Marina has become home to a group of sea lions. After you've enjoyed watching them eat, sleep, and play, you can learn more about these marine mammals at the **Sea Lion Center**. Note: This is separate from the aquarium, which charges admission. Sea Lion Center can be found at 203 Pier 39 (Beach St and the Embarcadero) 2 Beach St; San Francisco, CA 94133; Phone: (415) 705-5500; https://www.pier39.com

Presidio is a popular destination that mixes free and fee-based sites. Originally it was established by Spain at the same time the American colonies won their Independence from England. The United States seized the Presidio in 1847 during the Mexican-American War and it became a major U.S. military outpost. Today it is a 1,500-acre national park with museums, and free programs. The **Main Post** within the Presidio is a historic area that includes several attractions and memorials as well as a national cemetery. On its grounds is the **Presidio Visitor Center** with exhibits, maps, videos, and information on what to see and do. Open daily from 10 AM to 5 PM. Closed major holidays. **Presidio Officers' Club** is a museum and cultural center with exhibits tracing the Presidio's past and present as well as providing talks, free concerts, and events on the parade grounds. There's even an archaeology lab with periodic free tours. Admission is free. Open Tuesday through Sunday from 10 AM to 5 PM. For art lovers, the Presidio is home to the largest collection of **Andy Goldsworthy** sculptures on public view in North America. His works can be enjoyed via a three-mile loop along the Presidio's trail network. There's also the free **Tides Converge** galleries. Open weekdays from 8:30 AM to 5 PM. **Letterman Digital Arts Center** is home to both Yoda, immortalized as a life-sized bronze fountain, and Lucasfilm, which is open to the public during regular working hours. In the lobby, find props, memorabilia, costumes, and life-sized Darth Vader and Boba Fett statues. Presidio Visitor Center; 210 Lincoln Blvd; San Francisco, CA 94129; Phone: (415) 561-4323; https://www.presidio.gov

San Francisco Center for the Book offers a gallery of changing exhibits of artist books, prints, sculptural bookworks, and paper related artworks. Admission is free. Open daily from 10 AM to 5:30 PM. 375 Rhode Island St; San Francisco, CA 94103; Phone: (415) 565-0545; https://sfcb.org

San Francisco Railway Museum celebrates the city's iconic streetcars and cable cars. It features a full-sized replica of the motorman's platform from a 1911 San Francisco streetcar, plus historic artifacts, displays, photographs, and exhibits. Admission is free. Open Tuesday through Sunday from 10 AM to 5 PM. 77 Steuart St; San Francisco, CA 94105; Phone: (415) 974-1948; https://www.streetcar.org/museum

Truhlsen-Marmor Museum of the Eye promotes eye health through rotating exhibits on the ways virtual-reality is changing ophthalmology, the evolution of eye care, and how sight is being saved. Admission is free. Check website for days and times. 645 Beach St; San Francisco, CA 94109; Phone: (415) 561-8502; https://www.aao.org/about-the-museum

Wells Fargo Museum features a stagecoach that carried passengers and gold across the western plains, a display of gold dust and ore from California's Gold Country, and a special collection of Gold Rush letters. Open Monday through Friday from 9 AM to 5 PM. 420 Montgomery St; San Francisco, CA 94163; Phone: (415) 396-2619; https://www.wellsfargohistory.com/museums/san-francisco

San Jose, CA
History Park offers 32 original and reproduction homes, businesses, and landmarks, complete with paved streets, and running trolleys. Admission is free, except during special events. Closed holidays. Open Saturday and Sunday all year. Open daily in the summer. Senter Rd and Phelan Ave; San Jose, CA 95112; Phone: (408) 287-2290; http://historysanjose.org/wp/plan-your-visit/history-park

Ira F. Brilliant Center for Beethoven Studies is devoted solely to the life, works, and accomplishments of Ludwig van Beethoven (1770-1827) with the largest collection of Beethoven materials outside of Europe. Admission is free. Open Monday through Friday from 11 AM to 6 PM. Closes at 5 PM on Friday. Open Saturday from 1 PM to 5 PM. Closed major holidays. Dr. Martin Luther King Jr Library; Room 580; 1 Washington Sq; San Jose, CA 95192; Phone: (408) 808-2058; http://www.sjsu.edu/beethoven

San Jose Heritage Rose Garden delights with a world class collection of 3,000 plants including varieties of heritage, modern, and miniature roses. Admission is free. Open daily dawn to dusk. 438 Coleman Ave; San Jose, CA 95110; Phone: (408) 298-7657; http://www.heritageroses.us

San Jose Institute of Contemporary Art offers site-specific contemporary art installations. Admission is free. Open Tuesday through Friday from 10 AM to 5 PM and weekends from Noon to 5 PM. 560 S First St; San Jose, CA 95113; Phone: (408) 283-8155; https://www.sjica.org

Santa Clara, CA

The Intel Museum showcases the world's largest chipmaker and the micro-miniature world of computer chips. Admission is free. Open Monday through Friday from 9 AM to 6 PM and on Saturday from 10 AM to 5 PM. Note: They recommend calling in advance. Robert Noyce Bldg; 2200 Mission College Blvd; Santa Clara, CA 95054; Phone: (408) 765-5050; https://www.intel.com/content/www/us/en/company-overview/intel-museum.html

Sausalito, CA

Marine Mammal Center rescues, and treats sick and injured animals in their state-of-the-art veterinary facilities. The center is free to visit and open to the public daily from 10 AM to 4 PM except Thanksgiving, Christmas and New Year's Day. A guided tour will incur a fee. 2000 Bunker Rd; Sausalito, CA 94965; Phone: (415) 289-7325; http://www.marinemammalcenter.org/visiting-us

Sylmar, CA

Nethercutt Museum and Collection focuses on antique, classic, and special interest automobiles. The museum spans four floors displaying more than gorgeous cars. The music room showcases automated mechanical instruments, Swiss bird boxes, cylinder and disc music boxes, and grand pianos. Open to the public at no charge. The Nethercutt Museum is open for self-guided tours. The Collection is only available by guided tour, with advance reservations required. 15151 Bledsoe St; Sylmar, CA 91342; Phone: (818) 364-6464; http://www.nethercuttcollection.org/Home.aspx

Victorville, CA

California Route 66 Museum celebrates its Route 66 heritage with fun and whimsy, including photo opportunities in a '50s diner, and their VW Love Bus. Admission is free but donations are gratefully accepted. Open Monday and Thursday through Saturday from 10 AM to 4 PM. Open Sunday from 11 AM to 3 PM. 16825 South D St; Victorville, CA, 92395; Phone: (760) 951-0436; http://califrt66museum.org

Colorado

Arvada, CO
Arvada Center for the Arts and Humanities is a theater, music, dance, and art destination. The **Galleries at the Arvada Center** hosts art exhibitions across three galleries. It's free and open daily. Monday through Friday open from 9 AM to 6 PM. On Saturday from 10 AM to 6 PM and on Sunday from 1 PM to 5 PM. The galleries remain open until 7:30 PM on evenings with performances. https://arvadacenter.org/galleries. **Arvada Historical Museum** offers the actual 144-year-old Haines log house, furnished much as it would have been when Asahel and Abigail Haines and their children lived there. It's free to visit. The museum is open Monday through Friday 9 AM to 6 PM. Open Saturday from 10 AM to 5 PM and Sunday 1 PM to 5 PM. Closed major holidays and when the Arvada Center is closed. 6901 Wadsworth Blvd; Arvada, CO 80003; Phone: (720) 898-7200; https://arvadacenter.org/galleries/historical-museum

Boulder, CO
Celestial Seasonings Factory visits combine tours and tastings. Free tours are available Monday through Friday from 10 AM to 4 PM, Saturday from 10 AM to 4 PM, and on Sunday from 11 AM to 3 PM. Closed major holidays. 4600 Sleepytime Dr; Boulder, CO 80301; Phone: (303) 581-1202; http://www.celestialseasonings.com/visit-us

NCAR Tour explores the National Center for Atmospheric Research (NCAR) exhibits on weather and climate. There's also art-science galleries, and an outdoor weather trail. Visitors can take a self-guided tour or sign up for a free guided tour. The exhibits are open daily weekdays from 8 AM to 5 PM. Weekend and holidays from 9 AM to 4 PM. Public tours Monday, Wednesday, and Friday at Noon. 1850 Table Mesa Dr; Boulder, CO 80305; Phone: (303) 497-1000; https://scied.ucar.edu/visit

Buena Vista, CO
St. Elmo Townsite is a quasi-ghost town. Founded in 1880, nearly 2,000 people settled in this town when mining for gold and silver started. A general store opens seasonally for tourists, and the locals live nearby in newer houses. Most of the town is generally uninhabited, leaving the streets with its abandoned buildings for visitors. https://www.buenavistacolorado.org/history

Calhan, CO
Paint Mines Interpretive Park stretches over 750 acres, deriving its name from the colorful strata that provided clay to early Native Americans. The geology of the area is marked by spires and hoodoos created by erosion from wind and rain. Free

admission. Open daily dawn to dusk. 29950 Paint Mines Rd; Calhan, CO 80808; Phone: (719) 520-7529; https://communityservices.elpasoco.com/parks-and-recreation/paint-mines-interpretive-park

Colorado Springs, CO
U.S. Air Force Academy is known for its stunning chapel with 17 spires. The chapel is open to the public Monday through Saturday from 9:30 AM to 4:30 PM and on Sunday from 1 PM to 4:30 PM. Tours are available. Worship services are open to the public. Arnold Hall contains several military and academy exhibits. Open daily from 9 AM to 5 PM. Closed major holidays. 515 S Cascade Ave; Colorado Springs, CO 80903; Phone: (719) 635-7506 or (800) 888-4748; https://www.academyadmissions.com/visit-the-academy/self-guided-tours/visitor-center-information

Dr. Lester L. Williams Fire Museum includes over 3,000 items from fire plugs to hats and even children's fire-fighting toys, but the centerpiece of the museum is the actual equipment, including a 1898 Metropolitan Steamer, and a 1926 Ahrens Fox. Free admission. Open Monday through Friday from 8 AM to 4:30 PM. 375 Printers Pkwy; Colorado Springs, CO 80910; Phone: (719) 385-5950; http://www.williamsfiremuseum.com

Garden of the Gods is a spectacular park with 1,300 acres of sandstone formations, hiking trails, and a driving loop. Admission is free to both the park and the visitor center. Note: Visiting Rock Ledge Ranch Historic Site will incur a fee. Seasonal hours. 1805 N 30th St; Colorado Springs, CO 80904; Phone: (719) 634-6666; https://gardenofgods.com

Commerce City, CO
Rocky Mountain Arsenal National Wildlife Refuge is located just outside of Denver and delivers an interactive exhibit hall, and a discovery room with hands-on activities. There are floating boardwalks at Lake Mary, and Lake Ladora, and a self-guided 11-mile Wildlife Drive auto tour through the bison pasture, grasslands, wetlands, and woodlands. Admission is free. Open daily from sunrise to sunset. The visitor center is open Wednesday through Sunday from 9 AM to 4 PM. Closed on federal holidays. 6550 Gateway Rd; Commerce City, CO 80022; Refuge Phone: (303) 289-0232; https://www.fws.gov/refuge/Rocky_Mountain_Arsenal/visit/plan_your_visit.html

Cortez, CO
Notah Dineh Trading Company and Museum is the place to shop and admire museum-quality Native American art. Navajo rugs elevate weaving to a true art form, and the collection includes the largest known Two Grey Hills weaving in the world. In addition, the museum holds beautiful beaded leatherwear, fringed

dresses and leggings, and some historic firearms. On your way into the shop, along the parking lot wall, admire the mural *Navajo Flea Market* by James King. Open Monday through Saturday 9 AM to 5:30 PM. 345 W Main St; Cortez, CO 81321; Phone: (970) 565-9607; http://notahdineh.com/index.html

Denver, CO (See also Commerce City, CO and Morrison, CO)
Colorado State Capitol was modeled after the Capitol Building in Washington, D.C. and features white Colorado granite, rose onyx and marble, stained glass depictions of events and people integral to Colorado, and a gold-plated dome. There are exhibits, visitor galleries, and art. Tours are complimentary and offered hourly Monday through Friday 10 AM to 3 PM. You can take a self-guided tour Monday through Friday from 7:30 AM to 5 PM. Closed most legal holidays. 200 E Colfax Ave; Denver, CO 80203; Phone: (303) 866-2604; https://leg.colorado.gov/visit-learn

Denver Mint Facility fabricates circulating coins as well as the Denver portion of the annual uncirculated coin sets and commemorative coins. Visitors can take a free tour on a first-come, first-served basis. Note: Extensive prohibitions are listed on the website. Tours are limited to adults and children seven years and older. Pick up free tickets at Tour Information at the gift shop entrance. The ticket window opens at 7 AM Monday through Thursday. Closed observed federal holidays. The last tour is at 3:30 PM. Cherokee St; Denver, CO 80204; Phone: (303) 405-4761; https://competition.usmint.gov/visiting-the-united-states-mint-in-denver-colorado

Money Museum at the Federal Reserve Bank - Denver Branch offers currency dating back to 1775, and exhibits on the history of the Federal Reserve. Visitors will need a valid passport or state-issued ID but can walk in any time for a free self-guided tour. Open Monday through Friday from 9:30 AM to 4 PM. Closed bank holidays. 1020 16th St; Denver, CO 80202; Phone: (303) 572-2429; https://www.kansascityfed.org/moneymuseum?location=1

Englewood, CO
Gateway Classic Cars is a classic and exotic car dealership – one of several across the country. Their back showroom is filled with gorgeous classic cars and they welcome browsers. 14150 Grasslands Dr; Suite A; Englewood, CO 80112; Phone: (303) 872-4722; http://gatewayclassiccars.com

Estes Park, CO
Estes Park is the best base for exploring the front range of Rocky Mountain National Park, but you don't have to go into the park to do some hiking. Trailheads scattered throughout the area provide excellent and free hiking.
Lily Lake may be the perfect introduction to hiking in Colorado. It is a beautiful lake with three trails of varying degrees of difficulty. Note: The trail begins at the

9,090 feet elevation. Highway 7 near Mileposts 6 and 7, south of Estes Park; http://www.rmnp.com/RMNP-Areas-LilyLake.HTML

Evergreen, CO
Hiwan Heritage Park contains a 25-room log lodge, plus three other original buildings furnished with the original residents' belongings. Admission is free as are the guided tours. Museum is open Tuesday through Friday from Noon to 4 PM. Open Saturday and Sunday from Noon to 5 PM. 28473 Meadow Dr; Evergreen, CO 80439; Phone: (720) 497-7650; https://www.jeffco.us/1251/Hiwan-Heritage-Park

Fort Collins, CO
Budweiser Brewing Experience includes a free tour of the brewing and packaging of Budweiser beer. Tours are offered Thursday through Sunday from 11 AM to 4 PM. Visitors over 21 will be able to taste one of their beers as part of the tour. 2351 Busch Dr; Fort Collins, CO 80524; Phone: (970) 490-4691; http://www.budweisertours.com/locations/ft-collins-colorado.html

New Belgium Brewery started modestly in the basement of Jeff Lebesch after his beer epiphany in Belgium. Book the 90-minute tour online. Tours are free, starting at 11:30 AM and leave every hour until 4:30 PM. Beer sampling is included. 500 Linden St; Fort Collins, CO 80524; Phone: (970) 221-0524; http://www.newbelgium.com/Brewery/fort-collins

Swetsville Zoo is filled with the quirky and fun machinery-scrap sculptures of Bill Swets. He's been building these metal creatures for years. Although admission is free, donations are appreciated. Opens at 11 AM but visitors should call to verify. 4801 E Harmony Rd; Fort Collins, CO 80528; Phone: (970) 484-9509.

Fort Morgan, CO
Fort Morgan Museum offers permanent and temporary exhibits that showcase the museum's collection, plus traveling exhibits from other institutions. A model train layout depicts Fort Morgan's Main Street circa 1915. Admission is free. Open Monday 9 AM to 6 PM. Open Tuesday through Thursday from 9 AM to 8 PM. Open Friday and Saturday from 9 AM to 5 PM. 414 Main St; Fort Morgan, CO 80701; Phone: (970) 542-4011; https://www.cityoffortmorgan.com/238/Museum

Frisco, CO
Frisco Historic Park & Museum honors the town's heritage with a museum and park built from original structures including restored mining cabins, ranch homes, a log chapel, the original schoolhouse, and a jail. Admission is free. Open Tuesday through Sunday from 10 AM to 5 PM. Closed October 31st through November 2nd and Thanksgiving, Christmas, and New Year's Day. 120 Main St; Frisco, CO

80443; Phone: (970) 668-3428; https://www.townoffrisco.com/play/historic-park-and-museum/general-info/

Georgetown, CO
Alpine Hose No. 2 Georgetown Firefighting Museum houses uniforms, furnishings, fixtures, and photographs. No admission fee, however donations are appreciated. Open seasonally. 507 Fifth St; Georgetown, CO 80444; Phone: (303) 569-2840; https://www.historicgeorgetown.org/alpine-hose--2.html

Georgetown Energy Museum is a fully functioning and operational hydroelectric generating plant built in 1900. Admission is free with donations gratefully accepted. Open daily June through December from 11 AM to 5 PM. Open weekends during the off season. 600 Griffith St; Georgetown, CO 80444; Phone: (303) 204-9873; https://www.georgetownenergymuseum.org

Golden, CO
Colorado School of Mines Geology Museum offers an actual moon rock, plus fossils, gemstones, meteorites, and historic mining artifacts. There's even an outdoor geologic trail featuring outcrops with fossilized dinosaur tracks. Admission is free. Open Monday through Saturday from 9 AM to 4 PM. Open Sunday from 1 PM to 4 PM. Closed Thanksgiving, Christmas, and New Year's Day and may be closed during the university's winter break. General Research Laboratory (GRL) building; 1310 Maple St; Golden, CO 80401; Phone: (303) 273-3815; http://www.mines.edu/Geology_Museum

Rocky Flats National Wildlife Refuge is the place for ten miles of year-round hiking trails and wildlife viewing. Admission is free. Open daily from sunrise to sunset. Closed Thanksgiving, Christmas, and New Year's Day. 10801 Highway 93; Golden, CO 80402; Phone (303) 289-0232; http://www.fws.gov/refuge/rocky_flats

Guffey, CO
Rocky Mountain Wildlife Foundation provides sanctuary, rehabilitation, and environmentally natural housing for captive-born wolves and wolf dogs who have suffered from injuries, neglect, or abuse. There is no charge for visiting, however donations are greatly appreciated. Tours by appointment only. Note: Wear clothing that you don't mind getting dirty. Shoes or boots are required. All tours are private. Note: They recommend using their directions rather than a GSP. Phone: (719) 660-5480; https://www.rmwf.org/visit.html

Loveland, CO
Loveland Museum highlights both art and history. The art section is mix of free and fee-based but all the history exhibits are free. Open Tuesday through Friday

from 10 AM to 5 PM. Closes at 7 PM on Thursday. Open Saturday from 10 AM to 4 PM and Sunday from Noon to 4 PM. 503 N Lincoln Ave; Loveland, CO 80537; Phone: (970) 962-2410; https://www.lovelandmuseumgallery.org

Manitou Springs, CO

The town is famous for its springs and the incline cog railway. Pick up a map of the springs from the visitor center for a DIY tour. The Cog Railway is not free, but if you are a climber, you can take the steps upwards... as far as you feel you can go. The trail gains nearly 2,000 feet of elevation over less than one mile. Remember, you will have to go back down that same distance. Starting at 6400 feet above sea level. The trail is free and open from 6 AM to 6 PM. http://manitoumineralsprings.org/index.html

Manitou Springs Heritage Center creates exhibits focused on the history of Manitou and the area. Admission is free. Open Wednesday through Sundays 11:30 AM to 4:30 PM. 517 Manitou Ave; Manitou Springs, CO 80829; Phone: (719) 685-1454; http://www.manitouspringsheritagecenter.org

Morrison, CO (See also Denver, CO)

Red Rocks Park and Amphitheatre is the beautiful outdoor concert venue in the Denver area, but it is also a destination on its own. The visitor center features the geological and musical history of Red Rocks, the Performers Hall of Fame display, and free video screenings. The Colorado Music Hall of Fame is inside the Trading Post gift shop. Outside, short hikes wend through the park. It is free to visit. Of course, attending a concert will incur ticket fees as will a guided tour of the park. Open all year for free self-guided tours, beginning one hour before sunrise until one hour after sunset. Hours vary during the April to October concert season with early closures every day. 18300 W Alameda Pkwy; Morrison, CO 80465; Phone: (720) 865-2494; https://www.redrocksonline.com/the-park

Rye, CO

Bishop Castle started as a family home and grew to become a stone and iron castle. Three full stories of interior rooms include a Grand Ballroom, soaring towers, bridges with striking vistas, and a fire-breathing dragon. Admission is free because Jim Bishop hated it when as a child he couldn't go to the zoo or the ballpark because admission was too high. Donations are gratefully accepted, or purchase something in the gift shop. The Castle is always open. 12705 State Highway 165; Rye, CO 81069; Phone: (719) 564-4366; http://www.bishopcastle.org

Trinidad, CO

Ludlow Massacre Site and Memorial is announced by a tiny sign on I-25 but few know the story. The monument marks the site of the Ludlow Massacre that occurred on April 20, 1914 when the Colorado National Guard attacked and later burned a tent community of striking coal miners. The United Mine Workers of America (UMWA) erected a granite monument in memory of the miners and their families who died that day, and an exhibit recounts the history. County Road 44; Trinidad, CO 81082; http://www.santafetrailscenicandhistoricbyway.org/ludlow.html

Connecticut

East Canaan, CT
Beckley Furnace Industrial Monument preserves this 19th-century iron-making blast furnace constructed in 1847. There is no charge to visit. Docents are sometimes on the site in summer on Saturdays but the grounds are open all year during daylight hours. 140 Lower Rd; East Canaan, CT 06024; Phone: (860) 837-0270 (leave a message); http://beckleyfurnace.org

Groton, CT
Submarine Force Library & Museum is the only submarine museum operated by the United States Navy and offers the USS Nautilus, and a collection of submarine artifacts. Admission is free. Open Wednesday through Monday from 9 AM to 4 PM. One Crystal Lake Rd; Groton, CT 06340; Phone: (800) 343-0079; http://www.ussnautilus.org

Hartfort, CT
Connecticut State Capitol is a gold-domed Victorian Gothic building adorned with spires, statues, medallions, bas-reliefs, stained glass, and stenciling. Self-guided tours are available Monday through Friday from 8 AM to 5 PM. Free one-hour guided tours of the State Capitol and Legislative Office Building are also available. Check the website for tour information. Closed all major holidays. 210 Capitol Ave; Hartford, CT 06106; Phone: (860) 240-0222; https://wp.cga.ct.gov/CapitolTours

Museum of Connecticut History provides historic documents, including the State's original 1662 Royal Charter. Gun enthusiasts will enjoy the Colt's Patent Firearms Manufacturing Company Factory Collection, while the Mitchelson Coin Collection spans the 17th century to the present. Admission is free. Open Monday through Friday 9 AM to 4 PM. Open on Saturday from 9 AM to 2 PM. Closed state holidays. 231 Capitol Ave; Hartford, CT 06106; Phone: (860) 757-6535; http://museumofcthistory.org

Museum of Jewish Civilization recounts the broad history of Jewish civilization including the lives of the Jews across the world and in ancient Israel as well as Jewish life in Europe after the Holocaust. The museum is located inside the Mortensen Library in the Harry Jack Gray Center on the University of Hartford main campus. Admission is free. Open 11 AM Monday through Friday. On Tuesday closes at 1:30 PM. On Monday and Wednesday closes at 3 PM and on Thursday at 2 PM. 200 Bloomfield Ave; West Hartford, CT; Phone: (860) 768-5729; http://www.hartford.edu/a_and_s/greenberg/museum

Myths, Minds & Medicine explores the dramatic changes in the perception and treatment of people with mental illness. Artifacts, letters, and old photos illustrate medicine's well-intentioned, but sometimes misguided efforts. The voices of patients are part of the story through aural recreations of letters found in the archives. Free to the public. Open Monday through Friday from 9 AM to 5 PM. Institute of Living; Commons Building; 200 Retreat Ave; Hartford, CT 06114; Phone: (860) 545-4501; https://instituteofliving.org/about-us/myths-minds-medicine

New Haven, CT

Beinecke Rare Book & Manuscript Library is one of the world's largest buildings entirely dedicated to rare books and manuscripts. Highlights include one of the 48 existing copies of the Gutenberg Bible, and John James Audubon's Birds of America. There is no admission charge. Closed holidays and during university recesses. 121 Wall St, New Haven, CT 06511; Phone: (203) 432-2977; https://beinecke.library.yale.edu

Cushing Center & Yale Medical Library contains the efforts of pioneering neurosurgeon Harvey Cushing who recorded and documented each of his patients' stories, even retaining specimens removed in operations. There are 2,200 case studies dating from the late 1800s to 1936. Admission is free but visitors must register at the medical library's circulation desk first and receive a Cushing Center Proxy Card. The library is open Monday through Friday from 8 AM to 8 PM. Open on Saturday from 10 AM to 7 PM, and on Sunday from 9:30 AM to 8 PM. Cushing/Whitney Medical Library is in the sub-basement (two floors down from main level). Sterling Hall of Medicine; 333 Cedar St; New Haven, CT 06510; Phone: (203) 785-5352; http://library.medicine.yale.edu/cushingcenter/visiting

Yale Center for British Art is the largest collection of British art outside the United Kingdom from the Elizabethan period onward. The Center and its programs are free. Open Tuesday through Saturday from 10 AM to 5 PM and on Sunday from Noon to 5 PM. Center is closed on major holidays. 1080 Chapel St; New Haven, CT 06510; Phone: (203) 432-2800; https://britishart.yale.edu

Yale Collection of Musical Instruments permanently displays historic keyboard instruments including 28 clavichords, harpsichords, and pianos from the 16th through the 20th centuries. A smart phone audio tour features restored instruments in live performance. Admission is free with donations accepted. The collection is open September through July on Tuesday to Friday from 1 PM to 4 PM and on Sunday from 1 PM to 5 PM. Closed on national holidays, the month of August, and during Yale University recesses. 15 Hillhouse Ave; New Haven, CT 06511; Phone: (203) 432-0822; http://collection.yale.edu

New London, CT
Connecticut College Arboretum provides seasonal beauty all year with the landscaped grounds of the college campus as well as their plant collections, nature areas, and managed landscapes. There is no fee to visit. Open daily dawn to dusk. 270 Mohegan Ave (Rt 32); New London, CT 06320; Phone: (860) 439-5020; https://www.conncoll.edu/the-arboretum

Norwalk, CT
Norwalk City Hall Murals include 31 restored Works Progress Administration (WPA) murals from 1935 to 1941. The largest assemblage covers the three floors of City Hall. A self-guided tour is free. A docent led tour incurs a cost. 125 East Ave; Norwalk, CT 06851; Phone: (203) 854-3200; http://norwalkhistoricalsociety.org/images_2/Norwalk-WPA-Murals-Brochure-062015.pdf

Storrs, CT
Ballard Institute and Museum of Puppetry displays part of its over 2,500 puppets from all over the world. There's also books, manuscripts, posters, drawings, audio-visual materials, and photographs. There is no cost to visit the museum although there is a charge for their theatrical performances. Open Tuesday through Sunday from 11 AM to 7 PM. 1 Royce Cir; Storrs, CT 06268; Phone: (860) 486-8580; http://bimp.uconn.edu

Windsor, CT
Luddy/Taylor Tobacco Museum houses photographs, exhibits, and artifacts of the Connecticut Valley's tobacco industry. Free admission. Open Tuesday, Wednesday, Thursday, and Saturday from Noon to 4 PM. Northwest Park; 135 Lang Rd; Windsor, CT 06095; Phone: (860) 285-1888; http://www.tobaccohistsoc.org

Delaware

Dover, DE

Air Mobility Command Museum is dedicated to airlift and air refueling history, but the museum also displays 30 aircraft from cargo haulers, and fighters, to helicopters, and even presidential aircraft. The museum is located in the former Hanger 1301 in the building complex where secret military operations once took place. Admission is free. Guided tours are available. Open Tuesday through Sunday from 9 AM to 4 PM. Closed federal holidays except Veterans Day. Note: Access to the museum is only through the museum gate on Rt 9. 1301 Heritage Rd; Dover, DE 19902; Phone: (302) 677-5938; https://amcmuseum.org

Delaware State Capitol provides visitors with guided and self-guided tours of the legislative hall at no cost. State Capitol building is open to the public Monday through Friday from 8 AM until 4:30 PM. Tours are available Monday through Friday from 10 AM to 1 PM. In addition, tours can be taken on the first Saturday of each month and holidays from 9 AM to 4:30 PM, except Thanksgiving, Christmas, and New Year's Day. 411 Legislative Ave; Dover, DE 19901; Phone: (302) 739-9194; http://regulations.delaware.gov/Tour; https://legis.delaware.gov/Resources/PlanningAVisit

Johnson Victrola Museum traces the technology of early music. Eldridge Reeves Johnson founded the Victor Talking Machine Company in 1901. Exhibits include phonographs, recordings, memorabilia, and trademarks. Admission is free. Donations are appreciated. Open Wednesday through Saturday from 9 AM to 4:30 PM. Closed Easter, Thanksgiving, Christmas, and New Year's Day. 375 S New St; Dover, DE 19904; Phone: (302) 739-3262; http://history.delaware.gov/museums/jvm/jvm_main.shtml

Old State House served as Delaware's capitol until 1933. Admission is free. Donations appreciated. Open Monday through Saturday from 9 AM to 4:30 PM and Sunday from 1:30 PM to 4:30 PM. 25 The Green; Dover, DE 19901; Phone: (302) 744-5054; https://history.delaware.gov/sh_main

Woodburn, the official residence of the Governor of Delaware, is considered to be one of the finest Middle Period Georgian houses in Delaware. Admission is free. Tours are available Monday through Friday, 8:30 AM to 4:00 PM by appointment only. Tours must be scheduled at least 24 hours in advance. 151 Kings Hwy SW; Dover, DE 19901; Phone: (302) 739-5656 https://woodburn.delaware.gov

Milford, DE

Abbott's Mill Nature Center features trails through deciduous and Atlantic White Cedar woodlands. Sections of the trail include a handicap-accessible boardwalk that follows a stream to open meadows, picnic area, and a Garden for Wildlife. There's also a historic working gristmill and its 20-acre pond. Trails are open daily dawn to dusk. 15411 Abbott's Pond Rd; Milford, DE 19963; Phone: (302) 422-0847; https://www.delawarenaturesociety.org/centers/abbotts-mill-nature-center

Newark, DE

The **University of Delaware** offers three distinctly different collections free to the public. All are open Wednesday through Friday, and on Sunday from Noon to 5 PM. **Mineralogical Museum** displays 350 regional minerals. Penny Hall; 255 Academy St; Newark, DE 19716; Phone: (302) 831-4940; https://library.udel.edu/special/collections/mineralogical-museum. **Mechanical Hall Gallery** is the home of the Paul R. Jones Collection of African American Art. 30 N College Ave; Newark, DE 19716; Phone: (302) 831-8088; https://library.udel.edu/special/venues/mechanical-hall-gallery. **Old College Gallery** encompasses both a main gallery and the smaller West gallery, and curates between two and four exhibitions per year. 18 E Main St; Newark, DE 19716; Phone: (302) 831-6589; https://library.udel.edu/special/venues/old-college-gallery

Wilmington, DE

DuPont Environmental Education Center is 212 acres of freshwater tidal marsh adjoining the Christina River with its variety of wildlife. Open all year. The visitor center provides panoramic river and marsh views, plus a 10-acre ornamental garden, a quarter-mile handicap-accessible pond loop, and access to the seven-mile long Markell bike/hike trail. The visitor center is open Tuesday through Saturday from 11 AM to 5 PM and Sunday from Noon to 4 PM. Closed Thanksgiving, Christmas, and New Year's Day. 1400 Delmarva La; Wilmington, DE 19801; Phone: (302) 656-1490; https://www.delawarenaturesociety.org/centers/dupont-environmental-education-center

Florida

Florida is beloved by tourists who make Orlando and the beaches of this sandy-edged peninsula their destination. But Florida existed long before air-conditioning opened the state to tourists and snow-birds, and some of that history lives on.

Alachua, FL

Retirement Home for Horses at Mill Creek Farm saves and cares for elderly horses as well as retired police and military horses. Admission is technically not free – the price is two carrots. Visitors are welcomed on Saturday from 11 AM to 3 PM. 20307 NW CR 235A; Alachua, FL 32615; Phone: (386) 462-1001; https://millcreekfarm.org/visitor-information

Cape Coral, FL

Wicked Dolphin Artisan Rum Distillery sounds a bit like a rock group but this distillery goes for playful in name and drink. Tours are available Tuesdays, Thursdays, and Saturdays followed by rum sampling. Tours and tastings are free but reservations are required. 31 SW Third Pl; Cape Coral, FL 33991; Phone: (239) 242-5244; http://wickeddolphinrum.com/tours

Davenport, FL

Florida Sports Hall of Fame can be found in the Central Florida Visitor Center. It highlights athletes, coaches, and teams with memorabilia, collectibles and autographs, including NASCAR drivers Bobby and Donnie Allison. Free to visit. Open daily from 8 AM to 5 PM. 101 Adventure Ct; Davenport, FL 33837; Phone: (863) 420-2586; http://flasportshof.org/hall-of-fame

Daytona Beach and South Daytona, FL

Jackie Robinson Ballpark and Museum honors the contribution of baseball great Jackie Robinson who broke the color barrier in 1946 in this historic ballpark. The bronze statue of Robinson is on permanent display at the park's entrance but there's much more to see in the free outdoor museum. Open daily from 9 AM to 5 PM. Call if the gate is locked. 105 E. Orange Ave; Daytona Beach, FL 32114; Phone: (386) 257-3172; http://www.milb.com/content/page.jsp?ymd=20100223&content_id=8118488&sid=t450&vkey=team1

Museum of Racing History -- Living Legends of Auto Racing in the Sunshine Mall contains archival photos, engines, helmets, and other artifacts depicting the early days of racing. There's also a core collection of cars usually on display. There is no admission charge. Open Monday through Saturday from 10 AM to 5 PM. Note: They advise calling to confirm hours in the summer. 2400 S Ridgewood Ave; #36; South Daytona, FL 32119; https://livinglegendsofautoracing.com/museum

Southeast Museum of Photography is dedicated to photography and curates changing, limited run exhibits. Admission and events are free. Open Tuesday through Friday from 11 AM to 5 PM and on Wednesday until 6 PM. Open Saturday from 1 PM to 5 PM. Daytona State College; 1200 International Speedway; Daytona Beach, FL 32114; Phone: (386) 506-4475; https://www.smponline.org

DeLand, FL

African American Museum of the Arts centers on African American and Caribbean American culture and art. It is home to a permanent collection of more than 200 artifacts, including sculptures and ceremonial masks. Admission is free. Open Wednesday through Saturday from 10 AM to 4 PM. 325 S Clara Ave; DeLand, FL 32721; Phone: (386) 736-4004; https://www.africanmuseumdeland.org/aboutus.htm

DeLand Naval Air Station Museum, in a historic hanger, features exhibits of war-era archives and memorabilia, military vehicles, and aircraft. Admission is free with donations appreciated. Open Wednesday through Sunday from Noon to 4 PM. 910 Biscayne Blvd; DeLand, FL 32724; Phone: (386) 738-4149; http://www.delandnavalairmuseum.org

Gillespie Museum of Minerals features geology exhibits, displays on native ecosystems, minerals and mining, and fluorescent rocks. No admission fee. Open September through June on Tuesday through Friday from 10 AM to 4 PM. Closed during academic holidays and breaks. They advise checking the website for closures. 421 N Woodland Blvd; Unit 8403; DeLand, FL 32723; Phone: (386) 822-7330; https://www.stetson.edu/other/gillespie-museum

Homer and Dolly Hand Art Center exhibits Stetson University's extensive collection of art by Modernist painter Oscar Bluemner. All exhibitions are free. Open Monday through Wednesday, and Friday from 11 AM to 4 PM. On Thursday open from 11 AM to 6 PM. Open Saturday from Noon to 4 PM. Closed for all national holidays and holiday weekends as well as school-related breaks. 139 E Michigan Ave; DeLand, FL 32723; Phone: (386) 822-7262; https://www2.stetson.edu/hand-art-center

Memorial Hospital and Veterans Museum delivers eight different galleries and exhibits including a full operating room of the time period, mock pharmacy, and physicians examining room. There's also an array of electrical equipment, and WWI and WWII artifacts. The West Volusia Black Medical Gallery recognizes early medical professionals. Open Monday through Friday from Noon to 4 PM. Tours are free, though donations are accepted. 230 N Stone St; DeLand, FL 32720; Phone: (386) 490-6204; http://www.delandhouse.com/deland_memorial_hospital_museum.html

Eglin Air Force Base (near Valparaiso, FL)
Air Force Armament Museum displays weaponry from the early days of World War I through today's high tech planes and bombs. Vintage military aircraft, including the fastest plane ever built – the SR-71 Blackbird – are found outside. Admission is free. Open Monday through Saturday from 9:30 AM to 4:30 PM. Closed on federal holidays. Outdoor air park is open during daylight hours. 100 Museum Dr; Eglin Air Force Base, FL 32542; Phone: (850) 882-4062; http://www.afarmamentmuseum.com

Ellenton, FL
Judah P. Benjamin Confederate Memorial at Gamble Plantation Historic State Park is the only surviving antebellum mansion in South Florida. At the end of the Second Seminole War (1836-1842) the vanquished Seminoles were removed from Florida and the Armed Occupation Act was passed by Congress. The Act was similar to the Homestead Acts that opened the west to settlers. In 1843 Major Robert Gamble claimed his acreage. The United Daughters of the Confederacy bought and rehabilitated the house and furnished it in the style of a successful mid-19th century plantation. Admission is free but there is a charge for the guided tours. The park is opened daily all year from 8 AM until sunset. The visitor center with a museum is open Thursday through Monday from 9 AM to 5 PM. 3708 Patten Ave; Ellenton, FL 34222; Phone: (941) 723-4536; https://www.floridastateparks.org/park/Gamble-Plantation

Gainesville, FL
Florida Museum of Natural History offers permanent exhibits of Florida's fossils encapsulating 65 million years of Earth's history. Learn about some of the Museum's latest fossil research with images and specimens. There's also information on the area's waterways and wildlife as well as the people of early Florida. General admission is free, although there is a charge for featured exhibits and the Butterfly Rainforest. 3215 Hull Rd; Powell Hall; UF Cultural Plaza; Gainesville, FL 32611; Phone: (352) 846-2000; https://www.floridamuseum.ufl.edu

Samuel P. Harn Museum of Art features American paintings, African, and pre-Columbian collections, and contemporary works of art. Admission is free. Open Tuesday through Friday from 11 AM to 5 PM. Open Saturday from 10 AM to 5 PM. Open Sunday from 1 PM to 5 PM. Closed state holidays. 3259 Hull Rd; Gainesville, FL 32611; Phone: (352) 392.9826; http://www.harn.ufl.edu

Jacksonville, FL (See also St Augustine, FL)

Fort Caroline is part of the Timucuan Preserve, and describes the brief 16th century French presence in Florida. It summarizes some of the themes that dominated north Florida history from the contact between Native Americans and Europeans, to the battles between the French and Spanish. There's also hiking trails. Note: Bug repellent is recommended. The site is open daily from 9 AM to 5 PM. 12713 Fort Caroline Rd; Jacksonville, FL 32225; Phone: (904) 641-7155; https://www.nps.gov/timu/index.htm

Jacksonville Equestrian Center isn't exactly a free attraction, but this 2,000 acre facility regularly offers horse-focused free admission events. Note: The facility is sometimes used for fee-based events.
13611 Normandy Blvd; Jacksonville, FL 32221; Phone: (904) 255-4254; http://www.jaxequestriancenter.com/events

Kingsley Plantation features the oldest surviving plantation house in the state built circa 1798. There's an attached kitchen, barn, and even the remains of slave cabins. There is no cost to visit the plantation. The tour of the main house is also free, but only available on weekends. Reservations are suggested. The grounds are open daily from 9 AM to 5 PM. Closed Thanksgiving, Christmas, and New Year's Day. Note: The road to the plantation is unpaved but drivable. 11676 Palmetto Ave; Jacksonville, FL 32226; Phone: (904) 251-3537; https://www.nps.gov/timu/learn/historyculture/kp.htm

Sally Corporation calls itself *The Dark Ride Specialists* for its creation of rides in an indoor environment and through a series of scenes or tableaus with sound, light, animation, and special effects. They also create human, animal, and cartoon animatronic characters and shows. Free tours every Tuesday and Thursday from 9 AM until 1 PM. Reservations must be made in advance. Tours are open to individuals as well as groups. Note: No tours are offered June through August. 745 W Forsyth St; Jacksonville, FL 32204; Phone: (904) 355-7100; http://sallycorp.com/company/tours

The Keys

A region unto itself, joined by bridges to each other and the Florida peninsula, the Keys (from the Spanish cayo meaning small island) are laidback, quirky, and outdoorsy with a definitely tropical vibe.

Big Pine Key, FL

National Key Deer Refuge is home to the pint-size white-tailed deer known as Key Deer. But the over 9,000 acres making up the refuge are also home to 23 endangered and threatened plant and animal species. Visitors can view the wildlife at the observation platform at Blue Hole and along Mannillo Trail. The refuge is open all year but rangers and volunteers offer guided walks, bike rides, and kayak trips generally from December through March. Admission is free. The refuge is open daily from sunrise to sunset. The visitor center is open Monday through Saturday from 10 AM to 3 PM. 179 Key Deer Blvd; Big Pine Key, FL 33043; Phone: (305) 872-0774; https://www.fws.gov/refuge/National_Key_Deer_Refuge

Key West, FL

Key West is famous for Duval Street and Mallory Square. Both are fun to explore any time, but visit Mallory Square at its Sunset Celebration. The waterfront fills with visitors, locals, and performers. http://www.mallorysquare.com

Key West Cemetery is known for its fascinating headstones and its extensive system of above-the-ground graves. There are historic Catholic, and Jewish sections as well as the USS Maine Plot dedicated in 1900. The Los Martires de Cuba is a memorial for those who fought in the Cuban revolution. A free comprehensive self-guided tour map is available at the cemetery's front entrance. Office hours are Monday through Friday from 8:30 AM to 3:30 PM. You can download a self-guided tour map, with some quirky highlights: http://www.keywesttravelguide.com/key-west-cemetery-map-self-guided-tour 701 Pauline St; Key West, FL 33040; Phone: (305) 292-8177; http://www.cityofkeywest-fl.gov/department/division.php?structureid=62

Kissimmee, FL

Disney Wilderness Preserve started out as a heavily logged ranch, but has now been restored to a near pristine environment with 3,500 acres of wetlands that feed the headwaters of the Greater Everglades watershed. The preserve offers hiking trails leading to the shores of Lake Russell along with opportunities to view rare animal and bird species. There's a self-guided nature trail and a 2½-mile hiking trail. Admission is free. 2700 Scrub Jay Trail; Kissimmee, FL 34759; Phone: (407) 935-0002; https://www.nature.org/ourinitiatives/regions/northamerica/unitedstates/florida/placesweprotect/the-disney-wilderness-preserve.xml

Lakeland, FL

Polk Museum of Art at Florida Southern College has gathered works on modern and contemporary art as well as Ancient American, Asian, European Decorative, and African art. Admission is free. Open Tuesday through Saturday from 10 AM to 5 PM, and Sunday from 1 PM to 5 PM. 800 E Palmetto St; Lakeland, FL 33801; Phone: (863) 688-7743; https://polkmuseumofart.org

Polk's Nature Discovery Center at Circle B Bar Reserve started as a cattle ranch but today is home to a wide variety of plants and animals. The family-friendly Exhibit Hall introduces the habitats of central Florida. Admission is free. Open Tuesday through Saturday from 9 AM to 4 PM, and on Sunday from Noon to 4 PM. The trails are generally open daily dawn to dusk. 4399 Winter Lake Rd; Lakeland, FL 33803; Phone: (863) 668-4673; http://polknature.com/polk-nature-discovery-center

Melbourne Beach, FL

Archie Carr National Wildlife Refuge invites visitors to explore the diverse habitats of the barrier island. The center provides interactive exhibits, nature films, one-mile dune-to-lagoon nature trail, and an accessible ocean view boardwalk. There are no day use fees but a fee will be incurred at certain areas within Sebastian Inlet State Park. Open Tuesday through Sunday from 9 AM to 5 PM. Note: Guided turtle walks are available seasonally – the money collected from these fee-based tours help fund their activities. 8385 S US Hwy A1A; Melbourne Beach, FL 32951; Phone: (321) 723-3556; https://www.fws.gov/refuge/Archie_Carr/visit/plan_your_visit

Miami and Miami Beach, FL

Institute of Contemporary Art, Miami (ICA) highlights established contemporary artists though their permanent collection and exhibits. Free admission. Open Tuesday through Sunday from 11 AM to 7 PM. Free guided tours are available at 1 PM every day. You can reserve tickets online. 61 NE 41st St; Miami, FL 33137; Phone: (305) 901-5272; https://www.icamiami.org/visit

Patricia & Phillip Frost Art Museum curates unique exhibitions as well as displays from their permanent collection with an emphasis on Haitian and Cuban painting. Admission is free. Open Tuesday through Saturday from 10 AM to 5 PM, and on Sunday from Noon to 5 PM. Closed most legal and university holidays. 10975 SW 17th St; Miami, FL 33199; Phone: (305) 348-2890; https://frost.fiu.edu/visit/index.html

Little Haiti Cultural Complex showcases Haitian art, sculpture, and crafts. There's an art gallery and the Caribbean Marketplace with authentic Haitian art and crafts for sale. Admission is free to the gallery and marketplace. Open Monday through Friday 10 AM to 9 PM. Open Saturday from 10 AM to 4 PM. 212-260 NE 59th Terrace; Miami, FL 33137; Phone: (305) 960-2969; http://littlehaiticulturalcenter.com

Miami Beach Botanical Garden highlights native plants and trees. Visitors can also stroll through a Japanese garden. Admission is free although donations are appreciated. Open Tuesday to Sunday from 9 AM to 5 PM. Closed some major holidays. 2000 Convention Center Dr; Miami Beach, FL 33139; Phone: (305) 673-7256; https://www.mbgarden.org/visit/hours

Palm Coast, FL

Princess Park Preserve features a lodge that was once owned by a princess, and the story behind it is unusual and fascinating. There are free lodge tours Friday through Sunday at 2 PM. Admission to the park is free. The park is open daily from 7 AM to 6 PM for recreational activities. There's even horse trails. 2500 Princess Place Rd; Palm Coast, FL 32137; Phone: (386) 313-4020; http://www.flaglercounty.org/departments/princess_place_preserve/index.php

Pensacola, FL

Colonial Archaeological Trail is a collection of outdoor exhibits relating to the Spanish, British, and American occupations. http://www.historicpensacola.org/plan-your-visit/museums-properties/colonial-archaeological-trail

Museum of Naval Aviation features over 140 restored aircraft representing Navy, Marine Corps, and Coast Guard Aviation. Admission is free although the motion-based flight simulator, and 4D theater shows will incur charges. Located at Naval Air Station Pensacola, visitors are required to enter and exit through the West Gate off Blue Angel Parkway. The National Naval Aviation Museum shares its home with the United States Navy's **Blue Angels Flight Demonstration Squadron**. Visitors are invited to watch these pilots practice on most Tuesday and Wednesday mornings from March to November. Practice typically last about an hour and begins at 11:30 AM. Note: Pensacola is on Central Time. Admission to their practice is free. 1750 Radford Blvd; Pensacola, FL 32508; Phone: (800) 327-5002; http://www.navalaviationmuseum.org

Port Orange, FL

Dunlawton Plantation Sugar Mill Ruins certainly offers gardens and the ruins of sugar mills, but only Dunlawton offers dinosaurs peeking around ruins and trees. In the 1950s the land was home to a theme park called Bongoland, and some of the large faux creatures still remain. There is no admission charge. Open daily 8 AM to 5 PM. Closed Christmas, and New Year's Day. 950 Old Sugar Mill Rd; Port Orange, FL 32129; Phone: (386) 767-1735; http://www.dunlawtonsugarmillgardens.org

St. Augustine, FL (See also Jacksonville, FL)

Fort Matanzas National Monument Park was part of the give-and-take between the major players in colonizing the Americas. French, Spanish, British all took turns possessing the area. The fort offers free admission to tour the 18th century

Spanish fort. As a nice addition, a complimentary boat ride to the fort is included. Passes are issued from the Fort Matanzas Visitor Center (not the St. Augustine city visitor center) on a first come, first served basis. Open from 9 AM to 5:30 PM daily except Thanksgiving, and Christmas Day. The ferry runs hourly on the half-hour between 9:30 AM and 4:30 PM. 8635 A1A S; St. Augustine, FL 32080; Phone: (904) 471-0116; http://www.nps.gov/foma

St. Augustine Distillery offers free tours with tastings of all their artisan spirits, plus a small museum with historical and informative exhibits. Tours are offered daily from 10:30 AM to 5 PM. 112 Riberia St; St. Augustine, FL 32084; Phone: (904) 825-4962; http://staugustinedistillery.com/tours-rfp

Sarasota, FL
Drum Circle Distilling invites visitors for free tours and tastings of their Siesta Key Rum. They also make spiced and toasted coconut rums. Tours are currently offered daily except Thursdays. They recommend online registration and an arrival 15 minutes early. 2212 Industrial Blvd; Sarasota, FL 34234; Phone: (941) 702-8143; http://www.drumcircledistilling.com/Company/tours.html

Tallahassee, FL
The city's Art & Culture District offers more than 70 studios, galleries, and small shops. https://www.railroadsquare.com
Florida State Capitol is open for free self-guided tours Monday through Friday from 8 AM to 5 PM. Closed holidays. Self-guided tour information and pamphlets are available from the Florida Welcome Center. 400 South Monroe St; Tallahassee, FL 32399; Phone: (850) 488-6167; https://www.floridacapitol.myflorida.com/visitors/visiting_the_capitol

Governor's Mansion opens five state rooms of the mansion, plus the outdoor Manatee Sculpture Courtyard to visitors. The free public tours are available all year Monday through Friday from 10 AM to 4 PM but must be booked in advance. 700 N Adams St; Tallahassee, FL 32303; Phone: (850) 717-9345; http://www.floridagovernorsmansion.com/schedule_a_tour

Historic Capitol has been restored to its 1902 appearance. More than 250 artifacts in 21 rooms and three floors invite visitors to trace the evolution of Florida government from territorial days to the present. Self-guided tour pamphlets are available. Admission is free, however donations are appreciated. Open Monday through Friday from 9 AM to 4:30 PM. Open Saturday from 10 AM to 4:30 PM and Sunday and holidays from Noon to 4:30 PM. Closed on Thanksgiving, and Christmas Day. 400 S Monroe St; Tallahassee, FL 32399; Phone: (850) 487-1902; http://flhistoriccapitol.gov/Pages/VisitUs

Knott House Museum was built in 1843, probably by George Proctor, who was a free black builder. Attorney Thomas Hagner and his bride Catherine Gamble moved in the next year. The Knott family bought the house in 1928. Today it's a museum with furnishings from that time period. Admission is free. Donations accepted. Guided tours are offered Wednesday through Friday at 1 PM, 2 PM, and 3 PM. On Saturday tours are provided at 10 AM, 11 AM, Noon, 1 PM, 2 PM, and 3 PM. Closed the month of August for annual maintenance. 301 E Park Ave; Tallahassee, FL 32301; Phone: (850) 922-2459; http://www.museumoffloridahistory.com/about/sites/index.cfm

Meek Eaton Black Archives emphasizes records relating to the history of Africans and Black Americans. The museum component of the archives is open to the public Monday through Friday from 10 AM to 5 PM and Saturday from Noon to 4 PM. There is no admission fee. Museum tours are self-guided. F1lorida A&M University; 445 Gamble St; Tallahassee, FL 32307; Phone: (850) 599-3020; http://famu.edu/index.cfm?MEBA&Home

Museum of Florida History illuminates the past and present cultures of the state. Admission is free with donations appreciated. Open Monday through Friday from 9 AM to 4:30 PM. Open Saturday from 10 AM to 4:30, and Sunday and holidays from Noon to 4:30 PM. Closed Christmas Eve, Christmas Day, New Year's Eve, and New Year's Day. R.A. Gray Building; 500 S Bronough St; Tallahassee, FL 32399; Phone: (850) 245-6400; http://www.museumoffloridahistory.com/index.cfm

Supreme Court welcomes visitors to observe oral arguments held August through June typically during the first full week of each month. No appointment is necessary and self-guided tours are available. The courthouse is open Monday through Friday from 8 AM to 5 PM. Closed all holidays. 400 S Duval St; Tallahassee, FL 32399; Phone: (850) 921-9446; http://www.floridasupremecourt.org/education/index.shtml

Tampa, FL

Yuengling Brewery Tours are open to the public and free. Tours are currently offered Monday through Friday at 10:30 AM and 1 PM, and on Saturday at 10:30 AM and Noon. Enjoy free sampling at the brewery's biergarten after the tour. Note: Completely closed shoes are required. 11111 N 30th St; Tampa, FL 33612; Phone: (813) 972-8529; https://www.yuengling.com/visit-us

Vero Beach, FL

Pelican Island National Wildlife Refuge has wildlife viewing available from hiking trails, and observation platforms. Free wildlife tours are offered in winter on Wednesday from 8 AM to 10 AM. There is no fee to enjoy the refuge. Public areas are open daily from 7:30 AM until sunset. Note: Bring your own drinking water and bug repellant. Hwy A1A, south of Sebastian Inlet. Phone: (772) 581-5557; https://www.fws.gov/refuge/Pelican_Island

Georgia

Andersonville, GA

Andersonville National Historic Site preserves the former Camp Sumter, an infamous Confederate prisoner-of-war (POW) camp during the last year of the Civil War. Built to hold a maximum of 10,000 prisoners, instead it was cramped and overcrowded with more than 45,000 Union soldiers. Almost 30% died of exposure, and disease. Two sections of the stockade wall have been reconstructed. The site also contains the Andersonville National Cemetery, and the National Prisoner of War Museum which honors U.S. POWs in all wars. There is no entrance fee. Open daily from 8 AM to 5 PM, and the museum is open daily from 9:30 AM to 4:30 PM. Both are closed Thanksgiving, Christmas, and New Year's Day. 760 POW Rd; Andersonville, GA 31711; Phone: (229) 924-0343; https://www.nps.gov/ande/index.htm

Atlanta, GA

Atlanta Monetary Museum focuses on the Federal Reserve offering interactive exhibits explaining the story of money from barter to modern times, and the history of banking in America. Tours are self-guided and free, available Monday through Friday from 9 AM to 4 PM. Closed major holidays. Note: Adult visitors to the Monetary Museum will need to present a valid form of government-issued ID. 1000 Peachtree St NE; Atlanta, GA 30309; Phone: (404) 498-8500; https://www.frbatlanta.org/about/tours/museum.aspx

Clark Atlanta University Art Museum is home to a historical collection of African-American art, and murals by Hale Woodruff. It presents exhibitions and related programs placing African-American fine art within the context of key art movements and intellectual currents of the 20th and 21st centuries. Admission is free with donations accepted. Open Tuesday through Friday from 11 AM to 4 PM. The *Art of the Negro* mural series can be found in the Hale Aspacio Woodruff Atrium. It is open Monday through Friday from 9 AM to 5 PM. 223 James P. Brawley Dr, SW; Atlanta, GA 30314; Phone: (404) 880-8000; http://www.cau.edu/art-galleries

David J. Sencer CDC Museum explains the CDC's origins and history through documents, photographs, and objects from the CDC collection. Highlights include a wooden intelligence test, Dr. Joseph Mountin's microscope, an iron lung, and a ped-o-jet used in the campaign to eradicate smallpox. Admission is free. Open Monday through Friday from 9 AM to 5 PM, closing on Thursday at 7 PM. Closed federal holidays. 1600 Clifton Rd NE; Atlanta, GA 30329; Phone (404) 639-0830; http://www.cdc.gov/museum/index.htm

Fernbank Science Center and the Dr. Ralph L. Buice, Jr. Observatory houses the largest telescope in the southeastern United States. Free public observations are offered every Thursday and Friday evening from 9 PM (or dark) until 10:30 PM, weather permitting. Check the website for updates. The exhibit hall at the Fernbank Center is free to visit. Currently open Monday through Friday from Noon to 5 PM, closing on Thursday and Friday at 9 PM. Open Saturday from 10 AM to 5 PM. They recommend checking hours in advance as they vary through the year. Note: There is a fee for the planetarium show. 156 Heaton Park Dr; Atlanta, GA 30307; Phone: (678) 874-7102; http://www.fernbank.edu/fsc.html

Georgia State Capitol offers both self-guided and guided tours of the Capitol, including the Capitol Museum, and Hall of Valor. All are free of charge. While most of the exhibits are located on the fourth floor, memorials, and artwork highlighting Georgia's history can be found throughout the building. Open Monday through Friday from 8 AM to 5 PM. Closed Georgia state holidays. Note: All visitors aged 18 and older must show photo identification. 206 State Capitol; Atlanta, GA 30334; Phone: (404) 656-2846; http://www.libs.uga.edu/capitolmuseum

Martin Luther King Jr. National Historic Site includes the birthplace and grave of this famous civil rights leader. The grounds also include the Ebenezer Baptist Church, and the Freedom Hall Complex. Stop at the information desk for an orientation to the historic site, and to sign up for a Birth Home tour. There is no admission fee. The visitor center, the historic Ebenezer Baptist Church, and Freedom Hall are open daily from 9 AM to 5 PM. The Birth Home is open for ranger-led tours daily from 10 AM to 4 PM. 450 Auburn Ave NE; Atlanta, GA 30312; Phone: (404) 331-5190; https://www.nps.gov/malu/index.htm

Robert C. Williams Paper Museum preserves the history of paper and paper technology, from ancient Sumerian cuneiform tablets and Egyptian papyrus scrolls to the watermarked papers of Italy to the high-tech machinery of the modern paper industry. Admission is free. Open Monday through Friday from 9 AM to 5 PM. Closed all Georgia Tech holidays. In the Renewable Bioproducts Institute. 500 10th St NW; Atlanta, GA 30332; Phone: (404) 894-7840; http://paper.gatech.edu

Duluth, GA
Hudgens Center for Art and Learning displays rotating exhibits with works from their private collection as well as from local artists. Admission to the galleries is free. Open Tuesday through Saturday from 10 AM to 5 PM. Open late Thursday to 8 PM. 6400 Sugarloaf Pkwy; Building 300; Duluth, GA 30097; Phone: (770) 623-6002; https://thehudgens.org

Folkston, GA

Folkston Funnel is the main railroad artery in and out of Florida. The Folkston platform not only provides the view, but also a scanner to listen to radio traffic between trains. Visitors can stop by the restored Folkston depot, now a museum dedicated to railroad memorabilia. Admission is free. The funnel is always open. The museum is open Monday through Friday from 9 AM to 5 PM, and Saturday from 10 AM to 3 PM. Closed major holidays. 3795 Main St; Folkston, GA 31537; Phone: (912) 496-2536; https://charltoncountyga.us/239/Museum

Kennesaw, GA

Bentley Rare Book Museum highlights the diversity of the written and printed word in the English-speaking world, including Georgia authors, Cherokee language, and medieval manuscripts and special exhibits. Free to the public. Open Tuesday through Friday from 10 AM to 4 PM. It's on the ground floor of the Sturgis Library. 385 Cobb Ave; Kennesaw, GA 30144; Phone: (470) 578-6289; https://rarebooks.kennesaw.edu/index.php

Bernard A. Zuckerman Museum of Art presents works from Kennesaw State University's permanent art collection as well as exhibits of contemporary works. Free to the public. Open Tuesday through Saturday from 10 AM to 5 PM and on Sunday from Noon to 5 PM. May be closed during university holidays and summer/winter breaks. 492 Prillaman Way; Kennesaw, GA 30144; Phone: (470) 578-3223; https://arts.kennesaw.edu/zuckerman/index.php

Lilburn, GA

BAPS Shri Swaminarayan Mandir is a traditional Hindu mandir, or place of worship. Visually striking, the mandir is made of over 34,000 pieces of hand-carved Italian marble, Turkish limestone and Indian pink sandstone. The mandir is open to all and entrance is free. Visitors are invited to witness or participate in ceremonies and prayers. Open daily from 9 AM to 6 PM. Times of the rituals and ceremonies are listed on the website. Note: All clothing must cover shoulders and knees and they request that all personal belongings remain inside vehicles. There is a fee to rent the audio tape tour. 460 Rockbridge Rd NW; Lilburn, GA 30047; Phone: (678) 906-2277; https://www.baps.org/atlanta

Lithonia, GA

AWARE Wildlife Center rehabilitates Georgia's injured and orphaned native wild animals. Their free tours are held at 1 PM every Saturday and Sunday, weather permitting. Donations are always welcomed. No reservations needed. 4158 Klondike Rd; Lithonia, GA 30038; Phone: (678) 418-1111; http://www.awarewildlife.org/programs-tours

Macon, GA

Ocmulgee Mounds National Historical Park protects the 17,000-year-old Native American earth lodge and mounds. Ocmulgee Mounds had the largest archaeology dig in American history with over 800 people discovering 3 million artifacts. The park and the visitor center are open daily from 9 AM to 5 PM. Closed Christmas, and New Year's. Admission is free, except for some special events. 1207 Emery Hwy; Macon, GA 31217; Phone: (478) 752-8257 x222; https://www.nps.gov/ocmu/index.htm.

Rose Hill Cemetery opened in 1840 and is most noted for the members of the Allman Brothers band who are buried there. Gregg and Duane Allman, and founding bassist Berry Oakley all share a fenced in private area. The cemetery is open 24 hours a day. 1071 Riverside Dr; Macon, GA 31201; Phone: (478) 751-9119.

Marietta GA

Marietta Fire Department Museum dates back to the 1800s and displays fire service clothing, equipment, and antique apparatus as well as antique fire engines and fire-fighting equipment. Free to visit. Donations appreciated. Open Monday through Friday from 8 AM to 5 PM. Fire Station 1; 112 Haynes St; Marietta, GA 30060; Phone: (770) 794-5466; http://www.marietta.com/marietta-fire-museum

Peachtree City, GA

Dixie Wing WWII Aircraft Museum examines combat aircraft flown by all military services of the United States, and rare flying WWII and Korea warplanes. Admission is free. Open Tuesday, Thursday, and Saturday from 9 AM to 4 PM. 1200 Echo Ct; Peachtree City, GA 30269; Phone: (678) 364-1110; http://www.DixieWing.org

Plains, GA

Jimmy Carter National Historic Site encompasses the museum and visitor center in the Plains High School and includes a restored and furnished classroom, principal's office, and auditorium. Other rooms feature exhibits that describe the Carters' lives in Plains, including the post-presidency. The Plains Train Depot focuses on Carter's campaigns for State Senator, Governor of Georgia, and the 1976 Presidential Campaign. The Jimmy Carter Boyhood Farm was his home from the age of four until he started college. Admission to all are free. The site is open daily except Thanksgiving, Christmas, and New Year's Day. A guided walking tour of the Jimmy Carter Boyhood Farm is generally offered Saturday and Sunday at 1 PM. 300 N Bond St; Plains, GA 31780; Phone: (229) 824-4104; https://www.nps.gov/jica/index.htm

Sandy Springs, GA

Anne Frank in the World uses photographs and short films to illuminate the life of Anne Frank whose diary put a face to the children slain by the Nazis. The site includes a replica of Anne Frank's room where she hid from the Nazis. *Witness to the Holocaust: WWII Veteran William Alexander Scott III at Buchenwald* highlights World War II veteran and civil rights activist who served as a photographer in a segregated battalion of the United States Army and witnessed the liberation of the Buchenwald concentration camp. The exhibit is free and open to the public. Note: Parents may want to consider their children's age as both graphic images and disturbing themes are included. It is on the second level of the Parkside Shopping Center at the top of the stairs. Open Tuesday through Friday from 10 AM to 4 PM with 2 PM closing on Friday. Open Saturday and Sunday from Noon to 4 PM. 5920 Roswell Rd; Suite A-209; Sandy Springs, GA 30328; Phone: (770) 206-1558; https://holocaust.georgia.gov/anne-frank-world-1929-1945

Savannah, GA

Savannah has a free downtown transit system, spanning land and water. The Savannah Belles Ferry links River Street to Hutchinson Island by providing free passage across the Savannah River. https://www.catchacat.org/getting-around/ride-free-downtown

Bonaventure Cemetery has many famous residents and is known for its beauty, but it may be most famous for its role in the 1994 novel *Midnight in the Garden of Good and Evil* and the subsequent movie. There is never an admission charge. It is open daily from 8 AM to 5 PM. The Bonaventure Historical Society offers a limited schedule of free guided tours. You can also download an app for self-guided tours. Note: The cemetery is technically in nearby Thunderbolt. 330 Bonaventure Rd; Thunderbolt, GA 31404; Phone: (912) 651-6843; http://www.bonaventurehistorical.org

City Hall Tours highlight the building's history, architecture, and art. Monthly lunch-time tours are held the first Tuesday of each month at Noon. Tours are free, but space is limited and reservations are necessary. City Hall also hosts *Art in the Rotunda*, a rotating exhibit on the first floor featuring the work of local artists or highlighting local history. Open Monday through Friday from 8:15 AM to 5 PM. Closed city holidays. 2 E Bay St, Savannah, GA 31401; Phone: (912) 651-4212; https://www.savannahga.gov/557/City-Hall-Tours
https://www.savannahga.gov/1356/Programs-and-Exhibits

Ghost Coast Distillery embraces the spirit of Savannah with their free behind-the-scenes tour filled with stories about the city's history of drinks and revelry as well as how they create their hand-crafted spirits. Note: If you take the tour on a weekday you'll also see their video presentation. Tours available Tuesday through Saturday from Noon to 6 PM, and on Sunday from 1 PM to 4 PM. 641 Indian St; Savannah, GA 31401; Phone: (912) 298-0071; https://ghostcoastdistillery.com/visit-us

Savannah Botanical Gardens presents both formal and naturalistic plantings as well as a two-acre pond, amphitheater, nature trails, and an archaeological exhibit. Admission is free. Open Monday through Sunday from 8 AM to 8 PM. 1388 Eisenhower Dr; Savannah, GA 31406; Phone: (912) 355-3883; https://www.savannahbotanical.org

Sautee Nacoochee, GA
Gourd Place is a retail shop, but one with 200 gourds from 23 countries. They also have works by contemporary gourd artists. Open daily April through mid-December on Monday through Saturday from 10 AM to 5 PM, and Sunday from 1 PM to 5 PM. Closed Easter and Thanksgiving. 2319 Duncan Bridge Rd; Sautee Nacoochee, GA 30571; Phone: (706) 865-4048; http://gourdplace.com

Statesboro, GA
Museum on Main showcases the region's history through a partnership with Georgia Southern University to host traveling exhibits. Admission is free. Open Monday through Friday from 9 AM to 5 PM, closing on Friday at 4 PM. Open Saturday from 9 AM to 1 PM. 222 S Main St; Statesboro, GA 30458; Phone: (912) 489-1869; https://www.visitstatesboro.org/museum-on-main

Suwanee, GA
Everett's Music Barn hosts free live music on Saturday nights. Donations appreciated. Doors open at 6 PM every Saturday. Show starts at 8 PM. 4055 Stonecypher Rd; Suwanee, GA 30024; Phone: (770) 722-1276; http://www.everettsmusicbarn.net/home.html

Warner Robins, GA
Museum of Aviation – Georgia Aviation Hall of Fame displays some of their 85 historic U.S. Air Force aircraft, missiles, cockpits, and exhibits. Admission is free. Open daily 9 AM to 5 PM. Closed major holidays. 1942 Heritage Blvd; Warner Robins, GA 31088; Phone: (478) 926-6870; http://www.museumofaviation.org

Hawaii

Hawaii often confuses visitors by being a state made up of several islands, including one named Hawaii. The most popular island and the one hosting the state capitol is not Hawaii – it's Oahu. Thus, there's the state of Hawaii, the island named Hawaii (also known as the Big Island), and the famous beach (Waikiki) on an entirely different island. For an added bit of confusion, the official spelling of Hawaiian names can include an apostrophe which is a glottal stop and indicates a separate sound. The fully correct spelling for this state is Hawai'i but for simplicity the apostrophe has been omitted from island names. The four major islands are Hawaii, Kauai, Maui, and Oahu. Although there are other islands that make up Hawaii, these are the most popular. All state parks on Hawaii are free to visit.
https://hawaiistateparks.org

One important note about area codes. The (808) telephone area code is **not** a toll-free code – it covers the inhabited, developed and uninhabited areas of the Hawaiian Islands.

Island of Hawaii (The Big Island)
Captain Cook, HI
Royal Kona Coffee Center celebrates the coffee from the Kona region of Hawaii. The coffee center offers free tours and tastings. Visitors will see where Kona growers bring their coffee cherries to be processed and ultimately shipped to their facility on Oahu. Open daily, including holidays from 7:30 AM to 5 PM. 83-5427 Mamalahoa Hwy; Captain Cook, HI 96704; Phone: (800) 669-5633; http://royalkonacoffee.com/visit

Hilo, HI
Wailuku River State Park is two separate park areas in one. The popular **Boiling Pots** is a succession of big pools connected by underground flows making the waters roll and bubble as if boiling. The 80-foot **Rainbow Falls** is famous for the rainbow formed from its morning mist. Admission is free. Open daily during daylight hours. Both park sections are accessed via Waianuenue Avenue in downtown Hilo. Hilo, HI 96720; Phone: (808) 587-0400; http://dlnr.hawaii.gov/dsp/parks/hawaii/wailuku-river-state-park

Kailua-Kona, HI
Kaloko-Honokohau National Historical Park offers an ancient heiau (or temple) standing at the end of the beach. Guided tours and special programs are available at the visitor center, Hale Ho'okipa, located ½-mile north of the entrance to Honokohau Harbor. Admission to the park is free. Open daily from 8:30 AM to 4

PM. Hwy 19; Kailua-Kona, HI 96740; Phone: (808) 329-6881 x1329; https://www.nps.gov/kaho/index.htm

Kawaihae, HI
Pu`ukohola Heiau combines the romance of the Great King Kamehameha, an ancient temple, and sharks. Mailekini Heiau is a temple-turned-fort. Park rangers provide presentations, and guided tours of the grounds as staffing permits. No entrance fees. Open daily 7:30 AM to 5 PM. 62-3601 Kawaihae Rd; Kawaihae, HI; Phone: (808) 882-7218; https://www.nps.gov/puhe/index.htm

Keaau, HI
Mauna Loa Macadamia Nut Corporation invites visitors to tour the factory and enjoy free samples of Hawaii's favorite nut. The three-mile drive to the visitor center meanders through macadamia nut orchards. Open daily 8:30 AM to 5 PM. 16-701 Macadamia Rd; Keaau, HI 96749; Phone: (888) 628-6256 (Toll-free); https://www.maunaloa.com/visitor

Kealakekua, HI
Greenwell Farms offers complimentary daily tours of the coffee fields and processing plant from 9 AM to 4 PM. Free samples of various coffee products are provided. 81-6581 Mamalahoa Hwy; Kealakekua, HI 96750; Phone: (808) 323-2295; http://www.greenwellfarms.com/coffee-tour

Waimea, HI
Note: Also known as Kamuela, this town is different from Waimea on the island of Kauai with its famous canyon.
Lapakahi State Historical Park protects a 600-year old, partially restored ancient Hawaiian fishing settlement. A self-guided one-mile loop trail offers a glimpse of early Native Hawaiian life. There is no admission fee. Open daily 8 AM to 4 PM. Closed state holidays. 57-1686 Akoni Pule Hwy; Waimea, HI 96743; Phone: (808) 961-8311; http://dlnr.hawaii.gov/dsp/parks/hawaii/lapakahi-state-historical-park

Island of Kauai
Waimea, HI
Waimea Canyon State Park has been aptly compared to Arizona's Grand Canyon. The rim overlooks the deep, colorful gorge and provides a view of Ni'ihau Island. Open daily during daylight hours with no admission. The main road, Waimea Canyon Drive, leads to a lower lookout point and the main Waimea Canyon Overlook with views of Kauai's dramatic interior. Waimea Canyon Dr; Waimea, HI 96796; Phone: (808) 274-3444; http://dlnr.hawaii.gov/dsp/parks/kauai/waimea-canyon-state-park

Island of Maui
Lahaina, HI

This seaport town overflows with free attractions and the credit goes to the Lahaina Restoration Foundation. Not all of the sites are free but several important places are open at no cost. http://lahainarestoration.org/historic-sites

Hale Pa'ahao Prison was Lahaina's new prison in the 1850s and the list of unlawful infractions includes many behaviors that aren't criminalized today including Breaking the Sabbath. Admission is free. Open daily from 10 AM to 4 PM. 187 Prison St; Lahaina, HI 96761; Phone: (808) 661-3262; http://lahainarestoration.org/hale-paahao-prison

Hale Pa'i Printing Museum is the home of the first Hawaiian language newspaper. It printed the first newspaper west of the Rocky Mountains on February 14, 1834. Free admission. Open Monday through Wednesday from 10 AM to 4 PM. 980 Lahainaluna Rd; Lahaina, HI 96761; Phone: (808) 662-0560; http://lahainarestoration.org/hale-pai-museum

Lahaina Heritage Museum in the 150-year-old courthouse on Prison Street celebrates the history of the city. It's adjacent to Banyan Tree Park, another free site. The old prison in the basement is now an art gallery, but you can still see the original cells with their iron bars. Admission and tours are free. Open daily 9 AM to 5 PM. 648 Wharf St; Lahaina, HI 96761; Phone: (808) 661-3262; http://lahainarestoration.org/lahaina-heritage-museum

Lahaina Lighthouse sits at the end of Lahaina Harbor and is the oldest lighthouse in the Pacific. http://lahainarestoration.org/lahaina-lighthouse

Pioneer Mill Co was the first plantation to grow sugar commercially in Lahaina and the company built one of Hawaii's first sugar mills. The buildings have all been demolished but the 225-foot high, brick-and-concrete smokestack is still standing. Visitors can also see two locomotive engines (Lahaina and Launiupoko) used by the Pioneer Mill Co. Admission is free. Open during daylight hours. 275 Lahainaluna Rd; Lahaina, HI 96761; Phone: (808) 661-3262; http://lahainarestoration.org/pioneer-mill-smokestack-locomotives

Plantation Museum centers on West Maui's plantation era using artifacts and photos including displays of heirlooms, appliances, tools, and sports gear. Admission is free. Open daily 9 AM to 6 PM. On the upper level of the Wharf Cinema Center. 658 Front St; Lahaina, HI 96761; Phone: (808) 661-3262; http://lahainarestoration.org/plantation-museum

Island of Oahu

Oahu is the island with the biggest city, Honolulu, and the home of the state governmental agencies. It was the site of the attack on Pearl Harbor.

Haleiwa, HI

Pu'u o Mahuka Heiau State Historic Site shelters the largest heiau (religious site or temple) on Oahu. Visitors can only view the temple from outside the walls. Located about an hour north of Waikiki. There is no entrance fee. 59-818 Kamehameha Hwy; Haleiwa, HI 96712; Phone: (808) 587-0300; http://dlnr.hawaii.gov/dsp/parks/oahu/puu-o-mahuka-heiau-state-historic-site

Honolulu, HI

Hawai'i State Art Museum (HiSAM) offers art, special exhibitions, and a sculpture garden. All programs are free. 1 Capitol District Building; 250 S Hotel St; Second floor; Honolulu, HI 96813; Phone: (808) 586-9958; http://sfca.hawaii.gov/hisam/visitor-information

Hawai'i State Capitol offers self-guided tours. Pick up the brochure in Room 415. Open Monday through Friday from 7:45 AM to 6 PM. Closes at 4:30 PM when not in session. 415 S Beretania St; Honolulu, HI 96813; Phone: (808) 587-0478; https://governor.hawaii.gov/hawaii-state-capitol-tours

Honolulu Police Department's Museum showcases the evolution of law enforcement in Hawaii from the pre-Cook era to the present. Admission is free. Walk-ins are welcomed. Guided tours are available Monday through Friday from 9 AM to 3 PM. Closed state holidays. 801 S Beretania St; Honolulu, HI 96813; Phone: (808) 529-3111; http://honolulupd.org/community/index.php?page=museum

King Kamehameha V Judiciary History Center uses films, exhibits, and recreated rooms to present Hawaii's unique legal history, and the judicial process. All programs and tours are free. Open Monday through Friday from 8 AM to 4 PM. Closed holidays. 417 South King St; Honolulu, HI 96813; Phone: (808) 539-4999; http://www.jhchawaii.net/tours

Lion Coffee Company Tours take visitors through the process of turning raw beans into coffee. The tours are free and offered Monday through Friday at 10:30 AM and 12:30 PM. No tours on state or federal holidays. Roastery may not be in full operation on Friday afternoons. Free samples are included. Note: Visitors must wear closed toe shoes and all exposed jewelry must be removed. Children under the age of 12 are not allowed on the tours. 1555 Kalani St; Honolulu, HI 96817; Phone: (808) 843-4200; https://www.lioncoffee.com/tours

Pearl Harbor and the USS Arizona National Memorial is the National Monument is one of the most popular and sprawling attractions in Hawaii. It is free to enter but includes both free and fee-based places. Open daily from 7 AM to 5 PM. 1 Arizona Memorial Pl; Honolulu, HI, 96818; Phone: (808) 422-3399; https://www.nps.gov/valr/index.htm

USS Arizona Memorial experience is free. It includes a 23-minute documentary, boat ride to the memorial, time at the memorial, and the boat ride back. You can go to the visitor center on the day of your visit and attempt to get a walk-in ticket, but this is a very popular park. An alternative is to make a reservation on http://www.recreation.gov. There is a non-refundable $1.50 convenience fee per reserved ticket. If you choose to get a reservation, only use the .gov site. Commercial sites charge extra fees. Note: The Battleship Missouri, the USS Bowfin Submarine Museum & Park, and the Pacific Aviation Museum Pearl Harbor all charge a fee to visit. For more information: https://www.nps.gov/valr/planyourvisit/nearby-attractions.htm.

U.S. Army Museum Of Hawaii is housed in Battery Randolph, a massive reinforced concrete emplacement with roofs as much as 12 feet thick. Admission is free although donations are welcomed. There is a charge for the audio tour. The museum is open Tuesday through Saturday from 10 AM to 5 PM. Note: The museum is on the grounds of the Hale Koa Hotel and the Ft. DeRussy Recreation Center in Waikiki. 2131 Kalia Rd; Honolulu, HI 96815; Phone: (808) 955-9552; http://hiarmymuseumsoc.org

Kaaawa, HI
Ahupuaa O Kahana State Park was established as a living park interpreting Hawaiian values and lifestyle. There is no entrance fee. Open daily during daylight hours. 52222 Kamehameha Hwy; Kaaawa, HI 96730; Phone: (808) 587-0308; http://dlnr.hawaii.gov/dsp/parks/oahu/ahupuaa-o-kahana-state-park

Waimanalo, HI
Kaiwi State Scenic Shoreline offers a one-mile hike to a lookout above the historic lighthouse. The route offers views of the southeastern Oahu coastline. There is no fee to hike the trail. Makapuu Lighthouse Rd, Waimanalo, HI 96795; http://dlnr.hawaii.gov/dsp/parks/oahu/kaiwi-state-scenic-shoreline

Idaho

Arco, ID
Experimental Breeder Reactor-I (EBR-I) Atomic Museum invites visitors to see a nuclear reactor and learn how it generates electricity. Admission is free. Open daily from Memorial Day weekend through Labor Day weekend from 9 AM to 5 PM. Hwy 20/26; Arco, ID 83213; Phone (208) 526-0050; https://inl.gov/experimental-breeder-reactor-i

Almo, ID
City of Rocks National Reserve is situated at the south end of the Albion Mountains and features granite pinnacles, fins, and domes. The reserve is also known for its hiking, mountain biking, and bird watching. There is no fee to enter. Open 24 hours a day. The visitor center is open daily during peak season. Off-season it is open Tuesdays through Saturdays from 8 AM to 4:30 PM. Closed holidays. Note: roads may be impassable from November through April. Call the City of Rocks Visitor Center for the latest road conditions. Almo, ID 83312; Phone (208) 824-5901; https://www.nps.gov/ciro/index.htm

Ahsahka, ID
Dworshak Dam was a flood risk management project by the Army Corps of Engineers. Today it offers three floors of exhibits and a theater that plays several on-demand videos. The visitor center is free. Open daily from Memorial Day weekend through Labor Day weekend from 8:30 AM to 4:30 PM. Other times of the year open Monday through Friday. 1842 Viewpoint Rd, Ahsahka, ID 83520; Phone: (208) 476-1255; http://www.nww.usace.army.mil/Missions/Recreation/Dworshak-Dam-and-Reservoir/Dworshak-Visitor-Center

Boise, ID
Idaho Anne Frank Human Rights Memorial includes a life-sized bronze statue of Anne Frank as she peers out an open window. The walls of the memorial contain over 60 quotes from the world's humanitarian leaders. The memorial is free to visit and open 24 hours a day. Wassmuth Center for Human Rights; 777 S Eighth St; Boise, ID 83702; Phone: (208) 345-0304; http://wassmuthcenter.org

Idaho Black History Museum conserves historical photos, crafts, and other artifacts reflecting Black culture. The paintings of Idaho artist Pablo Rodriguez include *Slave to President* depicting the 400-year journey of Black Americans from enslavement to President of the United States. Admission is free with donations gratefully accepted. Open Tuesday from 10 AM to 3 PM. Open Wednesday and Thursday from 10 AM to 4 PM. Open Saturday from 11 AM to 4 PM. 508 Julia Davis Dr; Boise, ID 83702; Phone: (208) 789-2164; http://www.ibhm.org

Idaho Military History Museum presents military history with fighter jets, tanks, and armored personnel carriers showcasing all branches of the military with special focus on Idaho. Admission is free but donations are appreciated. Open Tuesday through Saturday from Noon to 4 PM. 4692 W Harvard St; Boise, ID 83705; Phone: (208) 272-4841; https://museum.mil.idaho.gov

Idaho Museum of Mining and Geology explains the state's geologic history and mining heritage. Admission is free. Open Wednesday through Sunday from Noon to 5 PM. Rock Identification with a Geologist takes place Wednesday through Friday from Noon to 4 PM. 2455 Old Penitentiary Rd; Boise, ID 83712; Phone: (208) 368-9876; https://www.idahomuseum.org

Idaho State Capitol fourth floor public galleries provide a view of the legislative proceedings and the House and Senate Chambers. Self-guided tours begin on the Garden Level with the central rotunda filled with educational panels about Idaho and state government. Open Monday through Friday from 6:30 AM to 7 PM. Open Saturday, Sunday, and holidays from 9 AM to 5 PM. 700 W Jefferson St; Boise, ID 83720; Phone: (208) 332-1012; https://legislature.idaho.gov/capitol

Franklin, ID
Historic Franklin was settled by the Mormons in 1860, making it the oldest city in Idaho. Several original buildings can be entered with no admission fee, although donations are appreciated. Open Memorial Day through Labor Day on Tuesday through Saturday from 11 AM to 3 PM. 111 E Main St; Franklin, ID 83237; Phone: (208) 646-2290; https://history.idaho.gov/hours-and-locations

Hagerman, ID
Hagerman Fossil Beds National Monument has the earliest record of Equus, the genus that includes all modern horses, donkeys, and zebras, proving that horses definitely evolved in North America. The Hagerman Horse, Equus simplicidens, dates back 3½ million years, sadly becoming extinct about 10,000 years ago. There is no fee to enter the visitor center, monument grounds, or to attend programs. Open daily Memorial Day through Labor Day from 9 AM to 5 PM. Winter hours are Thursday through Monday. Closed during all winter federal holidays. Note: There are no fossil quarries or places where you see fossils in the ground. 221 N State St; Hagerman, ID 83332; Phone: (208) 933-4105; https://www.nps.gov/hafo/index.htm

Hansen, ID (See also Twin Falls, ID)

Stricker Ranch & Rock Creek Station dates from 1865 and includes the Stricker House, Rock Creek Store, a pioneer cemetery, and outbuildings. This historic site was an early transportation center serving the Oregon Trail, Overland Mail Stage route, and the Kelton Freight Road. Admission and self-guided tours are free. Donations are greatly appreciated. Hours are limited. Open April to September on Sunday from 1 PM to 5 PM. 3715 E 3200 North; Hansen, ID 83334; Phone: (208) 423-4000; https://history.idaho.gov/stricker

Jerome, ID

Minidoka National Historic Site once held almost 13,000 men, women, and children imprisoned during World War II for being of Japanese descent. Visitors can walk the interpretive trail lined with 23 exhibit panels. It is free to visit. The grounds are open daily from sunrise to sunset. Construction of a permanent visitor center is underway. They advise checking the website for schedules and guided tours. 296 S 1400 E; Jerome, ID 83338; Phone: (208) 933-4100; https://www.nps.gov/miin/index.htm

Lapwai, ID

Nez Perce National Historical Park encompasses 38 sites across Idaho, Montana, Oregon, and Washington. There are no fees to visit any of the Nez Perce National Historical Park locations. The **Spalding Visitor Center** provides an introduction to the Nez Perce story and features a collection of clothing, tools, weapons, and ceremonial objects. From Memorial Day to Labor Day, the park staff provides special walks and talks. Located 11 miles east of Lewiston, ID. 39063 US-95; Lapwai, ID 83540; Phone: (208) 843-7009; https://www.nps.gov/nepe/learn/historyculture/the-spalding-site.htm

Murphy, ID

Historic Swan Falls Powerhouse Museum is part of Idaho Power's Swan Falls dam and powerhouse built in 1901 to supply electricity to nearby mines. The museum illuminates the area's early history and the development of the first hydroelectric dam on the Snake River. Admission is free. The museum is generally open mid-April through Labor Day on Saturday from 10 AM to 4 PM, and offers a free self-guided tour. Swan Falls Rd; Phone: (208) 388-669; https://www.idahopower.com/recreation/parks-and-campgrounds/swan-falls/swan-falls-tour-guidelines-information

Post Falls, ID

Buck Knives Factory offers free tours Monday through Thursday from January to November. The 45-minute tours take place at 10 AM, 12:15 PM, and 2 PM. Note: Fully closed shoes are required. Children must be at least seven-years-old.

Please call ahead for a reservation. 660 S Lochsa St; Post Falls, ID 83854; Phone: (800) 326-2825; https://www.buckknives.com/about/plant-tours

Soda Springs, ID
Captive Geyser was discovered during the drilling for a local swimming pool. The water is now capped and controlled by a timer allowing it erupt every hour on the hour reaching up 100 feet. Picture boards in the Geyser Park Visitor Center depict the history of the town. Enter on Main Street and First St S; Soda Springs, ID 83276; https://idahohighcountry.org/item/soda-springs-geyser

Twin Falls, ID (See also Hansen, ID)
Ten miles of developed trails throughout Twin Falls and along the scenic Snake River Canyon invite walkers, hikers, and bikers. Watch BASE jumpers leap from the Perrine Bridge. Access to the trails is at the north end of Washington St N, at the Twin Falls Visitor Center.

Herrett Center for Arts & Science presents a complete mammoth skeleton, fossils as well as contemporary art, and artifacts from ancient cultures. Admission to the museum is free. Note: Planetarium shows incur a cost. Open Tuesday and Friday from 9:30 AM to 9 PM. Open Wednesday and Thursday from 9:30 AM to 4:30 PM. Open Saturday from 1 PM to 9 PM. Closed federal holidays. 315 Falls Ave; Twin Falls, ID 83303; Phone: (208) 732-6655; http://herrett.csi.edu

Illinois

Alton, IL

National Great Rivers Museum uses interactive exhibits and theater presentations to explain the importance of the Mississippi River and the locks and dams that make it navigable. Operated by the U.S. Army Corps of Engineers, there is no charge for the museum or the tours. Open daily 9 AM to 5 PM. Tours are held 10 AM, 1 PM, and 3 PM. 2 Lock and Dam Way; Hwy 143; East Alton, IL 62024; Phone: (618) 462-6979; http://www.meetingoftherivers.org

Byron, IL

Byron Museum of History presents the area's history and its famous people through exhibits and programs. The museum complex also includes the historic Read House, which was on the Underground Railroad and is listed on the National Underground Railroad Network to Freedom. For sports fans there's the story of Albert Goodwill Spalding, the professional baseball player and famous sporting goods manufacturing founder. Admission is free. Open Wednesday through Saturday from 10 AM to 3 PM. Closed major holidays. 110 N Union St; Byron, IL 61010; Phone: (815) 234-5031; http://www.byronmuseum.org

Heritage Farm introduces visitors to early country life. Self-guided tours of the restored farm buildings are free. Guided tours will incur a cost. Open daily April through October on Monday through Friday from 8 AM to 4:30 PM, Saturday from 10 AM to 6 PM, and Sunday from 2 PM to 6 PM. 8059 N River Rd; Bryon, IL 61010; Phone: (815) 234-8535; http://www.byronforestpreserve.com/facilities/heritage-farm-museum.aspx

Carthage, IL

Kibbe Hancock Heritage Museum offers artifacts related to the history of Hancock County and western Illinois. The museum has acquired the collection of the Illinois Funeral Director's Funeral Customs Museum which includes the material and social history of the mortuary profession, and American funeral customs. Admission is free, although donations are gratefully accepted. Open Tuesday through Saturday from Noon to 4 PM, and Sunday from 1 PM to 4 PM. Closed major holidays. 306 Walnut St; Carthage, IL 62321; Phone: (217) 357-9552; https://kibbe.wordpress.com

Chicago, IL

Chicago has several public spaces that are delightful for residents and visitors. **Millennium Park** draws visitors for its larger-than-life public art, the Frank Gehry-designed Jay Prizker Pavilion, and the beauty of **Lurie Garden**. https://www.cityofchicago.org/city/en/depts/dca/supp_info/millennium_park.htm l. **Navy Pier** is a favorite place to shop, stroll, and play along the lake. Throughout the summer there are free events (as well as paid admission events). Opens at 10 AM daily with seasonal closings. 600 E Grand Ave; Chicago, IL 60611; Phone: (312) 595-7437; https://navypier.com **Riverwalk** runs along the Chicago River from Lake Shore Drive past Franklin to Lake Street providing views of the river and the stunning architecture of the city. https://www.chicagoriverwalk.us

Chicago Cultural Center was completed in 1897 as Chicago's first central public library. The south side of the building is graced by the world's largest stained glass Tiffany dome. On the north side is a 50,000 piece of glass domes designed by Healy & Millet. Self-guided tours are free. The building is open daily Monday through Friday from 10 AM to 7 PM and Saturday and Sunday from 10 AM to 5 PM. Closed all major holidays. They also offer free events, performances and art exhibitions. 78 E Washington St; Chicago, IL 60602; Phone: (312) 744-3316; https://www.cityofchicago.org/city/en/depts/dca/supp_info/chicago_culturalcenter .html

Clarke House Museum depicts family life in Chicago during the years before the Civil War. The house is now part of the Chicago Women's Park in the Prairie Avenue Historic District. Both admission and public tours are free. Tours are currently offered on Wednesday, Friday, and Saturday at 1 PM and 2:30 PM. 1827 S Indiana Ave; Chicago, IL 60616; Phone: (312) 744-3316; https://www.chicago.gov/city/en/depts/dca/supp_info/clarke_house_museum.htm l

Ed Paschke Art Center honors the artist who was born, raised, lived, and worked on Chicago's Northwest side. His art was influenced by Gauguin, Picasso, and Seurat but he maintained an interest in Outsider Art – the creative expression outside accepted cultural norms. Free admission, with donations welcomed. Open daily 10 AM to 7 PM. Closed major holidays. 5415 W Higgins Ave; Chicago IL 60630; Phone: (312) 533-4911; http://www.edpaschkeartcenter.org

Hyde Park Art Center curates over 20 exhibits highlighting contemporary artists who forge a link between art, and social and political discourse. Free and open Monday through Thursday from 9 AM to 8 PM. Open Friday and Saturday from 9 AM to 5 PM. Open Sunday from Noon to 5 PM. 5020 S Cornell Ave; Chicago, IL 60615; Phone: (773) 324-5520; http://www.hydeparkart.org

Lincoln Park Conservatory grows the thousands of plants needed for public parks. The conservatory showcases exotic plants in the Palm House, Fern Room, and Orchid House. Admission is free. Open daily 9 AM to 5 PM. 2391 N Stockton Dr; Chicago, IL 60614; Phone: (312) 742-7736; http://www.chicagoparkdistrict.com/parks/lincoln-park-conservatory

Lincoln Park Zoo invites visitors to a stroll along Nature's Boardwalk, enjoy the white-bearded, male De Brazza's monkey, watch owls and other birds of prey, and observe a colony of African penguins. Admission is free, although there is a charge for the train ride, carousel, and Penguin Encounter. Open daily at 10 AM with seasonal closings. 2001 N Clark St; Chicago, IL 60614; Phone: (312) 742-2000; http://www.lpzoo.org

Museum of Contemporary Photography (MoCP) creates exhibits of contemporary and traditional photography, including contemporary Asian photography. Admission is free. Open Monday through Saturday from 10 AM to 5 PM with extended hours on Thursday until 8 PM. Open Sunday from Noon to 5 PM. Closed all major and university holidays and when a new exhibit is installed. Located in Columbia College. 600 S Michigan Ave; Chicago, IL 60605; Phone: (312) 663-5554; http://www.mocp.org/index.php

National Museum of Mexican Art features one of the country's largest Mexican art collections including Día de los Muertos items, documentary photographs of 19th century Mexico and the Mexican Revolution, plus colonial religious art and contemporary multimedia installations. Admission is free. Open Tuesday through Sunday from 10 AM to 5 PM. 1852 W 19th St; Chicago, IL 60608; Phone: (312) 738-1503; http://nationalmuseumofmexicanart.org

National Museum of Puerto Rican Arts and Culture showcases traditional and contemporary Puerto Rican art and introduces visitors to the history, traditions, and culture of Puerto Rico. Free admission. Open Tuesday through Friday from 10 AM to 5 PM, and Saturday from 10 AM to 2 PM. 3015 W Division St; Chicago, IL 60622; Phone: (773) 486-8345; http://nmprac.org

National Veteran's Art Museum showcases the art of the military veterans – their perception and the reality of combat. In addition to their permanent collection the museum features changing exhibits. Free admission. Open Tuesdays to Saturdays 10 AM to 5 PM. 4041 N Milwaukee Ave; Chicago, IL 60641; Phone: (312) 326-0270; http://www.nvam.org

Revolution Brewing Tours and Tasting provides complimentary tours and tastings on a first come, first served basis. Tours are currently offered Wednesday through Friday at 6 PM and 7 PM, on Saturday hourly from 3 PM to 6 PM, and on Sunday hourly from 2 PM to 4 PM. Note: You must be 21 or older. They recommended you arrive early to put your name on the list. 3340 N Kedzie Ave; Chicago, IL 60618; Phone: (773) 588-CANS; https://revbrew.com/visit/brewery/tours

Smart Museum of Art specializes in paintings by old masters, furniture by Frank Lloyd Wright, and sculptures by Degas, Matisse, Rodin, and Henry Moore. The museum is located at the north end of the University of Chicago. Free admission. Open Tuesday through Sunday from 10 AM to 5 PM, with extended closing on Thursday until 8 PM. Closes during installations of new exhibits and on major holidays. 5550 S Greenwood Ave; Chicago, IL 60637; Phone: (773) 702–0200; http://smartmuseum.uchicago.edu

Dixon, IL (See also Moline, IL)

Best known for its connection to agricultural giant John Deere, the story starts here in 1837 when Deere set up his small blacksmith shop. His development of the first commercially successful steel plow created an agricultural revolution. **John Deere Historic Site** displays a replica of the original blacksmith shop. Visitors can also walk the grounds and tour the original Deere family home. Admission is free. Open March through December on Monday through Saturday from 9 AM to 5 PM. Open Sunday from Noon to 4 PM. Closed major holidays. Note: Grand Detour and Dixon refer to the same location. 8334 S. Clinton St; Dixon, IL 61021; Phone: (815) 652-4551; https://www.deere.com/en/connect-with-john-deere/visit-john-deere/historic-site

Evanston, IL

American Toby Jug Museum specializes in this unusual form of pottery. It's a jug dating back to the 1760s in the form of a seated person, or the head of a famous person. He is usually a heavy-set, smiling man holding a mug of beer and often wearing 18th century attire. This museum hosts its self-described "world's largest collection of Toby and Character Jugs." The museum also commissions their own jugs. Admission is free. Open Wednesday through Friday, and the first and third Saturday of the month from 10 AM to 5 PM. 910 Chicago Ave; Evanston, IL 60202; Phone: (877) 862-9687; http://www.tobyjugmuseum.com

Forest Park, IL

Showmen's Rest is a 750 plot section of Woodlawn Cemetery owned by the Showmen's League of America. It has a particularly sad origin. On June 22, 1918 an empty Michigan Central Railroad train plowed into the circus train when the engineer fell asleep. Many of the performers and show workers were killed. A Memorial Day service is held at Woodlawn Cemetery every year for those "performing now at the biggest of the Big Tops." 7600 W Cermak Rd; Forest

Park, IL 60130; Phone: (708) 442-8500;
http://www.showmensleague.org/showmens-rest

Freeport, IL
Lincoln-Douglas Debate Square was the location of the famous Lincoln-Douglas Debates of 1858 when both men were running for the United States Senate from Illinois. The key issue was whether slavery would be allowed in new territories of the United States. On August 27, 1858 the Freeport Doctrine, an important statement regarding slavery and states' rights, was proclaimed by Douglas. A series of waysides describe the events and ideas which led to the debates. There's also life-size statue *Lincoln and Douglas in Debate* by artist Lily Tolpo. 114 E Douglas St; Freeport IL 61032; Phone: (815) 233-1357; http://stephenson-county-il.org/directory/lincoln-douglas-debate-square

Fulton, IL
Fulton's Dutch Windmill was built to help control flooding, but now it's a fully functional mill that provides stone-ground flours for sale in the gift shop. Engineered and pre-fabricated in the Netherlands, it was shipped to the United States where Dutch millwrights assembled and installed it. Entrance to the windmill is free, but donations are appreciated. Open weekends in May and daily through the end of October. 415 10th Ave; Fulton, IL 61252; Phone (815) 589-3925; https://www.cityoffulton.us/city/fulton-directory/attractions/de-immigrant-windmill.html

Grand Detour, IL (See Dixon, IL)

Joliet, IL
Old Joliet Prison Park is the city's infamous prison. Now free and open to the public, it provides eight informational kiosks describing its history and inmates as well as its television/movie fame. Open daily dawn to dusk. 1125 Collins St; Joliet, IL 60432; Phone: (815) 723-9045; http://cityofjoliet.info/visitors/joliet-prison

Macomb, IL
Museum of Geology covers the world of rocks, minerals, and their economic uses. The museum also describes the origin and occurrence of coal, oil and gas, and how glaciers of the Ice Age formed the soils. Admission is free. Open Monday through Friday from 9 AM to 4:30 PM but closed Noon to 1 PM. Other times by special arrangement. First floor of Tillman Hall on the Western Illinois University campus. 115A Tillman Hall; 1 University Cir; Macomb IL 61455; Phone: (309) 298-1151; http://www.wiu.edu/cas/geology/museum.php

Metropolis, IL
Superman's Statue honors its fictional hometown son. On January 21, 1972, DC Comics declared Metropolis the *Hometown of Superman*. On June 9th of that year the Illinois State Legislature passed Resolution 572 that confirmed that honor. A 15-foot painted bronze statue of Superman stands on Superman Square at 111 E Fifth St. A statue of Noel Neill's Lois Lane stands a few blocks away on Eighth and Market Streets. There is a fee-based Superman Museum but there's no charge to take a selfie by the statues. Each year on the second weekend of June the city holds their annual Superman Celebration. https://www.supermancelebration.net

Moline and East Moline, IL (See also Dixon, IL)
Butterworth Center and Deere-Wiman House were both Deere family homes. Admission is free. Tours are available by appointment only during regular business hours Monday through Friday. Donations are welcome. For drop-in tour times call the center at (309) 743-2700.
Deere-Wiman House is at 817 11th Ave; Moline, IL 61265
Butterworth Center is at 1105 Eighth St; Moline, Illinois 61265
https://www.butterworthcenter.com/visitors

Harvester Works manufactures combines and front end equipment. The free tour of the Harvester Works is offered Monday through Friday at 8 AM, 10 AM, and 12:30 PM. Reservations must be made a minimum of 48 hours in advance. All participants must be at least 13 years old. Closed-toe shoes are required. Note: The website lists all the Deere tours available. 1100 13th Ave; East Moline, IL 61244; Phone: (800) 765-9588; https://www.deere.com/en/connect-with-john-deere/visit-john-deere/factory-tours

John Deere Pavilion displays everything from vintage machines to today's agricultural, construction and forestry equipment. Admission is free. Open Monday through Saturday from 9 AM to 5 PM and Sunday Noon to 4 PM. 1400 River Dr; Moline, IL 61265; Phone: (309) 765-1000; https://www.deere.com/en/connect-with-john-deere/visit-john-deere/pavilion

John Deere Seeding Group is open for free facility tours Monday through Friday at 8 AM, 10 AM, and 12:30 PM. All participants must be at least 13 years old. No sandals or open-toed shoes. All guests must wear long pants or a long skirt covering all skin. Reservations are required. 501 River Dr; Moline IL 61265; Phone: (800) 765-9588; https://www.deere.com/en/connect-with-john-deere/visit-john-deere/factory-tours

Normal, IL
University Galleries of Illinois State University features both emerging and established artists. All exhibitions and events are free. Open Monday through

Thursday from 9:30 AM to 5 PM, with extended hours on Friday to 8 PM. Open Saturday and Sunday from Noon to 4 PM. Hours may change in summer. 11 Uptown Cir; Suite 103; Normal IL 61761; Phone: (309) 438-5487; https://galleries.illinoisstate.edu

OFallon, IL (See also St. Louis, MO)

Gateway Classic Cars is a classic and exotic car dealership – one of several across the country. Browsers are welcomed. Open Monday through Saturday from 9 AM to 5 PM. 1237 Central Park Dr; OFallon, IL 62269; Phone: (618) 271-3000; http://gatewayclassiccars.com/locations?location=STL

Quincy, IL

All Wars Museum spans the American Revolution to the War on Terrorism. On the grounds of the Illinois Veteran's Home, the museum is free. Open March through early December on Tuesday through Saturday from 9 AM to 4 PM. Closed Noon to 1 PM. Open Sunday 1 PM to 4 PM. 1707 N 12th St; Quincy, IL 62301; Phone: (217) 222-8641; http://www.quincyivh.org/museum.html

Lincoln-Douglas Debate Interpretive Center recounts the story of these two influential men. The hours are generally Monday through Friday from 8:30 AM to 4:30 PM but visitors are advised to call first. 128 N Fifth St; Quincy, IL 62301; Phone: (217) 228-8696; https://www.hsqac.org

Rock Island, IL

Fryxell Geology Museum is home to a complete skeleton of a Platecarpus *sea serpent*, skulls of extinct creatures, and a 22-foot long skeleton of Cryolophosaurus, a large crested carnivorous dinosaur discovered in Antarctica in 1991. Admission is free. Open when classes are in session. Monday through Friday from 8 AM to 4:30 PM. Open Saturday and Sunday from 1 PM to 4 PM. 639 38th St; Rock Island, IL 61201; Phone: (800) 798-8100; http://www.augustana.edu/locations/fryxell-geology-museum/visiting

Rock Island Arsenal Museum highlights the people involved in Arsenal Island's history, the manufacturing processes used at Rock Island Arsenal, and the military equipment that was produced there. Note: Check the website for the listing of security requirements to visit this active military base. Admission is free. Open Tuesday through Saturday from Noon to 4 PM. 3500 North Ave; Rock Island, IL 61299; Phone: (309) 782-5021; http://www.arsenalhistoricalsociety.org/museum/index.html

Springfield, IL

Not only the home of the State Capitol, Springfield is also the location of several Lincoln sites, some of which are free to visit.

African American History Museum displays the stories of Black life in Central Illinois, past and present. There is no admission fee but donations are appreciated. Open Tuesday through Friday from Noon to 4 PM and Saturday from 10 AM to 5 PM. 1440 Monument Ave; Springfield, IL 62702; Phone: (217) 391-6323; https://spiaahm.org

Illinois State Capitol saw its first legislative session in 1877. Visitors can watch Illinois politics in action from balcony-level seating when the legislature is in session. Tours are offered every half hour on Monday through Friday from 8 AM to 4 PM. There are no tours from Noon to 1 PM. On Saturday and Sunday tours are offered every hour between 9 AM and 3 PM except from Noon to 1 PM. Sign up at the information desk. Closed some major holidays. 401 S Second St; Springfield IL 62701; Phone: (217) 782-2099; http://www.cyberdriveillinois.com/departments/physical_services/captioltours.html

Lincoln Depot was the last place Abraham Lincoln visited before leaving Springfield. The date was February 11, 1861. He left for Washington DC where he was assassinated four years later. The first floor houses a self-guided museum. The second story is the Noll Law Office. Admission is free. Open Monday through Friday from 10 AM to 4 PM. 930 East Monroe St; Springfield, IL 62701; Phone: (217) 544-8695; http://www.lincolndepot.org

Lincoln Home National Historic Site is a four-block restored to its 1860 appearance and contains twelve historic structures, including the only home Abraham Lincoln ever owned. There is no admission fee to the site. Visitors can take a self-guided tour of the neighborhood and the historic exhibits located throughout the area. Guided tours of the Lincoln home are free. Stop at the visitor center information desk for a ticket. Open daily from 8:30 AM to 5 PM. Closed some major holidays. 426 S Seventh St; Springfield, IL 62701; Phone: (217) 492-4241; https://www.nps.gov/liho/index.htm

Lincoln Memorial Garden contains plants native to the three states in which Abraham Lincoln lived; Kentucky, Indiana, and Illinois. The 100-acre site features six miles of trails, footbridges, a pond, and dozens of wooden benches inscribed with Lincoln quotes. Admission is free except during special events. Open all year sunrise to sunset. 2301 E Lake Shore Dr; Springfield, IL 62712; Phone: (217) 529-1111; http://lincolnmemorialgarden.org

Lincoln Tomb at Oak Ridge Cemetery features the granite monument that is the final resting place of Abraham Lincoln, his wife Mary, and three of their four sons. Lincoln's oldest son, Robert, is buried in Arlington National Cemetery. The tomb is open to the public and is free. Open daily 9 AM to 5 PM. Closed major holidays. 1500 Monument Ave; Springfield, IL 62702; Phone: (217) 782-2717; https://www2.illinois.gov/dnrhistoric/Experience/Sites/Central/Pages/Lincoln-Tomb.aspx

Urbana, IL
Wandell Sculpture Garden is set among 22 acres of recreated Illinois prairie and features works from local artists with ties to the University of Illinois. Free to visit and open daily from dawn to dusk. Windsor Rd and Race St; Urbana, IL 61801; Phone: (217) 367-1536; http://www.urbanaparks.org/parks/wandell-sculpture-garden

Wilmette, IL
Baha'í House of Worship for North America is open to the public with free admission. Stop in the visitor center and learn about the building and the Baha'i faith. Devotional programs of readings from the world's great scriptures are held in the auditorium daily at 9:15 AM and 12:30 PM. The welcome center is open daily from 10 AM to 5 PM. Note: Shoes and shirts are required. Modest dress is recommended. 100 Linden Ave; Wilmette, IL, 60091; Phone: (847) 853-2300; https://www.bahai.us/bahai-temple

Indiana

Anderson, IN
Gustav Jeeninga Museum of Bible and Near Eastern Studies highlights the Egyptian, Roman, Greek, Babylonian, Assyrian, and Israelite periods as they relate to the Bible. There is no admission fee. Open Monday through Friday from 8 AM to 5 PM. Note: Hours during the summer and the Christmas holiday may be irregular. The museum is located on the campus of Anderson University in the School of Theology. 1100 E Fifth St; Anderson, IN 46016; Phone: (765) 641-4428; https://www.anderson.edu/academics/jeeninga-museum

Bloomington, IN
IU Eskenazi Museum of Art displays ancient gold jewelry and African masks as well as paintings by Claude Monet and Pablo Picasso – over 45,000 objects representing nearly every art-producing culture throughout history. Admission is always free. Open Tuesday through Saturday at 10 AM. Tuesday through Thursday closes at 5 PM. On Friday and Saturday closes at 7 PM. Open Sunday from Noon to 5 PM. 1133 E Seventh St; Bloomington, IN 47405; Phone: (812) 855-5445; https://artmuseum.indiana.edu/index.html

Mathers Museum of World Cultures encourages understanding of the world's cultures, past and present. Highlights of their collection include photographs depicting Native American interactions with European Americans in the first quarter of the 1900s, an array of smoking pipes from Cameroon, and dress and adornment from North Africa, the Middle East, Central Asia, and South Asia. Admission is free. Open Tuesdays through Fridays from 9 AM to 4:30 PM, and on Saturdays and Sundays from 1 PM to 4:30 PM. Closed during Indiana University semester breaks. 416 N Indiana Ave; Bloomington, IN 47408; Phone: (812) 855-6873; https://mathersmuseum.indiana.edu

Wylie House Museum was built in 1835 by Andrew Wylie, first president of Indiana University and furnished as it might have looked in the 1840s when Dr. Wylie and his family lived there. Free guided tours are given on Tuesday through Saturday from 10 AM to 2 PM. Closed holidays and December to mid-January. 307 E Second St; Bloomington, IN 47401; Phone: (812) 855-6224; https://libraries.indiana.edu/wylie-house-museum

Fort Wayne, IN (See also New Haven, IN)
Hanson Observation Deck offers public viewing of the quarry in action. Visitors are invited to see how miners wrest limestone, and produce sand and gravel. 4529 Sand Point Rd; Fort Wayne, IN 46809

Historic Old Fort Wayne is a faithful reproduction of the post built by American troops under the command of Major John Whistler in 1815-1816. Located in a public park, the fort is always open to view but can only be visited during events, which are open to the public at no charge. Brochures are outside some of the buildings with information about the history of the fort, how each building would have been used, and a schedule for upcoming events. 1201 Spy Run Ave; Fort Wayne, IN 46805; Phone: (260) 437-2836; https://oldfortwayne.org

Franklin, IN

Johnson County Museum of History displays the early history of Johnson County, beginning 400 million years ago in the Paleozoic Era through to life in the 1950s. Admission is free. Open Tuesday through Friday from 9 AM to 4 PM, and Saturday from 10 AM to 3 PM. Call or see their online calendar for closings. 135 N Main St; Franklin, IN 46131; Phone: (317) 346-4500; http://www.johnsoncountymuseum.org

Indianapolis, IN

The canal in downtown Indianapolis is a three-mile loop perfect for biking and walking. Located in Indianapolis' Holliday Park, **Ruins** preserves the remains of a demolished New York skyscraper as though it was a work of classical art. **ArtsPark** invites visitors to enjoy interactive sculptures in a 12-acre open–air setting. More than 27 sculptures created by Indiana and internationally-known artists decorate the landscape. No admission charge. Open dawn to dusk. 820 E 67th St; Indianapolis, IN 46220; Phone: (317) 255-2464; http://www.indplsartcenter.org/exhibitions

Au Ho-nien Museum focuses on painting, poetry, and calligraphy by contemporary artist Au Ho-nien. His art combines traditional Chinese painting with Western perspective and techniques. There is no admission charge. Open daily in the Schwitzer Student Center. 1400 E Hanna Ave; Indianapolis, IN 46227; Phone: (317) 788-3253; https://www.uindy.edu/arts/au-ho-nien-museum

Indianapolis Art Center curates over 50 art exhibitions each year in its six art galleries. Admission is free. The center is open Monday through Friday 9 AM to 10 PM. Open Saturday 9 AM to 6 PM and Sunday Noon to 6 PM. Between semesters it is open Monday through Saturday from 9 AM to 6 PM and on Sunday from Noon to 6 PM. In the Marilyn K. Glick School of Art. 820 E 67th St; Indianapolis, IN 46220; Phone: (317) 255-2464; https://www.indplsartcenter.org

Indiana State Capitol offers free guided tours of the 1888 building and its architecture as well as the offices and chambers. The Statehouse is open Monday through Friday from 8 AM to 5 PM, and Saturday from 10 AM to 2 PM. Guided tours are offered Monday through Friday from 9 AM to 3 PM and on Saturday at 10:15 AM, 11 AM, Noon and 1 PM. 200 W Washington St; Indianapolis, IN 46204; Phone: (317) 233-5293; http://www.in.gov/idoa/2371.htm

Indiana State Police Museum depicts the history of the Indiana State Police from its inception in 1933 to present day. The museum's collection includes the death mask of the infamous John Dillinger, a 1938 Chevrolet police vehicle, and uniforms from different eras. Admission is free. Open Tuesday through Friday from 9 AM to 3 PM. 8660 E 21st St; Indianapolis, IN 46219; Phone: (317) 899-8293; https://www.in.gov/isp/museum.htm

Jeffersonville, IN

Schimpff's Confectionery Museum is also a shopping opportunity. On display are thousands of pieces of American candy memorabilia. The Candy Demonstration Area, Chocolate Dipping Room, and Candy Museum are open during normal store hours. Free tours may be available. Open Monday through Saturday from 10 AM to 5 PM. Closed major holidays. 347 Spring St; Jeffersonville, IN 47130; Phone: (812) 283-8367; http://schimpffs.com/index.html

Lafayette, IN

Art Museum of Greater Lafayette displays exhibits four times a year from its collection of 19th and 20th century American art focused on Indiana. Free admission. Open daily from 11 AM to 4 PM during exhibitions. Closed between exhibitions and on major holidays. 102 S 10th St; Lafayette, IN 47901; Phone: (765) 742-1128; http://www.artlafayette.org

Subaru of Indiana Automotive (SIA) offers a free, mile-long walk along an elevated catwalk through the facility. Reservations are required. Note: Skirts are highly discouraged and participants must be at least 10 years of age. Tours are offered at 11 AM on Monday, Wednesday and Friday. Check the site for black-out dates. 5500 State Rd 38 E (Exit 168 off I-65); Lafayette, IN 47905; Phone: (765) 449-6250; http://subaru-sia.wixsite.com/indiana/tour

Muncie, IN

David Owsley Museum of Art at Ball State University explores the visual arts from ancient cultures through the 20th century and across six continents. Admission is free. Open Monday through Friday from 9 AM to 4:30 PM. Open Saturday and Sunday from 1:30 PM to 4:30 PM. The museum is closed on major holidays, university holidays, and spring break. 2021 W Riverside Ave; Muncie, IN 47306; Phone: (765) 285-5242; http://cms.bsu.edu/web/museumofart

New Haven, IN (See also Fort Wayne, IN)

Star*Quest Observatory provides free stargazing for the public every clear Saturday night from April to November starting one hour after sunset and continuing for two hours. Trained volunteers work the observatory telescopes and are available to answer your questions. You may also bring your own telescope. Jefferson Township Park. 1720 S Webster Rd; New Haven, IN 46774; https://www.fortwayneastronomicalsociety.com/stargazing

Notre Dame, IN

Snite Museum of Art has amassed 29,000 works representing many of the principal cultures and periods of world art history. Admission is free. Open Tuesday through Friday from 10 AM to 5 PM and open on Thursday until 7:30 PM. Open Saturday from Noon to 5 PM. Closed major national holidays. 100 Moose Krause Cir; Notre Dame, IN 46556; Phone: (574) 631-5466; http://sniteartmuseum.nd.edu

Princeton, IN

Toyota Indiana Visitors Center actually drives visitors to see production in action. A tram takes you to a Body Weld shops to see hundreds of robots join steel parts with thousands of spot welds. Visitors also get to see cars being assembled and the quality checks by team members. The free tours are available Monday through Friday. Reservations required. Note: A valid photo ID is required for each adult. Long-sleeves, long pants, and closed-toe shoes are required for the plant tour. 4000 Tulip Tree Dr; Princeton, IN 47670; Phone: (888) 696-8211; https://www.tourtoyotaindiana.com/visitor-info

Richmond, IN

Take a self-guided tour to three locations featuring nearly 70 stained-glass windows by Louis Comfort Tiffany – First Presbyterian Church, St. Paul's Episcopal Church, and Morrisson-Reeves Library. The map is available at the Richmond Welcome Center. Learn more at: http://visitrichmond.org/listing/tiffany-stained-glass-trail

Hayes Arboretum features Indiana's old growth forest, acres of reforested woods, several miles of hiking trails and running paths, a museum, Indian mounds, ponds, fields, and wetlands. Free admission. Open Tuesday through Saturday from 9 AM to 5 PM. 801 Elks Country Club Rd; Richmond, IN 47374; Phone: (765) 962-3745; http://www.hayesarboretum.org

Joseph Moore Museum at Earlham College has amassed artifacts from Babylonian tablets to Roman lamps, stone tools from local Adena mounds, and an authentic Egyptian mummy. Admission is always free, donations are welcome. Open Monday, Wednesday, Friday, Saturday and Sunday from 1 PM to 5 PM. Currently offering Live Animal Encounters and Planetarium Shows at no charge.

Closed the Saturday of the school commencement, July 4th, Christmas Eve, Christmas Day, and New Year's Day. 801 National Rd W; Richmond, IN 47374; Phone: (765) 983-1303; http://www.earlham.edu/joseph-moore-museum

Richmond Rose All America Rose Selection Board (A.A.R.S.) Garden encourages visitors to experience the beauty of this flourishing 25-year-old garden that highlights over 100 varieties of All American Selections® Roses. There is no admission fee. Open daily from 6 AM to 11 PM. Glen Miller Park; 2519 E Main St; Richmond, IN 47374; Phone: (765) 962-3745; http://richmondrosegarden.com

Saint Mary-of-the-Woods, IN (See also Terre Haut, IN)
Shrine of Saint Mother Theodore Guerin honors Saint Mother Theodore (Saint Theodora), the foundress of the Sisters of Providence of Saint Mary-of-the-Woods. The rooms represent Mother Theodore's journey from France to Saint Mary-of-the-Woods, Indiana. Original artifacts include Saint Mother Theodore's writing desk, chaplet, prayer book, and shoes. Admission is free with donations appreciated. Open daily from 7 AM to 8 PM. 1 Sisters of Providence; Saint Mary-of-the-Woods, IN 47876; Phone: (812) 535-3131; https://spsmw.org/visit/must-sees/shrine-of-saint-mother-theodore-guerin

Shelbyville, IN
Grover Museum offers the Streets of Old Shelby, a village of the 1900-1910 era, and the *History of the Railroad in Shelby County* which features a diorama with running model trains. There's also three rotating galleries. Museum admission is free but donations are encouraged. Open Tuesday through Saturday from 10 AM to 5 PM. Closed some major holidays. 52 W Bdwy; Shelbyville, IN 46176; Phone: (317) 392-4634; http://grovermuseum.org

St. Joe, IN
Sechler's Pickles offers free plant tours from April through October on Monday through Thursday from 9 AM to 11 AM, and again from 12:30 PM to 3 PM. Note: Wear closed-toe shoes and no dangling jewelry. The showroom is open for pickle purchases Monday through Friday from 8:30 AM to 4:30 PM, and Saturday from 8:30 AM to Noon. Closed holidays. 5686 SR 1; St. Joe, IN 46785; Phone: (800) 332-5461; http://www.sechlerspickles.com/pages/contacts.html

Terre Haute, IN (See also Saint Mary-of-the-Woods, IN)
Clabber Girl Museum includes vintage items that look at the history of Clabber Girl. There's a delivery wagon, and an antique race car from the Indianapolis Motor Speedway as well as antique household items and kitchen appliances, vintage toys, and an old-fashioned coal generator. Admission to the museum is free. Open Monday through Friday from 8 AM to 5 PM. Open Saturday from 8

AM to 3 PM. 900 Wabash Ave; Terre Haute, IN 47807; Phone: (812) 478-7111; https://www.clabbergirl.com/museum-and-bake-shop-cafe/museum

Eugene V. Debs Museum is the former home of Eugene V. Debs and Katherine Metzel Debs. Debs was an activist, promoting workers' right to organize unions and to strike in order to protect their interests. The interior of the museum features many of Debs' possessions and other artifacts from his lifetime. Guided tours are available on a walk-in basis. The museum is open to the public and admission is free. Open Tuesday through Saturday from Noon to 5 PM. On the campus of Indiana State University. 451 N Eighth St; Terre Haute, IN 47807; Phone: (812) 232-2163; https://debsfoundation.org

Sheldon Swope Art Museum features American art including paintings, sculptures, and works on paper from the 19th century to the present. The major strength of collection is American Scene Painting of the 1930s and 1940s, and historic Indiana art. Admission is free. Open Tuesday through Sunday from Noon to 5 PM. Open late Friday until 8 PM. 25 S Seventh St; Terre Haute, IN 47807; Phone: (812) 238-1676; https://www.swope.org

Zionsville, IN
Antique Fan Collectors Museum houses 2,000 antique fans, some dating to the early 1880s. Highlights include the earliest battery-powered fans, water-powered fans, even steam- and alcohol-powered fans. The museum is hosted by Fanimation, Inc and admission is free. Open Monday through Friday 10 AM to 4 PM; 10983 Bennett Pkwy; Zionsville, IN 46077; Phone: (317) 733-4113; http://www.fanimation.com/museum

Iowa

Iowa has two very famous and very different sons – Grant Wood, and Captain James T Kirk – and the state celebrates both with sites that are free to visit. Grant Wood is one of the most famous of the painters of American Regionalism which focused on realistic scenes of rural and small-town America. In his most famous painting, American Gothic, a stern-looking man in farmers' overalls holds a pitchfork and an equally severe looking woman stands beside him. Captain James T. Kirk is the famous fictional Captain of the beloved Starship Enterprise whose five-year mission was "to explore strange new worlds, to seek out new life, and new civilizations. To boldly go where no man has gone before."

Iowa state parks do not charge an entrance fee. https://www.iowadnr.gov/Places-to-Go/State-Park

Ames, IA
Iowa State University offers several museums open to the public but all come with a suggested amount for a donation. Only the library offers truly free admission. There is significant public art on the grounds that is free to explore. Check the website for information on their not-quite free museums: https://www.museums.iastate.edu

Iowa State University Library celebrates Grant Wood. The Library is home to *Breaking the Prairie*, three panels in the Grant Wood Heritage Area of the Parks Library lower lobby. The panels depict the beginning of tillage in Iowa by the pioneers in the 1840s. But there's more than the thoughtful murals by Wood, the Library is a trove of paintings, sculptures, and scrolls. Although the library is generally open 7:30 AM to 2 AM, the hours may change during the year. 701 Morrill Rd; Ames, IA 50011; Phone: (515) 294-3642; http://www.lib.iastate.edu/about-library/art

Cedar Rapids, IA
Grant Wood Home and Studio was where the artist lived and painted from 1922 to 1935. His most famous work, American Gothic, was painted in this studio in 1930. No admission fee. Open April through December on Saturday and Sunday from Noon to 4 PM. 810 Second Ave SE; Cedar Rapids, IA 52403; Phone: (319) 366-7503; http://www.crma.org/Content/Grant-Wood/Grant-Wood-Studio.aspx

Council Bluffs, IA
Bob Kerrey Pedestrian Bridge connecting Council Bluffs to Omaha Nebraska's Riverfront is an s-curved, cable-stayed bridge boasting a striking, modern design.

At night multi-colored lights illuminate the structure. The bridge is the first pedestrian bridge to connect two states, with plaques highlighting the point over the Missouri River where the state lines meet. https://www.councilbluffs-ia.gov/2178/Bob-Kerrey-Pedestrian-Bridge.

Pottawattamie County Courthouse Lobby is another Grant Wood site. In 1927 he was commissioned to create murals for the Corn Room, and the Pioneer Room of the new Hotel Chieftain. The hotel was eventually sold and the murals removed. In 2000 the Bluffs Arts Council collected and restored pieces of the mural which are now displayed in the lobby of the county courthouse. 227 S Sixth St; Council Bluffs, IA 51503; Phone: (712) 328-5644; https://pottcounty-ia.gov/attractions/courthouse-art

Union Pacific Museum celebrates the glory days of train travel, especially when the Union Pacific Railroad was a major player. Reconstructed cars, railroad china, and authentic vintage Union Pacific uniforms recreate the travel experience. The museum's first floor has been dedicated to the building the Transcontinental Railroad. Admission is free but a guided tour will incur a small charge. Open Thursday through Saturday from 10 AM to 4 PM. 200 Pearl St; Council Bluffs, IA 51503; Phone: (712) 329-8307; http://www.uprrmuseum.org

Davenport, IA
Palmer Family and Chiropractic Museum honors the little known fact that Chiropractic Medicine was started in Davenport, Iowa by D. D. Palmer in the 1890s. The Palmer Family and Chiropractic Museum is located throughout the Palmer campus. Many of the exhibits are in the Vickie Anne Palmer Hall. Self-guided tour brochures are available in the lobby as well as the welcome center in the Academic Health Center building. Numerous skeletons and spinal columns exhibiting a variety of anomalies and pathologies as well as normal spines and skeletons are currently displayed in the Palmer Main Clinic and on the first floor of the David D. Palmer Memorial Health Sciences Library. The exhibits are free. Open 8 AM to 4:30 PM, Monday through Friday when classes are in session. Vickie Anne Palmer Hall; 115 W Seventh St; Davenport, IA 52803; Phone: (563) 884-5245; http://www.palmer.edu/about-us/history/palmer-family-chiropractic-museum

River Music Experience is primarily a venue for performances but their exhibits are free. Visitors can explore the music and musicians who created the roots of today's music from New Orleans to St. Paul and then to Chicago and beyond. Access a database with over 300 biographies, 1,000 audio files, and enjoy in-depth information and samples of America's music on America's river. RME also offers free live music in the on-site cafe from Noon to 1 PM on Monday through Friday.

129 N Main St; Davenport, IA 52801; Phone: (563) 326-1333; http://rivermusicexperience.org/About-Us/Exhibits

Des Moines, IA

Des Moines Art Center is a design collaboration by Eliel Saarinen, I. M. Pei, and Richard Meier. It is filled with 20th, and 21st century works of modern and contemporary art as well as examples from other styles and cultures including Japanese woodblock prints. Admission is free. Open Tuesday, Wednesday, and Friday from 11 AM to 4 PM. Open on Thursday from 11 AM to 4 PM. On Saturday open 10 AM to 4 PM and on Sunday from Noon to 4 PM. Closed major holidays. 4700 Grand Ave; Des Moines, IA 50312; Phone: (515) 277-4405; http://www.desmoinesartcenter.org

Iowa State Capitol sports a 23-karat gold dome flanked by four smaller domes. Inside, there's the governor's offices, legislature, and the old Supreme Court room. Open Monday through Friday from 8 AM to 5 PM and on Saturday from 9 AM to 4 PM. Free self-guided and formal tours available Monday through Saturday. Call for tour times. E Ninth St & Grand Ave; Des Moines, IA 50319; Phone: (515) 281-5591; https://www.legis.iowa.gov/resources/tourcapitol

John and Mary Pappajohn Sculpture Park is an extension of the Des Moines Art Center featuring sculptures in the park. Admission is free. Open sunrise to midnight. 1330 Grand Ave; Des Moines, IA 50309; Phone: (515) 277-4405; https://www.desmoinesartcenter.org/visit/hours-directions

State Historical Museum of Iowa showcases the state's accomplishments, contributions, and heritage. It includes an exhibit celebrating Iowa's movie legacy, and one that explores presidential candidates' journeys through the Iowa caucuses and beyond. Visitors can even discover the history of bicycling in Iowa. Admission is free. Open Monday through Saturday from 9 AM to 4:30 PM. 600 E Locust St; Des Moines, IA 50319; Phone: (515) 281-5111; https://iowaculture.gov/history/museum

Wells Fargo History Museum highlights an authentic Concord stagecoach, Wells Fargo treasure box, gold and money, and historic banking machines. Admission is free. Open Monday through Friday from 8:30 AM to 5 PM. Closed bank holidays. 666 Walnut St; Des Moines, IA 50309; Phone: (515) 245-8400; https://www.wellsfargohistory.com/museums/des-moines

World Food Prize Hall of Laureates, also known as the *Nobel Prize for Food and Agriculture*, honors global achievements in science, agriculture, and humanitarian efforts. Open free to the public on Tuesdays and Saturdays. Guided tours are available on Tuesday at 9 AM, 10:30 AM, Noon, and 1:30 PM. There are no guided tours on Saturday but the Hall is open 9 AM to 1 PM. 100 Locust St; Des Moines, IA 50309; Phone: (515) 245-3783; https://www.worldfoodprize.org

Eldon, IA

American Gothic House may be the most famous house in Iowa. Built in 1881 by Catherine and Charles Dibble, the farmhouse features a single oversized window and was made in a style called Carpenter Gothic. Wood was intrigued and decided to paint "the kind of people I fancied should live in that house." Tour the adjacent American Gothic House Center which showcases Grant Wood's life, and the history of the house. Admission is free. Open Tuesday through Saturday from 10 AM to 5 PM. Open Sunday and Monday from 1 PM to 4 PM. 301 American Gothic St; Eldon, IA 52554; Phone: (641) 652-3352; https://iowaculture.gov/history/sites/american-gothic-house

Forest City, IA

Winnebago Factory Tours are offered to the public at no cost April through October on Monday through Friday 9 AM and 1 PM. They recommend verifying the schedule in advance. Note: Closed toe shoes are required. 1045 South Fourth St; Forest City, IA 50436; Phone: (641) 585-6936 or (800) 643-4892; https://winnebagoind.com/company/visit

Okoboji, IA

Higgins Museum houses the largest collection of National Bank Note issues on permanent exhibit anywhere in the country. These notes provided credit to both the government and the public during the fifty year period between the Civil War and World War One. It is real currency, still redeemable by the Department of the Treasury. Admission is free. The museum is open Memorial Day through Labor Day on Tuesday through Sunday from 11 AM to 5:30 PM. 1507 Sanborn Ave; Okoboji, IA 51355; Phone: (712) 332-5859; http://www.thehigginsmuseum.org

Pella, IA

Klokkenspel features eight four-foot mechanical figures that perform to the music of a 147-bell carillon. It's a form of Glockenspiel clock that uses moving figurines to reenact a play or skit. 625 Franklin St; Pella, IA 50219; http://www.cityofpella.com/facilities/Facility/Details/7

Riverside, IA

Voyage Home Museum proves that the people of Riverside, Iowa have a sense of humor. In 1985 the city proclaimed itself the future birthplace of Captain James T. Kirk, the Captain of the Star Trek Enterprise. Even better, they did so with the agreement Gene Roddenberry who made the famous television series. The city has created the Star Trek Voyage Home Museum in what had been the Riverside History Museum and filled it with Star Trek exhibits as well as exhibits focused on the history of the town. Admission is free. Open Monday through Saturday at 10 AM. Closes at 3 PM on Monday and Wednesday. Closes at 4 PM on Tuesday, Thursday, Friday and Saturday. Open Sunday Noon to 4 PM. The city also holds a Trek Fest the last weekend of June. 361 W First St; Riverside, IA 52327; Phone: (319) 648-2226; https://the-voyage-home-museum.business.site

Walcott, IA
Iowa 80 Trucking Museum is the result of Iowa 80 Truckstop founder Bill Moon's passion for trucks. Currently there are over 100 antique trucks in the collection with 60 of them on display in the museum along with over 300 original signs, and 24 vintage gas pumps. Admission is free with donations appreciated. From Memorial Day to Labor Day open Monday through Saturday from 9 AM to 5 PM, and Sunday from Noon to 5 PM. The rest of the year it is open Wednesday through Saturday from 9 AM to 5 PM, and Sunday Noon to 5 PM. Closed some major holidays. 505 Sterling Dr; Walcott, IA 52773; Phone: (563) 468-5500; https://iowa80truckingmuseum.com

Waterloo, IA (See also East Moline, Illinois)
John Deere offers several free tours across the area. Participants must be at least 13 years of age. Closed toe shoes are required. Reservations are recommended. There are age restrictions, and video recording and photography are not permitted.
John Deere Drivetrain Operations include transmissions, front and rear axles, gears, and shafts. Tours are offered Monday through Friday at 1 PM. 400 Westfield Ave; Waterloo, IA 50701; Phone: (800) 765-9588; https://www.deere.com/en/connect-with-john-deere/visit-john-deere/factory-tours

John Deere Engine Works takes unfinished engine blocks, heads, and crankshafts and assembles them into John Deere diesel engines. Tours available Monday through Friday at 9:30 AM and 1 PM. 3801 W Ridgeway Ave; Waterloo, IA 50704; Phone: (800) 765-9588; https://www.deere.com/en/connect-with-john-deere/visit-john-deere/factory-tours

John Deere Factory Assembly Tours --Tractor Cab Assembly Operations lets visitors watch as tractors are assembled, painted, and made ready. This free tour is given Monday through Friday at 8 AM, 10 AM, and 1 PM. 3500 E Donald St; Waterloo, IA 50703; Phone: (319) 292-7668; (888) 453-5804 (Reservations); https://www.deere.com/en/connect-with-john-deere/visit-john-deere/factory-tours

John Deere Tractor & Engine Museum illustrates the history of John Deere tractors and engines at the site of the first John Deere tractor factory. Admission is free. Open Monday through Saturday from 9 AM to 5 PM. Open Sunday from

Noon to 4 PM. Closed some major holidays. 500 Westfield Ave; Waterloo, IA 50701; Phone: (319) 292-6126; https://www.deere.com/en/connect-with-john-deere/visit-john-deere/tractor-and-engine-museum

Kansas

Abilene, KS

Most people visit this prairie town for the fee-based Dwight D. Eisenhower Presidential Library & Museum, but there are two free attractions which offer additional reasons to visit.

Greyhound Hall of Fame answers the question "Why is Abilene the Greyhound Capital of the World." Learn more about this breed through displays from ancient times to the present, and meet the resident greyhounds. Admission is free. Open daily 9 AM to 4:45 PM. 407 S Buckeye; Abilene, KS 67410; Phone: (785) 263-3000; http://greyhoundhalloffame.com

Old Abilene Town depicts the Wild West in Abilene in the 1860s. Grounds include the Old Abilene Town Main Street. Free to visit. Open May through September with gun-fighting re-enacted on Saturday at Noon, 1:30 PM, and 3:30 PM, and on Sunday at 1:30 PM, and 3:30 PM. Check the website for current seasonal hours. 100 SE Fifth St; Abilene, KS 67410; http://oldabilenecowtown.com

Bonner Springs, KS

Moon Marble Company certainly sells marbles, but it also displays marbles as art, and offers free marble-making demonstrations. Open Monday through Saturday from 10 AM to 5 PM with demonstrations usually on Tuesday, Friday, and Saturday between 10:30 AM and 3 PM. 600 E Front St; Bonner Springs, KS 66012; Phone: (913) 441-1432; https://www.moonmarble.com

Dodge City, KS

Take a walking tour of the **Old Dodge City National Historic District**. The trail is marked with bronze sidewalk medallions and statuary to commemorate the city's many famous and infamous denizens. Pick up a trail map at the Dodge City Convention and Visitors Bureau Information Center. 400 W Wyatt Earp Blvd; Phone: (620) 225-8186; http://www.dodgecitytrailoffame.org/cms

Emporia, KS

Johnston Geology Museum at Emporia State University is home to 45 exhibits including the Hamilton Quarry Fossil Assemblage, an entire 320 million-year-old ecosystem complete with plants, insects, water scorpions, fish, amphibians, and other fossils. Admission is free. Open 8 AM to 10 PM Monday through Friday. Open on Saturday only when the university is in session. 14th and Merchant St; Emporia, KS 66801; Phone: (316) 341-5978; https://www.emporia.edu/~es/museum/museum.htm

Fort Scott, KS

Fort Scott was in active use from 1842-1873 and its exhibits, period furnishings, and living history programs tell the story of military life. The site preserves 11 original historic buildings. Others are reconstructions built on the original foundations. There is no fee to enter the park. Open daily 8:30 AM to 4:30 PM. Closed major holidays. Old Fort Blvd; Fort Scott, KS 66701; Phone: (620) 223-0310; https://www.nps.gov/fosc/index.htm

Fort Leavenworth, KS

Fort Leavenworth contains a national cemetery, Frontier Army Museum, monuments (including Buffalo Soldier Monument) and 19th century buildings. The museum is free to visit. Note: Start your visit at the Visitors Control Center. Drivers must have a valid license, registration, and proof of insurance. All passengers must also have an acceptable ID. Call for information on accepted IDs. The Control Center is open Monday through Friday from 5:30 AM to 4:30 PM, and weekends from 6:30 AM to 4:30 PM. Closed national holidays. 8 Sherman Ave; Fort Leavenworth, KS 66027; Phone: (913) 684-3600; https://home.army.mil/leavenworth/index.php/about/visitor-information

Junction City, KS

Milford Nature Center is a family-friendly place with dioramas lining the halls, and live animal exhibits featuring snakes, amphibians, turtles, and a large bird of prey. The Butterfly House exhibit is open from late May through early October, weather and butterflies permitting. Admission is free. Open Monday through Friday from 9 AM to 4:30 PM. Closed Thanksgiving, Christmas, and New Year's Day. April through September the center is also open weekends from 1 PM to 5 PM. 3415 Hatchery Dr; Junction City, KS 66441; Phone: (785) 238-5323; https://www.junctioncity.org/62/Milford-Nature-Center-Fish-Hatchery

Larned, KS

Fort Larned was an army post in the 1860s on the Santa Fe Trail. It's considered the nation's best-preserved and best-restored fort dating back to the Indian Wars. Admission is free. Regular guided tours are available from May to September. Open daily from 8:30 AM to 4:30 PM. Closed major holidays. 1767 KS Hwy 156; Larned, KS 67550; Phone: (620) 285-6911; https://www.nps.gov/fols/index.htm

Lawrence, KS

Spencer Museum of Art at the University of Kansas creates special exhibits in addition to their collections of American, Asian, and Contemporary art. Admission is free. Donations are welcome. Open Tuesday, Friday, and Saturday from 10 AM to 4 PM. Open Wednesday and Thursday from 10 AM to 8 PM. Open Sunday from Noon to 4 PM. Closed holidays. 1301 Mississippi St; Lawrence, KS 66045; Phone: (785) 864-4710; https://spencerart.ku.edu

Lindsborg, KS
Birger Sandzén Memorial Gallery shows the work of local, regional, and nationally recognized artists. Named for Birger Sandzén who has been called one of the Eight Wonders of Kansas in Art for his unique landscapes. Free admission with donations appreciated. Open Tuesday through Saturday from 10 AM to 5 PM and Sunday from 1 PM to 5 PM. Closed major holidays. 401 N First St; Lindsborg, KS 67456; Phone: (785) 227-2220; http://sandzen.org

Manhattan, KS
Marianna Kistler Beach Museum of Art at Kansas State University celebrates regional as well as international art. Admission is free. Open Tuesday, Wednesday, and Friday from 10 AM to 5 PM, Thursday from 10 AM to 8 PM. Open Saturday from 11 AM to 4 PM. Closed major holidays. 14th St & Anderson Ave; Manhattan, KS 66506; Phone: (785) 532-7718; http://beach.k-state.edu

Nicodemus, KS
Nicodemus National Historic Site was settled during the post-Civil War Reconstruction when formerly enslaved people headed to Kansas. It may be the oldest Black settlement west of the Mississippi River. The 1939 Township Hall, the visitor center, and the A.M.E. Church foyer are open to visitors. There is no fee to visit. The park is open June through the end of August. The visitor center is open all year on Monday through Saturday from 9 AM to 4:30 PM. Closed on federal holidays. 304 Washington Ave; Nicodemus, KS 67625; Phone: (785) 839-4233; https://www.nps.gov/nico/index.htm

Norton, KS
They Also Ran Gallery celebrates the presidential candidates who ran, but lost the election. The gallery was started in the 1960s by William Walter Rouse, who was inspired by the book *They Also Ran* by Irving Stone. Photos and plaques tell their stories and remind people that some of these candidates went on to achieve other glories. There is no admission fee. The gallery is part of the First National Bank. The gallery is open Monday through Friday 9 AM to 3 PM. 105 W Main; Norton, KS 67654; Phone: (785) 877-3341; http://www.theyalsoran.com/index.asp

Oakley, KS
Buffalo Bill Bronze Sculpture celebrates the birthplace of the *Legend of Buffalo Bill*. It was here in Logan County in 1868 that William F. Cody won his title of

Buffalo Bill in a buffalo-hunting contest. Located outside the Buffalo Bill Cultural Center and Visitor Center. 3083 US Hwy 83; http://www.buffalobilloakley.org

Overland Park, KS
Nerman Museum of Contemporary Art displays leading-edge contemporary art as well as items from their eclectic collection of modern sculpture, Latino art, clay pieces, and photographs. Admission is free. Open Tuesday, Friday, and Saturday from 10 AM to 5 PM. Open Wednesday and Thursday from 10 AM to 8 PM, and Sunday from Noon to 5 PM. The museum is located in Johnson County Community College. 12345 College Blvd; Overland Park, KS 66210; Phone: (913) 469-3000; http://www.nermanmuseum.org/index.html

Piqua, KS
Buster Keaton Museum answers the question – what connection did the famous comic actor have with tiny Piqua. Although he was born there on October 4, 1895, it wasn't until many years later when he and his wife were driving through Kansas that a connection was formed. Seeing a sign for Piqua, they decided to visit the place of his birth. The result of that spontaneous decision is the one-room museum, located in the Piqua water department. There are posters, articles, and photographs. A small collection of his movies on video tape are available for visitors to enjoy. Admission is free. Open Monday through Friday from 8 AM to 2 PM. Other hours by appointment. Rural Water District 1; 302 S Hill St; Piqua, KS 66761; Phone: (620) 468-2385; http://www.kansastravel.org/busterkeatonmuseum.htm

Russell, KS
Deines Cultural Center honors E. Hubert Deines (1894-1967), a printmaker known for his meticulous wood engraving. The permanent art collection includes all of his wood engravings as well as various works he collected during his lifetime. Admission is free. Open Tuesday through Friday from Noon to 5 PM, and on Saturday and Sunday from 1 PM to 5 PM. Closed holidays. 820 N Main St; Russell, KS 67665; Phone: (785) 483-3742; http://deinesculturalcenter.org/index.html

Topeka, KS
Brown v. Board of Education National Historic Site illuminates the history and people behind the turning-point decision of Brown v. Board of Education, which ended legal segregation in public schools. Admission is free. Open Monday through Saturday from 9 AM to 5 PM. Open Sunday in season. Closed Thanksgiving, Christmas, and New Year's Day. 1515 SE Monroe St; Topeka, KS 66612; Phone: (785) 354-4273; https://www.nps.gov/brvb/index.htm

Kansas State Capitol is free to visit, and the tours are also free, with reservations suggested. Open Monday through Friday from 8 AM to 5 PM. Open Saturday from 10 AM to 4 PM. Closed state holidays. 6425 SW Sixth Ave; Topeka, KS 66615; Phone: (785) 272-8681; http://www.kshs.org/p/kansas-state-capitol-plan-your-visit/18649

Mulvane Art Museum offers two sculpture gardens, an interactive laboratory for young visitors, and over 4,000 works of art. Admission is free. Open Tuesday from 10 AM to 7 PM and Wednesday through Friday from 10 AM to 5 PM. Open Saturday from 1 PM to 4 PM. Closed holidays. 1700 SW College Ave; Topeka, KS 66621; Phone: (785) 670-1010; https://washburn.edu/mulvane

Museum of the Kansas National Guard features the weapons, uniforms, and other artifacts carried or worn by Kansas Guardsmen from the Civil War to the War on Terrorism. These artifacts describe the life of Kansas citizen-soldiers and their missions. Outside, visitors can see displays of military equipment. Admission is free. Open Monday through Saturday from 10 AM to 4 PM. 125 SE Airport Dr; Topeka, KS 66619; Phone: (785) 862-1020; http://www.kansasguardmuseum.org

Wellington, KS

Chisholm Trail Museum hosts military items as well as artifacts from early local businesses, antique furniture, and items brought to the area by early pioneer wagons, and even by cowboys traveling the Chisholm Trail. Admission is free with donations appreciated. June through October it is open every day, except Tuesday, from 1 PM to 5 PM. In May and November it is open only on weekends. Closed for the season December through April. 502 N Washington; Wellington, KS 67152; Phone: (620) 326-3820; http://www.chisholmtrailmuseum.us

National Glass Museum highlights American-made glassware from the 1800s through the 1970s. No admission is charged, but they gratefully accept donations. Open Thursday and Friday from 11 AM to 4 PM and on Saturday from 10 AM to 2 PM, or by appointment. Closed January, February, and may be closed during March. 117 S Washington; Wellington, KS 67152; Phone: (620) 524-1553; http://www.ndga.net/museum.php

Wichita, KS

Great Plains Nature Center offers two miles of accessible trails through wetlands, prairie, and riparian habitats on the 240 acres of the Chisholm Creek Park. The park is open daily dawn to dusk. The visitor center provides a 2,200-gallon aquarium and other nature exhibits. Admission to the center is free. It is open Monday through Saturday from 9 AM to 5 PM except federal, state, and city holidays. 6232 E 29th St. N; Wichita, KS 67220; Phone: (316) 683-5499; https://gpnc.org

Keeper of the Plains is a towering steel sculpture by Kiowa-Comanche artist Blackbear Bosin. It stands at the confluence of the Arkansas, and Little Arkansas Rivers at 650 N Seneca St; Wichita, KS 67203

Wichita State University offers two free museums. The **Holmes Museum of Anthropology** specializes in prehistoric and historic ceramics and pottery. It also displays textiles and traditional clothing and weavings. The museum is free, donations are accepted. Open Monday through Friday from 1 PM to 5 PM. Closed June, July and August. Neff Hall; 1845 Fairmount; Wichita, KS 67260; Phone: (316) 978-7068; http://holmes.anthropology.museum. The **Ulrich Museum of Art** holds over 6,000 works of art, but is known for the Martin H. Bush Outdoor Sculpture Collection. The 80 works are spread across the 330-acre Wichita State University campus – always open and always free. The indoor galleries are also free. They are open Tuesday through Friday from 11 AM to 5 PM, and Saturday and Sunday from 1 PM to 5 PM. Closed major university holidays. 1845 Fairmount St; Wichita, KS 67260; Phone: (316) 978-3664; https://www.wichita.edu/museums/ulrich

Kentucky

Famous for its thoroughbred horses and its distilled spirits, Kentucky also surprises with its lesser known attractions. Admission to Kentucky State Parks is free although the museums on the grounds may charge a fee. https://parks.ky.gov

Bardstown, KY

Barton 1792 Distillery offers several free tours of the inner workings of bourbon distilling and ends with a complimentary tasting. Visitors must be 21 years of age to taste. Tours are offered Monday through Saturday from 9 AM to 4 PM. The last tour leaves at 3 PM. Register at the gift shop. 300 Barton Rd; Bardstown, KY 40004; Phone: (866) 239-4690; http://www.1792bourbon.com

Oscar Getz Museum of Whiskey History displays his 50 year collection of rare artifacts and documents concerning the American whiskey industry dating from pre-Colonial days. The museum also includes exhibits on Presidents Washington and Lincoln, plus authentic moonshine stills, antique bottles and jugs, and medicinal whiskey bottles. Admission is free although donations are appreciated. Note: Other museums at this location do charge a fee. From November through April open Tuesday through Saturday from 10 AM to 4 PM. Open Sunday from Noon to 4 PM. From May through October open Monday through Friday from 10 AM to 5 PM. Open Saturday from 10 AM to 4 PM, and Sunday Noon to 4 PM. Spalding Hall; 114 N Fifth St; Bardstown, KY; Phone: (502) 348-2999; http://www.whiskeymuseum.com

Berea, KY

Berea College provides full-tuition scholarships to all students. Proud of its tradition and mission, the college offers free tours focused either on a historic overview of the College and its most interesting buildings or their student crafts program showcasing broom craft, weaving, and woodcraft. Reservations are recommended and can be made online. 104 Main St; Berea, KY 40403; Phone: (859) 985-3197; https://www.berea.edu/visitor-center

Frankfort, KY

Buffalo Trace Distillery selected its name as a tribute to the buffalo. The 200-year-old distillery created their own signature Buffalo Trace Kentucky Straight Bourbon Whiskey. Several tours are offered free and all end with a tasting of some of their award-winning products. Tours offered Monday through Saturday from 9 AM to 4 PM and on Sunday from Noon to 3 PM. Note: They recommend calling (800) 654-8471 on the day of your visit for updated information. 113 Great

Buffalo Trace; Frankfort, KY 40601; Phone: (502) 696-5926;
http://www.buffalotracedistillery.com/visit-us/our-tours

Capital City Museum has two floors introducing visitors to political and personal life in Kentucky over the past 200 years. Admission is free. Open from 10 AM to 4 PM Monday through Saturday. 325 Ann St; Frankfort, KY 40601; Phone: (502) 696-0607; http://www.capitalcitymuseum.com

Josephine Sculpture Park has almost 70 works of art along 30 acres of walking paths. All sculptures are hands-on, so feel free to bring the children. Admission is free. Open daily from dawn until dusk. 3355 Lawrenceburg Rd; Frankfort, KY 40601; Phone: (502) 352-7082; https://josephinesculpturepark.org

Kentucky Governor's Mansion is open for tours Tuesday and Thursday morning from 9 AM to 11 AM, excluding some federal and all state holidays. All Governor's Mansion tours are free of charge. Note: They advise calling ahead to check availability and scheduling. 704 Capitol Ave; Frankfort, KY 40601; Phone: (502) 564-3449; https://governorsmansion.ky.gov/Pages/visit.aspx

Kentucky State Capitol offers visitors a Beaux Arts Style Capitol with murals of historic figures, and a collection of dolls dressed in replicas of Kentucky's First Lady inaugural gowns. If the legislature is in session, visitors can observe them in action. Open Monday through Friday from 8 AM to 4:30 PM. From April through October, the capitol also open on Saturday from 10 AM to 2 PM. 700 Capital Ave; Frankfort, KY 40601; Phone: (502) 564-3449; https://capitol.ky.gov/Pages/visitorinfo.aspx

Georgetown, KY
Toyota Kentucky is said to be America's first and the world's largest Toyota manufacturing facility Their free tour is available on weekdays. Register on the website. 1001 Cherry Blossom Way; Georgetown, KY 40324; Phone: (800) TMM-4485; http://www.tourtoyota.com/kentucky

Yuko-en on the Elkhorn features Bluegrass landscaping framed in a Japanese style stroll garden. Admission is free. Open daily dawn to dusk. 700 Cincinnati Rd; Georgetown, KY 40324; Phone: (502) 863-5424; http://www.yukoen.com

Hodgenville, KY
Abraham Lincoln Birthplace National Historical Park has both the first memorial to Lincoln and a symbolic replica of his birth place cabin. Another part of the park holds Abraham Lincoln Boyhood Home at Knob Creek. Admission to both sections is free. Start your visit at the visitor center at the Abraham Lincoln Birthplace. There you'll find exhibits including the original Lincoln Family Bible,

and *Abraham Lincoln: The Kentucky Years*, a 15-minute captioned film. **The First Lincoln Memorial** is built on the knoll above a spring where many believe the Lincoln cabin originally stood. A symbolic birth cabin honors the single-room log cabin where Lincoln was born on Sunday, February 12, 1809. Visits are self-guided from Labor Day to Memorial Day. Ranger led tours are available from Memorial Day until Labor Day. The visitor center, memorial building, and grounds open daily 9 AM to 5 PM. Closed on Thanksgiving, Christmas, and New Year's Day. 2995 Lincoln Farm Rd; Hodgenville, KY 42748; Phone: (270) 358-3137; https://www.nps.gov/abli/index.htm

Abraham Lincoln Boyhood Home at Knob Creek was Lincoln's home during his early years. The center is staffed daily from Memorial Day through Labor Day. Visitors have the opportunity to view a historical garden (summers only) and a replica log cabin. Self-guided walks are available. The grounds open daily during daylight hours. 7120 Bardstown Rd; Hodgenville, KY 42748; Phone: (270) 358-3137; https://www.nps.gov/abli/planyourvisit/boyhood-home.htm

Morehead, KY
Kentucky Folk Art Center has gathered nearly 1,400 pieces of art created by self-taught artists. These are displayed on a rotating basis in the center's first floor gallery. In the second floor gallery, the center presents changing exhibits of folk art, fine art, textiles, photography, and historical content. Admission is free. Open Monday through Saturday from 9 AM to 5 PM. 121 E Second St; Morehead, KY 40351; Phone: (800) 585-6781; http://www.moreheadstate.edu/kfac

Lexington, KY
Arboretum State Botanical Garden of Kentucky is free to visit with donations gratefully accepted. Open daily from dawn to dusk. 500 Alumni Dr; Lexington, KY 40503; Phone: (859) 257-6955; http://arboretum.ca.uky.edu

Art Museum at the University of Kentucky Singletary Center for the Arts has collected more than 4,800 Old Masters as well as American and Kentucky masterpieces. Free admission. Open Tuesday through Thursday from 10 AM to 5 PM. Open late on Friday to 8 PM. Open Saturday and Sunday from Noon to 5 PM. Closed university holidays. 405 Rose St; Lexington, KY 40506; Phone: (859) 257-5716; http://finearts.uky.edu/art-museum

Thoroughbred Park is divided into five major areas, each with a bronze statue or vignette from the world of racing. The bronze mares and foals, thoroughbreds, and jockeys, including the greats such as Willie Shoemaker, and Jerry Bailey are all heading towards the finish line. The artist is Gwen Reardon. Open 24 hours a day all year. 100 Midland Ave; Lexington, KY 40507; Phone: (859) 233-7299; https://www.visitlex.com/listing/thoroughbred-park/6048

Louisville, KY

Cave Hill Cemetery is noted for its lush landscaping, memorial art, and famous people who are interred there. The cemetery does offer fee-based formal tours, but if you just want to pay your respects to boxing great Muhammad Ali, this is his final resting place. "Float like a butterfly, sting like a bee." 701 Baxter Ave; Louisville, KY 40204; Phone: (502) 451-5630; http://www.cavehillcemetery.com

KMAC Museum highlights regional art and works for form a bridge between traditional folk art and contemporary art. Admission is free. Open Tuesday through Saturday from 10 AM to 6 PM. Open Sunday from 10 AM to 5 PM. Closed major holidays. 715 W Main St; Louisville, KY 40202; Phone: (502) 589-0102; https://www.kmacmuseum.org

Museum of the American Printing House for the Blind details the history of the education of people who are blind. Visitors can write their names using a mechanical braille writer and test their comprehension skills on computers equipped with talking software. The museum is open 8:30 AM to 4:30 PM Monday through Friday. Open Saturday from 10 AM to 3 PM. Free guided tours of the printing facility are also available, with donations gratefully accepted. The tours take place Monday through Thursday at 10 AM and 2 PM. Closed on major holidays and on Derby Day (the first Saturday in May).1839 Frankfort Ave; Louisville, KY 40206; Phone: (502) 895-2405; http://www.aph.org/museum/visit

Nicholasville, KY

Harry C. Miller Lock Collection and the Museum of Physical Security highlight safe locks, time locks, and key operated locks. Some of the time locks date back to the 1800s and feature ornate metalsmithing. Resident historians are ready to answer questions. Located in the Lockmasters Security Institute, the museum is free and open for tours Monday through Friday from 8 AM to 5 PM. 2101 John C Watts Dr; Nicholasville, KY 4035; Phone: (866) 574-8724; http://www.lsieducation.com/museum/index.html

Ravenna, KY

Fitchburg Furnace is composed of two stacks – Blackstone and Chandler. The site was once one of the largest charcoal-fired furnaces ever built and it was the only twin stack furnace in the world. Admission is free. A kiosk and interpretive signs are located at the site. 1875 Fitchburg Rd; Ravenna, KY 40472; Phone: (606) 723-2450; http://www.estillcountyky.net/fitchburg-furnace.html

Louisiana

Head to Louisiana for its vibrant cuisine, unique music, and an irrepressible love of life. And these free attractions.

Angola, LA

Angola State Penitentiary Museum documents 130 years of prison life. There is no fee to visit the museum. Open Monday through Thursday from 8 AM to 4:30 PM and on Friday from 8 AM to 5 PM. 17544 Tunica Trace (Hwy 66); Angola, LA 70712; Phone: (225) 655-2592; https://www.angolamuseum.org

Barksdale AFB, LA (See also Shreveport-Bossier City, LA)

Barksdale Global Power Museum highlights vintage aircraft including the venerable B-17 and B-24 bombers of World War II, and the P-51 Mustang. Inside six galleries present additional exhibits. Admission is free. Open Monday through Saturday from 9:30 AM to 4 PM. Closed Thanksgiving Day, Christmas Day, and New Year's Day. Note: Visitors must enter through Barksdale Air Force Base's North Gate on Northgate Road. Tell gate personnel you are visiting the museum and have the driver's licenses or state identifications of everyone in your vehicle above the age of 17. Check the website for more admission requirements, especially if you are coming from outside the USA. 88 Shreveport Rd; Barksdale AFB, LA, 71110; Phone: (318) 752-0055; http://www.barksdaleglobalpowermuseum.com

Bossier City, LA (See Shreveport-Bossier City, LA)

Baton Rouge, LA

Louisiana's Old State Capitol provides the Old State Capitol Museum of Political History, along with several changing exhibits. Don't miss the *Ghost of the Castle* about the history of the building. Admission is free. Open Tuesday through Friday from 10 AM to 4 PM. Open Saturday from 9 AM to 3 PM. 100 North Blvd; Baton Rouge, LA 70801; Phone: (225) 342-0500; http://www.louisianaoldstatecapitol.org/museum

Louisiana State Capitol is largely the story of flamboyant governor Huey Pierce Long. Not only was the construction of the building part of his political platform, it was part of his death. On September 10, 1935 Long was attacked within the walls of the building. The bullet holes can still be seen. Long was buried in the Capitol Gardens and there's a memorial on the grounds as well. The 27th floor observation area provides striking city views. There is no fee for admission. The Capitol is open daily from 8 AM to 4:30 PM except major holidays. 900 N Third

St; Baton Rouge, LA 70802; Phone: (225) 342-7317;
https://www.nps.gov/nr/travel/louisiana/cap.htm

LSU AgCenter Botanic Gardens is a collection of gardens, paths and walkways. The gardens are generally free to visit but there is a fee to see Windrush Gardens, and the Rural Life Museum. Open daily from 8 AM to 5 PM. Closed major holidays. 4560 Essen La; Baton Rouge, LA 70809;
Phone: (225) 763-3990; https://www.lsu.edu/botanic-gardens/gardens/gardens.php

LSU Museum of Natural Science highlights nine habitat dioramas constructed from 1955 to 1964 by the talented scientist and artist, Ambrose Daigre. The dioramas gave the illusion of a real scene being viewed through a window. The museum also has displays Louisiana wildlife. Free admission. Open Monday through Friday from 8 AM to 4 PM. Closed state holidays and at 2 PM on Fridays during the school year. 119 Foster Hall; Baton Rouge, LA 70803; Phone: (225) 578-2855; https://www.lsu.edu/mns

Bell City, LA

Southwest Louisiana National Wildlife Refuge Complex invites visitors to cross a boardwalk over a wildlife pond and enter the visitor center to explore the exhibits and films. Additional viewing options include a platform behind the center and nearby **Pintail Wildlife Drive** and boardwalk. No admission fee. The center is open Monday through Thursday from 7:30 AM to 4 PM, on Friday from 7:30 AM to 3 PM, and on Saturday from 9 AM to 4 PM. The wildlife drive is always open. 1428 Hwy 27; Bell City, LA 70630; Phone: (337) 598-2216; https://www.fws.gov/refuge/Cameron_Prairie/visit/plan_your_visit.html

Carville, LA

National Hansen's Disease Museum honors the first facility in the continental United States to isolate, and attempt to treat Hansen's disease – once known as leprosy. Today that complex is a national museum which recounts the story of the disease, those who were affected, and the medical staff who cared for them. Admission to the museum and the grounds is free. Open Tuesday through Saturday from 10 AM to 4 PM. Closed on federal holidays. There is also a nine-stop driving tour through the complex. Note: You will be entering a military base and must show valid ID at the gate. 5445 Point Clair Rd; Carville, LA 70721; Phone: (225) 642-1950;
https://www.hrsa.gov/hansensdisease/museum/index.html

Chalmette, LA

Jean Lafitte National Historical Park & Preserve - Chalmette Battlefield was the site of the Battle of New Orleans in the War of 1812. Visitors will see the Chalmette Monument, cannon replicas, and the Malus-Beauregard House.

Admission is free. The battlefield grounds and visitor center is open daily from 9 AM to 4:30 PM. 8606 W St. Bernard Hwy; Chalmette, LA 70043; Phone: (504) 281-0510; https://www.nps.gov/jela/chalmette-battlefield.htm

Chauvin, LA

Chauvin Sculpture Garden + Nicholls State University Art Studio preserves and protects the folk art of Kenny Hill, and displays the work of contemporary artists. Permanent collections include paintings, photographs, sculpture, and pottery created by local artists. Admission is free. Open Saturday and Sunday from 11 AM to 4 PM or by appointment. 5337 Bayouside Dr; Chauvin, LA 70344; Phone: (985) 594-2546; https://www.nicholls.edu/folkartcenter/folk.html

Defelice Marine Center invites visitors to meet their marine animals and learn about wetlands through their exhibits. There's also an observation tower and a pond boardwalk. Free to visit. Open daily from 8 AM to 4 PM. 8124 Hwy 56; Chauvin, LA 70344; Phone: (985) 851-2800; https://lumcon.edu/visit-and-directions

DeRidder, LA

Beauregard Museum exhibits handmade tools, artifacts from the timber industry, old photographs from the parish's history, Native American arrowheads and pottery, military memorabilia, antique furniture, musical instruments, and curiosities. Located in Kansas City Southern Depot the museum is free of charge and open Tuesday through Saturday from 10 AM to 4 PM. Closed all federal holidays. 120 S. Washington Ave; DeRidder, LA 70634; Phone: (337) 463-8148; http://www.cityofderidder.org/152/Beauregard-Parish-Museum

Lois Loftin Doll Museum features over 3,000 dolls from all over the world. Located inside the Tourist Commission Office. Admission is free. Open Monday through Friday from 9 AM to 4 PM. Closed major holidays. 313 W First St; DeRidder, LA 70634; Phone: (337) 463-5534; http://www.beauregardtourism.com/museums.html

Eunice, LA

Cajun Music Hall Of Fame and Museum celebrates this unique music through musical instruments, records, and albums of Cajun sounds. Admission is free. Open Tuesday through Saturday from 9 AM to 4:30 PM. 230 S CC Duson Dr; Eunice, LA 70535; Phone: (337) 457-6534; http://cajunfrenchmusic.org/hall-of-fame

Prairie Acadian Cultural Center is a unit of the Jean Lafitte National Historical Park and Preserve. Ranger programs, exhibits, artifacts, and films explain the history of the Acadians who settled the prairie region of southwest Louisiana. The Country Mardi Gras Exhibit displays costumes and photos, and special stations offer audio recordings. Free admission. Open Wednesday through Friday from 9:30 AM to 4:30 PM, and Saturday from 9:30 AM to 6 PM. Closed on federal holidays. Open on Mardi Gras. 250 Park Ave; Eunice, LA 70535; Phone: (337) 457-8499; https://www.nps.gov/jela/prairie-acadian-cultural-center-eunice.htm

Ferriday, LA

Delta Music Museum celebrates the uniquely American music of the Mississippi Delta and its gospel, blues, swamp pop, country, and rock 'n 'roll. The museum is free and open Wednesday through Friday from 9 AM to 4 PM. 218 Louisiana Ave; Ferriday, LA 71334; Phone: (318) 757-9999; http://www.deltamusicmuseum.com

Grambling, LA

Eddie G. Robinson Museum provides videos and interactive exhibits highlighting the achievements of "winningest coach in NCAA Division I football "and the over 200 players who went on to professional careers. Admission is free. Open Monday through Friday from 10 AM to 4 PM. Closed some state holidays. 126 Jones St; Grambling, LA 71245; Phone: (318) 274-2210; http://www.robinsonmuseum.com

Jennings, LA

Gator Chateau (Alligator House) at Louisiana Oil & Gas Park invites everyone to interact with live alligators at this home to rescued and orphaned baby alligators. There's mature alligators as well. Admission is free. Open Monday through Saturday from 9 AM to 5 PM. Closed some major holidays. Alligator feedings are held on Friday at 3:30 PM from June through September. 100 Rue de l' Acadie, (I-10 at Exit 64); Jennings, LA 70546; Phone: (337) 821-5521; http://www.jeffdavis.org/tourism/attractions/gator-chateau.html

Jonesville, LA

Catahoula National Wildlife Refuge invites viewing and photographing of wildlife from the observation tower overlooking a lake. Their wildlife drive parallels Cowpen Bayou and takes visitors through a bottomland hardwood forest where bobcat, white-tailed deer, and feral hogs can be seen. There's also bird watching along the dirt roads on the Bushley Bayou Unit. No admission fee. Open daylight hours throughout the year. 210 Catahoula NWR Rd; Jonesville, LA 71343; Phone: (318) 992-5261; https://www.fws.gov/refuge/Catahoula

Lacassine, LA

Bayou Rum Distillery is set on 22 acres with natural ponds, and a sugar cane field. Take a free tour to see how Bayou Rum is produced. Distillery tours are offered daily at 10 AM and 11 AM, then again hourly from 1 PM to 4 PM. 20909 Frontage Rd (I-10 at exit 48); Lacassine, LA 70650; Phone: (337) 588-5800; https://bayourum.com

Lafayette, LA

Acadian Cultural Center illuminates Louisiana history and culture – the origins, migration, settlement, and contemporary culture of the Acadians. Ranger programs, films, exhibits, and events focus on music, story-telling, dance, and food. Admission is free. Open Tuesday through Friday from 9 AM to 4:30 PM and Saturday from 8:30 AM to Noon. 501 Fisher Rd; Lafayette, LA 70508; Phone: (337) 232-0789; https://www.nps.gov/jela/new-acadian-cultural-center.htm

Lake Providence, LA

Louisiana State Cotton Museum offers the history of cotton farming in Louisiana with a farmhouse, tenant house, commissary, chapel, first electric cotton gin in Louisiana, and musical instruments of the Delta Blues. Admission is free. Open Tuesday through Saturday from 10 AM to 4 PM. Closed on holidays. 7162 Hwy 65 N; Lake Providence, LA 71254; Phone: (318) 559-2041; https://www.sos.la.gov/HistoricalResources/VisitMuseums/LouisianaStateCotton Museum/Pages/default.aspx

Monroe, LA

Black Bayou Lake Refuge provides a habitat for waterfowl, endangered wildlife as well as visiting and resident wildlife. Enjoy a mile-long nature trail through a variety of habitats and onto the wildlife pier that extends over Black Bayou Lake. There are no entrance fees. Open Monday through Friday from 8 AM to 4 PM. Open Saturday from 9 AM to 5 PM, and Sunday 1 PM to 5 PM. 480 Richland Pl; Monroe, LA 71203; Phone: (318) 387-1114; https://www.fws.gov/refuge/Black_Bayou_Lake

Chennault Aviation & Military Museum honors all veterans, and features exhibits on war from World War I through Iraq and Afghanistan. Admission is free. Open Tuesday through Saturday from 9 AM to 4 PM. Closed Thanksgiving, Christmas, and New Year's Day. 701 Kansas La; Monroe, LA 71203; Phone: (318) 362-5540; http://www.chennaultmuseum.org/visit.php

Masur Museum of Art focuses on regional artists. It also commissions series from individual artists. Admission is free. Open Tuesday through Friday from 9 AM to

5 PM, and Saturday from Noon to 5 PM. 1400 S Grand St; Monroe, LA 71202; Phone: (318) 329-2237; http://www.masurmuseum.org

Natchez, LA
Oakland Plantation – Cane River Creole National Historical Park features nearly 60 historic buildings, including the main house, pigeonniers, store, cook's cabin, overseer's house, tenant cabin, and various outbuildings. Guided tours are available. The park does not charge admission fees. Donations are accepted. All programs and events are free unless noted otherwise. 4386 Hwy 494; Natchez, LA 71456; Phone: (318) 352-0383; https://www.nps.gov/cari/index.htm

New Orleans, LA
Ansel M. Stroud Jr. Military History & Weapons Museum presents weapons and uniforms dating from the early 18th century through the present. The focus is on the citizen-soldiers of the Louisiana National Guard. On the grounds are tanks, fighter planes, and other examples of American firepower. No charge for admission. Donations welcome. Open Monday through Saturday from 10 AM to 4 PM. Closed major holidays. Note: Photo ID is required. Jackson Barracks Area C; 4209 Chenault Blvd; New Orleans, LA 70117; Phone: (504) 278-8664; https://geauxguardmuseums.com/about-the-museums

Madame John's Legacy is considered one of the best examples of French colonial architecture in North America. Visitors with a penchant for pottery will enjoy the display of more than 50 glazed ceramics pieces that was once part of Newcomb College. Admission is free. Open Tuesday through Sunday from 10 AM to 4:30 PM. Closed state holidays. 632 Dumaine St; New Orleans, LA 70116; Phone: (504) 568-6968; https://louisianastatemuseum.org/museum/madame-johns-legacy

New Orleans Glassworks & Printmaking Studio holds free glassblowing demonstrations and hosts open studio visits. Currently open Monday through Saturday from 10 AM to 5 PM. Call in advance to confirm scheduling as the hours vary by season. 727 Magazine St; New Orleans, LA 70130; Phone: (504) 529-7279; http://neworleansglassworks.com

New Orleans Jazz National Historical Park may be the only place in the country where a historical park refers not to a place, or a person, but to music. The park's primary visitor center is the starting point. You can find out about musical events in the city, and there are ranger-led demonstrations, talks, video documentaries, and live music both at both the visitor center and at the Old U.S. Mint. All facilities, programs, and special events are free and open to the public. The visitor center is open Tuesday through Saturday from 9 AM to 4:30 PM. Closed Mardi Gras and federal holidays. Note: Some free concerts are held at the New Orleans

Jazz Museum at the Old Mint. Visiting the museum will incur a fee, but there is no fee for the concerts sponsored by the Historical Park. Check with the park's visitor center for information on those free concerts. 916 N Peters St; New Orleans, LA 70130; Phone: (504) 589-4841; https://www.nps.gov/jazz/index.htm

Metairie Cemetery is one of New Orleans' famous above-ground cemeteries known for its eclectic memorial styles. You'll also find the graves of everyone from Confederate generals, U.S. Congressmen, famous jazz trumpeter Al Hirt, "King of Swing" Louis Prima, baseball Hall of Famer Mel Ott, and Ruth Fertel – the first woman licensed in Louisiana as a thoroughbred horse trainer. It is free to visit. Open daily 8:30 AM to 5 PM. 5100 Pontchartrain Blvd; New Orleans, LA 70124; Phone: (504) 486-6331; https://thecontemplativetraveler.wordpress.com/2016/11/25/cities-of-the-dead-metairie-cemetery-new-orleans-louisiana

Rosetree Blown Glass Studio and Gallery specializes in the creation of blown art glass in the Venetian style. The studio is free to visit. Open Monday through Friday from 10 AM to 5 PM. Note: Pedestrians will need to take the fee-based ferry across the Mississippi River from the French Quarter. It's also possible to drive across a vehicle-only bridge. 446 Vallette St; New Orleans, LA 70113; Phone: (504) 366-3602; https://rosetreegallery.com/contact

Sydney and Walda Besthoff Sculpture Garden displays over 60 sculptures including *Venus Victorius* by Pierre Auguste Renoir, *Reclining Mother and Child* by Henry Moore, and *Restrained* by Deborah Butterfield. Admission is free. Open daily. Closed all legal holidays. Guided tours are offered Friday, Saturday, and Monday at Noon. Note: There is an admission charge to the New Orleans Museum of Art, only the Sculpture Garden is free. One Collins C. Diboll Cir; New Orleans, LA 70124; Phone: (504) 658-4100; https://noma.org/sculpture-garden/background

Oil City, LA
Louisiana State Oil and Gas Museum interprets Louisiana's early oil industry history though photographs, films, and life-size dioramas. A collection of machinery, rigs, and equipment is on display next to the train depot. Free admission. Open Wednesday through Friday from 10 AM to 4 PM. 200 S Land Ave; Oil City, LA 71061; Phone: (318) 995-6845; https://www.sos.la.gov/HistoricalResources/VisitMuseums/LouisianaStateOilAndGasMuseum/Pages/default.aspx

Opelousas, LA
Le Vieux Village Historical Park & Heritage Museum includes a Creole home, a country store, and doctor's office from the early 19th century. The Venus House

was built using bousillage, a mixture of clay and grasses as the infill between the timbers of a half-timbered building. The tourist information center contains a display of historic photos, knives, guns, and other memorabilia tied to Jim Bowie, who once lived in Opelousas. The Orphan Train Museum, housed inside a restored train depot, illustrates the story of the children who came to Louisiana from New York between 1873 and 1929. Open Tuesday through Friday from 10 AM to 2 PM. Self-guided tours are available daily, and guided tours are offered free at 10 AM and 2 PM. 828 E Landry St; Opelousas, LA 70570; Phone: (337) 948-6263; http://cityofopelousas.com/tourist-info-center-le-vieux-village

Patterson, LA
Wedell-Williams Aviation and Cypress Sawmill Museum honors aviation pioneers Jimmie Wedell and Harry P. Williams who formed an air service in Patterson, Louisiana. The David J. Felterman Theater features a film of the 1932 Cleveland National Air Races. Although not conceptually related, the Cypress Sawmill Collection documents the history of the cypress lumber industry in Louisiana. Admission is free. Open Tuesday through Saturday from 9:30 AM to 4 PM. 118 Cotten Rd; Patterson, LA 70392; Phone: (985) 399-1268; http://louisianastatemuseum.org/museums/cypress-sawmill-collection-and-wedell-williams-aviation-museum

Plaquemine, LA
Plaquemine Lock State Historic Site presents an example of early hydraulic engineering design, and the historic significance of Bayou Plaquemine. There's a museum, visitor center, and open air pavilion with a display of various water craft used when the lock was operational. There is no charge for admission. Open Thursday, Friday, and Saturday from 9 AM to 5 PM. 57730 Main St; Plaquemine, LA 70764; Phone: (225) 687-7158; https://www.louisianatravel.com/articles/plaquemine-lock-state-historic-site

Shreveport-Bossier City, LA (See also Barksdale AFB, LA)
Louisiana State Exhibit Museum dates back to the massive public art program of the New Deal in 1939. Inside 23 dioramas depict Louisiana life in the 1940s. Another highlight is the four panel fresco on the North portico. LSEM's collection also includes Louisiana Native American artifacts, regional, and national history artifacts, original works by local artists, and natural history exhibits. Admission is free. Open Monday through Friday from 9 AM to 4 PM. Closed all state holidays. 3015 Greenwood Rd; Shreveport, LA 71109; Phone: (318) 632-2020; http://www.laexhibitmuseum.org

Meadows Museum of Art is notable for the 350 paintings, watercolors, and drawings of Indochina by the French Academic artist Jean Despujols, created between 1936 and 1938. There's also Inuit, Haitian, and African art. Admission is free. Open Monday through Saturday from 10 AM to 6 PM. Located in Centenary College of Louisiana. 2911 Centenary Blvd; Shreveport, LA 71104; Phone: (318) 869-5169; https://www.themeadowsmuseum.com

R.W. Norton Art Gallery sits on 40 acres of landscaped gardens and walking trails. Inside, visitors can peruse the museum's collection of more than 400 paintings as well as hundreds of sculptures, prints, decorative arts, and tapestries. The Norton owns a rare *Birds of America* by John James Audubon. There is no admission to view the grounds, the museum's art collection, or special exhibitions. The museum is open Wednesday and Thursday from 10 AM to 5 PM. Open Friday and Saturday from 10 AM to 7 PM. Open Sunday from 1 PM to 5 PM. Closed federal holidays. Gardens are open daily from 7 AM to 7 PM. 4747 Creswell Ave; Shreveport, LA 71106; Phone: (318) 865-4201; http://www.rwnaf.org

Shreveport Water Works Museum is both a National Historic Landmark and a National Historic Civil Engineering Landmark. Opened in 1887 as the city's first water plant, the entire physical plant (pumps, filters and other machinery) remains in place as a rare example of an intact steam water works. One of the buildings on the site also hosts the **Railroad Museum** with historic railroad artifacts. Free admission. Open Tuesday through Saturday from 10 AM to 4 PM. Open Sunday from Noon to 4 PM. 142 N Common St; Shreveport, LA 71101; Phone: (318) 221-3388; http://shreveportwaterworks.org/waterworks-museum

Southern University Museum of Art at Shreveport (SUMAS) focuses on the artistic, historical, and cultural contributions of African and American Blacks. Admission is free. Open Tuesday through Thursday from 10 AM to 5 PM. Open Friday from 9 AM to Noon. 610 Texas St, Shreveport, LA 71101; Phone: (318) 670-9631; http://www.susla.edu/page/university-museum

Spring Street Historical Museum can be found in one of Shreveport's oldest buildings and it retains its original interior and exterior. The museum's artifacts include vintage clothing dating back to 1835, antique toys, firearms and swords, photographs, antique maps, Persian rugs, and original 18th and 19th century furniture. The second-floor Victorian parlor is a step back in time to the late 1870s and 1880s. There is no admission fee, but they do accept donations. Open Tuesday through Saturday from 10 AM to 4 PM. Closed major holidays. 525 Spring St; Shreveport, LA 71101; Phone: (318) 424-0964; https://springstreetmuseum.org

Tallulah, LA
Tensas River National Wildlife Refuge encourages visitors to walk the Hollow Cypress boardwalk to the observation tower, and drive the Wildlife Drive, a 4½-

mile loop to see songbirds, and white-tailed deer. Admission is free. Open from 4 AM to 2 hours after sunset. The visitor center is open Monday through Friday from 8 AM to 4 PM. Closed all federal holidays. 2312 Quebec Rd; Tallulah, LA 71282; Phone: (318) 574-2664; https://www.fws.gov/refuge/Tensas_River

Thibodaux, LA
E.D. White Historic Site focuses on the history of the Bayou Lafourche area, with features on the Chitimacha Indians, Acadian settlers, slavery, sugar cane plantations, and the White family. Admission is free. Open Tuesday through Saturday from 10 AM to 4:30 PM. 2295 LA Hwy 1; Thibodaux, LA 70301; Phone: (985) 447-0915; https://louisianastatemuseum.org/museum/ed-white-historic-site

Jean Lafitte National Historical Park & Preserve, Wetlands Acadian Cultural Center offers free jam sessions with local musicians, history walks, and the story of Louisiana's bayou country. Admission is free. Open Monday and Tuesday from 9 AM to 7 PM and Wednesday through Friday from 9 AM to 5 PM. Closed federal holidays and Mardi Gras. 314 St. Mary St, LA Hwy 1; Thibodaux, LA 70301; Phone: (985) 448-1375; https://www.nps.gov/jela/wetlands-acadian-cultural-center.htm

Winnfield, LA
Louisiana Political Museum & Hall of Fame was created by an act of the Louisiana Legislature in 1987. If you haven't heard of Winnfield, it is likely you heard of three of its famous and controversial sons – Huey P. Long, Earl K. Long, and O.K. Allen. Earl Long's campaign vehicle is one attraction as is Huey P. Long's dining room. Admission is free. Open Monday through Friday from 9 AM to 5 PM. 499 E Main St; Winnfield, LA 71483; Phone: (318) 628-5928; http://www.lapoliticalmuseum.com/generalinformation.html

Maine

The famed Appalachian Trail starts in Maine. This 2,180+ mile long hiking trail traverses wild vistas, woodlands, and even the cultural landscape of the Appalachian Mountains. Although some access points are free to enter, the starting point in Maine is not free. Learn more about this historic and challenging trail at https://www.nps.gov/appa/index.htm

Augusta, ME

Augusta Nature Education Center invites the public to enjoy their network of trails for walking, biking, snowshoeing, cross-country skiing, photography, geocaching, and wildlife observation. Any non-motorized daylight activity is welcomed. Entrance is free. Open dawn to dusk. S Belfast Ave; Augusta, ME 04330; http://augustanaturecenter.org

Blaine House tours take visitors through the first floor rooms of the 1833 mansion and describes the historical background of teacher-turned-political leader, James G. Blaine. The tour also provides information about the official uses of the house as the Governor's residence. The tours are free and must be scheduled at least three days in advance. They are available Wednesday and Friday between 9 AM and 2:30 PM. Note: A security form must be submitted. 192 State St; Augusta, ME 04330; Phone: (207) 287-2301; https://mainestatemuseum.org/visit/blaine-house-and-state-house-tours

Maine State House is based on the design of the Capitol building of the state of Massachusetts. The reason for this odd fact is that at one time Maine was actually part of Massachusetts. The state didn't gain its independence until 1820. Walk-in visitors are welcome. The State House is open Monday through Friday from 8 AM to 5 PM. Guided tours run hourly between 9 AM and Noon. State St; Augusta, ME 04330; Phone (207) 287-1692; http://legislature.maine.gov/lio/security-screening/9120

Viles Arboretum (formerly the Pine Tree State Arboretum) offers six miles of trails as well as botanical and outdoor art exhibits. The Art Trail takes strollers through the largest permanent outdoor display of art in Maine. Admission is free. Grounds are open daily, dawn to dusk. The visitor center is open from 8 AM to 4:30 PM, Monday through Friday. 153 Hospital St; Augusta, ME 04330; Phone: (207) 626-7989; http://www.vilesarboretum.org

Bar Harbor, ME (See also Hulls Cove, ME)

Bar Harbor Historical Society Museum uses memorabilia, maps, antique clothing, and pictures to show the history of Bar Harbor. Admission is free. Open mid-June to October on Monday through Friday from 1 PM to 4 PM. Closed holidays. 33 Ledgelawn Ave; Bar Harbor, ME 04609; Phone: (207) 288-3807; http://www.barharborhistorical.org

George B. Dorr Museum of Natural History features dioramas of coastal Maine wildlife, and a tide pool tank with live sea stars, hermit crabs, snails, and other marine creatures. Admission is free with donations requested. Open Tuesdays through Saturdays from 10 AM to 5 PM. Closed in December. Please call to verify hours. 105 Eden St; Bar Harbor, ME 04609; Phone: (207) 288-5395; https://www.coa.edu/dorr-museum

Bangor, ME

Orono Bog Boardwalk is a one-mile boardwalk loop trail to the peat moss center of the Orono Bog. Admission is free. There are also free tours and talks. Open May until Thanksgiving weekend, or the first snowfall. From May through August open 7 AM to 6:30 PM. Opens later and closes earlier each month after that. Check website for the hours during your visit. The boardwalk is closed from December through April. Admission is free as are all tours (advance registration is required). Bog Walk, Orono, ME 04473; https://umaine.edu/oronobogwalk

University Of Maine Museum of Art centers on an extensive collections of original prints and photography. It also emphasizes modern and contemporary art by some of the world's most famous artists, and artists with significant ties to Maine. Admission is free. Open Tuesday through Saturday from 10 AM to 5 PM. 40 Harlow St; Bangor, ME 04401; Phone: (207) 581-3300; https://umma.umaine.edu

Brunswick, ME

Bowdoin College Museum of Art specializes in decorative arts, paintings, sculptures, and illustrations. Open free to the public on Tuesday through Saturday from 10 AM to 5 PM with later closing on Thursday to 8:30 PM. The museum is closed national holidays and during the school's December break. 9400 College Station; Brunswick ME 04011; Phone: (207) 725-3275; http://www.bowdoin.edu/art-museum

Peary MacMillan Arctic Museum & Arctic Studies Center hosts an unusual collection started by Donald B. MacMillan who amassed 9,000 images, movies, and objects from Greenland, Labrador, and Baffin Island. Today the holdings include historic Inuit artifacts as well as contemporary art and crafts from across the Arctic. Free admission. Open Tuesday through Saturday from 10 AM to 5 PM, and Sunday from 2 PM to 5 PM. Hubbard Hall at Bowdoin College. 9500 College Station; Brunswick, ME 04011; Phone: (207) 725-3416; http://www.bowdoin.edu/arctic-museum

Calais, ME

Saint Croix Island International Historic Site recounts the history of the French presence in North America. A short, accessible interpretive trail features bronze figures of the French and Passamaquoddy as well as displays that discuss historical events and the interaction of the two cultures. The park is free to visit and open all year during daylight hours. 84 Saint Croix Dr; Calais, ME 04619; Phone: (207) 454-3871; https://www.nps.gov/sacr/index.htm

Camden, ME

Merryspring Nature Center beckons with trails and theme gardens. Open free daily during daylight hours. 30 Conway Rd; Camden, ME 04843; Phone: (207) 236-2239; http://www.merryspring.org

Castine, ME

Wilson Museum began with geologist Dr. John Howard Wilson needing a place for his rocks and fossils. Today the museum displays tool-making artifacts and items from Africa, the Americas, and Bali. Admission is free, but there is a charge for guided tours of the John Perkins House. The Wilson Museum campus is open from the end of May through the end of September on Monday through Friday from 10 AM to 5 PM. Open Saturday and Sunday from 2 PM to 5 PM. 120 Perkins St; Castine, ME 04421; Phone: (207) 326-9247; http://www.wilsonmuseum.org

Ellsworth, ME

Woodlawn Park features a 1900s formal garden enclosed with a lilac hedge, designed in the Colonial Revival style. A cutting garden was added to provide fresh flowers for Woodlawn's afternoon teas. Admission is free. Open from dawn to dusk all year. There is a fee to tour the family home. 19 Black House Dr; Ellsworth, ME 04605; Phone: (207) 667-8671; https://woodlawnmuseum.com/visit-woodlawn

Fort Kent, ME

Fort Kent Blockhouse is the only fortification relating to the Aroostook War of 1838-1839 This was basically a border dispute between the British colony of New Brunswick and the U.S. State of Maine. Admission is free with donations gratefully accepted. Open daily from Memorial Day to Labor Day from 9 AM to 5

PM. Blockhouse Rd; Fort Kent, ME 04743; Phone: (207)768-8341;
https://www.nps.gov/maac/planyourvisit/blockhouse.htm

Hulls Cove, ME (See also Bar Harbor, ME)

Hulls Cove Sculpture Garden provides sculptures, flower gardens, and pathways adjacent to the fee-based Acadia National Park. Open to the public without charge daily all year from dawn to dusk. It's next to the **Old Tool Barn** known for its old tools, antiques, antiquarian books, paintings, and prints. Note: Some of the more fragile sculptures and many of the tools are put in storage for winter. 17 Breakneck Rd; Bar Harbor, ME 04609; Phone: (207) 288-5126;
http://www.davistownmuseum.org/TDMcircumTrail.htm

Kingfield, ME

Ski Museum provides the manufacturing and history of skis. Learn about Paris Manufacturing, and watch the video *From Tree to Ski* which explains how skis were manufactured in the 1930s. Their children's corner includes early ski figurines, skis, sleds, and toys. A replica of a *King & Dexter* ski shop includes tools that were used in the shop. Admission is free. Hours are subject to change with the availability of volunteers. Call or check the website for latest hours. 256 Main St; Kingfield, ME 04947; Phone: (207) 265-2023;
http://www.skimuseumofmaine.org/about

Lewiston, ME

Bates College Museum of Art honors the work of Marsden Hartley as well as Robert Indiana, who paid homage to Hartley through *The Hartley Elegies*. There's also contemporary African and Chinese photography, pre-Columbian sculpture and ceramics, and Japanese woodblock prints. Admission is free. Open Monday through Saturdays from 10 AM to 5 PM. Closed during installations. Olin Arts Center; 75 Russell St; Lewiston, ME 04240; Phone: (207) 786-6158;
https://www.bates.edu/museum

Ogunquit, ME

Ogunquit Heritage Museum at Captain James Winn House blends nature and history. Winding paths and wooded areas surround the circa 1780 building. Inside the Winn house there are exhibits and artifacts related to fishing and lobstering. Admission is free. Open June through October on Tuesday through Saturday from 1 PM to 5 PM. 86 Obeds La; Ogunquit, ME 03907; Phone: (207) 646-0296;
http://www.ogunquitheritagemuseum.com/AboutUs.html

Orono, ME

Hudson Museum is the repository of the Palmer collection – 550 tomb figures from the Colima, Jalisco, and Nayarit cultures of Western Mexico. The museum also holds the largest institutional collection of funerary art in the United States.

There is no admission fee. Open Monday through Friday from 9 AM to 4 PM. From September to May, the museum expands its hours to include Saturdays from 11 AM to 4 PM. Closed on major holidays. Collins Center for the Arts; University of Maine; 2 Flagstaff Rd; Orono, ME 04469; Phone: (207) 581-1904; https://umaine.edu/hudsonmuseum

Page Farm and Home Museum includes historic buildings, farm technologies, and artifacts of rural culture. There is no admission fee but donations are most welcome. Open Tuesday through Saturday from 9 AM through 4 PM. 5787 Museum Barn; Portage Rd; Orono, ME 04469; Phone: (207) 581-4100; https://umaine.edu/pagefarm

Portland, ME (See also South Portland, ME)
Institute of Contemporary Art (ICA) at Maine College of Art curates innovative exhibitions and public programs that showcase contemporary art by local, national, and international artists. Admission is free. Open Wednesday through Sunday from 11 AM to 5 PM, closing at 7 PM on Thursday. 522 Congress St; Portland, ME 04101; Phone: (207) 699-5025; https://www.meca.edu/about/institute-of-contemporary-art

Maine Jewish Museum offers contemporary art exhibitions featuring established, Jewish-connected, and Maine-connected artists. The museum also houses Jack Montgomery's photo exhibit of Holocaust survivors who settled in Maine as well as a permanent exhibition of Maine Jewish history. Admission is free. Open Monday through Friday from 10 AM to 2 PM and Sunday from 1 PM to 5 PM. 267 Congress St; Portland ME 04101; Phone: (207) 773-2339; https://mainejewishmuseum.org/art-exhibits

Spring Point Ledge Lighthouse can be found at the end of a 900-foot breakwater wall that borders the Atlantic Ocean. Visitors can take a short walk along the breakwater wall to visit the lighthouse. Free tours are available during summer, weekend open houses. 2 Fort Rd, South Portland, ME 04106; https://springpointlight.org

Presque Isle, ME
Air Museum illustrates the history and importance of the Presque Isle International Airport dating back to the 1930s. Located in the Main Terminal it's open when the airport is open. 645 Airport Dr; Presque Isle, ME 04769; Phone: (207) 764-2550; https://www.flypresqueisle.com/airport/amenities

Maysville Museum packs history into a small space with four major areas of focus – the Aroostook War, Presque Isle and the Civil War, Agri-CULTURE, and Presque Isle's rural one-room schoolhouses. No admission fee. Note: There is no public restroom. Open April through October on Monday through Saturday from 10 AM to 2 PM. 165 Caribou Rd; Presque Isle, ME 04769; Phone: (207) 762-1151; https://savingplaces.org/distinctive-destinations/the-maysville-museum

South Portland, ME (See also Portland, ME)

Maine Military Museum displays authentic artifacts of the military services from the Revolutionary War to Afghanistan and Iraq. A primary focus is on American Prisoners of War. There is no admission fee. From Memorial Day to Veteran's Day open Tuesday through Sunday from 11 AM to 5 PM. The rest of the year open Saturday and Sunday from 11 AM to 5 PM, and by request. 50 Peary Ter; South Portland, ME 04106; Phone: (207) 767-8227; https://mainemilitarymuseum.org

Solon, ME

South Solon Meetinghouse features the original 1842 podium, pews, choir loft, windows, and steeple. The interior of the South Solon Meeting House was elaborately painted between 1952 and 1957 by 13 artists from the nearby Skowhegan School of Painting and Sculpture. The building is always open to the public. South Solon Rd and Meetinghouse Rd; Solon, ME 04979; http://www.southsolonmeetinghouse.org

Waterville, ME

Colby College Museum of Art displays American art as well as a large collection of works by Alex Katz, and the Bernat Collection of Oriental Ceramics. Admission, gallery talks, lectures, and receptions are open to the public, free of charge. Open Tuesday through Saturday from 10 AM to 4 PM and Sunday from Noon to 4 PM. Closed major holidays. 5600 Mayflower Hill; Waterville, ME 04901; Phone: (207) 859-5600; http://www.colby.edu/museum

Wells, ME

Rachel Carson National Wildlife Refuge offers a one-mile loop meandering through pine woods with views of tidal salt marshes. The trail is open every day from dawn to dusk. The best time to view wildlife is at dawn and dusk. There are no entrance fees. Donations are accepted. Guides to refuge reptiles, amphibians, and mammals, and a bird list are available at headquarters which is open Monday through Friday from 8 AM to 4:30 PM. 321 Port Rd; Wells, ME 04090; Phone: (207) 646-9226; https://www.fws.gov/refuge/rachel_carson

Maryland

Annapolis, MD

Annapolis Maritime Museum preserves and displays the maritime heritage of Annapolis and the Chesapeake Bay. Admission is free with donations accepted. The museum offers both free and fee-based guided tours. Open Tuesday through Sunday from 11 AM to 3 PM. Closed major holidays. 723 Second St; Annapolis, MD 21403; Phone: (410) 295-0104; https://amaritime.org

Annapolis Junction, MD
Fort George G. Meade, MD

National Cryptologic Museum highlights the cryptologic profession and their machines, devices and the techniques. Admission is free. Open Monday through Friday from 9 AM to 4 PM. Open the first and third Saturday of the month from 10 AM to 2 PM. Closed federal holidays. 8290 Colony Seven Rd; Annapolis Junction, MD 20701; Phone: (301) 688-5849; https://www.nsa.gov/about/cryptologic-heritage/museum

Banneker-Douglass Museum was named for the Black scientist Benjamin Banneker and Black social crusader Frederick Douglass. The museum illuminates their lives as well as Black history in Maryland from 1633 to the present. The museum is free to visit. Open Tuesday through Saturday from 10 AM to 4 PM. 84 Franklin St; Annapolis, MD 21401; Phone: (410) 216-6180; http://bdmuseum.maryland.gov

Maryland State House was the site of George Washington's resignation as commander-in-chief of the Continental Army, and the ratification of the Treaty of Paris. The State House is open daily from 9 AM to 5 PM, except Christmas and New Year's Day. Self-guided tour information is available in the Office of Interpretation on the first floor. Note: Picture IDs are required for entrance and metal detectors are in operation. 100 State Cir; Annapolis, MD 21401; Phone: (410) 260-6445; http://msa.maryland.gov/msa/mdstatehouse/html/visitor.html

Mitchell Gallery at St. John's College hosts a diverse array of exhibitions and programs. All exhibitions and most programs are free. Open Tuesday through Sunday from Noon to 5 PM. Docent tours are held on Thursday from Noon to 3 PM. Mellon Hall; 60 College Ave; Annapolis, MD 21401; Phone: (410) 626-2556; https://www.sjc.edu/annapolis/mitchell-gallery

U.S. Naval Academy Museum welcomes visitors to two floors of exhibits on the history of sea power, the development of the U.S. Navy, and the role of the U.S. Naval Academy. Admission is free. Monday through Saturday open from 9 AM to

5 PM and Sunday from 11 AM to 5 PM. Closed Thanksgiving, Christmas, and New Year's Day. Note: All visitors 21 years of age or older must show a valid picture ID at the gate. See the list of acceptable forms of ID on their website. The museum advises checking the website for current security restrictions before planning a visit. King George St; Annapolis, MD 21402; Phone: (410) 293-2108; https://www.usna.edu/Museum

Baltimore, MD (See also Ellicott City, MD)

Baltimore Museum of Art is known for its 19th century, modern, and contemporary art, particularly works by Henri Matisse. General admission is free although some special exhibits will incur a cost. The museum is open Wednesday through Sunday from 10 AM to 5 PM. The sculpture garden is open Wednesday through Sunday 10 AM to dusk except during inclement weather. 10 Art Museum Dr; Baltimore, MD 21218; Phone: (443) 573-1700; https://artbma.org

Burying Grounds at Westminster Hall is the final resting place of Edgar Allan Poe, General Sam Smith, and General James McHenry. It is open free to the public from 8 AM to dusk. Plaques explain the history of the grounds and tell the biographies of the people buried there. Note: The Catacombs and Westminster Hall itself are only available with a fee-based tour. 500 W Baltimore St; Baltimore, MD 21201; Phone: (410) 706-7214; http://www.westminsterhall.org

Camden Yards Outdoor Sculptures celebrates six of the greatest Baltimore Orioles. Larger-than-life bronze sculptures of Frank Robinson, Earl Weaver, Jim Palmer, Eddie Murray, Cal Ripken, and Brooks Robinson are installed in the public park area outside the entrance to Camden Yards on Eutaw Street. Note: Eutaw Street is located between the Warehouse and the ballpark. Eutaw Street is open daily for visitors free of charge on nongame days. 333 W Camden St; Baltimore, MD 21201; Phone: (888) 848-BIRD (2473); https://baltimore.org/photo-tour/camden-yards-and-baltimore-orioles

Cylburn Arboretum is home to hundreds of specimen trees and plantings, gardens, wooded trails, and historic mansion. Cylburn Arboretum is free and open to the public all year but is closed Mondays and holidays. 4915 Greenspring Ave; Baltimore, MD 21209; Phone: (410) 367-2217; http://cylburn.org

Irish Railroad Workers Museum honors the immigrants escaping Ireland's famine of 1845-1853. The site consists of five alley houses where the immigrants who worked for the adjoining B&O Railroad lived. Two of the houses have become the museum. All public tours and museum visits are free. Open Friday from 11 AM to 3 PM and Saturday from 11 AM to 4 PM. They offer free Irish-inspired programs every second Saturday of the month. Note: The nearby B&O

Railroad Museum charges a fee. 918 and 920 Lemmon St; Baltimore, MD 21223; Phone: (410) 347-4747; http://www.irishshrine.org/index.html

Johns Hopkins Archaeological Museum has placed 700 archaeological objects from ancient Greece, Rome, Egypt, the Near East, and the ancient Americas in the custom-built museum facility within the Gilman atrium. The museum is currently free to visit. Guided tours will incur a cost. Fall and spring semesters, the museum is open Monday through Friday from 10:30 AM to 1:30 PM, however, visitors to Gilman Hall can walk the perimeter of the museum even when it is closed and see over 400 objects in their exterior facing cases. 150 Gilman Hall; 3400 N. Charles St; Baltimore, MD 21218; Phone: (410) 516-0383; http://archaeologicalmuseum.jhu.edu/learn/for-the-public

Living History Museum honors the critical role of nurses and chronicles the history of the profession. Admission is free. The museum is located on the second floor of the University of Maryland School of Nursing. Open Tuesday and Wednesday from 10 AM to 2 PM. Hours change during semester breaks and school holidays. 655 W Lombard St; Baltimore, MD 21201; Phone: (410) 706-0674; http://www.nursing.umaryland.edu/museum

Walters Art Museum invites visitors to enjoy a diversity of art from 19th century images of French gardens to Ethiopian icons, richly illuminated Qur'ans and Gospel books, and ancient Roman sarcophagi. Admission and walk-in tours are free. Open Wednesday through Sunday from 10 AM to 5 PM and on Thursday until 9 PM. Watch conservators at work every Friday, Saturday, and Sunday 12:30 PM to 4 PM. Closed major holidays. 600 N Charles St; Baltimore, MD 21201; Phone: (410) 547-9000; https://thewalters.org

Boonsboro, MD
Washington County Rural Heritage Museum includes several metal buildings, an outdoor homestead, and a village of authentic period buildings from the 1800s. Exhibits show early rural life, large pieces of farm equipment and farm implements, and pre-1940 modes of transportation. There is no admission charge, but donations are accepted. Open Saturday and Sunday from 1 PM to 4 PM. Closed on all holidays. Note: They recommend calling ahead or checking the website for any schedule updates prior to your visit. 7313 Sharpsburg Pike; Boonsboro, MD 21713; Phone: (240) 420-1714; http://www.ruralheritagemuseum.org/index.shtm

Bowie, MD
National Capital Radio and Television Museum has an extensive collection of old radio and TV literature, radio and television artifacts and working displays. Learn about Morse code, sound effects in old radio programs, and then hear some

of those programs. See the television showcased in the 1939 World's Fair. Admission is free but they welcome donations. Open Friday from 9 AM to 4 PM. Open Saturday and Sunday from Noon to 4 PM, and by appointment. 2608 Mitchellville Rd; Bowie, MD 20716; Phone: (301) 390-1020; http://ncrtv.org

Northampton Slave Quarters and Archaeological Park uses interpretive signs to describe the history and archaeology of the slave quarters. Admission is free. Open daily from sunrise to sunset. 10915 Water Port Ct; Bowie, MD 20721; Phone: (301) 627-1286; http://www.mncppc.org/3009/Northampton-Plantation-Slave-Quarters

Catonsville, MD
Benjamin Banneker Historical Park and Museum is dedicated to the life and times of Benjamin Banneker, often considered the first Black American man of science. The museum's exhibits chronicle his contributions as a largely self-taught mathematician, astronomer, and naturalist during the late 1700s. Admission is free. The grounds are open sunrise to sunset. The museum is open Tuesday through Saturday from 10 AM to 4 PM. May through October it is also open on Sunday from Noon to 4 PM. 300 Oella Ave; Catonsville, MD 21228; Phone: (410) 887-1081; https://visitoldellicottcity.com/item/benjamin-banneker-historical-park-and-museum

Chevy Chase, MD
Woodend Sanctuary is the headquarters of the Audubon Naturalist Society. The grounds are dotted with a wildflower meadow, meandering trails, a native plant garden, and an aquatic life pond. Admission is free. Trails are open daily dawn to dusk. 8940 Jones Mill Rd; Chevy Chase, MD 20815; Phone (301) 652-9188; https://anshome.org/visit

Church Creek, MD
Harriet Tubman Underground Railroad State Park and Visitor Center presents exhibits as well as the stories of Harriet Tubman's life and work. The grounds include a meditation garden, and nature trails. Admission is free. Open daily from 9 AM to 5 PM. Closed major holidays. 4068 Golden Hill Rd; Church Creek, MD 21622; Phone: (410) 221-2290; http://visitdorchester.org/harriet-tubman-ugrr-visitor-center

College Park MD
University of Maryland Art Gallery has gathered prints, drawings, paintings, sculptures, and photographs. Admission is free. Open Monday through Friday from 11 AM to 4 PM. Closed on all University of Maryland observed holidays. 2202 Parren J. Mitchell Art-Sociology Building; 3834 Campus Dr; College Park, MD 20742; Phone: (301) 405-2763; https://www.artgallery.umd.edu

Cumberland, MD

Allegany Museum collects artifacts, maps, photographs, motion picture film, video and audio oral histories from the greater Cumberland, Maryland area. Admission is free. Open mid-March through December on Tuesday through Saturday from 10 AM to 4 PM and on Sunday from 1 PM to 4 PM. 3 Pershing St; Cumberland, MD 21502; Phone: (301) 777-7200; https://alleganymuseum.org

C&O Canal National Historical Park and Visitors Museum focuses on the history of the C&O Canal and Cumberland. Explore a life size section of a canal boat. View exhibits on the canal's construction, cargo, mules, locks, and crew. Admission is free. From April through December, open daily 9 AM to 5 PM. In March open daily from 10 AM to 4 PM. Closed major holidays. 13 Canal St; Cumberland, MD 21502; Phone: (301) 722-8226; https://www.nps.gov/choh/planyourvisit/cumberlandvisitorcenter.htm

Ellicott City, MD (See also Baltimore, MD)

Part of the Baltimore metropolitan area, the town offers several historic buildings open to the public for free. The hours are limited and seasonal. Phone: (410) 313-0421; https://www.howardcountymd.gov/historicsites

Baltimore & Ohio Ellicott City Station Museum highlights the oldest surviving railroad station in America and the original terminus of the first 13 miles of commercial railroad in the country. The site features the main depot building, the freight house, a replica of the first horse-drawn passenger rail car, and a 1927 Caboose. Admission is free. Open Wednesday and Thursday from 10 AM to 3 PM, and Friday through Sunday from 10 AM to 5 PM. 3711 Maryland Ave; Ellicott City, MD 21043; Phone: (410) 313-1945; https://www.howardcountymd.gov/Baltimore-Ohio-Station-at-Ellicott-City

Ellicott City Colored School fulfilled an 1879 Maryland State law requiring that counties provide educational facilities for Black children. Today, the museum is focused on the history of Black Americans in Howard County. Admission is free. Tours are available May through December on Saturday and Sunday from 1 PM to 4 PM. 8683 Frederick Rd; Ellicott City, MD 21043; Phone: (410) 313-0421; https://www.howardcountymd.gov/HistoricSites

Firehouse Museum honors fire-fighting in the late 19th and early 20th centuries. The original building was designed to house the hand-drawn and horse-drawn fire equipment. Visitors can see fire apparatus, model toys, and a visual history of Howard County's Volunteer Fire Department. Admission is free. Tours are available May through December on Saturday and Sunday from 1 PM to 4 PM. 3829 Main St; Ellicott City, MD 21043; Phone: (410) 313-0421; https://www.howardcountymd.gov/HistoricSites

Patapsco Female Institute Historic Park was created in 1837 as an elegant finishing school for young women but with a unique twist – math and science were included in the curriculum. Admission is free. Tours are currently provided spring through fall on Saturdays and Sundays from 1 PM to 4 PM. 3655 Church Rd; Ellicott City, MD 21043; Phone: (410) 313-0421; https://www.howardcountymd.gov/patapscofemaleinstitute

Emmitsburg, MD
National Shrine of Saint Elizabeth Ann Seton honors the first American-born saint. The museum displays illustrations, anecdotes, and 19th century artifacts including her hand-written letters. Visitors can view a 12-minute film about her life. Pick up a map at the visitor center for a self-guided tour. Admission and self-guided tours are free. The Basilica and museum are open Monday through Saturday 10 AM to 4:30 PM and Sunday from Noon to 4:30 PM. The grounds and cemetery are open all year from dawn to dusk. Note: Guided tours of her home will incur a cost. 339 S Seton Ave; Emmitsburg, MD 21727; Phone: (301) 447-6606; https://setonshrine.org

Frederick, MD
Mount Olivet Cemetery/Francis Scott Key Monument welcomes visitors to explore interpretive exhibits, and take a self-guided tour of the notable individuals interred there. The most famous is Francis Scott Key, the man who wrote *The Star-Spangled Banner*. Pick up the brochure/map guide in advance from the information kiosk adjacent the Francis Scott Key Monument, or the mausoleum office lobby. 515 S Market St; Frederick, MD 21701; Phone: (301) 662-1164; http://www.mountolivetcemeteryinc.com/tourism--tours.html

Frostburg, MD
Frostburg Museum displays local history, including exhibits on the National Road, mining, family living, and technology. Admission is free with donations accepted. Open Tuesday through Saturday from Noon to 5 PM. 69 Hill St; Frostburg, MD 21532; Phone: (301) 689-1195; http://www.frostmuseum.org

Greenbelt, MD
Goddard Visitor Center demonstrates Goddard's innovative work in earth science, astrophysics, heliophysics, planetary science, engineering, communications and technology development. Free to visit. From September through June open Tuesday through Friday from 10 AM to 3 PM. Open Saturday and Sunday from Noon to 4 PM. July and August open one hour later during the week to 4 PM. No change in weekend hours. ICESat Rd; Greenbelt, MD 20771; Phone: (301) 286-3978; https://www.nasa.gov/centers/goddard/visitor/home/index.html

Hagerstown, MD

Washington County Museum of Fine Arts highlights American, 19th century European, and International art plus curated exhibitions from their permanent collection and special-themed displays. Free admission. Open Tuesday through Friday from 10 AM to 5 PM. Open Saturday from 10 AM to 4 PM and on Sunday from 1PM to 5 PM. Closed all major holidays. 401 Museum Dr; Hagerstown, MD 21740; Phone: (301) 739-5727; http://wcmfa.org

Laurel, MD

Dinosaur Park illuminates Maryland prehistory with this fossil site of 115 million-year-old remains of dinosaurs and other prehistoric animals. The fenced-in fossil area is only accessible during open houses and special events, but the interpretive garden is open daily from dawn to dusk. Admission is free. Open houses are held on the first and third Saturday of every month from Noon to 4 PM. Programs are free. 13100 Mid-Atlantic Blvd; Laurel, MD 20708; Phone: (301) 627-1286; http://www.mncppc.org/3259/Dinosaur-Park

Nanjemoy, MD

Ghost Fleet of Mallows Bay Park has been declared a national marine sanctuary to protect the collection of historic shipwrecks dating back to the Civil War as well as archaeological artifacts nearly 12,000 years old. It is considered the "largest assemblages of shipwrecks in the Western Hemisphere." Several can be seen stranded in the shallow water. Admission is free. Open daily 5:30 AM to dusk. Note: There is a free boat launch, and you can bring your own kayak to get a better view. 1440 Wilson Landing Rd; Nanjemoy, MD 20662; Phone: (301) 932-3470; https://www.charlescountyparks.com/parks/mallows-bay-park

Port Tobacco, MD

Port Tobacco Historic Village was once Maryland's second largest seaport. Explore the reconstructed courthouse and other historic buildings. Admission is free. From April through December open Wednesday through Sunday from 10 AM to 4 PM. From January through March open Thursday through Sunday from 10 AM to 4 PM. 8450 Commerce St; Port Tobacco, MD 20677; Phone: (301) 392-3418; https://www.charlescountymd.gov/locations/port-tobacco-courthouse

Potomac, MD

Glenstone is a private contemporary museum media melding art, architecture, and landscape. Outdoor sculptures are installed in a variety of settings. The Pavilions features changing exhibitions, and rooms dedicated to single artists. The Gallery is the original museum building and hosts changing exhibitions. Admission is always free. Open Thursday to Sunday from 10 AM to 5 PM. Visits should be scheduled in advance. 12100 Glen Rd; Potomac, MD 20854; Phone: (301) 983-5001; https://www.glenstone.org/visit/plan-your-visit

Prince Frederick, MD

Battle Creek Cypress Swamp is the northernmost bald cypress swamp in North America. Take a walk on the quarter-mile boardwalk trail along the Patuxent River. Exhibits offer an interactive look at local wildlife, and cultural history of the area. Admission is free. From Memorial Day through Labor Day open Monday through Friday from 9 AM to 4:30 PM, Saturday from 10 AM to 6 PM, and Sunday from 1 PM to 6 PM. Earlier closing on Saturday and Sunday the rest of the year. Grays Rd; Prince Frederick, MD 20378; Phone: (410) 535-5327; https://calvertparks.org/bccss.html

Rockville, MD

Glenview Mansion sits amid 28 acres and offers a six-room art gallery with rotating exhibitions by local, national, and international artists. Glenview Mansion is free and open to the public Monday through Friday from 8:30 AM to 4:30 PM. 603 Edmonston Dr; Rockville, MD 20851; Phone: (240) 314-8660; https://www.rockvillemd.gov/389/Glenview-Mansion

Meadowside Nature Center and its trails covers almost 500 acres. The grounds are open sunrise to sunset. The indoor and outdoor exhibits including raptors that cannot be released into the wild. The birds are located in enclosure behind the nature center. The nature center is open Tuesday through Saturday from 9 AM to 5 PM. A special talk is held on Saturday at 11:30 AM and Noon. There are no fees for the park. 5100 Meadowside La; Rockville, MD 20855; Phone: (301) 258-4030; https://www.montgomeryparks.org/parks-and-trails/rock-creek-regional-park/meadowside-nature-center

Salisbury, MD

Salisbury Zoo is home to a variety of birds and animals. Admission is always free with donations accepted. Open daily from 9 AM to 4:30 PM. Closed Thanksgiving, and Christmas Day. 755 S Park Dr; Salisbury, MD 21804; Phone: (410) 548-3188; https://salisburyzoo.org

Shady Side, MD

Captain Avery Museum explains the life and livelihood of a Chesapeake Bay waterman in the late 19th century. Admission is free. Open daily dawn to dusk. 1418 E W Shady Side Rd; Shady Side, MD 20764; Phone: (410) 867-4486; https://captainaverymuseum.org

Silver Springs, MD

National Museum of Health and Medicine, established during the Civil War, is now a center for the collection of archival materials, anatomical and pathological specimens, medical instruments and artifacts. Admission is free. Open daily from 10 AM to 5:30 PM. Closed Christmas. 2500 Linden La; Silver Spring, MD 20910; Phone: (301) 319-3300; http://www.medicalmuseum.mil/index.cfm

Upper Marlboro, MD
Columbia Air Center describes the history and events at the site of this early airport that was likely the first licensed Black-owned and operated airfield in America. No charge to visit. Open daily 8 AM to dusk. 16000 Croom Airport Rd; Upper Marlboro, MD 20772; Phone: (301) 627-6074; http://www.pgplanning.org/2002/Columbia-Air-Center

Mount Calvert Historical and Archaeological Park has gathered over 8,000 years of history and culture including an early colonial town, and an 18th and 19th century tobacco plantation. The museum provides *A Confluence of Three Cultures* displaying archeological finds. Admission is free. The site itself is open daily dawn until dusk. The house and museum exhibit are open April through October on Saturday from 10 AM to 4 PM and on Sunday from Noon to 4 PM. The excavations are open on most Saturdays from April through October. 16801 Mount Calvert Rd; Upper Marlboro, MD 20772; Phone: (301) 627-1286; http://www.pgparks.com/3007/Mount-Calvert-Historical-and-Archaeologi

Wheaton, MD
Brookside Gardens, within Wheaton Regional Park, includes their Aquatic Garden, the Woodland Walk, plus formal gardens. Admission is free. Open daily sunrise to sunset. The Conservatories are open 10 AM to 5 PM. 1800 Glenallan Ave; Wheaton, MD 20902; Phone: (301) 962-1400; https://www.montgomeryparks.org/parks-and-trails/brookside-gardens

Woodbine, MD
Days End Farm Horse Rescue provides daily farm tours with the opportunity to meet some of the horses and learn their stories. The free tours are offered from 9 AM to 4 PM. Donations are always appreciated. 1372 Woodbine Rd; Woodbine, MD 21797; Phone: (301) 854-5037; https://www.defhr.org/visit

Massachusetts

Amherst, MA

Beneski Museum of Natural History displays more than 1,700 specimens from dinosaur skeletons to minerals. Free admission. Open Tuesday through Friday from 11 AM to 4 PM, and on Saturday and Sunday from 10 AM to 5 PM. 11 Barrett Hill Dr; Amherst, MA 01002; Phone: (413) 542-2165; https://www.amherst.edu/museums/naturalhistory/visit

Mead Art Museum houses the Amherst College art collection, a diverse selection of ancient and modern paintings, sculptures, ceramics, furniture, textiles, and glassware. There are Russian modernist paintings, and West African art. Admission is free. Opens at 9 AM Tuesday through Sunday. Closing hours vary with the academic calendar. 41 Quadrangle Dr; Amherst, MA 01002; Phone: (413) 542-2335; https://www.amherst.edu/museums/mead/visit

University Museum of Contemporary Art specializes in works on paper – contemporary photographs, drawings, and prints. Admission is free. Open Tuesday through Friday from 11 AM to 4:30 PM, and on Saturday and Sunday from 2 PM to 5 PM. Closed on all academic breaks and state holidays. UMass Fine Arts Center; 151 Presidents Dr; Amherst, MA 01003; Phone: (413) 545-3672; https://fac.umass.edu/UMCA/Online

Andover, MA

Addison Gallery of American Art hosts a collection of American painting and photography, and presents several exhibitions a year. Admission to the museum and events is free. Open Tuesday through Saturday from 10 AM to 5 PM, with extended hours on Wednesday while classes are in session. Open Sunday from 1 PM to 5 PM. Closed national holidays and the month of August. Phillips Academy; 180 Main St; Andover, MA 01810; Phone: (978) 749-4015; https://addison.andover.edu

Boston, MA

Arnold Arboretum of Harvard University was designed by Frederick Law Olmsted, who also designed New York City's Central Park. Admission is free, as are the tours. Donations are appreciated. Open daily sunrise to sunset. The visitor center is open daily 10 AM to 5 PM. Closed Wednesdays and holidays. 125 Arborway; Boston, MA 02130; Phone: (617) 524-1718; https://www.arboretum.harvard.edu/visit

Boston Library offers free public daily tours highlighting both its art and architecture. Tours begin in the McKim Building vestibule, through the library's

Dartmouth Street entrance. One tour is offered daily but the schedule frequently changes. No tours are given on major holidays. 700 Boylston St; Boston MA 02116; Phone: (617) 536-5400; http://www.bpl.org/central/tours.htm

Coit Observatory hosts a Wednesday open night, weather permitting, to acquaint visitors with the night sky through telescopes and binoculars. Tickets are free but reservations are required. Note: Held outside and visitors are advised to dress warmly in winter. This is a program of the Astronomy Department of Boston University. 725 Commonwealth Ave; Boston, MA 02215; Phone: (617) 353-2625; https://www.bu.edu/astronomy/events/public-open-night-at-the-observatory

Commonwealth Museum traces the history of Massachusetts through the colonial, revolutionary, federal, and 19th century reform periods. *Tracing our Roots* tells the story of four Massachusetts families representing Native American, English, African-American, and Irish heritage. Admission is free. Open Monday through Friday from 9 AM to 5 PM. From Memorial Day through Labor Day, it is also open on weekends from 9 AM to 3 PM. Closed major holidays. State Archives Building; 220 Morrissey Blvd; Boston, MA 02125; Phone: (617) 727-9268; http://www.sec.state.ma.us/mus/index.html

Massachusetts State House is a repository of the state's history and features a dome coppered by Paul Revere in 1802. Self-tours and guided tours are available. The tours are given weekdays from 10 AM to 3:30 PM and are free of charge. The building is open from 8:45 AM to 5 PM. The Massachusetts State House is closed on weekends and holidays. Advance reservations are requested for conducted tours. 24 Beacon St; Boston, MA 02133; Phone: (617) 727-3676; https://www.sec.state.ma.us/trs/trsgen/genidx.htm

New England Holocaust Memorial consists of six towers which are internally lit to glow nightly. The number six recalls the millions of Jews killed in the Holocaust. Six also represents the number of main death camps; and the six years from 1939-1945 when the infamous *Final Solution* took place. This outdoor space is open and accessible to the public at all times. Carmen Park; 98 Union St; Boston, MA 02129; Phone: (617) 457-8755; http://www.nehm.org/visit/self-guided-tour

Brookline, MA
John Fitzgerald Kennedy National Historic Site invites visitors to tour the house where JFK was born. From mid-May through October, the site is open Wednesday through Sunday from 9:30 AM to 5 PM. Guided tours are offered on the hour and half hour starting at 10 AM. The last tour departs at 3:30 PM. Tours are free and offered first come, first served basis. 83 Beals St; Brookline, MA 02446; Phone: (617) 566-7937; https://www.nps.gov/jofi/index.htm

Cambridge, MA

The free attractions of Cambridge include several museums that are part of Harvard, but not all the Harvand museums are free. The ones included below charge no admission. For a listing of all museums visit: https://www.harvard.edu/on-campus/museums

Arnold Arboretum includes 281 acres and hosts garden-themed art shows. Stroll on your own or download a guide: https://www.arboretum.harvard.edu/visit/self-guided-tours. There is no admission charge, but donations are appreciated. Open sunrise to sunset. 125 Arborway; Boston, MA 02130; Phone: (617) 524-1718; https://www.arboretum.harvard.edu

Carpenter Center for the Visual Arts mounts curated exhibits in only building in North America designed by Swiss-born architect Le Corbusier. Admission is free. Open Tuesday through Sunday from Noon to 5 PM. Note: There is a charge for tickets to their films. 24 Quincy St; Cambridge, MA 02138; Phone: (617) 496-5387; https://carpenter.center

Collection of Historical Scientific Instruments focuses on scientific instruments made obsolete by new technologies. Spanning the fields of astronomy, navigation, horology, surveying, geology, calculating, physics, biology, medicine, psychology, electricity, and communication, visitors can trace how science has changed and grown. Admission is free. Open Sunday through Friday from 11 AM to 4 PM. Galleries may be closed for installations and some major holidays. 1 Oxford St; Cambridge, MA 02138; Phone: (617) 495-2779; https://chsi.harvard.edu

Ethelbert Cooper Gallery of African and African American Art features contemporary and historical installations. Admission is free. Open Tuesday through Saturday from 10 AM to 5 PM. Call or check the website to verify gallery opening. Located adjacent the Hutchins Center. 104 Mount Auburn St; Cambridge, MA 02138; Phone: (617) 496-5777; https://www.coopergalleryhc.org

Harvard Semitic Museum concentrates on Near Eastern artifacts, mostly from museum-sponsored excavations in Egypt, Iraq, Israel, Jordan, Syria, and Tunisia. Admission is free. Open Monday through Friday from 11 AM to 4 PM. Open Sunday from 11 AM to 4 PM. 6 Divinity Ave; Cambridge, MA 02138; Phone: (617) 495-4631; https://semiticmuseum.fas.harvard.edu

Harvard University Tours are student-led and provide a history of the university, general information, and a personal view on the student's individual experience. This outdoor walk may be cancelled in bad weather. The tour leaves from the Harvard Information Center in the Smith Campus. The tour is free. Registration begins one hour prior to departure time. Tours are generally offered Monday through Saturday from 9 AM to 5 PM. The online calendar provides day-by-day information. Smith Campus Center; 30 Dunster St; Cambridge, MA 02138; Phone: (617) 495-1573; https://www.harvard.edu/on-campus/visit-harvard

Longfellow House Washington's Headquarters National Historic Site preserves the home of the famous poet, Henry Wadsworth Longfellow. The house also served as headquarters for General George Washington during the Siege of Boston, July 1775. There is no fee to visit the gardens and grounds. Open every day dawn to dusk. Free tours of the house are offered seasonally starting in May. Note: Park staff recommends the use of public transportation as parking is extremely limited. 105 Brattle St; Cambridge, MA 02138; Phone: (617) 876-4491; https://www.nps.gov/long/index.htm

Charlestown, MA
National Historical Park Massachusetts contains several historically important sites. There are no fees at the federally or municipally owned sites however, privately owned partner sites charge a fee. **Bunker Hill** holds a special place in American history. On June 17, 1775, New England soldiers faced the British army for the first time in a battle that came to be called *The Battle of Bunker Hill*. Technically a British win, Colonial forces came together to fight hard against the British. The park's main exhibits are at the **Bunker Hill Museum** in the old Charlestown Branch building of the Boston Public Library. The **Bunker Hill Monument, Lodge, and Museum** are National Park Service sites with free admission. 43 Monument Sq; Charlestown, MA 02129; Phone: (617) 242-7275; https://www.nps.gov/bost/planyourvisit/bhm.htm

USS Constitution is also part of Boston National Historical Park located at the Charlestown Navy Yard. Open free of charge. Note: Everyone age 18 or older must present a valid federal of state-issued photo ID or a passport to board the ship. Currently open Wednesday through Sunday from 10 AM to 4 PM. Note: Although the ship is free to explore, a visit to the USS Constitution Museum requires a donation. 1 Constitution Rd; Charlestown, MA 02129; Phone: (617) 799-8198; https://www.navy.mil/local/constitution/visitor%20information.asp

Concord, MA
Minute Man National Historical Park encompasses the towns of Concord, Lincoln, and Lexington. Start at Minute Man Visitor Center and watch *The Road To Revolution*, a multimedia theater program that depicts Paul Revere's ride and the battles at Lexington Green, North Bridge, and along the Battle Road. Exhibits include a forty-foot mural that portrays the fighting between Colonists and British Regulars. There is no fee to visit. Free ranger-led programs are available. The visitor center is open daily from April through October from 9 AM to 5 PM. The grounds are open daily sunrise to sunset. 174 Liberty St; Concord, MA 01742; Phone: (978) 369-6993; https://www.nps.gov/mima/index.htm

Great Meadows National Wildlife Refuge offers a wildlife observation tower, platform, and direct access to the Concord River. Interpretive information and general information is posted on kiosks throughout the refuge. No admission fee. Open from sunrise to sunset. 179 Monsen Rd; Concord, MA 01742; Phone: (978) 443-4661; https://www.fws.gov/refuge/Great_Meadows/visit/plan_your_visit.html

Dalton, MA
Crane Museum of Papermaking invites visitors to explore the history of the oldest paper company in America. Exhibits focus on 200 years of papermaking and particularly on Crane papers that were made for currency, bonds, stock certificates, and stationery. Admission is free and they welcome children. Open Tuesday through Thursday from 1 PM to 5 PM, expanding in the summer to Monday through Friday from 1 PM to 5 PM. W Housatonic St; Dalton MA 01226; Phone: (413) 684-6380; http://www.crane.com/about-us/crane-museum-of-papermaking

Eastham, MA
Nauset Light – Cape Cod National Seashore offers free tours of one of the most photographed lighthouse on Cape Cod. Located within the Cape Cod National Coast, the tours are open-house style and include the opportunity to climb Nauset Light, visit the lookout room, and learn about its history. Admission is free but donations are welcomed. Lighthouse grounds are open daily. Upcoming tours are listed on the website. Visitors should park at Nauset Light Beach parking lot, across the street. Note: The keeper's house is privately owned. 120 Nauset Light Beach Rd; Eastham, MA 02642; Phone: (508) 240-2612; https://www.nausetlight.org/visit

Hyannis, MA
Cape Cod Potato Chips invites visitors to learn how their chips are made with free self-guided tours. Open Monday through Friday from 9 AM to 5 PM. Closed holidays. 100 Breeds Hill Rd; Hyannis, MA 02601; Phone: (888) 881-2447; https://www.capecodchips.com/about/factory-tour

Mashpee, MA
Lowell Holly offers walking trails among holly and rhododendron gardens as well as views of the large, freshwater Mashpee Pond and Wakeby Pond. Open daily, sunrise to sunset. South Sandwich Rd; Mashpee, MA 02563; Phone: (508) 636-4693; http://www.thetrustees.org/places-to-visit/cape-cod-islands/lowell-holly.html

Northampton, MA

Calvin Coolidge Presidential Library and Museum has papers, photographs, artifacts, and memorabilia associated with the political and personal life of Calvin Coolidge (1872-1933), the 30th President of the United States. Open Monday 9 AM to 5 PM, Tuesday from 1 PM to 5 PM, Wednesday from 4 PM to 9 PM, and Thursday from 1 PM to 5 PM. Forbes Library; 20 West St; Northampton, MA 01060; Phone: (413) 587-1011; https://forbeslibrary.org/calvin-coolidge-presidential-library-and-museum

Pittsfield, MA

Herman Melville Memorial Room at the Berkshire Athenaeum features books, pictures, letters, and memorabilia relating to Herman Melville while he was living in Pittsfield. Open Monday through Thursday from 9 AM to 9 PM. Open Friday 9 AM to 5 PM, and Saturday from 10 AM to 5 PM. Closes earlier weekdays in July and August. Closed holidays. Note: Melville's actual house, Arrowhead, is open only for fee-based guided tours. 1 Wendell Ave; Pittsfield, MA 01201; Phone: (413) 499-9486; http://www.pittsfieldlibrary.org/melville_room.html

Plymouth, MA

1749 Court House and Museum was built in 1749 and highlights Plymouth's history. It is the oldest wooden court house in America. Admission is free. Open daily June through early October. 1 Town Sq; Plymouth, MA 02360; Phone: (508) 830-4075; https://www.seeplymouth.com/things-to-do/1749-court-house-and-museum

Plymouth Rock at Pilgrim Memorial State Park is traditionally considered to be the place where the passengers of the Mayflower landed in the New World. From April through November interpreters share its history, answer visitors' questions, and provide guided walking tours. A replica of the Mayflower is normally moored at the park. No fee to experience this piece of history. Open sunrise to sunset. 79 Water St; Plymouth, MA 02360; Phone: (508) 747-5360; https://www.mass.gov/locations/pilgrim-memorial-state-park

North Adams, MA

North Adams Museum of History and Science invites the whole family to see over 25 permanent exhibits on three floors depicting life in North Adams and Massachusetts. There's also a model of the solar system, a train set, and a full size model of the Fort Massachusetts Barracks Room. Admission is free. From May through October open Thursday through Saturday from 10 AM to 4 PM and Sunday from 1 PM to 4 PM. November through April open Saturday from 10

AM to 4 PM and Sunday from 1 PM to 4 PM. Western Gateway Heritage State Park; Building 5A; State St; North Adams, MA 01247; Phone: (413) 664-4700; http://www.northadamshistory.org

Orleans, MA
French Cable Station Museum highlights the original Atlantic undersea telegraphic cables, instruments, maps, and assorted memorabilia. During World War I, General Pershing in France communicated with the U.S. government through this cable station. Museum is free with free guided tours available. Open June through September on Friday, Saturday, and Sunday from 1 PM to 4 PM. Last tour at 3:30 PM. Cove Rd and Rt 28; Orleans, MA 02653; Phone: (508) 240-1735; http://www.frenchcablestationmuseum.org

Quincy, MA
Quincy Homestead was the home for five generations of the Quincy family who had significant roles in early American history. Free tours are offered two Saturdays a month in June, July, and August. A donation is greatly appreciated. 34 Butler Rd; Quincy, MA 02169; Phone: (617) 742-3190; http://nscdama.org/quincy-homestead

Salem, MA
Salem Maritime National Historic Site encompasses several locations. Most park facilities, tours, and programs are free. The exception is the film *Salem Witch Hunt* shown at the visitor center which will incur a fee. Stop at the visitor center to register for the free tours of the Custom House and Narbonne House. 2 New Liberty St; Salem, MA 01970; Phone: (978) 740-1650. **Custom House** focuses on the tools of the Custom Service, the work of the Customs inspectors, and the office of famous American author Nathaniel Hawthorne. There's also the **Public Stores,** and the **Narbonne House**. The grounds, trails, docks, and outdoor exhibits are open 24 hours a day. The park's historic buildings, tours, and programs operate on a seasonal schedule. Each attraction has its own hours. 193 Derby St; Salem, MA 01970; Phone: (978) 740-1650; https://www.nps.gov/sama/index.htm

Salem Witch Trials Memorial was designed as a place of respect and reflection reminding visitors of the 20 individuals who were put to death in 1692. Accused of witchcraft, they literally died from the effects of ignorance and intolerance. Free to visit. Open from dawn till dusk. Liberty St (between Charter and Derby); Salem, MA 01970; Phone: (978) 740-1250; https://www.voicesagainstinjustice.org/memorial

Saugus, MA

Saugus Ironworks National Historic Site showcases early iron-working history, including waterwheels, forges, mills, and an historic 17th century home. The grounds are open daily. There is no fee to enter. The visitor center, museum, and buildings are open June through October on Wednesday through Sunday from 10 AM to 5 PM. Site tours are free and offered June through October. Visitors can also take a self-guided tour of the grounds. 244 Central St; Saugus, MA 01906; Phone: (781) 233-0050; https://www.nps.gov/sair/index.htm

Shrewsbury MA

Artemas Ward House Museum depicts over two centuries of everyday life. There is no admission charge. Open mid-April through the end of November on Wednesday through Saturday from 10 AM to 4 PM. Closed Noon to 1 PM. Also open by appointment. Closed major holidays. 786 Main St; Shrewsbury, MA 01545; Phone: (508) 842-8900; https://wardhouse.harvard.edu

South Hadley, MA

Joseph Allen Skinner Museum contains over 7,000 objects from minerals and fossils to tools and farm implements, 19th century souvenirs. Free and open from May through October on Wednesday and Sunday from 2 PM to 5 PM, and by appointment. 50 College St; South Hadley, MA 01075; Phone: (413) 538-2245; https://artmuseum.mtholyoke.edu/collection/joseph-allen-skinner-museum

Mount Holyoke College Art Museum crosses five continents and thousands of years of history. Highlights include ancient Mediterranean art, decorative art, contemporary art, photography, glass, and ceramics. Admission is free. Open Tuesday through Friday from 11 AM to 5 PM. Open Saturday and Sunday from 1 PM to 5 PM. Closed major holidays, and for installations during college breaks. Lower Lake Rd; South Hadley, MA 01075; Phone: (413) 538-2245; https://artmuseum.mtholyoke.edu

Springfield, MA

Springfield Armory National Historic Site was the nation's first armory and it preserves the world's largest historic U.S. military small arms collection, along with historic archives, buildings, and landscapes. From Memorial Day through the end of October the site is open daily from 9 AM to 5 PM. From November until Memorial Day weekend open Wednesday through Sunday from 9 AM to 5 PM. Closed Thanksgiving, Christmas, and New Year's Day. 1 Armory Sq; Springfield, MA 01105; Phone: (413) 734-8551; https://www.nps.gov/spar/index.htm

Waltham, MA

Gore Place is the historic house and estate of Massachusetts Governor Christopher Gore, and includes a small farm with sheep, goats, and poultry. There is no charge to visit the grounds or to take a self-guided tour. Pick up a free map at the carriage house during regular business hours. Open daily from dawn to dusk. Note: There is a fee for tours of the mansion. 52 Gore St; Waltham, MA 02453; Phone: (781) 894-2798; http://www.goreplace.org

Wellesley, MA

Davis Museum at Wellesley College was envisioned as a box of treasures that opens at each landing to reveal art from antiquity to contemporary. Admission is free. Note: There may be a charge for special exhibits. Open Tuesday through Saturday from 11 AM to 5 PM. Open Wednesday until 8 PM. Open Sunday from Noon to 4 PM. 106 Central St; Wellesley, MA 02481; Phone: (781) 283-2051; https://www.wellesley.edu/davismuseum

Wellesley College Botanic Garden is open daily from dawn to dusk. There is no charge to visit. Download a self-guided tour map from their website. 106 Central St; Wellesley, MA 02481; Phone: (781) 283-3094; https://www.wellesley.edu/wcbg/visit

Williamstown, MA

Williams College Museum Of Art emphasizes American, modern, and contemporary art. Admission is free. Open daily from 11 AM to 6 PM. 15 Lawrence Hall Dr; Williamstown, MA 01267; Phone: (413) 597-2429; https://wcma.williams.edu/visit

Woods Hole, MA

ArtsWorcester at the Davis Art Gallery exhibits local contemporary artists. Free to visit but open only during exhibitions on Tuesday through Thursday from Noon to 5 PM, and Friday and Saturday from Noon to 7 PM. Hours are weather-dependent. Printers Building; 44 Portland St (3rd floor); Worcester MA 01608; Phone: (508) 755-5142; http://artsworcester.org

Woods Hole Science Aquarium is the home of 140 species of marine animals found in the Northeast and Middle Atlantic waters. Bring the children to enjoy their Touch Tanks with lobsters, horseshoe crabs, sea stars (starfish), and other marine life. Seal feedings at 11 AM and 4 PM most days. Visitors are even allowed to go behind the scenes and watch staff at work. Free admission with donations are appreciated. Open Tuesday through Saturday from 11 AM to 4 PM. 166 Water St; Woods Hole, MA 02543; Phone: (508) 495-2001; http://aquarium.nefsc.noaa.gov/index.html

Michigan

Adrian, MI
Robinson Planetarium features a 30 foot dome and a Spitz A-3-P star projector. Free programs for all ages are scheduled throughout the year. William and Charles Sts; Adrian, MI 49221; Phone: (517) 264-3944; http://adrian.edu/campus-life/planetarium

Alpena, MI
Great Lakes Maritime Heritage Center and Thunder Bay National Marine Sanctuary preserves nearly 200 historic shipwrecks in and around the bay. The sanctuary is a popular destination for divers, snorkelers and kayakers. The Great Lakes Maritime Heritage Center explores the history and archaeology of these wrecks. Permanent exhibits feature a life-sized recreation of a Great Lakes schooner, and a shipwreck site. Free admission. Summer hours are 9 AM to 5 PM daily. Winter hours are Monday through Saturday from 10 AM to 5 PM and on Sunday from Noon to 5 PM. 500 W Fletcher St; Alpena, MI 49707; Phone: (989) 356-8805; https://thunderbay.noaa.gov/maritime/glmhc.html

Ann Arbor, MI
University of Michigan is a top destination for visitors, providing free museums, art on the campus, and unusual experiences. Note: The University of Michigan Museum of Art is also nominally free but requests a $10 donation. It's not included. **Carillon at Burton Tower** peals out a concert every weekday at Noon, when classes are in session. http://smtd.umich.edu/about/facilities/central_campus/burton/burton.htm The **Ann and Robert H. Lurie Carillon** on the North Campus plays a 30-minute recital at 1:30 PM every weekday when classes are in session. http://smtd.umich.edu/about/facilities/north_campus/lurie/lurie.htm

Detroit Observatory has been restored to its 1854 appearance retaining its original telescopes and mechanical systems. They host open houses on select Sundays where you can tour the building and chat with the docents. The Astronomy Department also hosts public viewing nights, weather permitting. Climbing stairs is required to reach the dome and telescope. 1398 E Ann St; Ann Arbor, MI 48109; Phone: (734) 764-3482; http://bentley.umich.edu/about/detroit-observatory

Kelsey Museum of Archaeology houses over 100,000 artifacts and works of art from ancient Egypt, Rome, Greece, and the Near East. The museum includes the largest collection of Greco-Roman Egyptian artifacts outside of Cairo. Open the drawers under display cabinets for even more items. A highlight of the museum is the large-scale reproduction of the famous Villa of the Mysteries murals from ancient Pompeii. Admission is free, but donations are welcomed. Open Tuesday through Friday from 9 AM to 4 PM. Open Saturday and Sunday from 1 PM to 4 PM. Entrance is on Maynard Street. 434 S State St; Ann Arbor, MI 48109; Phone: (734) 764-9304; http://www.lsa.umich.edu/kelsey

Matthaei Botanical Gardens has 11 outdoor gardens featuring bonsai, native, and medicinal plants. The conservatory is filled with plants from around the world. Admission is free. From Labor Day to mid-May open Monday and Tuesday from 10 AM to 4:30 PM. On Wednesday closes at 8 PM, and Thursday through Sunday closes at 4:30 PM. The rest of the year from mid-May to Labor Day open daily 10 AM to 8 PM. 1800 N. Dixboro Rd; Ann Arbor, MI 48105; Phone: (734) 647-7600; https://mbgna.umich.edu/matthaei-botanical-gardens/gardens

Museum of Natural History displays an extensive dinosaur exhibit plus Michigan wildlife, anthropology, geology, and a digital Planetarium. Visitors can observe actual working laboratories where U-M scientists are conducting research. Admission is free, donations are welcomed. Open daily 9 AM to 5 PM. Note: There is a charge for the Planetarium show. Ruthven Museums Building; 1109 Geddes Ave; Ann Arbor, MI 48109; Phone: (734) 764-0478; https://lsa.umich.edu/ummnh/visiting.html

Nichols Arboretum has created historically important collections of plants, but visitors can just enjoy nature. Admission is free. Open daily sunrise to sunset. 1610 Washington Hts; Ann Arbor, MI 48104
Phone: (734) 647-7600; https://mbgna.umich.edu/nichols-arboretum/displays-natural-areas

Stearns Collection of Musical Instruments displays selected musical instruments from its collection of over 2,500 pieces from all over the world. They can be seen in exhibition areas throughout the Earl V. Moore Building of the School of Music, Theatre & Dance, and in the Vesta Mills Gallery. Admission is free. Open Monday through Friday from 10 AM to 5 PM. E.V. Moore Building; 1100 Baits Dr; Ann Arbor, MI 48109; Phone: (734) 936-2891; https://smtd.umich.edu/research/stearns_collection/aboutthecollection.htm

Battle Creek, MI
Kingman Museum on the grounds of the Leila Arboretum holds three floors of exhibits and invites the public to walk through Michigan habitats, get an up-close look at how the human body works, and see exotic animals and insects. Admission to the museum is free. Note: They also have shows in the Digistar Planetarium, which will incur a fee. Open Saturday and Sunday from 10 AM to 4 PM. 175

Limit St; Battle Creek, MI 49037; Phone: (269) 965-5117;
http://www.kingmanmuseum.org

Leila Arboretum offers more than 2,000 species of trees and shrubs, many dating back to the 1920s. Admission is free. Open dawn to dusk. 928 W Michigan Ave; Battle Creek, MI 49017; Phone: (269) 969-0270; http://lasgarden.org/index.html

Concord, MI
Mann House and its furnishings illustrate typical family life in the 1880s. Admission is free. Generally open Memorial Day through Labor Day on Wednesday through Sunday from 10 AM to 5 PM. Open late on Friday to 6 PM. 205 Hanover St; Concord, MI 49237; Phone: (517) 373-1359; http://www.michigan.gov/mannhouse

Dearborn, MI (See also Detroit, MI)
Gateway Classic Cars is one of several classic and exotic car dealerships across the country that invite visitors to explore their collection. 15000 Commerce Drive N; Dearborn, MI 48120; Phone: (313) 982-3100; http://gatewayclassiccars.com/locations?location=DET

Detroit, MI (See also Dearborn, MI)
Famous for its Motor City history, the city also hosts a RiverWalk and the largest public market district. The **Detroit RiverWalk** and Dequindre Cut Greenway are open daily from 6 AM to 10 PM. Enjoy the just over one mile path through the city. http://detroitriverfront.org. The **Eastern Market** commercial district is a Michigan State Historic Site and the largest historic public market district in the United States. https://www.easternmarket.com/markets/taste-of-our-markets

Detroit Historical Museum depicts the city's first 200 years from French fur trading post to a major industrial center. There's even a recreation of the streets of Old Detroit. Admission is free. Open Tuesday through Friday from 9:30 AM to 4 PM. Open Saturday and Sunday from 10 AM to 5 PM. 5401 Woodward Ave; Detroit, MI 48202; Phone: (313) 833-1805; https://detroithistorical.org/about-us/our-museums/detroit-historical-museum

Detroit Library is known for its art and architecture as well as its special collections. Self-guided tours are free. The Detroit Public Library Friends Foundation offers free docent-led tours in the Fall. Open Tuesday and Wednesday from Noon to 8 PM. Open Thursday through Saturday from 10 AM to 6 PM. 5201 Woodward Ave; Detroit, MI 48202; Phone: (313) 481-1300; https://www.dplfound.org

General Motors Renaissance Center (GMRENCEN) offers free tours through the landmark building on Monday through Friday at Noon and 2 PM on a first-come basis. They advise arriving 10 minutes before the tour departure time. Register at the PURE DETROIT store located in Tower 400 on Level One. 100 Renaissance Center; Detroit, MI 48243; Phone: (313) 568-5624; http://gmrencen.com/play

Heidelberg Project is an outdoor art environment in the heart of an urban area. Artists take recycled materials and found objects and turn them into thought-provoking art. 3600 Heidelberg St; Detroit, MI, 48207; Phone (313) 458-8414; https://www.heidelberg.org/plan-your-visit

Lincoln Street Art Park & Sculpture Garden is not a traditional park, and it doesn't contain traditional art. And there's not much garden there either. It's more a space for folks to use thrown away items to construct large-scale sculptural pieces. There's also plenty of wall art (perhaps better known as graffiti). It is behind the Recycle Here! building on Holden Avenue. 5926 Lincoln St; Detroit, MI 48208; https://www.facebook.com/Lincoln-Street-Art-Park-179542518761761

N'Namdi Center for Contemporary Art covers more than a century of art in every genre, especially contemporary abstract paintings, with changing exhibits throughout the year. The N'Namdi Collection is considered one of the finest private collections of Black American art in the world. There is no fee to visit and most of their programming is free. Open Tuesday through Saturday from 11 AM to 6 PM. 52 E Forest Ave; Detroit, MI 48201; Phone: (313) 831-8700; http://nnamdicenter.org

Wayne State University (WSU) Planetarium highlights the planets, stars, galaxies, and other wonders of the universe. Public shows are free and currently held every Friday at 7 PM and 8:30 PM. Tickets are required and you'll need to show up at least 10 minutes before the show or the tickets will be released to other guests. Old Main Building; Room 0209; 4841 Cass Ave; Detroit, MI 48202; Phone: (313) 577-6455; https://planetarium.wayne.edu/about

Hickory Corners, MI
Midwest Miniatures Museum shows the world in miniature – scaled down models and diorama feature architectural styles and scenes that depict historical time periods. Admission is free with donations appreciated. Hours are highly seasonal, but open daily May through October. 6855 W Hickory Rd; Hickory Corners, MI 49060; Phone: (269) 671-4404; http://www.midwestminiaturesmuseum.com

W.K. Kellogg Manor House was the summer home of cereal pioneer W.K. Kellogg. The estate was built in 1925-1926 and includes not only the Tudor Revival building but a carriage house, greenhouse with potting shed, a caretaker's cottage, boathouse, an authentic Dutch windmill and gardens. Donated to Michigan State University, it's been restored and opened to the public. Self-guided tours are free and available Monday through Friday from 9 AM to 1 PM, and again from 1:30 PM to 4 PM. Guided tours will incur a fee. 3700 E Gull Lake Dr; Hickory Corners, MI 49060; Phone: (269) 671-2160; https://conference.kbs.msu.edu/manor-house/visit

Kalamazoo, MI
Kalamazoo Valley Museum uses artifacts, photographs, and documents to recount the history of the Valley. General admission to the museum is free. Special programs may incur a fee and there is a cost for the planetarium shows. Open Monday through Saturday from 9 AM to 5 PM. Open Sunday and some holidays from 1 PM to 5 PM. 230 N Rose St; Kalamazoo MI 49007; Phone: (269) 373-7990; https://www.kalamazoomuseum.org

Lansing and East Lansing, MI
Capitol Quarter Midget Association is dedicated to safe racing for kids. There is no admission charge to watch the races and all are welcome. Races run seasonally on most weekends during the summer. 16460 US Hwy 27; Lansing, MI 48906; Phone: (269) 484-4362; http://capitolquartermidgets.com

Eli and Edythe Broad Art Museum at Michigan State University blends historic, modern, and contemporary art. Free admission. Open Tuesday through Sunday from Noon to 7 PM. 547 E Circle Dr; East Lansing, MI 48824; Phone: (517) 884-4800; https://broadmuseum.msu.edu/visit

Fenner Nature Center offers four miles of trails, some featuring ponds and overlooks, plus specialized gardens. Admission is free. The park is open daily from 8 AM to dusk. The visitor center has seasonal hours. 2020 E Mount Hope Ave; Lansing, MI 48910; Phone: (517) 483-4224; https://mynaturecenter.org/visit/takeahike

Michigan 4-H Children's Gardens is open free to visit. The outdoor gardens are open daily from dawn to dusk. Indoor garden is open Monday through Friday from 8 AM to 4 PM. Open on Saturday and Sunday from 10 AM to 4 PM. 1066 Bogue St; East Lansing, MI 48824; Phone: (517) 353-0452; https://4hgarden.msu.edu/information/index.html

Michigan State Capitol invites the public to see the Rotunda and the Gallery of the Governors. Visits to the House and Senate galleries, the Governor's office, and the historic Supreme Court chamber are based on availability. Both self-guided and guided tours are free. Guided tours are generally available Monday through Friday from 9 AM to 4 PM and Saturday from 10 AM to 3 PM. Self-guided tours are available Monday through Friday. Closed holidays. Note: Guided tour times are subject to change daily based on staffing levels. 100 N Capitol Ave; Lansing, MI 48933; Phone: (517) 373-2353; http://capitol.michigan.gov/plantour

Michigan Supreme Court Learning Center is a museum-like education center with activities and exhibits, including a mock courtroom. Admission is free. Open Monday to Friday from 9 AM to 4 PM. Closed court holidays. Note: The Hall of Justice is a court building with security procedures. All adult visitors must present a government-issued photo ID and sign in to enter. 925 W Ottawa St; Lansing, MI 48915; Phone: (517) 373-7171; http://courts.mi.gov/education/learning-center/Pages/default.aspx

Marquette, MI
DeVos Art Museum at Northern Michigan University highlights regional, national, and international contemporary art. Admission to the museum and its events are free. Open Tuesday and Wednesday from 10 AM to 5 PM. Open Thursday and Friday from Noon to 8 PM. Open on Saturday and Sunday from Noon to 6 PM. 1401 Presque Isle Ave; Marquette, MI 49855; Phone: (906) 227-2235; http://art.nmu.edu/department/museum/index.htm

Mattawan, MI
Wolf Lake Hatchery Visitor Center teaches fishery science through displays, multi-media programs, and interpretive materials. Wander on your own or take a free guided tour of the hatchery. Memorial Day to Labor Day open Monday through Saturday from 10 AM to 6 PM and on Sunday from Noon to 6 PM. Closed Thanksgiving to March. Open the remaining months on Tuesday through Saturday from 10 AM to 4 PM and on Sunday from Noon to 4 PM. Admission is free. The Hatchery is an official Michigan Wildlife Viewing Area. 34270 CR 652; Mattawan, MI 49071; Phone: (269) 668-2876; http://www.michigan.gov/wolflakevc

Muskegon, MI
Carr-Fles Planetarium on the Muskegon Community College campus creates four new planetarium programs each year. The free shows are offered from late August through June every Tuesday and Thursday evening at 7 PM. Doors open at 6:45 PM. 221 S Quarterline Rd; Muskegon, MI 49442; Phone: (231) 777-0289; http://www.muskegoncc.edu/mathphysical-sciences/carr-fles-planetarium

Negaunee, MI

Michigan Iron Industry Museum highlights the state's iron mining industry, the different technologies developed by iron mining companies, and daily life in these communities. Admission is free. Donations are appreciated. May through October open daily from 9:30 AM to 4:30 PM. From November through April open Wednesday through Friday as well as the first Saturday the month from 9:30 AM to 4 PM. 73 Forge Rd; Negaunee, MI 49866; Phone: (906) 475-7857; http://www.michigan.gov/ironindustrymuseum

Saginaw, MI

Japanese Cultural Center, Tea House, and Gardens of Saginaw invites visitors to explore their three-acre garden with weeping cherry trees, authentic stone lanterns, hand crafted bamboo gates, an Asian-inspired gazebo, and an arching vermilion bridge over a winding stream. Guided tours and tea will incur a cost but it's free to explore the gardens on your own. Open April to October on Tuesday through Saturday from Noon to 4 PM. 527 Ezra Rust Dr; Saginaw, MI 48601; Phone: (989) 759-1648; http://www.japaneseculturalcenter.org

Marshall M. Fredericks Sculpture Museum is focused on the life and works of sculptor Marshall Fredericks known for his monumental figurative sculptures, public memorials and fountains, portraits, and animal figures. Admission is free with donations gratefully accepted. Guided tours are also available free of charge with advanced reservations. Open Monday through Friday from 11 AM to 5 PM and on Saturday from Noon to 5 PM. Saginaw Valley State University; 7400 Bay Rd; Saginaw, MI 48710; Phone: (989) 964-7125; http://marshallfredericks.org

Shiawassee National Wildlife Refuge offers several hiking tours, but it also provides the Wildlife Drive, the refuge's auto tour route. The drive is generally open from June through the end of September from sunrise to one hour before sunset but may be closed due to flooding, soft roads, or other special conditions. There is no entrance fee. 6975 Mower Rd; Saginaw, MI 48601; Phone: (989) 777-5930; https://www.fws.gov/refuge/Shiawassee

Minnesota

Among the special initiatives developed by Minnesota, their Sinfonia is a stand-out. Conductor Jay Fishman wanted to create a professional orchestra dedicated to bringing live classical music to underserved residents of Minnesota. These free events take place across the state. Call (612) 871-1701 or check http://www.mnsinfonia.org for more information.

Austin, MN

SPAM Museum celebrates the tinned meat product created and sold by Hormel since 1937. It was a food staple long before Monty Python made SPAM a household word. The museum features nine *SPAMtastic* galleries including its role in feeding U.S. troops as well as interactive games and photo opportunities. Admission is free. From October through March it is open Monday through Saturday from 10 AM to 5 PM and Sunday from 11 AM to 4 PM. Closed Mondays in January and February. From April through September it is open Monday through Saturday from 10 AM to 6 PM, and Sunday from 11 AM to 5 PM. Closed several major holidays. 101 Third Ave NE; Austin, MN 55912; Phone: (507) 437-5100; http://www.spam.com/museum

Sola Fide Observatory is open to the public on specified Saturdays throughout the year with free public programs introducing visitors to the wonders of the night sky. The observatory is owned and operated by volunteers from JC Hormel Nature Center. 180th St near 536th Ave; Austin, MN 55912; Phone: (507) 437-7519; http://www.hormelnaturecenter.org/sola-fide-observatory.html

Bemidji, MN

Paul Bunyan and Babe the Blue Ox calls to lovers of things that are large. In 1937 Bemidji wanted to have a tourist-attracting mascot for their first ever winter carnival. Paul Bunyan was soon joined by a Babe statue. Placed in a municipal park overlook the lake, Paul and Babe were wildly popular, and still are, now as a national historic landmark. The park is free and open every day. 300 Bemidji Ave N; Bemidji, MN 56601; https://www.bemidji.org/paul-bunyan-and-babe-the-blue-ox

Bloomington, MN

Normandale Community College's Japanese Garden shelters over 300 trees and shrubs set amid traditional Japanese garden elements – bridges, stone lanterns, islands, streams, and waterfalls. There is no admission fee. Note: There is a charge for their self-guiding brochure and there are fee-based guided tours. The Garden is open daily sunrise to sunset unless reserved for an event. 9700 France Ave S;

Bloomington, MN 55431; Phone: (952) 358-8200 or (800) 481-5412;
http://www.normandale.edu/community/japanese-garden

Blue Earth, MN
Green Giant Statue Park is home to the largest (and only) Green Giant statue. The big guy tops 55-feet tall and is the mascot of the Green Giant vegetable company. The company was actually started in Le Sueur about 60 miles away, but the photo op is in Blue Earth. 1126 Green Giant Ln; Blue Earth, MN 56013; Phone: (507) 526-3001; http://www.becity.org

Cloquet, MN
R. W. Lindholm Service Station is famous for its architect. Frank Lloyd Wright designed the station for oilman Ray Lindholm whose house Wright had designed in 1952. The station opened in 1958 and was added to the National Register of Historic Places in September, 1985 for its architectural significance. It features Wright's signature cantilever design with glass walls and copper canopy. 202 Cloquet Ave Cloquet, MN 55720; Phone: (218) 879-2279; http://www.cloquet.com/pages/community/f.l.-wright-gas-station.php

Cold Spring, MN
Third Street Brewhouse Tour is a free guided tour of the Brewhouse that includes beer samples in their Taproom. Tours are held Saturdays at 1 PM and 2 PM. Reservations required. Note: Tour participants must wear closed toe shoes. 219 Red River Ave; Cold Spring, MN 56320; Phone: (320) 685-3690; http://www.thirdstreetbrewhouse.com/tours

Collegeville, MN
St. John's Bible is the first hand-illuminated, hand-written Bible since the invention of the printing press. Calligrapher Donald Jackson, MVO, Scribe to the House of Lords and her majesty Queen Elizabeth II created the Bible with gold and platinum leaf on vellum, using hand-made inks and quills. He also developed the lettering used in the Bible. The Saint John's Bible Gallery features changing exhibitions of 28 original folios. The exhibition also includes rare books and manuscripts from the Hill Museum & Manuscript Library collections along with tools, materials and sketches used in making the Bible. There is no admission charge. Open for self-guided tours Monday through Friday from 10 AM to 4 PM. From June through mid-December open Saturdays from Noon to 4 PM. The public is welcomed to join the monks for the Liturgy of the Hours in the Abbey Church, walk the nature trails in their Arboretum, or along the shore of Lake Sagatagan. Visitors are advised to check the website for closings. Alcuin Library; 2835 Abbey Plaza; Saint John's University; Collegeville, MN 56321; Phone: (320) 363-2122; http://www.saintjohnsbible.org

Duluth, MN

Hawk Ridge Bird Observatory invites visitors to enjoy over four miles of hiking trails and explore geology, flora, and wildlife. There is no charge to visit or enjoy the public programs. From September through October naturalists are on site daily. Best time to visit is mid-August through November. Note: East Skyline Parkway is closed from December to early May. 3980 E Skyline Pkwy; Duluth, MN 55803; Phone: (218) 428-6209; http://www.hawkridge.org

Lake Superior Maritime Visitor Center in historic Canal Park provides the Duluth Ship Canal, Aerial Bridge, three replica cabins, a pilothouse, two-story steam engine, 50 scale models, and interactive displays. Always free. Donations accepted. Open daily at 10 AM with seasonal closings. 600 Canal Park Dr; Duluth, MN 55802; Phone: (218) 720-5260; https://www.lsmma.com

Minneapolis, MN (See also St. Paul, MN)

Frederick R. Weisman Art Museum was designed by Frank Gehry to be a building with two personalities. The conventional brick side faces the campus, but walk around and the building changes radically. Admission is free. Open Tuesday through Friday at 10 AM and closes at 5 PM except on Wednesday when it is open until 8 PM. Open Saturday and Sunday from 11 AM to 5 PM. The museum offers a one hour tour on Saturday and Sunday at 1 PM. 333 E River Pkwy; Minneapolis, MN 55455; Phone: (612) 625-9494; http://www.weisman.umn.edu

Midway Contemporary Art curates exhibitions of artists who are rarely shown in the United States. Admission is free. Open Wednesday through Saturday from 11 AM to 5 PM. 527 Second Ave SE; Minneapolis, MN 55414; Phone: (612) 605-4504; https://midwayart.org

Minneapolis Institute of Art offers works that span six continents, and about 20,000 years, going from ancient sculpture to contemporary photography. Admission is free for the main collection, although special exhibits may incur a fee. Open Tuesday through Saturday at 10 AM and closes at 5 PM except Thursday and Friday when it closes at 9 PM. Open Sunday from 11 AM to 5 PM. Closed several major holidays. 2400 Third Ave S; Minneapolis, MN 55404; Phone: (612) 870-3000; https://new.artsmia.org

Minneapolis Sculpture Garden showcases more than 40 works from the Walker Art Center's collections. Note: The Walker Art Center charges admission, only the sculpture garden is free to visit. Open daily from 6 AM to Midnight. 726 Vineland Pl; Minneapolis, MN 55403; Phone: (612) 375-7600; https://walkerart.org/visit/garden

Wells Fargo Museum presents its Midwestern heritage. Admission is free. Open Monday through Friday from 9 AM to 5 PM. Closed bank holidays. Sixth and Marquette; Minneapolis, MN 55479; Phone: (612) 667-4210; https://www.wellsfargohistory.com/museums/minneapolis

Moorhead, MN (See also Fargo, ND)

Rourke Art Gallery + Museum provides fine and folk art both ancient and modern. Admission is free. Open Friday through Sunday from 1 PM to 5 PM. 521 Main Ave; Moorhead, MN 56560; Phone: (218) 236-8861; http://www.therourke.org

New Ulm, MN

New Ulm's Glockenspiel is a free-standing carillon clock tower with 37 bells that chime each quarter hour. At Noon, 3 PM, and 5 PM the three-foot-high animated figures appear and move to the music as they depict the history of the city. From Thanksgiving until mid- January the glockenspiel depicts the nativity scene. 327 N Minnesota St; New Ulm MN 56073; http://www.newulm.com/visitors-community/things-to-do/attractions/glockenspiel-2

Red Wing, MN

Red Wing Shoe Company Museum is home to the world's largest boot. Standing over 20-feet tall, the boot is a size 638 ½. It is an actual giant boot using the same design and materials used to build the Red Wing classic style number 877. The free museum also features Norman Rockwell original art featuring footwear ads from the 1960s. Open Monday through Friday from 9 AM to 8 PM. Open Saturday 9 AM to 6 PM, and on Sunday from 11 AM to 5 PM. 315 Main St; Red Wing, MN 55066; Phone: (651) 388-6233; http://solutions.redwingshoes.com/WorldsLargestBoot

Richfield, MN

Wood Lake Nature Center features several wildlife viewing areas, and three miles of trails and boardwalks. The nature center and park is free, but there will be a charge for any naturalist-led activity. The park is open daily from sunrise to 11 PM. 6710 Lake Shore Dr; Richfield, MN 55423; Phone: (612) 861-9365; http://www.richfieldmn.gov/around-town/wood-lake-nature-center

Shafer, MN

Franconia Sculpture Park is filled with ever-changing exhibitions of monumental sculpture, many of which you are invited to touch. They offer an artist-in-residence program and the public is encouraged to visit these sculptors and discuss the artistic process. Entrance is free as are park events. There are also free tours on

Sundays at 2 PM from May through October. 29836 St Croix Trail; Shafer, MN 55074; Phone: (651) 257-6668; http://www.franconia.org

Saint Cloud, MN
Munsinger Clemens Gardens are two adjacent but different gardens. The Munsinger dates from the 1930s with WPA-constructed paths and garden areas refurbished and expanded in the 1980s. The Clemens is a formal garden developed in the 1990s. Admission is free. Open spring to fall from 7 AM to 10 PM. Riverside Dr SE; St. Cloud, MN 56301; Phone: (320) 257-5959; http://www.munsingerclemens.com

St. Paul, MN (See also Minneapolis, MN)
Landmark Center opened in 1902 as the Federal Court House and Post Office for the upper Midwest. Today visitors come for its cultural offerings, free museums, and tours. There are free public tours on Thursday at 11 AM and Sunday at Noon. Tours focus on the building's history, architecture, restoration, preservation as well as famous and infamous people. 75 W Fifth St; St. Paul, MN 55102. http://www.landmarkcenter.org/tours

The Landmark Center also hosts two unusual museums.
American Association of Woodturners Gallery offers the Gallery of Wood Art with the tools and techniques used in wood-working. Admission is free. Phone: (651) 484-9094; http://www.galleryofwoodart.org/Visiting.html

Schubert Club Museum introduces visitors to the history of music-making. Hear music boxes and phonographs dating back to 1900. Play and compare the mechanics of several keyboard instruments spanning four centuries. No admission charge. Staff is available to provide tours. Hours change seasonally. Check the website for current hours. Phone: (651) 292-3267; http://schubert.org/museum/about-the-museum

Minnesota Governor's Residence opens for free guided tours during the summer, and again in December. 1006 Summit Ave; St. Paul, MN 55105; Phone: (651) 201-3464; https://mn.gov/admin/governors-residence/tours

Minnesota State Capitol offers historic legislative chambers, and monumental public works of art. Admission to the State Capitol and self-guided tours are free. A donation of $5 per person is suggested if you take one of their guided tours. Open Monday through Friday from 8 AM to 5 PM. Open Saturday from 10 AM to 3 PM and on Sunday from 1 PM to 4 PM. 75 Rev Dr Martin Luther King Jr Blvd; St. Paul, MN 55155; Phone: (651) 296-2881; http://www.mnhs.org/capitol

Wayzata, MN

Minnetonka Center for the Arts is open to the public for free exhibits. Artwork is displayed throughout the facility and all classrooms have large glass windows so visitors can watch a studio in action. Open Monday through Saturday at 9 AM. Closes at 4 PM on Monday, Wednesday, Friday, and Saturday. Closes at 9:30 PM on Tuesday and Thursday. Note: Closes on Saturday at 1 PM mid-June through August. 2240 North Shore Dr; Wayzata, MN 55391; Phone: (952) 473-7361; http://www.minnetonkaarts.org

Mississippi

Bay St Louis, MS
Alice Moseley Folk Art & Antique Museum combines folk art with train history. Alice Mosely was a folk artist who began painting at age 65. She believed that art should tell a story. Over 50 of her paintings are on display in this free admission museum. Open Monday through Saturday from 10 AM to 4 PM. Closed major holidays.1928 Depot Way; Bay St Louis, MS 39520; Phone: (228) 467-9223; https://alicemoseley.com/the-museum

Bay St Louis Mardi Gras Museum delights visitors with over a dozen elaborate Mardi Gras costumes. No admission charged. Inside the historic train depot at 1928 Depot Way; Bay St Louis, MS 39520; Phone: (228) 463-9222; https://playonthebay.org/attractions

Biloxi, MS
Biloxi Fire Museum, located in a former firehouse, displays two of the five original fire bells, an 1880s hose cart, a 1908 American LaFrance steam fire engine, and a 1923 American LaFrance chain-driven fire engine. Admission is free. Donations appreciated. Open Saturday from 9 AM to 3 PM, and by appointment. 1046 E Howard Ave; Biloxi, MS 39530; Phone: (228) 435-6119; https://biloxi.ms.us/departments/fire-department/history

Biloxi Visitors Center highlights Biloxi's history and heritage from French explorer days to present through exhibits and films. 1050 Beach Blvd; Biloxi, MS 39530; Phone: (800) 245-6943; https://biloxi.ms.us/visitor-info/museums/visitors-center

Camp Shelby, MS
Mississippi Armed Forces Museum covers America's military history from the 1800s through the War on Terrorism using historic artifacts and documents, video, and recreations. A vehicle park offers aircraft, tanks, and field artillery. Free admission. Note: Enter through the North or South Gate from Highway 49. Visitors over the age of 16 must present a valid photo ID. Drivers must have a valid drivers license and may be required to present vehicle registration or proof of insurance. Admission is free. Open Tuesday through Saturday from 9 AM to 4 PM. Open Memorial Day, July 4th, and Veterans Day. Closed most other federal

and state holidays. Building 850; Forrest Ave W; Camp Shelby, MS 39407; Phone: (601) 558-2757; https://armedforcesmuseum.us/home

Columbus, MS
Tennessee Williams Home & Welcome Center is in the rectory of what had been St. Paul's Episcopal Church where his grandfather had served as rector. In 1993 the rectory was in jeopardy of being torn down until the city made it the town's Welcome Center, and moved it to its new site on Main Street. Visitors can take a free tour of the first home of legendary playwright Tennessee Williams. Open Monday through Saturday from 8:30 AM to 5 PM. 300 Main St; Columbus, MS 39701; Phone: (662) 328-0222; http://www.visitcolumbusms.org/places-to-visit/tennessee-williams-home-and-welcome-center-c-1875

Tenn-Tom Waterway Transportation Museum highlights the extensive lock and dam system and transportation artifacts. Headquartered in the Tennessee-Tombigbee Waterway Development Authority building, admission to the museum is free. Open Monday through Friday from 8 AM to 4 PM. 318 Seventh St N; Columbus, MS 39703; Phone: (662) 328-3286; https://www.tenntom.org/ttw-museum

Corinth, MS (See also Shiloh, TN)
Coca-Cola Museum at Corinth Coca-Cola Bottling Works features over 1,000 pieces of authentic Coca-Cola memorabilia, plus a large collection of historic machines. Admission is free. Open Monday through Friday from 8 AM to 4:45 PM. 601 Washington St; Corinth, MS 38834; Phone: (662) 287-1433; http://www.corinthcoke.com/museum

Shiloh National Military Park spans Corinth, MS and Shiloh, TN. It was site of one of the more brutal battles of the Civil War. Over 100,000 soldiers entered the battle and over 23,000 died. Shiloh National Military Park does not charge an entrance fee at either of its locations. Phone: (731) 689-5696; https://www.nps.gov/shil/index.htm

Corinth Battlefield Unit contains 14 historic sites associated with the siege, battle, and occupation of Corinth, Mississippi during the Civil War.
Corinth Civil War Interpretive Center is truly a must-see part of the park. It features interactive displays and multimedia presentations on the Battle of Shiloh and the Siege and Battle of Corinth. It chronicles the birth and growth of the United States, the rise of sectionalism, key events leading to the Civil War, and a symbolic representation of four years of war. Admission is free. Open from 8 AM to 5 PM daily except Thanksgiving, Christmas, and New Year's Day. 501 W Linden St; Corinth, MS 38834; Phone: (662) 287-9273;

https://www.nps.gov/shil/planyourvisit/corinth.htm;
https://www.nps.gov/shil/planyourvisit/things2do.htm

Corinth Contraband Camp illuminates a little known part of the Civil War. During the war, enslaved people fled to safety behind Union lines. A portion of the camp is preserved including quarter-mile walking path with six life-size bronze sculptures depicting life of camp residents. 800 N Parkway St; Phone: (662) 287-9273; Corinth, MS 38834; https://www.nps.gov/shil/planyourvisit/contrabandcamp.htm

Gautier, MS
Mississippi Sandhill Crane National Wildlife Refuge provides an observation deck overlooking the savanna. Stop by the visitor center for help finding the best places to see these magnificent birds. Staff also provides tours that run through fall and winter. Entrance is free as are all the programs. The refuge is open daily during daylight hours. The visitor center is open Monday through Saturday from 9 AM to 3 PM. Closed federal holidays. Note: In summer, insect repellent is advised as is closed-toe shoes. 7200 Crane La; Gautier, MS 39553; Phone: (228) 497-6322; https://www.fws.gov/refuge/Mississippi_Sandhill_Crane

Greenville, MS
Winterville Mounds features 12 prehistoric Native American mounds, two large plazas, and a museum. Admission is free. The visitors center is open Tuesday through Saturday from 9 AM to 5 PM. The grounds of the site are open daily from dawn until dusk. 2415 Hwy 1 N; Greenville, MS 38703; Phone: (662) 334-4684; http://www.mdah.ms.gov/new/visit/winterville-mounds

Gulfport, MS
Mississippi Coast Model Railroad Museum is home to the largest LEGO railroad display in Mississippi. There are multiple scale model train layouts as well as elevated and ground level G scale trains. Admission is free but donations are appreciated. Open Tuesday through Saturday from Noon to 5 PM. 504 Pass Rd; Gulfport, MS 39507; Phone: (228) 284-5731; https://www.mcmrcm.org

Hattiesburg, MS
University of Southern Mississippi Museum of Art exhibits pieces on loan from artists, museums, and galleries. Admission and receptions are free. Open Monday through Friday from 10 AM to 5 PM. The gallery is closed during exhibit installations and for all USM scheduled holidays. The Gallery of Art & Design is the primary exhibition space. George Hurst Building; 104 Southern Dr; Hattiesburg, MS 39406; Phone: (601) 266-5200; https://www.usm.edu/performing-visual-arts/museum-art.php

Jackson, MS

Greenwood Cemetery holds many notable Mississippians. Three downloadable walking tour maps are available: General Tour, African American Tour, and a Confederate Tour. Located at the intersection of West, Davis, Lamar, and George Streets. Jackson, MS 39202; Phone: (601) 362-4471; http://www.greenwoodcemeteryjackson.org/tours.html

Medgar Evers Home was the Evers home and the site of his assassination in 1963. Operated by Tougaloo College the home contains period furnishings, exhibits, and family photographs. There is no admission fee, but donations gratefully accepted. Visiting is by appointment only. 2332 Margaret Walker Alexander Dr; Jackson, MS 39213; Phone: (601) 977-7706 or (601) 977-7935; https://www.tougaloo.edu/library/archives-special-collections

Mississippi Governor's Mansion opens its historic section on Tuesday through Friday from 9:30 AM to 11 AM. Guided tours are given every half-hour beginning at 9:30 AM. Admission is free. Note: For security reasons public restrooms are not available. They recommend calling first to confirm tour hours. 300 E Capitol St; Jackson, MS 39201; Phone: (601) 576-6920; http://www.mdah.ms.gov/new/visit/governors-mansion

Mississippi Museum of Art offers curated shows but is best known for *Mississippi Story*, a thematic exhibition of artists with a connection to the state. Admission is free. Open Tuesday through Saturday from 10 AM to 5 PM. Open Sunday from Noon to 5 PM. 380 S Lamar St; Jackson, MS 39201; Phone: (601) 960-1515; http://msmuseumart.org/index.php/visit

Mississippi State Capitol invites visitors to view the Senate and House of Representatives when in session. Other highlights include the statue of *Blind Justice*, and four figures representing Mississippi history – two Native Americans, a European explorer, and a Confederate soldier. On the grounds visitors can see a replica of the original Liberty Bell, and the monument *Women of the Confederacy*. Self-guided and guided tours are free. Tours are given weekdays starting at 9:30 AM with the last tour beginning at 2:30 PM. Closed federal holidays. 400 High St; Jackson, MS 39201; Phone: (601) 359-3114; http://www.legislature.ms.gov/Pages/History.aspx

Old Mississippi State Capitol served as the Mississippi statehouse from 1839 until 1903. Significant legislative history was made there including the 1839 Married Women's Property Act, and Mississippi's secession from the Union in 1861. Free to visit. Open Tuesday through Saturday from 9 AM to 5 PM. Open

Sunday 1 PM to 5 PM. 100 State St; Jackson, MS 39201; Phone: (601) 576-6920; http://www.mdah.ms.gov/oldcap

Leland, MS
Jim Henson and the Birthplace of Kermit the Frog honors the man who created the Muppets and the beloved Kermit the Frog with exhibits and displays. There is no admission but donations are appreciated. Memorial Day through Labor Day open Monday through Saturday from 10 AM to 5 PM. Closes at 4 PM the rest of the year. 415 SE Deer Creek Dr; Leland, MS 38756; Phone: (662) 686-7383; http://birthplaceofthefrog.org

Lucedale, MS
Palestine Gardens creates a scale model of the land of the Bible during the time of Jesus. There's the River Jordan, ruins of Jericho, Bethlehem, and Jerusalem. There is no admission charge. They recommend calling ahead for current hours. 201 Palestine Gardens Rd; Lucedale, MS 39452; Phone: (601) 947-8422; https://www.facebook.com/pages/category/Religious-Organization/Palestine-Gardens-Replica-of-the-Holy-Land-169447236398924/

Meridian, MS
Key Brothers Aviation Exhibit celebrates the brothers who set a world endurance flight record of 27 days, breaking the previous record of 23 days. In order to stay aloft, they had to keep refueling the plane. Along with local inventor and mechanic A. D. Hunter, the Key brothers developed a valve for aerial refueling that became the industry standard for the United States military. The exhibit also reviews the history of aviation. Admission is free. At the Meridian Regional Airport. 2811 US Hwy 11 South; Meridian, MS 39307; Phone: (601) 482-0364; https://www.meridianairport.com/keybrothersaviationmuseum

Meridian Museum of Art displays works of renowned regional and Mississippi artists. Admission is free. Open Tuesday through Saturday from 11 AM to 4 PM. 628 25th Ave; Meridian, MS 39301; Phone: (601) 693-1501; http://www.meridianmuseum.org/index.html

Moss Point, MS
Grand Bay National Estuarine Research Reserve welcomes the spring and fall migration of Yellow Warblers, Redstarts, and Scarlet Tanager. There's 18,000 acres of pine savanna, salt marshes, bays and bayous as well as habitats unique to the coastal zone. Admission is free. The interpretive visitor center is open Monday through Friday from 9 AM to 3 PM. Public roads and trails open during daylight hours. 6005 Bayou Heron Rd; Moss Point, MS 39562; Phone: (228) 475-7047; http://grandbaynerr.org

Natchez, MS

Eudora Welty House and Garden interprets the life of the internationally acclaimed author. The Education and Visitors Center has permanent and temporary exhibits, and an orientation film. Free and open Tuesday through Friday from 8:30 AM to 5 PM. On the second Saturday of the month it is open from 8:30 AM to Noon. Tours of the house will incur a fee. 1109 Pinehurst St; Jackson, MS 39202; Phone: (601) 353-7762; http://www.mdah.ms.gov/welty

Grand Village of Natchez Indians features three prehistoric Native American mounds, a reconstructed Natchez Indian house, and museum. Admission is free. Open Monday through Saturday from 9 AM to 5 PM and on Sunday from 1:30 PM to 5 PM. 400 Jefferson Davis Blvd; Natchez, MS 39120; Phone: (601) 446-6502; http://www.mdah.ms.gov/new/visit/grand-village-of-natchez-indians

Historic Jefferson College, named in honor of President Thomas Jefferson, opened in 1811. Its most famous student was Jefferson Davis, who later became president of the Confederate States of America. Currently open by appointment. 16 Old North St; Natchez, MS 39120; Phone: (601) 442-2901; http://www.mdah.ms.gov/new/visit/historic-jefferson-college

Natchez National Historical Park chronicles the Natchez people of the American South and the development of the region. In addition to the visitor center there are two main places to visit within the park; Melrose Estate and William Johnson House. Phone: (601) 446-5790; https://www.nps.gov/natc/planyourvisit/things2do.htm

Natchez Trace Parkway meanders through three states with several free stops in Mississippi. At Milepost 261 signs at the **Chickasaw Village** describe the long-gone structures and history of the Chickasaw who once lived there. The abandoned town of **Rocky Springs** awaits visitors at Milepost 54.8. Milepost 41.5 is the site of **Sunken Trace**. A short trail allows you to walk on the Natchez Trace, literally sinking the soft ground. **Mount Locust Inn** at Milepost 15.5 dates back to 1820. Walking paths lead visitors past sites of the brick kiln, family cemetery, slave cemetery, and other plantation locations. Generally open from February through November. There is no cost to visit. https://www.nps.gov/natr/planyourvisit/placestogo.htm

Melrose Estate includes the grounds, outbuildings, and formal gardens as well as the mansion. The grounds and gardens are free to visit although a tour of the house will incur a fee. The grounds are open daily from 8:30 AM to 5 PM. 1 Melrose-Montebello Pkwy; Natchez, MS 39120. Phone: (601) 446-5790.

William Johnson House complex consists of the actual Johnson home and the adjoining McCallum House. William Johnson was a free Black barber, and the museum illuminates the life of free Blacks in the pre-Civil War south. There is no admission fee. Open Monday through Saturday from 9 AM to 5 PM. Closed from Noon to 1 PM for lunch. On Sunday open Noon to 5 PM. Closed on Thanksgiving, Christmas, and New Year's Day. 210 State St; Natchez, MS 39120; Phone: (601) 446-5790.

Ocean Springs, MS

Gulf Islands National Seashore – Davis Bayou Area has a two-mile trail through a coastal forest and local bayous. The William M. Colmer Visitor Center provides indoor exhibits about the shore and the islands. Free to visit. Open daily from 8:30 AM to sunset. Hwy 90 east of downtown Ocean Springs; Phone: (228) 875-9057 ext. 4100; https://www.gulfcoast.org/listings/gulf-islands-national-seashore-visitor-center-%26-campground/748

Oxford, MS

Burns-Belfry Museum chronicles African American history from slavery through Civil Rights. Other exhibits describe the history of the old Burns Church. Admission is free with donations appreciated. Open Wednesday, Thursday, Friday from Noon to 3 PM and on Sunday from 1 PM to 4 PM. Jackson Ave E; Oxford, MS 38655; Phone: (662) 281-9963; http://www.burns-belfry.com/index.php

LQC Lamar House Museum honors LQC Lamar best known for his involvement in national political affairs after the end of the Civil War, and his efforts to reconcile the North and South. Admission is free. Open Friday through Sunday from 1 PM to 4 PM. 616 N 14th St; Oxford, MS; Phone: (662) 513-6071; http://www.lqclamarhouse.com/index.php

University Museum combines 19th century scientific instruments, and an extensive collection of the work of Theora Hamblett, and native folk artist. Admission is free. Donations accepted. Open Tuesday through Saturday from 10 AM to 6 PM. Closed university holidays. The campus is also home to William Faulkner's home, Rowan Oak but there is a charge to visit the house. University Ave and Fifth St; Oxford, MS 38655; Phone: (662) 915-7073; https://museum.olemiss.edu/visit

Starkville, MS

Mississippi State University contains an excellent and diverse assemblage of free collections and museums with over a dozen galleries. https://www.museums.msstate.edu/public-galleries

The Mitchell Library offers three fascinating exhibits. 395 Hardy Rd; Starkville, MS 39762; Phone: (662) 325-7668; (662) 325-7679

The **Charles H. Templeton, Sr. Music Museum** displays his collection of musical instruments, recordings, and sheet music. Open Monday through Friday from 9 AM to 5 PM. Phone: (662) 325-6634; http://lib.msstate.edu/templeton/index.php **John Grisham Room** displays memorabilia and materials from the writings and achievements of this best-selling author, former Mississippi legislator, and MSU alumnus. Open Monday through Friday from 8 AM to 5 PM. Phone: (662) 325-6634; http://lib.msstate.edu/grisham; The **Ulysses S. Grant Presidential Library Museum and Reading Room** focuses on the correspondence, photographs, paintings, engravings, statues and other artifacts relating to the 18th President of the United States, Ulysses S. Grant. Open Monday through Friday from 7:30 AM to 5 PM. Phone: (662) 325-4552; http://www.usgrantlibrary.org/visit

Head to the Welcome Center for clocks and tours of the campus. The **Cullis & Gladys Wade Clock Museum** displays over 400 clocks and watches dating back as far as the early 1700s. Open Monday through Friday from 8 AM to 5 PM. 75 BS Hood Dr; Phone: (662) 325-5198; https://www.visit.msstate.edu/clockmuseum Phone: (662) 325-5198.

Oktibbeha Heritage Museum depicts the history of Starkville and the county through exhibits of Coca Cola memorabilia, Civil War and military display, and early medical and dental instruments. Admission to the museum is free, but donations are appreciated. Open Tuesday through Thursday from 1 PM to 4 PM. 206 Fellowship St; Starkville, MS 39759; Phone: (662) 323-0211; http://oktibbehaheritagemuseum.com/wordpress

Tupelo, MS

This city is famous for being the home town of Elvis Presley. Fans can enjoy Presley-themed wall murals, and a statue of the King himself based on a photo from his 1956 Homecoming Concert. The statue can be found at the Tupelo Fairgrounds at East Main Street in the Fairpark District. Conduct your own Presley tour by picking up a copy of the *Elvis Presley Driving Trail* at the Tupelo Convention & Visitors Bureau at 399 E Main St, Tupelo, MS 38804; Phone: (662) 841-6521; https://www.tupelo.net

Gumtree Museum of Art features several time-limited exhibits. Free admission. Open Tuesday through Friday from 10 AM to 4 PM. 213 W Main St; Tupelo, MS 38802; Phone: (662) 844-2787; https://gumtreemuseum.com

Private John Allen National Fish Hatchery provides birdwatching opportunities at the wildlife viewing area, and invites visitors to learn about raising the fish that stock public waters. No admission charged. Open Monday through Friday from 7 AM to 3:30 PM. 111 Elizabeth St; Tupelo, MS 38802; Phone: (662) 842-1341; https://www.fws.gov/southeast/private-john-allen

Vicksburg, MS

Famous as the site for the Civil War battle, the Vicksburg National Military Park requires an entry fee, but you can learn about local history at no cost.

Jesse Brent Lower Mississippi River Museum details life along the Mississippi River from the ways people have used the river, to living through the flooding. The M/V Mississippi IV has been made part of the museum. Admission is free. Open Monday through Saturday from 9 AM to 4 PM and on Sunday from 1 PM to 4 PM. 910 Washington St; Vicksburg, MS 39183; Phone: (601) 638-9900; http://www.lmrm.org

Waveland, MS

Waveland's Ground Zero Hurricane Museum derives its name from Waveland's unique position as Ground Zero for Hurricane Katrina. Located in a restored historic school this museum pays tribute to the people who lived through the devastation and rebuilt their lives. Admission is free, donations are accepted. Open Tuesday, Friday, and Saturday from 10 AM to 3 PM. 335 Coleman Ave; Waveland, MS 39576; Phone: (228) 467-9012; http://wavelandgroundzero.com

West Point, MS

Sam Wilhite Transportation Museum highlights transportation, from the narrow trails of Native Americans to today's modern highway system. Admission is free with donations accepted. Open Thursday through Saturday from 10 AM to 5 PM. 5 Depot Dr; West Point, MS 39773; Phone: (662) 494-8910; http://www.wpnet.org/index.php/attractions/wilhite_transportation

Missouri

Missouri is dotted with preserved historic towns, and their state parks offer free admission. https://mostateparks.com/

Altenburg, MO
Lutheran Heritage Center and Museum combines historic buildings with museum exhibits recounting the area's German heritage. Free admission. Open daily from 10 AM to 4 PM. 75 Church St; Altenburg, MO 63732; Phone: (573) 824-6070; https://lutheranmuseum.com

Arrow Rock, MO
Arrow Rock State Historic Site was once a busy river town. The site has a restaurant but there's also the Old Courthouse, and George Caleb Bingham's house. The visitor center highlights the history of Arrow Rock and Boone's Lick Country. Admission is free. The grounds are open daily from 7 AM to 10 PM. The visitor center is open from June through August from 10 AM to 5 PM. The remainder of the year it is open from 10 AM to 4 PM. Closed some major holidays. 39521 Visitor Center Dr; Arrow Rock, MO 65320; Phone: (660) 837-3330; https://mostateparks.com/park/arrow-rock-state-historic-site

Branson, MO
Shepherd of the Hills Fish Hatchery includes exhibits and displays, wildlife-viewing blind, and tower. The hatchery is free to visit. Guided tours are given weekdays from Memorial Day to Labor Day and self-guided tours are available the rest of the year. From September through May it is open Tuesday through Saturday from 9 AM to 5 PM. During June, July, and August it is open daily from 9 AM to 5 PM. Closed all state holidays. 483 Hatchery Rd; Branson, MO 65616; Phone: (417) 334-4865; https://nature.mdc.mo.gov/discover-nature/places/shepherd-hills-fish-hatchery

Butler, MO
Robert A. Heinlein Library Addition honors its famous son, science fiction writer Robert Heinlein. The library features memorabilia and original books, including *Starship Troopers* and *Puppet Master*. Although Heinlein may be most famous for *Stranger In a Strange Land* this prolific writer is an icon among fans of science fiction. The library is open Monday through Friday from 9:30 AM to 5:30 PM with a Thursday closing at 7 PM. Open Saturday from 9:30 to 1:30 PM. 100 W Atkison St; Butler, MO 64730; Phone: (660) 679-4321; http://www.butlerpubliclibrary.org/heinlein-room

Cape Girardeau, MO

Crisp Museum focuses on archaeology, history, and fine art. A video in the museum's theater highlights southeast Missouri's heritage. Located inside Southeast Missouri State University's River Campus. Admission is free. Open Monday through Friday from 9 AM to 5 PM with summer hours of 10 AM to 4 PM. Open weekends from 1 PM to 4 PM. Closed most major holidays. 518 S Fountain St; Cape Girardeau, MO 63701; Phone: (573) 651-2260; https://semo.edu/museum

Carthage, MO

Precious Moment's Chapel is noted for the paintings and stained glass windows by artist Sam Butcher depicting stories from the Bible. Free chapel tours and free admission. Open daily from 10 AM to 4 PM. Last tour begins at 3 PM. 4321 Chapel Rd; Carthage, MO 64836; Phone: (800) 543-7975; https://preciousmomentschapel.org

Columbia, MO

Missouri Historic Costume and Textile Collection at University of Missouri includes everything from 16th century textile fragments to 21st century apparel and accessories. Admission is free. Visitors are welcomed to view the current exhibit in Gwynn Hall, open Monday through Friday from 8 AM to 6 PM. Note: The hours follow the University calendar. Check the website to find out when the exhibitions are available. Department of Textile and Apparel Management; 137 Stanley Hall; Columbia, MO 65211; Phone: (573) 884-5001; http://tam.missouri.edu/MHCTC/exhibitions.html

Museum of Anthropology at University of Missouri holds the largest collection of prehistoric Missouri artifacts in the world. Visitors can also explore Missouri's pioneer and rural history as well as   collections from cultures from across the globe. The Grayson Archery Collection is considered the world's most comprehensive archery collection. Admission is free. Open Tuesday through Friday from 9 AM to 4 PM, and Saturday and Sunday from Noon to 4 PM. Closed university holidays. 115 Business Loop 70 W; Columbia, MO 65203; Phone: (573) 882-3573; https://anthromuseum.missouri.edu

Museum of Art and Archeology at University of Missouri invites visitors to wander through two floors of human history with a strong emphasis on Greek, Roman, and Near Eastern art works as well as ancient Egypt and Byzantium. Free admission. Open Tuesday through Friday from 9 AM to 4 PM, and Saturday and Sunday from Noon to 4 PM. Closed university holidays. 115 Business Loop 70 W; Columbia, MO 65203; Phone: (573) 882-3591; https://maa.missouri.edu

Stephens College Historic Costume Gallery holds two public exhibits a year. Admission is free but the hours are limited. Open Wednesday from Noon to 1 PM, Thursday from 5:30 PM to 8:30 PM, and Saturday and Sunday from Noon to 3 PM. Lela Raney Wood Hall; Mezzanine Floor; 6 N College Ave; Columbia, MO 65201; Phone: (573) 876-7220; https://www.stephens.edu/services/box-office/fashion

Cuba, MO

This Route 66 Mural City offers visitors a glimpse into Cuba's history. Their beautifully created murals depict conflicts between the troops of Confederate General Sterling Price and Union General Thomas Ewing in September 1864, a visit by Harry Truman, enjoying life along the river, a family taking an outing in an old car, families waving goodbye to soldiers, even a landing by Amelia Earhart. A restored Route 66 gas station makes Cuba one of the fun small towns to visit along the Mother Road. Brochures for self-guided tours are available at the visitor center at the junction of the N Service Road and I-44. Or download it here: http://cubamomurals.com/images/MuralCity.pdf http://cubamomurals.com

Diamond, MO

George Washington Carver National Monument includes both the birthplace of George Washington Carver and the cemetery where members of his family are buried. Carver once said, "If I know the answer you can have it for the price of a postage stamp. The Lord charges nothing for knowledge and I will charge you the same." Admission is free. The grounds are always open. The visitor center is open daily from 9 AM to 5 PM. Guided tours are available. Closed some major holidays. 5646 Carver Rd; Diamond, MO 64840; Phone: (417) 325-4151; https://www.nps.gov/gwca/index.htm

Eureka, MO

Route 66 State Park Visitor Center explores the history of America's Main Street. Located in Bridgehead Inn, a 1935 roadhouse on the site of the town of Times Beach, the visitor center records the history of the town, and the environmental cleanup after its exposure to dioxin. It also provides Route 66 memorabilia. Open daily March through November from 9 AM to 4:30 PM. Closed December through February as well as Easter and Thanksgiving. 97 N Outer Rd; Eureka, MO 63025; Phone: (636) 938-7198; https://mostateparks.com/park/route-66-state-park

Florida, MO

Mark Twain Birthplace State Historic Site includes Twain's two-room birthplace cabin with first editions of many of the Twain's works, a handwritten manuscript of *Tom Sawyer*, and many of the furnishings from his Connecticut home. Admission to the site and tours of the museum are free. A red granite monument in town marks the original location of the cabin. From April through October the site is open Monday through Thursday from 10 AM to 4 PM and on Friday and Saturday from 10 AM to 5 PM. Open Sunday from 1 PM to 5 PM. The rest of the year it is open only on Friday and Saturday from 10 AM to 4 PM . Closed some major holidays. Note: Mark Twain was born Samuel Clemens in 1935. 37352 Shrine Rd; Florida, MO 65283; Phone: (573) 565-3449; https://mostateparks.com/park/mark-twain-birthplace-state-historic-site

Fort Leonard Wood, MO

Mahaffey Museum Complex contains museums for three branches of the military; the Army, Engineer and Chemical, and Military Police. An open-air military vehicle museum is also on the grounds. There is also an authentic World War II company street complete with a chapel and supply building as well as housing and company headquarters. There are no fees to visit. Open Monday through Friday from 8 AM to 4 PM. Open Saturday from 10 AM to 4 PM. 495 South Dakota Ave; Fort Leonard Wood, MO 65473; Phone: (573) 596-0780; https://showmefortleonardwood.wordpress.com/2018/09/05/fort-leonard-wood-museum-complex

Gray Summit, MO

Purina Farms has barnyard animals, dogs, cats, and offers cow milking, wagon rides, hayloft activities, and daily dog shows. Admission is free except during special events. Open Wednesday through Sunday from 9:30 AM to 3:30 PM. In summer also open on Tuesday. 200 Checkerboard Dr; Gray Summit, MO 63039; Phone: (314) 982-3232; https://www.purina.com/purina-farms/visit/visiting-purina-farms

Hannibal, MO

Famous for being the home of Mark Twain (born Samuel Clemens), most of the Twain sites will incur a fee. Twain fans will also want to check out Florida, Missouri for more Twain places.

Hannibal History Museum uses photographs, artifacts, and interactive exhibits to illuminate the stories of famous Hannibal residents as well as the town's history. Closed in January and in February open by appointment only. March through October open daily. November and December closed on Tuesday and Wednesday. Admission is free. 200 N Main St; Hannibal, MO 63401; Phone: (573) 221-1819; http://www.hannibalhistorymuseum.com

Independence, MO

There is a fee to visit the Harry S. Truman National Historic Site, but history lovers can follow the *Truman Walking Trail*. The trail begins at the Truman Home Ticket Center at Main Street and Truman Road and takes you past 43 plaques embedded in the sidewalks throughout the National Historic Landmark

District. Brochures are available at key points along the route or download it: http://www.ci.independence.mo.us/comdev/HP_WalkingTours_Truman **Mormon Visitor Center** greets visitors with exhibits on Mormon settlers in Missouri between 1831 and 1839 as well as exhibits on the importance of families, messages from modern prophets and from the Book of Mormon. Admission is free. Open daily October through April from 10 AM to 7 PM. From May through September open daily from 9 AM to 9 PM and on Sunday from 10 AM to 9 PM. 937 W Walnut; Independence, MO 64050; Phone: (816) 836-3466; https://www.lds.org/locations/independence-visitors-center

Jefferson City, MO

Governor's Mansion Tours are available but advance reservations are required for all visitors. Tours are provided February through mid-May on Tuesday through Thursday from 10 AM to 1:45 PM, and again in September and October on Tuesday through Thursday from 9 AM to 11:30 AM. 201 W Capitol Ave; Jefferson City, MO 65101; Phone: (573) 751-2854; https://mostateparks.com/page/60074/tours

Jefferson Landing was a center of commerce with steamboats traveling between St. Louis and Kansas City docking in front of the **Lohman Building** (which now features an 1850s general store and warehouse). The nearby Union Hotel contains the **Elizabeth Rozier Gallery** with changing exhibits on Missouri history, art, and culture. There is no admission fee. Open from March through the first weekend in December on Tuesday through Saturday from 10 AM to 4 PM. 100 Jefferson St; Jefferson City, MO 65101; Phone: (573) 751-2854; https://mostateparks.com/page/55181/jefferson-landing-tours

Missouri State Capitol impresses visitors with Thomas Hart Benton's murals, and its location on a limestone bluff above the river. **Missouri State Museum**, located in the State Capitol, details the state's natural and cultural history. Free guided tours are held Monday through Friday starting at 9 AM with the last tour beginning at 3 PM. Saturday and Sunday tours start at 11 AM and 2 PM. Closed for one hour at Noon. No tours on major holidays. 201 W Capitol; Jefferson City, MO 65101; Phone: (573) 751-2854; https://mostateparks.com/page/55179/capitol-tours

Missouri Veterinary Medical Foundation Museum is dedicated solely to veterinary medicine with artifacts dating from the 16th century. There's also a hands-on children's learning center. Admission is free. Open Monday through Friday from 9 AM to 4 PM. Closed holidays. 2500 Country Club Dr; Jefferson City, MO 65109; Phone: (573) 636-8612; http://www.movma.org/page/Museum

Museum of Missouri Military History preserves Missouri's military history from the Revolutionary War to the present day. Military equipment is on display outside. You will need to show a photo ID at the center's main gate. Free admission. Open Tuesday through Saturday from 10 AM to 4 PM. 2405 Logistics Rd; Jefferson City, MO 65101; Phone: (573) 638-9603; http://www.moguard.com/public-affairs/museum-of-missouri-military-history

Supreme Court of Missouri welcomes visitors with free scheduled 30-minute guided tours Monday through Friday every half-hour from 9 AM to 11 AM, and from 2 PM to 3:30 PM. No tours are offered on public holidays, and when the Court is scheduled to hear oral arguments. Note: Visitors to the building are subject to security screening measures. 207 W High St; Jefferson City, MO 65101; Phone: (573) 751-7331; https://www.courts.mo.gov/page.jsp?id=100

Joplin, MO
Spiva Center for the Arts has free exhibitions and community events. Donations are gratefully accepted. Open Tuesday through Saturday from 10 AM to 5 PM. Closed most major holidays. 222 W Third St; Joplin, MO 64801; Phone: (417) 623-0183; https://spivaarts.org

Independence, MO
Independence is the birthplace of Harry Truman, but most of the locations associated with his life charge a fee to visit. One exception is the tour of the Truman Courthouse.
Truman Courthouse contains Truman's original office and courtroom from the late 1920s and early '30s. The Jackson County Historical Society holds free tours with days and times subject to change. 112 W Lexington Ave; Independence, MO 64050; Phone: (816) 252-7454; http://jchs.org/truman-courthouse

Kansas City, MO
Hallmark Visitors Center is open Monday through Saturday from 9:30 AM to 4:00 PM offering free self-guided behind-the-scenes tours. On Monday through Friday from 1 PM to 2 PM a writer, illustrator, designer, photographer, or sculptor is at the Hallmark Live exhibit to talk with visitors. Crown Center Complex; 2450 Grand Blvd; Kansas City, MO 64108; Phone: (816) 274-3613; http://www.hallmarkvisitorscenter.com

Kemper Museum of Contemporary Art features modern and contemporary works of art from around the world. Admission is free. Open Tuesday through Sunday at 10 AM, closes at 4 PM. Open until 9 PM on Thursday and Friday.

4420 Warwick Blvd; Kansas City, MO 64111; Phone: (816) 753-5784; https://www.kemperart.org

Money Museum at the Federal Reserve Bank of Kansas City offers a free look of the nation's financial system. Interactive exhibits include lifting a solid gold bar, adding your photo to the center of custom designed currency, and looking into a four-story cash vault. Admission is free. Open Monday through Friday from 9:30 AM to 4 PM. Closed bank holidays. Note: Visitors 18 and older must present a photo ID, state issued ID, or a passport. International visitors must present a valid passport. 1 Memorial Dr; Kansas City, MO 64198; Phone: (816) 881-2683; https://www.kansascityfed.org/moneymuseum

Nelson-Atkins Museum of Art provides art, architecture, and sculpture. Free to visit, although special exhibits incur a charge. Open Wednesday from 10 AM to 5 PM, and Thursday and Friday from 10 AM to 9 PM. Open Saturday and Sunday from 10 AM to 5 PM. 4525 Oak St; Kansas City, MO 64111; Phone: (816) 751-1278; https://nelson-atkins.org

Oak Ridge, MO
Pinecrest Azalea Gardens features both walking and driving paths. Free admission. Open only March through mid-May during daylight hours. 799 Torre La; Oak Ridge, MO 63769; Phone: (573) 979-1112; http://pinecrestazaleagardens.com

Pineville, MO
McDonald County Historical Society Museum recreates a courtroom, prosecutor's office, telephone room and drug store. The museum is free to visit with donations gratefully accepted. Open summers only on Friday and Saturday from 10 AM to 4 PM. 400 Main St; Pineville, MO 64856; Phone: (417) 223-7700; http://www.mcdonaldcohistory.org/museum.html

Rolla, MO
Ed Clark Museum of Missouri Geology provides minerals, rocks, fossils, even mammoth tusks. The museum also hosts a computer program that depicts earthquake occurrences. Admission is free. Open Monday through Friday from 8 AM to 5 PM. Closed federal and state holidays. 111 Fairgrounds Rd; Rolla, MO 65401; Phone: (573) 368-2100; https://dnr.mo.gov/geology/edclarkmuseum.htm

Missouri S&T Mineral Display holds over 4,000 minerals from over 92 countries. Admission is free. Open Monday through Friday from 8 AM to 4 PM.

129 McNutt Hall; Missouri S&T Campus; 1400 N Bishop; Rolla, MO 65401; Phone: (573) 341-4573; https://ggpe.mst.edu/mineral-collection

Sedalia, MO

Daum Museum of Contemporary Art specializes in works of contemporary art as well as special exhibits in nine galleries on three levels. Admission is free with donations welcomed. Open Tuesday through Friday from 11 AM to 5 PM and on Saturday and Sunday from 1 PM to 5 PM. 3201 W 16th St; Sedalia, MO 65301; Phone: (660) 530-5888; http://www.daummuseum.org

St. Charles, MO

Fast Lane Classic Cars delights lovers of classic cars with over 180 vehicles in two buildings. Free to visit. Open Monday and Friday from 9 AM to 7 PM, and Tuesday through Thursday from 9 AM to 6 PM. Open Saturday from 9 AM to 5 PM. 427 Little Hills Blvd; St Charles, MO 63301; Phone: (636) 940-9969; https://fastlanecars.com

Ste. Genevieve, MO

Felix Valle House State Historic Site hosts 18th and early 19th century buildings tracing the community's history from French and then Spanish control until finally becoming part of the United States via the 1803 Louisiana Purchase. Explore the grounds for free, but building tours will incur a fee. 198 Merchant St; Ste. Genevieve, MO 63670; Phone: (573) 883-7102; https://mostateparks.com/park/felix-valle-house-state-historic-site

St. Louis, MO (See also St. Charles, MO, and Valley Park, MO)

This tourist-friendly city offers **Forest Park**, home to many of the city's museums. Most offer free admission, although some special exhibits and experiences will incur a cost. **The Zoo** is free but most of the activities that appeal to children do cost: https://www.stlzoo.org/visit/hours-prices. **Saint Louis Science Center** offers free general admission but their special experiences will incur a significant fee including the shows and planetarium, simulators, and their Discovery Room. https://www.slsc.org/visit. The only museum that is completely free is Missouri History Museum listed below. Learn more about the museums and their fees at: https://www.forestparkforever.org/park-attractions

Anheuser-Busch Brewery is the largest and oldest brewery and the site of their free St. Louis General Brewery Tour. It is offered throughout the year. Note: For tour times, they advise checking at the reception desk. Tickets are free and are available on a first come, first served basis. If you wish to reserve a spot, there is a $5 fee. Note: There are several other specialized fee-based tours offered. 12th and Lynch St; St. Louis, MO 63118; Phone: (314) 577-2626; http://www.budweisertours.com

Bellefontaine Cemetery blends final resting places with historical significance, and a 314-acre arboretum. On select Saturdays from March through November visitors can take a free bus/trolley tour of the cemetery. They also offer free three-mile walking tours. Register to attend by reviewing their events calendar or calling the office. Self-guided tours are available daily from 8 AM through 5 PM. 4947 W Florissant Ave; St. Louis, MO 63115; Phone: (314) 381-0750; http://bellefontainecemetery.org

Calvary Cemetery invites visitors to pay tribute at the graves of Tennessee Williams, Gen. William Tecumseh Sherman, and Dred Scott as well as study the architecturally significant private mausoleums and monuments. A free self-guided historic tour pamphlet is available at the office and online. Open daily 8 AM to 5 PM. 5239 W Florissant Ave; St. Louis, MO 63115; Phone: (314) 792-7738; http://greatriverroad.com/stlouis/calvary.htm

Citygarden offers landscaping, public art, and its unique Video Wall which comes to life at night with movies, photography, and art videos. Admission is free. Open daily sunrise to 10 PM. Brochures are available in boxes located around the central walking paths in the park. 801 Market St; St. Louis, MO 63101; Phone: (314) 241-3337; http://www.citygardenstl.org

Contemporary Art Museum St. Louis curates themed exhibits. Admission is free. Open Wednesday through Sunday at 10 AM. Closes at 5 PM on Wednesday, Saturday and Sunday. Closes at 8 PM on Thursday and Friday. Closed major holidays and between exhibits. 3750 Washington Blvd; St. Louis, MO 63108; Phone: (314) 535-4660; http://camstl.org

Gateway Arch Museum traces the story of the Native Americans, explorers, pioneers, and rebels featuring 200 years of the westward expansion of the United States. The Museum at the Gateway Arch is free, and a ticket is not required to enter the museum or Arch visitor center. Open daily in winter from 9 AM to 6 PM and in summer from 8 AM to 10 PM. Note: You will need a purchased ticket to ride to the top of the Arch and to see the documentary movie. 11 N Fourth St; St. Louis, MO 63102; Phone: (314) 655-1600; https://www.archpark.org/visit/points-of-interest/museum-at-the-gateway-arch

Grant's Farm was named for Ulysses S. Grant who originally worked a portion of the land. The 1855 cabin Grant built was bought by August Busch Sr. in 1907 and moved to its present location. Admission is free, as are tram rides and all the shows. A few of the attractions will incur a fee. Note: There is a $12 parking fee. Grant's Farm is open seasonally, generally mid-April through the end of September. 10501 Gravois Rd; St. Louis, MO 63123; Phone: (314) 843-1700; http://www.grantsfarm.com/home.html

Holocaust Museum & Learning Center chronicles the history of the Holocaust interspersed with the personal accounts of survivors who immigrated to St. Louis. Photographs, artifacts, text panels, and audio-visual displays depict pre-war Jewish life in Europe, the rise of Nazism, and events of the Holocaust between 1933 and 1945. Admission is free. Open Monday through Thursday from 9:30 AM to 4:30 PM. Closes Fridays at 4 PM. Open Sunday 10 AM to 4 PM. Free, guided tours every Sunday at 10:30 AM. 12 Millstone Campus Dr; St. Louis, MO 63146; Phone: (314) 432-0020; https://www.jfedstl.org/direct-services/hmlc

Inside the Economy Museum at the Federal Reserve Bank is a family-friendly destination with interactive displays, games, sculptures, and videos. The museum is organized into five zones each devoted to a different aspect of the economic education. Admission is free. Open Monday through Friday from 9 AM to 3 PM. Closed holidays. 1 Federal Reserve Bank Plaza; Broadway and Locust St; St. Louis, MO 63166; Phone: (314) 444-7309; https://www.stlouisfed.org/inside-the-economy-museum

James S. McDonnell Prologue Room showcases the pioneers of aviation and their milestone events. Models of aircraft and spacecraft are also on display. Hundreds of scale models, dioramas, paintings, photographs and videos focus on the companies that make up the Boeing Company. Prologue Room is free to visit. Open for self-guided tours in June, July and August, on Monday through Friday from 9 AM to 4 PM. Building 100; 8905 Airport Rd; St Louis, MO 63134; Phone: (314) 232-6896; https://www.boeing.com/company/tours/prologue-room.page

Laumeier Sculpture Park offers 60 large-scale outdoor sculptures in a 105-acre park. Free and open daily, visitors are asked to first register at the visitor center located in the Adam Aronson Fine Arts Center. Although the sculpture park is open daily from 8 AM to sunset, the Fine Arts Center is open daily from 10 AM to 4 PM. 12580 Rott Rd; St. Louis, MO 63127; Phone: (314) 615-5278; http://www.laumeiersculpturepark.org

Mildred Lane Kemper Art Museum at Washington University specializes in contemporary art. Admission is free. Open Wednesday through Monday from 11 AM to 5 PM. Closed university holidays. 1 Brookings Dr; St. Louis, MO 63130; Phone: (314) 935-4523; http://www.kemperartmuseum.wustl.edu

Missouri History Museum offers both permanent and time-limited exhibits. Admission is free although there is a fee for some of their special exhibits. Open daily from 10 AM to 5 PM with extended hours on Tuesday until 8 PM. Closed Thanksgiving and Christmas Day. Lindell Blvd and DeBaliviere Ave; St. Louis, MO 63177; Phone: (314) 746-4599; http://mohistory.org

Moto Museum fills its galleries with motorcycles and related items spanning 1900 to 1975 and covering more than 20 countries The museum was created by motorcycle enthusiast Steve Smith. Admission is free although donations are appreciated. Open Monday from 9 AM to 3 PM. Open Tuesday through Friday from 9 AM to 4 PM. Closed for private events. Note: They recommend calling first. 3441 Olive St; St. Louis, MO 63103; Phone: (314) 446-1805; https://www.themotomuseum.com

Museum of Contemporary Religious Art examines the intersection of contemporary art and religious themes. Admission is free. Open only during exhibitions on Wednesday through Sunday from 11 AM to 4 PM, open until 7 PM on Thursday. Closed for some holidays. Check their website for current information. Saint Louis University; 3700 W Pine Blvd; St. Louis, MO 63103; Phone: (314) 977-7170; https://www.slu.edu/mocra

Old Courthouse was the site of the first two trials in the pivotal Dred Scott case in 1847 and 1850. It was also where Virginia Minor's case for a woman's right to vote came to trial in the 1870s. Tour this historic structure, and visit the restored courtrooms to learn more about the 19th century judicial system. The Courthouse features trial re-enactments and ranger-led tours. Free admission. Open daily. From Memorial Day through Labor Day open from 7:30 AM to 8 PM. The rest of the year open 8 AM to 5 PM. Closed Thanksgiving, Christmas, and New Year's Day. 11 N Fourth St; St. Louis, MO 63102; Phone: (314) 655-1600; https://explorestlouis.com/partner/old-courthouse

Samuel Cupples House is a Romanesque Revival home, built with 42 rooms and 22 fireplaces, with a gallery for SLU's collection of pre-1919 fine and decorative art. It also includes the extraordinary glass collection of Eleanor Turshin. Starting in the 1950s Turshin operated a jewelry factory. During her travels she became fascinated by art glass and amassed one of the world's best examples of art nouveau, and art deco glass with pieces from Steuben, Tiffany, Daum, and Lalique. Admission is free. Open Tuesday through Saturday from 11 AM to 4 PM. 3673 W Pine; St. Louis, MO 63103; Phone: (314) 977-6631; https://www.slu.edu/samuel-cupples-house

Schlafly Bottleworks invites visitors to come for the tour and enjoy the beer. Both are free. Tours are currently offered on Friday, Saturday, and Sunday. Note: You must wear completely closed shoes. Calling ahead to check tour times is strongly advised. 7260 Southwest Ave; St. Louis, MO 63143; Phone: (314) 241-2337; http://schlafly.com/tours

St. Louis Art Museum and Grace Taylor Broughton Sculpture Garden highlights international 20th century and contemporary sculpture. The garden features more than 400 trees arranged to form arboreal enclosures. The East Building contains more than 33,000 works from African American to Textile Arts. Admission to the museum is free although there is a fee for featured exhibitions (except on Fridays). Open daily from 6 AM to 10 PM. Closed Thanksgiving, and Christmas Day. 1 Fine Arts Dr; St. Louis, MO 63110; Phone: (314) 721-0072; http://www.slam.org

St. Louis University Museum of Art has amassed a core collection of work by modern masters. Fans of Dale Chihuly should note the display in the museum's contemporary gallery. Admission to the museum is free although guided tours may incur a cost. Open Wednesday through Sunday from 11 AM to 4 PM. The hours are subject to change during holiday breaks. Closed on national holidays. Visitors are advised to call ahead to check hours. 3663 Lindell Blvd; St. Louis, MO 63108; Phone: (314) 977-6631; https://www.slu.edu/sluma/index.php

Ulysses S. Grant National Historic Site at Whitehaven encourages visitors to watch the introductory film *Ulysses S. Grant: A Legacy of Freedom* in the visitor center theater, walk the historic trail, visit his famous home and outbuildings, and explore the museum located in the original stable. Entrance into the site is free. Visits inside the main house are also free, but visitors need to pick up a ticket available at the visitor center allowing access at a specific time. 7400 Grant Rd; St. Louis, MO 63123; Phone: (314) 842-1867; https://www.nps.gov/ulsg/index.htm

Springfield, MO
Springfield Art Museum started with American art from the 18th century but now includes art of the Midwest, as well as textiles, decorative arts, and pottery. Large-scale sculptures are exhibited throughout the grounds. Admission is free with donations appreciated. Open Tuesday through Saturday from 10 AM to 6 PM. Open late Thursday until 8 PM. Open Sunday from 1 PM to 5 PM. Closed city and national holidays. 1111 E Brookside Dr; Springfield, MO 65807; Phone (417) 837-5700; https://www.sgfmuseum.org

Valley Park, MO
World Bird Sanctuary protects over 200 non-releasable birds and more than 500 birds receiving medical care. Their Nature Center houses a variety of birds, mammals, and reptiles. Admission is free as are seasonal shows, demonstrations, and hiking trails, plus Keeper Chats every Saturday and Sunday at 11 AM. A guided tour will incur a cost as will interacting with the animals and birds. Open daily from 8 AM to 5 PM. Closed Thanksgiving, and Christmas Day. Note: Parts of the sanctuary may be closed periodically for private paid programs. 125 Bald Eagle Ridge Rd; Valley Park, MO 63088; Phone: (636) 225-4390; https://www.worldbirdsanctuary.org

Waynesville, MO

Old Stagecoach Stop depicts the building's history with each of its 10 rooms recreating a moment in time from stage stop and tavern to hospital during the Civil War. Admission is free. Open seasonally April through September on Saturday, from 10 AM to 4 PM. 106 N Lynn St; Waynesville, MO 65583; Phone: (573) 336-3561; http://oldstagecoachstop.org

Montana

This larger-than-life state is a known for wide open spaces, tough cowboys, and rugged beauty. Its eastern edge is part of the Great Plains while the western end is the Rocky Mountains. Fee-based National Parks pull in thousands of visitors a year and deserve their popularity. But if you know where to look, there's plenty of history, and beauty to be seen for free, and the independent spirit of the people make for some very unusual attractions.

The tourism season in Montana is generally June through September. Many small places close in the off-season or have limited hours. Always check before you go. Montana State Parks are only free for residents. Visitors will have to pay a fee. If you live in Montana, learn more about your free parks at http://stateparks.mt.gov

Big Sandy, MT
Big Sandy Historical Museum features historical items from the local area and early pioneer ranching days. No charge to tour the museum, located in the old Burlington Northern train depot, but it gratefully accepts donations. Open June through August on Tuesday through Saturday from 10 AM to 4 PM. Main St (Hwy 87); Big Sandy, MT 59520; Phone: (406) 378-2640; https://www.visitmt.com/listings/general/museum/big-sandy-historical-museum.html

Big Timber, MT
Crazy Mountain Museum offers a replica Norwegian stabbur (storehouse), a tipi, and a one-room schoolhouse as well as a 12-foot by 6-foot display of the town of Big Timber as it existed in 1907. Admission is free with donations gratefully accepted. Open Memorial Day through September on Monday through Saturday from 10 AM to 4:30 PM, and on Sunday from 1 PM to 4:30 PM. 2 S Frontage Rd; Big Timber, MT 59011; Phone: (406) 932-5126; http://crazymountainmuseum.com

Billings, MT
Montana Pro Rodeo Hall and Wall of Fame honors Montana professional cowboys and cowgirls who achieve national recognition in the sport of rodeo. The larger than life bronze statue, sculpted by Western Artist R. F. Rains, depicts Dan Mortensen, six-time World Champion Bronc Rider riding Tee Box. The memorial wall contains the names of previous professional rodeo champions. The statue is located at the entrance to the MetraPark Arena on the Yellowstone County Fairgrounds. There is no admission fee, and it can be viewed 24 hours a day. 308

Sixth Ave N; Billings, MT 59101; Phone: (406) 256-6515;
http://www.montanaprorodeo.org

Museum of Women's History casts a light on the lives of women in Montana
and beyond. Exhibits feature women from all walks of life, all professions, and all
ethnic groups, both local and international. Admission is free and donations are
gratefully accepted. Open Monday, Tuesday, and Thursday from 1 PM to 4 PM
or by appointment. 2822 Third Ave N; B3; Billings, MT 59101; Phone: (406)
248-2015; http://www.visitbillings.com/visit/171/Museum-of-Womens-History

Yellowstone County Museum contains over 15,000 artifacts celebrating
Montana's past including handcrafted saddles, rare firearms, pioneer wagons,
tribal bead work, and cowboy and western artifacts. Free admission. Open
Tuesday through Saturday from 10:30 AM to 5:30 PM. Closed the month of
January and holidays. 1950 Airport Terminal Cir; Billings, MT 59105; Phone:
(406) 256-6811; http://www.ycmhistory.org

Butte, MT
Mineral Museum is part of the Montana Bureau of Mines and Geology, and
offers rocks and minerals from Montana, the world, and even outer space – about
13,000 specimens of which about 1,000 are displayed at any one time. Free to
visit. Open daily mid-June through mid-September from 9 AM to 5 PM. The rest
of the year open weekdays from 9 AM to 4 PM. Closed major holidays. 1300 W
Park St; Butte, MT 59701; Phone: (406) 496-4414;
https://mbmg.mtech.edu/museum/museum.html

Broadus, MT
Powder River Historical Museum & Mac's Museum has gathered a diversity of
items from photos and books, to vintage autos, tractors and farm implements.
Mac's Museum is Mr. Mac McCurdy with a collection of over a thousand
arrowheads, birds' eggs, butterflies, geologic specimens, as well as about 20,000 sea
shells. Museum entrance is free. Open June through September on Monday
through Friday from 9 AM to 5 PM. 102 W Wilson; Broadus, MT 59317; Phone:
(406) 436-2977; https://www.visitmt.com/listings/general/museum/powder-river-
historical-museum-mac-s-museum.html

Browning, MT
Blackfeet Heritage Center & Art Gallery, owned and operated by the Blackfeet
Nation, exhibits and sells the work of more than 500 artists from 16 separate
North American tribes. There's also a baby Tyrannosaur skeleton that was found
on the Blackfeet reservation. Admission is free. Open daily June through October,
and weekdays in winter from 9 AM to 6: PM 333 Central Ave; Browning, MT

59417; Phone: (406) 338-5661; https://www.visitmt.com/listings/general/art-gallery/blackfeet-heritage-center-art-gallery.html

Chester, MT

Liberty County Museum provides exhibits on homesteading, farming, ranching, medicine, military, and business. Admission is free and donations are accepted. Open daily mid-May to Labor Day from 1 PM to 8 PM. 230 Second St E; Chester, MT 59522; Phone: (406) 759-5256; http://co.liberty.mt.us/museum

Chinook, MT

Bear Paw Battlefield and Blaine County Museum (See also Wisdom, MT – Big Hole National Battlefield Visitor Center) Critical to understanding the history of Native Americans and settlers is the story of the ongoing disputes between the Federal government and the Nez Perce and Chief Joseph. It started when several bands of Nez Perce resisted relocation from their traditional lands to a reservation in west-central Idaho. In 1855 the Nez Perce agreed to cede 7½ million acres of tribal land to the government while still retaining the right to hunt and fish. But when gold was discovered on the land, the rules changed. The ancestral lands allowed to the Nez Perce were severely reduced and the Nez Perce were required to move. Those who refused to relocate attempted to flee U.S. Army troops and reach sanctuary in Canada. They almost made it to safety, but following a five-day battle and siege, the Nez Perce ceased fighting. On October 5, 1877 Chief Joseph gave his immortal speech at Bear Paw "From where the sun now stands, I will fight no more forever." It was the final act in the Nez Perce war. They were only 40 miles away from the border and some did manage to escape to Canada. But for the rest it was a promise broken. It wasn't until 1885 that the Nez Perce were finally allowed to return to their homeland.

Blaine County Museum illuminates the battlefield events with historic artifacts found at the Bear Paw Battlefield, time-period photographs, and military equipment from the late1800s. There's also a twenty-minute multi-media presentation *Forty Miles from Freedom* recounting the events leading up to the Battle and Siege of the Bear Paw. Their exhibits also include prehistoric fossils from the area, and the remains of gigantic marine reptiles. No charge for admission. Open all year with seasonal hours. 501 Indiana St; Chinook, MT 59523; Phone: (406) 357.2590; http://www.blainecountymuseum.com

Bear Paw Battlefield commemorates the final battle of the Nez Perce War. The park is free to visit. A self-guided interpretive trail winds through the battlefield. The battlefield is open daily during daylight hours. Pick up a brochure/trail map at either the museum or the battlefield. Route 240; Chinook, MT 59523; Phone:

(208) 843-7009; https://www.nps.gov/nepe/planyourvisit/bear-paw-battlefield.htm

Deer Lodge, MT

Grant-Kohrs Ranch National Historic Site preserves a pioneer ranch, complete with original furnishings. Ranger-led programs are offered daily from Memorial Day through Labor Day. Tour the climate controlled storage facility and view some of the 35,000 items in the collection. Other tours include a guided visit to the ranch house and special ranger talks. There is no admission fee to the park or for their programs. Open daily from 9 AM to 5:30 PM Memorial Day through Labor Day. Closes at 4:30 the rest of the year. Closed Thanksgiving, Christmas, and New Year's Day. Call for off-season tour options. Exit 184 off I-90; Deer Lodge, MT 59722; Phone: (406) 846-2070 ext. 250; https://www.nps.gov/grko/index.htm

Ekalaka, MT

Carter County Museum highlights artifacts from Native American and early settlers of Carter County and the paleontology of the area There is no admission charge. Open all year on Monday through Friday from 9 AM to 5 PM. April through November also open Saturday from 9 AM to 5 PM and Sunday from 1 PM to 5 PM. December through May also open Saturday and Sunday from 1 PM to 5 PM. 306 N Main St; Ekalaka, MT 59324; Phone: (406) 775-6886; https://cartercountymuseum.org

Eureka, MT

Tobacco Valley Historical Village contains ten historic buildings and artifacts from the Tobacco Valley area covering the 1880s to the 1920s. Explore the general store, schoolhouse, library, church, two log cabins, hand-hewn house, railway depot, caboose, and fire tower. There is no admission charge although donations are appreciated. The museum is open Memorial Day through Labor Day from 1 PM to 5 PM. 4 Dewey Ave; Eureka, MT 59917; Phone: (406) 297-7654; http://www.tobaccovalleyhistory.org

Fort Peck, MT

Fort Peck Interpretive Center and Museum includes the two largest aquariums in Montana, and a life-size model of Peck's Rex – the Tyrannosaurus Rex that greets visitors in the lobby. Exhibits focus on the Charles M. Russell National Wildlife Refuge and Fort Peck Lake, as well as the construction history of Fort Peck Dam. There is no admission charge for either the Fort Peck Dam Interpretive Center or Museum or powerhouse tours. The center is open daily from May through September from 9 AM to 5 PM. The center is closed December through March. Reduced hours in October and November. Powerhouse tours are offered daily Memorial Day through September. No tours are available from October through Memorial Day. 157 Yellowstone Rd; Fort Peck, MT 59223; Phone: (406) 526-3493; https://www.fws.gov/refuge/Charles_M_Russell/visit/visitor_activities/FPIC.html

Gallatin Gateway, MT

Little Bear School House Museum features old school desks with ink wells and writing slates, a teacher's desk, authentic black boards, and books. There is no fee to visit the Little Bear School House Museum. Open Memorial Day through Labor Day on Friday, Saturday, and Sunday from 1 PM to 5 PM. 76200 Gallatin Rd; Gallatin Gateway, MT 59730; Phone: (406) 580-6228; https://www.facebook.com/littlebearschoolhousemuseum

Glendive, MT

Frontier Gateway Museum provides the history of Glendive through a blacksmith shop, two country stores, a buggy shed, a fire hall, a display of farm machinery, as well as a sheep wagon, log cabin and schoolhouse. Admission is free. Open Memorial Day to Labor Day on Monday through Saturday from 9 AM to 5 PM and on Sunday from 1 PM to 5 PM. 201 State St; Glendive, MT 59330; Phone: (406) 377-8168; http://www.frontiergatewaymuseum.org

Great Falls, MT

History Museum uses changing exhibits to recount the stories of the individuals and groups who have added to the diversity of the Central Montana region. Exhibits focus on military history, homesteading, and Glacier National Park. Admission is free. Open Tuesday through Friday from 10 AM to 5 PM. 422 Second St S; Great Falls, MT 59401; Phone: (406) 452-3462; http://www.thehistorymuseumgreatfalls.com

Paris Gibson Square Museum of Art features contemporary art with changing and permanent exhibitions. A highlight is the permanent exhibit of the unique figural sculptures of Lee Steen (1897-1975). These are truly stick figures, created from tree branches. His folk art once congregated in his yard, but they have now found a permanent home in this museum. The other permanent exhibit is by Great Falls artist Jean L. Price who creates dogtags for the soldiers lost in war. Admission is free. Open all year on Monday through Friday from 10 AM to 5 PM and Saturday from Noon to 5 PM. Closed major holidays. 1400 First Ave N; Great Falls, MT 59401; Phone: (406)727.8255; http://www.the-square.org

Helena, MT

Archie Bray Foundation for the Ceramic Arts is a treasure hunt for art. The 26 acres shelter ceramic artifacts and sculptures created by former resident artists as well as commissioned site-specific pieces. Tour the grounds for free during daylight hours, observe artists at work in the studios. A self-guided tour map is available in the mailbox in front of the Pottery. The North Gallery is open year-round. During the summer the Bray's Warehouse Gallery features work by current resident artists. Open Monday through Saturday from 10 AM to 5 PM and in June, July, and August it is also open on Sunday from 1 PM to 5 PM. 2915 Country Club Ave; Helena, MT 59602; Phone: (406) 443-3502; http://archiebray.org

Historic Reeder's Alley is the oldest intact piece of early Helena history and illuminates the lives of miners, the Chinese, and the men and women who sought their fortunes in Montana. Highlights include the Pioneer Cabin, reputed to be the oldest residence in Helena. Tours are available June, July, and August. The small extensions at the back of the Caretaker's House were used as *cribs* – tiny places where the women entertained the customers. The Yee Wau cabin next door is the only remaining Chinese-associated house in Helena. The Alley is open daylight hours. Reeder's Alley is located on South Park Avenue across from Pioneer Park. Phone: (406) 422-4727; https://reedersalley.com

Holter Museum of Art highlights artists who have captured the vistas and people of Montana. Admission is free. Open Tuesday through Saturday from 10 AM to 5:30 PM and on Sunday from Noon to 4 PM. 12 E Lawrence St; Helena, MT 59601; Phone: (406) 442-6400; https://www.holtermuseum.org

Montana Military Museum Fort Harrison takes visitors from 1805 through the 20th century. Admission and tours are free. Donations welcomed. Open Thursday from 9 AM to 4 PM and upon request. Note: Bring a Photo ID to enter the Fort. Fort Harrison Complex; 1956 Mt Majo St; Helena, MT 59602; Phone: (406) 324-3550; https://www.montanamilitarymuseum.org

Montana State Capitol invites visitors to explore on their own with booklets available at the information desk on the first floor of the Capitol. The most notable feature inside the Greek neo-classical building are the four circular paintings from 1902 surrounding the rotunda. They depict four archetypical people of Montana's early history – a native American (Chief Charlo), an explorer and fur trapper (Jim Bridger), a gold miner (Henry Finnis Edgar), and a cowboy (said to be inspired by the works of Western painter C.M. Russell). The capitol is open to visitors all year on Monday through Saturday from 8 AM to 5 PM. Note: There are fees associated with Montana Historical Society Museum and Original Governor's Mansion. 1301 E Sixth Ave; Helena, MT 59601; Phone: (406) 444-4789; https://mhs.mt.gov/education/capitoltours

Libby, MT

Libby Dam Visitor Center offers guided tours of the dam and powerhouse. One highlight is the massive 75-ton granite sculpture on the face of the Treaty Tower. Admission and tours are free. Open Memorial Day through Labor Day. The visitor center is open 9:30 AM to 6 PM. Tours are available at 10 AM, Noon, 2 PM and 4 PM. Hours vary after Labor Day and visitors are advised to call ahead for hours and tour availability. Note: Photo ID required for adults. 17877 Highway 37; Libby, MT 59923; Phone:(406) 293-5577; https://www.nws.usace.army.mil/Missions/Civil-Works/Locks-and-Dams/Libby-Dam/Information

Missoula, MT

Fort Missoula grounds are always open, always free and include an extensive collection of buildings – a total of 20 structures including the Noncommissioned Officer's Quarters (1878), Alien Detention Center Barracks (1940), Engine No.7 (1923), and the Library Car (1921) from the Anaconda Copper Mining Company. Visitors can enter any out-buildings with open doors as well as climb the lookout tower. For a map of the grounds visit: http://buildings.fortmissoulamuseum.org Note: There is a museum on the grounds that charges an admission fee, although residents of Missoula can visit the museum for free. 3400 Captain Rawn Way; Missoula, MT 59804; Phone (406) 728-3476; http://www.fortmissoulamuseum.org/index.php

Missoula Art Museum concentrates on the American West with an emphasis on contemporary Montana artists. Its signature collection is the Contemporary American Indian Art Collection. Admission and tours of the museum are free. Open Tuesday through Saturday 10 AM to 5 PM. 335 No Pattee; Missoula, MT 59802; Phone: (406) 728.0447; http://www.missoulaartmuseum.org

Montana Museum of Work History celebrates the innovation and work ethic with displays of antique firearms, steam and gas engines, automobiles, tools of all descriptions, logging, and mining equipment. Located within the Axmen retail store in Missoula. Admission is free. Open Tuesday through Friday from 8:30 AM to 5:30 PM and Saturday from 9 AM to 2 PM. 7655 U.S. Hwy 10 W; Missoula, MT 59808; Phone: (406) 728-7020; http://www.montanamuseumofworkhistory.com

Smokejumper Visitor Center honors those who jump out of planes and into forest fires. This is the largest base in the country and the visitor center explains the world of smokejumpers. There's an actual fire lookout from 1937 that visitors can explore. The tours look at the profession of smokejumping and enable visitors to learn about jump gear, parachutes, cargo, and aircraft. Tours are free. Open daily from Memorial Day through Labor Day from 8:30 AM to 5 PM. Call to schedule a tour at other times. 5765 W Broadway St; Missoula, MT 59808; Phone: (406) 329-4934; https://www.fs.fed.us/science-technology/fire/smokejumpers/missoula/center

Shelby, MT
Marias Museum of History and Art features early homestead history from dinosaur fossils to vintage toys. Rooms recreate a historic medical office, parlor, and country store. There's also memorabilia from the Dempsey-Gibbons heavyweight championship fight that was held on July 4, 1923 in the town of Shelby. Open June, July, and August on Monday through Friday from 1 PM to 7 PM and on Saturday from 1 PM to 4 PM. From September through May open only on Tuesday from 1 PM to 4 PM. 1129 First St N; Shelby, MT 59474; Phone: (406) 424-2551; http://toolecountymt.gov/museum.html

Sidney, MT
MonDak Heritage Center provides stories, artifacts, and photographs on local culture. The center also on displays the art of J.K. Ralston who celebrated the American West. Admission is free. Open Tuesday through Friday from 10 AM to 4 PM and Saturday from 1 PM to 4 PM. Note: there was an admission charge for several years but in 2019 the center was opened to the public to enjoy for free. 120 Third Ave SE; Sidney, MT 59270; Phone: (406) 433-3500; http://mondakheritagecenter.org

Terry, MT
Prairie County Museum and Cameron Gallery grew from the 1906 State Bank of Terry building to include the only steam heated outhouse west of the Mississippi, a pioneer homestead, the Burlington Northern train depot, an old red wooden caboose and the Evelyn Cameron Gallery. Admission is free with donations gratefully accepted. Open Memorial Day to Labor Day on Monday, Wednesday, Thursday, and Friday from 9 AM to 3 PM. Open on Saturday and Sunday from 1 PM to 4 PM. 101 S Logan Ave; Terry, MT 59349; Phone: (406) 635-4040; https://www.visitmt.com/listings/general/museum/prairie-county-museum-and-evelyn-cameron-gallery.html

Twin Bridges, MT
R. L. Winston Rod Company Factory offers free tours and the chance to try one of their rods out on their casting lawn. Open Monday through Friday from 8 AM to 5 PM with free tours at 11 AM. 500 S Main St; Twin Bridges, MT 59754; Phone: (406) 684-5674; https://winstonrods.com/about-winston/contact

Wibaux, MT

Pierre Wibaux Museum displays items from early-day settlers in this area and the story of Pierre Wibaux and his life. There's also a Montana Centennial Train Car which went to the World's Fair in New York in 1964, an antique barber shop, and a livery stable. Admission is free, and the museum also offers a free historic walking tour. Open Memorial Day to Labor Day on Monday through Saturday from 9 AM to 5 PM and Sunday from 1 PM to 5 PM. 112 E Orgain Ave; Wibaux, MT 59353; Phone: (406) 796-9969; https://www.visitmt.com/listings/general/museum/wibaux-museum.html

Winifred, MT

Winifred Museum features items from the town's early days and the Native tribes that predated it. They also display a collection of Tonka toys reputed to be the largest collection in the world. Admission is free, but donations are greatly appreciated. Open seasonally. Visitors are advised to call for current hours. 210 Main St; Winifred, MT 59489; Phone: (406) 462-5425; http://www.winifredmontana.com/winifred-museum

Wisdom, MT (See also Chinook, MT, the Bear Paw Battlefield, and Blaine County Museum)

Big Hole National Battlefield Visitor Center presents the complicated and tumultuous history of the Nez Perce. Relations that started out peacefully had become contentious by the 1870s. The Federal government demanded that the Nez Perce give up their lands in the Pacific Northwest and move to a reservation in Idaho, even though it was in violation of a previous treaty. A small band of Nez Perce Indians refused and lost the battle with the U.S. Army near the Big Hole River in Montana. With the goal of escaping to Canada, the Nez Perce made camp in the Big Hole Basin. On August 9, 1877 Colonel John Gibbon attacked. The cost to the Nez Perce was seen on August 10th. Almost 90 Nez Perce were dead (including women and children) along with 31 soldiers and volunteers. The remaining Nez Perce escaped, again trying to reach Canada. But two months later Colonel Nelson Miles decisively defeated the Nez Perce at the Battle of the Bear Paw Mountains (See Chinook, MT). The Big Hole National Battlefield was created to honor all who were there. The visitor center has exhibits, artifacts, and award winning 26 minute film *There is No Turning Back* about those events. There's also three self-guided trails and ranger-led tours and talks. Entrance to the battlefield is free. Open daily all year in summer from 9 AM to 5 PM and in winter from 10 AM to 5 PM. Closed federal holidays in October through February. 16425 Hwy 43 West; Wisdom, MT 59761; Phone: (406) 689-3155; https://www.nps.gov/biho/index.htm

Nebraska

Alliance, NE

Carhenge is a hybrid of Amarillo's Cadillac Ranch and England's Stonehenge. Jim Reinders conceived Carhenge as a memorial to his father. He covered 38 cars with grey paint and then placed them to reproduce Stonehenge in a circle about 96 feet in diameter. Admission is free but donations are appreciated. 2151 CR 59; Alliance, NE 69301; Phone: (308) 762-3569; http://carhenge.com

Dobby's Frontier Town depicts life in the small frontier town in the Nebraska Sandhills. Restored buildings and businesses are filled with antiques and tools. Admission is free with donations appreciated. Open daily May through October from 10 AM to 6 PM. 320 E 25th St; Alliance, NE 69301; http://dobbysfrontiertown.com/wordpress

Knight Museum and Sandhills Center proves history can be fascinating. It takes a broad view of local history presented through the lives of the people who lived there. Admission is free. In summer open daily Monday through Friday from 8 AM to 7 PM, Saturday from 10 AM to 6 PM, and Sunday from 1 PM to 5 PM. In winter open Monday through Friday from 8 AM to 5 PM and Saturday from 10 AM to 5 PM. 908 Yellowstone Ave; Alliance, NE, 69301; Phone: (308) 762-2384; https://knightmuseum.com

Beatrice, NE

Homestead National Monument of America uses interactive indoor exhibits and living history experiences to introduce visitors to the Homestead Act of 1862. The act transferred more than 270 million acres of land from federal to private ownership as hopeful farmers (including immigrants and freed slaves) spread across the land previously home to groups of Native Americans known today as the Plains Indians. The grounds include the Palmer-Epard cabin built in 1867, and the Freeman school (named after a local family) which was in use from 1872 until 1967. There is no fee to visit. Open daily, all year, except Thanksgiving, Christmas, and New Year's Day. The trails are open sunrise to sunset. From Memorial Day to Labor Day the Heritage Center and Education Center are open daily from 8:30 AM to 6 PM. The Freeman school is open daily from 1 PM to 4 PM. The rest of the year the center is open weekdays from 8:30 AM to 5 PM and weekends from 9 AM to 5 PM. The Freeman school is open upon request. 8523 W State Highway 4; Beatrice, NE 68310; Phone: (402) 223-3514; http://www.nps.gov/home

Crawford, NE

Fort Robinson State Park offers hiking, mountain biking, fishing on its over 22,000 acres as well as important history. It started a military post in 1874 and was the site of the notorious 1879 Cheyenne Outbreak. A band of Northern Cheyenne were being held at the fort. Fearing that they would be sent to Oklahoma (which had been declared Indian Territory) they tried to escape. Most were killed, and the few that survived were returned to the fort. Fort Robinson was also the site of the bayonet killing of the Oglala Sioux leader chief Crazy Horse. In fact you can stand where he was attacked and visit the building in which he died. The State Historical Society operates a fee-based museum but there are also restored or reconstructed buildings which interpret the fort's history that are free to visit. 3200 US Hwy 20; Crawford, NE 69339; Phone: (308) 665-2900; http://www.stateparks.com/fort_robinson_state_park_in_nebraska.html

Gering, NE

Scotts Bluff National Monument honors the pioneers who made the perilous crossing to the new lands of the west. The bluff was also a landmark for Native Americans as well as emigrants on the Oregon, California, and Mormon Trails. Stand at the summit (a shuttle is often available to bring visitors to the top of the overlook) and peer down at Mitchell Pass – the gateway to the West. Hike the trails, browse the exhibits in the museum, and watch the 12-minute video on the Oregon Trail. There is no entrance fee. The park grounds and trails are open from sunrise to sunset. The visitor center is open daily from 8 AM to 4:30 PM, and to 6 PM in summer. State Hwy 92 West; Gering NE 69341; Phone: (308) 436-9700; https://www.nps.gov/scbl/index.htm

Harrison, NE

Agate Fossil Beds National Monument stretches back well over 5 million years and contains bones preserved in one of the world's most significant Miocene Epoch mammal sites. The Daemonelix Trail features fossil exhibits, while the Fossil Hills Trail takes visitors around the historic early 1900s quarries that are the source for the monument's most famous fossil finds. The trails are open daily from dawn to dusk. Guides for both trails are located at the trailheads and in the visitor center. The video *The Fossil Hills* is shown on request. The Cook Collection consists of artifacts the Cook family received in the late 1800s and early 1900s from close family friends like Red Cloud, Chief of the Oglala Lakota. Admission is free. The visitor center is open daily 8 AM to 4 PM. Closed some major holidays. 301 River Rd; Harrison, NE 69346; Phone: (308) 668-2211; https://www.nps.gov/agfo/index.htm

Kearney, NE

Museum of Nebraska Art highlights works from artist-explorer George Catlin, and Thomas Hart Benton's original illustrations for the Oregon Trail. MONA also displays a collection of wildlife art by John James Audubon. The Cliff Hillegass Sculpture Garden presents outdoor art. Free admission. Open Tuesday to Saturday from 10 AM to 5 PM. Open Sunday from Noon to 5 PM. Closed major holidays. 2401 Central Ave; Kearney, NE 68847; Phone: (308) 865-8559; https://mona.unk.edu/mona

Lewellen, NE

Windlass Hill Trail offers a ½ mile loop walking trail winding up a steep hill that the pioneers had to traverse with their wagons. An exhibit tells the history of the area. Visitors can still see some of the wagon ruts. The grounds are open daily 8 AM to sunset. There is no charge to visit. Note: Windlass Hill is physically separate but a part of Ash Hollow State Historical Park which requires a fee to visit, and its visitor center charges an additional fee. Hwy 26; Lewellen, NE 69147; Phone: (308) 778-5651; https://www.alltrails.com/trail/us/nebraska/windlass-hill-trail

Lincoln, NE

National Museum of Roller Skating holds a collection of historical roller skates dating to 1819. The museum offers films, videotapes, and even costumes. Admission is free. Open Monday through Friday from 9 AM to 5 PM. 4730 South St; Lincoln, NE 68506; Phone: (402) 483-7551; http://www.rollerskatingmuseum.com

Nebraska History Museum explores 12,000 years of Nebraska history, with special themed exhibits ranging from quilting heritage to depictions of the Wild West. Admission is free. Open Monday to Friday from 10 AM to 5:30 PM. Open Saturday from 1 PM to 5:30 PM. 131 Centennial Mall N; Lincoln, NE 68508; Phone: (402) 471-4754; http://www.nebraskahistory.org/sites/mnh/exhibits.htm

Nebraska State Capitol is filled with murals dedicated to all the acts of daily heroism from nursing to fighting poverty, illness, as well as military service. The observation deck provides an impressive city view. Open daily Monday through Friday from 8 AM to 5 PM. Open Saturday and most holidays from 10 AM to 5 PM. Open Sunday from 1 PM to 5 PM. Tours are available on the hour except at Noon. 1445 K St; Lincoln, NE 68508; Phone: (402) 471–0448; http://capitol.nebraska.gov/visit

Sheldon Museum of Art curates themed exhibitions. Admission is free. Open Monday through Saturday from 10 AM to 5 PM, and open until 7 PM on Thursday and Friday. Open Sunday from Noon to 5 PM. Note: the museum closes on major holidays, during installation of new exhibits, and on the days of home football games. More than thirty of the museum's monumental sculptures are exhibited throughout the University of Nebraska campus. 1209 R St; Lincoln, NE 68508; Phone: (402) 472-2461; http://www.sheldonartgallery.org

Sunken Gardens uses over 30,000 individual annual plants to create a different visual experience each year. Admission is free, donations are accepted. Garden hours are 6 AM to 11 PM daily. S 27th St and Capitol Pkwy; Lincoln, NE 68502; Phone: (402) 441-8258; http://lincoln.ne.gov/city/parks /parksfacilities/publicgardens/sunken/index.htm

North Platte, NE

Cody Park Railroad Museum displays a Union Pacific 3977 and offers hands-on displays of historic railroad artifacts. Enjoy the fully restored railroad depot, several rail cars, and a caboose. Admission is free. Open daily all year with longer hours May through September. 1400 N Jeffers St; North Platte, NE 69101; Phone: (800) 955-4528; http://visitnorthplatte.com/attraction/cody-park-railroad-museum

Fort Cody Trading Post is part gift shop, part museum. Its Old West Museum includes a 20,000 piece hand-carved miniature replica of the Buffalo Bill Wild West Show. The scenes were created by Ernie and Virginia Palmquist over a 12 year period. There's also guns, chaps, boots, hats, and saddles. There's no charge to see the exhibits. Open every day, except Easter Sunday, Thanksgiving, Christmas, and New Year's Day. Extended hours in summer. 221 Halligan Dr; North Platte, NE 69101; Phone: (308) 532-0801; https://www.fortcody.com

Ogallala, NE

Boot Hill in Ogallala is set apart by its distinctive sculpture. Boot Hill is not an uncommon name for cemeteries in the West. The name came from the deaths of these men with their boots on – suddenly and likely violently. These graves, however, are watched over by bronze statue called *The Trail Boss*, a replica of the statue which was part of a larger tableau sculpted by Robert Summers for Pioneer Plaza in Dallas. Ogallala's Boot Hill was also the final resting place for women, and children. Sites of 24 burials have been identified and a pamphlet available at the entrance to the cemetery lists the names and a bit of their history. Corner of D and 10th Sts; Ogallala, NE 69153; https://nebraskatravelerguide.com/activity/boot-hill-cemetery

Omaha, NE

Bemis Center features solo and group exhibitions of artwork in all media by local, national, and international artists. Gallery admission is free with donations welcomed. Open Wednesday through Saturday from 11 AM to 5 PM with Thursday closing at 9 PM. 724 S 12th St; Omaha, NE 68102; Phone: (402) 341-7130; http://www.bemiscenter.org

Bob Kerrey Pedestrian Bridge connects Council Bluffs, IA to Omaha's Riverfront. The s-curved cable-stayed bridge boasts a striking, modern design. At night multi-colored lights are turned on. The bridge is the first pedestrian bridge to connect two states, with plaques highlighting the point over the Missouri River where the state lines meet. 705 Riverfront Dr; Omaha, NE 68102; Phone: (402) 444-5900; http://omaha.net/places/bob-kerrey-pedestrian-bridge

Hot Shops Art Center includes 50 art studios, four art galleries, three anchor hot shops including Crystal Forge, Bruning Sculpture, and Hot Shops Pottery. A visit to the art galleries, work spaces, and shops is free. Gallery events are generally held on the first Friday or Saturday evening of the month. 1301 Nicholas St; Omaha, NE 68102; Phone: (402) 342-6452; http://www.hotshopsartcenter.com/index.html

Joslyn Art Museum offers a diversified collection from ancient through modern and contemporary art as well as Native American, Asian, Western, and Latin art forms. General admission is free although there may be additional charge for some special exhibitions. They also offer free public tours. Open Tuesday through Saturday from 10 AM to 4 PM with extended hours on Thursday until 8 PM. Open Sunday 10 AM to 4 PM. Closed major holidays. 2200 Dodge St; Omaha, NE 68102; Phone: (402) 342-3300; https://www.joslyn.org

Mormon Trail Center Winter Quarters Historical Site is the location of a major interpretive center built by the LDS Church. The Mormon Pioneer Cemetery, which was a burial site for some of the pioneers who died at Winter Quarters, includes a monument called *Tragedy of Winter Quarters*, sculpted by Avard Fairbanks. Admission is free. Open daily. From October through March open Monday through Saturday from 10 AM to 6 PM and Sunday from Noon to 6 PM. The rest of the year open Monday through Saturday from 9 AM to 8 PM and Sunday from Noon to 8 PM. 3215 State St; Omaha, NE 68112; Phone: (402) 453-9372; https://www.lds.org/locations/mormon-trail-center-at-historic-winter-quarters

Nevada

Beatty, NV
Often considered to be the Gateway to Death Valley, the town of Beatty also offers several free attractions.

Beatty Museum & Historical Society preserves the history of the Beatty area, including the Bullfrog Mining District, and the ghost towns and attractions in the area. Admission is free. Donations welcomed. Open daily from 10 AM to 3 PM. 417 Main St; Beatty, NV 89003; Phone: (775) 553-2303; http://www.beattymuseum.org

Goldwell Open Air Museum hosts seven out-sized sculptures near the ghost town of Rhyolite. Admission is free and the desert location is always open. An on-site visitor center offers exhibits and original artwork. Generally open Monday through Saturday from 10 AM to 4 PM, except in summer when it usually closes by 2 PM. Four miles west of Beatty off Hwy 374; Phone: (702) 870-9946; http://goldwellmuseum.org

Rhyolite is one of the most photographed ghost towns in the West. It had a short but spectacular growth starting in 1905 which ended just a few years later. Kelly Bottle House was built out of medicine, beer, and whisky bottles. Restored for a Paramount Pictures film in 1926, the house still stands and is the oldest and largest bottle house in the United States. There is no admission fee. Rhyolite is four miles west of Beatty on SR 374 and is overseen by the Bureau of Land Management. Phone: (760) 786-3200; https://www.nps.gov/deva/learn/historyculture/rhyolite-ghost-town.htm

Boulder City, NV
Hoover Dam is an engineering marvel and the new bridge is the highest concrete-arch bridge in the world as of 2018. The recently opened Mike O'Callaghan-Pat Tillman Memorial Bridge was built to relieve congestion but has the additional value of allowing visitors to park and walk across the bridge for free. It had been possible to drive across US 93 and stop at the dam, but when the new bridge opened, traffic was rerouted. Drivers in Nevada can still take the US 93 Exit 2 and drive the old road to the dam but must pay a fee for parking at the dam. Drivers from Arizona will dead-end at the dam and then have to retrace the road back to continue the journey west. Although it is free to see the outside of the dam, there is a charge for tours and even to see the visitor center. https://www.usbr.gov/lc/hooverdam

Carson City, NV

Nevada State Capitol was built in 1870 with sandstone from the Nevada State Prison quarry. The capitol complex in the heart of Carson City includes the State Capitol, Legislative Building, Supreme Court, and State Library and Archives. The Nevada State Capitol is open free to the public for self-guided tours Monday through Friday from 8 AM to 5 PM. Closed holidays. 101 N Carson St; Carson City, NV 89701; Phone: (800) NEVADA-1; https://www.nps.gov/nr/travel/nevada/nev.htm

Stewart Indian School provided education and vocational skills to Native American youth from Nevada, California, Arizona, and New Mexico with the goal of promoting assimilation into American life and culture. Attendance was not always voluntary. The campus is open for self-tours with 20 points of interest. Use your cell phone to access recorded messages from alumni and employees about their personal experiences at the school. Before visiting, you can also download podcasts from: http://stewartindianschool.com/walking-trail. The campus itself is owned by the State of Nevada and is open free to the public. 5500 Snyder Ave; Carson City, NV, 89701; Phone: (775) 687-8333; http://stewartindianschool.com/museum

Elko, NV

California Trail Center highlights living-history events and exhibits. There is no admission charge, and all programs are free. Open Wednesday through Sunday from 9 AM to 4:30 PM. Closed Thanksgiving, Christmas, and New Year's Day. 1 Interpretive Center Way; off I-80, at Hunter Exit 292; Elko, NV 89801; Phone (775) 738-1849; https://www.blm.gov/visit/california-trail-interpretive-center; https://www.californiatrailcenter.org

Ely, NV

Garnet Hill is a designated rock hounding location and a favorite for collectors looking for garnets. Searchers can find these gems by carefully breaking up rocks, or exploring the surface and drainage sites. Bring your own hammer. Free to the public. Note: No water is available. Hwy 50; Ely, NV 89301; Phone (775) 289-1800; https://www.blm.gov/visit/garnet-hill

Fallon, NV

Churchill County Museum documents life in the region through fire trucks and steam rollers, furniture and clothing. Highlights include the Woodliff store, one of the oldest commercial buildings in Fallon, as well as an authentically recreated tule home, constructed with reeds. Admission is free. Open March through November on Tuesday through Sunday from 10 AM to 5 PM with Sunday closing at 3 PM. From December through February open Tuesday through Sunday from 10 AM to

4 PM with Sunday closing at 3 PM. 1050 S Maine St; Fallon, NV 89406; Phone: (775) 423-3677; http://ccmuseum.org

Grimes Point Prehistoric Rock Art Site holds rock writings and petroglyphs that can be viewed along a 1/4 mile, self-guided interpretive trail. Free admission. Open all year. Hwy 50; Fallon, NV 89406; Phone: (775) 885-6000; https://www.blm.gov/visit/grimes-point-hidden-cave-site

Hidden Cave Archaeological Area is part of Grimes Point. It has been excavated by archaeologists several times, uncovering a high proportion of broken artifacts, leading to speculation that 3,500 to 3,800 years ago, the cave was used as a cache. Free public tours are offered by the Churchill County Museum (see above) on the second and fourth Saturdays of each month, except when part of a federally recognized three-day weekend. http://ccmuseum.org/hidden-cave-tours

Hawthorne, NV
Mineral County Museum collects mining, fire, railroad equipment, and horse drawn vehicles as well as 1800s Mission Bells found in the desert. Admission is free. Open Monday through Saturday from 11 AM to 4 PM. 400 10th St; Hawthorne, NV 89415; Phone: (775) 945-5142; http://web2.greatbasin.net/~mcmuseum/index.html

Henderson, NV
Henderson Bird Viewing Preserve is on the eastern edge of the Pacific Migratory Flyway and its nine ponds are home to thousands of migratory waterfowl as well as its own resident desert birds. A paved path is approximately 3/4 of a mile long. Admission is free. Seasonal hours with a 6 AM opening (7 AM in winter) and a 2 PM close (shortened to Noon during the summer). Last entry is 30 minutes before closing. Note: This is a desert, always bring water. 350 E Galleria Dr at Moser Dr; Phone: (702) 267-4180; http://www.cityofhenderson.com/henderson-happenings/facilities/henderson-bird-viewing-preserve

Sloan Canyon National Conservation Area includes the Sloan Petroglyph Site, believed to hold more than 300 rock art panels with 1,700 individual design elements. There are no entrance fees. Note: The general consensus is that the hike to see the petroglyphs is quite strenuous. The Sloan Canyon NCA Visitor Contact Station is open daily October through May from 8 AM to 4:30 PM. From June through September, the Contact Station is open Friday through Sunday from 8 AM to 4:30 PM. North McCullough Wilderness, located in the Conservation Area, is open for hiking, horseback riding, and wildlife watching. Nawghaw Poa Rd, Henderson, NV 89052; Phone: (702) 515-5000; https://www.blm.gov/programs/national-conservation-lands/nevada/sloan-canyon-nca

Hiko, NV

Mt. Irish Archeological Site covers 640 acres and provides prehistoric rock art of the Native Americans who used the area 4,000 years ago. Interpretive trails and a trail guide is available at visitor register boxes. Additionally, visitors can enjoy viewing desert bighorn sheep, pronghorn antelope, mule deer, and a variety of bird species. There is no fee to visit. Logan Rd off Hwy 318; Hiko, NV 89017; Phone: (775) 726-8100; https://www.blm.gov/visit/search-details/262709/1

Las Vegas, NV (See Boulder City, NV for the Hoover Dam)

There are some surprising and free things to do in Las Vegas. The casinos have embraced both art and fun, in addition to the gaming.

ARIA Fine Art Collection features work by acclaimed painters, sculptors, and installation artists.
3730 S Las Vegas Blvd; Las Vegas, NV 89158; Phone: (877) 347-2742; https://aria.mgmresorts.com/en/amenities/aria-fine-art-collection.html

Bellagio's Gardens highlight horticulture as art. Although it is open all year, the gardens are closed between seasonal exhibits. Check the website for exact dates. https://bellagio.mgmresorts.com/en/entertainment/conservatory-botanical-garden.html The Bellagio also delights those passing by outside with its famous 15-minute fountain show synchronized to music. 3600 S Las Vegas Blvd; Las Vegas, NV 89109; Phone: (702) 693-7111; https://bellagio.mgmresorts.com/en/entertainment/fountains-of-bellagio.html

Caesars Palace Fall of Atlantis at the Forum recounts the fall of Atlantis using 9-foot tall statues. The Forum is open Sunday through Thursday from 10 AM to 11 PM and on Friday and Saturday from 10 AM to Midnight. 3570 S Las Vegas Blvd; Las Vegas, NV 89109; Phone: (702) 893-4800; https://www.caesars.com/caesars-palace/things-to-do/forum-shops

Circus Acts at Circus Circus are performed daily at the Carnival Midway Arcade. The show starts at 11:30 AM daily. Performances run hourly until just after midnight. 2880 S Las Vegas Blvd; Las Vegas, NV 89109; Phone: (702) 734-0410; https://circuscircus.mgmresorts.com/en/entertainment/circus-acts.html

Cosmopolitan WALLWORKS hosts the city's loveliest walls with its permanent art installation of graffiti murals. Some of the best-known street artists have turned concrete into art along the walls of the parking garage and stairwells. 3708 S Las Vegas Blvd; Las Vegas, NV 89109;
Phone: (702) 698-7000;
https://www.cosmopolitanlasvegas.com/resort/art/collection

Fremont Street is a bit of old Las Vegas and the site of the Fremont Street Experience with the neon signs provided by the Neon Museum (a fee-based museum). There are free concerts and overhead light shows generally starting after 6 PM. 425 Fremont St; Las Vegas, NV 89101; Phone: (702) 678-5600; https://vegasexperience.com

Flamingo's Wildlife Habitat is 15 acres filled with exotic birds, fish and turtles as well as Chilean flamingos. Free and open daily dawn to dusk. Pelican feedings 8:30 AM and 2 PM daily. 3555 S Las Vegas Blvd; Las Vegas, NV 89109; Phone: (702) 733-3349; https://www.caesars.com/flamingo-las-vegas/things-to-do/wildlife-habitat

Mirage Volcano erupts nightly to music on Sunday through Thursday at 8 PM and 9 PM. Friday through Sunday at 8 PM, 9 PM, and 10 PM. 3400 S Las Vegas Blvd; Las Vegas, NV 89109; Phone: (702) 791-7111; https://mirage.mgmresorts.com/en/amenities/volcano.html

Shelby Heritage Center and Carroll Shelby Store honors the legacy of Carroll Shelby, legendary automotive designer and race driver, best known for his involvement with the AC Cobra and Shelby Mustangs for Ford Motor Company. Open Monday through Friday from 9 AM to 6 PM. Open Saturday from 7 AM to 6 PM and on Sunday from 10 AM to 5 PM. Free guided tours are available Monday through Friday at 10:30 AM and 1:30 PM and on Saturday at 10:30 AM. 6405 Ensworth St; Las Vegas, NV 89119; Phone: (702) 942-7325; http://www.shelby.com

Silverton Casino Aquarium holds thousands of tropical fish, and a few Mermaids during their scheduled Mermaid Swims held Thursday through Sunday. The Silverton Casino Aquarium even offers a staff marine biologist to answers guests' questions during the feeding show which takes place daily at 1:30 PM and 4:30 PM. 3333 Blue Diamond Rd; Las Vegas, NV 89139; Phone: (702) 263-7777; https://silvertoncasino.com/amenities/aquarium

Sunset Stampede Laser Light and Water Show at Sam's Town chronicles the Western pioneer experience with music, dancing water, and a state-of-the-art laser light show. The show is free and occurs daily at 2 PM, 4 PM, 6 PM, 8 PM, and 10 PM on the main casino floor. 5111 Boulder Hwy; Las Vegas, NV 89122; Phone: (702) 456-7777; https://www.samstownlv.com/experience/mystic-falls

Wynn Lake of Dreams is hidden within the resort, but it's been described as four thousand lights, stunning holographics, and puppetry. Shows run nightly, every half hour beginning at 8 PM until 12:30 AM. 3131 S Las Vegas Blvd, Las Vegas,

NV 89109; Phone: (702) 770-7000;
https://www.wynnlasvegas.com/entertainment/lake-of-dreams

Nixon, NV
Pyramid Lake Paiute Tribe Museum & Visitors Center describes the heritage of the Paiute Native Americans who are one of the original tribes in Nevada area. Visitors will also learn why the Paiute people hold the lake and its surrounding landscape sacred. Other displays focus on Pyramid Lake's natural history and its residents. Admission is free. Wednesday through Sunday 10 AM to 4:30 PM. Note: Hours may change seasonally. 709 State St; Nixon, NV 89424; Phone: (775) 574-1088; https://pyramidlake.us/museum

Reno, NV
Downtown, and the Midtown District are home to more than 100 murals, painted by local, national and international artists. Follow this Art Spot Reno Midtown Reno Mural Tour map: https://www.visitrenotahoe.com/things-to-do/arts-and-culture/public-art/

W. M. Keck Earth Science and Mineral Engineering Museum collects minerals, ores, fossil specimens, and photographs, in addition to mining-related objects. One of the highlights is the exhibit on the Comstock Lode – the first major silver ore discovery in the U.S. and one which made immense fortunes for those involved. One of those who benefitted was John W. Mackay who commissioned Tiffany and Company of New York to design and produce a 1,250 piece set of sterling silver service for 24, which was completed in 1878. The museum is home to a significant portion of that dinner service. Admission is free. Open Monday through Friday from 9 AM to 4 PM, and the first Saturday of each month from Noon to 4 PM. Closed university holidays. University of Nevada at Reno; 1664 N. Virginia St; Reno, NV 89557; Phone: (775) 784-4528; https://www.unr.edu/keck

Virginia City, NV
Comstock Firemen's Museum includes historic fire apparatus and displays of artifacts and photographs including uniform shirts, ornate leather belts and leather helmets. Highlights include Nevada's oldest fire-fighting vehicle – 1839 Christian Hight four-wheel hand-drawn hose carriage, and other pieces from the late 1800s. Antique cast iron toys make up another part of the collection. Admission is free, but they appreciate donations. From May through October open daily from 10 AM to 4 PM. November and December open weekends only. 125 South C St; Virginia City, NV 89440; Phone: (775) 847-0717; http://www.comstockfiremuseum.com

New Hampshire

Brookline, NH

Andres Institute of Art is considered New England's largest outdoor sculpture park. Artists who come to the institute are encouraged to create and install their sculptures along walking trails scattered across 140 acres. It's free to explore although donations are appreciated. Open daily from dawn to dusk. Note: sturdy footwear is suggested for hiking the trails. 98 Rt 13; Brookline, NH 03033; Phone: (603) 673-8441; http://andresinstitute.org

Concord, NH

NH Audubon's McLane Center is a family-friendly place with exhibits, live animals, and several miles of hiking trails. Admission is free with donations appreciated. Trails are open daily from dawn to dusk. The raptor mews are accessible through the center courtyard and also open dawn to dusk. The visitors center is open Monday to Friday from 10 AM to 5 PM and Saturday from 10 AM to 4 PM. Closed on major holidays. 84 Silk Farm Rd; Concord, NH 03301; Phone: (603) 224-9909; http://www.nhaudubon.org/about/centers/mclane

New Hampshire State House is the oldest statehouse in which the legislature still sits in the original chambers. Stop by the visitor center for information on free tours. Open Monday through Friday from 8 AM to 4 PM. Note: The center is sometimes closed for lunch. 107 N Main St; Concord, NH 03301; Phone: (603) 271-2154; http://www.gencourt.state.nh.us/NH_Visitorcenter/default.htm

Durham, NH

Museum of Art at the University of New Hampshire creates exhibits from their ever-growing collection of paintings, photographs, Japanese wood block, African art, and sculptures. Free admission. Open September through May on Monday through Friday from 10 AM to 4 PM and open till 6 PM on Thursday. Open Saturday from Noon to 4 PM. Closed during the summer, university holidays, and during exhibition changes. 30 Academic Way; Durham, NH 03824; Phone: (603) 862-3712; https://cola.unh.edu/moa

Franconia, NH

Franconia Heritage Museum displays a fully furnished 1878 New England farmhouse. Admission is free, donations welcomed. Open from Memorial Day weekend through Columbus Day weekend on Saturdays from 1 PM to 4 PM or by appointment. 553 Main St; Franconia, NH 03580; Phone: (603) 823-5000; http://www.franconianh.org/heritage-museum.html

New England Ski Museum showcase ski pioneers, New England Olympians, the 10th Mountain Division, classic skis, and local legends. Open daily from 10 AM to 5 PM from Memorial Day through the end of ski season, usually early April. Closes some major holidays. 135 Tramway Dr; Exit 34B off I-93; Franconia, NH 03580; Phone: (603) 823-7177; http://newenglandskimuseum.org/visit

Greenland, NH
Great Bay Discovery Center treats visitors to exhibits about the Great Bay Estuary and the marine creatures that call it home. An accessible trail and boardwalk meanders through a variety of habitats. The Discovery Center is free and open from May through September on Wednesday through Sunday from 10 AM to 4 PM. Open weekends in October, and closed November through April. The grounds of Great Bay are open year round, dawn to dusk. 89 Depot Rd; Greenland, NH 03840; Phone: (603) 778-0015; https://www.greatbay.org/visit/index.htm

Hanover, NH
Hood Museum of Art in Dartmouth College highlights indigenous Australian contemporary art, a major archive of photojournalism, and fresco mural cycle *The Epic of American Civilization* (1932-34), by José Clemente Orozco. The museum is free as are their public programs. Open Wednesday from 11 AM to 5 PM, Thursday and Friday from 11 AM to 8 PM, and Saturday and Sunday from 11 AM to 5 PM. 6 E Wheelock St; Hanover, NH 03755; Phone: (603) 646-2808; https://hoodmuseum.dartmouth.edu/visit

Keene, NH
Horatio Colony House Museum is a restored 1800s New England family home representing three generations with original furnishing and decorative arts from around the world. Admission is free. May through mid-October open Wednesday through Sunday from 11 AM to 4 PM. Closed July 4th. Trails are available daily from dawn to dusk. 199 Main St; Keene, NH 03431; Phone: (603) 352-0460; http://horatiocolonymuseum.org

Meriden, NH
Aidron Duckworth Art Museum displays the artwork and writings of Aidron Duckworth in the building he turned into a home and studio. The museum is free to visit. Open May through October on Friday, Saturday, and Sunday from 10 AM to 5 PM. 21 Bean Rd; Meriden, NH 03770; Phone: (603) 469-3444; http://aidronduckworthmuseum.org

Moultonborough, NH
Loon Center and Markus Wildlife Sanctuary invites visitors to enjoy New Hampshire's loons and other wildlife through displays, exhibits, and videos. The 200-acre sanctuary includes forest, ponds, streams, and lake shore with two walking trails. Admission is free. The walking trails are open daily dawn to dusk.

Open daily from July through Columbus Day from 9 AM to 5 PM. From mid-May through June it is open Monday through Saturday 9 AM to 5 PM. The rest of the year it is open Thursday, Friday and Saturday from 9 AM to 5 PM. Check the website for holidays closings. 183 Lee's Mill Rd; Moultonborough, NH 03254; Phone: (603) 476-5666; https://www.loon.org/markus-wls.php

New Castle, NH
Fort Constitution State Historic Site is a popular picnic site but has history as well. It was originally Fort William and Mary. It fell into disrepair and was renamed Fort Constitution when renovations were completed in 1808. It is the ruins of this later fort that can be seen today. Open to the public year-round at no charge. US Coast Guard Station; 25 Wentworth Rd; New Castle, NH 03854; Phone: (603) 271-3556; https://www.nhstateparks.org/visit/historic-sites/fort-constitution-historic-site

New London, NH
Ice House Museum is Bill Kidder's special collection of automobiles and Americana – antique Ford automobiles, children's ride-on toys, steam whistles, padlocks, washing machines, auto parts, horse-drawn carriages, a town jail, a blacksmith shop, and a tinsmith shop. Admission is free. The museum is open seasonally from Memorial Day through Columbus Day on Tuesday and Thursday from 9 AM to 4 PM. Open Saturday from 9 AM to 2 PM. 91 Pleasant St; New London, NH 03257; Phone: (603) 526-9394; http://www.wfkicehouse.org/newsite

North Conway, NH
Eastern Slope Branch of the New England Ski Museum exhibits skiing history. Admission is free. Open daily from 9 AM to 4 PM. Note: There may be seasonal closures. 2628 White Mountain Hwy; North Conway, NH 03860; Phone: (603) 730-5044; http://newenglandskimuseum.org/eastern-slope-branch

Plymouth, NH
Museum of the White Mountains at Plymouth State University preserves, and promotes the history, environmental legacy, and the culture of the region. The Dan Noel collection includes rare glass-plate photographs, stereoscopic images, hotel ledgers, postcards as well as first edition books about the region. Frances "Dolly" MacIntyre Collection focuses on art by female artists in the 19th and 20th century. Admission is free. Open Monday through Friday from 10 AM to 5 PM and Saturday from 11 AM to 4 PM. Closed university holidays. 17 High St; Plymouth, NH 03264; Phone: (603) 535-3210; https://www.plymouth.edu/museum-of-the-white-mountains

Portsmouth, NH
Portsmouth Athenaeum is a library, gallery, and museum. It curates special exhibits as well as offering its own collections. Free and open to the public Tuesday through Saturday from 1 PM to 4 PM. The gallery is on the third floor. 6 Market Sq; Portsmouth, NH 03801; Phone: (603) 431-2538; https://portsmouthathenaeum.org

Sugar Hill, NH
Sugar Hill Historical Museum consists of two barns, a main building, and the Reid-Burpee house adjacent to the Carriage barn. On display are tools, horse-drawn carriages, folk-style paintings of old Sugar Hill, and a Benjamin Morrill tower clock as well as a growing collection of historic public signs and sleighs. Admission is free. Donations welcome. Open Memorial Day weekend through Columbus Day weekend on Friday and Saturday from 11 AM to 3 PM. 1400 NH-117; Sugar Hill, NH 03586; Phone: (603) 823-5336 http://www.sugarhillnh.org/library-and-museum/sugar-hill-historical-museum

Union, NH
Heritage Park Railroad Museum Campus includes the Freight House with the H/O scale model of the Boston & Maine Railroad line circa 1909, the restored Union Station with numerous exhibits, the restored 1902 Russell snow plow, and a B&M caboose. Exhibits are free. Open from late June to Columbus Day on Saturday and Sunday from Noon to 4 PM. The blacksmith shop is open most days and times when Heritage Park is open. 282 Main St; Union, NH 03887; Phone: (603) 224-2281 http://www.historicwakefieldnh.com/events--hours--directions.html

New Jersey

Atlantic City, NJ
Absecon Lighthouse is the state's tallest lighthouse and the original first-order Fresnel Lens is still in place at the top. Admission to the Keeper's House museum, exhibits, and grounds is free, although there is a fee to climb the lighthouse. Open daily July and August from 10 AM to 5 PM with an 8 PM closing on Thursday. The rest of the year open Thursday through Monday from 11 AM to 4 PM. Closed some major holidays. 31 S Rhode Island Ave; Atlantic City, NJ 08401; Phone: (609) 449-1360; http://www.abseconlighthouse.org

Bayville, NJ
Double Trouble Village -- Double Trouble State Park includes historic structures dating from the late 19th century through the early 20th century as well as woodland, cranberry bogs, creeks, and a nature trail. There is no entrance fee, but program fees may apply. The park grounds are open daily 8 AM to dusk. The interpretive center is generally open Wednesday through Sunday from 9 AM to 4 PM. Calling ahead is advised. Keswick Rd (CR 618) and Double Trouble Rd (CR 619); Bayville, NJ 08721; Phone: (609) 726-1191; http://www.njparksandforests.org/parks/double.html

Bridgeton, NJ
Bridgeton Hall of Fame All Sports Museum has gathered rare memorabilia as well as the Cincinnati Reds bat collection, and a Golden Glove from Hall of Fame legend Willie Mays. Admission is free. Open Thursday through Saturday from 10 AM to Noon and again from 1 PM to 3 PM or by appointment. 18 Burt St; Bridgeton, NJ 08302; Phone: (856) 451-7300; http://www.co.cumberland.nj.us/allsportsmuseum

Cohanzik Zoo is home to over 100 animals in modern, naturalistic exhibits. Admission is free with donations gratefully accepted. Open daily from 9 AM to 5 PM. Closes at 4 PM in fall and winter. 45 Mayor Aitken Dr; Bridgeton, NJ 08302; Phone: (856) 453-1658; http://cohanzickzoo.org

Brigantine, NJ
Marine Mammal Stranding Center Museum is the only rescue facility in the state that handles sick and injured marine life. Sea Life Museum features 25 life-sized replicas of marine mammals and fish. Educational displays explain the plight of marine animals that try to eat ocean debris. A TV monitor provides a live feed of animals in the hospital. During the summer there's an outdoor marine observation tank. It is free, although donations or a purchase in the gift shop are greatly appreciated. From June to early September it is open Tuesday through

Sunday from 10 AM to 4 PM. From early September through the end of May it is open only on Saturday and Sunday from 10 AM to 2 PM. 3625 Brigantine Blvd; Brigantine, NJ 08203; Phone: (609) 266-0538; https://mmsc.org

Camden, NJ
Walt Whitman House was the famous poet's home from 1884 until his death in 1892. It was here that Whitman became famous for his poem *Leaves of Grass*. The House contains an extensive collection of writings, photographs and memorabilia. Admission is free, however visits are by guided tour only. It is recommended that visitors call ahead to confirm hours and availability. 330 Mickle Blvd/Martin Luther King Jr. Blvd; Camden NJ 08103; Phone: (856) 964-5383; http://www.njparksandforests.org/historic/whitman/index.html

Cape May Court House, NJ
The town of Cape May Court House is separate from the more famous Cape May, located about 15 miles away.
Cape May Zoo is home to more than 550 animals, representing more than 250 species. Admission is free, although donations are appreciated. Additional activities may incur a fee. Open daily from 10 AM to 4:30 PM. Closed Christmas. 707 US 9; Cape May Court House, NJ 08210; Phone: (609) 465-5271; http://www.cmczoo.com/visit.php

Glassboro, NJ
Heritage Glass Museum highlights more than 200 years of South Jersey glass. Admission is free. Open Saturday from 11 AM to 2 PM and Wednesday from Noon to 3 PM. Closed Wednesdays in June, July, and August. 25 E High St; Glassboro, NJ 08028; Phone: (856) 881-7468; https://www.heritageglassmuseum.com

Rowan University Art Gallery showcases all forms of visual expression and new media. Free admission. Open Monday, Tuesday, and Wednesday from 10 AM to 5 PM, and Thursday, Friday, and Saturday from 10 AM to 7 PM. 301 W High St; Glassboro, NJ 08028; Phone: (856) 256-4521; https://sites.rowan.edu/artgallery

Hewitt, NJ
Long Pond Ironworks State Park contains the remains of an ironworking village with 18th and 19th century buildings as well as ruins of an industrial complex. There's also hiking trails and scenic overlooks. The park is free to enter. The Friends of Long Pond Ironworks offers tours with a suggested donation. Open daily from sunrise to sunset. The museum is open April through November on Friday, Saturday and Sunday from 9 AM to 4:30 PM. 1334 Greenwood Lake Tpk; Hewitt, NJ 07421; Phone: (973) 657-1688;

https://www.njparksandforests.org/parks/longpond.html;
http://longpondironworks.org

Highlands, NJ
Sandy Hook Unit, Gateway National Recreation Area invites visitors to take a stroll around Fort Hancock Historic Post and investigate the Sandy Hook lighthouse, keepers' quarters, and barn. **Fort Hancock** was part of the Army's permanent fortifications from the Spanish-American War to the age of nuclear missiles. Visitors may tour gun batteries and the historic post as well as the Sandy Hook Lighthouse. **Sandy Hook Lighthouse** is not only the oldest surviving lighthouse in the country, it is still in use. Lighthouse tours are available on a first come, first served basis. There are no entrance fees, but there are parking fees in summer from Memorial Day weekend to Labor Day. From November through March the park is open from 5 AM through 8 PM daily, open until 9 PM the rest of the year. The visitor center is open daily except major holidays. Note: It is located at the northern end of the Sandy Hook Unit of Gateway National Recreation Area on the grounds of Fort Hancock where parking is free. Rt 36; Highlands, NJ 07760; Phone: (732) 872-5970; https://www.nps.gov/gate/learn/historyculture/sandy-hook-places.htm

Twin Lights Historic Site is known for dual, although nonidentical, light towers. One flashes and the other is fixed but both look out over the bluffs. Twin Lights has free admission. Hours are seasonal although generally open weekends. Note: They advise calling to make sure they are open. Grounds are open from 9 AM to 4:30 PM. 2 Light House Rd; Highlands, NJ 07732; Phone: (732) 872-1814; http://www.twinlightslighthouse.com/index.html

Jersey City, NJ
Empty Sky 9/11 Memorial features twin stainless steel walls as a dramatic tribute to those who died at the World Trade Center on September 11, 2001. *Empty Sky* is engraved with the names of those killed in the attacks. This memorial is located in Liberty State Park, with views of the Manhattan skyline, the Statue of Liberty, and Ellis Island. The memorial and park are free of charge. Open daily from 6 AM to 10 PM. Liberty State Park; 1 Audrey Zapp Dr; Jersey City, NJ 07305; Phone: (201) 915-3403; http://nj911memorial.org/empty-sky

Lambertville, NJ
Howell Living History Farm demonstrates early farming practices from 1890 to 1910. Free admission, although special activities incur a cost. Open Saturday from 10 AM to 4 PM from the end of January through beginning of December. From early April through November open Tuesday through Friday from 10 AM to 4 PM and Sunday from Noon to 4 PM. The farm is closed on Easter and Mercer County holidays as well as most of December and January. Note: Call to verify

hours in the off season. 70 Woodens Ln; Lambertville, NJ 08530; Phone: (609) 737-3299; http://www.howellfarm.org

Lawrenceville, NJ
National Guard Militia Museum of NJ: Lawrenceville Annex features weapons, uniforms, and other equipment going back to the Civil War, plus over 100 small-scale military equipment models. About 15 tanks, vehicles, and cannon are displayed outside. Free admission. Open Tuesday, Friday, and Saturday from 9 AM to 3 PM. Artillery Armory; 151 Eggerts Crossing Rd; Lawrenceville, NJ 08648; Phone: (609) 530-6802; http://www.nj.gov/military/museum

Millville, NJ
Millville Army Air Field Museum honors the 10,000 men and women who received advanced gunnery training during WWII. The museum displays WWII aviation artifacts. The Link Trainer building houses a rare, fully-operational link trainer. Admission is free. Open from Tuesday through Sunday from 10 AM to 4 PM. 1 Leddon St; Millville, NJ 08332; Phone: (856) 327-2347; http://www.p47millville.org

New Brunswick, NJ
Rutgers University Geology Museum showcases a dinosaur trackway, an exhibit on the evolution of the human diet, a fully articulated mastodon skeleton, and mineral exhibits. Free admission. Mid-September to mid-May open Tuesday through Thursday from 10 AM to 5 PM, Friday from 10 AM to 4 PM, and Saturday from 10 AM to 2 PM. Limited summer schedule. Closed major holidays and school breaks. Geology Hall; 2nd Floor; 85 Somerset St; New Brunswick, NJ 08901; Phone: (848) 932-7243; http://geologymuseum.rutgers.edu/geology-museum

North Plainfield, NJ
Fleetwood Museum of Art and Photographica displays the camera collection of Benjamin Fleetwood – over 800 cameras, illustrating the 150 year evolution of camera design. The oil paintings of his wife, the Matilda Fleetwood are also on exhibit. The museum is in the Vermeule Community Center. No fees are charged. Open Saturdays from 10 AM until 4 PM and Sundays from 1 PM to 4 PM. Closed major holiday weekends. 614 Greenbrook Rd; North Plainfield, NJ 07063; Phone: (908) 756-7810; http://www.fleetwoodmuseum.com

Piscataway, NJ
East Jersey Old Town Village contains original, replicated, and reconstructed 18th and 19th century structures. Stroll through New Brunswick barracks, Runyon house, Williamson wheelwright shop, Fitzrandolph house, and Smalleytown schoolhouse. It's free to visit and many of the programs are also free.

Open Tuesday through Friday from 8:30 AM to 4:15 PM, and on Sunday from 1 PM to 4 PM. Closed holidays. Daily tour at 1:30 PM. 1050 River Rd; Piscataway, NJ 08854; Phone: (732) 745-3030; http://www.middlesexcountynj.gov/Government/Departments/BDE/Pages/East-Jersey-Olde-Towne-Village.aspx

Point Pleasant, NJ
New Jersey Museum of Boating invites the public to take a free guided tour of their extensive collection of maritime arts and artifacts. Open during the summer on Wednesday through Sunday from Noon to 4 PM. Johnson Boat Works Building 13; 1800 Bay Ave; Point Pleasant, NJ 08742; Phone: (732) 606-7605; http://njmb.org/about-the-museum

Princeton, NJ
Drumthwacket is one of the few state governor residences that isn't in the same town as the state capitol. Drumthwacket is open most Wednesdays for guided tours at 1 PM with the exception of the holidays and the month of August. Preregistration is required. There is no charge to tour Drumthwacket. 354 Stockton St; Princeton, NJ 08540; Phone: (609) 683-0057; http://drumthwacket.org

Einstein Museum is described the only permanent Albert Einstein exhibit in the United States. Oddly enough it is tucked into a back corner of Landau, a family run clothing store. It features photos, articles, artifacts, and information about the world's most famous physicist. Open during business hours, Monday through Saturday from 9:30 AM to 5:30 PM and Sunday from 9:30 AM to 4:30 PM. Landau; 102 Nassau St; Princeton, NJ 08542; Phone: (609) 924-3494; http://www.landauprinceton.com/einstein-museum

Princeton University Art Museum covers ancient to contemporary art. The exhibits are thematic as well as highlighting specific artists across all media. Always free. Open Tuesday through Saturday from 10 AM to 5 PM and open late on Thursday to 9 PM. Open Sunday from Noon to 5 PM. Closed major holidays. McCormick Hall; Elm Dr; Princeton, NJ 08544; Phone: (609) 258-3788; http://artmuseum.princeton.edu

Robbinsville, NJ
BAPS Shri Swaminarayan Mandir is a Hindu place of worship, and the largest in the United States. Made of Italian Carrara marble, the pieces were carved by artisans in India, then shipped to the United States where they were reassembled to create the mandir in Robbinsville. There is no admission fee. The grounds are open daily from 9 AM to 7:30 PM. The public is invited to observe the ceremonies. Check the website for times of the rituals. 112 N Main St;

Robbinsville, NJ 08561; Phone: (609) 918-1212; https://www.baps.org/Global-Network/North-America/Robbinsville.aspx

Sea Girt, NJ
National Guard Militia Museum of NJ explains how armed conflicts and military institutions have shaped the national and local experience. General admission is free. Open daily from 10 AM to 3 PM. Closed on state holidays. Sea Girt Ave and Camp Dr; Sea Girt, NJ 08750; Phone: (732) 974-5966; http://www.nj.gov/military/museum

Somerville NJ
Old Dutch Parsonage site holds both the parsonage and the Wallace House – the largest house built in New Jersey during the Revolutionary War. Admission is free. Open Wednesday to Saturday from 10 AM to 4 PM and on Sunday from 1 PM to 4 PM. 71 Somerset St; Somerville, NJ 08876; Phone: (908) 725-1015; http://www.njparksandforests.org/historic/olddutch-wallace/odwh-home.htm

Trenton, NJ
New Jersey State House provides free tours of the building's history, art, architecture, and the legislative process. The tours are offered Monday through Friday on the hour from 10 AM to 3 PM. On the first and third Saturday of the month tours are also held from Noon to 3 PM. Start your tour in the welcome center located in the Annex adjacent to the parking garage. Note: Everyone over the age of 18 must show a photo ID. 125 W State St; Trenton, NJ 08608; Phone: (609) 847-3150; http://www.njleg.state.nj.us/legislativepub/visiting_guided.asp

New Jersey State Police Museum & Learning Center informs visitors about crime scene investigation, the Lindbergh baby kidnaping, and the evolution of state police vehicles. Admission is free. Open Monday through Friday from 10 AM to 4 PM. Open Saturday by appointment. New Jersey State Headquarters; River Rd (Rt 175); Trenton, NJ 08628; Phone: (609) 882-2000; http://www.njspmemorialassociation.org/museum/museum.php

West Deptford, NJ
Gateway Classic Cars is a classic and exotic car dealership – one of several across the country. Browsers are welcome. Open Monday through Saturday from 9 AM to 5 PM. 1228 Forest Pkwy; Suite 200; West Deptford, NJ 08066; Phone: (856) 485-3750; http://gatewayclassiccars.com

New Mexico

New Mexico is not only the Land of Enchantment, it has serious nuclear history from both Los Alamos and the Trinity Site. But the state really shines when it comes to art and culture, with Native American, Latino, and Anglo traditions coming together to create a rich heritage. It also has serious road trip credentials – the Mother Road runs right through the state.

Albuquerque, NM

Albuquerque has a vibrant street art tradition with permitted murals throughout Downtown and Nob Hill. Some of the murals can be found on this website: https://www.murosabq.com. For one of the longest stretches of graffiti, head to the arroyo next to Acme Metals at 6142 Second St NW. It was once the site of a large invitation-only event that brought artists from around the country to paint the walls.

KiMo Theatre is one of the few examples of the short-lived, opulent Art Deco-Pueblo Revival Style blending elements of adobe architecture and motifs with soaring lines and linear designs of Art Deco. Open for free self-guided tours when the theater is not in use. Generally open Wednesday through Saturday from Noon to 6 PM. Sunday Noon to 3 PM. But hours can vary. Check the site's calendar to see if a free guided tour is available. http://www.kimotickets.com/calendar. 423 Central Ave, NW; Albuquerque, NM 87102; Phone: (505) 768-3522; https://www.cabq.gov/culturalservices/kimo

Petroglyph National Monument protects one of the largest petroglyph sites in North America. Stop by the visitor center and pick up a map. There are no entrance fees, however, the city does charge a small parking fee at one of the sites – Boca Negra Canyon. All other trails, and the visitor center are free to visit. Note: There are no petroglyph viewing trails at the visitor center but park staff can suggest trails to visit and provide driving directions. The visitor center is open daily 8:30 AM to 4:30 PM. Closed major holidays. Unser Blvd, NW at the Western Trail intersection; Albuquerque, NM 87120; Phone: (505) 899-0205 x335; https://www.nps.gov/petr/planyourvisit/placestogo.htm

Tingley Beach entices families with a beach surrounding its three fishing ponds and a model boat pond. If you want to fish you'll need to purchase a license. No admission fee. Open daily dawn to dusk. 1800 Tingley Dr SW; Albuquerque, NM 87102; Phone: (505) 768-2000; https://www.cabq.gov/culturalservices/biopark/tingley

University of New Mexico serves both students and residents with multiple museums. **Maxwell Museum of Anthropology** delivers a reconstructed cave setting complete with replicated ice-age drawings and several galleries to illuminate the cultural heritage of the Southwest. The museum is world-renowned for its holdings of art and artifacts from this region including prehistoric pottery. Admission is free, donations welcomed. Open Tuesday through Saturday from 10 AM to 4 PM. Closed major holidays. MSC01 1050; Anthropology Bldg; 500 University Blvd NE; Albuquerque, NM 87131; Phone: (505) 277-4405; http://maxwellmuseum.unm.edu **Meteorite Museum** offers more than 5,000 specimens of the museum with over 600 different meteorites. Admission is free but the museum often closes for the summer, lack of docents, and other reasons. Check the website for opening days and times. Northrop Hall; 500 University Blvd NE; Albuquerque, NM 87131; Phone: (505) 277-1644; http://meteorite.unm.edu/meteorites/meteorite-museum

Alamogordo, NM
Shroud Exhibit and Museum is a thoughtful and free museum presenting evidence to support the Shroud of Turin – the shroud in which Jesus was wrapped after he was crucified. Open Monday, Tuesday, Thursday, Friday and Saturday from 1 PM to 5 PM, and Sunday from 2 PM to 4 PM. 923 New York Ave; Alamogordo, NM, 88310; Phone: (575) 415-5206; http://shroudnm.com/Index.html

Alto, NM (See Ruidoso NM)

Angel Fire, NM
Vietnam Veterans Memorial was constructed for U.S. Marine Corps First Lieutenant Victor David Westphall III and the fifteen men who died with him on May 22, 1968 in Vietnam. The visitor center provides memorabilia and informational panels. There's also a chapel on the grounds. There is no entrance fee. Open 9 AM to 4 PM daily. The chapel is always open. 34 Country Rd; Angel Fire, NM 87710; Phone: (575) 377 6900; https://www.vietnamveteransmemorial.org

Artesia, NM
Artesia Historical Museum & Art Center exhibits photographs, Native American artifacts, and farm and ranch displays. Admission is free. Open Tuesday through Friday from 9 AM to 5 PM but closed for lunch from Noon to 1 PM. Open Saturday from 1 PM to 5 PM. 505 W Richardson Ave; Artesia, NM 88210; Phone: (575) 748-2390; https://www.artesianm.gov/154/Museum-Art-Center

Belen, NM

Belen Harvey House Museum presents Fred Harvey who revolutionized travel to and through the southwest by creating the eponymous Harvey House chain of restaurants and hotels, and Harvey Girls who staffed the restaurants. Admission is free with donations gratefully accepted. Open Tuesday through Friday from Noon to 5 PM. Occasional Saturday hours. Closed major holidays. 104 N First St; Belen, NM 87002; Phone: (505) 861-0581; http://www.belen-nm.gov/harvey-house-collection.aspx

Capitan, NM

Grave of Smokey Bear is located on the grounds of Smokey Bear Historical Park. There is an admission charge to enter the building, but the famous bear's grave is actually located behind that building with a plaque and sign. You can just follow the path around back to the grave. 118 W Smokey Bear Blvd; Capitan, NM 88316; Phone: (575) 354-2748; http://www.emnrd.state.nm.us/SFD/SmokeyBear/SmokeyBearPark.html

Carlsbad, NM

Carlsbad Museum & Art Center explores prehistory and history with Native American ceramics, from early Mogollon and Mesa Verde vessels to historic pueblo pottery. The McAdoo Collection highlights famous Taos artists. Admission is free but donations are welcomed. Open Tuesday through Saturday from 10 AM to 5 PM. 418 W Fox St; Carlsbad, NM 88220; Phone: (575) 887-0276; http://www.cityofcarlsbadnm.com/museum.cfm

Chimayo, NM

Santuario de Chimayo is considered the most important pilgrimage site in the United States. It is also one of the most beautiful, set against the breathtaking mountain background. Open daily from 9 AM to 5 PM (until 6 PM in summer). Mass takes place at 11 AM Monday through Saturday and at 10:30 AM and Noon on Sunday. The High Road to Taos town of Chimayo is also known for its weavers, and its deliciously robust red chile. 15 Santuario Dr; Chimayo, NM 87522; Phone: (505) 351-4889; https://www.nps.gov/nr/travel/american_latino_heritage/el_santuario_de_chimayo.html http://chimayo.us/PC/Points.html

Cimarron, NM

St. James Hotel is open for business as it has been for 140 years, complete with its fascinating and violent history. There's a video screening in the lobby and visitors can peek into some of the preserved historic rooms. Check out the bar where the likes of Jesse James imbibed, and sometimes shot up the ceiling. 617 S Collison Ave; Cimarron, NM 87714; Phone: (575) 376-2664; http://www.exstjames.com

Clayton, NM
Herzstein Memorial Museum explores another piece of the state's history – northern New Mexico in the 1930s, as well as the Santa Fe Trail, and (in)famous outlaws. There is no admission charge to visit the museum or for the monthly Historical Society programs, but donations are always welcome. Open Tuesday through Saturday 10 AM to 4 PM. Open until 5 PM May through August. 22 South Second St; Clayton, NM 88415; Phone: (575) 374-2977; https://www.claytonnm.org/the-herzstein-museum/

Cloudcroft, NM
This rugged mountain town is filled with forests and hiking trails. It is also breath-taking both for its beauty and the altitude – topping off at 9,000 feet. The Trestle Recreation Area provides day use hiking and biking. https://www.fs.usda.gov/Internet/FSE_DOCUMENTS/stelprdb5404319.pdf

Embudo, NM
Johnnie Meier Classical Gas Museum gathers everything automotive, and anything else that caught the attention of Johnnie Meier. Some of it valuable and collectible, others just fun to explore. There is no website, no admission, and no set hours. Located on the Low Road to Taos. 1819 Hwy 68; Embudo, NM 87531; Phone: (505) 852-2995.

Farmington, NM
Bisti/De-Na-Zin Wilderness Area delivers some of the most unusual scenery found in the Four Corners region. Known for its sandstone hoodoos, the heavily weathered rock forms of pinnacles, spires, and cap rocks. Check the website for explicit directions. It's located 36 miles south of Farmington – the nearest city. There are no fees to visit. Open all year. Note: It will be quite hot in summer. Always bring water. Phone: (505) 564-7600; https://www.blm.gov/visit/bisti-de-na-zin-wilderness

B Square Ranch houses a bit of everything including two museums, and a working farm and ranch. The **Bolack Museum of Fish and Wildlife** preserves over 2,500 specimens while the **Bolack Electromechanical Museum** features antique electrical, radio, communication, industrial, and agricultural artifacts. Free tours by appointment. Open Monday through Saturday from 9 AM to 3 PM. Closed major holidays. 3901 Bloomfield Hwy; Farmington, NM 87401; Phone: (505) 325-4275; http://www.bolackmuseums.com

E3 Children's Museum & Science Center has hands-on, science-related activities focused on Sound, Light, Magnetism, and Shadows. ArtTot's Turf is a special area for children five and under. Admission is free. Donations appreciated. Open Tuesday through Saturday from 10 AM to 5 PM. 302 N Orchard Ave;

Farmington, NM 87401; Phone: (505) 599-1425; https://www.fmtn.org/254/E3-Childrens-Museum-Science-Center

Fort Stanton, NM

Fort Stanton Historic Site summarizes over 155 years of history starting as a military garrison and ending as an World War II internment camp, with a stint as a tuberculosis hospital in between. Admission is free although donations are gratefully accepted. Open Monday through Saturday from 10 AM to 4 PM and Sunday from Noon to 4 PM. 104 Kit Carson Rd; Fort Stanton, NM 88323; Phone: (575) 354-0341; http://fortstanton.org

Fort Sumner, NM

Fort Sumner Historic Site/Bosque Redondo Memorial honors the Mescalero Apache and the Navajo who were evicted from their homes and forced to march hundreds of miles to the reservation. The story of the march and subsequent deaths are told in the memorial. Admission is free. Open Wednesday through Sunday from 8:30 AM to 4:30 PM. Closed major holidays. 3647 Billy the Kid Dr; Fort Sumner, NM 88119; Phone: (575) 355-2573; http://nmhistoricsites.org/bosque-redondo

Glen Rio, NM

Russell's Route 66 Museum combines the sale of gasoline with the owner's passion for classic cars. Stop for gas, and admire the historic car museum right inside the Travel Center. No charge to browse and enjoy. I-40 Exit 369; Phone: (575) 576-8700; http://www.russellsttc.com/gallery_museum.php

Grants, NM

El Malpais National Monument offers diverse landscapes and the opportunity for hiking, wildlife watching, and exploration of natural formations. There are no fees charged. There are several ways to reach El Malpais and each offers access to different sights and experiences. Monument trailheads are open from sunrise to sunset daily. The visitor center is open daily from 9 AM to 5 PM. Closed Thanksgiving, Christmas, and New Year's Day. I-40 exit 85; Phone: (505) 876-2783; https://www.nps.gov/elma/planyourvisit/gettingaround.htm; https://www.nps.gov/elma/index.htm

El Morro National Monument has been hydrating thirsty travelers for hundreds of years. Everyone from Ancestral Puebloans to present day tourists have stopped at the springs hidden at the base of a sandstone bluff. But there's more than water – unable to resist the easily carved stone, over 2,000 signatures, dates, messages, and petroglyphs decorate the base of the mesa. Hike the trails to view the inscriptions, water pool, pueblo ruins, and top of the promontory. The visitor center screens a 15-minute introduction to El Morro National Monument. The trails are open 9 AM to 5 PM in summer, and from 9 AM to 4 PM in winter. Closed major holidays. There is no fee to enter El Morro National Monument. Note: El Morro is about 40 miles west of Grants, which is the nearest major town to the monument. Hwy 53; Phone: (505) 783-4226 ext. 801; https://www.nps.gov/elmo/index.htm

Western New Mexico Aviation Heritage Museum answers the question – how did planes fly across the country before there was radio. The answer is that they followed the path indicated by a series of huge arrows, and a string of land-based lighthouses. New Mexico was part of the Los Angeles-Amarillo Airway route and two of those early buildings have been rehabilitated and turned into a tiny free museum. The hours are severely limited. The museum is currently open Saturdays from 9 AM to 1 PM, but the compound is open for a walking tour at other times. Visitors can also see the 51-foot airway beacon tower, and its electric-generator shed. Take I-40 Exit 79 or 81B to Old Route 66/NM 122 and drive into Milan. Directions are on the website. Grants-Milan Regional Airport; Airport Rd; Milan, NM 87020; Phone: (505) 287-4700; http://www.cibolahistory.org/airway-heritage-museum.html

Las Cruces, NM
Under the aegis of the **City of Las Cruces Museum System**, the city's museums are free and open to the public. They all share the same hours. Open Tuesday through Friday from 10 AM to 4:30 PM and Saturday from 9 AM to 4:30 PM. Closed major holidays. **Branigan Cultural Center** hosts changing cultural exhibits as well as educational programs, classes, and special events. 501 N Main St; Las Cruces, NM 88001; Phone (575) 541-2154; http://www.las-cruces.org/departments/quality-of-life/museum-system/branigan-cultural-center

Las Cruces Museum of Art hosts changing contemporary art exhibits. 491 N Main St Las Cruces, NM 88001; Phone: (575) 541-2137; http://www.las-cruces.org/departments/quality-of-life/museum-system/museum-of-art

Las Cruces Museum of Nature & Science features three permanent exhibits: Desert Life, Permian Trackways, and Light & Space exhibits. 411 N Main St; Las Cruces, NM 88001; Phone: (575) 522-3120; http://www.las-cruces.org/en/departments/quality-of-life/museum-system/museum-of-nature-and-science
Las Cruces Railroad Museum is located in an historic Santa Fe Railroad depot and describes the importance of the arrival of the Atchison Topeka & Santa Fe Railroad for the history of the city. 351 N Mesilla St; Las Cruces, NM 88005; Phone: (575) 647-4480; http://www.las-cruces.org/departments/quality-of-life/museum-system/railroad-depot-museum

Las Vegas, NM

Wander this historic city filled with architecture that dates back to the heyday of the railroad. Fans of the TV show Longmire will want to stand in **Las Vegas Plaza** where scenes from the popular show were filmed.

Castaneda Hotel is a historic Fred Harvey hotel located along Amtrak's Southwest Chief line. The hotel first opened in 1898 but was closed for many years. Totally renovated, it is now open to guests and those who just want to see a bit of the state's tourism past. Official tours will incur a fee. 524 Railroad Ave; Las Vegas, NM 87701; Phone: (505) 425-3591; http://castanedahotel.org

Dwan Light Sanctuary features 12 large prisms in the apses and ceiling which spread rainbows across the floor and walls. Named after designer and funder Virginia Dwan, the Dwan Light Sanctuary is open 6 AM to 8 PM daily. Visitors are requested to stop at the United World College (UWC) welcome center to register and receive a visitors pass. There is no charge, although donations are accepted. Forest 263 Rd; Las Vegas, NM 87701; Phone: (505) 454-4252; https://www.uwc-usa.org/page.cfm?p=528

Las Vegas National Wildlife Refuge offers wildlife viewing, hiking trails, an eight-mile scenic auto loop drive, and an observation deck. Use the Fred Quintana Overlook at Crane Lake for observing wildlife. There are no entrance fees. The refuge trails are open all year during daylight hours. The visitor center is open when staffing permits Monday through Thursday from 8 AM to 4:30 PM and Friday from 8 AM to 3:30 PM. Hwy 281; Las Vegas, NM 87701; Phone: (505) 425-3581; https://www.fws.gov/refuge/Las_Vegas

Los Alamos, NM

Los Alamos is famous for its role in developing the atomic bomb during World War II. You can download a walking tour of the major historical sites here: https://www.nps.gov/mapr/upload/Final-Brochure.pdf
The city of Los Alamos also has walking tour:
http://www.visitlosalamos.org/historic-walking-tour

Bradbury Science Museum presents science exhibits, including extensive information on the Manhattan Project and atomic bombs. This free museum is open Tuesday through Saturday from 10 AM to 5 PM, and Sunday and Monday from 1 PM to 5 PM. Closed major holidays. 1350 Central Ave; Los Alamos, NM 87544; Phone: (505) 667-4444; http://www.lanl.gov/museum/index.php

Los Alamos Nature Center encourages children and adults to learn about gardens, mud, and nature. Admission is free. Open Monday through Saturday from 10 AM to 4 PM with extended closing on Tuesday until 8 PM. Open Sunday from 1 PM to 4 PM. Closed on most major holidays. Note: There is a charge for the planetarium shows. 2600 Canyon Rd; Los Alamos, NM 87544; Phone: (505) 662-0460; http://peecnature.org

Manhattan Project National Historical Park is a work in progress. There are three areas at Los Alamos but only the visitor center is currently open. There is no entrance fee. From the end of May through October open daily 10 AM to 4 PM. November through April open Thursday through Monday from 10 AM to 3 PM. Closed Christmas and New Year's Day. 475 20th St; Los Alamos, NM 87544; Phone: (505) 661-6277; https://www.nps.gov/mapr/manhattan-project-los-alamos.htm

Lincoln, NM

Lincoln Historic Site is just about the entire town – 17 structures and outbuildings, seven of which are open year-round, and two more open seasonally. There is a fee to visit the museum, but it is free to stop in the visitor center and stroll the streets reliving Billy the Kid history. Note: There is only the most limited dining in town. Rt 380; Lincoln, NM 88338; Phone: (575) 653-4082; http://www.nmhistoricsites.org/lincoln

Madrid, NM

Driving along scenic Turquoise Trail (Rt 14) between Albuquerque and Santa Fe, the town of Madrid (pronounced MA-drid) was made famous in the movie Wild Hogs, but it has been luring tourists for far longer. The old coal mining town has been reborn as an artist community. Stop in the historic Mindshaft Tavern if you've a hankering for lunch.

Mountainair, NM

Salinas Pueblo Missions is actually three sites that represent a unique time in the area's history. Abo, Quarai, and Gran Quivara are now abandoned but they are reminders of the often conflicted relations between the Spanish, the people of the pueblos, and the Spaniards of Jewish descent who converted during the Inquisition. Visiting all the sites will take some driving, but visitors are rewarded with a more complete look at the life and history of the area. Entrance fees are not charged at any site. Open daily all year. Memorial Day to Labor Day open 9 AM to 6 PM closing at 5 PM the rest of the year. Closed Thanksgiving, Christmas, and New Year's Day. Closed during winter storms.
https://www.nps.gov/sapu/index.htm
From the town of Mountainair:
Abo: Ruins are nine miles west on US 60; ½ mile north on NM 513. Phone: (505) 847-2400.
Gran Quivira: Ruins are 26 miles south on NM 55. Phone: (505) 847-2770.

Quarai: Ruins are 8 miles north on NM 55 and 1 mile west. Phone: (505) 847-2290.

Pecos, NM
Pecos National Historical Park spans history and culture from ancestral Native American sites to the Civil War, and even actress Greer Garson. Entrance is free as are the guided ranger tours. From Memorial Day until Labor Day the park is open daily from 8 AM to 6 PM. Park is open daily in winter but with a 4:30 PM closing. Located 25 miles east of Santa Fe, New Mexico off Interstate 25. 1 Peach Dr; Pecos, NM 87552; Phone: (505) 757-7241; https://www.nps.gov/peco/index.htm

Portales, NM
Dalley Windmill Collection was the largest privately owned windmill collection in the nation until Bill and Alta Dalley donated it to the town of Portales. Today, the Dalley Windmill Museum is located on the fairgrounds near the intersection of U.S. 70 and Lime Street. Phone: (575) 356-5307; https://www.portales.com/dalley-windmill-museum

Jack Williamson Science Fiction Library in the Golden Library has one of the top science fiction collections in the world. It contains early 1900s pulp science fiction, correspondence, books, and even original manuscripts. Started with the personal collection of science fiction pioneer Jack Williamson, winner of the Hugo and Nebula awards and long associated with Eastern New Mexico University, the stellar collection was expanded by the donation of R. Duane and Kathryn Elms of Silver City. Their gift included one-of-a-kind items, first editions, signed editions and thousands of collectible publications. There is no admission fee. Open Monday through Friday from 8 AM to 5 PM. Closed major holidays and university breaks. Eastern New Mexico University; 1500 S Ave K; Portales, NM 88130; Phone: (575) 562-2624; https://my.enmu.edu/web/golden-library/special-collections/jack-williamson-science-fiction

Roswell, NM
Perhaps the most famous city in world for UFOs, Roswell also offers visitors art, aviation history, and beauty.
Anderson Museum of Contemporary Art features a diverse collection of modern art. Admission is free. Open Monday through Friday from 9 AM to 4 PM. Open on Saturday and Sunday from 1 PM to 5 PM. 409 E College Blvd; Roswell, NM 88201; Phone: (575) 623-5600; http://www.roswellamoca.org

Bitter Lake National Wildlife Refuge offers the 1/4 mile Butterfly Trail with information about butterflies and plants that attract them. There is an eight-mile wildlife drive and trails for spotting birds and dragonflies. Entrance is free. The visitor center hours are Monday through Friday from 8 AM to 4 PM. Note: They advise calling to verify. Refuge is open dawn to dusk. Located 10 miles northeast of Roswell. 4200 E Pine Lodge Rd; Roswell, NM 88201; Phone: (575) 625-4011; https://www.fws.gov/refuge/Bitter_Lake

Roswell Museum and Art Center offers the largest public collection of works by Peter Hurd and Henriette Wyeth. The two famous art families are connected to Roswell, and New Mexico. Peter Hurd was raised in Roswell, and he and his wife, Henriette Wyeth lived in nearby San Patricio. The exhibit *Made in New Mexico* is a semi-permanent exhibition highlighting the diverse art from the Native American potters, Spanish American santeros, and the Taos Art Colony. Admission is free. Open Tuesday through Saturday from 9 AM to 5 PM. Sunday and some holidays from 1 PM to 5 PM. Note: There is a fee for planetarium shows. 1011 N Richardson Ave; Roswell, NM 88201; Phone: (575) 624-6744; http://www.roswellmuseum.org

Walker Aviation Museum displays historical information about the base and the men and women who served there. Admission is free. Open Monday through Sunday from 9 AM to 4 PM. 1 Jerry Smith Cir; Roswell, NM 88203; Phone: (575) 347-2464; http://www.wafbmuseum.org

Ruidoso, NM
Ruidoso Downs Racehorse Hall of Fame celebrates quarter horse racing and the famous All-American Futurity, the richest quarter horse race in the United States. Located on the second floor at Ruidoso Downs near the entrance of the All American Turf Club the Hall of Fame displays a panoply of racing memorabilia and racing history. Admission is free. Hours are not listed, but the office staff will open the exhibits, and even provide a free tour upon request. 26225 Hwy 70; Ruidoso Downs, NM 88346; Phone: (575) 378-4431; http://www.raceruidoso.com/racehorse-hall-of-fame

Spencer Theater For The Performing Arts, designed by New Mexico architect Antoine Predock, is home to four major glass installations by Dale Chihuly. The theater offers free public tours on Tuesdays and Thursdays at 10 AM. Call the box office to make tour reservations. Note: The Spencer is actually located in the small nearby town of Alto. 108 Spencer Dr; Alto, NM 88312; Phone: (575) 336-4800; http://www.spencertheater.com/about.html

Santa Fe, NM
One of the best art experiences in the USA is to wander up and down **Canyon Road**. Santa Fe also holds several distinctive and popular art markets each year

which are definitely worth a visit. https://www.newmexico.org/events/big-annual-markets

109 East Palace was once a receiving station for Los Alamos. Everyone who received mail needed to keep the super-secret site secret, all mail was delivered to Santa Fe. A plaque commemorates the building's history.

Cathedral Basilica of St. Francis of Assisi is a gorgeous Romanesque cathedral constructed starting in 1869. 131 Cathedral Pl; Santa Fe, NM 87501; Phone: (505) 982-5619; https://www.cbsfa.org

New Mexico National Guard Museum began as a tribute to the veterans of the infamous Bataan Death March. The museum displays the history of that march as well as chronicling the horrific story of the 1,800 New Mexico soldiers, and the 900 who survived to return home. Free to visit. Open Tuesday through Friday from 10 AM to 4 PM. Closed major holidays. 1050 Old Pecos Trail; Santa Fe, NM 87505; Phone: (505) 474-1670; http://www.bataanmuseum.com

New Mexico State Capitol Roundhouse derives its name from its shape – the only round capitol building in the country. It combines elements of the three major New Mexican architectural styles – New Mexico Territorial style, Pueblo adobe architecture, and Greek Revival adaptations. It features nearly 600 artworks exhibited inside the State Capitol Complex as well as on the grounds. Open for self-guided tours on Monday through Friday from 7 AM to 6 PM. From Memorial Day through the last Saturday in August the capitol is also open for self-guided tours on Saturdays from 9 AM to 5 PM. . Guided tours by appointment. 490 Old Santa Fe Trail; Santa Fe, NM 87501; Phone: (505) 986-4589; https://www.nmlegis.gov/Visitors

Shidoni Bronze Gallery and Sculpture Gardens was once a foundry but has become huge gallery space and the outdoor sculpture garden. No charge to browse. Open Tuesday through Saturday from 10 AM to 5 PM. 508 Bishops Lodge Rd; Santa Fe, NM 87506; Phone: (505) 988-8001 ext. 120; http://www.shidoni.com/gallery.html

Tesuque Glassworks is filled with striking glass art, but visitors can also watch the daily glassblowing demonstrations and learn about the art of cast glass. There is no charge to visit. Open Monday through Sunday from 9 AM to 5 PM. 1510 Bishop's Lodge Rd; Tesuque, NM 87574; Phone: (505) 988-2165; http://www.tesuqueglass.com/index.html

Silver City, NM

Western New Mexico University Museum is home to the "largest, most comprehensive collection of scientifically excavated prehistoric Mimbres materials from a single Mimbres site." Mimbres bowls were made by people living in the Southwest from the late 10th to early 12th century and are known for the striking geometric patterns and imagery found on their black-on-white ceramics. Other collections focus on prehistoric Southwestern pottery and artifacts, including basketry; historic Maria and Julian Martinez San Ildefonso Pueblo pottery, and Santa Clara Pueblo pottery. There are also historic Navajo rugs, as well as historic photographs. Admission is free. Open Monday through Friday from 9 AM to 4:30 PM. Open Saturday and Sunday from 10 AM to 4 PM. Fleming Hall; 1000 W. College Ave; Silver City, NM 88062; Phone: (575) 538-6386; https://museum.wnmu.edu

Socorro, NM

Fort Craig Historic Site was once home to nearly 4,000 troops tasked with safeguarding the settlers from Apache, Navajo, and Comanche raid. It was also the site of the largest Civil War battle in the Southwest. Free to visit. Open daily during daylight hours. The visitor center is open Thursday through Monday 8 AM to 5:30 PM. Closed Thanksgiving, Christmas, and New Year's Day. Full directions on the website. Fort Craig is about 35 miles south of Socorro off I-25. Phone: (575) 835-0412; https://www.blm.gov/visit/fort-craig-historic-site

Sevilleta National Wildlife Refuge offers wildlife watching, hiking, and photography. There are no entrance fees. Open on Monday through Friday from 8 AM to 4:30 PM. Open Saturday spring through fall. Note: Visitors can park at the entry gate and walk in to enjoy the trails when the visitor center and gate are not open. 40 Refuge Rd (Exit 169 off of Interstate 25); Socorro, NM 87801; Phone: (505) 864-4021; https://www.fws.gov/refuge/Sevilleta

Trinity Site holds an important place in American and World War II history. It was the location of the world's first atomic bomb test on July 16, 1945. Trinity is only open twice a year – on the first Saturday in April and October. This event is free and open to the public. No reservations are required. Entrance is through the Stallion Gate open between 8 AM and 2 PM. Maps and full directions at: http://www.wsmr.army.mil/Trinity/Pages/DirectionsMaps.aspx Note: A shuttle bus takes visitors the McDonald Ranch where the bomb was actually assembled. Phone: (575) 678-1134; http://www.wsmr.army.mil/Trinity/Pages/Home.aspx

Taos, NM

Old Courthouse, built in 1934, is filled with galleries, shops, and the remains of the old jail. On the second floor there are several striking justice-themed murals commissioned by the Works Progress Administration (WPA). 104 N Plaza; Taos,

NM 87571; https://livingnewdeal.org/projects/old-taos-county-courthouse-phillip-murals-taos-nm

Rio Grande Gorge Bridge offers spectacular views of the river and the gorge created by the Rio Grande. Located about 10 miles northwest of Taos on Rt 64.
San Francisco de Asis was made famous by photographer Ansel Adams and artist Georgia O'Keeffe, and remains a striking structure dating back to 1771. The Spanish Colonial church is notable for its massive adobe buttresses. Located four miles south of Taos, in the village of Ranchos de Taos. Generally open daily from 10 AM to 4 PM. 60 St Francis Plaza; Ranchos De Taos, NM 87557; Phone: (575) 758-2754; https://www.nps.gov/nr/travel/american_latino_heritage/San_Francisco_de_Assisi_Mission_Church.html

Tesuque, NM (See Santa Fe, NM)

Tucumcari, NM
This Route 66 town showcases its history in wall murals. Pick up a map at the Chamber of Commerce at 404 W Route 66 Blvd; Tucumcari, NM 88401; Phone: (575) 461-1694; http://www.tucumcarinm.com

Watrous, NM
Fort Union National Monument contains the remains of the largest 19th century military fort in the region, part of the defense of the Santa Fe Trail and the settlers who came west. Ranger led guided tours of the monument and specialized talks are held every day during the summer season. There is no fee. Open daily 8 AM to 4 PM, closing at 5 PM in summer. Closed Thanksgiving, Christmas, and New Year's Day. Located off I-25 north, exit 366 at Watrous. NM 161; Phone: (505) 425-8025; https://www.nps.gov/foun/index.htm

White Oaks, NM
It's not precisely a ghost town – people do still live there. , but it isn't the booming gold mining town it had been. If it's open, the No Scum Allowed Saloon is famous throughout the state – for the name? For the beer? Who knows? It's open Wednesday through Sunday. https://noscumsaloon.com There are also historic buildings are open seasonally. Three miles north of Carrizozo on US Hwy 54. https://www.newmexico.org/places-to-visit/ghost-towns/white-oaks

New York

Albany, NY

Corning Tower Observation Deck at the top of the 42-story Corning Tower is the tallest building in New York State outside of New York City. Access to the observation deck is free. Open Monday through Friday from 10 AM to 3:45 PM. Take the dedicated elevator from on the Plaza level. Note: An adult must accompany children under 16 and you will need to present photo ID at the Corning Tower Security Station. Empire State Plaza; Albany, NY 12242; Phone: (518) 474-2418; https://www.albany.org/listing/corning-tower-observation-deck/1117

Empire State Plaza (ESP) welcomes visitors to learn the history of the plaza and former Governor Nelson A. Rockefeller. Enjoy the public art program with 92 paintings, tapestries, and sculptures located in the ESP concourse, buildings, and outdoor areas. Self-guided tours are available Monday through Friday from 8:30 AM to 5 PM. Free guided art tours are also available by appointment. To schedule a tour, call the Empire State Plaza Visitor Center at (518) 474-2418. https://empirestateplaza.ny.gov/tours/art-collection

New York State Capitol is said to resemble a giant French chateau. Walk-in tours of the capitol are held Monday through Friday at 10 AM, Noon, 2 PM , and 3 PM. There are no public tours on Sundays or holidays. Tours are free and begin at the Plaza Visitor Center & Gift Shop in the North Concourse, Empire State Plaza. State St and Washington Ave; Albany, NY 12224; Phone: (518) 474-2418; https://hallofgovernors.ny.gov/generic/VisitTheCapitol

New York State Executive Mansion has been home to the state's governors and their families since 1875. The free public tour takes visitors through the Executive Mansion covering past and present New York State governors, architectural history, furnishings, artwork, and the Mansion's present existence as a LEED-certified building. Tours are available by appointment only and reservations must be made at least two weeks in advance. A photo ID is required for all adults. 138 Eagle St; Albany, NY 12202; Phone: (518) 473-7521; https://www.governor.ny.gov/explore-governors-mansion

New York State Museum covers the art, science, and history of the state. Admission is free with donations accepted. Open Tuesdays through Sundays from 9:30 AM to 5 PM except major holidays. 2 Madison Ave; Albany, NY 12230; Phone: (518) 474-5877; http://www.nysm.nysed.gov

Throop Museum shows life in rural America during the 19th and early 20th centuries. It is located on the first floor of the Albany College of Pharmacy and Health Sciences, in the O'Brien Building. The **Manufacturing Museum**, set up to replicate a small mid-19th century laboratory, features the tools a pharmacist would use to produce larger quantities of medications that were sold to shops and doctors. There is no cost for admission, however the museum does not have set hours. Contact the College to arrange a visit. 106 New Scotland Ave; Albany, NY 12208; Phone: (518) 694-7279; https://www.acphs.edu/throop

Auburn, NY

Fort Hill Cemetery is the final resting place of Harriet Tubman, best known for her role as a conductor on the Underground Railroad. The sites associated with her charge a fee, but a visit to the cemetery is free. Grounds are open dawn to dusk. 19 Fort St; Auburn, NY 13021; Phone: (315) 253-8132; http://www.forthillcemetery.net

Buffalo, NY (See also Lewiston, NY; Niagara Falls, NY; and Niagara University, NY)

Buffalo City Hall Observation Deck offers panoramic views of Lake Erie and western New York from the 28th-floor deck. Admission is free. Open Monday through Friday from 8:30 AM to 4 PM. 65 Niagara Sq; Buffalo, NY 14202; Phone: (716) 852-3300; https://www.visitbuffaloniagara.com/businesses/buffalo-city-hall-observation-deck

Buffalo City Hall Tour is a free guided walking tour offered by Preservation Buffalo Niagara. The tour covers the history of the building, and the art deco architectural elements. The tours are held every weekday at Noon in the lobby of City Hall. No reservations required. Note: They also offer fee-based tours. 65 Niagara Sq; Buffalo, NY 14202; Phone: (716) 852-3300; https://preservationbuffaloniagara.org/tours

Freedom Wall celebrates 28 notable civil rights leaders from America's past and present Michigan Ave and E Ferry St, Buffalo, NY 14209; https://www.albrightknox.org/community/ak-public-art/freedom-wall

Peace Bridge welcomes pedestrians to enjoy views of the Niagara River, Lake Erie, and the Buffalo skyline. Crossing into Canada and back is free for pedestrians but photo ID is required. See the website for accepted identification. Access the bridge from the Peace Bridge parking lot off Busti Avenue. https://www.peacebridge.com/index.php/bicyclists-pedestrians/walk-the-bridge

Tifft Nature Preserve is noted for its birding, but it also offers five miles of trails through marsh and forest. Access to the grounds, boardwalks, and trails is free.

Donations are gratefully accepted. Open year-round from dawn to dusk. 1200 Fuhrmann Blvd; Buffalo, NY 14203; Phone: (716) 825-6397; https://www.tifft.org

Clinton, NY
Ruth and Elmer Wellin Museum of Art at Hamilton College offers exhibitions, programs, and events free to the public. Open Tuesday through Sunday from 11 AM to 5 PM. 198 College Hill Rd; Clinton, NY 13323; Phone: (315) 859-4396; https://www.hamilton.edu/wellin

Corning, NY
This city is synonymous with glass, and it certainly has the dazzling Corning Museum of Glass, which charges a fee for admission. But if you visit the town you can, enjoy some spectacular stained glass windows at no charge.
Christ Episcopal Church of Corning highlights nearly 85 stained glass sanctuary windows. Most of the older windows were produced by the Tiffany Glass and Decorating Company and by J. & R. Lamb Studios. Regular office hours are Monday through Friday from 9 AM to 4 PM, closing at Noon in July and August. Download their brochure on the windows: http://www.christepiscopalcorning.org/wp-content/uploads/bsk-pdf-manager/Stained_Glass_Brochure_for_Window_Booklet_32.pdf. 39 E. First St; Corning, NY 14830; Phone: (607) 937-5449; http://www.christepiscopalcorning.org

Highland Falls, NY
West Point Museum documents the history of warfare dating back to Egyptian times. The adjacent West Point Visitors Center displays information about cadet life. Exhibits focus on cadet daily life and include a full-scale barracks room and uniform room. Located in front of the West Point Thayer gate. Admission is free. The visitor center is open daily from 9 AM to 4:45 PM. The museum is open daily from 10:30 AM to 4:15 PM. Closed major holidays. Note: The only way to explore the grounds of West Point is through a fee-based tour. 2110 New South Post Rd; Highland Falls, NY 10996; Phone: (845) 938-3590; https://westpoint.edu/visiting-west-point/visitors-center https://history.army.mil/museums/IMCOM/westPoint/index.html

Ilion, NY
Remington Museum & Country Store celebrates their rifle-making since Eliphalet Remington made the first one in 1816. The free museum is part of the main factory. Hours change seasonally. Closed first two weeks in July and on

major holidays. Note: Entrance to museum is on Catherine St. 14 Hoefler Ave; Ilion, NY 13357; Phone: (315) 895-3304; https://www.remington.com/about-us

Kinderhook, NY

Martin Van Buren National Historic Site honors the man considered a major figure of the abolitionist movement and who stoutly defended Abraham Lincoln's policies during the Civil War. There are no fees to enter or to tour his home, but you do have to register at the visitor center. The visitor center is open daily in season from 9 AM to 4:30. Tours are available when the visitor center is open. Closes for the year in early December. Check the website or call. The grounds are open daily all year from 7 AM until sunset. 1013 Old Post Rd; Kinderhook, NY 12184; Phone: (518) 758-9689 x2011; https://www.nps.gov/mava/index.htm

Lewiston, NY (See also Buffalo, NY; Niagara Falls, NY; and Niagara University, NY)

Niagara Power Vista highlights the science and the power of energy generation. Exhibits include a Virtual Reality ride, hands-on experiments, and the geology of Niagara. You can even walk through a turbine. Admission is free. Open daily from 9 AM to 5 PM. Closed some major holidays. 5777 Lewiston Rd; Lewiston, NY, 14092; Phone: (716) 286-6661; https://www.nypa.gov/communities/visitors-centers/niagara-power-vista

Mount Vernon, NY (See also New York City, NY)

Saint Paul's Church National Historic Site has been a hospital, supply depot, and barracks for both armies in the Civil War. Its cemetery dates back to 1704. There is no fee to visit and the tours are also free. From early January through late June open Monday to Friday from 9 AM to 5 PM. Early July through late-December open Tuesday through Saturday from 9 AM to 5 PM. 897 S Columbus Ave; Mt. Vernon, NY 10550; Phone: (914) 667-4116; https://www.nps.gov/sapa/index.htm

Niagara Falls, NY (See also Buffalo, NY; Niagara University, NY; and Lewiston, NY)

Niagara Falls State Park is a gem of a park and always open. Although there is a fee for some of the attractions, there is no fee to enter. Visitors can marvel at the falls, enjoy the evening illumination, and hike the trails often leading to beautiful views. If you bring your passport, you can walk across the Rainbow Bridge to the Canadian side of the Falls. 332 Prospect St; Niagara Falls, NY 14303; Phone: (716) 278-1796; https://www.niagarafallsstatepark.com

Niagara University, NY (See also Buffalo, NY; Lewiston NY; and Niagara Falls, NY)

Castellani Art Museum focuses on prints, photographs, paintings, drawings, and sculpture dating largely from the 1850s to the present. Admission is free, although donations are gratefully accepted. Open Tuesday through Saturday from 11 AM to 5 PM and Sunday from 1 PM to 5 PM. 5795 Lewiston Rd; Niagara University, NY 14109; Phone: (716) 286-8200; http://www.castellaniartmuseum.org

New York City, NY

There is often confusion about what is and what is not New York City. The city is actually composed of five boroughs: The Bronx (The is part of its name), Brooklyn, Manhattan (the borough that most people associate with New York City), Queens, and Staten Island. The attractions are listed by borough. Although it is undeniably expensive to visit, New York City has a stellar array of free attractions. Enjoy one of the greatest cities in the world. Especially the free parts.

The Bronx

Bronx Museum of the Arts specializes in contemporary art by New Yorkers of Latin, Asian, and African descent. This free admission museum is open Wednesday through Sunday from 11 AM to 6 PM and open late on Friday to 8 PM. 1040 Grand Concourse; Bronx, NY 10456; Phone: (718) 681-6000; http://www.bronxmuseum.org

Judaica Museum + The Art Collection displays rotating exhibits of contemporary artists, explores themes from the permanent collection, and highlights Jewish art and culture. Located on the main floor of the Jacob Reingold Pavilion at the Hebrew Home at Riverdale. Free to visit. Open Sunday through Thursday from 10:30 AM to 4:30 PM. Note: Photo ID is required for admission to the grounds. 5901 Palisade Ave; Bronx, NY 10471; Phone: (718) 581-1000; https://www.riverspringhealth.org/art

Maritime Industry Museum at Fort Schuyler contains ship models, historic artifacts, and nautical photographs and prints illustrating history of seafaring and passenger ship lines. Admission is free. Open Monday through Saturday from 9 AM to 4 PM. State University of New York Maritime College Campus, 6 Pennyfield Ave; Bronx, NY 10465; Phone: (718) 409-7218, http://sunymaritime.edu/about/visiting-maritime/maritime-museum

Brooklyn

Coney Island is one of the most famous parts of Brooklyn – beloved for its boardwalk and amusement park. It will cost to enjoy the amusements, but it won't cost a dime to stroll the boardwalk and take in the decidedly quirky atmosphere. Learn more about the historic beach resort and its activities at: https://www.coneyisland.com/tourist-information.

BRIC House offers curated exhibitions and programs focusing on emerging and mid-career artists whose work reflects Brooklyn's diversity. Their calendar lists concerts and events. Note: Almost everything offered is free but the website lists both free and fee-based events and shows. 647 Fulton St; Brooklyn, NY 11217; Phone: (718) 683-5600; https://www.bricartsmedia.org

Brooklyn Bridge is completely free to stroll. There's even a pedestrian walkway to make it safer. The just over one-mile span connects Manhattan and Brooklyn and can be accessed from both sides. If you don't want to walk back, both boroughs have excellent public transportation. The Brooklyn entrance is Tillary Street and Boerum Place. From Manhattan, start your stroll across from the northeast corner of City Hall Park along Centre Street. https://www.nycgo.com/articles/guide-to-the-brooklyn-bridge

Brooklyn Navy Yard BLDG 92 is base's museum with three floors of exhibits related to the history and development of the Yard, and a gallery space. Admission is free. Open on Wednesday through Sunday from Noon to 6 PM. Note: Tours of the Brooklyn Navy Yard are fee-based. 63 Flushing Ave at Carlton Ave; Brooklyn, NY 11205; Phone: (718) 907-5932; https://brooklynnavyyard.org/visit/bldg-92

Coney Art Walls – The Outdoor Museum of Street Art is curated by Joseph Sitt and Jeffrey Deitch. Free to the public. Open daily in summers from Noon to 8 PM. 3050 Stillwell Ave; Brooklyn, NY 11224; Phone: (212) 529-5055; http://coneyartwalls.com

Green-Wood Cemetery dates back to 1838 and is the final resting place of famous New Yorkers. It also features Brooklyn's highest point at Battle Hill. Once a site of the Revolutionary War, it is now marked with a seven-foot statue of the Minerva, goddess of wisdom, but also war and commerce. Pick up a free map at any of the entrances. Admission to Green-Wood is free at all times, but their talks and trolley tours will incur a fee. 500 25th St; Brooklyn, NY 11232; Phone: (718) 210-3080; https://www.green-wood.com/2010/visit-on-your-own

Harbor Defense Museum details the history and evolution of NYC's coastal defense systems. It is the only army museum in the City, and presents military artifacts from the Revolutionary War to World War II. Admission is free. Open Tuesday through Friday from 10 AM to 4 PM. Fort Hamilton; 230 Sheridan Loop; Brooklyn, New York 11252; Phone: (718) 630-4349; https://home.army.mil/hamilton/index.php/about/Garrison/harbor-defense-museum

Manhattan

9/11 Museum and Memorial honors and memorializes those who died in the terrorist attacks. The museum charges admission, but the Memorial is open free of charge. Covering eight of the 16 acres at the World Trade Center, the names of every person who died in the terrorist attacks of both February 26, 1993 and September 11, 2001 are inscribed in bronze around the twin memorial pools. Although the world remembers the attack of 9/11, far fewer are aware of the 1993 bombing of the WTC and the six people who died on that day. But New York remembers. The memorial is open to the public daily from 7:30 AM to 9 PM. 180 Greenwich St; New York, NY 10048; Phone: (212) 312-8800; https://www.911memorial.org

42nd Street Library: The New York Public Library's Stephen A. Schwarzman Building is guarded by world famous marble lions *Patience* and *Fortitude*. The Library is not only a scholarly resource but a surprising tourist destination filled with exhibits and unusual galleries. You can certainly wander on your own, but the library's docent-led free tours are an excellent way to see highlights. The one-hour tours are currently held at 11 AM and 2 PM on Monday through Saturdays, and at 2 PM on Sundays. Tours meet at the reception desk in Astor Hall and are available on a first come, first served basis. Note: The Schwarzman Building is closed on Sundays in July and August. 476 Fifth Ave; New York, NY 10018; Phone: (917) 275-6975; https://www.nypl.org/about/locations/schwarzman/visitor-guide

African Burial Ground National Monument includes four exhibit areas, and a 40-person theater. The site started as a burial ground in the 17th or 18th century, but was rediscovered in 1991 when excavation began for a federal office building. Admission is free. Donations are gratefully accepted. Open Tuesday through Saturday from 10 AM to 4 PM. Closed Thanksgiving, and Christmas Day. The outdoor memorial has the same hours but is closed in winter from November through March. Ted Weiss Federal Building; 290 Broadway; New York, NY 10005; Phone: (212) 637-2019; https://www.nps.gov/afbg/index.htm

American Folk Art Museum considers its collection to be the nation's premier assemblage of American folk art from the 18th century through the present. Works include giant weather vanes to Amish quilts, toys, and carousel animals. Admission is free. Open Tuesday through Thursday from 11:30 AM to 7 PM and Friday from Noon to 7:30 PM. Open Saturday at 11:30 AM to 7 PM and on Sunday from Noon to 6 PM. 2 Lincoln Square – Columbus Ave between 65th and 66th St; New York, NY 10023; Phone: (212) 595- 9533; http://folkartmuseum.org

Battery Park City Parks was created from landfills from development of lower Manhattan. The construction of the Twin Towers (destroyed in the terrorist attack on 9/11/ 2001) created tons of excavated material that grow into one of the city's spectacular parks. The 25 acres at the south end of Manhattan works its way up the west side of the city along the Hudson River, with spectacular views of the Statue of Liberty. It is a landscape of public art, restored and relocated historic monuments, gardens, grass, trees, and paths all free and open to the public. The Battery Bikeway links the east and west sides of lower Manhattan. Without a doubt, this is one of the gems of the city. And, totally free to wander. http://thebattery.org; https://bpcparks.org/visit/map

Castle Clinton National Monument was constructed between 1808 and 1811 in preparation for the War of 1812 against England. Today it's the ticket office for the Statue of Liberty. There is no fee to enter Castle Clinton National Monument and take a 20-minute ranger-guided tour. Tours are currently offered Monday through Sunday at 10 AM, Noon, 2 PM, and 3:30 PM. Note: Public transportation is the best option. Battery Park; New York, NY 10004; Phone: (212) 344-7220; https://www.nps.gov/cacl/index.htm

Central Park is easily the city's most famous and iconic park – the huge green heart of the city. The Central Park Conservancy offers free and fee-based guided tours. Visit their website for the offerings and how to join the walk.
http://www.centralparknyc.org/tours/#guided_tours_tab
They also offer free downloadable guides if you prefer to stroll. Available in English, French, and Spanish.
http://www.centralparknyc.org/tours/#self_tours_tab

City Hall has been home to New York City's government since 1812. Free tours take visitors to see its cupola-topped marble hall, and the governor's room. Reservations are recommended. The minimum age for tours is 9-years-old or 4th grade. Tour information is subject to change and visitors should check the website for updated information on tour days and times. Broadway and Murray St; New York, NY 10007; Phone: (212) 788-2656;
http://www1.nyc.gov/site/designcommission/public-programs/city-hall/about-city-hall.page

Fashion Institute of Technology rotates exhibits selected from its collection. The garments date from the 18th century and the accessories including shoes and textiles, date from the 5th century. Admission to exhibitions is free as are their gallery tours and talks. Open Tuesday through Friday from Noon to 8 PM and on Saturday from 10 to 5 PM. Closed major holidays. See their Visitor Guidelines for prohibited items: https://www.fitnyc.edu/museum/visit/guidelines.php. Seventh Ave at 27 St; New York, NY 10001; Phone: (212) 217-4558;
https://www.fitnyc.edu/museum/index.php

Federal Hall National Memorial is the site of New York City's 18th century City Hall and where John Peter Zenger was jailed, tried, and acquitted of libel for exposing government corruption in his newspaper. You can take a self-guided tour or one of the free tours offered by park rangers. Open Monday through Friday from 9 AM to 5 PM. Closed major holidays. 26 Wall St; New York, NY 10005; Phone: (212) 825-6990; https://www.nps.gov/feha/index.htm

Federal Reserve Bank of New York offers free guided tours to the public Monday to Friday at 1 PM and 2 PM except bank holidays. Hours are subject to change. Note: Reservations and printed tickets are required for entry and visitor should arrive 30 minutes early. Bring a photo ID. The name must match your reservation. 44 Maiden La; New York, NY 10045; https://www.newyorkfed.org/aboutthefed/visiting.html

General Grant National Memorial is the burial site of the 18th President of the United States, Ulysses S. Grant, and his wife Julia Dent Grant. Grant is credited with battlefield actions that led to Union victories in the Battles of Vicksburg, and Chattanooga. This ultimately led to the surrender of Robert E. Lee at Appomattox, ending the Civil War. After his presidency, Grant settled in New York City. A permanent exhibit addresses some of the major events in President Grant's life. The visitor center and memorial are free. Open Wednesday through Sunday from 9 AM to 5 PM. Riverside Park; Riverside Drive and 122nd St; New York, NY 10027; Phone: (212) 666-1640; https://www.nps.gov/gegr/index.htm

Governors Island National Monument (Manhattan-Brooklyn) is a seasonal destination offering tours of Fort Jay, Castle Williams, and Dock 102 as well as demonstrations of historic weapons and special events. There is no charge to visit the island or the national monument, but there is a charge for ferry transportation. Ferries leave from Battery Maritime Building at 10 South Street in Manhattan, and from Pier 6 Brooklyn Bridge Park in Brooklyn. Phone: (212) 825-3045; https://www.nps.gov/gois/index.htm

Grand Central Terminal is a popular destination on its own for exploring, dining, drinking, and shopping. Make sure to look up and see the beautifully restored ceiling glittering with the stars of the constellations. Grand Central Partnership offers a free tour of the Grand Central neighborhood that surveys many of the architecturally and historically significant sights. Check their website for current information: http://www.grandcentralpartnership.nyc/things-to-do/tours 89 E 42nd St; New York, NY 10017; Phone: (212) 340-2583; http://www.grandcentralterminal.com/what-to-see

Hamilton Grange National Memorial honors Alexander Hamilton who briefly lived in Harlem when it was a rural neighborhood. The house has been relocated to Saint Nicholas Park. Admission to the house and all tours are free. The visitor center is open Wednesday through Sunday except Thanksgiving and Christmas Day. Tours are offered at 10 AM, 11 AM, and 2 PM. Self-guided hours are Noon to 1 PM and again at 3 PM to 4 PM. Note: Backpacks, large bags, purses, and camera bags are prohibited in the period rooms. 414 W 141st St; New York, NY 10031; Phone: (646) 548-2310; https://www.nps.gov/hagr/index.htm

Hebrew Union College: Jewish Institute of Religion Museum and the Sigmund R. Balka Collection highlights Jewish art during the 19th and 20th centuries, complemented by ancient pottery from archaeological digs. Admission is free. Open Monday through Thursday from 9 AM to 5 PM and on Friday until 3 PM. Note: Current government issued photo ID required for security. 1 W 4th St; New York, NY 10012; Phone: (212) 824-2218; http://huc.edu/research/museums/huc-jir-museum-new-york

Hispanic Museum and Library covers nearly every aspect of art and culture in Spain – as well as Portugal, Latin America, and the Philippines. There's also a collection of prints and photographs documenting the architecture, peoples, and customs of Spain and Latin America. Admission is free. The museum is currently closed for renovation. Call or visit the website for updates. 613 W 155th St; New York, NY 10032; Phone: (212) 926-2234; http://hispanicsociety.org/visit/visitor-information

Houdini Museum of New York at Fantasma Magic displays several hundred objects that were used and personally belonged to Harry Houdini (born Erik Weisz). An animatronic Houdini even escapes from a straitjacket dangling from the ceiling. Admission is free. Open Monday through Saturday from 10 AM to 6 PM and on Sunday from 10 AM to 5 PM. 213 W 35th St; Suite 401; New York, NY 10001; Phone: (212) 244-3633; http://www.houdinimuseumny.com/visit

Juilliard School is world-famous for the achievements of its students, and the quality of their performances. Juilliard hosts hundreds of dance, drama, music, and cross-divisional performances every year, and some of those performances are free. Go to their Performance calendar. For "performance type" scroll down and select "free." 155 W 65th St; New York, NY 10023; Phone: (212) 799-5000; https://www.juilliard.edu/stage-beyond/performance-calendar

Miriam and Ira D. Wallach Art Gallery at Columbia University focuses on the contemporary artists of the Columbia campus and community. Admission is free. Open Wednesday through Friday from Noon to 8 PM. Open on Saturday and Sunday from Noon to 6 PM. Closed major holidays. Enter on W 125th Street, just west of Broadway. 615 W 129th St; Phone: (212) 854-6800; https://wallach.columbia.edu

Museum of Street Art (MoSA) at CitizenM Bowery Hotel resurrects one of the city's gone, but not forgotten landmarks. The famed 5 Pointz site has been destroyed but 20 graffiti artists collaborated in the painting of the CitizenM hotel's staircase turning it into a vertical exploration of street art. It's free but a visit should be booked in advance. 189 Bowery; New York, NY 10002; Phone: (212) 372-7274; https://www.citizenm.com/mosa

National Museum of the American Indian explores the diversity of Native American people. Admission is free. Open daily from 10 AM to 5 PM and on Thursday to 8 PM. Closed Christmas Day. 1 Bowling Green; New York, NY 10004; Phone: (212) 514-3700; http://nmai.si.edu/visit/newyork

Night Court serves the city that (almost) never sleeps. Night Court is open from 5 PM to 1 AM handling about 70 to 90 cases a night. It has become a major tourist destination and is free and open to the public. Note: Stay off your cell phone. You can be held in contempt of court if you fail to respect the proceedings. New York Criminal Court Building; 100 Centre St; New York, NY 10013; Phone: (646) 386-4500

Poet House invites the public to experience their exhibits of the physical and visual manifestation of poetry as well as works by visual artists. Free admission. Open Tuesday through Friday from 11 AM to 7 PM and on Saturday from 11 AM to 6 PM. 10 River Terrace; New York, NY 10282; Phone: (212) 431-7920; https://poetshouse.org/programs-events/exhibitions

Rockefeller Center beckons with art, beautiful gardens, and ever-changing exhibits and art displayed on the grounds. Open 7 AM to Midnight. Tours will cost, but it is free to take your own self-guided tour: https://www.rockefellercenter.com/blog/2016/08/18/art-route-rock-center; https://www.rockefellercenter.com/whats-happening
630 Fifth Ave; New York, NY 10111; Phone: (212) 332-6868

Schomburg Center for Research in Black Culture, part of the New York City public library system, focuses exclusively on African-American, African Diaspora, and African experiences. Named after Arturo Alphonso Schomburg whose collection formed the core, admission is free although donations are welcomed. Opened Monday through Saturday from 10 AM to 6 PM. 515 Malcolm X Blvd (at 135th St); New York, NY 10037; Phone: (917) 275-6975; https://www.nypl.org/events/tours/schomburg

St. Patrick's Cathedral is the landmark Neo-Gothic building and a highlight of a visit to New York City both for its beauty and religious importance. Guided tours are available on a limited schedule, but self-guided tours are always available.

Tours are free but donations are welcomed. You can download a tour brochure here: https://saintpatrickscathedral.org/documents/2015/3/Cathedral%20Tour%20and%20Map.pdf

St. Patrick's is also a parish church and mass is held daily. Fifth Ave at 51st St; New York, NY 10022; Phone: (212) 753-2261; https://saintpatrickscathedral.org

Theodore Roosevelt Birthplace National Historic Site is the early home of the 26th President of the United States, born and raised in New York City. Five of the rooms are open for free guided tours. There are no self-guided tours. Tours are available on the hour from 10 AM to 4 PM. Note: There is no Noon tour. 28 East 20th St; New York, NY 10003; Phone: (212) 260-1616; https://www.nps.gov/thrb/index.htm

Queens

Queens County Farm Museum surprises visitors with historic buildings, greenhouses, an orchard and even farm animals, all in the middle of the borough of Queens. It is the longest continuously farmed site in New York State. Admission is free, except during public events. Open daily from 10 AM to 5 PM. Closed major holidays. 73-50 Little Neck Pkwy; Queens, New York 11004; Phone: (718) 347-3276; http://www.queensfarm.org

Socrates Sculpture Park was transformed from a dump site to an art location with installations and light shows. Admission to the park's grounds, exhibitions, and programs is free, as is the self-guided tour. Socrates is open daily from 9 AM to sundown. Visitors can pick up information in the box on the Park's main gate at the intersection of Vernon Boulevard and Broadway. 32-01 Vernon Blvd; Queens, NY 11106; Phone: (718) 956-1819; https://socratessculpturepark.org

Staten Island

Staten Island Ferry takes commuters and tourists between Lower Manhattan and Staten Island. As part of the trip you will find a spectacular view of the Statue of Liberty, the vistas of New York Harbor and the Manhattan skyline. The ferry docks at the St. George Ferry Terminal. The ferry is free and is the best deal in NYC. It runs 24 hours a day, every day. Note: vehicles are not permitted – pedestrians only. Pick up the ferry on Staten Island at 1 Bay Street, and in Manhattan at 4 Whitehall Street.
http://www.siferry.com/index.html
http://www.nyc.gov/html/dot/html/ferrybus/staten-island-ferry.shtml

Snug Harbor Cultural Center & Botanical Garden is a mix of free and fee-based attractions. The fee-based places are the Newhouse Center for Contemporary Art, the New York Chinese Scholar's Garden, and the Connie Gretz Secret Garden.

The other gardens are free to visit. These include CSF Tuscan Garden modeled after the Villa Gamberaia in Florence, the White Garden filled with plants that have either gray green foliage or pure white blossoms, Rose Garden, the Allée, and the Perennial Garden. The main campus is open daily from dawn until dusk. 1000 Richmond Ter, Staten Island, NY 10301; Phone: (718) 425-3504; https://snug-harbor.org

North Blenheim, NY
Blenheim-Gilboa Visitors Center describes the unique engineering of a pumped-storage power facility through interactive, hands-on exhibits. Open daily from 10 AM to 5 PM. On the grounds is Lansing Manor, an 18th century home with authentic furnishings and antiques. There's 10 large rooms on two floors, plus a below-ground kitchen and other utility rooms. The manor is does not charge admission. Open daily except Tuesday from May through October for guided tours available from 10 AM to 5 PM. 1378 Rt 30; North Blenheim, NY 12131; Phone: (800) 724-0309; https://www.nypa.gov/communities/visitors-centers/blenheim-gilboa-visitors-center

Poughkeepsie, NY
Frances Lehman Loeb Art Center/Vassar College charts the history of art from antiquity to modern times. Admission is free. Open Tuesday through Saturday from 10 AM to 5 PM, open late Thursday to 9 PM. Open Sunday from 1 PM to 5 PM. Closed some major holidays and winter break. 124 Raymond Ave; Poughkeepsie, NY 12604; Phone: (845) 437-5237; https://fllac.vassar.edu

Sleepy Hollow, NY
Sleepy Hollow Cemetery is the final resting place for several famous residents including Washington Irving, author of the Legend of Sleepy Hollow, and labor leader Samuel Gompers. Known for its sculpture, stained glass windows, and lovely views, entrance is free. The cemetery provides a free map at the office and at the south gate, adjacent to the Old Dutch Church. Open Monday through Friday from 8 AM to 4:30 PM. Open Saturday and Sunday from 8:30 AM to 4:30 PM. Note: Special tours and events may incur a fee. 540 N Broadway; Sleepy Hollow, NY 10591; Phone: (914) 631-0081; http://sleepyhollowcemetery.org

Utica, NY
Museum of Art Munson-Williams-Proctor Arts Institute offers 19th century through contemporary American fine arts, 19th century American decorative arts, and paintings from the Hudson River School. Admission to this 1800s Italianate mansion museum is free although special exhibitions may have a fee. Open Tuesday through Saturday from 10 AM to 5 PM. Sunday from 1 PM to 5 PM. In July and August the Institute is also open Monday from 10 AM to 5 PM. 310 Genesee St; Utica, NY 13502; Phone: (315) 797-0000; http://www.mwpai.org

North Carolina

Ashville, NC

Asheville Distilling Company invites visitors to their tasting room on Friday and Saturday for free tours and tastings. Tours start at 5 PM. Note: Visitors must be at least 18 years of age to sample the spirits, although they can go on the tour. 12 Old Charlotte Hwy; Asheville, NC 28803; Phone: (828) 575-2000; https://ashevilledistilling.com

Aurora Fossil Museum encourages would-be archeologists to dig through their unique Pits of the Pungo filled with material containing fossils or fossil traces. Note: Bring your own trowel, sifter, and plastic bags for your finds. Head to the museum for fossil exhibits. There is no admission charge. Open Monday through Saturday from 9 AM to 4:30 PM. From March through Labor Day also open Sunday from 12:30 PM to 4:30 PM. Closed major holidays. 400 Main St; Aurora, NC 27806; Phone: (252) 322-4238; http://aurorafossilmuseum.org

Botanical Gardens of Asheville focuses on Southern Appalachian plants. There is no admission charge, but donations are appreciated. The gardens are open daily during daylight hours. The visitor center is open from April through November on Monday through Saturday from 10 AM to 4 PM and Sundays from Noon to 4 PM. From November through early December it is open daily from 11 AM to 3 PM. Closed the rest of the year. 151 W T Weaver Blvd; Asheville, NC 28804; Phone: (828) 252-5190; https://ashevillebotanicalgardens.org

Moog Factory was founded by electronic genius Robert Moog (1934-2005) who created the music synthesizer that bears his name. The Moog Factory offers free factory tours weekdays at 10:30 AM and 3:30 PM, but you must call ahead. If you just want to play one of these musical marvels, visit the Moog store and try out instruments currently in production. The store is open Monday through Friday from 10 AM to 6 PM, and Saturday from Noon to 5 PM. 160 Broadway St; Asheville, NC 28801; Phone: (828) 251-0090; https://www.moogmusic.com/content/visit-moog

Beaufort, NC

North Carolina Maritime Museum is one of three North Carolina Maritime Museums. The Beaufort museum hosts the artifacts from infamous pirate Blackbeard's wrecked flagship, the Queen Anne's Revenge. You'll find cannons, grenades, belt buckle, beads and special exhibits. Learn about boat-building at the Harvey W. Smith Watercraft Center. Free admission. Donations appreciated. Open weekdays from 9 AM to 5 PM. Open Saturday from 10 AM to 5 PM and

Sunday from 1 PM to 5 PM. 315 Front St; Beaufort, NC 28516; Phone: (252) 504-7740; https://ncmaritimemuseumbeaufort.com

Chapel Hill, NC
Ackland Art Museum has a special focus on Asian art, drawings, prints, and photographs as well as North Carolina pottery. The Ackland organizes more than a dozen special exhibitions a year. Free admission. Open Wednesday through Saturday 10 AM to 5 PM. Sunday 1 PM to 5 PM. The University of North Carolina at Chapel Hill; 101 S Columbia St; Chapel Hill, NC 27514; Phone: (919) 966-5736; https://ackland.org

Charlotte, NC
Billy Graham Library describes Billy Graham's journey from farm boy to religious leader. Free admission. Open Monday through Saturday from 9:30 AM to 5 PM. The last tour begins at 3:30 PM. Closed major holidays. 4330 Westmont Dr; Charlotte, NC 28217; Phone: (704) 401-3200; https://billygrahamlibrary.org

Charlotte Botanical Gardens at University of North Carolina are three garden sites with sixteen collections on display from Asian plantings to native wildflowers. Inside the greenhouse there's carnivorous plants and orchids. Admission to the greenhouse and gardens is free, but donations are appreciated. The gardens are open daily during daylight hours. The greenhouse is open Monday through Saturday from 10 AM to 3 PM and Sunday from 1 PM to 4 PM. 9090 Craver Rd; Charlotte, NC 28262; Phone: (704) 687-0721; https://gardens.uncc.edu

Wells Fargo History Museum highlights gold mining in North Carolina and includes a model of an 1889 Wachovia Bank branch from Winston-Salem. Admission is free. Open Tuesday through Saturday except bank holidays. Tours are available but must be booked ahead. 401 S Tryon St; Charlotte, NC 28202; Phone: (704) 715-1866; https://www.wellsfargohistory.com/museums/charlotte

Creswell, NC
Somerset Place offers a look at pre-Civil War plantation life. Seven original 19th century buildings are preserved including a reconstructed overseer's house, a plantation hospital, and cabins where enslaved families lived. Admission is free and donations appreciated. Open Tuesday through Saturday from 9 AM to 5 PM. Closed major holidays. 2572 Lake Shore Rd; Creswell, NC 27928; Phone: (252) 797-4560; https://historicsites.nc.gov/all-sites/somerset-place

Currie, NC
Moores Creek National Battlefield holds particular interest to those of Scottish descent. On February 27, 1776 Loyalist forces charging Moores Creek Bridge met and were defeated by North Carolina Patriots including Scottish Highlanders. It

was to be the last broadsword charge by the Highlanders, and the first major victory for the Patriots in the American Revolution. The battlefield site is free to visit and open daily from 9 AM to 5 PM. The visitor center is open Tuesday through Saturday from 9 AM to 5 PM. The park is closed on all federal holidays. 40 Patriots Hall Dr; Currie, NC 28435; Phone: (910) 283-5591; https://www.nps.gov/mocr/index.htm

Durham, NC
Bennett Place was the site of the largest troop surrender of the Civil War when Confederate General Johnston and Union General Sherman met at a farmhouse midway between their armies. No admission fees. Open Tuesday through Saturday 9 AM to 5 PM. Donations are accepted and appreciated. Note: Research has indicated that the correct spelling should actually be Bennitt. 4409 Bennett Memorial Rd; Durham, NC 27705; Phone: (919) 383-4345; https://historicsites.nc.gov/all-sites/bennett-place

Duke Homestead was the farm of Washington Duke, whose sons founded the American Tobacco Company. Visitors will see a museum of tobacco history with demonstrations of early farming techniques and manufacturing processes. Admission is free. Open Tuesday through Saturday from 9 AM to 5 PM. Closed most major holidays. Daily guided tours begin 15 minutes past the hour from 10:15 AM until 3:15 PM. 2828 Duke Homestead Rd; Durham, NC 27705; Phone: (919) 477-5498; https://historicsites.nc.gov/all-sites/duke-homestead

Historic Stagville includes the remnants of the one of the largest plantations in North Carolina. Visitors can see the original 1851 slave quarters, the 1860 barn, and a family house constructed in 1787. Admission is free. Guided tours are available Tuesday through Saturday at 11 AM, 1 PM, and 3 PM. Self-guided tours are also available however the historic structures are only open for guided tours. They recommend calling ahead as staffing limitations can cause a tour to be cancelled. 5828 Old Oxford Hwy; Durham, NC 27712; Phone: (919) 620-0120; http://www.stagville.org

Edenton, NC
Edenton National Fish Hatchery provides visitors with a scenic boardwalk, 36 ponds, holding house, and an aquarium. Admission is free. Open all year Monday through Friday from 7 AM to 3:30 PM. Open weekends and holidays from August through November. 1102 W Queen St; Edenton, NC 27932; Phone: (252) 482-4118; https://www.fws.gov/edenton

Fayetteville, NC
Airborne and Special Operations Museum (ASOM) starts in 1940 with the U.S. Army Parachute Test Platoon and ends with today's airborne and special

operations units. Admission is free although some individual experiences will incur a fee. Open Tuesday through Saturday from 10 AM to 5 PM. Open Sunday from Noon to 5 PM. Closed federal holidays. 100 Bragg Blvd; Fayetteville, NC 28301; Phone: (910) 643-2778; https://www.asomf.org/visit-the-museum

Fayetteville Area Transportation and Local History Museum displays the area's history through the early 20th century. Admission is free. Open Tuesday through Saturday from 10 AM to 4 PM. 325 Franklin St; Fayetteville, NC 28301; Phone: (910) 433-1457; https://fcpr.us/facilities/museums/fayetteville-area-transportation-and-local-history-museum

Fayetteville State University Planetarium take visitors on a tour of the solar system. Shows are free but you must register online. Lyons Science Building; Fayetteville State University; 1200 Murchison Rd; Fayetteville, NC 28301; Phone: (910) 672-1111; https://www.uncfsu.edu/community/planetarium

Museum of the Cape Fear Historical Complex includes the museum building with more than 400 years of history, the 1897 Poe house, and the historic Arsenal Park with the remains of an ordnance factory that served both the Federal and Confederate governments. Admission is free. Open Tuesday through Saturday from 10 AM to 5 PM. Open Sunday from 1 PM to 5 PM. Guided tours of the 1897 Poe house are also available at no cost. Closed major holidays. 801 Arsenal Ave; Fayetteville, NC 28305; Phone: (910) 500-4240; https://museumofthecapefear.ncdcr.gov/

North Carolina Veterans Park displays dog tags from each North Carolina member of the military who was killed in action from WWII to today. Admission is free. Open daily from 8 AM to dusk. 300 Bragg Blvd; Fayetteville, NC 28301; Phone: (910) 433-1457; https://fcpr.us/parks-trails/parks/north-carolina-veterans-park

Farmville, NC
May Museum and Park presents the history of Farmville from colonial times through current day. The museum displays a rotating exhibit of 19th and 20th century quilts culled from their collection. Free admission with donations are appreciated. Open Tuesday and Thursday from 9 AM until 2 PM. 3802 S Main St; Farmville, NC 27828; Phone: (252) 753-6725; http://farmvillenc.gov/departments/may-museum-park

Gibsonville, NC
Charlotte Hawkins Brown Museum named after the woman who helped transform the lives of more than 2,000 Black American students through Palmer Memorial Institute, a day and boarding school. Visitors can explore the historic

structures and learn more at the visitor center. Admission is free with donations appreciated. Open Tuesday through Saturday from 9 AM to 5 PM. Closed most major holidays. 6136 Burlington Rd; Gibsonville, NC 27249; Phone: (336) 449-4846; https://historicsites.nc.gov/all-sites/charlotte-hawkins-brown-museum

Greensboro, NC
Guilford Courthouse National Military Park was the site of a turning point in the Revolutionary War's Southern Campaign. It is recommended all visitors start their tour at the visitor center. Visitors can watch a 30-minute video about the battle. Artifacts and exhibits explain the course of the Southern Campaign Free admission. Open daily from 8:30 AM to 5 PM. Closed on Thanksgiving, Christmas, and New Year's Day. 2332 New Garden Rd; Greensboro, NC 27410; Phone: (336) 288-1776; https://www.nps.gov/guco/planyourvisit/battlefield-visitors-center.htm

Hatteras, NC
Hatteras Graveyard of the Atlantic Museum derives its name from the appellation given to the Outer Banks of North Carolina for its numerous shipwrecks. The museum highlights this history with artifacts recovered from the shipwrecks, including one of the famous German Enigma machines used to create "unbreakable" codes in WWII. Learn about piracy, including the infamous Anne Bonny and Blackbeard. Free admission with donations gratefully accepted. From the first Monday in April through the end of September the museum is open Monday through Saturday from 10 AM to 5 PM. Closes at 4 PM the rest of the year. Closed state holidays. 59200 Museum Dr; Hatteras, NC 27943; Phone (252) 986-0720; https://graveyardoftheatlantic.com

Hertford, NC
Jim "Catfish" Hunter Museum honors the pitcher for the Oakland Athletics who ultimately signed with the Yankees, but Hertford was his home town. The museum is in the Chamber building and contains memorabilia from his high school days, Kansas City, and Oakland Athletics, the New York Yankees, and his Hall of Fame induction. Free admission, but donations welcomed. Open March through December on Tuesday through Friday from 10:30 AM to 4:30 PM. Perquimans County Visitors Center; 118 W Market St; Hertford, NC 27944; Phone: (252) 426-5657; http://www.visitperquimans.com

Midland, NC
Reed Gold Mine was the site of the first documented gold find in the United States. North Carolina Historic Sites has restored portions of the underground tunnels for guided tours and established a visitor center with exhibits of gold and historical mining equipment. No fee is charged for admission or tours of the mine. There is a fee for gold panning which is available April through the end of

October, weather permitting. The mine is open Tuesday through Saturday from 9
AM to 5 PM. Closed most major holidays. 9621 Reed Mine Rd; Midland, NC
28107; Phone: (704) 721-4653; https://historicsites.nc.gov/all-sites/reed-gold-
mine

Outer Banks
A spit of land that is a summer haven and a beach-goer's delight, there are several
small towns along its shore.

Nags Head, NC
Jockey's Ridge State Park protects the tallest living sand dune on the Atlantic
coast. The visitor center includes a museum, and 360-foot boardwalk with exhibits
explain the dune's ecology. There are no entrance fees. Open daily all year at 8
AM, the visitor center opens at 9 AM. 300 W Carolista Dr; Nags Head, NC
27959; Phone (252) 441-7132; https://www.ncparks.gov/jockeys-ridge-state-park

Ocracoke, NC
British Cemetery of Ocracoke honors British seamen who died protecting the sea
lanes from German attacks. The ground was given to the British so that these men
may be buried in British soil. No admission. 234 British Cemetery Rd; Ocracoke,
NC 27960; http://www.offbeattravel.com/british-cemetery-outerbanks.html

Old Fort, NC
Mountain Gateway Museum expresses mountain lifestyle and history through
videos, self-guided exhibits of folk medicine, and traditional crafts including how
moonshine was made. There's also two log cabins built in the 1800s. Free
admission with donations accepted. Open Tuesday to Saturday from 9 AM to 5
PM and on Sunday from 2 PM to 5 PM. Closed all state holidays. 24 Water St;
Old Fort, NC 28762; Phone: (828) 668-9259;
http://www.mountaingatewaymuseum.org

Pineville, NC
President James K. Polk Historic Site examines the significant events of the 11th
President of the United States, including the Mexican-American War, settlement
of the Oregon boundary dispute, and the annexation of California. The visitor
center features a film on Polk's life and on his family. A reconstructed log house,
with separate kitchen, and barn is on the grounds. There is no fee to visit,
although donations are appreciated. Open Tuesday through Saturday from 9 AM
to 5 PM. Closed most major state holidays. 12031 Lancaster Hwy; Pineville, NC
28134; Phone: (704) 889-7145; https://historicsites.nc.gov/all-sites/president-
james-k-polk

Pinnacle, NC

Horne Creek Farm features the Hauser family's original farm house, and outbuildings appropriate to a tobacco farm including a curing barn and a corn crib There's no fee to visit, but special events will incur a fee. Open Tuesday through Saturday from 9 AM to 5 PM. Closed most major holidays. 308 Horne Creek Farm Rd; Pinnacle, NC 27043; Phone: (336) 325-2298; https://historicsites.nc.gov/all-sites/horne-creek-farm

Raleigh, NC

Ellen Mordecai Garden was recreated from first-hand descriptions of the family's kitchen garden in the letters and memoir of daughter Ellen Mordecai. The garden features the vegetables, herbs, and flowers that were grown in the 1800s. It is open daily during daylight hours. Although there is no fee to visit the garden, there is a fee to tour the Mordecai House. A small, one-story house that's a replica of birthplace of Andrew Johnson, 17th President of the United States is also on the site. Grounds are accessible anytime. 1 Mimosa St; Raleigh, NC 27604; Phone: (919) 857-4364; https://www.visitnc.com/listing/KyaG/ellen-mordecai-garden

North Carolina Museum of Art offers art inside and out, including 30 Rodin sculptures and the 164-acre Museum Park. Admission to the museum's permanent collection and museum park is free, although there is a fee for some exhibitions and programs. The museum is open Tuesday through Thursday from 10 AM to 5 PM and on Friday until 9 PM. Open Saturday and Sunday from 10 AM to 5 PM. Closed some holidays. The park is open daily, including holidays, from dawn to dusk. 2110 Blue Ridge Rd; Raleigh, NC 27607; Phone: (919) 839-6262; http://www.ncartmuseum.org

North Carolina Museum of History shows 14,000 years of North Carolina history through curated exhibits. Admission is free. The museum is open Monday through Saturday from 9 AM to 5 PM and Sunday open from Noon to 5 PM. Closed some major holidays. 5 E Edenton St; Raleigh, NC 27601; Phone: (919) 807-7900; https://www.ncmuseumofhistory.org/

North Carolina Museum of Natural Sciences is home to specimens across zoology, geology, and paleontology. Highlights include the first dinosaur ever found with a fossilized heart, whale skeletons, and wall of live snakes. Admission is free with donations accepted. Open Monday through Saturday from 9 AM to 5 PM and on Sunday from Noon to 5 PM. 11 W Jones St; Raleigh, NC 27601; Phone: (919) 733-7450; https://naturalsciences.org/visit.

North Carolina State Capitol has been restored to its original 1840 appearance and is open for free self-guided tours Monday through Saturday from 9 AM to 5 PM and free guided tours on Saturday at 11 AM and 2 PM. Closed major holidays. 1 E Edenton St; Raleigh, NC 27601; Phone: (919) 733-4994; https://historicsites.nc.gov/all-sites/n-c-state-capitol

Raleigh Municipal Rose Garden offers a year-round display of hybrid teas, floribundas, grandifloras, miniatures, and antique roses surrounded by an arboretum of evergreen and deciduous trees. Free admission. Open daily from sunrise to sunset. 301 Pogue St; Raleigh, NC 27607; Phone: (919) 821-4579; https://raleighlittletheatre.org/visit-us/rose-garden

Southport, NC
North Carolina Maritime Museum in Southport focuses on the maritime history of the lower Cape Fear River. Shipwrecks, piracy, the Civil War, fishing, and hurricanes are all on display. Admission is free with donations accepted. Open Tuesday through Saturday from 9 AM to 5 PM. 204 E Moore St; Southport, NC 28461; Phone: (910) 457-0003; https://www.southport-nc.com/nc-maritime-museum.html

Weaverville, NC
Zebulon B. Vance Birthplace features his two-story log cabin, an original 1790s slave cabin, and five outbuildings furnished as it would have been in the 1830s. Zebulon Baird Vance was a Confederate soldier, governor of North Carolina, congressman, and U.S. senator. Admission is free with donations appreciated. Open Tuesday through Saturday from 9 AM to 5 PM. Closed most major holidays. 911 Reems Creek Rd; Weaverville, NC 28787; Phone: (828) 645-6706; https://historicsites.nc.gov/all-sites/zebulon-b-vance-birthplace

Wilson, NC
Vollis Simpson Whirligig Park is at the intersection of engineering and art. After serving in World War II, Simpson started to create large whirligigs made of salvaged metal that moved with the wind. They are now on display free of charge. Open daily, including holidays, from 5 AM to Midnight. 301 S. Goldsboro St; Wilson, NC 27893; Phone: (252) 243-8440; https://www.wilsonwhirligigpark.org

Winston-Salem, NC
Historic Bethabara Park offers the oldest standing church with attached residence in North America, active archaeological sites, a reconstructed colonial village, French and Indian War palisade fort as well as community and medicinal gardens. Grounds are open daily all day and are free to visit. Note: There is a charge for guided tours, the visitor center, and exhibit buildings. 2147 Bethabara Rd; Winston-Salem, NC 27106; Phone: (336) 924-8191; http://www.cityofws.org/Departments/Recreation-Parks/Historic-Bethabara

Museum of Anthropology (MOA) invites discovery of ancient and modern artifacts from cultures around the world Admission is free with donations gratefully accepted. Open Tuesday through Saturday from 10 AM to 4:30 PM. Wake Forest University; 1834 Wake Forest Rd; Winston-Salem, NC 27106; Phone: (336) 758-5282; https://moa.wfu.edu

Southeastern Center for Contemporary Art (SECCA) combines art and gardens. Admission is free. Open Wednesday through Saturday from 10 AM to 5 PM, closes on Thursday at 8 PM. Open Sunday from 1 PM to 5 PM. Closed on major holidays. 750 Marguerite Dr; Winston-Salem, NC 27106; Phone: (336) 725-1904; http://www.secca.org

North Dakota

Alexander, ND

Lewis and Clark Trail Museum features homesteader necessities, farming implements, and other historic items. The three-story 1914 schoolhouse contains the museum, while the grounds are home to a sheep herder's wagon, a homestead-era cook car, and a log cabin. Admission to the museum is free with donations appreciated. Open Monday, Tuesday, and Thursday through Saturday from 10 AM to 5 PM. Open Sunday Noon to 5 PM. 102 Indiana Ave E; Alexander, ND 58831; Phone: (701) 828-3595;
http://www.ndtourism.com/alexander/attractions/lewis-and-clark-trail-museum

Bismarck, ND

Former Governors' Mansion State Historic Site has been restored to its 1893 appearance including features that show how the restoration was done. Admission is free with donations welcome. From mid-May through mid-September open Monday through Friday from 10 AM to 5 PM. Open Saturday and Sunday from Noon to 4 PM. Open the rest of the year by appointment. The grounds are open year round. 320 E. Avenue B; Bismarck, ND 58505; Phone: (701) 328-9528;
http://www.history.nd.gov/historicsites/fgm/index.html

North Dakota State Capitol is a 1933 Art Deco building open for free tours all year. Both guided and self-guided tours are available. Tours are hourly on the hour Monday through Friday between 9 AM and 3 PM. Noon tours are not available. Memorial Day through Labor Day there are additional tours on Saturday and Sunday. 600 E Boulevard Ave; Bismarck, ND 58505; Phone: (701) 328-2480;
https://www.nd.gov/omb/public/state-capitol-information

North Dakota State Museum traces North Dakota's history starting with the land's geologic formation 600 million years ago. Located on the same grounds as the State Capital. Admission is free. Open Monday through Friday from 8 AM to 5 PM. Open Saturday and Sunday from 10 AM to 5 PM. 612 E Boulevard Ave; Bismarck, ND 58505; Phone: (701) 328-2666; https://statemuseum.nd.gov

Cavalier, ND
Pembina County Museum and Pioneer Machinery Museum comprises 11 buildings including a church, an 1882 homestead, 1930s barn, blacksmith shop, granary, and more. Free admission. Open daily Memorial Day to Labor Day from 1 PM to 5 PM. Open the rest of the year by appointment only. 13572 N Dakota 5; Cavalier, ND 58220; Phone: (701) 265-4941; http://www.ndtourism.com/cavalier/museums/pembina-county-museum-and-pioneer-machinery-museum

Coleharbor, ND
Audubon National Wildlife Refuge shelters about 250 species of birds. Enjoy bird-watching along an eight-mile route that winds along the lake's shoreline. An auto tour brochure corresponds with numbered signs. The visitor center introduces visitors to the wildlife and the habitats of the refuge. There are no fees. Open all year Monday through Friday from 8 AM to 4:30 PM. Closed federal holidays. 3275 11th St NW; Coleharbor, ND 58531; Phone: (701) 442-5474; https://www.fws.gov/refuge/audubon

Fargo, ND (See also Moorhead, MN)
Celebrity Walk of Fame celebrates the famous in cement. Garth Brooks, Neil Diamond, KISS, Maury Wills, Debbie Reynolds, and Governor Jesse Ventura have all left their mark. Located outside the Fargo-Moorhead Visitors Center. Open 24 hours a day. 2001 44th St S; Fargo, ND 58103; Phone: (701) 282-3653; https://www.fargomoorhead.org/what-to-do/celebrity-walk-fame

Plains Art Museum exhibits national and regional 20th and 21st century art. Admission is free. Open Tuesday, Wednesday and Friday from 11 AM to 5 PM. Open late Thursday until 9 PM. Open Saturday from 10 AM to 5 PM. 704 First Avenue N; Fargo, ND 58102; Phone: (701) 551-6100; http://plainsart.org

Roger Maris Museum honors the legendary Roger Maris who hit 61 homers to break Babe Ruth's single-season home run record. Maris didn't want a museum, but relented on the condition that it would be free and open to the public. Located in the West Acres Mall, the museum opened in 1984, the year before Maris died. The video room screens historic footage with actual Yankee Stadium seats from the Maris era. Memorabilia from his youth and Major League playing days are also on display. Open daily. West Acres Mall; 3902 13th Ave S; Fargo, ND 58103; Phone: (701) 282-2222; http://www.westacres.com/roger-maris.php

Jamestown, ND
Stutsman County Courthouse is the state's oldest surviving courthouse. Noted for its Gothic Revival Style, and for its pressed metal interior, it is said to have the most complete collection of pressed tin in North Dakota. Free admission,

donations welcome. Open Memorial Day through Labor Day on Wednesday through Sunday from 10 AM to 5 PM. 504 Third Avenue SE; Jamestown, ND 58401; Phone: (701) 328-2666; http://history.nd.gov/historicsites/stutsmancc/index.html

Mayville, ND
Rainbow Garden and Sculpture Walk offers seven themed gardens including a children's garden. Sculptures are set amid the blooms. Admission is free. Open during daylight hours. 367 Third St SW (Hwy 200); Mayville, ND 58257; Phone: (701) 786-3160; http://www.rainbowgardenmayville.com

Minot, ND
Scandinavian Heritage Park is dedicated to five Nordic countries: Denmark, Finland, Iceland, Norway, and Sweden. Among the highlights of this outdoor museum are a 240-year-old log house from Norway, a replica stabbur (farm building), 27-foot-tall Swedish Dala horse, and a Gol Stave Church museum. All free to visit and enjoy. Donations gratefully accepted. The outdoor park is open daily but several buildings are closed in winter. 1020 S Bdway; Minot, ND 58702; Phone: (701) 852-9161; https://scandinavianheritage.org

Pembina, ND
Pembina State Museum features two exhibit galleries describing the history of the area with fossils, prehistoric tools, and fur trade items. The museum also explains the frontier forts. Free admission for the exhibits but there is a fee to visit the observation tower. Open Monday through Saturday from 9 AM to 5 PM. Open Sunday from 1 PM to 5 PM. 805 Hwy 59; Pembina, ND 58271; Phone: (701) 825-6840; http://history.nd.gov/historicsites/pembina/index.html

Regent, ND
Hettinger County Historical Society Museum includes pioneer dioramas with antiques, and tool and farm machinery collections. On the grounds is a rural church, schoolhouse, variety store, and local blacksmith's shop. Admission is free with donations appreciated. Open Memorial Day through Labor Day from Noon to 5 PM except closed Sunday. Open by appointment the rest of the year. 21 Main St; Regent, ND 58650; Phone: (701) 563-7798; http://hettingercomuseum.org

Riverdale, ND
Garrison Dam & Lake Sakakawea is a popular place to hike, fish and bird-watch, but the hatchery also encourages visitors to learn about the fish production process. Admission is free. Memorial Day through Labor Day the visitor center and aquarium are open 8 AM to 8 PM. Daily tours are held at 11 AM and 1 PM. The rest of the year the hatchery is open 8 AM to 3:30 PM. Closed on federal

holidays. 201 First St; Riverdale, ND 58565; Phone: (701) 654-7411; https://www.fws.gov/mountain-prairie/fisheries/garrisonDam.php

Stanton, ND

Knife River Indian Villages offers a full scale reconstructed Earthlodge, Hidatsa garden, and drying racks. The museum screens a 15-minute orientation film about the life of Buffalo Bird Woman who lived at the Knife River Indian Villages. Visitors can also learn about the history and culture of the Hidatsa people and decorative arts of Northern Plains Indians. There is no entrance fee. The park is open all year. The visitor center and earth lodge have seasonal hours. Open Memorial Day through Labor Day from 9 AM to 5 PM. The rest of the year open 8 AM to 4:30 PM. Closed major holidays. Park trails and grounds are open daily from sunrise until sunset. 564 CR 37; Stanton, ND 58571; Phone: (701) 745-3300; https://www.nps.gov/knri/index.htm

St. Michael, ND

Sullys Hill National Game Preserve on the south shore of Devils Lake enables visitors to search for bison and elk herds with observation decks along a four-mile route. There's also birding, and hiking. A fee is no longer required to enter Sullys Hill National Game Preserve. The refuge is open daily from 8 AM to sunset. Note: The Sullys Hill Overlook and the Devils Lake Vista Loop are closed during the winter. The visitor center is open June through August on Tuesday through Sunday from Noon to 4 PM. Closed federal holidays. Visitors access the refuge via Hwy 57. 2107 Park Dr; St. Michael, ND 58301; Phone: (701) 766-4272; https://www.fws.gov/refuge/Sullys_Hill_National_Game_Preserve

Washburn, ND

Fort Clark Historic Site recounts the cholera and smallpox epidemics that ravaged the Mandan people, and later the Arikara. A brochure interprets archeological features representing the ruins of houses, graves, storage pits, and the trading posts. An observation deck is also available. Free admission, donations welcome. Open from mid-May through mid-September. N Dakota 200 Alt W; Phone: (701) 328-3508; http://www.history.nd.gov/historicsites/clark

Walhalla, ND

Gingras Trading Post State Historic Site is the 1840s home and trading post of Antoine Blanc Gingras, restored to its original appearance. Interpretive panels and exhibits about Gingras, his heritage, and the fur trade are located in the restored house. Grounds with outdoor interpretive signs are open all year. Free admission. Donations welcomed. 12801-12899 105th ST NE; Walhalla, ND 58282; Phone: (701) 549-2775; http://history.nd.gov/historicsites/gingras/index.html

Williston, ND

Fort Union Trading Post National Historic Site has been reconstructed for self-guided tours as well as seasonal living history programs. The Bodmer Overlook trail takes visitors to the location where famed artist Karl Bodmer painted *The Assiniboine at Fort Union* in the 1830s. There is no fee to enter. Open daily except major holidays. Located in two time zones, Fort Union operates on Central Time (CT). Memorial Day through Labor Day open daily from 8 AM to 6:30 PM. Labor Day to Memorial Day open daily from 9 AM to 5 PM. 15550 Hwy 1804; Williston, ND 58801; Phone: (701) 572-9083; https://www.nps.gov/fous/index.htm

Ohio

Bowling Green, OH
Bowling Green Wind Farm features the four wind turbines that generate electricity for Bowling Green and its electric co-op. An informational computerized kiosk provides information on these towering turbines. Corner of Route 6 and Tontogany Rds; Bowling Green, OH 43402; Phone: (419) 354-6246; https://www.bgohio.org/departments/utilities-department/wind-turbines

Burton, OH
Century Village Museum contains 20 historically accurate buildings, more than 15,000 museum artifacts, and a working farm. The grounds are free and open daily sunrise to sunset. Guided tours of the buildings will incur a cost. 14653 E Park St; Burton, OH 44021; Phone: (440) 834-1492; http://www.centuryvillagemuseum.org

Cambridge, OH
Mosser Glass, Inc. offers tours of the factory explaining the process of forging beautiful hand-pressed glassware. Free tours are available Monday to Friday from 8:45 AM to 9:45 AM and again from 11 AM to 2 PM. No tours from the end of December through early January. Check the site for exact dates. 9279 Cadiz Rd; Cambridge, OH 43725; Phone: (866) 439-1827; https://mosserglass.com/factory-tours

Canton, OH
Harry London/Fannie May Chocolate Factory Tours take visitors behind the scenes to learn the step-by-step process used to craft their chocolates. Tours are free and depart hourly Monday through Thursday from 10 AM to 4 PM. 5353 Lauby Rd; North Canton, OH 44720; Phone: (800) 321-0444; https://www.fanniemay.com/about/chocolate-tours

Cincinnati, OH
Cincinnati Art Museum spans 6,000 years of art. General admission is free, but there is a fee for the traveling exhibitions. Open Tuesday through Sunday from 11 AM to 5 PM. Open Thursday until 8 PM. Closed Thanksgiving, and Christmas

Day. 953 Eden Park Dr; Cincinnati, OH 45202; Phone: (877) 472-4226; http://www.cincinnatiartmuseum.org

Skirball Museum in Cincinnati is one of the oldest repositories of Jewish cultural artifacts in America. Its signature exhibit *An Eternal People: The Jewish Experience* portrays the cultural, historical, and religious heritage of the Jewish people. Admission is free. Note: A current government issued photo ID required for security. Open Tuesday and Thursday from 11 AM to 4 PM and Sunday from 1 PM to 5 PM. 3101 Clifton Ave; Cincinnati, OH 45220; Phone: (513) 487-3098; http://huc.edu/research/museums/skirball-museum-cincinnati

William Howard Taft National Historic Site describes the life of the 27th President of the United States. Taft was born and raised in Cincinnati in a two-story Greek Revival home that is now a Historic Site. There are no entrance fees. Guided tours are offered daily every 30 minutes from 8:30 AM to 4:45 PM. The last tour leaves at 4 PM. 2038 Auburn Ave; Cincinnati, OH 45219; Phone: (513) 684-3262; https://www.nps.gov/wiho/index.htm

Circleville, OH

Ted Lewis Museum introduces visitors to the life of Circleville's jazz musician and entertainer Ted Lewis (born Theodore Leopold Friedman). He was famous for his signature question "Is everybody happy?" In addition to his memorabilia visitors can watch some of Lewis' performances in the Ted Lewis Theater including *On the Sunny Side of the Street*, and his famous routine, *Me and My Shadow*. Admission is free. Open Friday and Saturday from 1 PM to 5 PM. Closed holidays. 133 W Main St; Circleville, OH 43113; Phone: (740) 477-3630; https://www.tedlewismuseum.org

Cleveland, OH (See also Rocky River, OH)

Cleveland Cultural Gardens invites visitors to a collection of public gardens in Rockefeller Park. Drive through the 276 acres of woodland with over 30 distinct gardens honoring the ethnic groups who have contributed to the heritage of Cleveland and the USA. Phone: (216) 220-3075; www.clevelandculturalgardens.org

Cleveland Museum of Art provides a buffet of art. Admission is free, although some special exhibitions may carry a charge. Open Tuesday through Sunday from 10 AM to 5 PM, closing at 9 PM on Wednesday and Friday. Closed major holidays. 11150 East Blvd; Cleveland, OH 44106; Phone: (216) 421-7350; http://www.clevelandart.org

Dittrick Museum of Medical History of Case Western Reserve University, is home to surgical instruments and medical equipment, microscopes, nursing uniforms, historical contraceptive devices, and turn of the century x-ray equipment. No admission charged. Open Monday through Friday from 10 AM to 4 PM. Open Saturday from 10 AM to 2 PM. The Cleveland Medical Library Association; 11000 Euclid Ave; Cleveland, OH 44106; Phone: (216) 368-3648; https://artsci.case.edu/dittrick/museum

Learning Center and Money Museum is filled with hands-on, interactive exhibits about personal finance, economics, and the history of money. Admission and tours are free. Note: Visitors age 16 and older must present a valid driver's license, school ID, or other photo identification. Open Monday through Thursday from 9:30 AM to 2:30 PM. Closed bank holidays and special events. Federal Reserve Bank of Cleveland, 1455 E Sixth St; Cleveland, Ohio 44114; Phone: (216) 579-3188; https://www.clevelandfed.org/learningcenter/visit-us.aspx

Transformer Station is an offshoot of Cleveland Museum of Art and mounts cutting edge contemporary art projects. Admission to the gallery is free but there is a fee to attend concerts and performances. Open Wednesday through Sunday from 11 AM to 5 PM. Closed during installations. Check the website before you visit. 1460 W 29th St; Cleveland, OH 44113; Phone: (216) 938-5429; https://www.transformerstation.org

Columbus, OH

Billy Ireland Cartoon Library & Museum is considered the world's largest collection of materials related to cartoons and comics, including original art, books, magazines, comic books, archival materials, and newspaper comic strip pages and clippings. Admission is free. Open Tuesday through Sunday from 1 PM to 5 PM. Closes for new installations. Ohio State University; 110 Sullivant Hall; 1813 N High St; Columbus, OH 43210; Phone: (614) 292-0538; http://cartoons.osu.edu

Grange Audubon Insurance Center is a sanctuary for birds and nature lovers. It is located within Scioto Audubon Metro Park. Explore native plant demonstration gardens, and the LEED Gold Certified Green building. Free admission. Open Tuesday through Thursday from 10 AM to 5 PM. Open Friday and Saturday from 10 AM to 3 PM. Open Sunday from Noon to 5 PM. 505 W Whittier St; Columbus, OH 43215; Phone: (614)545-5475; http://grange.audubon.org/visit

Ohio Capitol Square includes the Ohio statehouse, Senate building and atrium. Free guided tours are offered Monday through Friday every hour on the hour beginning at 10 AM. The last tour begins at 3 PM. Guided tours are offered on Saturday and Sunday at Noon, 1 PM, 2 PM, and 3 PM. Note: The Ohio statehouse is open to the public on the weekends, but the House and Senate chambers are only available during guided tours. All tours depart from the Map

Room. Plan on arriving at least five minutes before the hour. 1 Capitol Square; Columbus, OH 43215; Phone: (614) 752-9777; http://www.ohiostatehouse.org/visit/public-tours

Ohio Designer Craftsmen/Ohio Craft Museum creates five major exhibitions each year, as well as smaller exhibits from the permanent collection of fiber, metal, jewelry, clay, wood, and mixed media art. Admission is free. Open Monday through Friday from 10 AM to 5 PM. Open Saturday and Sunday from 1 PM to 4 PM. Closed major holidays. 1665 W Fifth Ave; Columbus, OH 43212; Phone: (614) 486-4402; http://ohiocraft.org

Ohio Statehouse Museum encourages visitors to learn about the workings of the state government. Admission is free. Open Monday through Friday from 9 AM to 5 PM. Open Saturday and Sunday from Noon to 4 PM. Closed on state holidays. 1 Capitol Square; Columbus, OH 43215; Phone: (888) 644-6123; http://www.ohiostatehouse.org/museum/museum-education-center

Orton Geological Museum highlights its fossil collections, minerals, and rocks from Ohio and around the world. Open free Monday through Friday from 9 AM to 5 PM. School of Earth Sciences; 155 S Oval Mall; Ohio State University; Columbus, OH 43210; Phone: (614) 292-6896; https://ortongeologicalmuseum.osu.edu

Topiary Park delights with a unique 3-D topiary interpretation of Georges Seurat's famous painting *A Sunday Afternoon on the Isle of La Grande Jette*. It is the only known topiary representation of a painting and has 54 human figures, eight boats, three dogs, a monkey and a cat—each made from yew trees. Admission is free. The park is open daily from sunrise to sunset. 480 E Town St; Columbus, OH 43215; Phone: (614) 645-0197; https://www.facebook.com/topiarypark

Dayton, OH (See also Miamisburg, OH and Wright-Patterson AFB, OH)
Cox Arboretum is a one of the highlights of the admission-free MetroPark system. One highlight is the Butterfly House. Open May through October from 8 AM to 10 PM, peak season is considered to be the months of July and August. There's also a Children's Maze and beautiful gardens. The park is open from April through October from 8 AM to 10 PM, closes at 8 PM the rest of the year. 6733 Springboro Pike; Dayton, OH 45449; Phone: (937) 275-7275; https://www.metroparks.org/butterfly-house

Dayton Aviation Heritage National Historical Park spans the city of Dayton and Wright-Patterson Air Force Base and includes both free and fee-based sites. Only the free sites are included below.

Paul Laurence Dunbar Historic House is in the historic district and describes the life of the poet, writer, and lyricist. Dunbar bought the house for his mother in 1904, and he lived there with her until his death in 1906. Open Friday, Saturday, and Sunday from 10 AM to 4 PM. Closed Thanksgiving, Christmas, and New Year's Day. Tours take place throughout the day and admission is free. Start your visit at the visitor center entrance on Edison Street. 16 S Williams St; Dayton, OH 45402; Phone: (937) 225-7705; https://www.nps.gov/daav/planyourvisit/paul-laurence-dunbar-house-historic-site.htm

Wright Cycle Company documents the Wright Brothers transition from bicycle builders to airplane builders. Free admission. From March through October open daily from 9 AM to 5 PM. November through February open Wednesday through Sunday from 9 AM to 5 PM. Closed Thanksgiving, Christmas, and New Year's Day. 22 S Williams St; Dayton, OH 45402; Phone: (937) 225-7705; https://www.nps.gov/daav/planyourvisit/placestogo.htm

Wright-Dunbar Interpretive Center is located in the building where the Wright Brothers operated their printing business, and highlights the lives of the Wright Brothers and Orville's high school classmate, poet Paul Laurence Dunbar. Admission is free. From March through October open daily from 9 AM to 5 PM. November through February open Wednesday through Sunday from 9 AM to 5 PM. It is advised to check the website for current hours. Closed Thanksgiving, Christmas, and New Year's Day. 16 S. Williams St; Dayton, OH 45402; Phone: (937)225-7705; https://www.nps.gov/daav/index.htm

Wright Memorial is also on the grounds. The 17 foot obelisk of pink granite was dedicated on August 19, 1940, Orville's 69th birthday.

Woodland Historic Cemetery & Arboretum is a historic garden cemetery and the final resting place of Wilbur and Orville Wright, poet Paul Laurence Dunbar, Matilda and Levi Stanley (Queen and King of the Gypsies), writer Erma Bombeck, inventor Charles F. Kettering, and other historical Dayton figures. The 1889 chapel features original Tiffany windows depicting woodland themes from literature and a rendition of *The Messiah*. The cemetery offers self-guided tours. Many of their guided themed walks are free (donations gladly accepted). 118 Woodland Ave; Dayton, OH 45409; Phone: (937) 228-3221; http://www.woodlandcemetery.org/tours-and-events

Findlay, OH

Mazza Museum is dedicated to original art from picture books. Over 11,000 pieces in six galleries include favorites like Dr. Seuss and Patricia Polacco, but also new artists and their works. Free admission. Open Wednesday through Friday from Noon to 5 PM and Saturday from 1 PM to 4 PM. 201 College St; Findlay, OH 45840; Phone: (419) 434-4560; https://www.mazzamuseum.org

Jackson Center, OH

Airstream Factory invites visitors to learn more about the iconic RV with its distinctive aluminum design. Free walking tours are offered Monday through Friday beginning at 2 PM. Meet in the lobby of the Airstream Factory Service Center. Note: Airstream is expanding and there will be no tours from December 1, 2019 through the end of April 2020. Check the website for updated information. 419 W Pike St; Jackson Center, OH 45334; Phone: (877) 596-6111; https://www.airstream.com/company/tours

Fostoria, OH

From 1887 to 1920 this city produced some of the finest glass in the United States.

Glass Heritage Gallery is the destination for lovers of historic glass. Most of the 1,000 pieces in the gallery are on loan. Each case has a sign designating the manufacturer and the name or number of the pattern. No admission charge. In March open Thursday, Friday, and Saturday from 10 AM to 3 PM. April through December open Tuesday through Saturday from 10 AM to 4 PM. Closed January and February. 109 N Main St; Fostoria, OH 44830; Phone: (419) 435-5077; http://www.glasspass.org/glassheritate.htm

Iron Triangle Rail Park derives its name from the three mainline double tracks which cross each other and form a triangle around the rail park. The park provides a 360-degree unobstructed view of the over 100 freight trains on all of the surrounding rails. 499 S Poplar St; Fostoria, OH 44830; http://www.fostoriairontriangle.com

Greenville, OH

KitchenAid Mixer Factory offers free cooking demonstrations, and vintage KitchenAid artifacts and products at their museum. There is no charge to visit. Open Monday through Saturday from 9 AM to 6 PM. Plant tours are currently suspended but may be reinstated. They recommend calling toll free (800) 961-0959 for latest tour information. 423 S Broadway; Greenville, OH 45331; https://www.kitchenaid.com/experience-retail-center/

Howland, OH

Butler Institute of American Art Trumbull Branch features temporary exhibitions throughout the year as well as multiple permanent works of art inside and around the grounds. The Butler charges no admission fee. Open Wednesday through Sunday from 11 AM to 4 PM. Closed major holidays. 9350 E Market St; Warren, OH 44484; Phone: (330) 609-9900; https://butlerart.com

Huber Heights, OH

Carriage Hill MetroPark highlights farm life in the 1880s. Exhibits, demonstrations, reconstructed and historical buildings, and even period farm animals recreate agrarian life. The farm, and visitor center are free to visit. Hours are highly seasonal but all farm facilities are closed on Monday, and on Thanksgiving, Christmas and New Year's Day. 7800 E Shull Rd; Huber Heights, OH 45424; Phone: (937) 275-7275; https://www.metroparks.org/historical-farm

Lima, OH

Lincoln Park Railway Exhibit is the home of the Nickel Plate 779, the last steam engine ever built in Lima, Ohio. There's also a luxury private car, built in 1883, and a Nickel Plate caboose built in 1882. Open for outdoor viewing from dawn to dusk adjacent to the Indiana & Ohio Railroad. 199 S Shawnee St; Lima, OH 45804; Phone: (419) 221-5195; http://www.cityhall.lima.oh.us/Facilities/Facility/Details/10

Lockington, OH

Lockington Locks is considered one of the best preserved stair step canal locks in Ohio. Lock 1 has been restored to illustrate the history and importance of the canals in western Ohio. The remaining visible locks are maintained as a vestige of the canal system and an example of 19th century civil engineering. Admission is free. Open daily during daylight hours. Museum Trail and Cross Trail; Lockington, OH 45356; Phone: (800) 752-2619; https://www.ohiohistory.org/visit/museum-and-site-locator/lockington-locks

Marblehead, OH

Marblehead Lighthouse is the oldest lighthouse in continuous operation on the Great Lakes. From Memorial Day weekend through Labor Day Marblehead Lighthouse is open daily from Noon to 4 PM. Tours are offered on weekdays during the summer months and on select Saturdays. The museum and the lighthouse is free to visit but there is a charge to climb the lighthouse staircase. The Keeper's House and Livesaving Station museums are open the same hours as the lighthouse and are free to visit. 110 Lighthouse Dr; Marblehead, OH 43440; Phone: (419) 734-4424; http://parks.ohiodnr.gov/marbleheadlighthouse https://www.marbleheadlighthouseohio.org

Marysville, OH

Honda Heritage Center and Plant Tour offers two different tours, both free of charge. A self-guided tour of the center is available and reservations are suggested. Guided tours are available Tuesday, Thursday, and Friday from 10 AM to 4 PM and on Wednesday from Noon to 5 PM. Note: Guests under age 18 must be accompanied by an adult. Adults will need a government issued photo ID for check-in upon arrival. Fully enclosed shoes are required for the plant tour. Further, they advise that skirt/shorts must be knee length or longer for plant tour. 24025 Honda Pkwy; Marysville, OH 43040; Phone: (937) 644-6888; http://www.hondaheritagecenter.com/tours

Massillon, OH
Joseph J. and Helen M. Sommer Wildlife Conservation Center features rotating displays and exhibits. Outdoors there is housing for non-releasable wildlife that permanently live at the center. Both areas are open to visitors with free admission. Open Monday to Saturday from 8:30 AM to 4 PM. Sippo Lake Park; W 800 Genoa Ave NW; Massillon, OH 44646; Phone: (330) 477-0448; https://starkparks.com/wildlife-conservation-center

Massillon Museum preserves and reflects the legacy of Massillon and the region, particularly the legacy of football's legendary Paul Brown. A highlight is the Immel Circus – a 100-square foot miniature circus with 2,620 separate pieces. The Massillon Museum is free to visit, donations appreciated. Open Tuesday through Saturday from 9:30 AM to 5 PM and Sunday from 2 PM to 5 PM. 121 Lincoln Way E; Massillon, OH 44646; Phone: (330) 833-4061; http://www.massillonmuseum.org

Miamisburg, OH (See also Dayton, OH and Wright-Patterson AFB, OH)
Dayton-Wright Brothers Airport (KMGY) honors the Wright Brothers and the Wright Company where the famous brothers built the first mass-produced airplane – the original Wright "B" Flyer. Highlights include displayed aircraft, and the Wright B look-alike being built to modern standards with modern materials and components. Admission is free. Open Tuesday, Thursday, Saturday from 9 AM to 2:30 PM. 10550 Springboro Pike; Miamisburg, OH 45342; Phone: (937) 885-2327; http://www.wright-b-flyer.org

Newton Falls, OH
Newton Falls covered bridge is the oldest covered bridge still in service in Ohio and the only one in the state with a covered pedestrian walkway. It is located on Arlington Road.

Oak Harbor, OH
Sportsmen's Migratory Bird Center at the Magee Marsh Wildlife Area displays more than 300 mounted animals. A walking trail circles the ponds while a 40-foot observation tower provides a view of the area. The marsh is considered one of the top song bird spots in North America. Free to visit. The center is open Monday through Friday 8 AM to 3 PM. From April to September it is also open Saturday and Sunday from 8 AM to 3 PM. 13229 W State Route 2; Oak Harbor, OH

43449; Phone: (419) 898-0960; http://wildlife.ohiodnr.gov/public-hunting-fishing-wildlife-viewing-areas/sportsmens-migratory-bird-center-magee-marsh

Oberlin, OH

Oberlin College Allen Memorial Art Museum is noted for its 19th century paintings, sculptures, and decorative artwork displayed in an Italian Renaissance-style building. There's also a gallery for modern and contemporary art. Admission is free. Open Tuesday through Saturday from 10 AM to 5 PM and on Sunday from 1 PM to 5 PM. Closed some major holidays. 87 N Main St; Oberlin, OH 44074; Phone: (440) 775-8665; http://www2.oberlin.edu/amam

Oxford, OH

Hefner Museum of Natural History explores biology and natural history with a special focus on southwest Ohio. Admission is free. Open Monday through Friday from 9 AM to 4 PM. Closed university holidays. Miami University; Upham Hall, Room 100; 100 Bishop Cir; Oxford, OH 45056; Phone (513) 529-4617; http://miamioh.edu/cas/academics/centers/hefner-museum

Miami University Art Museum and Sculpture Park features exhibits in five galleries, plus three acres of scenic sculpture park grounds. Admission is free with donations accepted. Open Tuesday through Friday from 10 AM to 5 PM. Open Saturday from Noon to 5 PM. Closed university holidays. 801 S Patterson Ave; Oxford, OH 45056; Phone: (513) 529-2232; http://www.miamioh.edu/cca/art-museum

Rocky River, OH (See also Cleveland, OH)

Cowan Pottery Museum derives its name from potter R. Guy Cowan and his associates who created pieces starting in 1913 in Lakewood, Ohio and later moved to Rocky River, Ohio. There is no admission fee. Open Monday through Thursday from 9 AM to 9 PM. Open Friday and Saturday from 9 AM to 6 PM. During the school year also open Sunday 1 PM to 5 PM. Rocky River Public Library; 1600 Hampton Rd; Rocky River, OH 44116; Phone: (440) 333-7610; http://www.rrpl.org/cowan/index.html

St Clairsville, OH

Belmont County Sheriff's Residence Museum uses the restored 1888 residence to illuminate the lives and history of the people of Belmont County. Each of its eight rooms features a different community. Admission is free. Open May through November on Saturday and Sunday from 10 AM to 4 PM. 101 E Main St; St Clairsville, OH 43950; Phone: (740) 298-7020; https://www.facebook.com/Belmont-County-Sheriffs-Residence-Museum-1185341321589237

Sylvania, OH

Fossil Park encourages visitors to become fossil hunters. The fossils come from Hanson Aggregate, the Midwest's large working quarries, and contains fossils from the Devonian period. Although you can't use tools, you can keep anything you find in the soft shale. Admission and fossil hunting are free. Open daily Memorial Day to the end of October from 11 AM to 4 PM. Staff is there on weekends Memorial Day to Labor Day to answer questions. 5675 Centennial Rd; Sylvania, OH 43560; Phone: (419) 882-8313; http://www.olanderpark.com/olanderpark/fossil-park

Heritage Center Museum/Cooke-Kuhlman Home preserves the doctor's office, exam room, bedroom, and parlor as they were when Dr. Cooke lived and practiced here. Free admission. Open March through early December on Saturday and Sunday from 1 PM to 4 PM. Closed holidays. 5717 N Main St; Sylvania, OH 43560; https://heritagesylvania.org/our-attractions/cooke-kuhlman

Historical Village includes original and recreated historic buildings which traces the early history and community life. 5717 Main St; Sylvania, OH 43560; Phone: (419) 517-5533; https://heritagesylvania.org/plan-your-visit/visitor-information

Lathrop House was owned by abolitionists and was a stop on the road to freedom for escaping enslaved people. Admission is free. Open only April through early November on Sundays from 1 PM to 4 PM, or by appointment. Closed holidays. 5416 Main St; Sylvania, OH 43560; https://heritagesylvania.org/our-attractions/lathrop-house

Toledo, OH

Toledo Botanical Garden covers over 60 acres of display gardens and a two-acre urban farm. Admission is free except during some special events. Open daily from 7 AM to dark. 5403 Elmer Dr; Toledo, OH 43615; Phone: (419) 270-7500; https://metroparkstoledo.com/explore-your-parks/toledo-botanical-garden

Toledo Botanical Garden Artisan Village is a community of local artists who share studio space in the botanical garden. The website provides a calendar link for special events, classes, and demonstrations. https://artvillage419.org

Toledo Museum of Art invites visitors to enjoy 35 galleries in six buildings on 32 acres including the Georgia and David K. Welles Sculpture Garden, and the new Glass Pavilion. Free admission although tickets to special exhibits may incur a fee. Open Tuesday and Wednesday from 10 AM to 4 PM. On Thursday and Friday open from 10 AM to 9 PM. Open Saturday from 10 AM to 5 PM and Sunday from Noon to 5 PM. 2445 Monroe St; Toledo, OH 43620; Phone: (800) 644-6862; http://www.toledomuseum.org

Urbana, OH
Champaign Aviation Museum, located at the Grimes Field Airport, displays World War II aircraft including a B-25 Mitchell two engine WWII bomber fully restored and flying. Free admission with donations are appreciated. Open Tuesday through Saturday from 10 AM to 4 PM. 1652 N Main St; Urbana, OH 43078; Phone: (937) 652-4710; http://www.champaignaviationmuseum.org

Utica, OH
Velvet Ice Cream Factory Tour is a free 30-minute walking tour highlighting the origin of the 100 year old company, and the seven steps in making this dessert. May through October tours are available beginning at 11 AM. Closed November through April. 11324 Mt. Vernon Rd; Utica, OH 43080; Phone: (800) 589-5000; http://www.velveticecream.com/

Warren, OH
Neil Armstrong First Flight Memorial Lunar Module is a half-scale replica of the Apollo 11 lunar module at the site where astronaut Neil Armstrong took his first airplane ride at the age of six. The replica is 13 feet tall and 12 feet wide and weighs about two tons. Open daily from 10 AM to 5 PM. There is no admission charge. 2487 Parkman Rd NW; Warren, OH, 44485; Phone: (330) 898-3456; http://www.firstflightwarren.org

Wellston, OH
Buckeye Furnace features a reconstructed charcoal-fired iron blast furnace, along with its original stack built in 1852. There's also a reconstructed casting shed, charging loft where iron ore, limestone, and charcoal were loaded into the furnace, and the engine house which contained a steam-powered compressor. Free admission. Open Saturday and Sunday from Noon to 4 PM. 123 Buckeye Park Rd; Wellston, OH 45692; Phone: (800) 860-0144; https://www.ohiohistory.org/visit/museum-and-site-locator/buckeye-furnace

Wilmington, OH
Meriam R. Hare Quaker Heritage Center preserves the local, regional, and national history of the Religious Society of Friends. The Heritage Center is located at Wilmington College and includes a traditional Quaker meetinghouse. Admission is free. Open Monday through Thursday from 11 AM to 4 PM and some Fridays. College and Douglas Sts; Wilmington, OH 45177; Phone: (937) 481-2456; https://www.wilmington.edu/the-wilmington-difference/qhc

Wright-Patterson AFB Dayton, OH (See also Miamisburg, OH and Dayton, OH)
Huffman Prairie Flying Field Interpretive Center is part of Dayton Aviation Heritage National Historical Park. It hosts exhibits focusing on the Wright

brothers' development of the world's first practical airplane at Huffman Prairie in 1904 and 1905, and the accomplishments of Wright-Patterson Air Force Base. Admission is free. March through October open daily from 9 AM to 5 PM. From November through February open Wednesday through Sunday from 9 AM to 5 PM. Closed Thanksgiving, Christmas, and New Year's Day. 2380 Memorial Rd; Wright-Patterson Air Force Base, OH 45433; Phone: (937) 425-0008; https://www.nps.gov/daav/learn/historyculture/huffman-prairie-flying-field.htm

National Museum of the United States Air Force hosts more than 360 aerospace vehicles and missiles, many rare and one-of-a-kind. Admission to the museum is free although there is a charge for the theater and flight simulators. Also on the grounds is the Air Park which features aircraft exhibits, and a reproduction of the 1942 standard control tower. The museum is open daily from 9 AM to 5 PM. Closed on Thanksgiving, Christmas, and New Year's Day. 1100 Spaatz St; Wright-Patterson AFB, OH 45433; Phone: (937) 255-3286; https://www.nationalmuseum.af.mil/Visit

Youngstown, OH

Butler Institute of American Art preserves works of art in all media in a setting designed by McKim, Mead and White. The Beecher Center wing is devoted to new media and electronic art. Special exhibits are offered throughout the year. The Butler charges no admission fee. Open Tuesday through Saturday from 11 AM to 4 PM. Open Sunday from Noon to 4 PM. Closed major holidays. 524 Wick Ave; Youngstown, Ohio 44502; Phone: (330) 743-1107; https://butlerart.com

Oklahoma

Oklahoma, designated as Indian Territory by the U.S. government before the Civil War, was the destination for Native Americans who were forcefully removed (or enticed to leave) their original land to make way for settlers and expansion. Many lost their lives along the way, but the history of the state is intertwined with the history of the surviving Native American populations.

Anadarko, OK

Heritage Museum displays railroad memorabilia, photographs of early Anadarko settlers, historic Native American items, Civil War documents, and old military uniforms, as well as a grocery store and a pioneer doctor's office. Free admission. Open Tuesday through Saturday from 8 AM to 5 PM. Closed legal holidays. 311 E Main St; Anadarko, OK 73005; Phone: (405) 247-3240; http://www.cityofanadarko.org/departments/museum/index.php

National Hall of Fame for Famous American Indians is a self-guided walking tour among 41 bronze busts of famous Native Americans including Sequoyah, Captain Black Beaver, Sitting Bull, Geronimo, and Pocahontas. Free admission. The outdoor statuary area is always open. The visitor center is open Monday through Saturday from 9 AM to 5 PM and Sundays from 1 PM to 5 PM. 901 E Central Blvd; Anadarko, OK 73005; Phone: (405) 247-5555; https://americanindianhof.com

Southern Plains Indian Museum displays items of western Oklahoma Native American groups – historic clothing, shields, weapons, baby carriers, and toys as well as artwork by contemporary Indian artists and artisans. Free admission. Open Tuesday through Friday from 10 AM to 4:30 PM. Closed on all federal holidays. Note: They recommend calling ahead to confirm hours. 801 E Central Blvd; Anadarko, OK 73005; Phone: (405) 247-6221; https://www.doi.gov/iacb/SouthernPlainsIndianMuseum

Ardmore, OK

Greater Southwest Historical Museum highlights different aspects of history including early carriages, saddles, even soapbox derby cars, and Ardmore's first fire engine. Admission is free. Open Tuesday through Saturday from 10 AM to 5 PM. Closed holidays. 35 Sunset Dr; Ardmore, OK 73401; Phone: (580) 226-3857; http://gshm.org

Bartlesville, OK

Bartlesville Area History Museum offers interactive displays, photography, and artifacts. One of the museum's most popular attractions is an animatronic Frank Griggs, pioneer photographer who spent seven decades documenting Bartlesville life. Admission is free. Open Monday through Friday from 8 AM to 4 PM. Closed holidays. 401 S Johnstone Ave; Fifth Floor; Bartlesville, OK 74003; Phone: (918) 338-4294; http://www.bartlesvillehistory.com

Phillips 66 Museum is the story of Frank Phillips, and Phillips 66 petroleum industry empire told through exhibits and displays. Admission is free. Open Monday through Saturday from 10 AM to 4 PM. 410 Keeler; Bartlesville, OK 74003; Phone: (855) 631-8687; https://www.phillips66museum.com

Broken Bow, OK

Forest Heritage Center exhibits antique forestry tools, wood art, and homestead memorabilia. The highlight may be the 14 large dioramas capturing moments of the area's history. There's also a historically furnished 100-year-old, one-room cabin. Free admission. Open daily from 8 AM to 5 PM. Beavers Bend State Park; N US Hwy 259; Broken Bow, OK 74728; Phone: (580) 494-6497; http://www.forestry.ok.gov/fhc

Catoosa, OK

Arkansas River Historical Society Museum focuses on the history of the Arkansas River, river navigation, steamboat lore, and archeology. There's also a motorized model of a lock and dam. Entrance is free, donations are accepted. Open Monday through Friday from 8 AM to 4:30 PM. 5350 Cimarron Rd; Catoosa, OK 74015; Phone: (918) 266-2291; http://www.aopoa.net/history/museum.htm

Blue Whale is a beloved Route 66 icon. Built by Hugh S. Davis who envisioned the whale as part of a fun swim in the pond. It still stands – 20 feet tall and 80 feet long. 2680 N Hwy 66; Catoosa, OK 74015; http://bluewhaleroute66.com

Carnegie, OK

Kiowa Tribal Museum presents the history of the Kiowa people through artist-created murals. There's also a Sundance teepee. Free admission. Open Monday through Friday from 8 AM to 4:30 PM. 100 Kiowa Way; Hwy 9 W; Carnegie, OK 73015; Phone: (580)654-6366; https://kiowatribe.org/museum

Chelsea, OK

Ed Galloway Totem Pole Park is another of Oklahoma's stellar Route 66 stops. Ed Galloway spent his retirement years creating a monument to the American Indian built of stone, concrete, and imagination. This folk art icon is home to the world's largest concrete totem pole. The Fiddle House displays Galloway's hand-crafted fiddles and other inlaid wood artifacts. Located about 3½ miles east of U.S. Route 66. Admission is free. The grounds are open all year. Fiddle House is open daily March through December from Noon to 5 PM. Special appreciation goes to Rogers County Historical Society for preserving this folk art masterpiece. 21300 OK-28 A; Chelsea, OK 74016; Phone: (918)-342-1169; http://www.rchs1.org/totem-pole-park

Cheyenne, OK

Museums in Cheyenne City Park depict the settlement of the area in the late 1800s. Antique cars, trucks, and farm machinery are on display, along with a one-room school house, and an original 1900s restored log cabin. No admission charged, donation box available. Open seasonally March through October on Tuesday through Saturday from 10 AM to 4 PM. 107 Pioneer Pkwy; Cheyenne, OK 73628; Phone: (580)497-3882; http://www.rogermills.org/Museums/Museums_Pioneer.htm

Washita Battlefield National Historic Site recalls the November 27, 1868 surprise dawn attack on a Cheyenne village led by Lt. Colonel George Armstrong Custer. The visitor center screens a 27-minute film depicting the events leading up to the attack. The park is free to visit. The center is open daily from 8 AM to 5 PM. Closed major holidays. 18555 OK-47 Alt; Cheyenne, OK 73628; Phone: (580) 497-2742; https://www.nps.gov/waba/index.htm

Claremore, OK

Belvidere Mansion is part restaurant and part museum in a 1907 Victorian mansion. The second floor contains two historically furnished living quarters, a bathroom, archive room, and gift shop. A self-guided tour of the Belvidere Mansion is free. Open Tuesday through Saturday from 11 AM to 2 PM. 121 N Chickasaw Ave; Claremore, OK 74017; Phone: (918) 342-1127; http://www.belvideremansion.com

JM Davis Arms & Historical Museum has been described as "the largest privately-held firearms collection in the world." There are over 12,000 firearms, and thousands of non-firearm artifacts ranging from Old West saddles and spurs, beer steins, World War I posters, as well as a replica of an 1840s gunsmith shop. Admission is free, and donations are accepted. Open Tuesday through Saturday from 10 AM to 5 PM. 330 N JM Davis Blvd; Claremore, OK 74017; Phone: (918) 341-5707; http://www.thegunmuseum.com

Colcord, OK

Talbot Research Library & Museum includes a blacksmith shop, post office building, and general store. Free admission. Open Wednesday through Saturday

10 AM to 4 PM. 500 S Colcord Ave; Colcord, OK 74338; Phone: (918) 326-4532; http://www.talbotlibrary.org

Enid, OK
Simpson's Old Time Museum & Movie Studio is known for its extensive Western paraphernalia and antique collection. It's also been the location for a number of western films. Visitors can tour the movie set, complete with a saloon, hotel room, and old jail. Memorabilia, baseball collectibles, train sets, and wide range of military items are displayed around the museum. Free to visit. Open Monday through Saturday from 8 AM to 11 AM and then from 1 PM to 4 PM. 228 E Randolph Ave; Enid, OK 73701; Phone: (580) 234-4998; http://www.skeletoncreekproductions.com/m-museum.html

Frederick, OK
Pioneer Heritage Townsite is comprised of a general store, Horse Creek school building, and other sites that recreate life on the plains of Southwest Oklahoma in the 1920s. Admission is free. Donations are accepted. Open Tuesday through Saturday from 11:30 AM to 2:30 PM. Closed major holidays. 201 N Ninth St; Frederick, OK 73542; Phone: (580) 335-5844; http://www.tillmanokhistory.org/townsite_museum.html

Fort Sill, OK (See also Lawton, OK)
Fort Sill National Historic Landmark & Museum is a 19th century frontier army post of about 50 buildings. It's best known as the home of Geronimo during his later years. Geronimo was a prominent Apache leader who fought against forced reservation life. Never allowed to return to the land of his birth, he died at the Fort Sill hospital. Admission is free. Open Tuesday through Saturday from 9 AM to 5 PM. Closed major holidays. Note: Adults must have an approved form of identification. Follow the instructions on https://sill-www.army.mil/vcc to determine if you need a pass and how to obtain one. Call (580) 442-9603/9605 for further information. 435 Quanah Rd; Fort Sill, OK 73503; Phone: (580) 442-5123; http://sill-www.army.mil/museum/FSNHLM/index.html

Foyil, OK (See Chelsea, OK for Totem Pole Park)

Goodwell, OK
No Man's Land Museum chronicles the experiences of settlers in an area that no state would claim. It was soon given the name of *No Man's Land*. Admission to the museum is free. Open in summer on Tuesday through Saturday from 10 AM to Noon and again from 1 PM to 4 PM. Call to verify hours at other times of year. 207 W Sewell St; Goodwell, OK 73939; Phone: (580) 349-2670; http://www.nmlhs.org/museum.html

Hugo, OH

Mount Olivet Cemetery is the final resting place for circus performers and circus owners in a special area called Showmen's Rest. It is known for the unique headstones and gravesites. Trice and S 8th St; Hugo, OK 74743; Phone: (580) 326-9263; https://www.travelok.com/listings/view.profile/id.5187

Idabel, OK

Museum of the Red River is home to art, artifacts, and natural science specimens including the Oklahoma State Dinosaur. Admission is free. Open Tuesday through Saturday from 10 AM to 5 PM and Sunday from 10 AM to 3 PM. Closed national holidays. 812 E Lincoln Rd; Idabel, OK 74745; Phone: (580) 286-3616; https://www.museumoftheredriver.org

Jackson Center, OK

Airstream Factory Tour invites visitors to take a 3/4-mile walk through the Airstream factory, and see how their famous trailers and touring coaches are made. The tours are free and offered Monday through Friday at 2 PM starting in the lobby of the Service Center. Due to the plant's expansion no tours are available through April 2020. Tours are expected to resume after that date. Note: No sandals or open-toed shoes allowed. 419 W Pike St; Jackson Center, OH 45334; Phone: (877) 596-6111; http://www.airstream.com/company/tours

Jet, OK

Salt Plains National Wildlife Refuge welcomes over 300 species of birds who visit seasonally. It's also the site for the unique selenite crystals. No entrance fee. Stroll the nature trails, boardwalks, and overlooks. The refuge is open all year during daylight hours. The visitor center is open Monday through Friday from 7:30 AM to 4 PM. Closed on federal holidays. Digging for crystals is permitted, but only from April through mid-October. 71189 Harper Rd; Jet, OK 73749; Phone: (580) 626-4794; https://www.fws.gov/refuge/salt_plains

Lawton, OK (See also Fort Sill, OK)

Comanche National Museum & Cultural Center explains the religion, culture, and military history of the Comanche, including the 17 men who were among the legendary Code Talkers of World War II. A special exhibit recreates the sights and sounds of a Comanche buffalo hunt. Admission is free. Open Monday through Friday from 8 AM to 5 PM and Saturday from 10 AM to 2 PM. 701 NW Ferris Ave; Lawton, OK 73507; Phone: (580) 353-0404; http://www.comanchemuseum.com

Miami, OK

Route 66 Vintage Iron Motorcycle Museum offers their collection of over 40 vintage motorcycles and memorabilia. Free admission, donations appreciated.

Open May through October on Monday through Saturday from 10 AM to 6 PM and Sunday from Noon to 5 PM. November through April it is open Monday through Saturday from 10 AM to 6 PM. 128 S Main St; Miami, OK 74354; Phone: (918) 542-6170; https://www.route66vintageiron.com/

Muskogee, OK
Ataloa Lodge Museum was built in 1932 on the campus of historic Bacone College. Its holdings include a large Kachina doll collection, as well as Civil War memorabilia. There is no charge for admission although donations are appreciated. Open by appointment only. 2299 Old Bacone Rd; Muskogee, OK 74403; Phone: (918) 781-7283; http://www.bacone.edu/ataloa-lodge/plan-a-visit

Norman, OK
National Weather Center offers free walking tours of the facility. All tours require a reservation. All persons and packages are subject to inspection. Foreign visitors have additional requirements. 120 David L Boren Blvd; Norman, OK 73072; Phone: (405) 325-3095; http://www.ou.edu/nwc/visit/tours

University of Oklahoma's Fred Jones Jr. Museum of Art displays their Weitzenhoffer collection of French Impressionism, as well as traditional and contemporary art and other media from the 16th century to the present. Admission is free. Open Tuesday through Saturday from 10 AM to 5 PM. Open Sunday 1 PM to 5 PM. Closed university holidays. 555 Elm Ave; Norman, OK 73019; Phone: (405) 325-3272; http://www.ou.edu/fjjma

Oklahoma City, OK
45th Infantry Division Museum uses military artifacts to illuminate the military history of Oklahoma's 45th Infantry Division of the National Guard. One highlight is the Reaves Firearm Collection of infantry and cavalry weapons from the Revolutionary War to the Vietnam War. Admission is free. Donations are appreciated. Open Tuesday through Friday from 9 AM to 4:15 PM. Open Saturday from 10 AM to 4:15 PM, and Sunday from 1 PM to 4:15 PM. 2145 NE 36th St; Oklahoma City, OK 73111; Phone: (405) 424-5313; http://45thdivisionmuseum.com

American Pigeon Museum & Library educates the public about pigeons including their importance in war efforts. Admission is free. Open Friday and Saturday from 10 AM to 4 PM and by appointment. 2300 NE 63rd; Oklahoma City, OK 73111; Phone: (405) 478-5155; http://www.theamericanpigeonmuseum.org

Centennial Land Run Monument is a 45-statue homage to the men and women who sought the newly opened lands in what today is Oklahoma. The date was

April 22, 1889 and 50,000 people, with a flag clutched in their hands, raced to stake their claims. Located at the south end of the Bricktown Canal, the monument is a city park and is free and open 24 hours a day. 200 Centennial Ave; Oklahoma City, OK 73102; http://landrun.marbleart.us

Martin Park Nature Center & Trail features a hands-on nature center, three hiking trails, a bird observation wall, and a watch tower. General admission is free. The park is open daily April through September from 5 AM to 9 PM. Open daily from October through March from 5 AM to 6 PM. The visitor center is open Tuesday through Sunday from 9 AM to 6 PM. Closed city holidays. 5000 W Memorial Rd; Oklahoma City, OK 73142; Phone: (405) 297-1429; https://www.okc.gov/departments/parks-recreation/martin-park-nature-center

Oklahoma Contemporary Arts Center is the home of the Eleanor Kirkpatrick Gallery featuring the work of emerging, nationally, and internationally recognized Oklahoma artists. Free admission. Open Monday through Saturday from 9 AM to 10 PM. Open Sunday from 11 AM to 6 PM. 3000 General Pershing Blvd; Oklahoma City, OK 73107; Phone: (405) 951-0000; http://www.oklahomacontemporary.org

Oklahoma Governor's Mansion is open for tours but reservations are required. Call to reserve a tour. 820 NE 23rd; Oklahoma City, OK 73105; Phone: (405) 528-2020; http://www.fomok.org/tours.php

Oklahoma Railway Museum welcomes visitors to explore locomotives, passenger cars, cabooses, freight cars, and a steam engine. Admission is free. Open Thursday, Friday, and Saturday from 9 AM to 5 PM. Note: Fee-based train rides are held on the first and third Saturdays of the month, April through August. 3400 NE Grand Blvd; Oklahoma City, OK 73111; Phone: (405) 424-8222; https://www.oklahomarailwaymuseum.org

Oklahoma Sports Hall of Fame and Jim Thorpe Museum contains artifacts and memorabilia of legendary athlete and Oklahoma Native American, Jim Thorpe. Considered one of the most versatile athletes of modern sports, the highlight of his career was his stellar performance winning gold medals in the 1912 Olympic Games. Free admission. Open Tuesday through Saturday from 10 AM to 5 PM. 20 S Mickey Mantle Dr (NW Corner of the Chickasaw Bricktown Ballpark); Oklahoma City, OK 73104; Phone: (405) 427-1400; https://www.oklahomasportshalloffame.org

Oklahoma State Capitol features Greco-Roman architecture and murals, restored stained glass, tribal flag plaza, and changing art exhibits. Guided tours are available hourly Monday through Friday from 9 AM to 3 PM except Noon. Self-guided tours are available at other times including Saturday and Sunday from 9 AM to 4

PM. 2300 N Lincoln Blvd; Oklahoma City, OK 73105; Phone: (405) 521-3356; https://www.okhouse.gov/Information/CapitolTours.aspx

Porcelain Art Museum is located at the World Organization of China Painters and displays hand-painted china from around the world. Admission is free and donations accepted. Open Monday through Thursday from 8 AM to 4 PM. 2700 N Portland Ave; Oklahoma City, OK 73107; Phone: (405) 521-1234; http://www.wocporg.com

Red Earth Art Center is home to a rotating collection of traditional and contemporary fine art, pottery, basketry, textiles, and beadwork. There is no charge to visit. Open Monday through Friday from 10 AM to 5 PM. 6 Santa Fe Plaza; Oklahoma City, OK 73102; Phone (405) 427-5228; https://www.redearth.org

Okmulgee, OK
Muscogee Creek Council House Museum provides information on early tribal leaders, the tribes' role in the Civil War, and items brought along the infamous Trail of Tears. Admission is free with donations accepted. Open Tuesday through Friday from 10 AM to 4 PM and Saturdays from 10 AM to 3 PM. 106 W Sixth St; Okmulgee, OK 74447; Phone: (918) 756-2324; http://okmulgeetourism.com/creek-council-house-museum

Oologah, OK
Will Rogers Birthplace Ranch has livestock, and a peacock, but visit for the White House on the Verdigris – the birth home of Will Rogers known for his humor, wisdom, and roping skills. Listen to Will Rogers Jr. describe life on the ranch. Free admission, donations accepted. Mid-November to February open Wednesday through Sunday from 10 AM to 5 PM. From March through mid-November open only on Saturday and Sunday from 10 AM to 5 PM. Closed on Thanksgiving, and Christmas. 9501 E 380 Rd; Oologah, OK 74053; Phone: (918) 341-0719; http://www.okhistory.org/sites/wrranch

Pawhuska, OK
Tallgrass Prairie Preserve provides hiking trails, and a scenic drive through the largest protected tallgrass prairie in the USA. It is home to white-tailed deer, coyotes, and buffalo herds. Free admission. The preserve is open daily from dawn to dusk. 15316 CR 4201; Pawhuska, OK 74056; Phone: (918) 287-4803; https://www.nature.org/ourinitiatives/regions/northamerica/unitedstates/oklahoma/placesweprotect/tallgrass-prairie-preserve.xml

Osage Nation Museum tells Osage history and culture through objects from the permanent collection. Admission is free. Donations are accepted. Open Tuesday through Saturday from 8:30 AM to 5 PM. Closed federal holidays. 819

Grandview Ave; Pawhuska, OK 74056; Phone: (918) 287-5441;
https://www.osagenation-nsn.gov/museum

Ponca City, OK
Conoco Museum focuses on Oklahoma's oil boom days with interactive displays, a 40-seat movie theater, and a replica development laboratory. Free admission. Open Monday through Saturday from 10 AM to 5 PM. Closed major holidays. 501 W South Ave; Ponca City, OK 74601; Phone: (580) 765-8687; https://www.conocomuseum.com/EN/Pages/index.aspx

Poncan Theatre has one of the world's largest collections of hand-painted lobby art including original movie posters for films from 1931 to 1937. Free to enjoy when the theater is open. Generally open weekday afternoons from 1 PM to 5 PM and one hour prior to show times. Donation-based guided tours are also available. 104 E Grand Ave; Ponca City, OK 74601; Phone: (580)765-0943; https://www.poncantheatre.org

Ripley, OK
Washington Irving Trail Museum is devoted to history's forgotten treasures. Highlights include a 37-pound meteorite, a fulgurite created by lightning, a six-gauge double barrel percussion shotgun, and an 1832 Eli Terry mantel clock with wooden works. Also included is a hand-made stars and bars Civil War Confederate flag with bullet holes. Admission is free. Open Wednesday through Saturday from 11 AM to 5 PM and on Sunday from 1 PM to 5 PM. Note: It is advised to call first to make sure the museum will be open. 3918 S Mehan Rd; Ripley, OK 74062; Phone: (405) 624-9130; http://www.washingtonirvingtrailmuseum.com

Sallisaw, OK
14 Flags Museum honors Oklahoma's sometimes turbulent multi-cultural history and the influence of 14 separate Native American nations. The grounds shelter historic structures dating back to when the Cherokee settlers began arriving in the early 1830s. The oldest property is the Lattimore cabin, which was built in 1835. The second cabin was built by Judge Franklin Faulkner sometime during the 1840s after he married a Cherokee woman and was forced to migrate into Oklahoma on the Trail of Tears. Free admission. Open daily during daylight hours. 400 E Cherokee St; Sallisaw, OK 74955; Phone: (918) 775-2608; https://www.exploresouthernhistory.com/sallisawmuseum.html

Shattuck, OK
Shattuck Windmill Museum & Park preserves 63 authentic restored windmills used from the 1850s to the 1950s spread out over the four-acre park. Reconstructed and relocated buildings, including a general store, reflect life in 1900s. Free admission. Outdoor museum open daily during daylight hours. The

store is open Monday through Saturday from 10 AM to 4 PM. 1100 E 11th St; Shattuck, OK 73858; Phone: (580) 938-5291; http://www.shattuckwindmillmuseum.org

Shawnee, OK
Citizen Potawatomi Nation Cultural Heritage Center preserves and showcases the Anishinabe Potawatomi oral traditions, early way of life, conflict, and forced removals. Free admission. Open Monday through Friday from 8 AM to 5 PM and on Saturday from 10 AM to 3 PM. 1899 S Gordon Cooper Dr; Shawnee, OK 74801; Phone: (405) 878-5830; http://www.potawatomiheritage.com

Tishomingo, OK
Chickasaw National Capitol Building overlooks the town of Tishomingo and served as the Chickasaw National Capitol until 1906. Admission is free. Open Monday through Friday from 8 AM to 5 PM and Saturday from 10 AM to 4 PM. Tours are available Tuesday through Friday. 411 W Ninth St; Tishomingo, OK 73460; Phone: (580) 371-9835; https://www.chickasaw.net/Our-Nation/Locations/Chickasaw-National-Capitol.aspx

Tulsa, OK
Elsing Museum features the rock collection of Willard Elsing – minerals, natural crystal formations, and intricate Oriental sculptures. Free admission. Open Wednesday through Saturday from 1:30 PM to 4:30 PM. Oral Roberts University; 7777 S Lewis Ave; Tulsa, OK 74171; Phone: (918) 495-6262; http://www.oru.edu/the-elsing-museum

John Hope Franklin Reconciliation Park recounts the history of Black Americans and the town of Tulsa with focus on the 1921 riot. The park is named after the civil rights leader who thought it was important to tell this often forgotten history. Free admission. Open daily 8 AM to 8 PM. 321 N Detroit Ave; Tulsa, OK 74103; Phone: (918) 295-5009; https://www.jhfcenter.org/reconciliation-park

Oklahoma Jazz Hall of Fame at the Jazz Depot honors jazz, blues, and gospel musicians in the state of Oklahoma. The museum displays photographs, biographical information, artifacts, and memorabilia. Admission to the museum is free. Open Monday through Friday from 9 AM to 5 PM. Free Jazz Jams on Tuesday from 6 PM to 8 PM, followed by Blues Jams from 8 PM to 10 PM. Free Jazzwich live music every Friday from 11:30 AM to 1 PM. Other events may incur a fee. 111 E First St (Upper Level); Tulsa, OK 74103; Phone: (918) 928-5299; http://www.okjazz.org

Tulsa Garden Center offers a historic mansion with free guided tours, the municipal rose garden, and several other specialty gardens. Admission is free. Open Tuesday through Saturday from 8:30 AM to 4 PM. 2435 S Peoria Ave; Tulsa, OK 74114; Phone: (918) 576-5155; https://www.tulsagardencenter.org

Tulsa Art Deco Museum is located inside Art Deco Philcade Building and highlights the short-lived but distinctive design. Items range from functional pieces for the home to advertising artwork. Admission is free. Open whenever the lobby is open, generally weekdays with some Saturday hours. Hours are subject to change. 511 S Boston Ave; Tulsa, OK 74120; Phone: (918) 417-6544; http://tulsaartdecomuseum.com

Tuskahoma, OK
Choctaw Nation Museum Oklahoma Capitol Museum served as the Capitol of the Choctaw Nation until 1907. The museum displays focus on Choctaw history before European contact, the Trail of Tears, Choctaw life in Oklahoma, the Light horsemen, the Choctaw Code Talkers, and Choctaw basketry. Admission is free. Open Monday through Friday from 8 AM to 4:30 PM. Closed holidays. Council House Rd; Tuskahoma, OK 74574; Phone: (918) 569-4465; http://www.choctawnationculture.com/museum/choctaw-nation-capitol-museum.aspx

Tuttle, OK
Braum's Family Farm is home to one of the largest dairy operations in the world. Tours take visitors through life on the farm, a processing plant, and bakery. Tours and ice cream samples are free of charge. Reservations are required. Tours held Monday through Friday at 9 AM and 11 AM. 491 CS 2880; Tuttle, OK 73089; Phone: (405) 228-4604; https://www.braums.com/tour-braums

Wewoka, OK
Seminole Nation Museum interprets the history and culture of the Seminole Nation of Oklahoma from their origin in the Southeast, through the Florida Everglades, to the Indian Territory now known as Oklahoma. There are historic photographs, and interpretive exhibits. Admission is free, donations are encouraged. Open Monday through Saturday from 10 AM to 5 PM. Closed federal holidays. 524 S Wewoka; Wewoka, OK 74884; Phone: (405) 257-5580; https://www.seminolenationmuseum.org

Woodward, OK
Plains Indians and Pioneers Museum is also the town's visitor center and highlights its history. Exhibits include a bank, homesteader cabin, saloon, jail, photo studio, and newspaper office. Native American history is represented through exhibits featuring the Cheyenne and Arapaho. Admission is free. Open

Tuesday to Saturday 10 AM to 5 PM. 2009 Williams Ave; Woodward, OK 73801; Phone: (580) 256-6136; http://www.nwok-pipm.org

Yukon, OK
Express Clydesdales Ranch introduces visitors to the beloved Clydesdale – imported from Clydesdale, Scotland. Admission is free. The Clydesdale barn is open Tuesday through Saturday from 10 AM to 5 PM and Sunday from 12:30 PM to 5 PM. Closed all major holidays. 12701 W Wilshire Blvd; Yukon, OK 73099; Phone: (405) 350-6404; http://www.expressclydesdales.com

Oregon

Ashland, OR

Ashland Art Center showcases the work of local artists with two levels of studios in which the artists' work is displayed and offered for sale. Talk to a working artist, enjoy the ever-changing displays. Admission is free. Open daily 10 AM to 6 PM. 357 E. Main St; Ashland, OR 97520; Phone: (541) 482-2772; https://www.ashlandartcenter.org

Schneider Museum of Art - Southern Oregon University creates bimonthly exhibits focusing on contemporary visual arts. Free docent-led tour every Tuesday at 12:30 PM. Note: The museum closes between exhibitions. Free admission. Open Monday through Saturday from 10 AM to 4PM. 555 Indiana St; Ashland, OR 97520; Phone: (541) 552-6245; http://sma.sou.edu

Astoria, OR

Hanthorn Cannery Museum depicts 130 years of community, and cannery history. The company eventually became Bumble Bee Seafoods. The museum is housed at Pier 39 and is the oldest remaining processing plant on the lower Columbia River. There is no admission charge, though donations are appreciated. Open daily from 9 AM to 6 PM. 100 39th St; Astoria, OR 97103; Phone: (503) 468-6725; https://canneryworker.org

Beaverton, OR

Cooper Mountain Nature Park offers visitors 3½ miles of trails through a variety of habitats ranging from conifer forest to prairie to oak woodlands. There is no admission charge. Open daily from dawn to dusk. 18895 SW Kemmer Rd; Beaverton, OR 97007; Phone: (503) 629-6350; .http://www.thprd.org/parks-and-trails/detail/cooper-mountain-nature-park

VintageTek preserves vintage instruments, memorabilia, and photographs from Tektronix, a local electronics company founded in 1945. Admission is free with donations are accepted. Open Thursday through Saturday at 10 AM. Closes Thursday at 6 PM, and Friday and Saturday at 4 PM. 13489 SW Karl Braun Dr; Beaverton, OR 97077; Phone: (503) 644-0161; https://vintagetek.org

Bend, OR

Pilot Butte State Scenic Viewpoint has seven miles of trails that wind around an extinct volcano. Reach the summit of the 480-foot butte by a mile-long nature trail or a mile-long paved road. Interpretive panels illuminate the geography, geology, and natural history of the region. There are no fees associated with this

park. 1310 NE Hwy 20; Bend, OR 97701; Phone: (541) 388-6055;
https://oregonstateparks.org/index.cfm?do=parkPage.dsp_parkPage&parkId=33

Cascade Locks, OR
Bonneville Lock & Dam, in the heart of the Columbia River Gorge, introduces visitors to the cultural history of the region, dam construction, the development of navigation along the Columbia River, and the life-cycles of salmon and Pacific lamprey. A rooftop observation deck provides a panoramic view of the Columbia River Gorge. Free admission. Open daily from 9 AM to 5 PM. Bonneville Lock and Dam; Cascade Locks, OR 97014; Phone: (541) 374-8820;
http://www.nwp.usace.army.mil/Locations/ColumbiaRiver/Bonneville.aspx

Coos Bay, OR
Marshfield Sun Printing Museum features the original equipment of The Sun newspaper (1891-1944) and exhibits on local history. Admission is free. Donations accepted. Open from Memorial Day through Labor Day on Tuesday through Saturday from 1 PM to 4 PM. 1049 Front St; Coos Bay, OR 97420; Phone: (541) 269-0215; https://www.marshfieldsunprintingmuseum.org

Corvallis, OR
William L Finley National Wildlife Refuge provides a sanctuary for wintering waterfowl, wading birds, and shorebirds. Trails provide views of the different habitats. There are no fees to visit the park. Open from sunrise to sunset. The visitor center is off Finley Refuge Road and is open Monday through Friday from 8 AM to 4 PM and Saturday and Sunday from 10 AM to 4 PM. Closed on all federal holidays. Highway 99W; Corvallis, OR 97333; Phone: (541) 757-7236; https://www.fws.gov/refuge/william_l_finley

Eugene, OR
Owen Rose Garden features more than 4,500 roses from 400 varieties in a setting along the Willamette River in Riverfront Park. There is no admission fee. 300 N Jefferson St; Eugene, OR 97401; Phone: (541) 682-4800; https://www.eugene-or.gov/Facilities/Facility/Details/124

Fossil, OR (See also Mitchell, OR and Kimberly, OR)
John Day Fossil Beds – Clarno Palisades shelters fossils still embedded in rocks. The Palisades were formed 54 to 40 million years ago. The 1/4 mile loop Trail of Fossils is the only trail where visitors can see these fossils. There are no visitor entrance fees. Open year-round during daylight hours. Highway 218 between the towns of Fossil and Antelope; Phone: (541) 987-2333; https://www.nps.gov/joda/planyourvisit/clarno.htm

Grants Pass, OR

Grants Pass Museum of Art offers special limited-time exhibitions. General admission is free. Open Tuesday through Saturday from 10 AM to 5 PM. 229 Southwest G St; Grants Pass, OR 97526; Phone: (541) 479-3290; https://www.gpmuseum.com

Gresham, OR

Gresham Japanese Garden, also called Tsuru Island, is a 40-year-old Japanese garden with broadleaf evergreens, pines, and azaleas. Located within the 21-acre Main City Park. Free and open sunrise to sunset. 219 S Main Ave; Gresham, OR 97030; Phone: (503) 969-4386; http://greshamjapanesegarden.com

Joseph, OR

Old Chief Joseph Gravesite is adjacent Nez Perce National Historical Park. It is the burial site of Chief Joseph, the famous Nez Perce leader who refused to sell his Wallowa homeland and sign the 1863 Treaty. It is said that before he died in 1871, he told his son to defend his homeland and people. "My son, never forget my dying words, this country holds your father's body. Never sell the bones of your father and mother." The entire area is part of the ancestral homeland of the Nez Perce. There are no fees to visit the park. Hwy 82, north of Wallowa Lake. Phone: (208) 843-7009; https://www.nps.gov/nepe/planyourvisit/visit-old-chief-joseph-gravesite.htm

Kimberly, OR (See also Fossil, OR and Mitchell, OR)

John Day Fossil Beds – Sheep Rock Unit is one of the three locations for John Day Fossil Beds and showcases claystone layers dating 32 to 7 million years ago. Thomas Condon Paleontology Center has fossil exhibits and offers the opportunity to see scientists at work. There are no entrance fees. The outdoor areas, trails, and overlooks are open year-round during daylight hours. The Paleontology Center is open daily in summer from 9 AM to 5 PM, opening one hour later at 10 AM the rest of the year. Closed major holidays. 32651 Hwy 19; Kimberly, OR 97848; Phone: (541) 987-2333; https://www.nps.gov/joda/planyourvisit/sr-unit.htm

Lowell, OR

Lowell Covered Bridge Interpretive Center features a self-guided interpretive display on Oregon's covered bridges. Pioneer St and Hwy 58 at Lowell. https://www.ci.lowell.or.us/parksrec/page/lowell-covered-bridge-interpretive-center

Milwaukie, OR

Bob's Red Mill Tour invites visitors to learn about stone grinding whole grains on a free guided tour of the manufacturing facility. Watch the action through viewing windows and enjoy a free sample. Tours start at 10 AM on Monday through Friday. No tours on major holidays. 13521 SE Pheasant Ct; Milwaukie, OR 97222; Phone: (800) 349-2173; https://www.bobsredmill.com/tour-our-world-headquarters.html

Mitchell, OR (See also Fossil, OR and Kimberly, OR)

John Day Fossil Beds – Painted Hills is one of the three locations for John Day Fossil Beds. It preserves the history of climate change as well as specializes in leaf fossils 39 to 30 million years old. Boardwalks take you alongside the colorful clay hills. There is no fee to visit the park. Open year-round during daylight hours. Off Hwy 26; Bear Creek Rd; Mitchell, OR 97750; Phone: (541) 987-2333; https://www.nps.gov/joda/planyourvisit/ptd-hills-unit.htm

Oregon City, OR (See also Vancouver, WA)

McLoughlin House Unit of Fort Vancouver National Historic Site has been restored to tell the story of John McLoughlin, known as the Father of Oregon. There is no fee to visit and the house is open Fridays and Saturdays from 10 AM to 4 PM. Free public tours are available hourly throughout the day. Closed from mid-December through mid-February. Park grounds are open daily from dawn until dusk. Open Friday and Saturday from 10 AM to 4 PM. Free tours are available. 713 Center St; Oregon City, OR 97045; Phone: (503) 656-5151; https://www.nps.gov/fova/learn/historyculture/mcloughlin-house.htm

Oregon City Municipal Elevator connects two neighborhoods in Oregon City; downtown, and the historic McLoughlin neighborhood. The elevator is free to the public leading to the upper portion with an observation deck. Open Monday through Saturday from 7 AM to 7 PM and Sunday from 10 AM to 7 PM. 814 Main St; Oregon City, OR 97045; Phone: (503) 994-6633; https://www.downtownoregoncity.org/elevator

Philomath, OR

Benton County Historical Society operates a museum with over 120,000 photographs, historical documents, textiles, clothing, farm implements, and scientific instruments. A highlight is the Cockrell quilts incorporating different styles and techniques from the Revolutionary to the Civil War. Admission is free with donations welcomed. Open Tuesday through Saturday from 10 AM to 4:30 PM. 1101 Main St; Philomath, OR 97370; Phone: (541) 929-6230; http://www.bentoncountymuseum.org

Portland, OR

Hoyt Arboretum conserve endangered species of trees and shrubs from six continents with 12 miles of hiking trails. Located in Washington Park. Free admission. Open daily 5 AM to 10 PM. 4000 SW Fairview Blvd; Portland, OR 97221; Phone: (503) 865-8733; https://www.hoytarboretum.org

International Rose Test Garden is the oldest public rose test garden in the United States. The garden is free. Open daily 7:30 AM to 9 PM with free tours daily at 1 PM from Memorial Day weekend through Labor Day weekend. Located in Washington Park. 400 SW Kingston Ave; Portland, OR 97205; Phone: (503) 823-3636; https://www.portlandoregon.gov/parks/finder/index.cfm?action=viewpark&propertyid=1113

Japanese American Historical Plaza commemorates the people who were deported to inland internment camps during World War II. Their story is told in engraved poetry mounted on a series of stones. Open daily from 5 AM to Midnight. In March to April 100 cherry trees bloom around the monument. North of Burnside Bridge. Phone: (503) 224-1458; http://www.oregonnikkei.org/plaza.htm

Portland Police Museum features permanent and rotating exhibits including historic photos and uniforms, firearms collections, and an old jail cell. Admission is free. Open Tuesday through Friday from 10 AM to 3 PM. 1111 SW Second Ave; Portland, OR 97204; Phone: (503) 823-0019; Portland, OR 97204; https://portlandpolicemuseum.com/index.html

Portland Puppet Museum charges for the performances, but opens its door for free to their museum exhibits. Their newest exhibit features over 100 fairy tale characters from across Europe, Asia, and the United States. Open Thursday through Sunday from 2 PM to 8 PM. 906 SE Umatilla St; Portland, OR 97202; Phone: (503) 233-7723; http://www.puppetmuseum.com

Powell's City of Books calls itself the largest independent new and used bookstore in the world. Free tours are held on Sunday at 10 AM and 4 PM. Open 9 AM to 11 PM daily. 1005 W Burnside St; Portland, OR 97209; Phone: (800) 878-7323; https://www.powells.com/locations/powells-city-of-books

Vacuum Museum features 300 machines mounted on a wall in Stark's Vacuum Portland store. See the two-person-operated Busy-Bee – one pumped, one vacuumed. Admission is free. Open Monday through Friday from 8 AM to 6 PM, on Saturday from 9 AM to 6 PM, and Sunday from 10 AM to 5 PM. 107 NE Grand Ave; Portland, OR 97232; Phone: (503) 232-4101; http://starks.com/vacuum-museum

Wells Fargo Center exhibits the Cal-Oregon Stage line, and river boats of the Columbia River. Free admission. Open Monday to Friday from 9 AM to 6 PM. 1300 SW Fifth Ave; Portland, OR 97201; Phone: (503) 886-1102; https://www.wellsfargohistory.com/museums/portland

Prospect, OR
Prospect State Scenic Viewpoint offers visitors a hiking trail leading to Pearsony Falls, the Rogue River gorge and Mill Creek Falls. There are no fees to visit the park. Mill Creek Dr; Prospect, OR 97536; Phone: (541) 560-3334; https://oregonstateparks.org/index.cfm?do=parkPage.dsp_parkPage&parkId=22

Roseburg, OR
Winchester Dam Fish Ladder is dotted with viewing windows where visitors can observe fish species. Free to visit. Open daily from 7 AM to 7 PM. NE Stephens St; Roseburg, OR 97470; Phone: (503) 947-6000; https://www.dfw.state.or.us/fish/fish_counts/winchester_dam.asp

Salem, OR
Oregon Capitol is open for free self-guided visits from 8 AM to 5 PM weekdays. Closed all major holidays. Pick up a brochure of building highlights as well as information about exhibits and artwork, at the information kiosk on the first floor. 900 Court St NE; Salem, OR 97301; Phone: (503) 986-1388; https://www.oregonlegislature.gov/capitolhistorygateway/Pages/Tours.aspx

Salem's Riverfront Carousel was carved by local volunteers who created the hand-carved horses. The artisans demonstrate wood-carving in two workshops on the grounds. Generally open Monday through Thursday from 10 AM to 1 PM. Note: They suggest calling first. There is a charge to ride the carousel. 101 Front St NE; Salem, OR 97301; Phone: (503) 540-0374; http://salemcarousel.wixsite.com/salemcarousel/carvingexhibits

Salem SenateAires Men's Chorus welcomes visitors to their weekly rehearsals held Thursday evenings from 7:30 PM to 10:30 PM. Note: Call first to make sure they are rehearsing. Salem First Presbyterian Church; 770 Chemeketa St NE; Salem, OR 97301; Phone: (971) 208-7135; http://senateaires.org/visit-us

Springfield, OR
Springfield Museum features historical and artistic exhibits. Admission is free. Open Thursday through Saturday from 11 AM to 4 PM. Closed major holidays. 590 Main St; Springfield, OR 97477; Phone: (541) 726-2300; http://www.springfield-museum.com/

The Dalles, OR

The Dalles Dam Visitor Center provides interactive displays, a short film on the dam, and fish migrating up the fish ladder. No fees are charged. Open daily from Memorial Day to Labor Day from 9 AM to 5 PM. Open Friday through Sunday the rest of the year. 3545 Bret Clodfelter Way; The Dalles, OR 97058; Phone: (541) 296-9778; http://www.nwp.usace.army.mil/The-Dalles

Fire Museum is located in City Hall which was the original fire department. Admission is free. Open Monday through Friday from 8 AM 5 PM. Closed major holidays. 313 Court St; The Dalles, OR 97058; Phone: (541) 296-5481; http://www.ci.the-dalles.or.us/node/78

Tillamook, OR

Cape Meares National Wildlife Refuge and Lighthouse offers old-growth forest, and cliffs overlooking the ocean. The park is free to visit. Open daily from dawn to dusk. The Cape Meare's lighthouse, considered the shortest lighthouse on the Oregon Coast, is located at the north end of Three Capes Scenic Route. Admission is free. Open from April through October. 3500 Cape Meares Loop; Tillamook, OR 97141; Phone: (503) 842-2244; https://www.fws.gov/refuge/Cape_Meares

Tillamook Cheese Factory opens its factory for a self-guided tour through videos, displays, and kiosks. It's free, including cheese samples. Open daily from 8 AM to 6 PM from late September through mid-June. Open daily all year. Open from 8 AM to 6 PM on Sunday through Thursday and 8 AM to 8 PM on Friday through Saturday. Closed Thanksgiving, and Christmas Day. 4175 Hwy 101 N; Tillamook, OR 97141; Phone: (503) 815-1300; https://www.tillamook.com

West Linn, OR

Rogerson Clematis Garden at Luscher Farm contains the most comprehensive collection of clematis within a public garden in North America -- 1800 individual clematis representing over 800 distinct species. The collection contains unique and rare plants, as well as historic varieties and the newest hybrids. Admission is free. Open daily from dawn to dusk. 125 Rosemont Rd; West Linn, OR 97068; Phone: (971) 777-4394; https://www.rogersonclematiscollection.org

Wolf Creek, OR

Golden State Heritage Site was once a 19th century mining town noteworthy for the total absence of saloons. Visitors can explore the historic buildings including a church, a former residence, a shed, and a structure that once housed a post office

and store. There are no fees. Coyote Creek Rd; Wolf Creek, OR 97497; Phone: (541) 528-1118;
https://oregonstateparks.org/index.cfm?do=parkPage.dsp_parkPage&parkId=189

Pennsylvania

Alburtis, PA

Lock Ridge Furnace Museum is one of only two remaining furnaces that were in operation in central and eastern Pennsylvania in 1876. It harbors the furnace room, the former weighmaster's house, partial ruins of Furnace No. 8, and several associated buildings. Numbered signs allow visitors to take a self-guided tour. Admission is free. Open daily from 9 AM to 5 PM. Guided tours are offered from 1 PM to 4 PM on Saturdays and Sundays from May to September. 525 Franklin St; Alburtis, PA 18011; Phone: (610) 435-1074; http://www.lchs.museum/HistoricSites.htm

Beaver Falls, PA

Air Heritage Museum hosts almost a dozen heritage airplanes, aviation related displays from the early days of aviation to the present, and military artifacts. The museum is free and open Monday through Saturday from 10 AM to 5 PM. Closed major holidays. Located at the Beaver County Airport; 35 Piper St; Beaver Falls, PA 15010; Phone: (724) 843-2820; http://airheritage.org/about-the-museum

Allentown, PA

Haines Mill was originally built in 1760, reconstructed in 1909, and operated until 1956. The mill is open for free public tours on Saturday and Sunday from May through September from 1 PM to 4 PM. 3600 Haines Mill Rd; Allentown, PA 18104; Phone: (610) 435-4664; https://www.lehighcounty.org/Departments/Parks-And-Recreation/Our-Parks/Cedar-Creek-Parkway-East

Bradford, PA

Zippo/Case Museum invites visitors to take a self-guided tour of the repair clinic and the 14 custom-made Zippo street lighters that line the driveway to the building. Admission is free. Open Monday through Saturday from 9 AM to 5 PM and Sunday from 11 AM to 4 PM. 1932 Zippo Dr; Bradford, PA 16701; Phone: (814) 368-1932; https://www.zippo.com/pages/zippo-case-museums

Carlisle, PA

U.S. Army Heritage and Education Center main gallery features *The Soldier Experience* highlighting the history of the U.S. Army from the Spanish-American War to current missions. The outdoor Army Heritage Trail provides interactive and full-scale military exhibits including a Cobra helicopter, and a WWI trench system. The USAHEC is free to visit. Open Monday through Saturday from 10 AM to 5 PM and Sunday from Noon to 5 PM. Other exhibit buildings have shortened hours. The trail is open from dawn to dusk. 950 Soldiers Dr; Carlisle, PA 17013; Phone: (717) 245-3972; https://ahec.armywarcollege.edu/visit.cfm

Coplay, PA

Saylor Park Cement Kilns were built in 1893. The restored and stabilized kilns now house a free-admission outdoor cement industry museum. Open daily all year. 245 N Second St; Coplay, PA 18037; Phone: (610) 435-1074; http://www.lchs.museum/HistoricSites.htm

Erie, PA

Presque Isle State Park is a day-use park along a coastline peninsula into Lake Erie. The **Tom Ridge Environmental Center** offers interactive exhibits, a 75-foot glass-enclosed tower, and an orientation movie. Admission is free. The park is open daily sunrise to sunset. The center is open daily from 9 AM to 5 PM. Closed Thanksgiving, Christmas, and New Year's Day. 301 Peninsula Dr; Erie, PA 16505; Phone: (814) 833-7424; https://www.dcnr.pa.gov/StateParks/FindAPark/PresqueIsleStatePark/TRECPI/Pages/TRECPI.aspx/index.html

Fairfield, PA (See Also Gettysburg, PA)

Strawberry Hill Nature Preserve offers over 600 acres and over 60 species of birds. There is no fee to visit the nature preserve. Donations are gratefully accepted. Trails are open daily from dawn to dusk. 1537 Mt Hope Rd; Fairfield, PA 17320; Phone: (717) 642-5840; http://strawberryhill.org

Farmington, PA

Fort Necessity National Battlefield was the site of the opening action of the 1754 French and Indian War which ultimately ended French power in Colonial America. The twenty-minute movie *Road of Necessity* introduces the park story. Visit the reconstructed fort where the war began and nearby Mount Washington Tavern which is now a self-guided museum focusing on life along the National Road. The entrance fee to Fort Necessity National Battlefield ended in 2016. It is now free. The battlefield is open daily sunrise until sunset. Talks, tours, and historic weapons demonstrations are offered during the summer months. The visitor center is open daily from 9 AM to 5 PM. Mount Washington Tavern is open daily May through October from 10 AM to 4 PM. 1 Washington Pkwy; Farmington, PA 15437; Phone: (724) 329-5512; https://www.nps.gov/fone/index.htm

Gallitzin, PA

Allegheny Portage Railroad celebrates the 1834 opening of a direct route between Philadelphia and Pittsburgh. Tour the Engine House No. 6 Exhibit Shelter and the first floor of the Lemon house, restored to its 1840s appearance. The Lemon house is generally open daily from 9 AM to 5 PM from mid-April to mid-November. Hours are limited during winter. The grounds and trails of the park are open daily all year from sunrise to sunset. 110 Federal Park Rd; Gallitzin, PA 16641; Phone: (814) 886-6150; https://www.nps.gov/alpo/index.htm

Gardners PA

Appalachian Trail Museum celebrates everyone who has done this famous trail, either full or in part. About 13,000 photos of hikers can be viewed. A reconstruction of the shelter built by Earl Shaffer, the first person to walk the entire trail in 1948, is on display. There's also exhibits devoted to early founders of the trail, Benton MacKaye and Myron Avery, as well as some of the early thru-hikers. Located in an old grist mill at Pine Grove Furnace State Park admission is free, although donations are welcomed. The museum is open seasonally from the end of August to the end of October. Check the website for hours which are updated each year. 1120 Pine Grove Rd; Gardners, PA 17324; Phone: (717) 486-8126; https://www.atmuseum.org/about.html

Gettysburg, PA

Destination Gettysburg offers self-guided walking tour brochures at the Information Center or mailed by request. 571 W Middle St; Gettysburg, PA 17325; Phone: (717) 334-6274; (800) 337-5015; https://www.destinationgettysburg.com

Gettysburg Lincoln Railroad Station, built in 1859, served as a field hospital, a departure point for thousands of soldiers, and the place where President Lincoln was greeted when he came to deliver his Gettysburg Address. The station is free to visit. Open Friday through Sunday from March through May, and again in September and October from 10 AM to 5 PM. Open daily from Memorial Day through Labor Day from 10 AM to 5 PM. 35 Carlisle St; Gettysburg, PA 17325; Phone: (717) 338-1243; https://www.destinationgettysburg.com/members/historic-gettysburg-train-station.asp

Gettysburg National Military Park may be one of the most crucial Civil War sites. The Battle of Gettysburg and the Union victory came at a ferocious cost. It is considered the Civil War's bloodiest battle prompting President Abraham Lincoln's moving Gettysburg Address. Entrance to the park is free as are the ranger-guided programs. Note: Admission is charged for the museum, cyclorama, and the film. Guided tours and a visit to the home of Gettysburg attorney David Wills also incurs a charge. The grounds are open daily from April to October from 6 AM to 10 PM. The rest of the year the grounds are open daily from 6 AM to 7 PM. 1195 Baltimore Pike (Rt 97); Gettysburg, PA 17325; Phone: (717) 334-1124; https://www.nps.gov/gett/index.htm

Rupp House History Center provides a look at civilian life during the Civil War, and the soldiers who fought in and around Gettysburg. The lower level of the house is free to visit. Open from April through November on Friday and Saturday from Noon to 8 PM and on Sunday from Noon to 5 PM. Open some holidays. 451 Baltimore St; Gettysburg, PA 17325; Phone: (717) 339-2159; http://www.gettysburgfoundation.org/rupp-house

Sachs Covered Bridge at Water Works Road is a piece of Civil War history. Walking across it puts visitors on the bridge that was used by both armies before and after the Battle of Gettysburg. Closed to vehicles, this is now a pedestrian crossing over Marsh Creek. Phone: (717) 334-6274.

Hanover, PA
Hanover Pennsylvania Pretzel Bakery offers free tours and pretzels. Note: Everyone participating must be able to climb stairs. Tours are conducted on Tuesday, Wednesday, and Thursday all year. Reservations are required at least 24 hours in advance. To schedule a tour call (800) 233-7125 Ext 28592 on Monday through Friday from 9 AM to 5 PM. 1350 York St (Rt 116); Hanover, PA 17331; Phone: (717) 632-4477; https://www.snydersofhanover.com/tour-snyders-of-hanover

Harrisburg, PA
Art Association of Harrisburg presents in-house exhibitions of regional, national and international artwork. The gallery is free to visit. Open Monday through Thursday from 9:30 AM to 9 PM and on Friday and Saturday from 10 AM to 4 PM. Open Sunday from 2 PM to 5 PM. 3211 N Front St; Suite 301-A; Harrisburg, PA 17110; Phone: (717) 231-7788; http://www.artassocofhbg.com/index2.htm

Fort Hunter invites strolls along the river and the old towpath of the Pennsylvania Canal. Admission to the park is free. Take a self-guided tour of the historic buildings and the old estate. Tours of the mansion will incur a fee. The grounds are open 8 AM to dusk. 5300 N Front St; Harrisburg, PA 17110; Phone: (717) 599-5751; https://forthunter.org

Governor's Residence is open for public tours on Tuesday and Thursday from 9:30 AM to 2 PM. Tours are conducted by docents at no charge. Reservations are required at least one week in advance. No tours are available August and November. 2035 N Front St; Harrisburg, PA 17102; Phone: (717) 787-1192; https://www.residence.pa.gov/Tours/Pages/default.aspx

Pennsylvania State Capitol is filled with art, architecture, and history. The free tour starts every half hour Monday through Friday from 8:30 to 4 PM. On weekends and most holidays tours are offered at 9 AM, 11 AM, 1 PM, and 3 PM. Self-guided tours are available weekdays only. Closed Easter Sunday, Thanksgiving, Christmas, and New Year's Day. Note: Visitors are advised to check for schedule changes. Commonwealth Ave; Harrisburg, PA 17120; Phone: (800) 868-7672; http://www.pacapitol.com/plan-a-visit/tours.cfm

Jim Thorpe, PA
Jim Thorpe Memorial and Grave Site is in a bit of an unexpected location. The legendary athlete and Olympic gold medalist was born in Oklahoma and never set foot in Pennsylvania. Visitors can see the grave and learn more about his life and death. Note: Each year in May the town holds a birthday celebration. North Street (Rt 903); Jim Thorpe, PA 18229; https://www.jimthorpe.org/; https://en.wikipedia.org/wiki/Jim_Thorpe.

Lancaster, PA
Demuth Museum focuses on the works of Lancaster-born artist Charles Demuth, but also lets visitors stand in his studio and look out at the garden that inspired his floral watercolors. Admission is free with donations encouraged. Open Tuesday through Saturday at 10 AM. Closes at 4 PM except Friday when it closes at 6 PM. Open Sunday from Noon to 4 PM. The museum is closed between exhibitions. Note: They recommend calling to confirm hours. 120 E King St; Lancaster, PA 17602; Phone: (717) 299-9940; http://www.demuth.org

Phillips Museum of Art at Franklin & Marshall College delivers a permanent collection focused on decorative arts, Pennsylvania German culture and exhibitions from contemporary artists. Admission is free. Open Tuesday, Wednesday and Friday from Noon to 4 PM, and Thursday from 2 PM to 6 PM. Open Saturday and Sunday from Noon to 4 PM. Closed for school breaks during new installations. 623 College Ave; Lancaster, PA 17604; Phone: (717) 358-3849; https://www.fandm.edu/phillips-museum

Nazareth, PA
Martin Guitar Museum and Factory melds music history, culture, and craftsmanship showcasing 170 guitars that parallel their six generation history. The

museum is free to visit. Open Monday through Friday from 8 AM to 5 PM. The public tours are free and follow the making of a guitar from rough lumber to finished musical instrument. Note: There are also fee-based tours. Closed-toe shoes are recommended. Tours are available Monday through Friday between 11 AM and 2:30 PM. 510 Sycamore St; Nazareth, PA 18064; Phone: (610) 759-2837; https://www.martinguitar.com/about/visit-us

Orrtanna, PA

Mister Ed's Elephant Museum sells candy, peanuts, and fudge are available but the elephant-themed museum is free to visit. Mister Ed's Elephant Museum features more than 12,000 figures, circus souvenirs, political paraphernalia, and toys. Open daily from 10 AM to 6 PM. 6019 Chambersburg Rd; Orrtanna, PA 17353; Phone: (717) 352-3792; https://www.mistereds.com/

Philadelphia, PA

With about 4,000 painted walls, Philadelphia is a perfect city for people who love outdoor mural art. Their Mural Arts program is the nation's largest public art initiative. Their tours are fee-based but you can find the wall murals you want to visit using their online map: https://map.muralarts.org Or, download their map here: https://www.muralarts.org/self-guided

Carpenters' Hall was the site of the 1774 meeting to support a trade embargo against England, one of the first unified acts of defiance against the King. The delegates' chairs and the original banner carried during the 1788 Constitutional parade are displayed. Free to the public. Open Tuesday through Sunday from 10 AM to 4 PM. Note: Closed on Tuesday in January and February. Closed Christmas, Thanksgiving, and New Year's Day. 320 Chestnut St; Philadelphia, PA 19106; Phone: (215) 925-0167; http://www.carpentershall.org

Dream Garden features Tiffany glass and Maxfield Parrish art with a 15 by 49-foot mosaic of more than 100,000 pieces of favrile glass reproducing the Parrish painting. The work has been displayed since 1916. It is free to visit in the lobby of the Curtis Center. The lobby is open Monday through Friday from 8 AM to 6 PM and on Saturday from 10 AM to 1 PM. 601 Walnut St; Philadelphia, PA 19106; Phone: (215) 238-6450; http://www.ushistory.org/tour/dream-garden.htm

Edgar Allan Poe National Historic Site was Poe's home for six years, often considered to be his most prolific years. The home is unfurnished, the exhibits are located in the adjacent house. Admission is free. Open Friday through Sunday from 9 AM to 5 PM but closed for lunch from Noon to 1 PM. 532 N Seventh St; Philadelphia, PA 19123; Phone: (215) 965-2305; https://www.nps.gov/edal/index.htm

Fireman's Hall is dedicated to the art and science of firefighting. Displays of firefighting equipment illustrate how firefighters control blazes. See mock-ups of recreation areas, dressing rooms, and a chief's room. Learn about the fire marks that people affixed to their homes to indicate which insurance company was protecting them. Admission is free with donations appreciated. Open Tuesday through Saturday from 10 AM to 4 PM. Closed city holidays. 147 N Second Street, Philadelphia, PA 19106; Phone: (215) 923-1438; http://www.firemanshallmuseum.org/

Independence Hall is considered the most significant historical site in the country. It is the birthplace of the USA. Both the Declaration of Independence and U.S. Constitution were debated and signed here, establishing the universal principles of freedom and democracy. Admission is free, although timed entry tickets are required except in January and February. Tickets can be obtained on the morning of your visit at the Independence Visitor Center which is open daily 8:30 AM to 6 PM. Tickets can also be reserved in advance online or by phone however a convenience fee applies. Independence Hall is open daily from 9 AM to 5 PM and until 7 PM in summer. Hours of other historical buildings and facilities change seasonally. Closed some major holidays. Most of the park grounds are open 24 hours a day to pedestrians. 143 S Third St; Philadelphia, PA 19106; Phone: (215) 965-2305; https://www.nps.gov/inde/index.htm

Institute of Contemporary Art curates exhibits center on contemporary art and culture. Admission is free. Open Wednesday through Sunday from 11 AM to 6 PM. Open later on Wednesday to 8 PM. 118 S 36th St; Philadelphia, PA 19104; Phone: (215) 898-7108; https://icaphila.org

Liberty Bell Center presents the facts and the myths surrounding the nation's most famous bell. The 2,080-pound mostly copper structure is a good photo-op with Independence Hall in the background. Admission is free. Open daily from 9 AM to 7 PM in summer, open until 5 PM the rest of the year. 526 Market St; Philadelphia, PA 19106; Phone: (215) 965-2305; https://www.nps.gov/inde/planyourvisit/libertybellcenter.htm

President's House: Freedom and Slavery in the Making of a New Nation is an open-air exhibit next to the Liberty Bell Center at the remains of the nation's first executive mansion. The display focuses on where Presidents George Washington and John Adams lived as well as nine enslaved people who served the first President. Admission is free. The exhibit is open daily from 7 AM to 10 PM. 524 Market St; Philadelphia, PA 19106; Phone: (215) 965-2305; https://www.nps.gov/inde/learn/historyculture/places-presidentshousesite.htm

Ryerss Museum & Library highlights generations of family heirlooms, paintings, sculpture, decorative art, and an array of Asian art and artifacts. Admission is free.

Open Friday through Sunday from 10 AM to 4 PM. 7370 Central Ave; Philadelphia, PA 19111; Phone: (215) 685-0544; https://www.ryerssmuseum.org/museum

Science History Institute uses items from the Institute's collections to show how chemistry influences daily life. The museum also hosts various temporary and rotating exhibitions. Admission is free. Open Tuesday to Saturday from 10 AM to 5 PM. 315 Chestnut St; Philadelphia, PA 19106; Phone: (215) 925-2222; https://www.sciencehistory.org/museum

Shoe Museum is part of Temple University School of Podiatric Medicine and displays a selection from its collection on the sixth floor of the TUSPM main building. Highlights include a pair of 200-year-old French *sabots*, the wooden shoes that gave birth to the expression *sabotage,* and Egyptian burial sandals. Admission to the museum is free, but visits must be scheduled in advance. 148 N Eighth St; Philadelphia, PA 19107; Phone: (215) 625-5243; https://podiatry.temple.edu/about/shoe-museum

U S Mint shows the process of minting coins. View interactive displays depicting the many presidential and honorary commemoratives designed at the mint as well as early coining equipment, and rare and historic coins. All tours are free and self-guided. No reservations are necessary. Open Monday through Friday from 9 AM to 4:30 PM. Also open Saturday from Memorial Day through Labor Day and on Memorial Day and Labor Day Mondays. Closed most major holidays. 151 N Independence Mall E; Philadelphia, PA 19106; Phone: (215) 408-0112; https://www.usmint.gov/about/mint-tours-facilities/philadelphia/tour-information

Wells Fargo History Museum features a Concord city-style stagecoach, traditional clothing, and an interactive Wells Fargo agent. Admission is free. Open Monday through Friday from 9 AM to 5 PM. 123 S Broad St; Philadelphia, PA 19109; Phone: (215) 670-6123; https://www.wellsfargohistory.com/museums/philadelphia/

Pittsburgh, PA
Allegheny Observatory University of Pittsburgh is open to the public for free tours April through the end of October on either Thursday or Friday, depending on the month. Reservations are required. Call (412) 321-2400 Monday through Friday between the hours of 1 PM and 5 PM. All tours begin at 8 PM and last until approximately 10 PM. A short slide or film presentation is shown followed by a walking tour of the building. Department of Physics & Astronomy; 159 Riverview Ave; Pittsburgh, PA 15214; http://www.pitt.edu/~aobsvtry/tours.html
Frick Pittsburgh provides garden walks, the museums' collection of art, and their Car and Carriage Museum. Admission to the Frick grounds, Car and Carriage

Museum, greenhouse, and museum's permanent collection is free. Note: There are fees for other tours and special exhibitions. The Frick is open Tuesday through Sunday from 10 AM to 5 PM and open late on Friday to 9 PM. 7227 Reynolds St; Pittsburgh, PA 15208; Phone: (412) 371-0600; https://www.thefrickpittsburgh.org

Society for Contemporary Craft highlights craft materials such as clay, fiber, metal, paper, and wood by international, national and regional artists. Admission is free. Open Monday through Saturday from 10 AM to 5 AM, closing Friday at 4 PM. 2100 Smallman St; Pittsburgh, PA 15219; Phone: (412) 261-7003; https://contemporarycraft.org

Pottsville, PA
Yuengling & Son Brewery, Museum and Gift Shop invites visitors to discover the hand-dug caves that were used for beer fermentation before refrigeration, their iconic brew house with stained glass ceiling, and how they survived Prohibition. Tours are free for all ages but valid ID will be required if you wish to sample beer after the tour. Note: Completely closed shoes are required for the tour. From January through March tours are offered Monday through Friday on the hour from 10 AM to 2 PM and until 3 PM the rest of the year. Closed major holidays. 420 Mahantongo St; Pottsville, PA 17901; Phone: (570) 628-4890; https://www.yuengling.com/visit-us/#tab_pottsville-pa

Scranton, PA
Steamtown National Historic Site at the former Scranton yards of the Delaware, Lackawanna and Western Railroad (DL&W) features history and technology museums, special exhibits, and movies. Walking tours of the locomotive shop are offered. There are about 20 locomotives and 75 pieces of rolling stock. The park stopped charging admission in 2017. Train rides will incur a fee. Open daily from 9 AM to 5 PM. Closed Thanksgiving, Christmas, and New Year's Day. 350 Cliff St; Scranton, PA 18503; Phone: (570) 340-5200; https://www.nps.gov/stea/index.htm

Stoystown, PA
Flight 93 National Memorial honors the passengers and crew of Flight 93. On Tuesday morning, September 11, 2001, the U.S. came under attack when four commercial airliners were hijacked and used to strike ground targets within the United States of America. The actions of the 40 passengers and crew aboard Flight 93 thwarted the attack on the U.S. Capitol at the cost of their lives. The Tower of Voices is conceived as a monumental, 93-foot tall musical instrument preserving the memory and the heroism of those on Flight 93. There is no entrance fee for Flight 93 National Memorial. Grounds are open sunrise to sunset, year around, including all holidays, weather permitting. The visitor center is open daily 9 AM

to 5 PM. Closed Thanksgiving, Christmas, and New Year's Day. Note: The entrance to the memorial is located on US Route 30. 6424 Lincoln Highway; Stoystown, PA 15563; Phone: (814) 893-6322; https://www.nps.gov/flni/index.htm

York, PA
Harley-Davidson Vehicle Operations offers their free Classic Factory Tour focused on the Harley-Davidson's assembly line and fabrication areas. Exhibits detail the manufacturing and assembly processes of the factory. Only the Classic tour is free. Tours are offered Monday through Friday from 8 AM to 2 PM. No tours on major holidays and during production changes. 1425 Eden Rd; York, PA 17402; Phone: (717) 852-6590; https://www.harley-davidson.com/us/en/about-us/visit-us/yorkpa.html

Rhode Island

Block Island, RI

It's not possible to reach Block Island by car. There are no bridges, and either a ferry ride via BI Express Ferry, or a plane ride is necessary. Once you arrive, the 28 miles of walking trails preserved by the Nature Conservancy are free to visit. https://www.nature.org/en-us

Charleston, RI

Star Gazing at Frosty Drew Observatory is open to the public every Friday night all year for free stargazing and astronomy. The program starts at sunset or 6 PM, whichever comes later. Donations gratefully accepted. Frosty Drew Observatory has no telephone. Check the website for current information. Located in Ninigret Park. 61 Park La; Charlestown, RI 02813; https://frostydrew.org/events/StargazingNights.

Jamestown, RI

Beavertail State Park and Lighthouse offers striking coastline vistas from the park's overlooks and hikes along the coastline. **Beavertail Lighthouse and Museum** is open seasonally. There is no admission fee. From mid-June through Labor Day open daily from 10:30 AM to 4:30 PM. Note: There is a charge to climb the tower. Beavertail Rd; Jamestown, RI 02835; Phone: (401) 884-2010; https://www.beavertaillight.org/visitor-information

Jamestown Historical Society Museum displays exhibits on the town's history. Admission is free. Open from mid-June through Labor Day on Wednesday through Sunday from 1 PM to 4 PM. From Labor Day to Columbus Day the museum is open on weekends from 1 PM to 4 PM. Open by appointment anytime. 92 Narragansett Ave; Jamestown, RI 02835; Phone: (401) 423-7202; https://jamestownhistoricalsociety.org/ptv-detail-jamestown-museum

Jamestown Windmill stands three-stories high on Windmill Hill. Its domed cap holds the sails and can turn any direction to capture the wind. It is free to visit. Open the end of June to mid-October on Friday, Saturday, and Sunday from 1 PM to 4 PM and by appointment. Located in the Windmill Hill Historic District. North Rd; Jamestown, RI 02835; Phone: (401) 423-7202; https://jamestownhistoricalsociety.org/ptv-detail-windmill

Middleton, RI

Boyd's Wind Grist Mill is an opportunity to see and photograph a historic wind grist mill. Located in a small park with no admission charge. Open sunrise to sunset. Access to the inside of the mill is limited, however there are informational signs on the exterior. Paradise Valley Park; Prospect Ave; Middletown, RI 02842; Phone: (401) 849-1870; https://www.middletownhistoricalsociety.org/boyds-mill

Prescott Farm is a colonial farm site with a 1812 windmill, historic buildings, gardens, and walking trails. This site is free and open daily to the public from dawn to dusk. There is a fee for tours. 2009 W. Main Rd; Middletown, RI 02842; Phone: (401) 846-4152 ext. 123; https://www.newportrestoration.org/prescottfarm/#visit

Sachuest Point National Wildlife Refuge offers three miles of trails, plus viewing platforms for year-round birdwatching, unobstructed views of the refuge, and even a photography blind. Refuge volunteers frequently provide guided tours throughout the year. Admission is free. The visitor center is open daily from 10 AM to 4 PM. 769 Sachuest Point Rd; Middletown, RI 02842; Phone: (401) 619-2680; https://www.fws.gov/refuge/Sachuest_Point

Narragansett, RI
Point Judith Lighthouse is on Coast Guard Station Point Judith. Visitors can walk the grounds and take photographs of the lighthouse. 1470 Ocean Rd; Narragansett, RI 02882; Phone: (401) 789-0444; https://www.visitrhodeisland.com/listing/point-judith-lighthouse/886

Newport, RI
Known for the opulent mansions lining Cliff Walk, there is not much free in Newport, but its Old Quarter – Historic District covers 250 acres in the center of town with intact colonial buildings dating from the early and mid-18th century. It is free to walk the district but admission to the buildings will likely incur a charge. Download a walking map here: https://newporthistory.org/newports-old-quarter
Ballard Park offers two 19th century quarries and a diverse array of native and introduced plants plus access to the 54 acre wildlife refuge. Admission is free. Open sunrise to sunset. 21 Hazard Rd; Newport, RI 02840; Phone: (401) 619-3377; https://www.visitrhodeisland.com/listing/ballard-park/2760/

Cliff Walk remains a free and favorite place to stroll with the ocean on one side and the stunning, Gilded Age mansions on the other. Open all year from sunrise to sunset. http://www.cliffwalk.com

Fort Adams State Park preserves the large coastal fortification that had been active from 1841 through the first half of the 20th century. Tours of the fort will incur a fee, but the park is open free from sunrise to sunset for swimming, strolling, enjoying the views of the fort, harbor, and bay. 90 Fort Adams Dr; Newport, RI 02840; Phone: (401) 841-0707; http://www.riparks.com/Locations/LocationFortAdams.html

Providence, RI

Perhaps the most striking attraction in Providence is **WaterFire** – the award-winning sculpture by Barnaby Evans installed on the three rivers of downtown Providence. The glowing bonfires are a major draw for visitors. Check their website for scheduled lightings: https://waterfire.org

Pinwheel Tourism currently provides free walking tours of the city. They call it the Welcome to Providence Downcity Walking Tour, but they hope that if you enjoy the tour, you will pay what you believe it was worth. Tours are held Thursday through Sunday at 10 AM, and at Noon on the weekends. The tour is about two hours and covers less than 2½ miles. It begins at the back steps of the State House at 82 Smith Street. They offer free registration on the website. https://pinwheelprovidence.com

Newport has its Cliff Walk, but Providence offers **Benefit Street** filled with colonial buildings. https://www.visitrhodeisland.com/listing/benefit-streets-mile-of-history/97

Bannister Gallery at Rhode Island College presents eight to ten art exhibitions each year in traditional media as well as contemporary site specific, and video projects. Exhibits and events are free and open to the public. Open during the academic year on Monday through Friday from Noon to 8 PM. Roberts Hall, 124; 600 Mt Pleasant Ave; Providence, RI 02908; Phone: (401) 456-9765; http://www.ric.edu/bannister/Pages/About-Bannister-Gallery.aspx

David Winton Bell Gallery in the List Art Building of Brown University hosts four to five major exhibitions as well as maintaining a permanent collection of contemporary art and works on paper. Admission is free. Open Monday, Tuesday, Wednesday, and Friday from 11 AM to 4 PM; Thursday from 1 PM to 9 PM and Saturday and Sunday from 1 PM to 4 PM. Closed major holidays. 64 College St; Providence, RI 02912; Phone: (401) 863-2932; https://www.brown.edu/campus-life/arts/bell-gallery

Haffenreffer Museum of Anthropology in Manning Hall of Brown University documents Native arts of the Americas, Africa, and Southeast Asia. Admission is free. Open Tuesdays through Sundays from 10 AM to 4 PM. Closed university holidays. 21 Prospect St; Providence, RI 02912; Phone: (401) 863-2065; https://www.brown.edu/research/facilities/haffenreffer-museum/haffenreffer-manning-hall

Providence Athenaeum has more than books, although they certainly have a fascinating collection. Their offerings include busts, paintings, prints, sculptures, and an Egyptian cabinet. Self-guided tours are free, plus free staff-guided tours are held on Friday at 2 PM and Saturday at 11 AM. Open Monday through Saturday at 10 AM. Closes at 7 PM Monday through Thursday, and at 6 PM on Friday and Saturday. Open Sunday 1 PM to 5 PM. Shorter hours in summer and closed Sunday. 251 Benefit St; Providence, RI 02903; Phone: (401) 421-6970; https://providenceathenaeum.org

Providence College Galleries operate across Providence College's campus focusing on exhibitions and public programs emphasizing contemporary art, and cultural activities that intersect several disciplines. The two galleries that comprise the initiative are **Hunt-Cavanagh Gallery** at Hunt–Cavanagh Hall and the **Reilly Gallery** at the Smith Center for the Arts. Admission is free. The galleries are open during exhibitions on Wednesday through Saturday from Noon to 6 PM. Closed college holidays. 63 Eaton St; Providence, RI 02918; Phone: (401) 865 2400 http://pcgalleries.providence.edu

Providence Public Library offers free guided tours of the classic Venetian Renaissance building March through November on the first and third Tuesday of each month at 10:30 AM. 225 Washington St; Providence, RI 02903 Phone: (401) 455-8000; https://www.provlib.org/visit-us/historic-library-tours

Rhode Island Charter Museum, on the first floor of the Rhode Island State House, opens priceless documents and artifacts dating back to the 17th century to the public, including the original Royal Charter of 1663. The Charter Museum is free and open Monday through Friday from 8:30 AM until 4:30 PM. Closed major holidays. 82 Smith St; Providence, RI 02903; Phone: (401) 222-3983; http://sos.ri.gov/divisions/Civics-And-Education/charter-museum

Rhode Island State House was designed by noted architectural firm McKim, Mead, and White, which also designed many of the Newport mansions. Visiting the state house is free as are the tours. A self-guided tour brochure is available in the visitor center, gift shop, and in the State House Library. Open Monday through Friday from 8:30 AM to 4:30 PM. Closed on holidays. 82 Smith St; Providence, RI 02903; Phone: (401) 222-3983; http://sos.ri.gov/divisions/Civics-And-Education/State-House-Tour

Roger Williams National Memorial presents the story of Roger Williams who founded Rhode Island based on his belief of freedom of religion for all. The visitor center features an exhibit and a short film. The grounds of the National Memorial also includes a number of exhibits. There is no fee to visit. Open Monday through Sunday 9 AM to 5 PM but closed Mondays and Tuesdays in winter. Closed major holidays. 282 N Main St; Providence, RI 02903; Phone: (401) 521-7266; https://www.nps.gov/rowi/index.htm

Shakespeare's Head Building and Garden is an office building deriving its name from the Colonial era when the building was a print shop and post office with a sign featuring the head of Shakespeare. It's also known as the John Carter house. Behind the building is a 1939 Colonial Revival garden that is free and open to the public during daylight hours. 21 Meeting St; Providence, RI 02903; Phone: (401) 831-7440; http://ppsri.org/about/buildings

Wakefield, RI

Glass Station invites the public to watch glass blowers at work at no charge. Open Monday through Thursday from 10 AM to 6 PM, Friday and Saturday from 10 AM to 7 PM, and Sunday from 12:30 PM to 4:30 PM. 446 Main St; Wakefield, RI 02879; Phone: (401) 788-2500; https://www.theglassstationstudio.com/

Westerly, RI

People's Museum at the Westerly Armory in the historic National Guard armory contains artifacts from both the community and the military. There is no charge for tours. Open Mondays and Thursdays from 9 AM to 4 PM, and some holiday Mondays. 41 Railroad Ave; Westerly, RI 02891; Phone: (401) 596-8554; http://westerlyarmory.com

South Carolina

Aiken SC

Aiken County Historical highlights the history of the area. On the grounds there is a 1890s one-room schoolhouse and a log cabin built in 1808. No cost to visit, although donations are accepted. Open Tuesday through Saturday from 10 AM to 5 PM. Sunday from 2 PM to 5 PM. 433 Newberry St SW; Aiken, SC 2980; Phone: (803) 642-2015; https://discoversouthcarolina.com/products/1828

Aiken Thoroughbred Racing Hall of Fame and Museum celebrates Aiken's role in horse racing and the 40 champion thoroughbreds which have trained there. Admission is free, donations are welcomed. Open Tuesday through Friday, and Sunday from 2 PM to 5 PM. Open Saturday from 10 AM to 5 PM. Note: located on the grounds of Hopelands Gardens. 135 Dupree Pl; Aiken, SC 29801; Phone: (803) 642-7631; https://www.aikenracinghalloffame.com/index.html

Hopelands Gardens features regional flowers plus wetlands ponds and boardwalks. Free admission. Open 10 AM to sunset. 135 Dupree Pl; Aiken, SC 29801; Phone: (803) 642-7650; https://www.visitaikensc.com/whattodo/detail/hopelands_gardens

Anderson, SC

Anderson County Museum depicts the diverse history of the area through exhibits including the county fair and an authentic field kitchen used by the military. Free admission, donations accepted. Open Tuesday from 10 AM to 7 PM. Open Wednesday through Saturday from 10 AM to 4 PM. 202 E Greenville St; Anderson, SC 29621; Phone: (864) 260-4737; https://andersoncountymuseum.org/visit

Beaufort, SC

Parris Island Museum presents Port Royal's military role from the American Revolution to the Civil War and ultimately to the present. Additional exhibits include the site of French and Spanish colonies between 1562 and 1587. Note: Be prepared to show a driver's license, proof of vehicle insurance, and proof of vehicle registration. Admission is free. Open daily from 10 AM to 4:30 PM. Closed major holidays. 111 Panama St; Beaufort, SC 29902; Phone (843) 228-2951; http://parrisislandmuseum.com

Blacksburg, SC

Kings Mountain National Military Park preserves the site of the battle of Kings Mountain, fought October 7, 1780. This battle has been considered a turning point in the Revolutionary War in the South. The visitor center includes a 26-

minute film, exhibit area, and 1½ mile battlefield trail. There is no admission fee. Open daily from 9 AM to 5 PM. From Memorial Day to Labor Day extended Saturday and Sunday hours, closing at 6 PM. Closed major holidays. Note: The park recommends the use of the directions provided on the website. 2300 Park Rd; Blacksburg, SC 29702; Phone: (864) 936-7921; https://www.nps.gov/kimo/index.htm

Charleston, SC

Avery Research for African American History & Culture is on the site of the former Avery Normal Institute, a hub for Charleston's African-American community from 1865 to 1954. It presents exhibitions from its archival art and manuscripts, and of artists from South Carolina and throughout the African diaspora. The center offers public tours daily. Admission is free with donations welcomed. Open Monday through Friday from 10 AM to 5 PM. Closed from 12:30 PM to 1:30 PM. Note: The Avery has been closed for renovations. Check the website for opening information, including any change in admission policy. 125 Bull St; Charleston, SC 29401; Phone: (843) 953-7609; https://avery.cofc.edu

Citadel Museum depicts the history of the Military College of South Carolina from its founding in 1842 to the present. It is located on the third floor of the Daniel Library. Exhibits on the first and second floors feature cadet life and alumni achievements. The Citadel Museum is open during library hours. Monday through Friday from 7:30 AM to 5 PM, Saturday from 9 AM to 3 PM, and Sunday from Noon to 5 PM. Citadel parades are generally held on Fridays and are free and open to the public. Check http://www.citadel.edu/root/parade-schedule for the current parade information. 171 Moultrie St; Charleston, SC 29409; Phone: (843) 953-7573; https://library.citadel.edu/museum

Halsey Institute of Contemporary Art curates special-themed exhibitions. Admission is free. Open only during exhibitions on Monday through Saturday from 11 AM to 4 PM. Open until 7 PM on Thursdays. 161 Calhoun St; Charleston, SC 29401; Phone: (843) 953-4422; http://halsey.cofc.edu

Jewish Heritage Collection documents the Jewish experience in South Carolina from colonial times to present day and includes oral histories, manuscripts, artifacts, photographs, genealogies, memoirs, and home movies. Open free to the public in Special Collections on the third floor of the College of Charleston's Addlestone Library. Open Monday through Friday from 9 AM to 5 PM. 205 Calhoun St; College of Charleston; Charleston, SC 29401; Phone: (843) 953.8016; http://jhc.cofc.edu

Mace Brown Museum of Natural History at College of Charleston displays almost 1,000 fossils including dinosaur bones, Oligocene mammals of North America, mosasaurs, cave bears, Pleistocene mammals of the Carolinas, ocean life through time, and fossil plants. Admission is free. Open Thursday through Tuesday from 11 AM to 4 PM. School of Sciences and Mathematics; 202 Calhoun St; Charleston, SC 29401; Phone: (843) 953-3967; http://geology.cofc.edu/natural-history-museum

Clemson, SC

Home of Clemson University which offers the public two free attractions.
Bob Campbell Geology Museum (BCGM) highlights include a saber-tooth tiger, complete skull of Tyrannosaurus rex, and one of the largest collections of faceted gemstones in the southeastern states. Admission is free but donations are encouraged. Open Monday through Sunday from 10 AM to 5 PM. 140 Discovery La; Clemson, SC 29634; Phone: (864) 656-4600; https://www.clemson.edu/public/geomuseum

South Carolina Botanical Garden hosts an official American Hosta Society Display Garden, a 70-acre arboretum, miles of nature trails and streams, specialized gardens, and the most comprehensive collection of native plants in the Southeast. Admission is free. Gardens are open daily from dawn to dusk. Visitor center is open daily from 10 AM to 5 PM. Closed Clemson University holidays, and home football game Saturdays. 150 Discovery La; Clemson, SC 29634; Phone: (864) 656-3405; https://www.clemson.edu/public/scbg

Columbia, SC

Governor's Mansion, built in 1855, is open for free tours by appointment on Tuesday, Wednesday, and Thursday. Visitors can also enjoy the gardens which cover a city block. Gates are open weekdays from 9:30 AM to 4:30 PM. 800 Richland St; Columbia, SC 29201; Phone: (803) 737-1710; http://www.scgovernorsmansion.org

McKissick Museum of the University of South Carolina is home to gemstones, and mineral specimens, plus butterflies, quilts and other household textiles, art glass, alkaline-glazed stoneware, Catawba pottery, and the Charles T. (Bud) Ferillo, Jr. Collection of political memorabilia. Free to visit. Open Monday through Friday from 8:30 AM to 5 PM and Saturday from 11:00 AM to 3 PM. Closed all university and state holidays. 1501 Pendleton St; Columbia, SC 29201; Phone: (803) 777-7251; https://sc.edu/study/colleges_schools/artsandsciences/mckissick_museum/index.php

South Carolina Law Enforcement Officers Hall of Fame describes the history of South Carolina law enforcement through 12 exhibit areas. Admission is free. Open

Monday through Friday from 8:30 AM to 5 PM. Closed state holidays. 5400 Broad River Rd; Columbia, SC 29212; Phone: (803) 896-8199; https://scdps.sc.gov/hof

South Carolina Military Museum preserves the heritage of the South Carolina National Guard through objects from the late 17th century to today's Gulf War on Terror. Outside are larger vehicles and equipment. Museum admission is free, although donations are appreciated. Tours are available. Note: You will need a valid photo ID to enter. Open Monday through Saturday from 10 AM to 4 PM. Closed on state holidays and during some Saturdays of University of South Carolina's home games. 1 National Guard Rd; Columbia, SC 2920; Phone: (803) 299-4440; http://scmilitarymuseum.com

South Carolina State House is open for both self-guided and guided tours. During the legislative session (January to May) tours are offered every half hour beginning at 9:30 AM and ending at 3:30 PM. Tours are not offered at Noon or 12:30 PM. From June to December tours are available every hour on the half hour beginning at 9:30 AM and ending at 3:30 PM. Tours are not offered at 12:30 PM during these months. The State House is also open for tours on some Saturdays. Visitors enter the State House through the public entrance on the Sumter Street side of the building. 1100 Gervais St; Columbia, SC 29201; Phone: (803) 734-2430; https://southcarolinaparks.com/education-and-history/state-house

Florence, SC
Florence County Museum highlights Colonial period artifacts through Civil War, and items from the Florence Stockade prison camp. Their art collection includes eight works by 20th century Black American artist and Florence native, William H. Johnson, and the Wright Collection of Southern Art. Admission is free. Open Tuesday through Saturday from 10 AM to 5 PM with extended hours on Thursday until 7 PM. Open Sunday from 2 PM to 5 PM. 111 W Cheves St; Florence, SC 29501; Phone: (843) 676-1200; http://www.flocomuseum.org

Gaffney, SC
Cowpens National Battlefield is famous for the classic military tactic that was used there during the Revolutionary War. Known as a *double envelopment* or the *pincer movement*, military forces simultaneously attack both sides of an enemy formation. The partially paved 1 1/3 mile trail includes wayside exhibits and monuments. An almost 4 mile road (one way) travels the perimeter of the battlefield and includes wayside exhibits, parking areas with short trails to the Green River Road, and the circa 1828 Robert Scruggs log house. The visitor center screens the 18-minute video *Cowpens: A Battle Remembered* – an 18-minute show depicting the events of the battle. Admission is free. Open daily 9 AM to 5 PM.

4001 Chesnee Hwy; Gaffney, SC 29341; Phone: (864) 461-2828;
https://www.nps.gov/cowp/index.htm

Georgetown, SC
Hobcaw Barony is one of only ten Colonial baronies. The Discovery Center
provides exhibits specific to the Hobcaw Barony and its unique history and
ecology. Subjects include the Colonial era, slavery, and life in Friendfield Village,
one of the 19th century slave villages at Hobcaw Barony. Admission to the
Discovery Center Museum is free, but donations are appreciated. Access to the
16,000 acres is only by fee-based guided tours and programs. 22 Hobcaw Rd;
Georgetown, SC 29440; Phone: (843) 546-4623;
http://hobcawbarony.org/visit/hobcaw-barony-discovery-center

Greenville, SC
Greenville County Museum of Art is home to the world's largest public
collection of watercolors by iconic American artist Andrew Wyeth. The GCMA
also holds paintings and prints by contemporary artist Jasper Johns. The museum's
Southern Collection highlights works with ties to the South, including a collection
of antebellum clay vessels created by enslaved artisan David Drake. Admission is
free. Open Wednesday through Saturday from 10 AM to 5 PM and Sunday from
1 PM to 5 PM. Closed major holidays. 420 College St; Greenville, SC 29601;
Phone: (864) 271-7570; http://gcma.org

Greer, SC
BMW Zentrum will take you through BMW's history in aircraft, motorcycles,
and automobiles. There is also a virtual factory tour where viewers watch a BMW
being made from the car's perspective. The museum is free to visit, but there is a
charge to tour the factory. The museum is open Monday through Friday from
9:30 AM to 5:30 PM. 1155 Hwy 101 S; Greer, SC 29651; Phone: (888) tour-
BMW (868-7269); https://www.bmwusfactory.com/zentrum/general-
information/zentrum-information

Hartsville, SC
Hartsville Museum combines local history with special exhibits of art, both
indoors and out. No admission charge. Donations accepted. Open Monday
through Friday from 10 AM to Noon and from 1 PM to 5 PM. Open Saturday
from 10 AM to 2 PM. 222 N Fifth St; Hartsville, SC 29550; Phone: (843) 383-
3005; https://hartsvillemuseum.org

Mount Pleasant, SC
Charles Pinckney National Historic Site tells the story of Charles Pinckney, a
principal author and a signer of the United States Constitution. The site is the
remains of Snee Farm, his rice and indigo plantation. A1828 Low Country cottage

is a museum with films, exhibits, and archaeology displays. The ½ mile walking trail offers descriptions of the existing house, archeological excavations, and agricultural history. There are no entrance fees. Open Wednesday through Sunday from 9 AM to 5 PM. Closed major holidays. 1254 Long Point Rd; Mount Pleasant, SC 29464; Phone: (843) 881-5516; https://www.nps.gov/chpi/index.htm

Myrtle Beach, SC
Franklin G. Burroughs-Simeon B. Chapin Art Museum in a converted beach house mounts exhibitions from its permanent collection of regional artwork and historical maps. Free admission, donations gratefully accepted. Open Tuesday through Saturday from 10 AM to 4 PM. Open Sunday from 1 PM to 4 PM. Closed major holidays. 3100 S Ocean Blvd; Myrtle Beach, SC 29577; Phone: (843) 238-2510; http://myrtlebeachartmuseum.org

Ninety Six, SC
Ninety Six National Historic Site tells of the struggles of settlers in the area through a paved one-mile walking trail with wayside signs, a reconstructed siege works, stockade fort, original 1781 Star Fort, and town site. There are no fees to visit. Donations are accepted. The park offers ranger-led tours throughout the year. Stop at the visitor center for maps and information. Open Wednesday through Sunday from 9 AM to 4 PM. Their website notes that if you park outside the front gate you may visit the park grounds from daylight to dusk. 1103 Hwy 248; Ninety Six, SC 29666; Phone: (864) 543-4068; https://www.nps.gov/nisi/index.htm

North Augusta, SC
Living History Park presents demonstrations of Colonial life. Admission and all events are free. The park is open daily dawn to dusk. 299 W Spring Grove Ave; North Augusta, SC 29841; Phone: (803) 979-9776; http://www.colonialtimes.us

Rock Hill, SC
Comporium Telephone Museum mixes the history of the town of Rock Hill with history of communication. Free admission. Open Monday, Wednesday, Friday, and Saturday from 10 AM to 2 PM. Closed major holidays and two weeks at Christmas. 117 Elk Ave; Rock Hill, SC 29730; Phone: (803) 324-4030; https://about.comporium.com

Spartanburg, SC
The town's **Chapman Cultural Center** provides two different free places to visit. Both are open Tuesday through Saturday from 10 AM to 5 PM and on Sunday from 1 PM to 5 PM. Closed most major holidays. 200 E Saint John St; Spartanburg, SC 29306. **Spartanburg Art Museum** is devoted exclusively to

contemporary art with four to five exhibits a year. Phone: (864) 582-7616; https://www.spartanburgartmuseum.org **Spartanburg Regional History Museum** includes area furniture, locally made pottery, hand-crafted quilts and samplers, and other artwork. Phone: (864) 596-3501; http://www.spartanburghistory.org/aboutmuseum

Wadmalaw, SC

Charleston Tea Plantation is billed as America's only tea factory. Their production building has been designed with a gallery that runs down the length of the facility. Videos explain the tea-making process. There is no charge for the tour. Open daily from 10 AM to 4 PM. Late opening on Sunday from Noon to 4 PM. Factory tour begins every 15 minutes on the quarter hour. Note: There is a trolley tour that incurs a charge. Wadmalaw Island is about 15 miles south of Charleston. 6617 Maybank Hwy; Wadmalaw Island, SC 29487, Phone: (843) 559-0383; http://www.charlestonteaplantation.com/factory-tours

Walterboro, SC

Walterboro Wildlife Sanctuary includes over 800 acres with boardwalks and bridges as well as biking and walking trails for viewing nature, and wildlife. Free admission. Open dawn to dusk. 399 De Treville Rd; Walterboro, SC 29488; Phone: (843) 538-4353; https://www.walterborosc.org/walterboro-wildlife-sanctuary

South Dakota

Aberdeen, SD

Dacotah Prairie Museum welcomes visitors with exhibits from their permanent collection and short term shows. The Hatterscheidt Wildlife Gallery, on the museum's first floor, features over 55 mounted specimens from North America, Africa, and India. Admission is free with donations appreciated. Open Tuesday through Friday from 9 AM to 5 PM. Open Saturday and Sunday from 1 PM to 4 PM. 21 S Main St; Aberdeen, SD 57401; Phone: (605) 626-7117; http://www.brown.sd.us/dacotah-prairie-museum/home

Brookings, SD

South Dakota Agricultural Heritage Museum, part of South Dakota State University, has gathered an eclectic collection of tractors and implements, household furnishings, small tools, toys, and even a replica of a 1915 farmhouse. Free admission. Open Monday through Saturday from 10 AM to 5 PM. Sunday hours are seasonal. Closed state holidays. 977 11th St; Brookings, SD 57007; Phone: (605) 688-6226; http://www.agmuseum.com

Chamberlain, SD

Akta Lakota Museum & Cultural Center honors the Lakota culture through historical and artistic exhibits. Admission is free. Open daily May through October on Monday through Saturday from 8 AM to 6 PM, and on Sunday from 9 AM to 5 PM. From November through April open Monday through Friday from 8 AM to 4:30 PM. Closed national holidays. Located in St. Joseph's Indian School. 1301 N Main St; Chamberlain, SD 57325; Phone: (800) 798-3452; http://aktalakota.stjo.org

Dignity of Earth and Sky is a stunning impressive sculpture of a standing Native American woman. The 50-foot high stainless steel statue by South Dakota artist Dale Lamphere honors the women of the Lakota and Dakota Nations. She can be found at the Lewis & Clark Interpretive Center at the Chamberlain rest area on Interstate 90 between Exits 263 and 265. Admission to the center is free. Open daily from 8 AM to 5 PM. Phone: (605) 734-4562; http://www.chamberlainsd.com/area-culture/dignity-lewis-and-clark-interpretive-center/

Deadwood, SD

Famous as the place where Wild Bill Hickok met his end, the fatal poker game took place on August 2, 1876 in Nuttal & Mann's saloon when poker loser Jack McCall shot Hickok in the back of the head. The saloon was later renamed the No. 10 Saloon. Although there is a No. 10 Saloon in Deadwood, it is not the original. In fact, the original building no longer exists. Anyone paying homage to Wild Bill needs to visit 624 Lower Main St, the location of the original Nuttal & Mann's saloon.

Gettysburg, SD

Dakota Sunset Museum displays the 40-ton Sacred Medicine Rock with embedded human prints, Civil War exhibit, Native American dress, and antique furnishings, barbershop, blacksmith shop, general store, and one-room school house. Admission is free with donations accepted. In June, July, and August open on Monday through Saturday from 1 PM to 5 PM. From September to May open Tuesday through Saturday from 1 PM to 5 PM. 205 W Commercial Ave #104; Gettysburg, SD 57442; Phone: (605) 765-9480; http://www.dakotasunsetmuseum.com

Hill City, SD

Civilian Conservation Corps Museum of South Dakota celebrates the CCC, one of the most successful and popular of President Franklin Delano Roosevelt's New Deal programs, through photos and artifacts. Generally open Monday through Friday from 9 AM to 4 PM. Seasonal hours match that of the Hill City Visitor Information Center. 23935 Hwy 385, Hill City, SD 57745; Phone: (605) 574-2368; https://www.southdakotaccc.org

Hot Springs, SD

Wind Cave National Park is home to bison, elk, and other wildlife, and preserves several historic buildings. There are no fees to drive through or hike in the park. Note: There are fees to explore Wind Cave. The park is open daily. Wind Cave Visitor Center is opened daily 8 AM to 4:30 PM with expanded hours during the summer. Closed Thanksgiving, Christmas, and New Year's Day. Note: They recommend using the directions on the website rather than following a GPS. 11 miles north of Hot Springs off U.S. Hwy 385; Phone: (605) 745-4600; https://www.nps.gov/wica/index.htm

Keystone, SD

Mount Rushmore National Memorial is one of the most popular parks in the system. The Lincoln Borglum Visitor Center screens *Mount Rushmore, The Shrine*. Museum exhibits tell the story of Gutzon Borglum, the creation of Mount Rushmore, and the workers who assisted him. Gutzon Borglum's studio where he worked from 1939 to 1941 is on the grounds. Dominating the park are the carvings of George Washington, Thomas Jefferson, Theodore Roosevelt, and Abraham Lincoln. There is no admission fee, but there is a $10 mandatory fee to park. Facilities are open daily all year with the exception of December 25th. Parking garage and grounds are open 5 AM to 11 PM. 13000 Highway 244;

Keystone, SD 57751; Phone: (605) 574-2523;
https://www.nps.gov/moru/index.htm

Kimball, SD

South Dakota Tractor Museum has gathered historic tractors, automobiles, and restored farm machinery as well as an old windmill, blacksmith shop, and a barn full of horse-driven farm equipment. The museum charges no admission. Donations are welcomed. Open daily in summer from 9 AM to 5 PM and on Sunday from 1 PM to 5 PM. 117 Cemetery Rd (Exit 284 off I-90); Kimball, SD 57355; Phone: (605) 778-6421; https://www.facebook.com/sdtractor

Mitchell, SD

Corn Palace is likely one of the most unusually decorated buildings in the country, less from the onion domes and minarets that characterizes its design, and more from the mural panels created from corn. Each year a new theme is chosen and the outdoor murals are redone in the new motif, but always in colors and varieties of corn and corn cobs. The building is a community center and theater, and visitors are welcome to stroll past the outside, and view the historic murals inside. Free public tours are given during the summer.. The hours for the building are seasonal, but generally open daily from 8 AM to 5 PM. Closed major holidays. 612 N Main St; Mitchell, SD 57301; Phone: (605) 995-8430; https://cornpalace.com/176/Public-Tours

McGovern Legacy Museum honors George and Eleanor McGovern, alums of Dakota Wesleyan University. It describes McGovern's life as a senator and his run for the presidency. Admission is free. Open when the library is open, generally Monday through Friday from 8 AM to 5 PM. 1201 McGovern Ave; Mitchell, SD 57301; Phone: (605) 995-2937; https://www.mitchellsd.com/list/member/mcgovern-legacy-museum-7201

Philip, SD

Minuteman Missile National Historic Site is actually three different places along Interstate 90, two of which are free of charge. The **Visitor Center** focuses on the history of the arsenal of nuclear missiles sited in the Great Plains. It's located north side of exit 131 off I-90. **Missile Silo Delta-09** contains a fully operational Minuteman Missile, one of 150 spread across western South Dakota. It is located on the south side of exit 116 off I-90. **Launch Control Facility Delta-01** can only be visited as part of a fee-based ranger-led tour. The visitor center and Delta-09 are free to visit. The visitor center is open daily from 8 AM to 4 PM. Delta-09 is open daily from 9 AM to 3 PM, weather permitting. The park is closed Thanksgiving, Christmas, and New Year's Day. Phone: (605) 433-5552; https://www.nps.gov/mimi/index.htm

Pierre, SD

South Dakota National Guard Museum started as a small military museum and grew to become a repository for memorabilia and historical documents pertaining to the South Dakota National Guard. Admission is free. Open Monday through Friday from 9 AM to 4 PM. Closed major holidays. 301 E Dakota Ave; Pierre, SD 57501; Phone: (605) 773-2475; https://sdnationalguardmuseum.sd.gov

State Capitol Tours are primarily self-guided with brochures available. The capitol building is open Monday through Friday from 8 AM to 7 PM. On weekends and holidays open from 8 AM to 5 PM. Open to 10 PM Thanksgiving week through the end of the legislative session. Guided tours are also available but must be scheduled 48 business hours in advance. 500 E Capitol; Pierre, SD 57501; Phone: (605) 773-3688; https://boa.sd.gov/capitol/capitol-tour-office.aspx

Pine Ridge, SD

Heritage Center at Red Cloud Indian School highlights the Lakota heritage with 10,000 pieces of the Native American contemporary and historical Lakota paintings, textiles, traditional art, historical items, pottery, and sculpture. Admission is free, with donations much appreciated. From Labor Day to Memorial Day open Tuesday through Saturday from 9 AM to 5 PM. From Memorial Day to Labor Day open Monday through Saturday from 8 AM to 6 PM. Open Sunday and holidays from 10 AM to 5 PM. 100 Mission Dr; Pine Ridge, SD 57770; Phone: (605) 867-8257; https://www.redcloudschool.org/museum

Rapid City, SD

Visitors to historic downtown Rapid City are greeted by life-size bronze statues of our nation's past presidents which have been placed along the city's streets and sidewalks. https://www.visitrapidcity.com/things-to-do/city-presidents

Chapel In The Hills is unusual for its design, based on the famous Norwegian Borgund stave church. There is no admission fee but donations are very appreciated. From May through September the chapel and museum are open daily from 8 AM until dusk. Worship services are open to the public each evening at 7:30 PM during the summer months. 3788 Chapel La; Rapid City, SD 57702; Phone: (605) 342-8281; http://www.chapel-in-the-hills.org/index.html

Museum of Geology at the South Dakota School of Mines and Technology invites exploration of paleontology and mineralogy through its collections of gems, fossils, and skeletons. The museum also has an interactive children's zone. Admission is free. Donations are always appreciated. From Memorial Day through Labor Day open Monday through Saturday from 9 AM to 6 PM. Closed Independence Day. From Labor Day through Memorial Day open Monday through Saturday from 8:30 AM to 4 PM. Closed federal holidays. Located on the

3rd floor of the O'Harra Bldg; 501 E Saint Joseph St; Rapid City, SD 57701; Phone: (605) 394-2467; https://www.sdsmt.edu/Academics/Museum-of-Geology/Home

South Dakota Air and Space Museum showcases over 30 vintage military aircraft ranging from World War II bombers to the modern-day B-1. Admission to the museum is free as are the docent-led museum tours. Note: There is a charge for the seasonally offered guided tours of the base. From June through early September the museum is open daily from 8:30 AM to 6 PM. Closes at 4:30 PM the rest of the year. 2890 Davis Dr; Rapid City, SD 57706; Phone: (605) 385-5189; http://www.sdairandspacemuseum.com

Storybook Island Playground offers more than 100 storybook, nursery rhyme, and fairytale settings. Admission is free although there is a fee to ride the train, carousel, and the bounce. Open daily Memorial Day weekend through Labor Day weekend from 9 AM to 7 PM. 1301 Sheridan Lake Rd; Rapid City, SD 57702; Phone: (605) 342-6357; https://storybookisland.org

Redfield, SD
Historic Chicago and Northwestern Railroad Depot Museum holds railway memorabilia, artifacts, objects, documents, and pictures depicting the influence of the railroad at the turn of the century. Free admission with donations accepted. Open May through December on Tuesday through Saturday from 10 AM to 4 PM and on Sunday from 1 PM to 4 PM. Open January through April by appointment only. 715 W Third St; Redfield, SD 57469; Phone: (605) 472-4566; http://tourism.redfield-sd.com/c&nw-rr-depot

Sioux Falls, SD
Every year a new set of sculptures is chosen to line the **Sculpture Walk** in downtown Sioux Falls. Each piece remains on display for a full year and the public is encouraged to vote for their favorites. https://sculpturewalksiouxfalls.com
Eide/Dalrymple Gallery mounts about nine exhibits a year including European and American original prints in the Midwest. The Carl Grupp collection includes works of Picasso, Chagall, Winslow Homer, Whistler, Matisse, and Rouault. Admission is free. From September through May open Monday through Friday from 10 AM to 5 PM, and on Saturday from 1 PM to 4 PM. From June through August open Monday through Friday from Noon to 4 PM. Closed campus holidays. Augustana University; Center for Visual Arts; 30th St and S Grange Ave; Sioux Falls, SD 57197; Phone: (605) 274-4609; http://www.augie.edu/eidedalrymple-gallery

Old Courthouse Museum was the largest courthouse between Chicago and Denver when it was completed in 1893. As a museum it offers three floors of regional history exhibits. The second floor features its restored circuit courtroom and law library. Admission is free. Open Monday through Friday from 8 AM to 5 PM with late closing on Thursday at 9 PM. Open Saturday from 9 AM to 5 PM and Sunday Noon to 5 PM. Closed on major holidays. 200 W Sixth St; Sioux Falls, SD 57104; Phone: (605) 367-4210; https://www.siouxlandmuseums.com/home-page/old-courthouse-museum-exhibits

Pettigrew Home and Museum is the 1889 Queen Anne-style home of South Dakota's first senator, Richard Pettigrew. Free admission. Open May through September on Monday through Saturday from 9 AM to 5 PM and Sunday from Noon to 5 PM. The rest of the year open daily from Noon to 5 PM. Closed on major holidays. 131 N Duluth Ave; Sioux Falls, SD 57104; Phone: (605) 367-7097; https://www.siouxlandmuseums.com/home-page/pettigrew-home-museum

Spearfish, SD
D.C. Booth Historic National Fish Hatchery and Archives invites visitors to feed fish from above and watch them from below through the underwater viewing windows. Admission is free and the grounds are open daily from dawn to dusk. Inside the hatchery and museum visitors can view the fish production process with historic objects from hatcheries throughout the country. The Booth house features period furnishings and Booth family memorabilia including the only federal fisheries railcar exhibit in the country. Fisheries Boat #39, a wooden Great Lakes-style cabin cruiser, tells about early hatchery workers who went on expeditions to Yellowstone National Park to collect trout eggs and bring them back to the hatchery. Admission is free. The hatchery grounds are open dawn to dusk all year. Open daily from mid-May through the end of September. Guided tours through the historic buildings are available through September from 9 AM to 6 PM. 423 Hatchery Cir; Spearfish, SD 57783; Phone: (605) 642-7730; http://dcboothfishhatchery.org

Wall, SD
Wall Drug has morphed from a simple country drug store to a roadside attraction – all because owner Dorothy Hustead thought to offer travelers free ice water. Visitors can enjoy their extensive Western and illustration art collection. The ice water is still free. Open daily from 7 AM to 6 PM. 510 Main St; Wall, SD 57790; Phone: (605) 279-2175; http://www.walldrug.com

Tennessee

Great Smoky Mountains National Park straddles Tennessee and North Carolina. The park highlights the beauty of ancient mountains, and offers places to explore southern Appalachian mountain culture. Its 384 miles of road offers over 90 historic structures and four visitor centers – Cades Cove, Oconaluftee, Sugarlands, and Clingmans Dome. There is no charge to enter the park or see the visitor centers. Phone: (865) 436-1200; https://www.nps.gov/grsm/index.htm

Brownsville, TN

West Tennessee Delta Heritage Center celebrates the music, cotton, and beauty of the Tennessee Delta. There are three fresh water aquariums, a portion of the Felsenthal Lincoln Collection (one of the largest privately-owned collections on Abraham Lincoln in the Southeast), the West Tennessee Music Museum, and the West Tennessee Cotton Museum. For music history, enjoy a free self-guided tour of the **Tina Turner Museum**, once the Flagg Grove School which was attended by a young Anna Mae Bullock who later became known as Tina Turner. In addition to costumes, gold records, and her high school yearbook, the museum has preserved an authentic chalkboard, desks and benches. Self-guided tours are free of charge but there is a fee for guided tours. Donations gratefully accepted. **"Sleepy" John Estes** home also has free admission. April through September open Monday through Saturday from 9 AM to 6 PM and Sunday from 10 AM to 5 PM. October through March open Monday through Saturday 9 AM to 5 PM and Sunday from 1 PM to 5 PM. Closed Easter Sunday and Christmas Day. 121 Sunny Hill Cove; Brownsville, TN 38012; Phone: (731) 779-9000; http://www.westtnheritage.com/index.html

Byrdstown, TN

Cordell Hull Birthplace State Park honors U.S. Secretary of State under President Franklin Roosevelt who played a pivotal role in the creation of the United Nations. Visitors can tour a refurbished representation of the log cabin where he was born and a museum with Hull's personal items, including a replica of his 1945 Nobel Peace Prize. It is free to visit. Open Memorial Day weekend to Labor Day from 9 AM to 5 PM. From Labor Day to Memorial Day weekend it is open 9 AM to 4:30 PM. 300 Cordell Hull Memorial Dr; Byrdstown, TN 38549; Phone: (931) 864-3247; https://tnstateparks.com/parks/cordell-hull-birthplace

Chattanooga, TN

Made famous by the song, the Chattanooga Choo-Choo the former railroad station was once owned and operated by the Southern Railway. Today it is the Chattanooga Choo Choo Hotel at 1400 Market Street, and listed on the National Register of Historic Places. The Pullman train cars on the grounds have been repurposed into hotel rooms.

River Gallery Sculpture Garden in the Bluff View Art District is located on two acres overlooking the Tennessee River. The area includes a formal garden, meditation area, and an informal garden with a recycling mountain stream. 400 E Second St; Chattanooga, TN 37403; https://www.river-gallery.com/sculpture-garden

Sculpture Fields at Montague Park features 27 world renowned large-scale sculptures. Free to visit. Open daily from dawn to dusk. 1800 Polk St; Chattanooga, TN 37408; Phone: (423) 266-7288; https://www.sculpturefields.org

Clarksville, TN

Don F. Pratt Memorial Museum covers the history of the 101st Airborne Division, the *Screaming Eagles*, from the early 1940s to present. An outdoor park displays military aircraft and equipment highlighted by a fully restored C-47 aircraft. Admission is free. Open Tuesday through Saturday from 9:30 AM to 4:30 PM. Closed Christmas, and New Year's Day. 5702 Tennessee Ave; Clarksville, TN 42223; Phone: (270) 798-3215; http://fortcampbell.com/museums/don-f-pratt-museum

Fort Defiance Interpretive Center has been a hub of activity for more than two centuries, from the original Native Americans to the Civil War. Admission is free. Spring and summer open Monday through Saturday from 10 AM to 5 PM and on Sunday from 1 PM to 5 PM. The rest of the year it is open Monday through Saturday from 10 AM to 4 PM and Sunday from 1 PM to 4 PM. 120 Duncan St; Clarksville, TN 37040; Phone: (931) 472-3351; http://www.cityofclarksville.com/index.aspx?page=161

Cleveland, TN

Red Clay State Historic Park was the last seat of Cherokee government before the tribe's forced march on the Trail of Tears. The site includes forts and pens where the Cherokee were held awaiting removal. The James F. Corn Interpretive Facility contains exhibits on the 19th century Cherokee, the Trail of Tears, Cherokee art, a video theater, and a small library. Admission to all Tennessee State Parks is free. The visitor center is open in summer on Tuesday through Saturday from 9 AM to 5:30 PM. Open on Sunday and Monday from 1 PM to 5:30 PM. In winter open from 8 AM to 4:30 PM. 1140 Red Clay Park Rd SW; Cleveland, TN 37311; Phone: (423) 478-0339; https://tnstateparks.com/parks/red-clay

Clinton, TN
Green McAdoo Cultural Center honors the 12 young people from East Tennessee who desegregated Clinton High School and helped change history with their courage. If you want to understand the Civil Rights struggle – start here with the *Jim Crow* era in the South. Visitors will learn about the local 1950 lawsuit, McSwain et al vs. Anderson County, and its relationship to the landmark 1954 U.S. Supreme Court decision in Brown vs. Board of Education. Admission is free. Open Monday through Saturday from 10 AM to 5 PM. 101 School St; Clinton, TN 37717; Phone: (865) 463-6500; http://www.greenmcadoo.org/about-the-center

Collegedale, TN
Lynn H. Wood Archaeological Museum at Southern Adventist University displays artifacts from Egypt, Babylonia, Persia, Syria-Palestine, Greece, Cyprus, and Anatolia. Admission is free. Open Monday through Thursday from 9 AM to Noon and again from 1 PM to 5 PM. Open Friday from 9 AM to Noon. Open Saturday and Sunday from 2 PM to 5 PM. Closed summers and university breaks. 4881 Taylor Cir; Collegedale, TN 37315; Phone: (423) 236-2030; https://www.southern.edu/administration/archaeology/visit_us.html

Cookeville, TN
Cookeville Depot Museum is a repository for Tennessee Central Railway artifacts. A 1913 Baldwin steam engine, 1920s classic red caboose, 1960s caboose, and two small track cars are on the grounds. Admission is free. Open Tuesday through Saturday from 10 AM to 4 PM. 116 W Broad St; Cookeville, TN 38501; Phone: (931) 528-8570; https://www.cookevilledepot.com

Cumberland Gap, TN
Little Congress Bicycle Museum represents 41 years of collecting unique bicycles by R.E. McClanahan II. Admission is free. Open daily from 8 AM to 8 PM. 807 Llewellyn St; Cumberland Gap, TN 37724; Phone: (423) 869-9993; https://www.bicyclemuseum.net/default.html

Dayton, TN
Scopes Trial Museum & Rhea County Courthouse details the 1925 trial that placed Dayton on the legal world-map. Tennessee had just passed the Butler Act making it illegal to teach evolution in public schools. Mr. John T. Scopes, a teacher at Rhea Central High School, deliberately violated the law, and the famous trial followed. The courthouse has been renovated back to its original appearance and a museum showcasing the Scopes Trial was built in the courthouse basement. Admission is free. Open Monday through Friday from 8:30 AM to 4:30 PM. Open Saturday in April through November from 11 AM to 3 PM. 1475 Market

St; Dayton, TN 37321; Phone (423) 775-6171;
https://www.rheacountyheritage.com

Dunlap, TN

Dunlap Coke Ovens Park and Museum offers a real slice of coke mining history.
The beehive ovens are the remnants of a coke production facility dating back to
the early 1900s. The museum honors the history of the people who mined the fuel
through photos and artifacts. Visitors can explore the ovens, and hike the 3,900
foot incline to the top of the mountain where the digging for coal took place.
Admission is the grounds and the museum is free, with donations accepted. The
grounds are open all year dawn to dusk. The museum is open summer weekends
only on Saturday from 10 AM to 4 PM and Sunday Noon to 4 PM (CST). Note:
Each year they run the Dunlap Coke Ovens-Bluegrass Jam Band /Festival on the
first Saturday in June and the Friday night preceding it. The fee-based event
benefits the museum. Mountain View Cir; Dunlap, TN 37327; Phone: (423)
949-2156; http://cokeovens.com

Eva, TN

Tennessee River Folklife Interpretive Center and Museum features the lifeways
and customs of the people on the Tennessee River. Located in the Nathan Bedford
Forrest State Park. Admission is to the park and the museum is free with donations
gratefully accepted. Open daily 8 AM to 4:30 PM. 1825 Pilot Knob Rd; Eva, TN
38333; Phone: (731) 584-2128; https://tnstateparks.com/parks/nathan-bedford-
forrest

Farragut, TN

Farragut Museum preserves the heritage of this historical community and Admiral
David Glasgow Farragut, first admiral of the U.S. Navy, known for his statement,
"Damn the torpedoes, full speed ahead." Admission is free. Open Monday,
Tuesday, Thursday, and Friday from 10 AM to 4:30 PM. Open Wednesday from
8 AM to 5 PM. 11408 Municipal Center Dr; Farragut, TN 37934; Phone: (865)
966-7057; https://townoffarragut.org/186/Farragut-Museum

Gatlinburg, TN

Arrowmont School of Arts & Crafts welcomes visitors to the campus, and the
artwork of local, national, and international artists. Works in the permanent
collection are on display throughout the grounds and buildings all year. Galleries
are free of charge. Open Monday through Friday from 8:30 AM to 5 PM and on
Saturday from 8:30 AM to 4 PM. 556 Parkway; Gatlinburg, TN 37738; Phone:
(865) 436-5860; https://www.arrowmont.org

Grand Junction, TN

National Bird Dog Museum houses art, photography, and memorabilia about field trials, shooting sports, and over forty breeds of bird dogs. Admission is free with donations appreciated. Open Tuesday through Friday from 9 AM to 4 PM. Open Saturday from 10 AM to 4 PM, and on Sunday from 1 PM to 4 PM. Closed major holidays, including Mother's Day. 505 TN-57; Grand Junction, TN 38039; Phone: (731) 764-2058; http://www.birddogfoundation.com/index.php

Greeneville, TN

Andrew Johnson National Historic Site interprets the life and legacy of the 17th President and his presidency from 1865 to 1869. Johnson was the only self-taught president and he held nearly every political office available at the time. Several major locations and a visitor center comprise the site. There is no fee for admission or tours. Start at the visitor center open daily from 9 AM to 5 PM. 101 N College St; Greeneville, TN 37743. Next door the **Memorial Building** houses the presidential museum, as well as Andrew Johnson's original **1830s Tailor Shop**. The **Early Home** is at 201 E Depot St. The **Homestead** is at 209 S Main St. Guided tours are normally available daily but tickets must be picked up at the visitor center. In addition, Johnson and his family are buried at the **Cemetery** at 121 Monument Ave. The park, with the exception of the National Cemetery, is closed Thanksgiving, Christmas, and New Year's. Phone: (423) 638-3551; Greeneville, TN 37743; https://www.nps.gov/anjo/index.htm

Humboldt, TN

West Tennessee Regional Arts Center is the home of several collections of paintings, sculpture, lithographs, and porcelain. Admission is free with donations gratefully accepted. Open Monday through Friday from 9 AM to 4:30 PM. Closed on holidays. Note: Hours may be limited during June and July. 1200 Main St; Humboldt, TN 38343; Phone: (731) 784-1787; http://www.wtrac.tn.org

Jackson, TN

Cypress Grove Nature Park invites strolling along a mile of winding, elevated boardwalk through a cypress forest, as well as observing wildlife from the Rockwell Observation Tower. The Aerie Trail Raptor Center is a sanctuary for injured hawks, eagles, owls and other birds of prey. Admission to the park is free. Open daily. In spring and summer open 8 AM to 7 PM. In fall and winter open at 8 AM until 5 PM. 866 Airways Blvd (Highway 70 W); Jackson, TN 38301; Phone: (731) 425-8316; http://www.jacksonrecandparks.com/leagues/custom_page.cfm?leagueID=0&clientID=3046&pageID=558

Nashville, Chattanooga & Saint Louis Depot & Railroad Museum includes photos, artifacts, and memorabilia of the various railroad lines. A 1947 dining car and two cabooses are on the grounds. The Jackson Area Model Railroad Club has created a HO scale model railroad of the city and runs daily tours. Admission is free. Open Monday through Saturday from 10 AM to 3 PM. 582 S Royal St; Jackson, TN 38301; Phone: (731) 425-8223; http://www.jacksonrecandparks.com/leagues/custom_page.cfm?clientid=3046&leagueid=0&pageid=1112

Kingston, TN
Fort Southwest Point is a pioneer-era fort reconstructed on its original site. Visitor center houses a museum containing excavated artifacts. Admission is free. Open Tuesday through Saturday from 10 AM to 4 PM. 1226 S Kentucky St; Kingston, TN 37763; Phone: (865) 376-3641; https://www.roanetourism.com/vendor/14/fort-southwest-point

Knoxville, TN
Beck Cultural Exchange Center preserves and displays local and regional Black American history and has amassed copies of old Black weekly newspapers dating back to 1878. Admission is free. Open Tuesday through Saturday from 10 AM to 6 PM. Closed between Christmas and New Year's. 1927 Dandridge Ave; Knoxville, TN 37915; Phone: (865) 524-8461; http://www.beckcenter.net

Emporium Center for Arts & Culture showcases local and regional artists. Admission is free. Open Monday through Friday from 9 AM to 5 PM. Closed major holidays. 100 S Gay St; Knoxville, TN 37902; Phone: (865) 523-7543; https://www.knoxalliance.com

Ewing Gallery of Art and Architecture rotates exhibits several times a year. Located on the first floor of the Art and Architecture Building on the Knoxville campus, the gallery is free. Open Monday through Friday from 10 AM to 5 PM, closes at 7:30 PM on Thursday. Open Sunday from 1 PM to 4 PM. Closed national holidays and between exhibitions. 1715 Volunteer Blvd; Knoxville, TN; 37996; Phone: (865) 974-3200; https://ewing-gallery.utk.edu

Girl Scout Museum at Daisy's Place has gathered vintage Girl Scout uniforms, and badges as well as International Girl Scout, and Girl Guide items. Located inside the Knoxville Service Center. Admission is free. Generally open Monday through Friday from 9 AM to 5 PM. Closed major holidays. Visitors are advised to call to check the hours. 1567 Downtown West Blvd; Knoxville, TN 37919; Phone: (800) 474-1912; http://www.girlscoutcsa.org/en/our-council/gs-museum.html

Knoxville Museum of Art holds some of America's most well-known miniature diorama groups as part of the Thorne Rooms, but it also offers special exhibits focused on glass art, and the arts in Tennessee. Admission is free. Open Tuesday through Saturday from 10 AM to 5 PM and on Sunday from 1 PM to 5 PM. Closed major holidays. 1050 World's Fair Park Dr; Knoxville, TN 37916; Phone: (865) 525-6101; https://www.knoxart.org

McClung Museum of Natural History & Culture highlights the geologic, historical, and artistic past of Tennessee as well as cultures from around the globe. Admission is free. 1327 Circle Park Dr; Knoxville, TN 37996; Phone: (865) 974-2144; https://mcclungmuseum.utk.edu

Memphis, TN
A. Schwab's Dry Goods Store is the only remaining original business on Beale Street. It dates back to 1876 and its three floors are filled with store relics, voodoo powders, Memphis music, and retro toys. Open Monday through Thursday from Noon to 6 PM and to 8 PM on Thursday. Open Friday and Saturday from 10 AM to 9 PM and Sunday from 11 AM to 6 PM. 163 Beale St; Memphis, TN 38103; Phone: (901) 523-9782; https://a-schwab.com

Art Museum of the University of Memphis curates temporary exhibitions of contemporary art and culture alongside selections from their permanent collections. Egyptian antiquities and African art are exhibited in dedicated galleries. Admission is free. Open Monday through Saturday from 9 AM to 5 PM. Closed university holidays and between exhibitions. 3750 Norriswood Dr; 142 Communication & Fine Art Building; Memphis, TN 38152; Phone: (901) 678-2224; https://www.memphis.edu/amum

Elmwood Cemetery is an example of a garden cemetery. It's also an official Bird Sanctuary and Arboretum with several gardens on the grounds. The Victorian Carpenter Gothic Cottage serves as the visitor center. Free admission. Open daily from 8 AM to 4:30 PM. 824 S Dudley St; Memphis, TN 38104; Phone: (901) 774-3212; http://www.elmwoodcemetery.org

Mud Island Riverwalk offers a scale replica of the Lower Mississippi River from Cairo, Illinois, to just south of New Orleans, Louisiana. Stroll through six states marked with cities, bridges, and historic markers ending with the Gulf of Mexico. Riverwalk is free to visit. Open dawn to dusk. Note: Visiting the Mississippi River Museum will incur a fee. 125 N Front St; Memphis, TN 38103; https://www.memphisriverparks.org/parks/mud-island

Sidewalk of Stars at the Orpheum Theatre commemorates the appearances of legendary entertainers dating back to Harry Houdini, Mae West, John Philip Sousa, George Burns, and Gracie Allen. 203 S Main St; Memphis, TN 38103; Phone: (901) 525-7800

Milan, TN

West Tennessee Agricultural Museum describes the history of agriculture and agrarian life in West Tennessee. Admission is free. Open Monday through Friday from 8 AM to 4 PM. Closed holidays. 3 Ledbetter Gate Rd; Milan, TN 38358; Phone: (731) 686-8067; http://milan.tennessee.edu/museum

Murfreesboro, TN

Cannonburgh Village represents approximately 100 years of early Tennessee life from the 1830s to the 1930s. The village contains many of the buildings and businesses that would make up a town including gristmill, school house, a telephone operator's house, a doctor's office, a general store, and a blacksmith shop. Self-guided tours are free. Open seasonally. May through November open Tuesday through Saturday from 9 AM to 4 PM. Open Sunday from 1 PM to 4 PM. 312 S Front St; Murfreesboro, TN 37129; Phone: (615) 890-0355; http://www.murfreesborotn.gov/164/Cannonsburgh-Village

Stones River National Battlefield memorializes one of the bloodiest conflicts of the Civil War. Although the battle produced important gains for the Union it came at a tremendous cost. There are no fees to visit. Grounds are open daily from sunrise to sunset. Park rangers and volunteers offer guided tours of the battlefield on a regular basis from May through October. The visitor center offers a museum and a movie about the battle. It is open from 9 AM to 5 PM daily. Closed Thanksgiving and Christmas Day. 1563 N Thompson La; Murfreesboro, TN 37129; Phone: (615) 893-9501; https://www.nps.gov/stri/index.htm

Nashville, TN

Fort Nashborough was built to protect settlers from armed incursions by Native Americans hostile to their expansion into the area. The exterior of the fort's log cabins and block houses were rebuilt with historically accurate construction. The new fort and interpretive center is free to visit. Open daily from 9 AM to 4 PM. Riverfront Park; 170 First Ave N; Nashville, TN 37201; https://www.nashville.gov/Parks-and-Recreation/Historic-Sites/Fort-Nashborough.aspx

Fort Negley was the largest inland fort built in the United States during the Civil War. Admission to the park is free and open year round from dawn to dusk for self-guided walking tours. The visitor center provides interactive exhibits and two 20-minute videos covering the 1862 surrender of Nashville and the building of Fort Negley. During June, July, and August the visitor center is open Tuesday through Thursday from Noon to 4 PM, and on Friday and Saturday from 9 AM to 4 PM. From September through May it is open Tuesday through Saturday but with shortened hours. The **Vulcan Materials Company Fossils @ the Fort** encourages visitors to search for 400 million-year-old fossils sourced from one of their quarries. 1100 Fort Negley Blvd; Nashville, TN 37203; Phone: (615) 862-8470; https://www.nashville.gov/Parks-and-Recreation/Historic-Sites/Fort-Negley.aspx

Military Branch of the Tennessee State Museum explores America's conflicts, beginning with the Spanish-American War in 1898 and ending with Vietnam War. There is no admission charge. Open Tuesday through Saturday from 10 AM to 5 PM. Closed major holidays. War Memorial Building; Legislative Plaza; 301 Sixth Ave N; Nashville, TN 37243; Phone: (615) 741-2692; https://tnmuseum.org/military-branch

Tennessee Agricultural Museum collects home and farm artifacts from the 19th and early 20th centuries. Exhibited in a renovated plantation barn, the museum features a woodworking collection, wagons and large equipment such as a Jumbo steam engine. There's also log cabins, a farm house, one-room school, and a blacksmith shop. Self-guided tours are free. Special events will incur a charge. Open Monday through Friday from 9 AM to 4 PM. Closed on state holidays. Note: May close during inclement weather. 404 Hogan Rd; Nashville, TN 37220; Phone: (615) 837-5197; http://tnagmuseum.org

Tennessee Residence became the official governor's home when the state purchased the property in 1949. Tours are offered free at 10 AM on Tuesday and Thursday and by appointment from mid-March through mid-November. 882 Curtiswood Ln S, Nashville, TN 37204; Phone: (615) 741-2784; https://www.tn.gov/residence/about-the-residence.html

Tennessee State Capitol is open for free guided tours Monday through Friday on the hour from 9 AM to 3 PM. There is no Noon tour. All tours begin at the information desk on the first floor. Closed weekends and state holidays. 600 Dr Martin L King, Jr Blvd/Charlotte Ave; Nashville, TN 37208; Phone: (800) 407-4324; https://tnmuseum.org/state-capitol

Tennessee State Museum concentrates on artifacts related to the state's history and include art, furniture, textiles, and photographs produced by Tennesseans. There is no admission charge. Open Tuesday, Wednesday, Friday, and Saturday from 10 AM to 5 PM and on Thursday to 8 PM. Open Sunday from 1 PM to 5 PM. Closed major holidays. 1000 Rosa Parks Blvd at Jefferson St; Bicentennial Capitol Mall State Park; Nashville, TN 37208; Phone: (615) 741-2692; https://tnmuseum.org

Vanderbilt University Fine Arts Gallery presents exhibitions of Eastern and Western art from antiquity through modern and contemporary art. Admission to the gallery is free. During the academic year open Monday through Friday from

11 AM to 4 PM. Open weekends from 1 PM to 5 PM. In summer open Tuesday through Friday from Noon to 4 PM and Saturday from 1 PM to 5 PM. The gallery closes for school breaks and changes in museum installations during the academic year. Cohen Memorial Hall; 1220 21st Ave S; Nashville, TN 37203; Phone: (615) 322-0605; https://www.vanderbilt.edu/gallery/visit

Norris, TN
Lenoir Historical Complex in Norris Dam State Park includes the Lenoir Museum, an 18th century grist mill, and a threshing barn recreating life before the Tennessee Valley Authority built Norris Dam. There's also an antique barrel organ with 110 wood pipes that plays ten different tunes. Admission is free. The Lenoir Museum is open all year on Wednesday through Sunday from 9 AM until 5 PM. The grist mill is open April through October on Wednesday through Sunday from 9 AM to 4:30 PM. 2121 Norris Freeway; Norris, TN 37828; Phone: (865) 494-9688; https://tnstateparks.com/parks/activity-detail/norris-dam-interpretive-programs

Oak Ridge TN
It's not possible to tour the famous Oak Ridge facility for free. Public bus tour of the Department of Energy's Oak Ridge will incur a fee. More information at: https://amse.org/bus-tours

International Friendship Bell was the first monument between a U.S. Manhattan Project city and Japan. It serves as an expression of hope for everlasting peace. Free to visit. Open daily dawn to dusk. 1401 Oak Ridge Turnpike; Oak Ridge, TN 37830; Phone: (865) 425-3450; http://friendshipbell.com

K-25 Interpretive Center overlooks the original site with pictures, historic displays, and a video. K-25 was the site where gaseous diffusion uranium enrichment technology was pioneered as well as being one of the enrichment locations. Open daily from dawn till dusk. Highway 58; Oak Ridge, TN 37830; http://k-25virtualmuseum.org

University of Tennessee Forest and Arboretum spans 250 acres with 800 species of trees, shrubs, and flowering plants threaded by four nature trails. Admission is free. The arboretum grounds are open for walking daily from 8 AM until sunset. Note: The parking lot is accessible during office hours, but is subject to restrictions after office hours on weekdays, weekends, and holidays. 901 S Illinois Ave: Oak Ridge, TN 37830; Phone: (865) 483-3571; https://utarboretumsociety.org

Pall Mall, TN
Sergeant Alvin C. York State Historic Park pays tribute to one of the most decorated soldiers of World War I. The visitor center is modeled after York's

general store and displays artifacts from World War I, and exhibits on Sgt. York's life. Visitors can watch *Legacy in Action*, a 15-minute video narrated by Walter Cronkite, on Sgt. York and the history of the site. The visitor center is free to visit and open daily from 8 AM to 4:30 PM. Tours of the York home will incur a fee. The grounds also include a reproduction of a World War I trench. A half-mile hiking trail leads to the Wolf River cemetery where Sgt. York and his wife, Miss Gracie, are buried. 2609 N York Hwy; Pall Mall, TN 38577; Phone: (931) 879-6456; https://tnstateparks.com/parks/sgt-alvin-c-york

Rocky Top, TN

Coal Creek Mine Museum honors the history of the miners that lived, worked, and died in the explosions at Coal Creek, Fraterville, and Briceville, Tennessee. Photos show the inside and outside of the mines after the explosion. Admission is free with donations gratefully accepted. Open Tuesday through Saturday from 10 AM to 4 PM. 216 N Main St; Rocky Top, TN 37769; Phone: (865) 426-7914; http://www.coalcreekminersmuseum.com

Trenton, TN

Trenton Teapot Museum delights with over 500 pieces dating from 1750 to 1860. The porcelain veilleuses in the collection, although often referred to as teapots, were made as food warmers. Admission is free and the exhibit is open from 9 AM to 5 PM Monday through Friday. Trenton City Hall; 309 College St; Trenton, TN 38382; Phone: (731) 855-2013; http://www.teapotcollection.com/teapot/teapot-information/museum

Texas

From March 2, 1836, to February 19, 1846 the Republic of Texas fought for and gained its independence from Mexico. Eventually the citizens of the new republic decided that becoming part of the USA would protect them from continuing war with Mexico, but Texas never forgot its roots as the independent Republic of Texas.

Abilene, TX

Named *Storybook Capital of America*, this charming town is filled with statues from children's literature. Stroll through downtown Abilene and you'll encounter characters from Dr. Seuss' classics, as well as Dino Bob, Jack Frost, and the Three Little Kittens. The list keeps growing. Finding all these sculptures is the best kind of scavenger hunt. http://storybookcapitalofamerica.com/storybook-sculptures/

Center for Contemporary Arts presents more than 20 different exhibits of regional art, international photography, and award-winning short films. Admission is free. Open Tuesday through Saturday from 11 AM to 5 PM. Open until 9 PM on Thursday. 220 Cypress St; Abilene, TX 79601; Phone: (325) 677-8389; https://www.center-arts.com

Fort Phantom Hill was one of the second line of forts laid out in the early 1850s to protect the westward-moving frontier of Texas settlement. Fort Phantom Hill is part of the Texas Forts Trail offering three original stone buildings including an intact stone powder magazine, a stone guardhouse, and an almost-intact commissary or warehouse. Also on the grounds are foundations from the original fort. Free to visit and tours are self-guided. Open daily from dawn until dusk. 10818 FM 600; Abilene, TX 79601; Phone: (325) 677-1309; http://fortphantom.org

National Center for Children's Illustrated Literature creates exhibitions of award-winning children's book illustrations. Admission is free. Open Tuesday through Saturday from 10 AM to 4 PM. 102 Cedar St; Abilene, TX 79601; Phone: (325) 673-4586; http://www.nccil.org

Adrian, TX

The geo-mathematical midpoint of Route 66, and the town's motto is: "When you're here, you're halfway there." Travelers take their photo in front of the sign that reads, *1,139 miles to Chicago-1,139 miles to Los Angeles.* **Midpoint Café** is a time capsule with a retro look of the 1950s. 305 W Historic Rt 66; Adrian, TX 79001; Phone: (806) 538-6379; https://www.facebook.com/MidpointCafe

Anderson, TX
Fanthorp Inn State Historic Site depicts 19th century life at an early Texas stagecoach stop and family home. There is no entrance fee. Open for public tours on Saturday and Sunday from 9 AM to 3:30 PM. 579 S Main St; Anderson, TX 77830; Phone: (936) 873-2633; https://tpwd.texas.gov/state-parks/fanthorp-inn

Archer City, TX
Booked Up Inc is a must stop for fans of author Larry McMurtry, who is the owner and founder, and native son of the city. Open Thursday through Saturday from 1 PM to 5 PM. 216 South Center; Archer City, TX 76351; Phone: (940) 574-2511; https://www.bookedupac.com

Alamo, TX
Lower Rio Grande Valley National Wildlife Refuge offers visitors trails and observation decks for wildlife watching, hiking, and wildlife photography throughout its nearly 40,000 acres. It is considered one of the most biologically diverse national wildlife refuges in the system. Note: The Lower Rio Grande Valley National Wildlife Refuge, which is free to visit, shares its headquarters and a visitor center with the entrance to the fee-based Santa Ana National Wildlife Refuge. Open daily from sunrise to sunset. The refuge is located seven miles south of Alamo, Texas, on FM 907. U.S. Hwy 281; Phone: (956)784-7500; https://www.fws.gov/refuge/Lower_Rio_Grande_Valley

Albany, TX
Old Jail Art Center offers its permanent collection of modern drawings, paintings and prints by American and contemporary British artists. There's also Asian, and pre-Colombian art as well as an outdoor sculpture courtyard. Admission is free. Open Tuesday through Saturday from 10 AM to 5 PM. Closed major holidays. 201 S Second St; Albany, TX 76430; Phone: (325) 762-2269; http://theojac.org

Alpine, TX
Museum of the Big Bend on the campus of Sul Ross State University focuses on history and cartography as well as art, and archaeology. Admission is free. Open Tuesday through Saturday from 9 AM to 5 PM and on Sunday from 1 PM to 5 PM. Closed on major holidays. Note: The museum is located at the northeast corner of the campus and can be reached only via Entrance Four from Harrison Street. 400 N Harrison St; Alpine, TX 79832; Phone: (432) 837-8143; http://www.museumofthebigbend.com

Amarillo, TX
Amarillo Museum of Art (AMoA) features permanent and temporary exhibits. Collections include American photography, paintings, prints, drawings, and

sculptures as well as the Price Collection of Asian Art. On the campus of Amarillo College, admission is free. Open Tuesday through Friday from 10 AM to 5 PM and Saturday and Sunday from 1 PM to 5 PM. Closed major holidays. 2200 S Van Buren; Amarillo, TX 79109; Phone (806) 371-5050; http://www.amarilloart.org

Cadillac Ranch is the product of eccentric millionaire Stanley Marsh 3 (he doesn't like the Roman numeral III) and the Ant Farm, a San Francisco art collective. The site consists of ten graffiti-covered cars half-buried in a pasture along eastbound I-40 between exits 60 and 62. Exit onto the frontage road, then enter the pasture through an unlocked gate.

Harrington House includes a collection of decorative and fine arts. Vintage gowns and dresses of Mrs. Harrington from the 1930s to the 1970s are displayed as well as changing exhibits. There is no charge for admission. Tours are offered May through December on Tuesdays and Thursdays. Call to reserve a time. 1600 S Polk St; Amarillo, TX 79102; Phone: (806) 374-5490; https://www.harringtonhousehistorichome.org

RV Museum @ Jack Sisemore Traveland was started by Jack (father) and Trent (son) Sisemore who began collecting and restoring unusual vintage RVs over 25 years ago. Enter through the main showroom. The museum is free. Open Monday through Friday from 9 AM to 5 PM and Saturday from 9 AM to 4 PM. Closed major holidays. 4341 Canyon Dr; Amarillo, TX 79110; Phone (806) 358-4891; http://www.rvmuseum.net

Texas Air and Space Museum honors the Panhandle's history of flight through documents, historic aircraft, newspaper articles, exhibits, and photos dating back to the beginning of English Field Airport. Free admission, donations accepted. Open Monday through Saturday from 9 AM to 4 PM. On the grounds of the Rick Husband Amarillo International Airport. 10001 American Dr; Amarillo, TX 79111; Phone (806) 335-9159; http://www.texasairandspacemuseum.org

Texas Pharmacy Museum invites visitors to see a restored early 20th century pharmacy displaying tools of the trade and pharmacy products. Admission is free. Guided tours are held Tuesday through Thursday from 10 AM to Noon and 1:30 PM through 4 PM. Closed major holidays. Texas Tech University Health Sciences Center; School of Pharmacy; 1300 S Coulter; Amarillo, TX 79106; Phone: (806) 414-9269; https://www.ttuhsc.edu/pharmacy/museum

Vintage Autohaus & Imports entices car enthusiasts with classics, vintage, muscle, and European cars. No admission charged. Open Monday through Friday from 8 AM to 6 PM and Saturday 9 AM to 5 PM. Note: Must be 16 years and older. 8201 Amarillo Blvd W; Amarillo, TX; Phone: (806) 359-9600; http://www.vaitx.com

Austin, TX

Austin Nature and Science Center at Zilker Park offers activities and wildlife exhibits, as well as a child-friendly Dino Pit. Free admission. Open Monday through Saturday from 9 AM to 5 PM and Sunday from Noon to 5 PM. 2389 Stratford Dr; Austin, TX 78746; Phone: (512) 974-3888; http://www.austintexas.gov/department/austin-nature-and-science-center

Brush Square Museums presents different pieces of Austin and Texas history. **Susanna Dickinson Museum** preserves the home and legacy of the Alamo survivor, Susanna Dickinson. The **O. Henry Museum** was the home of the famed late short story writer born William Sidney Porter. The **Austin Fire Museum** rounds out the trio. Admission is free. All museums are open Wednesday through Sunday from Noon to 5 PM. 409 E Fifth St; Phone: (512) 472-1903; http://www.brushsquaremuseums.org

Elisabet Ney Museum displays the portrait collection created by 19th century German sculptor Elisabet Ney. Admission is free to visit her historic home and studio. Open Wednesday through Sunday from Noon to 5 PM. 304 E 44th St; Austin, TX 78751; Phone: (512) 974-1625; http://www.austintexas.gov/Elisabetney

George Washington Carver Museum and Cultural Center exhibits Black American historical and cultural material with Juneteenth as a permanent exhibit. Admission is free. Open Monday through Friday 10 AM to 6 PM with closing Thursday at 9 PM. Open Saturday from 10 AM to 4 PM. 1165 Angelina St; Austin, TX 78702; Phone: (512) 974-4926; http://www.austintexas.gov/carvermuseum

Governor's Mansion Tours are available to the public by reservation. Note: All visitors must pass a background security screening. Visitors must provide their name, date of birth, and government identification information at least a week in advance of their tour. To schedule a tour call (512) 305-8524. 1010 Colorado St, Austin, TX 78701; Phone: (512) 463-5518; https://tspb.texas.gov/prop/tgm/tgm/mansion.html

Harry Ransom Center at the University of Texas houses a rare Gutenberg Bible, literary manuscripts, the Watergate papers, and the world's first photograph. Exhibition galleries are free with donations encouraged. Open weekdays from 10 AM to 5 PM, open until 7 PM on Thursday. Open Saturday and Sunday from

Noon to 5 PM. 300 W 21st St; Austin, TX 78712; Phone: (512) 471-8944; https://www.hrc.utexas.edu

Texas Capitol Complex offers a 30-minute guided tour on the history of the building as well as self-guided tours. All are free. These tours run from Monday through Friday from 8:30 AM to 4:30 PM. On Saturday from 9:30 AM to 3:30 PM and on Sunday from Noon to 3:30 PM. Pick up a free self-guided tour pamphlet from the Capitol Information and Guide Service room or the Capitol Visitors Center. The building and grounds are open weekdays from 7 AM to 10 PM and on weekends from 9 AM to 8 PM. 1100 Congress Ave; Austin, TX 78701; Phone: (512) 463-4630; https://tspb.texas.gov/prop/tc/tc/capitol.html

Texas Capitol Visitors Center details Texas history through exhibits and videos. Open Monday through Saturday from 9 AM to 5 PM and Sunday from Noon to 5 PM. 112 E 11th St; Austin, TX 78701; Phone: (512) 305-8400; https://tspb.texas.gov/prop/tcvc/cvc/cvc.html

Texas Military Forces Museum at Camp Mabry explores the history of the Lone Star State's militia and volunteer forces from 1823 to 1903, when the Congress created the National Guard. Admission to the museum is free. Open Tuesday to Sunday 10 AM to 4 PM. 2200 W 35th St; Austin, TX 78763; Phone: (512) 782-5659; http://texasmilitaryforcesmuseum.org

Texas State Cemetery introduces visitors to the final resting places of Stephen F. Austin as well as many notable individuals. Both self-guided and free guided tours are available. Reservations are required. The grounds are open daily from 8 AM to 5 PM. The office is open Monday through Friday from 8 AM to 5 PM. 909 Navasota St; Austin, TX 78702; Phone: (512) 463-0605; https://tspb.texas.gov/prop/tsc/tsc/cemetery.html

Beaumont, TX
Art Museum Southeast Texas highlights painting, sculpture, prints, photographs, as well as folk and decorative arts of the 19th through 21st centuries, with an emphasis folk art. A gallery is dedicated to the folk art of Beaumont self-taught artist Felix "Fox" Harris. Admission is free with donations accepted. Open Monday through Friday from 9 AM to 5 PM. Open Saturday from 10 AM to 5 PM and on Sunday from Noon to 5 PM. Closed major holidays. 500 Main St; Beaumont, TX 77701; Phone: (409) 832-3432; https://amset.org

Beaumont Botanical Gardens & Warren Loose Conservatory offers visitors the Bert and Jack Binks Horticultural Center, and the Warren Loose Conservatory. Themed gardens showcase camellias, modern and antique roses, bromeliads and many native plants. Admission is free and donations are welcomed. The botanical gardens are open daily from 6 AM to 9 PM. The Warren Loose Conservatory is open Monday and Tuesday, and again on Thursday and Friday from 9 AM to 4 PM. It is also open Saturday and Sunday from 1 PM to 5 PM. Closed holidays. 6088 Babe Zaharias Dr; Beaumont, TX 77705; Phone: (409) 842-3135; http://beaumontbotanicalgardens.org

Edison Museum focuses on science and history as well as the life and inventions of Thomas Edison. Admission is free. Open Monday through Friday from 9 AM to 2 PM. Closed holidays. 350 Pine St; Beaumont, TX 77701; Phone: (409) 981-3089; http://www.edisonmuseum.org

Fire Museum of Texas is also the headquarters for the Beaumont Fire Department. Designated as he Official Fire Museum of Texas this child-friendly place encourages children to dress up like firefighters and take a photo with a life-size Smokey Bear. There's also several pieces of historic fire-fighting equipment. Admission is free. Open Monday through Friday from 8 AM to 4:30 PM. 400 Walnut St; Beaumont, TX 77701; Phone: (409) 880-3927; http://www.firemuseumoftexas.org

Brazoria, TX
San Bernard National Wildlife Refuge offers an auto tour route, trails, and boardwalks in a 45,730-acre wildlife conservation area along the coast of Texas. The nine-mile San Bernard Auto Tour covers a diversity of habitats. There is no entrance fee. Open daily sunrise to sunset. 6801 CR-306; Brazoria, TX 77422; Phone: (979) 964-3639; https://www.fws.gov/refuge/San_Bernard

Brenham, TX
Blue Bell invites you to see how they make ice cream from their observation deck and learn more in the visitor center. The observation deck is open Monday through Friday from 8 AM to 2 PM but they advise calling as hours are subject to change. 1101 S Blue Bell Rd; Brenham, TX 77833; Phone: (800) 327-8135; https://www.bluebell.com/the-little-creamery

Brownsville, TX
Palo Alto Battlefield preserves the grounds of the May 8, 1846 military action – the first major conflict in a border dispute that became the Mexican American War. Guided programs at Palo Alto Battlefield and Resaca de la Palma Battlefield begin in December and run through March. The visitor center hosts exhibits as well as provides brochures and trail guides. There is no fee to enter the park or attend park programs and events. The park and the visitor center is open daily

from 8 AM to 5 PM. 7200 Paredes Line Rd; Brownsville, TX 78526; Phone: (956) 541-2785 x333; https://www.nps.gov/paal

Conroe, TX
Lone Star Monument and Historical Flag Park honors the Texas fight for independence from Mexico. A 14-foot-tall bronze statue of *The Texian* stands in the center, surrounded by the 13 battle and rally flags of the Texas Revolution. 104 I-45 N; Conroe, TX 77301; https://texasflagpark.com

Cuero, TX
DeWitt County Historical Museum offers visitors a family home, and a two-room log cabin as well as an old-fashioned garden. Admission is free. Open Tuesday through Friday from 10 AM to Noon and again from 1 PM to 4 PM. 312 E Broadway; Cuero, TX 77954; Phone: (361) 275-6322; https://www.cityofcuero.com/444/DeWitt-County-Historical-Museum

Pharmacy and Medical Museum of Texas started as a pharmacy and drugstore. The interior includes the original 1889 wall cabinets, display counters and the pharmacist's preparation bench in their original locations. The first floor has been restored and holds items from the late 1800s through the early 1900s. Admission is free. Open Monday through Saturday from 10 AM to 3 PM. 114 E Main St; Cuero, TX 77954; Phone: (361) 485-8090; https://www.pharmacyandmedicalmuseum.org/home

Dallas (See also Fort Worth, TX and Grapevine, TX)
Crow Museum of Asian Art is a trove of beautiful Asian art displayed as curated exhibits. Sculptures are displayed in the outdoor courtyard. Admission is free. Donations appreciated. Open Tuesday through Sunday from 11 AM to 5 PM. Closed Independence Day, Thanksgiving Day, Christmas Eve, Christmas Day, and New Year's Day. 2010 Flora St; Dallas, TX 75201; Phone: (214) 979-6430; https://crowcollection.org

Dallas Art Museum is one of the major art attractions of the Dallas area. General admission to enjoy their extensive art collection is free. Special exhibits will incur a fee. Don't miss the Conservation Gallery with its windows into the restoration area. Open Tuesday through Saturday at 11 AM. Closes at 5 PM except for Thursday when it closes at 9 PM. Closed Thanksgiving, Christmas, and New Year's Day. 1717 N Harwood St, Dallas, TX 75201; Phone: (214) 922-1200; https://www.dma.org

Dealey Plaza National Historic Landmark District is the location where President John F. Kennedy was assassinated on July 22, 1963. Dealey Plaza encompasses three streets – Main Street, Elm Street, and Commerce Street. The plaza itself is open to the public. Note: The Sixth Floor Museum at Dealey Plaza charges admission. https://www.jfk.org/the-assassination/history-of-dealey-plaza One block east is the **John F. Kennedy Memorial Plaza** between Main and Commerce streets. https://www.jfk.org/the-assassination/history-of-john-f-kennedy-memorial-plaza

Federal Reserve Bank of Dallas offers guided tours to walk-in visitors at 10 AM on Wednesdays. No reservations are required. Admission and tours are free. Historical currency, founding of the Federal Reserve Bank as well as its role in the economy are highlighted. Self-guided tours are also available. Open Monday through Friday from 10 AM to 4 PM. Closed bank holidays. Note: All United States visitors are required to present a valid government-issued photo ID. International visitors must present a valid passport. 2200 N Pearl St; Dallas, TX 75201; Phone: (214) 922-5267; https://www.dallasfed.org

Freedman's Memorial honors a community of former slaves established after the Civil War. Over 1,000 graves were relocated. Sculptures by David Newton chronicles African Americans and their descendants' journey from slavery to emancipation. Free to enter. Open daily. Corner of Lemmon Ave and North Central Expressway, Dallas, TX 75223; http://texaslaketrail.com/plan-your-adventure/historic-sites-and-cities/sites/freedmans-cemetery-memorial

Pioneer Plaza features a re-creation of a cattle drive in bronze with longhorn steers being driven by three cowboys on horses. Free to visit. Near the Pioneer Cemetery at the corner of Griffin and Young Street. https://www.visitdallas.com/things-to-do/venue/view/6851/Pioneer-Plaza.html

El Paso, TX
The Border Patrol Museum is the only museum in the U.S. dedicated to agents of the Border Patrol. The museum is free and open Tuesdays through Saturdays from 9 AM to 5 PM. The staff are volunteers from the Border Patrol who are happy to answer questions and point out highlights. 4315 Woodrow Bean Transmountain Rd; El Paso, TX 79924; Phone: (915) 759-6060; https://borderpatrolmuseum.com

El Paso Museum of History and the Touch City Digital History Wall entrances visitors with its Digital Wall. The huge 35 feet display accesses the growing database of images, maps, and videos exploring El Paso's past and present. It is the only one in the United States and the largest in the world. Five galleries inside the museum explore the rich culture and history of El Paso. Admission is free although there is a fee for special exhibits. Open Tuesday through Saturday from 9 AM to 5 PM and Thursdays to 9 PM. Open Sunday from Noon to 5 PM.

Closed city holidays. 510 N Santa Fe St; El Paso, TX 79901; Phone: (915) 212-0320; http://history.elpasotexas.gov

Fort Bliss Museum and the Old Ironsides Museum details the history of the 1st Armored Division from its organization before World War II until the present day. Exhibits include over 40 tanks and other armored vehicles. Museum is free. Open Monday through Friday from 9 AM to 4 PM and Saturdays from 10 AM to 3 PM. 1735 Marshall Rd; El Paso, TX 79906; Phone: (915) 855-4677; https://www.bliss.army.mil/museum

UTEP Centennial Museum and Chihuahuan Desert Gardens focuses on the natural and cultural history of the Chihuahuan desert, the largest desert in North America, and includes a botanical garden dedicated to its flora. Admission is free. Open Monday through Saturday from 10 AM to 4:30 PM. The gardens are open daily from dawn to dusk. Closed on holidays and during UTEP football home games. The **Lhakhang** (or temple) is also on UTEP's Centennial Plaza. It is open on Wednesday from 11 AM to 1 PM. 500 W University Ave (at Wiggins Rd); El Paso, TX 79968; Phone: (915) 747-5565; https://www.utep.edu/centennial-museum

Fredericksburg, TX
Fort Martin Scott was the first U.S. military post on the western frontier of Texas. Explore the grounds and the buildings, both original and reproduced. Admission is free. Donations are gladly accepted. Open Thursday through Monday from 10 AM to 5 PM. 1606 E Main St; Fredericksburg TX 78624; Phone: (830) 217-3200; http://www.ftmartinscott.org/plan-your-visit.html

Frisco, TX
Texas Sculpture Garden features four acres showcasing contemporary sculptures by Texas artists. Free to the public. Open daily dawn to dusk. Interior artwork is open to visitors on weekdays 9 AM to 5 PM. 6801 Gaylord Pkwy; Frisco, TX 75034; Phone: (972) 377-1100; https://www.texassculpturegarden.org

Fritch, TX
Alibates Flint Quarries area was popular as far back as 13,000 years ago when mammoth-hunting humans sought the best stones for their tools. The visitor center provides exhibits, and an 11-minute film about the monument. Note: The quarry itself can only be accessed by a ranger guided program which are offered seasonally. There are no entrance fees and ranger-guided tours and programs are free. The Alibates visitor center is open daily from 9 AM to 4 PM. Closed Thanksgiving, Christmas, and New Year's Day. Located 35 miles north of

Amarillo. 37084 Alibates Rd; Fritch, TX 79036; Phone: (806) 857-6680; https://www.nps.gov/alfl/index.htm

Fort Hood, TX
1st Cavalry Division Museum details the history of the division from units that participated in the Civil War up to its current operations in Iraq and Afghanistan. There are life size dioramas and 10 acres of outdoor exhibits. Admission is free. Open Monday through Friday from 9 AM to 4 PM. Open Saturday from 10 AM to 4 PM and Sunday and holidays from Noon to 4 PM. Note: Visitors without military credentials must get a base pass from Fort Hood's Marvin Leath Visitors Center. U.S. Hwy 190 on T.J Mills Blvd; Fort Hood, TX 76545; Phone: (254) 287-9909; https://history.army.mil/museums/fieldMuseums/fortHood_1stCav/index.html

Fort Sam Houston, TX (See San Antonio, TX)

Fort Worth, TX (See also Dallas, TX)
Amon Carter Museum of American Art fulfills Amon Carter's wish for a free art museum with world-class art. The museum includes works by Frederic Remington and Charles Russell, and American art into the 20th century. Admission and tours of the museum are free. Open Tuesday through Saturday from 10 AM to 5 PM, closing Thursday at 8 PM. Open Sunday from Noon to 5 PM. Closed major holidays. 3501 Camp Bowie Blvd; Fort Worth, TX 76107; Phone: (817) 738-1933; http://www.cartermuseum.org

JFK Tribute was dedicated May 29, 2012 in General Worth Square as a memorial to the 35th President of the United States, John F. Kennedy. Located outside what was the Texas Hotel, the statue sits atop the site where President Kennedy made his last public speech. The 8-foot-tall bronze statue is flanked by a granite wall that includes photographs and quotes from John F. Kennedy's presidential term. General Worth Sq; 916 Main St; Fort Worth, TX 76102; Phone: (817)870-1692; http://www.jfktribute.com

Kimbell Art Museum offers its permanent collection free to visit. Special exhibits incur a fee. Open Tuesday through Thursday from 10 AM to 5 PM, Friday from Noon to 8 PM, Saturday from 10 AM to 5 PM and Sunday from Noon to 5 PM. 3333 Camp Bowie Blvd; Fort Worth, TX 76107; Phone: (817) 332-8451; https://www.kimbellart.org

Monnig Meteorite Gallery at Texas Christian University hosts samples from more than 2,300 different meteorites. Admission to the gallery is free. Open Monday through Friday from 1 PM to 4 PM, and Saturday from Noon to 4 PM.

Sid Richardson Science Building; 2950 W Bowie St; Texas Christian University; Fort Worth, TX 76109; Phone: (817) 257-6277; https://monnigmuseum.tcu.edu

Sid Richardson Museum exhibits permanent and special collections of paintings by some of the best known and loved Western artists, most notably Frederic Remington and Charles M. Russell. Free admission. Take a free docent-guided tour on Tuesdays and Saturdays at 2 PM. 309 Main St; Fort Worth, TX 76102; Phone: (817) 332-6554; https://www.sidrichardsonmuseum.org

Western Currency Visitor Center takes visitors through the process of printing the nation's currency. Tours are free. A tour wand is available for the blind and visually impaired. No photos are permitted. Open Tuesday through Friday from 8:30 AM to 5:30 PM. 9000 Blue Mound Rd; Fort Worth, TX 76131; Phone: (817) 231-4000; https://www.moneyfactory.gov/fortworthtxtours.html

Fredericksburg, TX
Wildseed Farms has been growing fields of wildflowers for over 35 years. There is no charge for admission. Walking trails are open daily from 9:30 AM to 5:30 PM. 100 Legacy Dr; Fredericksburg, TX 78624; Phone: (800) 848-0078; https://www.wildseedfarms.com

Galveston, TX
Galveston Arts Center offers curated, rotating contemporary art exhibits in a historic building on Galveston's Strand. Free admission. Open Tuesday through Saturday from 11 AM to 5 PM and Sunday from Noon to 5 PM. 2127 Strand; Galveston, TX 77550; Phone: (409) 763-2403; https://www.galvestonartscenter.org

Galveston-Port Bolivar Ferry takes travelers between Galveston Island and the Bolivar Peninsula. The free ferry service operates 24 hours a day and is provided by the Texas Department of Transportation (TxDOT). It is the only way drivers can cross the waterway between Bolivar Peninsula and Galveston Island. Find the ferry at Galveston Landing at 1000 Ferry Rd North; Galveston, TX 77550. At Bolivar Landing, find the ferry at 123 Texas Hwy 87; Port Bolivar, TX 77650; Phone: (409)795-2230; https://www.txdot.gov/driver/travel/ferry-schedules.html

Gonzales, TX
This museum-rich town has five museums in the Texas History Museum District. Some are free, others require a fee. The free museums are included below.
DuBose Gun Collection at the Robert Lee Brother Jr. Library is the collection of Charles DuBose and includes over 700 weapons, plus holsters, militaria, helmets, and swords. Free to the public. Open Monday from 11 AM to 7 PM, and Tuesday through Friday from 9 AM to 5 PM. Open Saturday 9 AM to Noon. 301

St Joseph St; Gonzales, TX 78629; Phone: (830) 672-6315;
https://www.gonzales.texas.gov/p/departments/library/431

Eggleston House is furnished to depict Texas pioneer life. Visitors can step onto the porch and activate recordings that describe the building, and illuminate two rooms. Admission is free with donations greatly appreciated. Open Tuesday through Saturday from 10 AM to Noon and 1 PM to 5 PM, and on Sunday from 1 PM to 5 PM. 1303 St Louis St; Gonzales, TX 78629; https://www.gonzalestx.travel/business/eggleston-house

Gonzales County Jail Museum was built in 1887 and features a rebuilt gallows, original cells as well as sheriff's and jailer's quarters. Free to visit with donations greatly appreciated. March through December open Tuesday through Saturday from 10:30 AM to 3:30 PM. In January and February open Thursday through Saturday from 10:30 AM to 3:30 PM. 414 St. Lawrence St; Gonzales, TX 78629; Phone: (888) 672-1095; https://gonzalestexas.com/museums

Gonzales Memorial Museum commemorates the soldiers from Gonzales who died in the Alamo and displays the *Come and Take It* cannon that fired the first shot for Texas Independence. Other objects reflect early life in Gonzales. Free of charge, donations are appreciated. Open Monday through Saturday from 10 AM to 5 PM. Closed from Noon to 1 PM. Open Sunday from 1 PM to 5 PM. 414 Smith St; Gonzales, TX 78629; Phone: (830) 672-6350; https://gonzalestexas.com/museums

Grapevine, TX (See also Dallas, TX and Fort Worth, TX)
Strolling through this town is a joy but definitely head to the Glockenspiel Clock Tower at 636 S Main Street and read about the free show put on by the gun fighting figures at the top of the tower.
https://www.grapevinetexasusa.com/listing/grapevine-glockenspiel-clock-tower/4108

Gateway Classic Cars is an exotic car dealership, one of several across the country, but their back showroom is filled with gorgeous classic cars. Browsers are welcomed. 1250 Mustang Dr; DFW Airport, TX 76051; Phone: (817) 310-9400; http://gatewayclassiccars.com/locations?location=DFW

Grapevine Historical Museum highlights the cultural and family life of early Grapevine residents through photos and artifacts. Admission is free. Open Tuesday through Friday from 10 AM to 4 PM. Open Saturday from 10 AM to 4 PM, and Sunday from Noon to 4 PM. 206 W Hudgins St; Grapevine, TX 76051; Phone: (817) 410-3526; https://grapevinehistory.weebly.com

Houston, TX

Art Car Museum celebrates cars as its own art form with elaborate and artfully constructed cars, low riders, and mobile contraptions as well as revolving exhibitions by local, national, and international artists. Free admission. Open Wednesday through Sunday from 11 AM to 6 PM. Closes during new installations. 140 Heights Blvd, Houston, TX 77007; Phone: (713) 861-5526; http://artcarmuseum.com

Blaffer Art Museum is the University of Houston's laboratory for the visual arts and contemporary culture with an emphasis on emerging and under-represented artists. Admission is always free. Open Tuesday through Saturday from 10 AM to 5 PM. 4173 Elgin St; Houston, TX 77204; http://blafferartmuseum.org

Contemporary Arts Museum curates exhibits as well as offering outdoor sculptures as part of their *Art Outside the Box* initiative. Admission is free. Open Tuesday through Friday from 10 AM to 7 PM closing Thursday at 9 PM. Open Saturday from 10 AM to 6 PM, and Sunday from Noon to 6 PM. Closed major holidays. 5216 Montrose Blvd; Houston, TX 77006; Phone: (713) 284-8250; https://camh.org

Cullen Sculpture Garden complements sculptures by Louise Bourgeois, Dan Graham, Henri Matisse, and Auguste Rodin with native trees, bamboo, and flowering crepe myrtle. Admission is free. Open daily 9 AM to 10 PM. 1001 Bissonnet St; Houston, TX 77006; Phone: (713) 639-7300; https://www.mfah.org/visit/cullen-sculpture-garden

Houston Arboretum and Nature Center incorporates several gardens from wildlife to urban. A raised walkway presents views of Buffalo Bayou, and the forest canopy. Free admission. Open daily from 7 AM to dusk. 4501 Woodway Dr; Houston, TX 77024; Phone: (713) 681-8433; https://houstonarboretum.org

Houston Center for Contemporary Craft emphasizes craft materials as art – primarily clay, fiber, glass, metal, wood, and even found and recycled materials. Visit the Artist Hall to meet some of the artists in their studios. Admission is free. Open Wednesday through Saturday from 10 AM to 5 PM. Open Sunday from Noon to 5 PM. Closed major holidays. 4848 Main St; Houston, TX 77002; Phone: (713) 529-4848; https://www.crafthouston.org

Houston Museum of African American Culture exhibits the work of four artists in the greater Houston area. Admission is free. Open Tuesday to Saturday from Noon to 5 PM. 4807 Caroline St; Houston, TX 77004; Phone: (713) 526-1015; http://hmaac.org

Lawndale Art Center features almost 500 artists in an Art Deco building. Admission is free. Open Wednesday, Thursday and Friday from Noon to 6 PM. Open Saturday from 11 AM to 5 PM, and Sunday from Noon to 3 PM. Closed major holidays. 4912 Main St; Houston, TX 77002; Phone: (713) 528-5858; https://lawndaleartcenter.org

Menil Collection features art distributed across the campus, with the main building displaying art from the prehistoric to the present day. Their Cy Twombly Gallery is located next door. Admission is free. Donations are appreciated. Open Wednesday through Sunday from 11 AM to 7 PM. 1533 Sul Ross St; Houston, TX 77006; Phone: (713) 525-9400; https://www.menil.org

Moody Center for the Arts at Rice University is both an art gallery and performance space. Admission to the gallery portion is free. Open Tuesday through Saturday from 10 AM to 5 PM. Closed holidays. Note: Use Campus Entrance 8 at the intersection of University Boulevard and Stockton Street. Houston, TX 77005; Phone: (713) 348-ARTS; https://moody.rice.edu

M/V Sam Houston Boat Tour is a free 90-minute round-trip, educational tour along the Houston Ship Channel. It focuses on the story of the port and maritime industry. Reservation are required and can be made online. Tours are available at 10 AM on Tuesday through Saturday and at again at 2:30 PM on Tuesday, Wednesday, and Friday. Sam Houston Landing; 7300 Clinton Dr, Houston, TX 77020; Phone: (713) 670-2631; https://porthouston.com/sam-houston-boat-tour

Station Museum offers several changing shows each year featuring sculptures, drawings, videos, and photographs. Admission is free. Open Wednesday through Sunday from 11 AM to 6 PM. 1502 Alabama St; Houston, TX 77004; Phone: (713) 529-6900; http://stationmuseum.com

Johnson City, TX (See also Stonewall, TX)

Best known as the hometown of President Lyndon B. Johnson, the town was actually named for his pioneer ancestors. There are several free LBJ-themed places to visit.

Lyndon B. Johnson National Historical Park chronicles story of the 36th President beginning with his ancestors. There is no fee to visit. Donations are gratefully accepted. Sites open for visitors include the **Johnson settlement** where Lyndon Johnson's grandfather and great-uncle established a cattle droving business. There's a log cabin, barns, cooler house, and windmill still standing. **President Johnson's boyhood home** is furnished in the early to mid-1920s period, depicting a rural Texas lifestyle of 75 years ago. The **Visitor Center** features exhibits, artifacts, and an award-winning 14-minute film. Note: The Texas White House is currently closed due to structural concerns. Check the website for latest information. 100 Ladybird La; Johnson City, TX 78636 Phone: (830) 868-7128; https://www.nps.gov/lyjo/index.htm

Katy, TX
Johnny Nelson Katy Heritage Museum features vintage farming equipment and artifacts from the town's agricultural and pioneering history. Admission is free. Open every Thursday through Sunday from 11 AM to 5 PM. 6002 George Bush Dr; Phone: (281) 574-8618; http://cityofkaty.com/rededication-of-katy-heritage-museum

Lackland Air Force Base, TX (See also San Antonio, TX)
The Airman Heritage Museum preserves Air Force history. The museum is free to visit and open to the public, but visitors must call first for information on base access. Open Wednesday and Friday from 9 AM to 3 PM. Open Thursday from 10:30 AM to 5:30 PM and Saturday from 10 AM to 2 PM. Closed all federal holidays. 2051 George Ave (Bldg 5206); JBSA Lackland AFB, TX 78236; Phone: (210) 671-8200; https://myairmanmuseum.org/the-museum

Lake Jackson, TX
Lake Jackson Historical Museum focuses on the history of Lake Jackson including the prehistoric era, the plantation era, development of the area's petrochemical industry, and the founding of modern Lake Jackson. Admission is free. Open Tuesday through Saturday from 10 AM to 4 PM. 249 Circle Way; Lake Jackson, TX 77566; Phone: (979) 297-1570; http://lakejacksonmuseum.org

Sea Center Texas combines a marine aquarium, fish hatchery, and a nature center. Self-guided visitor center and wetland tours are available. Reservations are required for guided hatchery tours. Admission is free, with donations appreciated. Open Tuesday through Saturday from 9 AM to 4 PM, Sunday from 1 PM to 4 PM. 302 Medical Dr; Lake Jackson, TX 77566; Phone: (979) 292-0100; https://tpwd.texas.gov/fishing/sea-center-texas

Langtry, TX
Judge Roy Bean Visitor Center is a combination rest stop and heritage center telling the story of the infamous Hanging Judge. Admission is free. Open daily 8 AM to 5 PM. US 90 at State Loop 25/Torres Ave; Langtry, TX 78871; Phone: (432) 291-3340; https://www.txdot.gov/inside-txdot/division/maintenance/sra-locations.html

La Porte, TX
San Jacinto Battleground State Historic Site brings back the days of 1836, when Texian troops surprised the Mexican army, routing them in only 18 minutes. Tour the San Jacinto Museum of History in the base of the San Jacinto Monument. Exhibits detail more than 400 years of early Texas history. Admission to the monument and museum is free. Note: There is an admission fee for the

observation floor, the movie, and special museum exhibits. Open daily 9 AM to 6 PM. Closed major holidays. 3523 Independence Pkwy S; La Porte, TX 77571; Phone: (281) 479-2431; https://tpwd.texas.gov/state-parks/san-jacinto-battleground

Lockhart, TX
SW Museum of Clocks & Watches honors time-keeping with rare and historically significant horological pieces from around the world, spanning three centuries. Free admission. Open Saturday from 10 AM to 4 PM. 109 E San Antonio St; Lockhart, TX 78644; Phone: (512) 658-3853; http://www.swmuseumofclocks.org

Lubbock, TX
Buddy Holly Statue and West Texas Walk of Fame is a memorial to Lubbock's beloved son, and other West Texas singers and entertainers. Holly's statue is at 19th St and Crickets Ave, across from the Buddy Holly Center (which charges an admission fee). Born Charles Hardin Holley, he was laid to rest in **City of Lubbock Cemetery** at 31st St and Teak Ave where fans still pay their respects. Inside the gate to the right is a road that leads to his grave on the left side of the road. The headstone spells his name the way it was ... Holley. http://civiclubbock.com

Lubbock Lake Landmark is an archaeological, and natural history preserve and a unit of Museum of Texas Tech University. Enjoy a half-mile stroll around the Landmark's central research compound. Inside the visitor center exhibits examine the tools and methods of the investigators as well as the fascinating history that they have uncovered. Free to the public. Open Tuesday through Saturday from 9 AM to 5 PM and Sunday from 1 PM to 5 PM. 2401 Landmark Dr; Lubbock, TX 79415; Phone: (806) 742-1116; http://www.depts.ttu.edu/museumttu/lll

Museum of Texas Tech University showcases its holdings in anthropology, fine arts, clothing and textiles, history, natural sciences, and paleontology. Admission is free. Open Tuesday through Saturday from 10 AM to 5 PM and Sunday from 1 PM to 5 PM. 3301 Fourth St; Lubbock, TX 79415; Phone: (806) 742-2490; http://www.depts.ttu.edu/museumttu

National Ranching Heritage Center takes visitors through the history of ranching in West Texas from late 1700s through the mid-1900s. The self-guided walk along the paved looped path goes past almost 50 buildings, each an example of how early settlers met the challenges of living on the range. Printed maps and smartphone app are available free. Admission is free with donations encouraged. Note: The 30-minute trolley tour will incur a cost. Open Monday through

Saturday from 10 AM to 5 PM and Sunday from 1 PM to 5 PM. 3121 Fourth St; Lubbock, TX 79409; Phone: (806) 742-0498; http://www.depts.ttu.edu/nrhc

Luckenbach, TX
Made famous in 1977 by the song *Luckenbach, Texas (Back to the Basics of Love)* the town is more like the personal property of Hondo Crouch and his friends who throw it open for people to come and enjoy music – both free and fee-based performances. Children are welcomed. US 290 to Farm to Market 1376; Phone (830) 997-3224; http://www.luckenbachtexas.com/events

Lufkin, TX
Museum of East Texas melds art and history. Admission is free. Open Tuesday through Friday from 10 AM to 5 PM, and Saturday through Sunday from 1 PM to 5 PM. 503 N Second St; Lufkin, TX 75901; Phone: (936) 639-4434; http://www.metlufkin.org

Texas Forestry Museum is everything about the past, present, and future of trees. Exhibits include Sawmill Town, Paper Mill, Money Trees, a logging train, fire tower, and Urban Wildscape Trail. There is no charge to visit. Donations gratefully accepted. Open Monday through Saturday from 10 AM to 5 PM. Closed major holidays. 1905 Atkinson Dr; Lufkin, TX 75901; Phone: (936) 632-9535; https://www.treetexas.com/about

McLean, TX
McLean-Alanreed Area Museum is on the historic Route 66 through the Texas Panhandle. Mementos of early settlers include rooms furnished in pioneer style, local history, and records of the World War II German prisoner-of-war camp. Admission is free with donations gratefully accepted. Open March through December on Tuesday through Friday from 10 AM to 4 PM. Note: There is no web presence for this museum. The town also has a historic Route 66 filling station at 219 Gray St. If you didn't see it on the way into town, ask at the museum how to find it. 116 Main St; Phone: (806) 779-2731

Nacogdoches, TX
Durst Taylor House and Gardens interprets the 1840 to 1860 time period and includes a fully functioning smokehouse, blacksmith shop, and chicken coop as well as heirloom gardens and a sugarcane mill. 304 North St; Nacogdoches, TX 75961; Phone: (936) 560-4443; https://www.ci.nacogdoches.tx.us/693/Durst-Taylor-Historic-House-and-Gardens

Old Stone Fort at Stephen F. Austin State University was never actually a fort, although it did serve other functions. Today it is a museum illuminating the history of east Texas, especially from 1690 to the overthrow of the Mexican government in 1836 by Texas revolutionists. Admission is free. Open Tuesday through Saturday from 9 AM to 5 PM and Sunday from 1 PM to 5 PM. 1808 Alumni Dr N; Nacogdoches, TX 75962; Phone: (936) 468-2408; http://www.sfasu.edu/stonefort

Sterne Hoya Museum & Library details Texas history through the lens of the Sterne and Hoya families. Tours are free, donations welcomed. Open Tuesday through Saturday from 10 AM to 4 PM. 211 S. Lanana St; Nacogdoches, TX 75961; Phone: (936) 560-5426; http://www.ci.nacogdoches.tx.us/index.aspx?NID=696

Nederland, TX
There are two free attractions in this small Texas town near the Louisiana border. Both share the same address, and website. Admission to both is free. 1500 Boston Ave; Nederland, TX 77627; https://nederlandtx.com/museums
La Maison Des Acadiens pays tribute to early French settlers of the area, and was built as a replica of an early Acadian home. Phone: (409) 722-0279. **Dutch Windmill Museum** was constructed as a tribute to the town's Dutch settlers. The first floor of the museum honors the late Tex Ritter, the country-and-western music star who called Nederland home. Phone: (409) 723-1545.

Odessa, TX
Ellen Noel Art Museum features rotating exhibitions of historical and contemporary art, and a sculpture and sensory garden. Admission is free. Open Tuesday through Saturday from 10 AM to 5 PM and Thursday to 8 PM. Open Sunday from 2 PM to 5 PM. Closed holidays. 4909 E University Blvd; Odessa, TX 79762; Phone: (432) 550-9696; https://www.noelartmuseum.org

Parker House Ranching Museum details the Parker family story as well as ranching history through period furnishings and exhibits. Admission is free. Open Friday from 10 AM to 4 PM and Saturday from 10 AM to 3 PM. 1118 Maple Ave; Odessa, TX 79761; Phone: (432) 335-9918; http://texaspecostrail.com/plan-your-adventure/historic-sites-and-cities/sites/parker-house-ranching-museum

Presidential Archives and Leadership Library and Bush Family Home documents the history of the Presidency. It also features one of the world's largest collection of campaign memorabilia. The home of the 41st and 43rd Presidents has been restored to how it would have looked Christmas morning in 1948 when George W. was two years old. The Dishong Collection features antique dolls dressed in miniature replicas of the First Ladies' gowns. Admission is free with donations accepted. Open Monday through Friday from 8 AM to 5 PM. 4919 E

University Blvd; Odessa, TX 79762; Phone: (432) 363-7737;
https://shepperdinstitute.com/presidential-archives

Stonehenge Replica reaches a height of 19 feet and can be accessed for free at any time by visitors to the University of Texas of the Permian Basin. Near the Visual Arts Studios. 4901 E University; Odessa, TX 79762;
https://www.utpb.edu/about/docs/utpbcampusmap.pdf

Orange, TX

Shangri La Gardens has gathered over 300 types of plants and a wide variety of wildlife. Free admission. Open Tuesday through Saturday from 9 AM to 5 PM. Closed all major holidays and the last week of December. 2111 W Park Ave; Orange, TX 77630; Phone: (409) 670-9113;
http://starkculturalvenues.org/shangrilagardens

Stark Museum of Art houses a collection of 19th and 20th century Western American art focused on the land, people, and diverse wildlife of the American West plus rare books and manuscripts. Admission is free. Open Tuesday through Saturday from 9 AM to 5 PM. Closed all major holidays as well as the last week of December. 712 Green Ave; Orange, TX 77630; Phone: (409) 886-2787;
http://starkculturalvenues.org/starkmuseum

Pampa, TX

Freedom Museum USA represents all branches of the United States Armed Forces through official and private memorabilia from military and civilian sources. Free admission with donations appreciated. Open Tuesday through Saturday from Noon to 4 PM. 600 N Hobart St; Pampa, TX 79065; Phone: (806) 669-6066;
http://www.freedommuseumusa.com

Pasadena, TX

Heritage Park & Museum is comprised of the original homes of two of the early settlers of the area. The Pomeroy, and the Park families' houses contain vintage furniture and clothing from the 1900s. Admission is free. Open Tuesday through Friday 9:30 AM to 2:30 PM. 204 S Main; Pasadena, TX 77506; Phone: (713) 472-0565; http://pasadenahistoricalsociety.org/?page_id=2

Pearland, TX

Delores Fenwick Nature Center highlights their freshwater, native fish aquarium as well as live animal exhibits. Admission is free although special programs and workshops will incur a fee. Free weekly programming for children is offered Wednesday, Thursday, and Friday. 5750 Magnolia Pkwy; Pearland, TX 77584;

Phone: (281) 652-1960; https://www.pearlandtx.gov/departments/parks-recreation/facilities/delores-fenwick-nature-center

Plano, TX
Interurban Railway Station Museum has been restored to its 1908 condition and displays memorabilia of railway and Plano history. Admission is free with donations accepted. Open Monday through Friday from 10 AM to 2 PM and on Saturday from 1 PM to 5 PM. 901 E 15th St; Plano, TX 75074; Phone: (972) 941-2117; https://interurbanrailwaymuseum.org

Port Bolivar, TX (See Galveston, TX)

Rockport, TX
Fulton Mansion & Education and History Center provides a look at the life of an affluent family in the late 1800s. Admission is free with donations greatly appreciated. Open Tuesday through Saturday from 10 AM to 4 PM and Sunday from 1 PM to 4 PM. 317 S Fulton Beach Rd; Rockport, TX 78382; Phone: (361) 729-0386; http://www.thc.texas.gov/historic-sites/fulton-mansion-state-historic-site

San Angelo, TX
International Waterlily Collection represents the passion of Ken Landon who propagates and hybridizes water lilies to create this stellar assemblage. There is no charge to visit. Open daily. Note: Best time for viewing is from April to October. Civic League Park; 2 S Park St; San Angelo, TX 76903; Phone: (832) 274-3377; http://www.internationalwaterlilycollection.com

San Antonio, TX (See also Lackland Air Force Base, TX)
Alamo is the site of the famous battle for Texas independence from Mexico. It started in December, 1835 when a group of volunteer soldiers occupied the former Franciscan mission. Two months later, on February 23, 1836, a Mexican force began a siege. Ultimately the Texans lost the battle, but not the war. Entrance to the Alamo Church and grounds is free. Open daily September through May from 9 AM to 5:30 PM. Open end of May through early September from 9 AM to 7 PM. Closed Christmas. 300 Alamo Plaza; San Antonio, TX 78205; Phone: (210) 225-1391; http://www.thealamo.org

Fort Sam Houston Museum recounts the history of Fort Sam Houston from its beginning in 1845 to the present day through artifacts, images, and stories. The larger evolution of American military installations, medical service and training is also described. Note: Use the Walters Street gate, north of Interstate 35. Museum visitors without a DoD ID card must stop at the Visitor Center at that gate. All visitors 18 years or older must present a picture ID card. Call the visitor center for more information. Admission is free. Open Tuesday through Friday from 10 AM to 4 PM and Saturday from Noon to 4 PM. Fort Sam Houston, TX 78234; Phone: (210) 221-2651; https://history.army.mil/museums/fieldMuseums/FSHMuseum/index.html

Fort Sam Houston US Army Medical Museum displays medical equipment, uniforms, and vehicles representing the entire period of service of the Army Medical Department from 1775 to the present. There is no charge for admission. Open Tuesday through Thursday from 9 AM to 4 PM, and Friday from 9 AM to Noon. Note: The closest entrance to the museum is through the Military Police checkpoint at the corner of Stanley and Harry Wurzbach Roads off I-410. All individuals in the vehicle must show a picture ID to enter Fort Sam Houston. 2310 Stanley Rd; Fort Sam Houston, TX 78234; Phone: (210) 226-0265; https://ameddmuseum.amedd.army.mil

Friedrich Wilderness Park is home to rare birds and orchids, plus walking trails. Admission is free. Donations accepted. Open daily 7:30 AM to sunset. 21395 Milsa Rd; San Antonio, TX; Phone: (210) 207-3780; https://hikesa.org/friedrich-wilderness-park

Japanese Tea Garden features walkways, stone arch bridges, an island, and a Japanese pavilion all in a former quarry in Brackenridge Park. Free to the public. Open daily from 8 AM to sunset. 3875 N St Mary's St; San Antonio, TX 78212; Phone: (210) 207-3050; http://saparksfoundation.org/japanese-tea-garden

San Antonio Art League and Museum combines paintings, drawings, prints, and photographs with ceramics and sculptures. Free admission. Open Tuesday through Saturday from 10 AM to 3 PM. 130 King William St; San Antonio, TX 78204; Phone: (210) 223-1140; https://www.saalm.org

San Antonio Missions were often a refuge for the people seeking escape from disease, drought, and attacks from Apache. The four missions are: Mission Concepcion at 807 Mission Rd; Mission San Jose at 6701 San Jose Dr; Mission San Juan Capistrano at 9101 Graf Rd; and Mission Espada at 10040 Espada Rd. Note: The Alamo is not part of the San Antonio Missions National Historical Park. Park Rangers and volunteers offer free guided tours of the four mission that make up the trail. Phone: (210) 932-1001; https://www.nps.gov/saan

San Marcos, TX

Central Texas Wing-Commemorative Air Force is housed in a 1943 vintage wooden hangar and is home to historic aircraft including a B-25 Mitchell Bomber, the only flying Bell P-39 fighter plane in the western hemisphere, and a newly restored C-45. The Stokes Library has one of the largest collections of military books – many out of print. Admission is free, however donations are gratefully accepted. Open Monday, Wednesday, Friday, and Saturday from 9 AM to 4 PM.

1841 Airport Dr; Building 2249; San Marcos, TX 78666; Phone: (512) 396-1943; https://www.centraltexasswing.org

LBJ Museum of San Marcos focuses on the years 1927 to 1930 that President Johnson spent in San Marcos at Southwest Texas State Teachers College, now Texas State University. Free admission. Open Thursday through Saturday from 10 AM to 5 PM and Sunday from 10 AM to 3 PM. 131 N Guadalupe St; San Marcos, TX 78666; Phone: (512) 353-3300; https://lbjmuseum.com

Wimberley Glass Works invites visitors to watch artisans create art glass. Open Wednesday through Saturday from 10 AM to 4 PM and Sunday Noon to 4 PM. Closes at 3:30 PM from end of May through the end of August. Closed Easter, Thanksgiving, Christmas, and New Year's Day. 6469 Ranch Rd 12; San Marcos, TX 78666; Phone: (512) 393-3316; https://wgw.com/pages/demonstrations

Wittliff Collections at Texas State University centers on the photography of the Southwest and Mexico, and also includes literary archives of Southwestern writers. Costumes, props, and memorabilia from the mini-series *Lonesome Dove* are on permanent display. Admission is free. Open Monday through Friday from 8:30 AM to 4:30 PM. Closed major holidays. Note: Hours change during holidays, university breaks, and interim sessions. 601 University Dr; Albert B. Alkek Library; 7th floor; San Marcos, TX 78666; Phone (512) 245-2313; https://www.thewittliffcollections.txstate.edu

Shamrock, TX
This is another of the Route 66 towns that once welcomed travelers. Several Art Deco buildings have been restored including a gas station and the U-Drop Inn which is currently the Visitor Information Center.

Stonewall, TX (See also Johnson City, TX)
The **LBJ Ranch and Visitor Center** offers a self-driving tour of the ranch. Pick up a map and free permit. An audio CD is also available for purchase. The Texas White House is not currently open for its tours fee-based tours. Free ranger-guided tours of the grounds are being offered. Hwy 290; Stonewall, TX 78671; Phone: (830) 868-7128; https://www.nps.gov/lyjo/index.htm

Sulphur Springs, TX
Leo St. Clair Music Box Collection began when the Belgian royal family gave Leo St. Clair a music box. Today there are over 150 pieces open to the public in the Sulphur Spring Library. Video clips show the music boxes in operation. Admission is free. Donations accepted. Open Monday through Friday from 9 AM to 6 PM and Saturday from 9 AM to Noon. 611 N Davis St; Sulphur Springs, TX

75482; Phone: (903) 885-4926;
http://www.sulphurspringstx.org/visitors/things_to_do.php

Southwest Dairy Center recreates a dairy barn, complete with silo, and a 1930s kitchen. Admission is free with donations accepted. Open Monday through Friday from 9 AM to 4 PM. 1210 Houston St; Civic Center Complex; Sulphur Springs, TX 75482; Phone: (903) 439-6455;
https://southwestdairyfarmers.com/pages/museum

Sweetwater, TX
National WASP WWII Museum refers to country's first female squadron, formed in 1942. The Army had a crucial need for pilots to deliver newly built trainer aircraft to the flight schools in the South. The 28 experienced civilian female pilots volunteered. Admission is free. Open Tuesday through Saturday from 10 AM to 5 PM and Sunday from 1 PM to 5 PM. 210 Avenger Field Rd (Off I-20 at 210 Loop 170); Sweetwater, TX 79556; Phone: (325) 235-0099;
https://waspmuseum.org

Texarkana, TX (See also Texarkana, AR)
Texarkana is a city split between eastern Texas and Arkansas.
Regional Arts Center features visual arts, including national touring, juried and invitational exhibitions. The exhibits are free to view. Open Tuesday through Saturday from 10 AM to 4 PM. Closed major holidays. 321 W Fourth St; Texarkana, TX 75504; Phone: (903) 792-8681;
http://trahc.org/exhibits-and-events

Vega, TX
This Route 66 town offers the restored 1924 Magnolia Gas Station. Visitors are invited to peer into the windows if it's closed. 222 N Main St; Vega, TX 79092.

Waco, TX
Martin Museum of Art highlights the McMullen-Connally Family Collection featuring the California School of Watercolor that flourished in the 1930s and 1940s. Admission is free. Open Tuesday through Saturday from 10 AM to 5 PM. Open Sunday from 1 PM to 5 PM. Hooper-Schaefer Fine Arts Center; 60 Baylor Ave; Waco, TX 76707; Phone: (254) 710-6371;
http://www.baylor.edu/martinmuseum

Masonic Grand Lodge features a museum on the history of Freemasonry in Texas. Both self-guided and guided tours are available. Admission is free. Open Monday through Friday from 8:30 AM to 4 PM. Museum tour times are offered every half-hour from 9 AM to 1:30 PM except for lunch. 715 Columbus Ave;

Waco, TX 76701; Phone: (254) 753-7395; https://grandlodgeoftexas.org/library-and-museum

Texas Scottish Rite Library & Museum (Lee Lockwood Library) consists of three floors of exhibits tracing the beginnings of Freemasonry in Europe, its migration to North America, and its entry into Texas. There's also American, Texas, and local history. Free admission. Open Monday, Wednesday, and Friday from 10 AM to 2 PM. 2801 W Waco Dr; Waco, TX 76701; Phone: (254) 754-3942; http://texasbrazostrail.com/plan-your-adventure/historic-sites-and-cities/sites/texas-scottish-rite-library-museum-lee-lockwood

Washington, TX
Washington on the Brazos State Historic Site sits on 293 acres of park land and is crucial to understanding Texas history. It was on this site on March 2, 1836 that delegates came together to formally declare their independence from Mexico. From that day until 10 years later the Republic of Texas proudly existed as a separate and unique nation. Several attractions charge a fee to enter, however, the site itself is free to wander and several of the buildings have signs providing information. The **Visitor Center** offers a free gallery with interactive exhibits and original artifacts that highlight key events in the birth of the Republic of Texas. The rotunda in the gallery's center pays homage and recognition to the 59 men who signed the Texas Declaration of Independence. The visitor center is open daily 9:30 AM to 5 PM. 23400 Park Road 12; Washington, TX 77880; Phone: (936) 878-2214; http://wheretexasbecametexas.org

Wichita Falls, TX
Museum of North Texas History offers Native American pottery, oil drilling models, and the Bill Carter collection of handmade, highly detailed replicas of naval vessels. Heritage Hall features 500 western hats known as *Nat's Hats*. Admission is free. Donations are welcome. Open Tuesday through Saturday from 10 AM to 4 PM. Closed major holidays. 720 Indiana Ave; Wichita Falls, TX 76307; Phone: (940) 322-7628; https://www.museumofnorthtexashistory.org/home.html

Wichita Falls Museum of Art at Midwestern State University focuses on American art, including original lithographs, etchings, mezzotints, drawings, watercolors, pastels, and photography. Admission is free. Open Tuesday through Saturday from 10 AM to 5 PM. 2 Eureka Cir; Wichita Falls, TX 76308; Phone: (940) 397-8900; http://www.wfmamsu.org

Utah

Southern Utah is filled with spectacular scenic byways. Note: Although most byways are free, some will require a fee if you plan to stop and park your car. Here are links to listing and descriptions of these roads:

https://www.visitutah.com/things-to-do/road-trips/scenic-byways;
https://www.fhwa.dot.gov/byways/states/UT;
https://www.visitcedarcity.com/scenic-byways-backways/

Blanding, UT

Mule Canyon Ruin shelters well preserved Ancestral Puebloan remains including a kiva and tower as well as a block of rooms. There is no admission fee. The site is open year round. Located about 20 miles south and west of Blanding, UT off Highway 95. Phone (435) 587-1500; https://www.blm.gov/visit/mule-canyon-ruins

Bluff, UT

Bluff Fort creates window into life on the river in the 1880s with one of the original cabins and replicas of other buildings. There's also a Navajo Hogan and Ute teepee. Admission to Bluff Fort is free. Open all year on Monday through Saturday from 9 AM to 5 PM. Closed major holidays. 550 E Black Locust Ave; Bluff, UT 84512; Phone: (435) 672-9995; http://www.hirf.org/fort.html

Hovenweep National Monument is composed of six ancient villages along a 20-mile expanse of mesa tops and canyons at the Utah-Colorado border. Start at the visitor center where you can explore the Square Tower group stretching along Little Ruin Canyon. There is no entrance fee. Hovenweep is open daily, year-round from sunrise to sunset. There are other groups of ruins that can be visited but you must obtain the map at the visitor center. Visitor center is generally open daily from 9 AM to 5 PM. Closed on Tuesday and Wednesday from mid-October through the end of March. Note: Follow the directions on the website rather than rely on a GPS. Phone: (970) 562-4282 x10; https://www.nps.gov/hove/index.htm

Valley of the Gods offers the scenery of Monument Valley on land owned by the Bureau of Land Management (BLM). The seven-mile loop brings pinnacles, monoliths, and buttes. Entrance to the Valley of the Gods is free. The road is unpaved graded gravel and sand accessible for non 4-wheel drive vehicles in dry weather. Hwy 163, 15 miles west of Bluff, UT. Phone: (435) 587-1500; https://bluffutah.org/valley-of-the-gods

Brigham City, UT

Bear River Migratory Bird Refuge and the James V. Hansen Wildlife Education Center offers birding opportunities and views, including a 12-mile auto tour and 1½ miles of trails around the Wildlife Education Center. There is no charge to visit the refuge. Open Tuesday through Friday from 8 AM to 4 PM and the 2nd and 4th Saturday of the month from 10 AM to 4PM. Auto loop is open daily from sunrise to sunset. I-15 exit 363; Brigham City, UT 84302; Phone: (435) 734-6425; https://www.fws.gov/refuge/Bear_River_Migratory_Bird_Refuge

Corinne, UT

ATK Thiokol Rocket Garden displays a complete booster for the space shuttle as well as and rockets from the middle of the century to the 2000s. Free to the public. Open daily in front of their building. 9160 Ut-83; Corinne, UT 84307; Phone: (435) 863-3511; https://www.facebook.com/pages/ATK-Promontory-Rocket-Garden/152364854812457

Robert Smithson's Spiral Jetty comes and goes with the rainfall. Using over 6,000 tons of black basalt rocks and earth from the site, Smithson formed a coil 1,500 feet long and 15 feet wide that winds counterclockwise into the water. The artwork has been donated to Dia Art Foundation. There is no address or phone number, but the Dia website has complete driving directions. https://www.diaart.org/visit/visit/robert-smithson-spiral-jetty

Cedar City, UT

Garth and Jerri Frehner Museum of Natural History features southwestern Utah's history and natural resources. Admission is free. Open Tuesday through Friday from 10:30 AM to 4:30 PM. Science Addition Building; 351 W University Blvd; Cedar City, UT 84720; Phone: (435) 865-8547; https://www.suu.edu/cose/museum

Southern Utah Museum of Art, on the campus of Southern Utah University, features the artwork of regional artists known for their landscapes as well as emerging and distinguished artists from around the country. SUMA is free. Open Tuesday through Saturday from 11 AM to 5 PM and Thursdays from 11 AM to 8 PM. Closed during all Southern Utah University holidays. 13 S 300 W; Cedar City, UT 84720; Phone: (435) 586-5432; https://www.suu.edu/pva/suma

Delta, UT

Great Basin Museum is the story of Millard County and nearby areas. Admission is free. From November through March open Thursday from 1 PM to 5 PM and Friday and Saturday from 10 AM to 5 PM. Summer hours are Monday through Saturday from 10 AM to 5 PM. 45 W Main; Delta, UT 84624; Phone: (435)

864-5013; http://millardcounty.com/index.php/events-festivals/great-basin-museum

Topaz Museum highlights the internment of Americans of Japanese ancestry during WWII. There is no admission fee, but donations are encouraged. Although few buildings remain, the site still has the foundations, concrete-lined excavations, and other ground-level features. The monument is at 10750 W 4500 N. Note: A visit to the museum first is suggested. Museum is open Monday through Saturday from 11 AM to 5 PM. 55 W Main; Delta, UT 84624; Phone: (435) 864-2514; http://www.topazmuseum.org

Fairview, UT
Fairview Museum of History and Art includes sculptures, regional art, and regional history depicted through historical portraits, photographs, diverse historical collections, and a model of a mammoth unearthed at the Mammoth Discovery Site. There is no charge for admission. Open April through October from 11 AM to 5 PM. November through March open Tuesday through Saturday from Noon to 4 PM. 85 N 100 E; Fairview, UT 84629; Phone: (435) 427-9216; http://fairviewmuseum.org

Hill Air Force Base, UT (See also Ogden, UT)
Hill Aerospace Museum displays historic and modern United States Air Force aircraft, missiles, munitions, and artifacts. It is also the site of the Utah Aviation Hall of Fame. Admission is free. Open Monday through Saturday from 9 AM to 4:30 PM. 7961 Wardleigh Rd; Hill AFB, UT 84056; Phone: (801) 825-5817; https://www.hill.af.mil/Home/Hill-Aerospace-Museum

Hyrum, UT
Hardware Ranch Wildlife Management Area offers wildlife viewing, hiking, and other outdoor recreation. The visitor center provides expansive views of the big meadow and opportunities to learn about Rocky Mountain Elk, and other wildlife species. Note: Visitor center is only open during the winter elk viewing season, generally December through February. Admission is free although sleigh rides are available in winter for a fee. Note: There is no food or fuel available. Blacksmith Fork Canyon Rd; Hyrum, UT 84319; Phone: (435) 753-6168; https://wildlife.utah.gov/hardware-visit.html

Layton, UT
Great Salt Lake Shorelands Preserve provides a handicapped-accessible one-mile loop boardwalk with 34 interpretive exhibits highlighted by a 30-foot viewing tower. Admission is free with donations appreciated. April through September open from 7 AM to 8 PM. Open 8 AM to 5 PM the rest of the year. Note: Mosquito repellent is advised. 41 S 3200 W; Layton, UT 84041; Phone: (801)

531-0999; https://www.nature.org/en-us/get-involved/how-to-help/places-we-protect/the-great-salt-lake-shorelands-preserve

Logan, UT
Cache Museum - Daughters of Utah Pioneers showcases artifacts, pictures, and histories of the early settlers of Cache Valley. Free admission. Open June, July, and August on Tuesday through Friday from 11 AM to 5 PM, and Saturday from 10 AM to 1 PM. Open on Wednesday and Thursday from 11 AM to 6 PM the rest of the year. Closed major holidays. 160 N Main St; Logan, UT 84321; Phone: (435)752-5139; http://cachedupmuseum.org/index.html

USU Geology Museum exhibits meteorites, rocks, and minerals with an emphasis on the geology of Utah and the Logan area. Note: Children under the age of 15 must be accompanied by a parent or teacher. Free admission. Open Monday through Friday from 8 AM to 5 PM. Closed on Utah State University holidays. Geology Building; Room 203; 4505 Old Main Hill; USU Campus; Logan, UT 84322; Phone: (435) 797-1273; http://www.geology.usu.edu/information/geology-museum

Moab, UT
Moab Museum of Film and Western Heritage is part of Red Cliffs Lodge, a working ranch and rustic inn as well as the site for early films. The museum houses memorabilia from the early films to the present. Movie and western ranching themes are also present throughout the ranch resort. The museum is self-guided and open to the public daily at no charge. Milepost 14, Highway 128; Moab, UT 84532; Phone: (866) 812-2002; http://redcliffslodge.com/property/moab-museum-film-western-heritage

Ogden, UT (See also Hill Air Force Base, UT)
Ogden Botanical Gardens invites visitors to explore specimen trees, shrubs, and flowering plants in 11 acres along the Ogden River. Admission is free. Generally open daily from 9 AM to 7 PM. 1750 Monroe Blvd; Ogden, UT 84401; Phone: (801) 399-8080; http://www.ogdenbotanicalgardens.org

Orem, UT
Roots of Knowledge Installation at Bingham Gallery Utah Valley University is a stained glass mosaic that depicts and interprets world history starting with the dawn of humanity. It highlights major inventions, important figures, and major world events incorporating actual rocks, fossils, coins, meteorite, petrified wood, and coral. Free and open to the public during library hours. Docents are available to assist drop-in visitors from Monday through Friday from 9 AM to 8 PM and on Saturdays from 11 AM to 5 PM. Note: The stained glass installation relies on exterior lighting so it is best viewed during daylight hours. 800 W University

Pkwy; Orem, UT 84058; Phone: (801) 863-8840; https://www.uvu.edu/rootsofknowledge

Park City, UT

Kimball Art Center curates exhibits across the arts. It is free and open Monday through Friday from 10 AM to 5 PM. Open Saturday and Sunday from Noon to 5 PM. 1401 Kearns Blvd; Park City, UT 84060; Phone: (435) 649-8882; https://kimballartcenter.org

Utah Olympic Park Museums are free attractions located within Utah Olympic Park. The Joe Quinney Winter Sports Center is home to the **Alf Engen Ski Museum** which uses touch screen displays, videos, virtual reality ski theater, games and topographical maps to show the ways people ski. The **George S. and Dolores Doré Eccles Salt Lake 2002 Olympic Winter Games Museum** explores the Olympic Games through a gallery of visual highlights and artifacts. Both are free and open daily from 9 AM to 6 PM. Closed Thanksgiving and Christmas. 3419 Olympic Pkwy; Park City, UT 84098; Phone: (435) 658-4240; https://engenmuseum.org

Provo, UT

Brigham Young University opens its doors to museums with free admission. **BYU Museum of Art** displays exhibits from its permanent collection as well as traveling shows and exhibitions organized by museum curators. General admission is free, but some special exhibitions require a paid ticket. Open Monday through Saturday at 10 AM with seasonal closing hours. Closed major holidays including Pioneer Day. N Campus Dr; Provo, UT 84602; Phone: (801) 422-8287; http://moa.byu.edu

Monte L. Bean Life Science Museum looks at the unique characteristics of planet Earth and how those characteristics sustain life. A highlight is their fiberglass globe with the most current NASA Satellite images. Admission is free and the museum holds free public shows on weekdays at 1 PM and 3 PM during the months of June, July, and August. Open Monday through Friday from 10 AM to 9 PM and Saturday from 10 AM to 5 PM. 645 E 1430 N; Provo, UT 84602; Phone: (801) 422-5050; http://mlbean.byu.edu

Museum of Peoples and Cultures curates special exhibits with free general admission. There is a charge for tours, specific programs, and events. Open Monday through Friday from 9 AM to 5 PM, closing Tuesday at 7 PM. Summer hours are 9 AM to 5 PM. Closed major holidays. 2201 N Canyon Rd; Provo, UT 84602; Phone: (801) 422-0020; http://mpc.byu.edu/home.html

Rockville, UT
Grafton Ghost Town is an abandoned frontier town originally settled by Mormons in 1859. It isn't easy to find but the area is worth exploring. The old Grafton cemetery is nearby. Grafton Heritage Partnership Project is working on restoring the buildings. Turn onto Bridge Road from UT-9 in Rockville. Directions are on the website. Phone (435) 635-2133; http://graftonheritage.org

Salt Lake City, UT
There is extensive Mormon history and sites in Salt Lake City as well as other free sites to explore.
Beehive House was the home of Brigham Young and other Church leaders. Today it is a museum displaying objects belonging to Young and his family. Admission is free. Open daily from 10 AM to 6 PM. 67 E S Temple; Salt Lake City, UT 84150; Phone: (801) 240-2681; https://www.templesquare.com/explore/beehive-house

Chase Home Museum of Utah Folk Art displays the state-owned collection of contemporary folk art. Admission is free. Open in winter on Wednesday through Friday from 11 AM to 4 PM. Open in summer on Tuesday through Saturday from 11 AM to 4 PM. Liberty Park; 1150 S Constitution Dr; Salt Lake City, UT 84105; Phone: (801) 533-5760; https://artsandmuseums.utah.gov/venues

Clark Planetarium features three floors of hands-on, interactive exhibits on space, and beyond including black holes, and possible alien landscapes. Admission to the exhibits is free. Admission to the Hansen Dome and Northrop Grumman IMAX Theatres will incur a fee. Open daily at 10:30 with varied closing hours. Closed Thanksgiving and Christmas Day. 110 S 400 W; Salt Lake City, UT 84101; Phone: (385) 468-7827; https://slco.org/clark-planetarium

Daughters of Utah Pioneers Memorial Museum celebrates Utah's pioneer heritage with six floors of exhibits. No admission fee. Open Monday through Saturday from 9 AM to 4 PM. 300 N Main St; Salt Lake City, UT; 84103; Phone: (801) 532-6479; http://www.dupinternational.org/index.php

Deuel Pioneer Log Home is one of the only two remaining original structures built when the Mormons arrived in the Salt Lake Valley in July 1847. Restored and furnished with authentic artifacts to show the lifestyle of the Mormon pioneers. View the inside through the cabin's door and windows. Free admission. 35 N W Temple; Salt Lake City, UT 84150; Phone: (801) 916-7000; http://mormonhistoricsites.org/deuel-log-home

Fort Douglas Military Museum showcases the history of Fort Douglas and U.S. military with hundreds of weapons, uniforms, and other items. The grounds display cannons, helicopters, and armored vehicles. Free of charge with donations welcomed. Open Tuesday through Saturday from Noon to 5 PM. Closed major holidays. 32 Potter St; Salt Lake City, UT 84113; Phone: (801) 581-1251; https://www.fortdouglas.org/visit

Gilgal Sculpture Garden incorporates 12 original sculptures and over 70 stones engraved with scriptures, poems, and literary texts. There is no admission fee. Open daily from April through September from 8 AM to 8 PM. October through March open 9 AM to 5 PM. Closed major holidays. 749 E 500 S; Salt Lake City, UT 84102; Phone: (801) 972-7860; http://gilgalgarden.org

Governor's Residence was built in 1902 as the home of mining magnate Thomas Kearns. Tours are free and offered during June, July, August, and December by the Utah Heritage Foundation. Tours are held on Thursday from 1 PM to 4 PM, excluding holidays. Note: Advanced reservations are required. Call (801) 533-0858 ext. 104 at least 24 hours in advance. 603 E S Temple; Salt Lake City, UT 84102; https://preservationutah.org/experience/take-a-tour/guided-tours/item/11-kearns-utah-governors-mansion

International Peace Gardens represents countries around the word through architecture and displays. Free admission. Open May through September from dawn until dusk. 1060 S 900 W, Salt Lake City, UT 84104; Phone: (801) 972-7800; http://www.internationalpeacegardens.org

Museum of Church History uses interactive media, films, and demonstrations as well as artifacts and art to explain the history of the Church of Jesus Christ of Latter-day Saints. Free admission. Open Monday through Friday from 9 AM to 9 PM and Saturday from 10 AM to 5 PM. Closed major holidays. 45 N W Temple; Salt Lake City, UT 84150; Phone: (801) 240-4615; https://www.templesquare.com/explore/church-history-museum

Tabernacle Choir has been provides a weekly live broadcast, *Music and the Spoken Word*. The broadcast and weekly choir rehearsals are free and open to the public. Children must be at least eight years of age. Note: Check the schedule at: https://www.templesquare.com/explore/tabernacle-choir

Temple Square can be explored through free tours provided by the Church of Jesus Christ of Latter-day Saint. Tours start on the hour at the flagpole west of the Temple, in the center of the square. Tours are available January through April tours from 9 AM to 7 PM, from May through October until 8 PM, and from November and December until 4 PM. https://www.templesquare.com/tour

Utah State Capitol was constructed between 1912 and 1916 using granite from nearby Little Cottonwood Canyon. The beehive, a symbol of the state of Utah, is featured in the building's interior, exterior, and grounds. Several historic buildings surround the capitol. Free guided and self-guided tours are available. Tours begin on the hour between 9 AM and 4 PM on Monday through Friday, with the exception of state holidays. The capitol is open for self-guided tours on Monday through Friday from 7 AM to 8 PM ending on Friday at 6 PM. Tours are held on Saturday, Sunday, and holidays from 8 AM to 6 PM. 350 N State St; 120 State Capitol; Salt Lake City, UT 84114; Phone: (801) 538-1800; https://utahstatecapitol.utah.gov/visitors-tours/visitors-center

Springville, UT

Springville Museum of Art is known for its collection of twentieth-century Russian and Soviet art. Admission is free. Donations are greatly appreciated. Open Tuesday through Saturday from 10 AM to 5 PM, and Wednesday to 9 PM. Closed major holidays. 126 E 400 S; Springville, UT 84663; Phone: (801) 489-2727; http://www.smofa.org

Vernal, UT

Dry Fork Petroglyphs cover 200 feet of cliff accessible via two self-guided trails. Note: The petroglyphs are located on the privately owned McConkie Ranch. Visitors are requested to respect both the glyphs and the land. There is no admission fee but donations accepted. Open daylight hours all year. 6228 McConkie Rd; Vernal, UT 84078; Phone: (435) 789-6932; http://www.flaminggorgecountry.com/Dry-Fork-Petroglyphs

Uintah County Heritage Museum features displays of the pioneers, Native Americans, miners, soldiers, lawmen, and outlaws who shaped the history of the Uinta Basin. It's also known for its porcelain doll collection representing First Ladies. The doll collection was created by sculptor Phyllis Juhlin Park. Free admission. Donations gratefully accepted. Open Monday through Thursday from 9 AM to 6 PM. Open until 7:30 PM June through August. Open Friday from 9 AM to 6 PM and Saturday from 10 AM to 4 PM. Closed major holidays. 155 E Main; Vernal, UT 84078; Phone: (435) 789-7399; https://www.uintahmuseum.org

Wellinton, UT

John Jarvie Property has long been used by Native Americans, fur trappers, and travelers. Buildings on the property are reconstructions of those owned and used by John Jarvie and include a general store, blacksmith shop, and a two-room dugout where John and his wife Nellie lived temporarily. The dugout was one of the three major hideouts along the aptly named Outlaw Trail. A small cemetery is also on the property. Guided tours are offered daily May through October from 10

AM to 5 PM. Note: It is advised to contact the either the Park Ranger Office at (435) 885-3307 or the Vernal Field Office at (435) 781-4400 to check days and hours. https://www.blm.gov/learn/interpretive-centers/john-jarvie-historic-ranch

Vermont

Barre, VT

Hope Cemetery is famous for the superb craftsmanship and unique designs carved in granite telling the story of the lives and deaths of the people buried there. No entrance fee. Open daily 7 AM to 5 PM. 201 Maple Ave; Barre, VT 05641; Phone: (802) 476-6245; http://vermonter.com/hope-cemetery

Rock of Ages Granite Quarry manufactures the renowned Barre granite. The visitors center screens a video about the quarrying and manufacturing processes as well as displays historic photos and exhibits. Admission is free. Visitors can also watch from an observation deck as the artisans craft the granite. Open from May through October on Monday through Saturday from 10 AM to 4 PM. Closed on holidays and associated days, and July 4th. Note: They also offer a fee-based guided quarry tour. 558 Graniteville Rd; Barre, VT 05654; Phone: (802) 476-3119; https://rockofages.com/tourism

Burlington, VT

Burlington Earth Clock consists of 14 stones in a ring aligned like a compass. Stand in the center and look west to the Adirondack Mountains. The five stones on that side are positioned to mark the horizon where the sun sets at the Solstices, Equinoxes, and the mid-points between those times of the year. The center of the circle is a sundial made of flat granite causing your shadow to tell the time of day. Open sunrise to sunset. Note: There is a seasonal fee for parking. On the Island Line Trail at Oakledge Park; Flynn Ave; Burlington, VT 05401; http://circlesforpeace.orghttps://www.burlingtoncityarts.org/art-public-places

Perkins Museum of Geology offers exhibits and hands-on activities. The museum is free of charge. Open when the university is in session on Monday through Friday from 9 AM to 4 PM. Summer and vacation hours are variable. Visitors are advised to call before coming. Note: Visitors are welcome to collect samples from a pile of waste rocks behind Delehanty Hall as well as add their unwanted specimens. Delehanty Hall; University of Vermont; Trinity Campus; 180 Colchester Ave; Burlington, VT 05405; Phone: (802) 656-8694; https://www.uvm.edu/perkins

East Montpelier, VT (See also Montpelier, VT)

Bragg Farm Sugar House visits include a free guided tour of the family operated maple farm. Open daily from 8:30 AM to 6 PM. 1005 VT Rt 14 N; East Montpelier, VT 05651; Phone: (802) 223-5757; https://braggfarm.com/visit.html

Fairfield, VT

Chester Arthur Historic Site honors the Fairfield-born 21st President of the United States who became President upon the death of James Garfield in September 1881. A granite monument stands next to a small two-room yellow house set back from a gravel road. The building was recreated using an old photograph as a guide and contains interpretive exhibits. Admission is free with donations appreciated. Open from July through mid-October on Saturday and Sunday from 10 AM to 5 PM. 4588 Chester Arthur Rd; Fairfield, VT 05455; Phone: (802) 828-3051; https://historicsites.vermont.gov/directory/arthur

Glover, VT

Bread & Puppet Museum has assembled one of the largest collections of puppets and masks in the world. The puppets recreate scenes from bygone theatrical shows. The collection fills two floors in the barn, spills out into the woodshed, across to the Cheap Art bus, and onto the walls of the Paper-Mache Cathedral behind the barn. Admission is free with donations welcomed. The museum is open daily from June through October from 10 AM to 6 PM as well as before and after evening fee-based performances. There is a museum tour every Sunday at 1 PM during July and August. 753 Heights Rd; Glover, VT 05839; Phone: (802) 525-3031; http://breadandpuppet.org/museum

Museum of Everyday Life is perhaps the only one celebrating humble items of daily life. Special exhibits have explored objects such as the safety pin, and the match, as well as the importance of the lock and key. Open daily from 8 AM to 8 PM, it is described as a *self-service museum* – turn on the lights when you enter, and turn off the lights when you leave. Donations are accepted at the door. Note: The space is not heated. Rt 16 about 5½ miles south of Glover. 3482 Dry Pond Rd; Glover, VT 05839; http://museumofeverydaylife.org

Manchester, VT

Southern Vermont Arts Center highlights the contributions of the original founders of the Southern Vermont Artists with 1,000 paintings, etchings, and sculptures. Admission is free. Open on Tuesday through Saturday from 10 AM to 5 PM and Sunday from Noon to 5 PM. 930 SVAC Dr; Manchester, VT 05254; Phone: (802) 362-1405; https://www.svac.org

Middlebury, VT

Middlebury College Museum of Art offers Asian art, photography, 19th century European and American sculpture, and contemporary prints. Sculptures are sited in various locations around the campus. Admission to the museum is free of charge. Open Tuesday through Friday from 10 AM to 5 PM. Open Saturday and Sunday from Noon to 5 PM. Closed all college holidays. Mahaney Center for the

Arts; 72 Porter Field Rd; Middlebury, VT 05753; Phone: (802) 443-5007; http://museum.middlebury.edu

Montpelier, VT (See also East Montpelier, VT)

Green Mount Cemetery is known for the art of its headstones and memorials. Open sunrise to sunset. 250 State St; Montpelier, VT 05602; Phone: (802) 223-5352; https://enjoyburlington.com/place/greenmount-cemetery

Morse Farm Maple Sugarworks provides free sugar house tours and tasting, multimedia displays in a woodshed theater, a nature trail, country store, and an outdoor farm life museum. Open daily all year. Opens at 9 AM, closing times vary seasonally. Closed Thanksgiving and Christmas. 1168 County Rd; Montpelier, VT 05602; Phone: (800) 242-2740; https://www.morsefarm.com/visit-us

T.W. Wood Gallery highlights American art, and art of central Vermont. Admission is free. Open Tuesday through Saturday from Noon to 4 PM. Located in the Center for Arts and Learning. 46 Barre St; Montpelier, VT 05602; Phone (802) 262-6035; https://www.twwoodgallery.org

Vermont State House has an interesting story. Montpelier became the capitol of Vermont because its citizens voted to privately fund the construction of the state's legislature. This building is the third state house and opened in 1859. Open Monday through Friday 7:45 AM to 4:15 PM. Open Saturday mid-July to mid-October from 11 AM to 3 PM. Closed state holidays. Visitors can take a self-guided tour when the building is open. An informative brochure of the Capitol building and their audio tour are available free of charge. Free guided tours are held July through mid-October on Monday through Friday from 10 AM to 3:30 PM and Saturday from 11 AM to 2:30 PM. 115 State St; Montpelier, VT 05602; Phone: (802) 828-1411; https://vtstatehouse.org

Norwich, VT

Sullivan Museum and History Center covers the history of Norwich University including artifacts and artwork, and the achievements of its alumni going back to 1819. Admissions is free. During the academic year open Monday through Friday from 8 AM to 4 PM and Saturday from 11 AM to 4 PM. 158 Harmon Dr; Northfield, VT 05663; Phone: (800) 468-6679; http://www.norwich.edu/museum

South Royalton, VT

Joseph Smith Birthplace Memorial describes Joseph Smith's family and his early life in New England. Smith published the *Book of Mormon* and is the founder of the Church of Jesus Christ of Latter-Day Saints. Start at the visitor center and then explore the other parts of the site. Guided tours are available at no charge. Some features of the historic site are self-guided. From May through October open Monday through Saturday from 9 AM to 7 PM and on Sunday from 1:30 PM to 7 PM. The rest of the year closes two hours earlier. Special hours during Christmas. 357 LDS Ln; South Royalton, VT 05068; Phone: (802) 763-7742; https://history.lds.org/article/historic-sites/vermont/south-royalton/what-to-expect-when-you-visit-the-joseph-smith-birthplace-memorial

St. Johnsbury, VT

St. Johnsbury Athenaeum features an extensive collection of American and European artists from the late 18th century to the mid 19th century including the famous Hudson River School. Open Monday, Wednesday, and Friday from 10 AM to 5:30 PM, Tuesday and Thursday from Noon to 7 PM, and Saturday from 10 AM to 3 PM. 1171 Main St; St. Johnsbury, VT 05819; Phone: (802) 748-8291; https://www.stjathenaeum.org

Stowe, VT

Helen Day Art Center holds exhibits, art classes, and festivals. Gallery entrance is free with donations accepted. Open Tuesday through Saturday from 10 AM to 5 PM. Gallery is closed between exhibitions. 90 Pond St; Stowe, VT 05672; Phone: (802) 253-8358; https://www.helenday.com

Waterbury, VT

Green Mountain Coffee° offers through interactive displays and videos. Cafe brews a daily variety of free samples. Open Monday through Friday from 7 AM to 5 PM. Open Saturday and Sunday from 8 AM to 5 PM. Closed some major holidays. 1 Rotarian Pl; Waterbury, VT 05676; Phone: (877) 879-2326; https://www.keurig.com/content/greenmountaincoffee-store

Woodstock, VT

Sugarbush Farm offers sampling their flavors of cheese plus maple syrup tastings. The maple syrup display is open all year although actual maple syrup season is in March and April. Open daily from 9 AM to 5 PM. Closed Thanksgiving and Christmas. During the winter and early spring call ahead for hours and road conditions. 591 Sugarbush Farm Rd; Woodstock, VT 05091; Phone: (802) 457-1757; https://sugarbushfarm.com/visit-the-farm

Virginia

Alexandria, VA

Fort Ward Museum & Historic Site is the best preserved of the Union forts and batteries which protected Washington, DC during the Civil War. The museum offers exhibits on Civil War topics, interpretive programs, and tours. There's also exhibits on Alexandria during the Civil War. Admission is free. Donations welcome. Museum is open Tuesday through Saturday from 10 AM to 5 PM and Sunday from Noon to 5 PM. Closed major holidays and adverse weather conditions. The park is open daily from 9 AM to sunset. 4301 W Braddock Rd; Alexandria, VA 22304; Phone: (703) 746-4848; https://www.alexandriava.gov/FortWard

Arlington, VA

Arlington House and the Robert E. Lee Memorial honors Lee for his role in promoting reconciliation after the Civil War. Arlington House has been restored to its historic 1860 appearance and is open for self-guided tours. The Robert E. Lee Museum at Arlington House contains exhibits and artifacts about Robert E. Lee and his family. Slave quarters are on the grounds for a look at the other side of plantation living. There is no fee to visit. Open daily from 10 AM to 4 PM with extended hours in summer (April through September) from 9 AM to 6 PM. Closed major holidays. Located at Arlington National Cemetery; Arlington, VA 22211; Phone: (703) 235-1530; https://www.nps.gov/arho/index.htm

Arlington National Cemetery is the final resting place for John F. Kennedy, the Tomb of the Unknown Soldier, and the Challenger Memorial. There is no charge to visit the cemetery, but the bus tour will incur a fee. Note: It is not possible to drive onto the grounds. Open daily. April through September open from 8 AM to 7 PM. Closes at 5 PM from October through March. Memorial Ave; Arlington, VA 22211; Phone: (877) 907-8585; https://www.arlingtoncemetery.mil

DEA Museum and Visitors Center encompasses the history of the Drug Enforcement Administration and the impact of drug addiction. Its collection has more than 2,000 objects ranging from old patent medicine bottles to modern drug concealment containers. Free admission. Open Tuesday through Saturday from 10 AM to 4 PM. Closed on federal holidays. 700 Army Navy Dr; Arlington, VA 22202; Phone: (202) 307-3463; https://deamuseum.org

National Inventors Hall of Fame Museum recounts the tales behind the famous inventors, the stories of iconic brands, and the inventions that changed the world. Other topics focus on the importance of intellectual property and damage of counterfeit products. Admission is free. Open Monday through Friday from 10

AM to 5 PM and Saturday from 11 AM to 3 PM. Closed some major holidays. 600 Dulany St; Alexandria, VA 22314; Phone: (571) 272-0095; http://www.invent.org/honor/hall-of-fame-museum

U.S. Marine Corps War Memorial – Iwo Jima Memorial represents the heroism of the Marines and those who have fought beside them. The statue reproduces the photograph taken by Joe Rosenthal of the Associated Press. Sculptor Felix W. de Weldon later constructed a scale model and then a life-size model of the image. Parking may be subject to restrictions The memorial grounds are open year-round from 6 AM until Midnight. The memorial is located on Arlington Ridge along the axis of the National Mall. Phone: (703) 289-2500; https://www.nps.gov/gwmp/planyourvisit/usmc_memorial.htm

Big Stone Gap, VA
Harry W. Meador Coal Museum was named after Harry W. Meador, an advocate of the coal mining industry who rose from union laborer to the Vice President of Coal Development. The museum displays photographs, mining equipment and tools, office equipment, coal company items, and a small dentist office from the early 1900s. Admission is free. Open Wednesday through Saturday from 10 AM to 5 PM and Sunday from 1 PM to 5 PM. E Third St and Shawnee Ave; Big Stone Gap, VA 24219; Phone (276) 523-9209; http://www.bigstonegap.org/attract/coal.htm

Chantilly, VA
Steven F. Udvar-Hazy Center is part of the Smithsonian's National Air and Space Museum, displaying thousands of aviation and space artifacts, including a Lockheed SR-71 Blackbird, a Concorde, and the Space Shuttle Discovery. Visitors can also view the Mary Baker Engen Restoration Hangar from a glassed-in mezzanine. Admission is free and the museum offers free docent tours daily. Some attractions will incur a cost. 14390 Air and Space Museum Pkwy; Chantilly, VA 20151; Phone: (703) 572-4118; https://airandspace.si.edu/udvar-hazy-center

Charlottesville, VA
Fralin Museum of Art at the University of Virginia highlights European and American painting, photography, works on paper, African art, and American Indian art. Admission is free. Donations are welcomed. Open Tuesday through Saturday from 10 AM to 5 PM. Open late Thursday to 7 PM. Open Sunday from Noon to 5 PM. Closed some major holidays. 155 Rugby Rd; Charlottesville, VA 22903; Phone (434) 924-3592; http://uvafralinartmuseum.virginia.edu

Kluge-Ruhe Aboriginal Art Collection is the largest collection of Indigenous Australian art outside Australia, with objects and paintings created by Aboriginal and Torres Strait Islander artists from different regions of Australia. Admission is free. There is a free guided tour every Saturday at 10:30 AM. Open Tuesday through Saturday from 10 AM to 4 PM. Open late on Thursday to 8 PM. Open Sunday 1 PM to 5 PM. Closed most major holidays. 400 Worrell Dr; Charlottesville, VA 22911; Phone (434) 244-0234; https://kluge-ruhe.org

Leander McCormick Observatory at the University of Virginia is open on the first and third Friday night of every month (except holidays) year round. View celestial objects through the historic 26-inch McCormick Refractor and other smaller telescopes (weather permitting), tour the observatory, hear a presentation by an astronomer, and see the exhibits. No tickets are required and advanced reservations are not necessary. Hours are seasonal. Call to verify before you visit. University of Virginia; McCormick Rd; Charlottesville, VA 22904; Phone: (434) 243-1885; http://astronomy.as.virginia.edu/public-outreach/observatory-public-night-program

Christiansburg, VA
Duncan Imports and Classic Cars displays classic cars from many different eras as well as Japanese domestic right-hand-drive vehicles. There is no admission to admire their cars. Open Monday through Friday from 8:30 AM to 5 PM and Saturday from 9 AM to 2 PM. 2300 Prospect Dr; Christiansburg, VA 24073; Phone: (540) 808-6433; http://www.duncanimports.com/used-inventory/index.htm

Falls Church, VA
Tinner Hill Historic Park is on the site of the home of Joseph and Elizabeth Tinner who fought the segregation laws that cut through their community and which led to the first rural branch of the NAACP. The Zig Zag Monument follows the original location of the segregation line. Admission is free. Open daily from dawn until dusk. 106 Tinner Hill Rd; Falls Church, VA 22042; Phone: (703) 729-0596; https://www.tinnerhill.org

Farmville, VA
Robert Russa Moton Museum honors the first non-violent student demonstration (1951) which lead to the ground-breaking Brown v. Board of Education of Topeka. The 1951 Moton Student Strike produced three-fourths of the plaintiffs in that famous case. The Supreme Court ultimately declared state laws establishing separate public schools for black and white students to be unconstitutional. Admission is free. Open Monday through Saturday from Noon to 4 PM. 900 Griffin Blvd; Farmville, VA 23901; Phone (434) 315-8775; http://www.motonmuseum.org

Ferrum, VA

Blue Ridge Institute & Museum curates exhibits on life in Appalachia emphasizing lifeways and folkways. Admission is free. Spring, fall, and winter open Monday through Saturday from 10 AM to 4 PM. From mid-May to mid-August open Monday through Saturday from 10 AM to 5 PM and Sunday from 1 PM to 5 PM. Note: There is a fee to visit the seasonally open Farm Museum across the road. 20 Museum Dr; Ferrum, VA 24088; Phone: (540) 365-2121; http://www.ferrum.edu/blueridgeinstitute

Fort Monroe, VA

Fort Monroe - Casemate Museum chronicles over 400 years of social and military history including the Contraband Decision of 1861 which determined that escaped slaves were contraband and could not be returned to their owners. The cell where Jefferson Davis was imprisoned after the Civil War is also recreated. Admission is free. Open October through April on Tuesday through Sunday from 10:30 AM to 4:30 PM. May through September open daily from 10:30 AM to 4:30 PM. Closed major holidays. 20 Bernard Rd; Fort Monroe, VA 23651; Phone: (757) 788-3391; https://fortmonroe.org/visit/casemate-museum

Fredericksburg, VA

The battle of Fredericksburg is considered to be one of the most one-sided battles of the Civil War. General Robert E. Lee faced Major General Ambrose Burnside on the heights behind the city, and lost badly. Union casualties were more than twice that of the Confederate troops. Visitors to the park can take a self-guided driving tour stopping at both Union and Confederate locations along the way. https://www.nps.gov/frsp/planyourvisit/maps.htm

Chatham Manor played a vital role in the Civil War as a Union headquarters, hospital, and soup kitchen. It is now the headquarters of Fredericksburg and Spotsylvania National Military Park offering five rooms of exhibits. Park volunteers give tours of the buildings. A 12-minute film is shown on the history of Chatham and a 32-minute film explains the Fredericksburg civilian experience during the Civil War. Entrance to the park and all buildings is free. The Manor is located about 1½ miles from the visitor center. 120 Chatham Ln; Fredericksburg, VA 22405; Phone: (540) 693-3200; https://www.nps.gov/frsp/learn/historyculture/chatham.htm

Fredericksburg Battlefield Visitor Center provides look through the exhibits. Open daily 9 AM to 5 PM. Take a self-guided walking tour of the Sunken Road, and a self-guided driving tour of the battlefields. Note: there is a cost to watch a 22-minute orientation film. 1013 Lafayette Blvd, Fredericksburg, VA 22401; Phone: (540) 693-3200.

Galax, VA

Blue Ridge Music Center provides free *Mid-Day Mountain Musicians* in the visitor center breezeway from Noon to 4 PM. Visitor center is open the month of May on Thursday through Monday, and open daily from the end of May through beginning of November. The Music Center is also home to the free interactive *Roots of American Music* museum exhibit. Blue Ridge Parkway @ Milepost 123; Galax, VA 24333; Phone: (276) 236-5309; http://blueridgemusiccenter.org

Hardy, VA

Booker T. Washington National Monument presents exhibits on the life of Booker T. Washington in the visitor center. The Plantation Trail is a ¼ mile loop through reconstructions of the 19th century farm buildings. Admission is free. Open daily from 9 AM to 5 PM. Closed Thanksgiving, Christmas, and New Year's Day as well as during inclement weather. 12130 Booker T. Washington Hwy; Hardy, VA 24101; Phone: (540) 721-2094; https://www.nps.gov/bowa/index.htm

Lexington, VA

Lee Chapel and Museum contains Lee's office and an exhibition focused on the contributions to education made by George Washington, and Robert E. Lee as well as changing exhibits. Admission is free with donations appreciated. From April through October open Monday through Saturday from 9 AM to 5 PM. Open Sunday from 1 PM to 5 PM. Closes at 4 PM the rest of the year. Also closed Easter Sunday, Thanksgiving recess, and Christmas through New Year's Day. Washington & Lee University; 100 N Jefferson St; Lexington, VA 24450; Phone: (540) 458-8768; https://www.wlu.edu/lee-chapel-and-museum

Stonewall Jackson Memorial Cemetery offers the tomb of the famous Confederate General. Open daily from sunrise to sunset. Maps of the cemetery may be obtained at the Lexington Visitor Center at 106 E Washington Street. The cemetery is located at 316 S Main St; Lexington, VA 24450; Phone: (540) 463-3777; https://www.virginia.org/listings/HistoricSites/StonewallJacksonMemorialCemetery

Virginia Military Institute is the nation's oldest state-supported military college. The museum has items related to Jackson's Civil War years. The Henry Stewart Collection includes antique firearms. The museum is open daily from 9 AM to 5 PM. Free cadet guided tours are offered daily at Noon, dependent on cadet availability. Meet in the lobby of the VMI Museum in Jackson Memorial Hall, Level 200. Dress parades are held throughout the school year on Friday at 4:15

PM, weather permitting. Call ahead to confirm the parade schedule, and availability of cadet tours. 415 Letcher Ave; Lexington, VA 24450; Phone: (540) 464-7334; https://www.vmi.edu/museums-and-archives/vmi-museum

Luray, VA

Luray Singing Tower, officially known as the Belle Brown Northcott Memorial, contains a carillon of 47 bells. Free recitals are held throughout the spring, summer, and fall. A tour of the upper tower incurs a cost, and requires climbing 108 steps. The carillon is situated in a park opposite Luray Caverns. Northcott Dr; Luray, VA 22835; Phone: (540) 742-7273; http://www.luraysingingtower.com/about.html

Manassas, VA

Manassas National Battlefield Park offers several opportunities to explore its history from a fiber-optic battle map to self-guided driving tours, and ranger guided walking tours. The Brawner Farm Interpretive Center and the historic Stone House are both open seasonally. Entrance to Manassas National Battlefield Park is free. All programs and buildings are free with donations accepted. Visitor center is open daily from 8:30 AM to 5 PM. Closed on Thanksgiving, and Christmas Day. The park is open daily from dawn to dusk. 6511 Sudley Rd; Manassas, VA 20109; Phone: (703) 361-1339; https://www.nps.gov/mana/index.htm

Mount Jackson, VA

Route 11 Potato Chips Factory invites visitors to watch the making of potato chips through large windows in their retail store. There are no walk-through tours. Free and open to the public Monday through Saturday from 9 AM to 5 PM. Closed on major holidays. 11 Edwards Way; Mount Jackson, VA 22842; Phone (540) 477-9664; http://www.rt11.com/viewing

Orange, VA

Ellwood Manor is part of the Fredericksburg and Spotsylvania National Military Park. It offers the family cemetery where General Stonewall Jackson's arm is buried as well as the story behind the interment of his limb. Historic Ellwood Manor features two rooms of exhibits about the house and the Battle of the Wilderness as well as a recreated headquarters scene. Volunteers staff the building, lead tours, and answer questions on Saturday and Sunday from 10 AM to 5 PM in season. At other times visitors can park outside the gate and walk onto the grounds. 36380 Constitution Hwy; Orange, VA 22960; Phone: (540) 693-3200; https://www.nps.gov/frsp/learn/historyculture/ellwood.htm

Richmond, VA

Capitol Square encompasses 12 acres and includes the State Capitol, Executive Mansion, and statuary. The entrance is at Ninth and Grace Streets The grounds are open daily from 6 AM to 11 PM.
https://virginiacapitol.gov/index.php/virginia-state-capitol/capitol-square/

Chimborazo Hospital Medical Museum is part of Richmond National Battlefield Park and focuses on the Confederate medical story, containing exhibits on medical equipment and hospital life in the 1860s. There is no admission fee. Generally opened 9 AM to 5 PM. Winter hours are Wednesday through Sunday from 9 AM to 4:30 PM. Closed major holidays. 3215 E Broad St; Richmond, VA, 23223; Phone: (804) 226-1981;
https://www.nps.gov/rich/learn/historyculture/chimborazo.htm

Executive Mansion is the home of the governor and family. Three of the original buildings on the grounds remain; the main house, cookhouse, and the carriage house. Tours are free and given Tuesday, Wednesday, and Thursday from 10 AM to Noon and again from 2 PM to 4 PM. Capitol Square, Richmond, VA 23224; Phone: (804) 358-5511; https://www.executivemansion.virginia.gov

Institute for Contemporary Art at Virginia Commonwealth University curates several exhibits each year. Free and open to the public although there may be a charge associated with some of the events. Open Tuesday through Sunday from 10 AM to 6 PM. Open late Wednesday to 8 PM. 601 W Broad St; Richmond, VA 23220; Phone: (804) 828-2823; https://icavcu.org

Maggie L. Walker National Historical Site commemorates the life of Maggie L. Walker, a Black American woman who was the first female founder/president of a chartered bank in the United States. There is no admission fee. Open Tuesday through Saturday from 9 AM to 5 PM. Closed major holidays. Ranger-guided tours start each hour from 10 AM to 4 PM. There is also a 20-minute film, *Carry On: The Life and Legacy of Maggie Lena Walker*. 600 N Second St; Richmond, VA 23219; Phone: (804) 771-2017; https://www.nps.gov/mawa/index.htm

Tredegar Iron Works was the Confederacy's leader in the production of artillery, ammunition, and war-related materials. Part of Richmond National Battlefield Park, it houses the visitor center with three floors of exhibits including a map room, displays on the Richmond military and home front, and the Park's orientation film to Richmond's battlefields. Open daily from 9 AM to 5 PM. The grounds contain machinery and related exhibits that address more than 100 years of iron-making. 470 Tredegar St; Richmond, VA, 23223; Phone: (804) 226-1981; https://www.nps.gov/rich/index.htm

University of Richmond Museum is comprised of three museums and galleries that display an array of art, artifacts, and natural history specimens; **Joel and Lila Harnett Museum of Art**, the **Joel and Lila Harnett Print Study Center**, and the **Lora Robins Gallery of Design from Nature**. All the university museums are free and are open Sunday through Friday from 1 PM to 5 PM. Closed for university events and holidays as well as semester breaks. They recommend checking the dates for each exhibition prior to visiting. University of Richmond; Richmond, VA 23173; Phone: (804) 289-8000; https://museums.richmond.edu

Virginia Museum of Fine Arts has an expansive permanent collection, with particular emphasis on Black American art, Fabergé and Russian decorative arts, and photography. Admission is free, although some of the special exhibits will require fee-based tickets. Free walk-in tours are given daily, excluding holidays, and are subject to docent availability. Open daily from 10 AM to 5 PM and on Thursday and Friday until 9 PM. 200 N Arthur Ashe Blvd; Richmond, VA 23220; Phone: (804) 340-1400; https://www.vmfa.museum

Virginia State Capitol was designed by Thomas Jefferson in 1785. Brochures for self-guided tours are available for download and at the information desk inside the Bank Street entrance. The Capitol building is open to visitors Monday through Saturday from 9 AM to 5 PM and Sundays from 1 PM to 5 PM. Closed major holidays. 1000 Bank St; Richmond, VA 23219; Phone: (804) 698-1788; https://virginiageneralassembly.gov/virginiaStateCapitol.php

Roanoke, VA
Roanoke is home to the **Roanoke Star**, the largest, free-standing illuminated star in the world. Perched atop Mill Mountain on Mill Mountain Parkway, it overlooks the surrounding valley and Blue Ridge Mountains. https://www.playroanoke.com/the-roanoke-star/
Community Arboretum on the campus of Virginia Western Community College features ten separate gardens and plant collections. Free admission. Open daily from sunrise to sunset. 3094 Colonial Ave SW; Roanoke, VA 24015; Phone: (540) 857-6388; http://www.virginiawestern.edu/arboretum/index.php

Eleanor D. Wilson Museum at Hollins University features artwork in a variety of media – paintings, photographs, and works on paper. Located on the first floor of the Richard Wetherill Visual Arts Center. Admission is free. Open Tuesday through Sunday from Noon to 5 PM and Thursday to 8 PM. Hollins University; 8009 Fishburn Dr; Roanoke, VA 24020; Phone: (540) 362-6532; https://www.hollins.edu/museum/index.shtml

Taubman Museum of Art exhibitions are drawn from collections around the world, regional artists, and the museum's permanent collection of American art from the 19th and early 20th centuries. Do not miss their rotating exhibit of the gorgeous jeweled purses of Judith Leiber. Free general admission although some special exhibits charge a fee. Open Wednesday through Saturday from 10 AM to 5 PM and Sunday from Noon to 5 PM. Closed major holidays. 110 Salem Ave SE; Roanoke, VA 24011; Phone: (540) 342-5760; https://www.taubmanmuseum.org

Spotsylvania, VA
Spotsylvania County Museum emphasizes the Battle of Spotsylvania, and the life of early Woodland Indians through artifacts, photographs and documents. There is no admission fee. The museum is open daily from 9 AM to 5 PM. Closed some major holidays. 9019 Old Battlefield Blvd; Spotsylvania, VA 22553; Phone (540) 507-7278; http://spotsylvaniamuseum.org

Triangle, VA
National Museum of the Marine Corps, adjacent to Quantico Marine Corps Base, focuses on the history of the Marines. There are aircraft suspended from the ceiling and tanks in the lobby. Interactive exhibits simulate boot camp. Visitors can test rifle skills with a laser-designated target acquisition M-16 at the rifle range. Admission is free as are the docent-led tours. Open daily from 9 AM to 5 PM except Christmas Day. 18900 Jefferson Davis Hwy; Triangle, VA 22172; Phone: (800) 397-7585; https://www.usmcmuseum.com

Woodford, VA
Stonewall Jackson Shrine at Fredericksburg & Spotsylvania National Military Park preserves the plantation office building where the famous General died. He was mistakenly shot by his own men on the night of May 2, 1863 at the Battle of Chancellorsville, dying of pneumonia on May 10th. The National Park Service has augmented some of the items used during Jackson's stay with other pieces and reproductions from the era to recreate the scene. Admission is free. Open Saturday, Sunday and Monday from 9 AM to 5 PM. 12019 Stonewall Jackson Rd; Woodford, VA 22580; Phone: (804) 633-6076; https://www.nps.gov/frsp/learn/historyculture/jds.htm

Washington, DC

This is probably the most budget-friendly destination in the country, if you ignore the high price of hotels and food. All government-sponsored destinations are free, your tax dollars working for you, plus numerous museums and art galleries. The DC tourism site is excellent, conveniently listing all these places.
https://washington.org/free-things-to-do

Nonetheless, here are a few gems that are free, and perhaps a bit under-the-radar.

Belmont-Paul Women's Equality National Monument explores the legacy of Alice Paul, and the 20th century women's rights movement. Admission is free. Open Wednesday through Sunday from 9 AM to 5 PM with free guided tours offered throughout the day. 144 Constitution Ave NE; Washington, DC 20002; Phone: (202) 543-2240; https://www.nps.gov/bepa/index.htm

Carter G. Woodson Home National Historic Site honors the work of Carter G. Woodson who co-founded the Association for the Study of Negro Life and History, Inc., now known as the Association for the Study of African American Life and History, Inc. (ASALH). The site focuses on the contributions of Black Americans to American history, and culture. Admission is free. Open Thursday, Friday, and Saturday from 9 AM to 5 PM. 1538 Ninth St NW; Washington, DC 20001; Phone: (202) 426-5961; https://www.nps.gov/cawo/index.htm

Congressional Cemetery was the first truly national burial ground. There is no admission fee. Open to the public daily from dawn to dusk. Note: Cars are not allowed in the cemetery, but visitors are welcomed to walk around the grounds and explore the history. 1801 E St SE; Washington, D.C. 20003; Phone: (202) 543-0539; https://congressionalcemetery.org

Culture House DC (Blind Whino) is a neighborhood church turned psychedelic arts collective. It features visual, musical, culinary, and performance arts. Their iconic exterior is the work of HENSE, also known as Alex Brewer. The inside is free to visit Saturday and Sunday from Noon to 5 PM and Wednesday from 5 PM to 8 PM. 700 Delaware Ave SW; Washington, DC 20024; Phone: (202) 554-0103; https://www.culturehousedc.org/visit

Folger Shakespeare Library Reading Room holds what maybe the world's largest Shakespeare collection. Admission is free. Open Monday through Saturday from 10 AM to 5 PM. Closed Thanksgiving, and Christmas Day. Guided weekend tours are also free, although reservations are required. 201 E Capitol St SE; Washington, DC 20003; Phone: (202) 544-4600; https://www.folger.edu/reading-room-tour

Ford's Theatre National Historic Site is a rare place to visit, presenting the complete story of the assassination of Abraham Lincoln, the 16th President of the United States. He was shot in Ford's Theatre on April 14, 1865. Mortally wounded, Lincoln was carried across the street to Petersen's boarding house. On April 15, 1865, President Lincoln died in the Petersen House. Ford's Theatre National Historic Site protects the theater, and Petersen House, and includes a museum about the assassination. Admission is free. Open daily except Thanksgiving, and Christmas Day. A purchased ticket is required to attend performances, rehearsals and special events at Ford's Theatre. In most cases the Petersen House will remain open even if the theater is closed for a performance. Ford's Theatre National Historic Site is open for tours from 9 AM to 5 PM. Note: Tickets are required to tour the historic site. These tickets are free, however there is a $3 fee if you want to reserve a specific time. To reserve a ticket call (888) 616-0270 or visit http://www.fords.org/visit/historic-site. 511 10th St NW; Washington, DC 20004; Phone: (202) 426-6924; https://www.nps.gov/foth/index.htm

Franciscan Monastery of the Holy Land in America reproduces Holy Land shrines in their garden. Daily tours of the church and seasonal tours of gardens are available. Admission and guided tours are free with donations greatly appreciated. Gardens and the shrines are open daily from 9 AM to 4:45 PM. 1400 Quincy St NE; Washington, DC 20017; Phone: (202) 526-6800; https://myfranciscan.org/visit

Mary McLeod Bethune Council House was the first headquarters of the National Council of Negro Women (NCNW) and was Mary McLeod Bethune's last home in Washington, DC. Bethune was the first person in her family born free, and the only person in her family with a formal education. She founded the Daytona Normal and Industrial School for Negro Girls in 1904. Today Bethune-Cookman College in Daytona is a fully accredited university. The Council House is free and open to the public for free tours on Thursday, Friday, and Saturday between 9 AM and 4 PM. 1318 Vermont Ave NW; Washington, DC 20005; Phone: (202) 673-2402; https://www.nps.gov/mamc/index.htm

National Bonsai & Penjing Museum at the U.S. National Arboretum is the world's first bonsai museum. There is no charge for admission to the arboretum or the museum. Open daily from 10 AM to 4 PM. Closed federal holidays. The U.S.

National Arboretum has slightly different hours and is open daily from 8 AM to 5 PM. Closed Christmas Day. 3501 New York Ave NE; Washington D.C. 20002; Phone: (202) 396-3510; https://www.bonsai-nbf.org/bonsai-museum

Rock Creek Cemetery combines lush landscaping, famous sculptures, and notable history as Washington's oldest cemetery dating back to 1719. Open daily from 8 AM to 7 PM including holidays. The cemetery office is open Monday through Friday from 9 AM to 5 PM. The office is closed on all holidays. 201 Allison St NW; Washington, DC 20011; Phone: (202) 726.2080; https://www.stpaulsrockcreek.org/cemetery

Washington State

North Cascades National Park encompasses a significant portion of the state, offering jagged peaks crowned by more than 300 glaciers and cascading waters. There is no fee to enter North Cascades National Park. Although private companies offer fee-based activities, the park provides interpretive programs, ranger-led walks and talks throughout the summer at no cost. See the details for each area of the park: https://www.nps.gov/noca/index.htm

Ashford, WA
Ex-Nihilo Sculpture Park, meaning roughly "something created from nothing," showcases the artwork of Dan Klennert who creates recycled iron sculptures. There is no admission but donations are definitely appreciated. The outdoor park is open all year. 22410 WA-706; Ashford, WA 98304; https://visitrainier.com/ex-nihilo-sculpture-park

Bainbridge Island, WA
The Bainbridge Island Japanese American Exclusion Memorial is an outdoor exhibit remembering the internment of Japanese Americans from Bainbridge Island. Open daily. Pritchard Park; 4192 Eagle Harbor Dr; Bainbridge Island, WA 98110; Phone: (206) 855-9038; http://bijaema.org/visit

Bainbridge Island Museum of Art features contemporary art and craft of the Puget Sound region. Admission is free. Open daily from 10 AM to 6 PM. 550 Winslow Way E; Bainbridge Island, WA 98110; Phone: (206) 842-4451; https://www.biartmuseum.org

Bellingham, WA
The city offers a 42-stop self-guided Downtown Bellingham Historic Walking Tour. Tour booklets are available at the Bellingham Visitor Center 904 Potter St; Bellingham, WA 98229; Phone: (360) 6713990.

Western Washington University Western Gallery and Outdoor Sculpture Collection presents temporary exhibitions concentrating on national and international art as well as Northwest paintings. The Outdoor Sculpture Collection showcases 29 pieces created by some of the world's best loved sculptors. Both the gallery and sculpture garden are free to the public. The Western Gallery is open Monday through Friday from 10 AM to 4 PM and Saturday from Noon to 4 PM. Museum closings follow the university calendar. The Outdoor Sculpture Collection is open at all times to the public. Washington University; 516 High St; Bellingham, WA 98225; Phone: (360) 650-3963; https://westerngallery.wwu.edu/sculpture

Bellevue, WA
Kelsey Creek Farm retains a country life with ponies, sheep, chickens, pigs, and ducks in a 1930s farm setting. There are no entrance fees. Open daily from 9:30 AM to 3:30 PM. 410 130th Pl SE; Bellevue, WA 98008; Phone: (425) 452-7688; http://www.farmerjayne.com

Blaine, WA
Alaska Packers Association Cannery Museum explains the history of processing salmon in an original cannery building using a scale model fish trap, antique machinery, gallery of historic photos, and an original 29-foot Bristol Bay sailboat. Admission is free with donations welcomed. Open Memorial Day through September on Friday, Saturday, Sunday from 1 PM to 5 PM. 9261 Semiahmoo Pkwy; Blaine, WA; Phone: (360) 371-3558; http://www.draytonharbormaritime.com/apa.html

Bremerton, WA
Bug (and Reptile) Museum Gift Shop is the place if you or your family love live bugs. There's a giant ant farm, and a microscope to help see the ants at work. Special glasses simulate the way bugs see the world. Admission is free. Open daily 10 AM to 5 PM. 1118 Charleston Beach Rd W; Bremerton, WA 98312; http://www.bugmuseum.com

Elandan Gardens beckons lovers of bonsai. These miniature trees are set among ponds, waterfalls, sculptures, and gardens. The site is shared with Elandan Interiors and the studio of sculptor Will Robinson. Open November through April on Friday, Saturday, and Sunday from 10 AM to 4 PM. 3050 W State Hwy 16; Bremerton, WA 98312; Phone: (360) 373-8260; http://www.elandangardens.com

Everett, WA
Jetty Island is a human-created island and park just off the Everett waterfront. A free daily summer ferry transports visitors across the Snohomish River from July 5th through Labor Day. It is the only way on and off the island. You can pick up boarding passes at the Jetty Island kiosk at Jetty Landing Park. Return passes can be picked up once you arrive at the Jetty. Monday through Friday from 9 AM to 5 PM. Phone: (425) 257-8304; http://www.portofeverett.com/marina/facilities/jetty-island

Schack Art Center curates exhibits from locally and internationally known and emerging artists. Visitors can also watch professional glassblowers at work. Admission to the gallery is free. Open Monday through Friday from 10 AM to 6 PM. Open Saturday from 10 AM to 5 PM and on Sunday from Noon to 5 PM.

Closed major holidays. 2921 Hoyt Ave; Everett, WA 98201; Phone: (425) 259-5050; https://www.schack.org

Federal Way, WA
Pacific Bonsai Museum displays 50 to 60 of the museum's 150 bonsai in an open air museum. Admission is free but donations greatly appreciated. Open Tuesday through Sunday from 10 AM to 4 PM. Closed major holidays. Note: Museum may close during inclement weather. 2515 S 336th St; Federal Way, WA 98003; Phone: (253) 353-7345; http://www.pacificbonsaimuseum.org

Fife, WA
Fife History Museum illustrates the impact of Native American, Swiss, Italian, Japanese, Scandinavian and Dutch groups on the area. Museum admission is always free. Open Wednesday, Thursday, and Friday from 11 AM to 4 PM. 2820 54th Ave E; Fife, WA 98424; Phone: (253) 896-4710; http://www.fifehistorymuseum.org

Friday Harbor, WA
San Juan Island National Historical Park offers both vistas and history. In 1859 the United States and Great Britain nearly went to war over possession of the island. The so-called Pig War started when an American settler shot a British pig on the island claimed by both nations. This resulted in two distinct camps – the American Camp and the English Camp. Hike the trails. Learn about the park's historic and prehistoric periods with artifacts from both camps. There is no fee to enter San Juan Island National Historical Park however the island can only be reached by air or ferry service and will incur that cost. American Camp: 4668 Cattle Point Rd; Friday Harbor, WA 98250; Phone: (360) 378-2240. British Camp: 3905 W Valley Rd; Friday Harbor, WA 98250; (360) 378-4409; https://www.nps.gov/sajh/index.htm

Grand Coulee, WA
Grand Coulee Dam includes major hydroelectric power generating plants and rises 350 feet above the river. The visitor center explores the construction, impact, and the generation of hydroelectricity. A free tour provides a look at some of the dam's inner workings. The visitor center is open daily from 9 AM to 5 PM, with extended hours between Memorial Day and end of September. During the summer season enjoy the laser light show *One River, Many Voices*. Closed major holidays. WA-155; Grand Coulee, WA 99133; Phone: (509) 633-9265; https://www.usbr.gov/pn/grandcoulee/visit

Granger, WA
Hisey Park began with the construction of dinosaur statues designed to attract tourists to the small town. Today the people of Granger have built over thirty

sculptures and created an annual Dino-in-a-Day celebration each June. Originally restricted to Hisey Park, some of these prehistoric creatures have moved into town itself. 219 Main St; Granger, WA 98932; http://www.grangerwashington.org/visiting

Hanford, WA (See Richland, WA for the Manhattan Project Site)

Molson, WA

Molson Schoolhouse & Ghost Town has quite a controversial history that visitors can explore with no fee. Donations are gladly accepted. The Schoolhouse Museum highlights the history of the town and is open from daily Memorial Day to Labor Day from 10 AM to 5 PM. The Old Molson Ghost Town is an outdoor collection of pioneer buildings and equipment open daylight hours from April to November, weather permitting. Located 15 miles from Oroville, WA. 539 Molson Rd; Molson, WA 98844; Phone: (509) 485-3292 http://www.molsonmuseums.org

Mukilteo, WA

Mukilteo Lighthouse displays items from its first 100 years. Admission is free, donations appreciated. The lighthouse is open April through September on Saturday and Sunday from Noon to 5 PM. The grounds are open all year. 608 Front St; Mukilteo, WA 98275; http://mukilteohistorical.org/visit

Olympia, WA

Washington State Capitol Campus includes parks and government buildings. Outdoors sites are open every day, all year round. Some of the buildings are open to the public while others can only be viewed as part of a tour. Two of the best places to tour are the Governor's Mansion and Washington State Capitol building. **Governor's Mansion** is the oldest standing building on the Capitol Campus and home to Washington's governors since 1910. It has been fully restored and furnished with many antiques from the American Federal period. The mansion is open for free public tours on Wednesday afternoons by reservation which must made at least 24 hours in advance. 416 14th Ave SE; Olympia, WA 98504; https://des.wa.gov/services/facilities-leasing/capitol-campus/tours

Washington State Capitol offers guided tours of the Legislative Building. These are free and offered daily Monday through Friday from 10 AM to 3 PM and on Saturday and Sunday from 11 AM to 3 PM. Closed Thanksgiving, the day after Thanksgiving, Christmas, and New Year's Day. Visitors can also explore the memorials, gardens, and special events. 416 Sid Snyder Ave SW; Olympia, WA 98504; Phone: (360) 902-8880;

https://www.experienceolympia.com/explore/things-to-do/attractions/top-visitor-attractions/washington-state-capital-tours

WET Science Center presents games and activities designed for children ages 10 and up as well as adults. Admission is free. Open Monday through Saturday from 10 AM to 4 PM. 500 Adams St NE; Olympia, WA 98501; Phone: (360) 664-2333; https://www.wetsciencecenter.org

Yashiro Japanese Garden brings traditional garden design to the urban landscape. Admission is free. Open daily dawn to dusk. 1010 Plum St SE; Olympia, WA 98501; Phone: (360) 753-8380; http://olympiawa.gov/city-services/parks/parks-and-trails/yashiro-japanese-garden

Redmond, WA
Microsoft Visitor Center features diverse topics including the future of AI, Minecraft, and Microsoft company history. Generally open Monday through Friday. Website lists the hours a week at a time. 15010 NE 36th St; Bldg 92; Redmond, WA 98052; Phone: (425) 703-6214; https://www.microsoft.com/en-us/visitorcenter/default

Renton, WA
Greenwood Memorial Park is the resting place of Jimi Hendrix. The grounds also include his memorial. 350 Monroe Ave NE; Renton, WA 98056; Phone: (425) 255-1511; https://www.dignitymemorial.com/funeral-homes/renton-wa/greenwood-memorial-park-funeral-home/2480

Richland, WA
Hanford Nuclear Site was the world's first full-scale plutonium production reactor created as part of the top secret Manhattan Project during World War II. Free four-hour tours are offered Monday through Saturday except during the winter months. Register for tours online. 2000 Logston Blvd; Richland, WA 99354; Phone: (509) 376-1647; http://manhattanprojectbreactor.hanford.gov

LIGO Hanford Observatory includes one of only two gravitational wave detectors in the U.S. Self-guided visits of exhibits, and hardware displays are available Monday, Tuesday, Thursday, and Friday from 10 AM to 4 PM, and on Wednesday from 9 AM to 2 PM. Free walking tours offered on the second Saturday of each month at 1:30 PM and at 3:30 PM. In addition a LIGO staff member gives a public talk at 3 PM. Reservations are not required. 127124 N Route 10; Richland, WA 99352; Phone: (509) 372-8106; https://www.ligo.caltech.edu/WA/page/lho-drop-ins;

https://www.ligo.caltech.edu/WA/page/lho-public-tours

Salkum, WA

Cowlitz Salmon Hatchery depicts the life cycle of salmon. Visitors can view spawning salmon from September to mid-January. Facilities for raising chinook and coho salmon include incubation equipment, salmon sorting and fish loading machinery, a fish ladder, and a barrier dam. Admission is free. The visitor center is open every day 7 AM to 3:30 PM. 199 Salmon Ln; Salkum, WA 98582; https://www.mytpu.org/tacomapower/fish-wildlife-environment/cowlitz-river-project/cowlitz-fisheries-programs/cowlitz-salmon-hatchery.htm

Seatac, WA

Highline Botanical Garden contains display gardens, woodlands, and trails. Free to the public. Open daily dawn to dusk. 13735 24th Ave S; SeaTac, WA 98168; Phone: (206) 391-4003; https://highlinegarden.org

Seattle, WA

Amazon Headquarters Tours offers several ways to see its headquarters in downtown Seattle. They advise checking the website for most recent days and times. **Understory** is their free public visitor center that showcases their approach to an urban office through self-guided museum-style exhibits. It is open Monday through Saturday from 10 AM to 8 PM and Sunday from 11 AM to 7 PM. 2101 Seventh Ave; Seattle, WA 98121; https://www.seattlespheres.com/visit-understory. **Spheres** is Amazon's plant-filled biodome workspace. Open two Saturdays a month from 10 AM to 6 PM and reservations are required. All adults (ages 18+) must present a valid government issued identification card to the reception desk. 2111 7th Ave; Seattle, WA 98121; https://www.seattlespheres.com/the-spheres-weekend-public-visits. Finally, **Headquarter tours** are guided tours of several of the buildings on their Seattle campus. These free tours are available on Tuesday and Thursday at 10 AM and 2 PM. Advance reservations are required. 2111 Seventh Ave; Seattle, WA 98121; https://www.seattlespheres.com/visit-hq

Bill & Melinda Gates Foundation shows the foundation's work developing local and global programs. Free to visit. Open Tuesday through Saturday from 10 AM to 5 PM. Drop-in public tour at 2 PM. Closed major holidays. 440 Fifth Ave N; Seattle, WA 98109; Phone: (206) 709-3100 Ext. 7100; https://discovergates.org

Frye Art Museum displays rotating collections of 19th and 20th century American, French, and German paintings and sculptures. Free admission and free tours throughout the week. Open Tuesday through Sunday from 11 AM to 5 PM. Open late Thursday until 7 PM. 704 Terry Ave; Seattle, WA 98104; Phone: (206) 622-9250.https://fryemuseum.org/visit

Hiram M. Chittenden (Ballard) Locks is one of the nation's busiest locks. Open to ship traffic 24 hours a day the locks provide a transportation route for thousands of commercial vessels and pleasure craft. Free guided tours are available. The visitor center is open daily May through September from 10 AM to 6 PM. Open the rest of the year on Thursday through Monday from 10 AM to 4 PM. Note: The large lock will be periodically closed for repairs. The Carl S. English Jr. Botanical Gardens is an English-style landscape garden with over 1500 varieties of plants from around the world. Open free daily from 7 AM to 9 PM. 3015 NW 54th St; Ballard, WA 98107; Phone: (206) 783-7059; https://www.nws.usace.army.mil/Missions/Civil-Works/Locks-and-Dams/Chittenden-Locks

Historic Theatre Tours of the Paramount, the Moore, and the Neptune are offered free by the nonprofit Seattle Theatre Group. **Paramount Theatre** tours are held on the first Saturday of every month. Meet at the main entrance of the theater by 10 AM on the corner of Ninth and Pine. **Moore Theatre** tours are held on the second Saturday of every month also at 10 AM starting at the main entrance on the corner of Second and Virginia. **Neptune Theatre** tours are held on the third Saturday of every month starting at 10 AM at the corner of NE 45th St and Brooklyn. Phone: (206) 682-1414; https://www.stgpresents.org/tours

Klondike Gold Rush National Historical Park Washington– Seattle Unit describes the world's last gold rush and the role played by Seattle in outfitting prospectors on their way to Alaska. The park is located within the historic Cadillac Hotel and includes a visitor center and museum. Three different 20-25 minute films follow the stories of hopeful prospectors. Admission to the park is free as are the ranger-led tours. The park is open daily from 10 AM to 5 PM opening at 9 AM from Memorial Day to Labor Day. Closed Thanksgiving, Christmas, and New Year's Day. 319 Second Ave S; Seattle, WA 98104; Phone: (206) 220-4240; https://www.nps.gov/klse/index.htm

Kubota Garden is a 20-acre Japanese garden with paths, ponds, and waterfalls. Free to the public. Open daily during daylight hours. 9817 55th Ave S; Seattle, WA 98118; Phone: (206) 725-5060; http://www.kubotagarden.org/visit/about-the-garden

Olympic Sculpture Park features over a dozen large-scale sculptures set against the backdrop of Puget Sound and the Olympic Mountains. Admission is free. Open daily sunrise to sunset. Note: The Seattle Art Museum charges a fee to visit. Only the sculpture park is free. 2901 Western Ave; Seattle, WA 98121; Phone: (206) 654-3100; http://www.seattleartmuseum.org/visit/olympic-sculpture-park

Spokane, WA

Spokane offers a self-guided Sculpture Walk that meanders through Riverfront Park. Then take the Centennial Trail towards the University District for dozens of other art installations.
https://my.spokanecity.org/riverfrontspokane/sightseeing/sculpture-walk

Gonzaga University presents two museums open free to the public.

Crosby House Museum focuses on 20th century singer and actor Harry Lillis (Bing) Crosby, a native of Spokane and alumnus of Gonzaga. Crosby's childhood home was built in 1911 and still stands at its original location. The main floor houses over 200 Crosby items including gold records, trophies, awards, and his Oscar for *Going My Way* (1944). The museum is free. Open Monday through Friday from 10 AM to 4 PM. Open Saturday from 1 PM to 4 PM. Closed major holidays. 508 E Sharp Ave; Spokane, WA 99258; Phone: (509) 313-4064; https://www.gonzaga.edu/student-life/arts-culture/crosby-museum.

Jundt Art Museum holds a permanent collection by old masters (Dürer, Rembrandt, Goya, and Delacroix) as well as modern masters (Rodin, Picasso, Chihuly, and Warhol). Special exhibitions by local, regional, national, and international figures across the media are also offered. Admission and programs are free. Open Monday through Saturday from 10 AM to 4 PM. 200 E Desmet Ave; Spokane WA 99258; Phone: (509) 313-6843; https://www.gonzaga.edu/student-life/arts-culture/jundt-art-museum

John A. Finch Arboretum borders Garden Springs Creek and grows native and cultivated plants. Admission is free. Arboretum grounds are open daily from dawn to dusk. 3404 W Woodland Blvd; Spokane, WA 99224; Phone: (509) 363-5466; https://my.spokanecity.org/urbanforestry/programs/finch-arboretum

Tacoma, WA

Walking through downtown Tacoma is the perfect way to view several installations by world-famous glass artist Dale Chihuly. Don't miss his Bridge of Glass between Dock Street and Pacific Avenue. Another stop is Union Station. The rotunda of the federal courthouse is open to the public and has a several pieces by Chihuly on view. Note: You may be requested to show a photo ID to gain entrance. https://www.tacomaartmuseum.org/chihuly

McChord Air Museum at McChord Air Force Base includes attack jets, bombers, transport planes, fighter jets and other military aircraft. The museum also has a restoration hangar for old planes. Admission is free. Donations welcomed. Open Wednesday through Friday from Noon to 4 PM. Closed Thanksgiving, Christmas, and New Year's Day. Note: Non U.S. Citizens cannot enter the Joint Base Lewis McChord without being sponsored by a U.S. DoD cardholder. Check the website or call for the ID requirements to access the base. McChord Air Force

Base; Tacoma, WA 98438; Phone: (253) 982-2485;
http://www.mcchordairmuseum.org

Port of Tacoma Observation Tower Viewing Platform provides views of the harbor and the opportunity to watch its ships. Admission is free. The tower is open to the public 24 hours a day. 1 Sitcum Way; Tacoma, WA 98421; Phone: (253) 383-5841; https://www.portoftacoma.com/community/explore-port

Tacoma Historical Society Exhibit Center traces the city's growth from the first Euro-American settlement through its emergence as a major city. Admission is free. Open Wednesday through Saturday from 11 AM to 4 PM. 919 Pacific Ave; Tacoma, WA 98402; Phone: (253) 472-3738; https://www.tacomahistory.org/visit

Tacoma Telephone Pioneers Museum exhibits vintage telephones including crank type old sets and the first cordless telephone from the 1961 Seattle World's Fair. There is no admission charge but they gratefully accept donations. Open Thursday from 8 AM until Noon. Call to verify hours. 757 S Fawcett Ave; Tacoma, WA 98402; Phone: (253) 627-2996; http://www.scn.org/telmuseum

W.W. Seymour Botanical Conservatory is one of only three public Victorian-style conservatories on the West Coast, known for its distinctive 12-sided central dome. It is home to more than 250 species of exotic tropical plants. Free admission with donations appreciated. Open Tuesday through Sunday from 10 AM to 4:30 PM. Closed major holidays. 316 S G St; Tacoma, WA 98405; Phone: (253) 404-3975; https://www.metroparkstacoma.org/conservatory-always-in-bloom

Union Gap, WA

Central Washington Agricultural Museum displays horse drawn equipment and early mechanical farm machinery as well as homestead and cabin replicas. Free admission with donations accepted. The grounds are open daily from dawn to dusk. The buildings are open April through October on Tuesday through Saturday from 10 AM to 4 PM and Sunday from 1 PM to 4 PM. Also on the grounds is the Olde Yakima Letterpress Museum listed below. 4508 Main St; Union Gap, WA 98903; Phone: (509) 457-8735; http://centralwaagmuseum.org/default.asp

Olde Yakima Letterpress Museum has no admission fee but is only open on Saturday from 10 AM to 4 PM with early 2 PM closing on the second and fourth Saturday. Phone: (206) 719-4979; http://oldeyakimaletterpressmuseum.org/index.html

Uniontown, WA

Artisans at the Dahmen Barn is a three-story structure with artists working out of 10 studios. No admission fee. Open Thursday through Sunday from 10 AM to 6 PM with early closing at 4 PM in January and February. Closed major holidays. Note: There is a fee for classes. 419 N Park Way; Uniontown, WA 99179; Phone: (509) 229-3414; http://www.ArtisanBarn.org

Vancouver, WA (See also Oregon City, OR)

Fort Vancouver National Historic Site spans the states of Oregon and Washington. The London-based Hudson's Bay Company established Fort Vancouver in 1825 as the headquarters of the company's interior fur trade. The site has change from a frontier fur trading post to a military fort and now encompasses several unique sites. There is free admission to the Fort Vancouver Visitor Center, and the Pearson Air Museum (see below). There is a fee to enter the Reconstructed Fort Site. The McLoughlin House Unit of Fort Vancouver NHS is free to enter, but it is located in Oregon City, OR. Open Tuesday through Saturday from 9 AM to 5 PM. Closed some major holidays. 1501 E Evergreen Blvd; Vancouver, WA 98661; Phone: (336) 816-6230; https://www.nps.gov/fova/index.htm

Pearson Air Museum provides a detailed look into the golden age of aviation at Pearson Field. Admission is free. Open Tuesday through Saturday from 9 AM to 5 PM. 1115 E Fifth St; Vancouver, WA 98661; Phone: (360) 816-6232; Phone: (360) 816-6232; https://www.nps.gov/fova/learn/historyculture/pearson.htm

Walla Walla WA

Donald Sheehan Gallery at Whitman College promotes art through exhibits and its Davis Collection of Asian Art. Admission is free. Hours dependent on school calendar. Open September through end of May on Tuesday through Friday from Noon to 5 PM, and Saturday and Sunday from Noon to 4 PM. Open by appointment only during the summer. Olin Hall; Isaacs Ave; Walla Walla, WA 99362; Phone: (509) 527-5992; https://www.whitman.edu/sheehan/Sheehan_Contact.html

Whitman Mission National Historic Site focuses on Marcus and Narcissa Whitman's religious mission to the Cayuse Nation. The 1847 attack on the Whitmans impacted the lives of the peoples of the Columbia Plateau for decades. But the situation turned out to be more complicated. There is no fee to enter Whitman Mission National Historic Site. The park grounds are open daily from sunrise to sunset. The visitor center is open daily. From Memorial Day weekend through Labor Day weekend open from 9 AM to 4:30 PM. Open the rest of the year on Wednesday through Sunday from 9 AM to 4 PM. Open Memorial Day, July 4th and Labor Day. 328 Whitman Mission Rd; Walla Walla, WA 99362; Phone: (509) 522-6360; https://www.nps.gov/whmi/index.htm

Winthrop, WA

North Cascade Smoke Jumper Base explains smokejumping – parachuting into remote and rugged terrain to combat wildfires. The base provides free tours from June through September from 10 AM to 5 PM. Please call ahead during off season to arrange a tour. 23 Inter-City Airport Rd; Winthrop, WA 98862; Phone: (509) 997-2031; http://www.northcascadessmokejumperbase.com/take-a-tour. Learn more about smokejumpers here: https://www.fs.fed.us/science-technology/fire/smokejumpers

West Virginia

This was once coal-mining country and that history is woven through many of the places to visit. There's also been fabrication of glass products which adds another dimension to the complex history of the state.

Charleston, WV

Governor's Mansion is open for free tours, but advance reservations are required. Tours begin at the Tours and Information Desk at the Lower Rotunda of the State Capitol Building on Thursday and Friday mornings, starting at 9 AM. Call for reservations. 1716 Kanawha Blvd; Charleston, WV 25305; Phone: (304) 558-4839; http://www.wvculture.org/museum/tours-all.html

West Virginia State Capitol is modeled after the U.S. Capitol dome, though it's actually five feet taller, and gilded in almost pure gold. Guided tours are available at no cost Monday through Friday every half hour (except Noon to 1 PM). Limited touring on Saturdays. Tours of the WV Supreme Court Chambers require advance reservation. To schedule a tour, please call (304) 558-2601. 1900 Kanawha Blvd E; Charleston, WV 25305; Phone: (304) 558-4839; http://www.wvculture.org/agency/capitol.html

West Virginia State Museum collects, preserves and displays items of West Virginia history, culture, art, paleontology, archaeology, and geology. Admission to the museum is free. Open Tuesday through Saturday from 9 AM to 5 PM. Capitol Complex; 1900 Kanawha Blvd E; Charleston, WV 25305; Phone: (304) 558-0220; http://www.wvculture.org/museum/State-Museum-Index.html

Elkins, WV

Stirrup Gallery of Davis & Elkins College starts with the Darby Collection with stone age tools and ends with crafted glass, wooden and metal objects of the early 20th century. In between there are guns, and pottery. Admission is free. Halliehurst Mansion; Davis & Elkins College; 100 Campus Dr; Elkins, WV 26241; Phone: (304) 637-1900; https://www.dewv.edu/arts-entertainment/stirrup-gallery

Green Bank, WV

The Green Bank Observatory is the home of the Robert C. Byrd Green Bank Telescope, the world's largest fully steerable radio telescope. Larger radio telescopes exist but they are not movable. Although there's a charge to take a tour of the facility, the **Science Center Exhibit Hall** is free and offers interactive exhibits exploring the electromagnetic spectrum, radio science, and the observatory history.

The Science Center is open Thursday through Monday from 10 AM to 6 PM. 155 Observatory Rd; Green Bank, WV 24944; Phone: (304) 456-2150; http://greenbankobservatory.org/visit

Helvetia, WV
Fasnacht Mask Museum provides a bit of Switzerland in West Virginia. Part of the celebration of Fasnacht is to make and wear your own ornate masks to scare away Old Man Winter. The most popular and best masks are saved in the free museum, located in Kultur Haus. This all-purpose building also houses the Helvetia General Store, Post Office, and Alpen Lodge. Note: This is a remote hamlet in Randolph County south of Buckhannon, and southwest of Elkins. Helvetia, WV 26224; Phone: (304) 924-9100; http://helvetiawv.com

Huntington, WV
Museum of Radio and Technology traces radio history from the 1920s to the 1950s with vintage radios and equipment as well as ham radios, and military radios. Admission is free with donations appreciated. Open on Saturday from 10 AM to 4 PM and on Sunday from 1 PM to 4 PM. Open on most Fridays from 10 AM to 4 PM from late spring to early fall. Closed major holidays. 1640 Florence Ave; Huntington, WV 25701; Phone (304) 525-8890; https://www.mrtwv.org

Lansing, WV (See also Nuttallburg, WV)
Canyon Rim Visitor Center New River Gorge has become base jumping headquarters as people from all over the world come to either jump off the bridge, or watch others hurl themselves into space. The visitor center provides a two-mile view into the park and down to one of the world's oldest rivers. The exhibit room is filled with photographs and displays on the people and towns of the gorge as well as the natural history of the area. An auditorium offers two videos. Take the short hiking trail and descend into the gorge on a wooden boardwalk. There is no fee to enter. Open daily from 9 AM to 5 PM. Closed major holidays. 162 Visitor Center Rd; Lansing, WV 25862; Phone: (304) 574-2115; https://www.nps.gov/neri/index.htm

Logan, WV
Museum In The Park features artwork and historical items from the collection of the West Virginia State Museum. One of the museum's permanent exhibits is the Buffalo Creek Disaster. This was the worst industrial disaster in the history of Logan County. It happened on Saturday, February 26, 1972 when coal waste dams collapsed releasing 132 million gallons of toxic waste water. There is no admission fee. Open Wednesday through Saturday from 10 AM to 6 PM and Sunday from 1 PM to 6 PM. Generally closed January through March. 860 Wolfpen Hollow Rd; Logan, WV 25601; Phone: (304)792-7229; http://www.wvculture.org/museum/MITPmod.html

Madison, WV

Bituminous Coal Heritage Foundation Museum preserves the heritage of the southern WV coal fields through miner's tools, photographs, company records and other pieces of the state's mining history. There's a simulated coal mine with replica tools from the 1940s. There is no fee to tour the museum. Donations are appreciated. Open Monday, Thursday, Friday, and Saturday from Noon to 5 PM. 347 Main St; Madison, WV 25130; Phone: (304) 369-0316; http://wvcoalmuseum.org

Milton, WV

Blenko Glass Company started in 1893 and is still family owned and operated. Known for their hand-blown art glass the company offers a free museum and free self-guided tours. Enjoy demonstrations from their observation deck. Open Monday through Friday from 9 AM to 2:15 PM Note: The artisans are out to lunch from Noon to 12:30 PM. 9 Bill Blenko Dr; Milton, WV 25541; Phone: (304) 743-9081; https://blenko.com/visit-blenko

Morgantown, WV

Art Museum of WVU features Chinese scroll paintings, Japanese prints, contemporary ceramics, African ritual objects, textiles and jewelry as well as artworks by James Edward Davis. Admission is free. Open Wednesday and Thursday from 3:30 PM to 7:30 PM and on Friday from 12:30 PM to 4:30 PM. Open Saturday and Sunday from 12:30 PM to 4:30 PM. Hours change during holidays and university breaks. 2 Fine Arts Dr; Morgantown, WV 26506; Phone: (304) 293-2141; https://artmuseum.wvu.edu

Royce J. and Caroline B. Watts Museum at West Virginia University highlights the artifacts and archival materials from the mining and petroleum industries, including mine rescue equipment, canary cages, and model oil derricks. Admission is free. Open Monday, Wednesday, Friday and Saturday from 1 PM to 4 PM. Closed major holidays. 401 Evansdale Dr; Morgantown, WV 26506; Phone: (304) 293-4609; https://wattsmuseum.wvu.edu/home

West Virginia Botanic Garden at Tibbs Run Preserve is 85 acres of woods with four miles of trails. Admission to the garden is free, but donations are welcome. Open daily from dawn to dusk. 1061 Tyrone Rd; Morgantown, WV 26508, Phone: 304-322-2093; https://www.wvbg.org

Moundsville, WV (See also Wheeling, WV)

Grave Creek Mound is roughly 2,000 years old. Visit the Delf Norona Museum for artifacts and displays about prehistoric life in West Virginia. Admission to the museum is free. Open Tuesday through Saturday from 9 AM to 5 PM. 801

Jefferson Ave; Moundsville, WV 26041; Phone: (304) 843-4128;
http://www.wvculture.org/museum/GraveCreekmod.html

Nuttallburg, WV (See also Lansing, WV)

New River Gorge National River shelters the remains of the once-active town of Nuttallburg which began in 1870 when England-born entrepreneur John Nuttall started buying land. The town flourished until coal mining ended in 1958. In 1998 the family gave the land to the National Park Service. It is considered one of the most intact examples of a coal mining complex in West Virginia. Find directions and information on the town on the NPS website. There is no fee to enter New River Gorge National River. Phone: (304) 465-0508; https://www.nps.gov/neri/learn/historyculture/nuttallburg.htm

Talcott, WV

Great Bend Tunnel is one of the locations reputed to be the site of the contest between the beloved folk hero John Henry and a steam powered drill to prove worth of using men rather than machines. According to legend, John Henry won the epic battle, only to die in victory with his hammer in his hand. It is generally agreed that John Henry was born a slave, worked as a laborer for the railroads after the Civil War, and died in his 30s, leaving behind a young wife and a baby. The tunnel is also the future home of the **John Henry Historical Park** and hosts a statue of John Henry. WV-12; Talcott, WV 25951; http://www.johnhenryhistoricalpark.com; https://www.nps.gov/neri/learn/historyculture/john-henry-and-the-coming-of-the-railroad.htm

Weston, WV

Museum of American Glass preserves the history of the glass industry in West Virginia and the USA, displaying examples glass going back to the 1800s. It is also the home of the National Marble Museum. Admission is free. Open Monday through Saturday from 9:30 AM to 5 PM, and on Sunday from 1 PM to 5 PM. 230 Main Ave; Weston, WV 26452; Phone: (304) 269-5006; http://www.magwv.com

Wheeling, WV (See also Moundsville, WV)

West Virginia Independence Hall focuses on the Civil War and West Virginia's statehood. Tours of the museum are free. Open Tuesday through Saturday from 9 AM to 5 PM. Closed major holidays. 1528 Market St; Wheeling, WV 26003; Phone: (304) 238-1300 or (800) CALLWVA; http://www.wvculture.org/museum/WVIHmod.html

Whitesville, WV

Upper Big Branch Coal Mine Memorial honors the coal miners killed and injured in the 2010 explosion. The roadside memorial plaza is made up of three distinct sections and reminds visitors of the human cost that West Virginians have paid to wrest coal from the ground to power this country. 38175 Coal River Rd; Whitesville, WV 25209; Phone: (304) 837-3962; http://www.ubbminersmemorial.com

Wisconsin

There's a lot to love about America's Dairyland but one of the most delightful surprises is the abundance of water skiing shows that are completely free. Wherever you are planning to go in Wisconsin, there is likely to be one of these summer-only shows nearby. They are listed at the end of this chapter.

Alma, WI

Wings Over Alma Nature & Art Center in the midst of the Upper Mississippi River National Wildlife & Fish Refuge hosts bald eagles, herons, migrating waterfowl, songbirds and seasonal winged visitors. It provides a viewing deck of the Mississippi River by Lock & Dam #4. Artwork by local and regional artists is on display. Admission is free. Open daily from 10 AM to 5 PM. Closed Thanksgiving, and Christmas Day. 118 N Main St; Alma, WI 54610; Phone: (608) 685-3303; http://www.wingsoveralma.org

Ashland, WI

Northern Great Lakes Visitor Center offers a looped 2/3-mile boardwalk trail that winds through the cedar and tamarack wetlands, a five-story observation tower, and wildlife viewing platform. Free admission. Hosted or sponsored programs at the Northern Great Lakes Visitor Center may require a registration fee. Open daily 9 AM to 5 PM. Note: The adjacent to Whittlesey Creek National Wildlife Refuge is a fee-based national refuge. 29270 County Hwy G; Ashland, WI 54806; Phone: (715) 685-9983; https://nglvc.org

Babcock, WI

Sandhill State Wildlife Area is studded with marshes, woods, bison herds, and a variety of birds. Best time to view the Sandhill cranes is mid-October, but other birds can be viewed at other times of the year. The area also has driving trails and observation towers. Admission is free. Open April through October but visitors are advised to phone ahead for exact dates. 1715 CR X; Babcock, WI 54413; Phone: (715) 884-2437; http://dnr.wi.gov/topic/lands/WildlifeAreas/sandhill

Baraboo, WI

Famous for its circus history, Circus World charges a fee, but visitors can see some animals for free at the local zoo.

Ochsner Park and Zoo is home to over 17 different animal species and accepts animals born in captivity from licensed zoos and those not releasable in the wild due to injury. Open daily at 8:30 AM with seasonal closing hours. Admission is always free. 903 Park St; Baraboo, WI 53913; Phone: (608) 355-2760; https://www.facebook.com/ochsnerparkzoo

Beloit, WI

Logan Museum of Anthropology includes artifacts from over 123 countries and 480 cultural groups. The Shaw Gallery on the museum's second floor has small exhibits located in study drawers in the center of the gallery. Stroll the perimeter of the two story, glass enclosed building to view pre-Columbian ceramics, North American ethnographic objects and a large basketry collection as well as the curatorial staff at work. Free admission. Open 11 AM to 4 PM Tuesday through Saturday. Closed university holidays. Beloit College; 700 College St; Beloit, WI 53511; Phone: (608) 363-2677; https://www.beloit.edu/logan

Belmont, WI

First Capitol was the site of Wisconsin's first territorial legislature and includes two of the buildings restored to 1836 appearances. Inside are exhibits on early territorial Wisconsin and the first territorial legislature. Free admission. Open weekends during the summer from 10 AM to 4 PM. 18904 County Hwy G; Belmont, WI 53510; Phone: (608) 987-2122; https://firstcapitol.wisconsinhistory.org

Brillion, WI

Brillion Nature Center features wildlife in marsh, pond, forest, and prairie habitats. A boardwalk leads to a large viewing platform on the marsh. Wisconsin fish, reptiles, and amphibians can be viewed inside the nature center. A restored prairie is home to over 50 species of wildflowers. Admission is free. Trails are open daily from dawn until dusk. Open Monday through Friday from 9 AM to 3 PM. Naturalist led programs incur a fee. W1135 Deerview Rd; Brillion, WI 54110; Phone: (920) 756-3591; http://www.brillionnaturecenter.net

Bristol, WI

Pringle Nature Center conducts various free ongoing nature programs, exhibits, and interactive learning stations. There are hiking trails, plus cross country skiing and snow shoeing on all trails as appropriate. Snow shoes may be available for rent. Admission is free. Open April through November on Tuesday through Sunday from 9 AM to 4 PM. Note: They advise calling ahead during winter to make sure they are open. 9800 160th Ave; Bristol, WI 53104; Phone: (262) 857-8008; http://www.pringlenc.org

Green Bay, WI

Bay Beach Wildlife Sanctuary lets visitors discover nature through educational displays, live animal exhibits, and six miles of trails. This park is free and open to the public daily all year. The visitor center is open from 8 AM to 7:30 PM, closing at 4:30 from mid-September to mid-April. 1660 E Shore Dr; Green Bay, WI 54302; Phone: (920) 391-3671; http://www.baybeachwildlife.com

Janesville, WI

Helen Jeffris Wood Museum Center provides rotating exhibit galleries with a permanent exhibit on Pauline Pottery and Pickard China. Pauline Jacobus was a painter of porcelain and an art potter. Pickard China was known for its creation of art pieces. Admission is free. Open Wednesday through Saturday from 10 AM to 3 PM and Thursday until 4 PM. Open Sunday from Noon to 3 PM. Note: The center is also the ticket agency for fee-based tours of the Lincoln-Tallman House. 426 N Jackson St; Janesville, WI 53548; Phone: (608) 756-4509; http://www.rchs.us/sites/helen-jeffris-wood-museum-center

Kenosha, WI

Dinosaur Discovery Museum owns one of the most complete known fossil records. Visitors can learn what dinosaurs looked like, what they ate, how they behaved, and view replicas of Tyrannosaurus rex, Gallimimus, and Ceratosaurus. There is no admission fee. Donations are accepted. Open Tuesday through Sunday from Noon to 5 PM. Note: Guided tours will incur a cost. 5608 10th Ave; Kenosha, WI 53140; Phone: (262) 653-4450; https://museums.kenosha.org/dinosaur

Gateway Classic Cars is one of several classic and exotic car dealerships across the country and they welcome browsers. Admission is free. Open Monday through Saturday from 9 AM to 5 PM. 9949 58th Pl; Suite 400; Kenosha, WI 53144; Phone: (262) 891-4253; http://gatewayclassiccars.com/locations?location=MWK

Kenosha County Historical Society includes the **Kenosha History Center** which focuses on Kenosha County history with three exhibit galleries; and the **Southport Light Station Museum** which is a restored Light Keeper's home and lighthouse. Both are free to visit with donations appreciated. The history center is open Tuesday through Friday from 10 AM to 4:30 PM. Open Saturday from 10 AM to 4 PM and Sunday from Noon to 4 PM. Both floors of the **Lighthouse Keeper's Home** have been restored to a 1908 time period. There's an extensive collection of documents covering the Underground Railroad and walking tours of Underground Railroad Stations. **Southport Light Station Museum** is open seasonally from mid-May to the end of October. Open Thursday, Friday, and Saturday from 10 AM to 4 PM. Open Sunday from Noon to 4 PM Closed major holidays. Note: There is a charge to tour the top of the Southport Lighthouse. 220 51st Pl; Kenosha, WI 53140; Phone: (262) 654-5770; http://www.kenoshahistorycenter.org/index.html

Kiel, WI

Henning's Cheese, Inc is a 4th-generation family-owned cheese factory with free samples and the opportunity to watch cheese being made through viewing windows and live video feed. There's also a small display of historic cheese making equipment. Open Monday through Friday from 7 AM to 4 PM and Saturday from 8 AM to Noon. Closed major holidays. 20201 Point Creek Rd; Kiel, WI 53042; Phone: (920) 894-3032; http://www.henningscheese.com/cheese_store_museum.html

Kohler, WI

Kohler's "Industry in Action" Factory Tour brings visitors through the manufacturing stages that create everything from china lavatories to 6-foot cast iron tubs. Note: Participants must be at least 14 years old. Closed toe footwear must be worn on the tour. Advanced reservations are required. The free tours take place Monday through Friday at 8:30 AM. 101 Upper Rd; Kohler, WI 53044; Phone: (920) 457-3699; https://www.us.kohler.com/us/Industry-in-Action-Factory-Tours/content/CNT400040.htm

Madison, WI

Allen Centennial Garden highlights thematic gardens from around the world. Admission is free. The gardens are open daily dawn to dusk. 620 Babcock Dr; Madison, WI 53706; Phone: (608) 262-8406; https://allencentennialgarden.org/index.php

Chazen Museum of Art presents temporary exhibitions in the three dedicated galleries. The balance of the exhibit space is devoted to the Chazen's permanent collection spanning history, culture, media, and genre. Admission is free. Open Tuesday through Friday from 9 AM to 5 PM closing Thursday at 9 PM. Open Saturday and Sunday from 11 AM to 5 PM. Closed major holidays. 750 University Ave; Madison, WI 53706; Phone: (608) 263-2246; https://www.chazen.wisc.edu/

Ingersoll Physics Museum invites visitors to explore concepts ranging from mechanics and magnetism to modern physics. Historical scientific instruments are on display along the corridors of Chamberlin Hall. Museum is free. Donations are appreciated. Open Monday through Friday from 8 AM to 4 PM. Closed legal holidays. Chamberlin Hall; 1150 University Ave; Madison, WI 53706; Phone: (608) 262-4526; https://www.physics.wisc.edu/ingersollmuseum

Madison Museum of Contemporary Art has a core collection of American prints, photographs, and drawings but also includes paintings, sculptures, and the works of innovative artists. Free admission. Open Tuesday through Thursday from Noon to 5 PM, Friday from Noon to 8 PM, Saturday from 10 AM to 8 PM, and Sunday from Noon to 5 PM. 227 State St; Madison, WI 53703; Phone: (608) 257-0158; http://www.mmoca.org

University of Wisconsin Geology Museum, Madison is perfect for families offering glowing minerals, meteorites, and fossils as well as 120,000 geological and paleontological specimens. Admission is free. Open Monday through Friday from 8:30 AM to 4:30 PM and Saturday from 9 AM to 1 PM. Closed major holidays. 1215 W Dayton St; Madison, WI 53706; Phone: (608) 262-1412; http://geoscience.wisc.edu/museum

Washburn Observatory at UW-Madison Astronomy Department offers free public observing on the first and third Wednesday of each month. During June through August a Wednesday viewing is added to the schedule, weather permitting. Note: The dome is open to the outside. Dress appropriately. The Washburn Observatory Dome does not have a phone line. Find the latest information on their twitter feed: https://twitter.com/Washburn_Obs. 1401 Observatory Dr; Madison, WI 53706; http://www.astro.wisc.edu/the-public/public-observing-at-washburn/?Washburn

Wisconsin Executive Residence is a classical revival-style 1921 mansion with tours that include a brief history of the residence and a view of the main rooms on the first floor. Visitors can also stroll through the seven formal gardens and enjoy a view of Lake Mendota. Free docent-led tours are offered mid-June through the end of August on Thursday from 1 PM to 3 PM. Open house holiday tours are offered in December. 99 Cambridge Rd; Madison, WI 53704; Phone: (608) 246-5501; http://wisconsinexecutiveresidence.com

Wisconsin State Capitol is open to the public weekdays from 8 AM to 6 PM as well as weekends and holidays from 8 AM to 4 PM. Free tours are offered daily, except on major holidays. The sixth floor museum and observation deck are open during the summer months. 2 E Main St; Madison, WI 53702; Phone: (608)266-0382; http://tours.wisconsin.gov/pub/Content.aspx?p=Capitol%20Tour

Manitowoc, WI

Rahr West Art Museum specializes in 19th century paintings as well as displays porcelains, Chinese ivory carvings, and international antique dolls. No admission fee but donations gratefully accepted. Open Tuesday through Friday from 10 AM to 4 PM. Open Saturday and Sunday from 11 AM to 4 PM. 610 N Eighth St; Manitowoc, WI 54220; Phone: (920) 686-3090; http://www.manitowoc.org/1006/Rahr-West-Art-Museum

Marshfield, WI

Wildwood Park & Zoo highlights animals and birds from North America with key exhibits on mountain lions, wolves, deer, bison, and Sandhill cranes as well as a state-of-the-art bear exhibit. Admission is free, but donations are always welcome. Open daily at 7:30 AM. Closings are seasonal. 608 W 17th St; Marshfield, WI 54449; Phone: (715) 384-4642; http://ci.marshfield.wi.us/visitors/wildwood_zoo

Middleton, WI

National Mustard Museum has more than 5,000 varieties of this popular condiment. Gibbons Collection displays everything mustard from mustard pots to antique tins, jars, and vintage advertisements. Admission is free but donations or purchases of mustard in their gift shop are appreciated. Open daily from 10 AM to 5 PM. Closed Easter, Thanksgiving, Christmas, and New Year's Day. 7477 Hubbard Ave; Middleton, WI 53562; Phone: (608) 831-2222, (800) 438-6878; https://mustardmuseum.com/the-mustard-museum

Milwaukee, WI

Watching the **Calatrava-designed wings** open, flap, and close at the Milwaukee Art Museum is a free experience. Entering the museum will incur a fee, but it is impressive to watch the sweeping steel wings of the Burke Brise Soleil sunscreen open at 10 AM, flap at Noon, and close at 5 PM when the museum closes. View the spectacle at 700 N Art Museum Dr; Milwaukee, WI 53202; https://mam.org. **RiverWalk** is more than a scenic stroll along the Milwaukee River. It's also home to RiverSculpture, an outdoor gallery that includes both permanent pieces and temporary changing installations. https://milwaukeeriverwalkdistrict.com

American Geographical Society Library at University of Wisconsin-Milwaukee preserves over one million items including maps, atlases, photographs, slides, Landsat images, and digital spatial data. The library organizes thematic displays as well as offers a permanent selection of globes, maps, photographs, and cartographic instruments. Free admission. Open Monday through Friday from 8 AM to 4:30 PM. UWM Libraries; Third Floor; East Wing; 2311 E Hartford Ave; Milwaukee, WI 53211; Phone: (414) 229-6282; https://uwm.edu/libraries/agsl/exhibits

Basilica of St. Josephat was built in the Polish Cathedral style of church architecture and modeled after St. Peter's Basilica in Rome. It features one of the largest copper domes in the world. The visitor center is located in the Pope John Paul II Pavilion on the west side of the Basilica and open Monday through Saturday from 9 AM to 4 PM. Walking tour brochures are available. There is also a free exhibit of images and information detailing the story of the Basilica on the lower level of the Pavilion. Formal tour presentations of the Basilica are regularly held after the 10 AM Mass on Sundays. Admission and tours are free. 2333 S Sixth St; Milwaukee, WI 53215; Phone: (414) 902-3523; https://www.thebasilica.org/visit

Haggerty Museum of Art provides an array of exhibits and a full calendar of free performances, workshops, and gallery talks. Admission is free. Open Monday through Saturday from 10 AM to 4:30 PM. Open late on Thursday until 8 PM. Sunday open from Noon to 5 PM. N 13th and Clybourn Sts; Marquette University; Milwaukee, WI 53233; Phone: (414) 288-1669; http://www.marquette.edu/haggerty/index.php

Milwaukee Institute of Art & Design holds the Brooks Stevens Gallery, and the Frederick Layton Gallery which both offer curated and themed exhibits. MIAD's galleries are free and open Monday through Saturday from 10 AM to 5 PM. 273 E Erie St; Milwaukee, WI 53202; Phone: (888) 749-MIAD; https://www.miad.edu/miad-galleries-overview

Stone Creek Coffee Factory Tour is a Farm-to-Cup tour covering coffee growing seasons to the art of specialized roasting. The free tour takes place every Sunday at Noon at the Factory Café. 422 N Fifth St; Milwaukee, WI 53203; Phone: (414) 270-1008; http://www.stonecreekcoffee.com/tours

Minocqua, WI
Northwoods Wildlife Center works to rehabilitate wildlife and educate the public about their importance and needs. There is no admission cost, but donations are greatly appreciated. In summer open Monday through Saturday from 10 AM to 4 PM. In spring and fall open Monday through Saturday from 10 AM to 2 PM. December through February open Monday through Friday from 10 AM to 2 PM. They advise calling to confirm hours. 8683 S Blumenstein Rd; Minocqua, WI 54548; Phone: (715) 356-7400; http://northwoodswildlifecenter.org/education.html

Mount Horeb, WI
Wally Keller Tool Museum is part of the Duluth Trading Co. and features over 3,000 vintage tools, dating back to the early 1800s. Admission is free. Open Monday through Wednesday from 9 AM to 6 PM. Open late Thursday through Saturday until 8 PM. Open Sunday 11 AM to 5 PM. 100 W Main St; Mount Horeb, WI 53572; Phone: (608) 437-8655; https://www.duluthtrading.com/locations/?StoreID=001

Neenah, WI
Bergstrom-Mahler Museum of Glass holds the largest, most representative collection of glass paperweights in the world. There's also Germanic drinking

vessels, and jaw-dropping contemporary glass sculpture. Free admission. Open Tuesday through Saturday from 10 AM to 4:30 PM. Open Sunday from 1 PM to 4:30 PM. 165 N Park Ave; Neenah, WI 54956; Phone: (920) 751-4658; http://bmmglass.com

Peshtigo, WI

Harmony Arboretum presents a hardwood forest, winding walking trails, a restored prairie, and demonstration gardens. The Master Gardeners' display and demonstration garden is a three-acre area within the Arboretum. It is always free and open to the public. N3890 County E; Peshtigo, WI 54157; https://marinette.uwex.edu/horticulture/harmony-arboretum

Phillips, WI

Wisconsin Concrete Park highlights over 200 embellished concrete and mixed media folk art sculptures. Built between 1948 and 1964 by self-taught artist Fred Smith, the life-size and larger-than-life sculptures of people, animals, and events (both real and imagined) are installed throughout this Price County park. There is no admission charge. Open year round during daylight hours. Self-guided tour brochures are available on site for a donation. N8236 WI-13; Phillips, WI 54555; Phone: (715) 339-7282; https://wisconsinconcretepark.org

Pleasant Prairie, WI

Jelly Belly Visitor Center invites visitors to ride the Jelly Belly train through the candy warehouse and learn how Jelly Belly jelly beans are made. Free samples. Note: This is not a factory tour and they occasionally offer fee-based activities. Rides are free to the public daily from 9 AM to 4 PM. 10100 Jelly Belly La; Pleasant Prairie, WI 53158; Phone: (262) 947-3800; https://www.jellybelly.com/Wisconsin-Warehouse

Portage, WI

Visit over 50 **barn quilts** in a self-guided tour throughout the Columbia County countryside. Read the stories of the quilts and download the map at: https://columbia.uwex.edu/family-living/barn-quilts-3 Phone: (608) 742-9680
Museum at the Portage uses artifacts, maps, and photographs to capture the history of Wisconsin's third oldest settlement. Visitors can also see the study of author Zona Gale, the first woman to win the Pulitzer Prize for Drama in 1921. There is no charge for admission to the museum, though donations are welcomed. Open spring and fall on Thursday through Saturday from 1 PM to 4 PM. Open June through August on Tuesday through Saturday from 1 PM to 4 PM. 804 MacFarlane Rd; Portage, WI 53901; Phone: (608) 742-6682; http://portagemuseum.org

Poynette, WI

MacKenzie Center highlights the history of logging, the importance of conservation, an arboretum, and an 80-foot tall observation tower. A wildlife exhibit is home to animals native to Wisconsin. All of the animals in the exhibit were injured, orphaned or raised in captivity and cannot be released into the wild. Admission to the Center is free, but donations appreciated. The grounds are open all year dawn to dusk. The exhibits are open daily from the first full weekend in May through the last full weekend in October from 10 AM to 4 PM. From November through April open Monday through Friday from 10 AM to 4 PM. W7303 CR CS; Poynette, WI 53955; Phone: (608) 635-8105; http://dnr.wi.gov/education/mackenzie

Prairie du Chien, WI

Mississippi River Sculpture Park & Interpretive Center highlights five life-size bronze statues of people who have shaped Prairie du Chien: Chief Black Hawk; Dr. William Beaumont, father of gastroenterology; the Victorian Lady, representing tourists who enjoy the area; Julian Coryer, a voyageur; and Emma Big Bear, who earned her living in the mid-20th century with traditional Ho-Chunk crafts. Additional historic figures are planned. Admission is free. Open all year. 191 W Blackhawk Ave; Prairie du Chien, WI 53821; Phone: (608) 326-7207; http://www.statuepark.org

Racine, WI

SC Johnson offers free tours of their two Frank Lloyd Wright buildings. Note: If scheduling visits to SC Johnson headquarters and Wingspread allow sufficient travel time. https://www.scjohnson.com/en/a-family-company/architecture-and-tours/visit-sc-johnson-here-are-all-the-details-to-plan-your-tour

S C Johnson headquarters is the only Frank Lloyd Wright corporate headquarters that is still in use. A gallery features Frank Lloyd Wright-focused exhibits, films, and a replica twin-engine S-28 amphibian plane. Tours are available Thursdays through Sunday. Reservations required: https://reservations.scjohnson.com/SelectDate.aspx

Wingspread is one of Frank Lloyd Wrights' iconic, Prairie-style homes. Designed for H.F. Johnson, Jr. and his family, the Johnson Foundation provides free public tours. Reservations are required. For the Wingspread reservations: https://reservations.scjohnson.com/SelectDate.aspx

Sheboygan Falls, WI

Aviation Heritage Center of Wisconsin invites visitors to learn the history of the Hmong T-28 – the Hmong pilots who flew the North American T-28 Trojan and other aircraft in support of American CIA covert operations in Laos. It is the only exhibit of its kind in the nation. There's also simulators that were used to train Air Force pilots. There is no admission fee and donations are appreciated. Open Wednesday through Friday from 11 AM to 4 PM. Open Saturday and Sunday from Noon to 5 PM. Sheboygan County Airport; N6191 Resource Dr; Sheboygan Falls, WI 53085; Phone: (920) 467-2043; http://www.ahcw.org

Gardens of the John Michael Kohler Arts Center has ten galleries as well as more than 35 sculptures. The center also offers the unusual artist-created public toilets. Admission is always free. Gardens are open to the public during daylight hours. The center is open daily at 10 AM. On Monday, Wednesday and Friday it closes at 5 PM. Tuesday and Thursday it closes at 8 PM. On Saturday and Sunday open from 10 AM to 4 PM. 608 New York Ave; Sheboygan, WI 53081; Phone: (920) 458-6144; https://www.jmkac.org

Stevens Point, WI
Annette and Dale Schuh Riverfront Arts Center features changing exhibits. Admission is free. Open Tuesday through Friday from 11 AM to 5 PM. Open Saturday and Sunday from 11 AM to 3 PM. 1200 Crosby Ave; Stevens Point, WI 54481; Phone: (715) 343-6251; http://www.stevenspoint.com/index.aspx?nid=170

UW-Stevens Point Museum of Natural History seeks to bring natural history to life through large dioramas depicting environments from North America as well as Africa. There's also an extensive display depicting the Menominee Nation's Clan system, and even information on the Passenger Pigeon. Admission is always free. Hours change with the academic calendar. 900 Reserve St; Stevens Point, WI 54481; Phone: (715) 346-2858; https://www.uwsp.edu/cols-ap/museum/Pages/default.aspx

Stoughton, WI
Livsreise – Norwegian Heritage Center focuses on the Norwegian immigration to Wisconsin in the late 1800s and how it is part of the universal story of immigration featuring the experiences of the people who chose to emigrate. Visitors can also research their Norwegian family genealogy. *Livsreise*, which means *life's journey*, is free to the public. Open Tuesday through Saturday from 9:30 AM to 4:30 PM. 277 W Main St; Stoughton, WI 53589; Phone: (608) 873-7567; http://www.livsreise.org

Sturgeon Bay, WI
Door County Historical Museum educates about the early settlers, the area's orchards, and its industries. *Seasons of Life* wildlife diorama features over 100 native species. The family-friendly Pioneer Fire Station showcases historic fire trucks and a hands-on jail cell. Admission is free with donations appreciated. Open

daily May through October from 10 AM to 4:30 PM. 18 N Fourth Ave; Sturgeon Bay, WI 54235; Phone: (920) 743-5809; http://map.co.door.wi.us/museum

Three Lakes, WI
Ed's Northwoods Petroleum Museum illustrates the history of the petroleum industry with over 3,000 items including: pumps, signs, and cars. Admission is free with donations appreciated. Museum is open all year, generally Tuesday through Saturday Noon to 2 PM, but visitors are advised to call first to confirm. "Don't be shy, I live 2 minutes from the Museum and I am happy to oblige," says Ed. 7626 Highway 45 N; Three Lakes, WI 54562; Phone: (715) 617-0566; http://northwoodspetroleummuseum.org

Wausau, WI
Leigh Yawkey Woodson Art Museum curates exhibitions from Art Nouveau glass and Japanese ceramics, to quilt and fiber art. The museum has a permanent collection of historic and contemporary paintings, graphics, and sculptures primarily focusing on birds. The gardens are dotted with sculptures. Free admission. Open Tuesday through Friday from 9 AM to 4 PM. Open Saturday and Sunday from Noon to 5 PM. 700 N 12th St; Wausau, WI 54403; Phone: (715) 845-7010; https://www.lywam.org

Water Ski Shows Across Wisconsin
Wisconsin's many lakes have inspired outdoor public water shows. Times are limited, but if you amble down by the water in these towns you'll be entranced by the prowess of these water-based athletes. All the shows listed are free. Check the website for the latest schedule, which is subject to change.

Crandon, WI uses Lake Lucerne as the backdrop for the Crandon water ski show at the Water's Edge Lodge. 4140 County Road W; Crandon, WI 54520; Phone: (262) 365-3258; http://cwshows.knottlane.com/?page_id=799

Crivitz, WI has the Twin Bridge Water Ski Team preforming on the High Falls Flowage. Shows are held from end of June through mid-August (except for State Tournament dates) at 6:30 PM. They suggest bringing lawn chairs or blankets and particularly sunglasses. Stephenson Town Park; 315 Louisa St; Crivitz, WI 54114; Phone: (715) 927-3363; http://www.twinbridgewaterskiteam.com

Janesville, WI features its Rock Aqua Jays Water Ski team. Shows are held at the Rock Aqua Jay stadium Memorial Day through Labor Day and last 70 minutes (with a 10 minute intermission). Donations are encouraged, or perhaps the purchase of a souvenir t-shirts. 600 N Parker Dr; Janesville, WI 53545; Phone: (608) 757-3171; Phone: 800-487-2757; http://www.rockaquajays.com

La Crosse, WI invites watchers to the River City Water Ski Team Shows held at Airport Beach on Fisherman's Rd from mid-June to mid-August. They promise a bit of comedy as well. Fishermans Rd; French Island; La Crosse, WI 54603; Phone: (608) 792-2860; http://www.rivercitywaterski.com/index.html

Minocqua, WI offers the Min-Aquabat Water Ski team with new acts added each year. Shows held mid-June to mid-August. 400 W Park Ave; Minocqua, WI 54548; Phone: (715) 356-5266, (800) 446-6784; http://www.min-aquabats.com

Muskego Water, WI delights with the Bugs Water Ski Show which takes place at Idle Isle Park on Wednesday from Memorial Day through Labor Day. Bring a blanket or lawn chair for seating. W182S6666 Hardtke Dr; Muskego, WI 53150; Phone: (414) 698-6257; https://www.facebook.com/Waterbugs

Twin Lakes, WI has its Aquanuts performing shows from Memorial Day through Labor Day at Lance Park in Twin Lakes. 55 Lance Dr; Twin Lakes, WI 53181; Phone: (262) 877-2348; http://www.aquanutwatershows.com

Rome, WI features the Shermalot Show Team. Catch their show from Memorial Day through Labor Day at the Lake Arrowhead Dam. 15th Ave; Rome, WI 54457; Phone: (715) 513-6230; http://www.shermalotskiteam.com/about.html

Wrightstown, WI hosts the Waterboard Warriors Water Ski Show Team featuring four-tiered pyramids, bare-knuckled barefooting, and hydrofoil acrobatics. Mueller Park; 660 Washington St; Wrightstown, WI 54180; Phone: (920) 445-8829; http://www.waterboardwarriors.org

Wyoming

The most well-known and popular national and state parks charge an entrance fee. But there are places that offer some of the same thrilling scenery but without the cost. Several are not only free and informative, but also fun, and quirky.

Shoshone National Forest was America's first national forest and is filled with rugged peaks, steep cliffs, alpine plateaus and meadows, and the ghost town of Kirwin. Open free. Phone: (307) 527-6241; https://www.fs.usda.gov/main/shoshone/home; Find maps and visitor information here: https://www.fs.usda.gov/main/shoshone/maps-pubs

Casper, WY

Independence Rock, along the Oregon trail, is noted for its historic graffiti – the names and dates of people who passed by in search of a new life in the frontier. Located about 35 miles south of Casper on State Highway 220. http://www.ultimatewyoming.com/sectionpages/sec5/extras/independencerock.html http://wyoparks.state.wy.us/pdf/Brochure/IndependenceRock.pdf

National Historic Trails Interpretive Center encourages visitors to explore the stories of some of the half-million pioneers as they followed the Oregon, California, Mormon, and Pony Express Trails between 1841 and 1868. Start at the visitor center with their award-winning film *Footsteps to the West* and the eight galleries and exhibits. Admission is free. Open Tuesday through Saturday from 9 AM to 4:30 PM. Extended hours in summer. Closed major holidays. 1501 N Poplar St; Casper, WY 82601; Phone: (307) 265-8030; http://nhtcf.org

Tate Geological Museum houses over 3,000 fossil and mineral specimens. The highlight is their 11,600 year old Mammoth, nicknamed Dee, who stands almost 14 feet. Visitors can watch the museum's technicians work on the fossils and even step up to the window and ask questions of the staff. The Dino Den contains hands-on activities for children. The museum is free. Open Monday through Friday from 9 AM to 5 PM. Open Saturday and holidays from 10 AM to 4 PM. 125 College Dr; Casper, WY 82601; Phone: (307) 268-2447; https://www.caspercollege.edu/tate-geological-museum

Werner Wildlife Museum displays birds, fish, and animals plus an interactive area for children, and garden with bird feeding station. The museum and all events are free and open to the public. Open Monday through Friday from 9 AM to 4:30

PM. 405 E 15th St; Casper, WY 82601; Phone: (307) 235-2108;
https://www.caspercollege.edu/werner-wildlife-museum

Cheyenne, WY
This wild-west town offers the seasonal **Cheyenne Gunslingers Performances**
which generally takes place from early June through the end of July. Catch the
show at 15th St and Pioneer Ave. Phone: (307) 286-7906;
https://www.facebook.com/CheyenneGunslingers

Big Boy Steam Engine 4004 is the world's largest and powerful steam
locomotives, and one of the eight remaining Big Boys on display throughout the
country. Open daily. Holliday Park at 17th and Morrie Ave. Phone: (307) 637-
6423; https://www.cheyenne.org/listing/big-boy-steam-engine/116

Cheyenne Botanic Gardens and the Paul Smith Children's Village is a two-in-
one attraction sharing a location. Both are free and open Tuesday through
Saturday from 10 AM to 5 PM and on Sunday from Noon to 5 PM. Main
grounds are open daily from dawn to dusk. Closed some holidays. 710 S Lions
Park Dr; Cheyenne, WY 82001. **Cheyenne Botanic Gardens** host nine acres of
thematic landscapes ranging from xeriscape to lush. Their historic Century Plaza
displays the state's oldest locomotive. Phone: (307) 637-6458;
https://www.botanic.org. The **Children's Village** is filled with interactive activities
– gravity powered water works, farmers windmill, solar pumps, and hand powered
pumps. Phone: (307) 637-6349; https://www.botanic.org/discover/childrens-
village

Cowgirls of the West Museum and Emporium uses western and historical
memorabilia to present the history and legends of the women who helped claim
the west. The Emporium helps support the museum. No admission fee. The
Cowgirls Theatre screens the documentary film *Oh! You Cowgirl!* Open only in
summer on Tuesday through Friday from 10 AM to 4 PM and Saturday from 10
AM to 3 PM. 203 & 205 W 17th St; Cheyenne, WY, 82001; Phone: (307) 638-
4994; http://www.cowgirlsofthewestmuseum.com/index.asp

Historic Governor's Mansion can be explored through self-guided tours. Pick up
a brochure with a detailed description of each room. There is no fee to visit. Open
June through September on Monday through Saturday from 9 AM to 5 PM and
Sunday from 1 PM to 5 PM. Mid-January to May open Wednesday through
Saturday from 9 AM to 5 PM. Note: Closed October through mid-November and
again Christmas through mid-January. 300 E 21st St; Cheyenne, WY 82001;
Phone: (307) 777-7878; http://wyoparks.state.wy.us/index.php/places-to-
go/historic-governors-mansion

NCAR-Wyoming Supercomputing Center (NWSC) delivers exhibits on weather, climate, supercomputing, and atmospheric research. Admission is free. Open Monday through Friday from 8 AM to 5 PM. Open Saturdays from 10 AM to 4 PM. Closed holidays. 8120 Veta Dr; Cheyenne, WY 82009; Phone: (307) 996-4321; https://nwsc.ucar.edu/visitor-center

Wyoming State Capitol is open for building tours and displays on the state's wildlife and culture. Open Monday through Friday from 8:30 AM to 4:30 PM. 200 W 24th St; Cheyenne, WY 82001; Phone: (307) 777-7220; https://www.travelwyoming.com/listing/cheyenne/wyoming-state-capitol

Wyoming State Museum is the repository for Native American history, Wyoming's flora and fauna, and the state's mining industry, particularly coal. Wyoming's dinosaur graveyard and some of the state's earliest prehistoric residents are featured. Free admission. Open Monday through Saturday from 9 AM to 4:30 PM. Closed state and federal holidays. Barrett Building; 2301 Central Ave; Cheyenne, WY 82002; Phone: (307) 777-7022; http://wyomuseum.state.wy.us

Cody, WY

Buffalo Bill Dam & Visitor Center includes exhibits and a short film. Visitors are welcomed to walk to the top of the dam. Admission is free. Open daily from May through September on Monday through Friday from 8 AM to 6 PM. Open Saturday and Sunday from 9 AM to 5 PM. 4808 N Fork Hwy; Cody, WY 82414; Phone: (307) 527-6076; https://www.bbdvc.com

Dug Up Gun Museum specializes in firearms and presents over a thousand relic guns and other weapons spanning major conflicts from the American Revolution to World War II. Admission is free. Open daily May through September from 9 AM to 9 PM. 1020 12th St; Cody, WY 82414; Phone: (307) 587-3344; http://www.codydugupgunmuseum.com

Encampment, WY

Grand Encampment Museum preserves the town's history with over a dozen buildings filled with artifacts representing the timber, mining, and agricultural history of the valley. The Lora Webb Nichols collection highlights life on the frontier. A dedicated photographer, her images chronicled the lives of women, children, miners, and ranchers. Admission is free with donations appreciated. Open summers on Tuesday through Saturday from 9 AM to 5 PM and Sunday from Noon to 4 PM. In winter, usually open weekdays from 10 AM to 4 PM but visitors are advised to call first. The nearest large town is Riverside in the southeast corner of the state. 807 Barnett Ave; Encampment, WY 82325; Phone: (307) 327-5308; http://gemuseum.com

Guernsey, WY

Guernsey Ruts were worn in the soft sandstone, some up to five feet deep. Groups following the Oregon Trail shared the same route at this point including trappers, those hauling freight, prospectors seeking gold in California, and Mormons on their way west. There is no charge to visit the site. Open daily. http://mormonhistoricsites.org/guernsey-ruts-national-historic-landmark-guernsey-wyoming

Kemmerer, WY

Fossil Butte National Monument preserves fossilized fishes, insects, plants, reptiles, birds, and mammals that were once part of a subtropical environment. The visitor center displays some of these specimens. Ranger-led programs are available in summer and upon request other times of year. Note: Fossil Butte has several trails but the park cautions that hikers won't be able to see fossils on any of these trails. There is no fee to visit. Open daily spring and fall from 8 AM to 4:30 PM. Open until 6 PM daily in summer. The site is closed on Sunday from December through February. The monument is 9 miles west of Kemmerer on U.S. Highway 30. Follow the signs to the visitor center. 864 Chicken Creek Rd; Kemmerer, WY 83101; Phone: (307) 877-4455; https://www.nps.gov/fobu/index.htm

Fort Laramie, WY

Fort Laramie National Historic Site was established as a private fur trading fort in 1834, but soon became the largest and best known military post on the Northern Plains. The visitor center screens a 18-minute orientation film. The site hosts 12 restored buildings dating from 1849 to the late 1880s. Admission is free. Morning and afternoon programs and guided tours into the furnished buildings are available in summer. The park grounds are open daily from sunrise until sunset. The Fort Museum and Visitor Center is open daily 9 AM to 7 PM from Memorial Day to Labor Day. The rest of the year open 8 AM to 4:30 PM. Closed Thanksgiving, Christmas, and New Year's Day. Best reached from I-25. 965 Grey Rocks Rd; Fort Laramie, WY 82212; Phone: (307) 837-2221 x3002; https://www.nps.gov/fola/index.htm

Green River, WY (See also Rock Springs, WY)

Seedskadee National Wildlife Refuge is a major attraction for those who want to go birding and wildlife watching along the extensive trail system, boardwalks, and observation decks. There are no entrance fees. Grounds are open ½ hour before sunrise to ½ hour before sunset. The visitor center is open Monday through Friday from 7:30 AM to 4:30 PM. Closed federal holidays. Visitors are encouraged to call to see if the office is open. Seedskadee Rd; Green River, WY 82935; Phone: (307) 875-2187; https://www.fws.gov/refuge/Seedskadee

Hulett, WY

Hulett Museum & Art Gallery offers a buffet of the area's history and art. A cook-stove, wagon, tools of the ranching trade, a collection of both rifles and pistols, and dinosaur bones. Admission is free. Open in summer Monday through Friday from 8 AM to 5 PM and Saturday from 10 AM to 2 PM. In winter open Monday through Friday from 8 AM to 4 PM. 115 N Hwy 24; Hulett, WY 82720; Phone: (307) 467-5292; http://www.visithulett.com/index.php/members/shopping/14-hulett-museum-art-gallery

Jackson, WY

Jackson Town Square, located near the intersection of Broadway and Cache Streets, is marked by an elk antler archway at each of the four entrance points. Each arch contains about 2,000 elk antlers, which were shed by the residents of the nearby National Elk Refuge.

National Elk Refuge is the seasonal refuge for the Jackson elk herd as well as bison, bighorn sheep, pronghorn, mule deer, and trumpeter swans. Much of the refuge is off limits, but visitors can drive along Elk Refuge Road, which begins at the end of E Broadway Avenue in Jackson. Winter season, between November and April, is the best time to view elk and other wildlife. There is no fee to enter the refuge, or to drive the road which is open daily 24 hours a day. The historic Miller Ranch is open from the end of May through the middle of September. Note: The refuge offers fee-based sleigh ride tours each winter. https://www.fws.gov/refuge/National_Elk_Refuge

Laramie, WY

University of Wyoming Art Museum features European and American paintings, prints, sculpture, and drawings. One highlight is their special collection of the work of Ichiro, the largest single-artist netsuke (miniature sculpture) collection in the U.S. There's also Japanese wood block prints, and Persian miniature paintings. There is no admission fee. Open Tuesday through Saturday from 10 AM to 5 PM. Open late Thursday until 7 PM. Closed some major holidays. 2111 Willett Dr; Laramie, WY 82071; Phone: (307) 766-6622; http://www.uwyo.edu/artmuseum

University of Wyoming Geological Museum is highlighted by a 75-foot Apatosaurus skeleton that dominates the museum's exhibit hall. Another fossil on display is Big Al, the most complete Allosaurus ever found. But the museum also offers its lab dedicated to fossil preparation as a working exhibit. Admission is free.

Open Monday through Saturday from 10 AM to 4 PM. 200 N Ninth St; Laramie, WY 82072; Phone: (307) 766-2646; http://www.uwyo.edu/geomuseum/index.html

Lovell, WY
Pryor Mountain Wild Mustang Center educates visitors about the wild mustangs of Colonial Spanish American heritage. There is no fee to enter the area or the visitor center. The public is welcomed to stop by and learn how and where to best view the wild horses. Note: There is a fee for formal tours. Highway 14A; Lovell, WY 82431; Phone: (307) 548-9453; http://www.pryormustangs.org

Moorcroft, WY
West Texas Trail Museum displays pieces of its history from a chuck wagon to items from Robinson Mercantile. Admission is free. Donations are gladly accepted. Open Monday through Friday from 9 AM to 5 PM. Closed holidays. 100 E Weston St; Moorcroft, WY 82721; Phone: (307) 756-9300; http://westtexastrailmuseum.com

Pine Bluffs, WY
Texas Trail Museum mixes historic buildings and collected artifacts to depict the history of southeastern Laramie County. Visit the exhibit hall then tour the oldest school house in Laramie County, a decommissioned Catholic church, the Walker Boarding House, a Union Pacific caboose with railroad memorabilia, and the Bowser homestead house. There is no entrance fee, but donations are greatly appreciated. Open seasonally from May through September on Wednesday through Saturday from 9 AM to 4 PM and Sunday from 1 PM to 4 PM. 201 W Third St; Pine Bluffs, WY 82082; Phone: (307) 245-3713; http://www.facebook.com/TexasTrailMuseum

Powell, WY
Homesteader Museum celebrates the town's rich history through artifacts, historic buildings, and photographs. Climb a caboose, explore an original homestead, and peer inside a sheep herders wagon and an outhouse. No admission fee. From April through Memorial Day open Tuesday through Friday from 10 AM to 4 PM. From end of May through December open until 5 PM. June through September open Saturday from 10 AM to 2 PM. Closed January through March. 324 E First St; Powell, WY 82435; Phone: (307) 754.9481; http://homesteadermuseum.com

Rawlins, WY
Carbon County Museum has exhibits highlighting its cattle and sheep ranching heritage as well as mining. The Sweetwater school house is also on display. Admission is free. Open Tuesday through Saturday from 10 AM to 6 PM. 904 W

Walnut; Rawlins, WY 82301; Phone: (307) 328-2740;
http://www.carboncountymuseum.org

Rock Springs, WY (See also Green River, WY)

Killpecker Sand Dunes Open Play Area invites hiking, dune buggy riding, dirt biking, and ATV activities. Killpecker is the second largest active sand dune field in the world and is a non-fee area. BLM provides complete directions on their website. Phone: (307) 352-0256; https://www.blm.gov/visit/killpecker-sand-dunes-open-play-area-campground

Pilot Butte Wild Horse Scenic Tour along the 24-mile self-guided stretch can begin in either Green River or Rock Springs. Travelers should plan on approximately 90 minutes to complete the tour, most of which is on a gravel road. Watch for wild horses between Rock Springs and 14-Mile Hill across the top of White Mountain. This is a fee-free area. Phone (307) 352-0256; https://www.blm.gov/visit/pilot-butte-wild-horse-scenic-tour

Western Wyoming Community College hosts dinosaurs, natural history exhibits, and the Weidner Wildlife Museum. 2500 College Dr; Rock Springs, WY 82902; Phone: (307) 382-1600; https://www.westernwyoming.edu/about/visit. **Weidner Wildlife Museum** is the wildlife collection of Roger A. and Jeanne A. Weidner – nearly 125 species of mounted animals. There is no admission fee. Open Monday and Wednesday from 10 AM to 1 PM. Open Tuesday and Thursday from 1 PM to 4 PM. Closed school holidays. The campus is also home to **Easter Island** statues known as Moai that adorn the back lawn and the walking track area of the campus. They are nine concrete replicas. And, of course, five life-sized **dinosaurs** that are replicas of the earliest residents of the area are located around campus.

White Mountain Petroglyphs features hundreds of figures etched into the stone surface dating back 200 to 1,000 years. Some of the figures depict what might be bison and elk hunts. Other figures portray horses, and even a warrior figure. The Bureau of Land Management recommends that travelers visit the site in a vehicle with high clearance, and during good weather. There are no facilities at White Mountain Petroglyphs so bring food and especially water, and make sure your gas tank is full. There is no admission fee. Open all year, weather permitting. Hwy 191 N (26 miles northeast of Rock Springs); Rock Springs, WY 87120; Phone: (307) 352-0256; http://wyoshpo.state.wy.us/wyomingheritage//whiteMtnPetroglyphs.html

Sheridan, WY

The Don King Museum displays three decades of the King family's memorabilia. Saddles line the walls, but there's also stuffed bears, moose, and elk as well as wagons, coaches, Native American artifacts, guns, Western tack, and original artwork. The museum is part of King's Saddlery. Admission is free. Open Monday through Saturday from 8 AM to 5 PM. 184 N Main St; Sheridan, WY 82801; Phone: (307) 672-2702; http://www.kingssaddlery.com/museum.htm

Sundance, WY

The Sundance Kid and Crook County Museum remembers Harry A. Longabaugh, better known as the Sundance Kid, and his many illegal activities. He was eventually tried, convicted, and sentenced to 18 months hard labor at the Crook County jail in Sundance. Visiting the museum is free and provides artifacts and history about the area and the people who settled there. Hours vary by season. The statue of The Kid resting in a cell is outside the museum and can be seen any time. 309 E Cleveland St; Sundance, WY 82729; Phone: (307) 283-3666; https://www.facebook.com/crookcountymuseum